RESETTING THE COORDINATES

AN ANTHOLOGY OF PERFORMANCE ART IN AOTEAROA NEW ZEALAND

RESETTING THE COORDINATES

EDITED BY
CHRISTOPHER BRADDOCK
IOANA GORDON-SMITH
LAYNE WAEREA AND
VICTORIA WYNNE-JONES

MASSEY UNIVERSITY PRESS

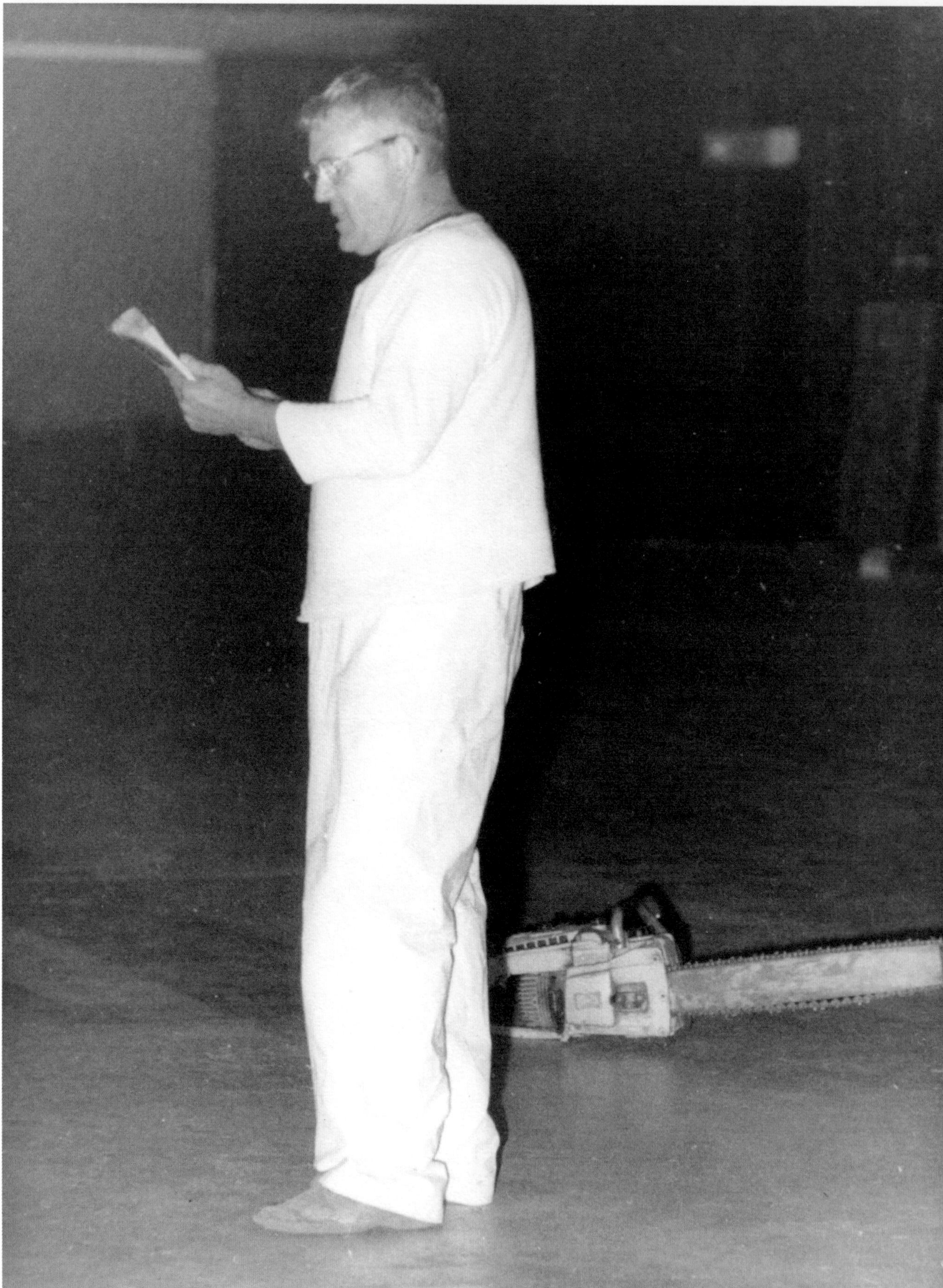

Jim Allen during a performance of *Poetry for Chainsaws, Pavilion K*, Epsom Showgrounds, Tāmaki Makaurau, Auckland, 1974. *Courtesy Michael Lett Gallery and the Allen family*

We dedicate this book to Jim Allen (1922–2023), who passed away on 9 June 2023 at the age of 100, not long after he had finished co-writing Chapter 3 with his close friend, artist James Charlton. Jim was a central figure in the development of conceptual post-object and performance art in Aotearoa New Zealand. His legacy as an arts educator and artist, both here and in Australia, lives on in the generations of artists who have taken inspiration from his prolific sculptural and performance innovations and his dedication to the teaching and learning of artistic practice.

INTRODUCTION

RESETTING THE COORDINATES

Christopher Braddock, for the editors

Resetting the Coordinates is the first anthology of performance art of Aotearoa New Zealand. From foundations in post-object art of the 1970s, feminist performance art in the 1980s, the growth in powerful Māori and Moana[1] performance in the 1990s, and the dynamic, diverse and inclusive scene of the 2010s and 2020s, the wide-ranging nature of this book makes it a taonga for artists, researchers and readers, benefiting tangata whenua, tangata moana and tangata Tiriti.

As the title asserts, this anthology contributes to an alternative history of New Zealand art.[2] It 'resets the coordinates' and questions dominant narratives in two ways: first, by affirming performance art as a significant part of New Zealand's turn towards international and contemporary artistic concerns, especially in the 1970s and 1980s; and second, by exploring Indigenous Māori and Moana approaches to performance that make performance art in Aotearoa different from anything else in the world.

The four editors welcome the eighteen writers who have contributed to this book. In tapping a rich vein in Aotearoa's art history, we want to honour the past and give space to new writers and practitioners, especially those asserting mātauranga Māori and Pasifika knowledge, actively endorsing and pursuing the principles of Te Tiriti o Waitangi, and paying attention to values of partnership, participation and protection.[3]

This introduction is chronological. It maps key shifts in performance art in Aotearoa while highlighting the contents of each chapter. Many chapters reference a number of time periods within our half-century overview. As a result, the linear chronology is interrupted by patches of non-linear temporality. *Resetting the Coordinates* does not set out to secure any concise history and is not a *catalogue raisonné* of all performance art over fifty years. In the words of art writer and critic Wystan Curnow, 'Such histories miss, or, worse, lose, the plot.' To Curnow's mind, a plot is a conspiracy, 'itself a box, in the thrall of its preordained outcomes, the ends of its narratives and arguments'.[4]

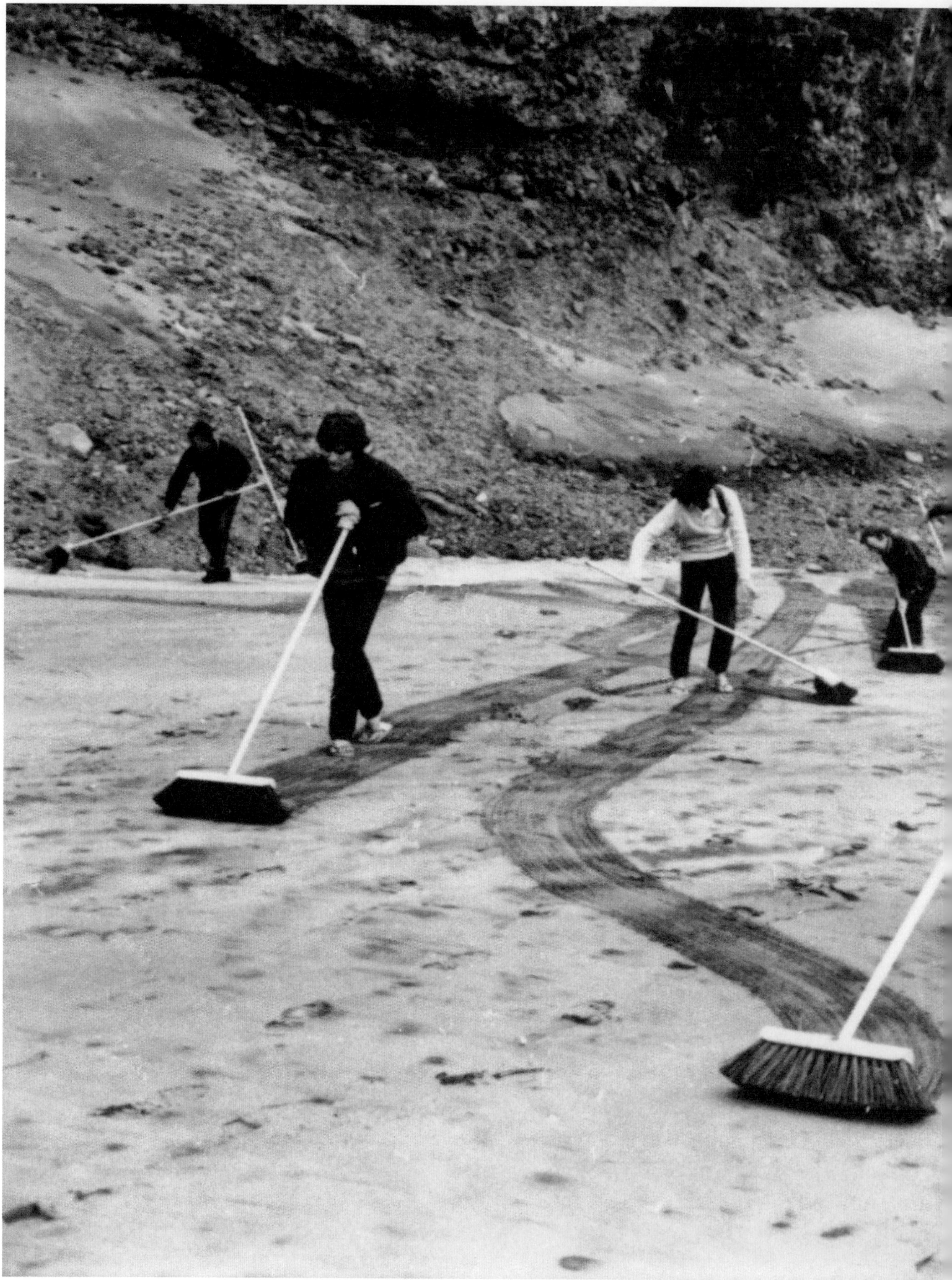

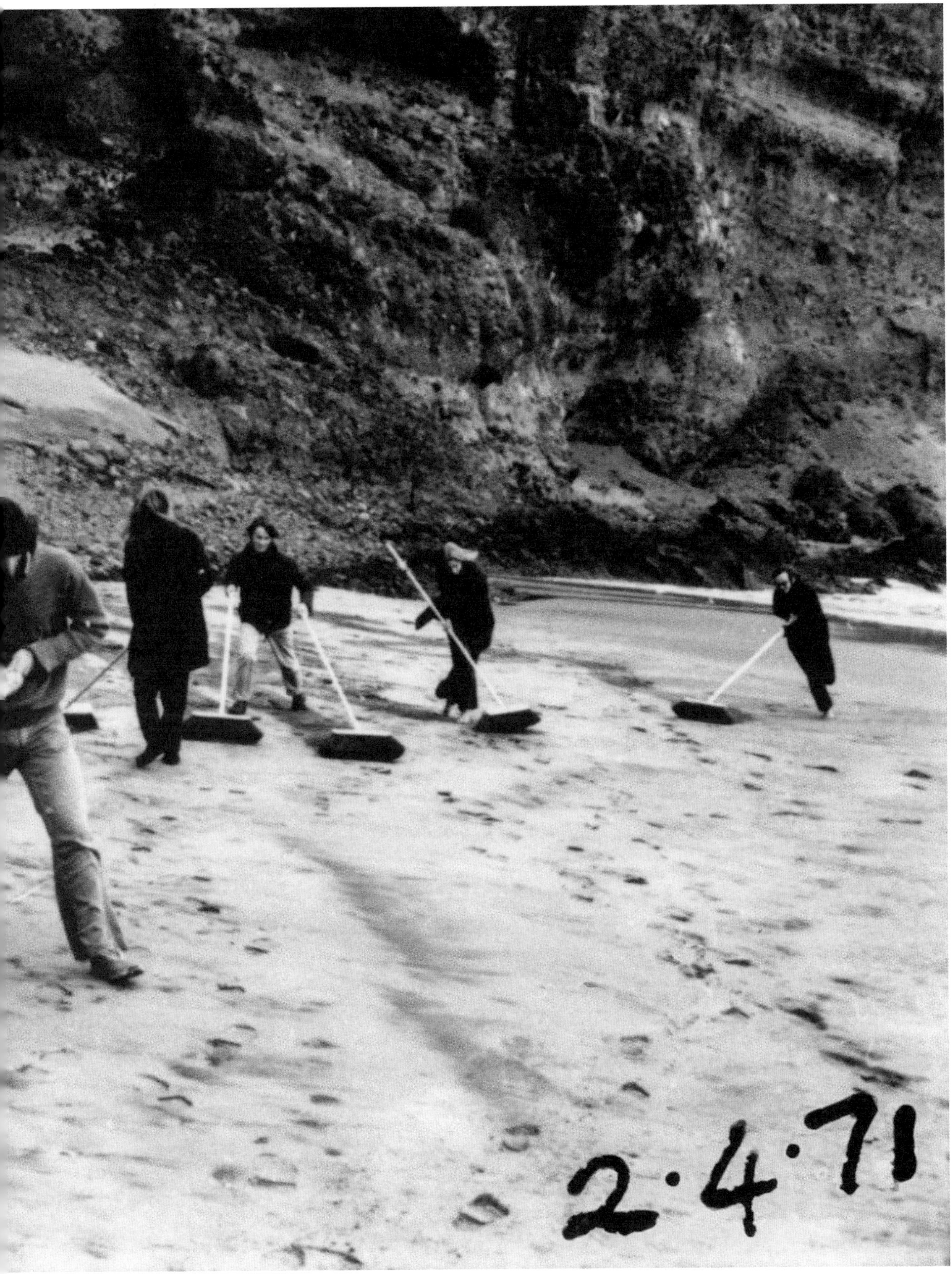
2·4·71

PART ONE: 1970–91
SETTING THE SCENE IN THE 1970S

PREVIOUS: Philip Dadson, *Purposeless Work 1: Beach sweeping*, 1971. *Photo by Jim Allen*

If, on 2 April 1971, you had journeyed out across the unsealed metal roads to the west coast of the Tāmaki Makaurau Auckland region of the North Island of Aotearoa New Zealand, venturing as far as the remote Karekare Beach, to the north of Whatipu Beach and the great Manukau Harbour and south of Piha Beach, you would have come across the mystifying scene of ten people arduously sweeping the beach with long-handled yard brooms. Karekare is a long, black, iron-sand beach. Quite a lot of sweeping to do, then.

According to his art school lecturer Jim Allen, twenty-five-year-old sound and performance artist Phil Dadson had returned to Elam School of Fine Arts at the University of Auckland after 'a year off' in Europe to study with Cornelius Cardew.[5] As described by Andrew Clifford and Rachel Shearer in Chapter 6 of this book, Dadson then established an Aotearoa splinter group of Cardew's Scratch Orchestra (soon to evolve as Dadson's From Scratch), which Allen recalls first performed in the lecture theatre at Elam.[6]

In this hothouse moment of what was to become known in New Zealand and Australia as post-object art, Allen recalls a beach 'swept with yard brooms [involving] groups of people knitted together in common endeavour'.[7] Allen was one of the sweepers (and photographers), along with other sculpture staff, Dadson himself, and a number of Dadson's student colleagues at Elam, including Maree Horner, Malcolm Ross, Nigel Brown and Bryony Dalefield.

The sweepers arrived at Karekare in the late morning and swept, as Dadson describes it, 'from late morning thru to mid'ish afternoon . . . as long as it took from one end to t'other'.[8] As noted by Blair French in his survey of performance art of the 1970s (Chapter 1), *Purposeless Work 1: Beach sweeping* (1971) was the first in a series of 'purposeless work' projects, a category inspired by Cardew and Scratch Orchestra activity. Dadson recalls: 'This was work for the sake of the work, no particular purpose, no rewards' across a 'pointless-to-sweep stretch of beach' in 'communion with the elements and the place'.[9]

I write this, fifty-three years on, from my art school office at Auckland University of Technology (AUT), having just returned from a studio 'crit. session' with second-year students. Toni Lochead, a promising performance art student, has made an artwork titled *Stopping the Tide* (2023). Dressed in a bright green bodysuit, Lochead mopped the incoming tide at Te Atatū Peninsula beach in Tāmaki Makaurau with a standard domestic mop, to halt rising sea levels. Deploying forms of humour and futility in the public sphere, Lochead approaches climate activism by scaling problems down to tasks that she can perform.[10] She was unaware of Dadson's 1971 performance. On my smart phone, I googled 'purposeless work' while she looked on with surprise, noting the artwork for her blog.

As an art educator and artist, I am aware of how preoccupied our current art students are with the 'now', accentuated by social media platforms. My hope is that this anthology will encourage further interest and research into a range of performance art practices in Aotearoa. It joins recent projects like Natasha Conland's significant 2018 exhibition, *Groundswell: Avant-garde Auckland 1971–79*, at Auckland Art Gallery Toi o Tāmaki and Christina Barton and Gregory Burke's 2023 exhibition at Te Pātaka Toi Adam Art Gallery, *In Relation: Performance works by Peter Roche & Linda Buis 1979–1985* (the subject of Chapter 5 in this book), which were focused case studies of moments in Aotearoa's post-object and performance art history. Without these efforts, students will continue to suffer from the historical amnesia that leaves them unaware of the practices that have taken place on their doorstep. We hope not.

The Waitākere Ranges and Karekare Beach were features in the poetry of Allen Curnow, father of Wystan Curnow. The Curnows built a holiday home on Lone Kauri Road near Karekare Beach in the early 1960s.[11] Young Wystan would have known the place well. Allen Curnow's poem 'Looking West, Late Afternoon, Low Water' dates from the 1990s and begins with a curiously current concern for climate change: 'Our beach was never so bare. Freak tide,/ system fault, inhuman error, will it// never stop falling? . . . A wall of pale green glass miles above/ head high alongside, complete with fish// crossing . . .'[12]

When Wystan Curnow returned to New Zealand in 1970 after doctoral study in the United States, he found himself in a country where 'painting was the dominant medium, landscape the dominant subject, and national identity the dominant idea'.[13] By mainstream accounts, artists were *painting* the landscape, not sweeping it. That country is now immeasurably different. When invited by the *New Zealand Listener* to write a review of Auckland's first 100 years, Curnow began with a mention of Dadson's *Purposeless Work 1: Beach sweeping*, noting the importance of the beach for New Zealanders: 'The beach is a line between land and sea, society and not-society, this country and the great elsewhere.' He contrasted Dadson's artwork with what he called the 'ulterior motives' and 'bad faith' of organised outdoor sport, saying that Dadson's art celebrated the beach: 'the ebb & flow, come & go of currents, air & water & stone & to neither impose nor impinge upon its nature'.[14]

Curnow's pivotal position when recounting the first decade and more of this book's story is found in his dedication to what was referred to at the time as post-object art.[15] Curnow began writing art criticism in the early 1970s 'largely out of an intense interest in post-object art'[16] and due to Jim Allen's inspirational advocacy of contemporary art at Elam.[17] He attended 'crit. Sessions' at Elam, and noted: 'recruiting me as house critic was one of many things he [Allen] did to make the School the base of a scene'.[18]

We are honoured to include a chapter in this book co-written by Jim Allen and his friend, artist James Charlton. Chapter 3, 'Getting It Straight', grew from conversations between the two men about re-enactments of Allen's performance art practice; Charlton had assisted in re-enactments of Allen's *Contact* (1974) at the Govett-Brewster Art Gallery in 2010 and at Artspace Aotearoa in Tāmaki Makaurau in 2011. *Contact*'s semi-mythical status for subsequent generations of artists is based partly on a reprisal of Allen's work by Michael Lett Gallery in Tāmaki Makaurau. Their chapter here discusses Allen's views on the drawbacks and benefits of re-enactments and offers insight into the planning and realisation of *Contact*.

1973: ECONOMIC CRISIS AND POLITICAL UPHEAVAL

The 1970s was a decade of extraordinary economic crisis coupled with political protest. Global economies were reeling from the oil shocks of 1973 and 1978–79. New Zealand relied heavily on imported oil, and soaring oil prices resulted in a worsening balance of payments coupled with increased unemployment and inflation. Britain joined the European Economic Community in 1973, and within four years New Zealand's exports of butter and cheese there had halved.[19] In 1973, Prime Minister Norman Kirk ordered the naval frigate *Otago*, with a cabinet minister on board, to enter the French nuclear testing zone at Mururoa Atoll in the South Pacific.[20] The publicity, together with a successful case in the world court, forced French nuclear tests underground. Robert Muldoon became prime minister in 1975, and by 1976 the country was in recession.

Since the early 1970s Dadson has been a key proponent of group, collaborative and improvisational performance art practices, and as such has had a huge influence over the art scene.[21] Dadson's From Scratch gave its first public performance at the inaugural Sonic Circus festival at Victoria University of Wellington in 1974. Eight years later, on 27 September 1982 at Auckland Town Hall, they performed the preview performance of their nuclear protest work *Pacific 3, 2, 1, Zero (Part 1)*, which was destined for the 1982 Paris Art Biennale. As Andrew Clifford and Rachel Shearer describe in Chapter 6, 'Sound and Performance Cultures in Aotearoa', the group's arrangement of PVC pipe percussion racks imitated the symbol for nuclear disarmament, and their vocals resembled a protest chant that comprised the names of islands across Te Moana-nui-a-Kiwa, including Mururoa.[22] I witnessed this performance at the age of twenty, and it confirmed my desire to be an artist. I recall vividly the energy of the performers (Geoff Chapple, Wayne Laird, Don McGlashan and Dadson) in their combined lament for and warning of impending nuclear disaster, and the dynamic sculptural installation that was, quite literally, *being performed.*

In 1973 the poet Hone Tūwhare convened what was to be the first of the annual hui of the Māori Artists and Writers Society (later Ngā Puna Waihanga), held in that first year at Te Kaha marae in the Eastern Bay of Plenty.[23] Thereafter, with prominent Māori artist Para Matchitt as president, annual marae-based hui showcased the often ground-breaking work of Māori visual, performing and literary artists within an inclusive, affirming cultural environment.[24] Also during this period, the 1975 Māori land march or hīkoi led by Ngāpuhi leader Whina Cooper protested the loss of Māori land. On arrival at Parliament in Te Whanganui-a-Tara on 13 October, the marchers presented a petition with 60,000 signatures. In the same year, the Treaty of Waitangi Act established the Waitangi Tribunal, which, for the first time, gave Te Tiriti o Waitangi recognition in New Zealand law.

Standing on the shoulders of these remarkable predecessors, contemporary Māori and Moana performance artists have pursued dynamic forms of performance art that are explored in no fewer than 12 chapters of this book. These include Chapter 8 by Layne Waerea and Chapter 10 by Lana Lopesi and Waerea, the latter exploring the emergent, adaptive and fluid nature of lived social difference in Māori and Moana performance art. Both of these chapters trace whakapapa to the activist 'performances' of the 1970s (and earlier) and relate Māori and Moana artistic performance to concepts such as whakapapa, gafa, mana, mana motuhake and mau.

1976: NEW ART

It was in this financial crisis, coupled with dynamic political and cultural activity, that Curnow and Allen co-edited the 1976 publication *New Art: Some recent New Zealand sculpture and post-object art*, which included the artworks of Phil Dadson, Bruce Barber, Don Driver, Kieran Lyons, Greer Twiss, Leon Narbey, Maree Horner and Allen, as noted by Allen and Charlton in Chapter 3 of this book. *New Art* was a landmark publication for New Zealand in that it included new ways of writing about art, such as transcriptions of tape-recorded interviews and discussions, thus expanding how artworks and performances might be contextualised.[25]

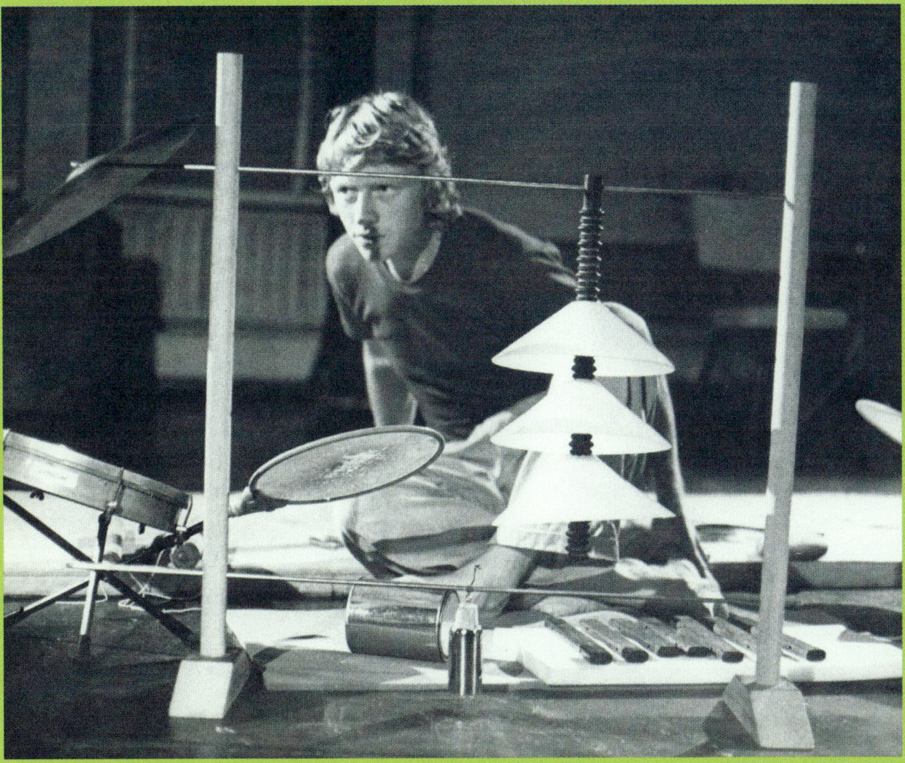

Philip Dadson performing with From Scratch at Sonic Circus in Wellington, 1974. *Courtesy the From Scratch Archive. Photo by Ian McDonald*

As Blair French discusses in Chapter 1, in *New Art* Curnow included his 25 June 1973 text 'Mt Eden Crater Performance', on the work of Bruce Barber, whose performance was part of *Solar Plexus*, an annual winter solstice dawn-to-dusk drumming event in the crater of Maungawhau Mount Eden, initiated by Dadson in 1970 (discussed in Chapter 6).[26] This was Curnow's first attempt at in situ experimental writing, which allowed him to become immersed in the experiences of the works he encountered; 'a stream-of-consciousness, phenomenological account' as Robert Leonard writes.[27] By Curnow's account, the text is a poetic collage account that 'enacts the relation of Barber's performance to language'.[28] Put another way, it enacts the performance through writing *as* performance:

> Cover-cover . . . the filling with . . . pip, pip (electronic) . . . New York . . . great crater at my feet . . . beyond the North rim: cranes, the inner harbour, the North Shore and the islands are sharply outlined dark shapes . . . 10.25, Saturday morning, June 25, day following winter-solstice . . . and so on . . . the pudding has? . . . cover-cover . . . sky a light blue, morning mist mostly dissipated by now leaving behind some low-lying cloud in the . . . the bowl carefully with . . . the bowl carefully with . . . the sun's warmth, it's a good day . . .

Curnow's broken phrases responded to what he was hearing and seeing and deliberately challenged the division between critic, writer, audience, performer and documentation — which is characteristic of the performance art discussed throughout this book. As explored in Chapter 5 by Christina Barton and Gregory Burke on the performance art of Peter Roche and Linda Buis, and in Chapter 13 by myself and Victoria Wynne-Jones, on secret, unannounced performances, Curnow emphasised a shift from viewers as passive observers to viewers as persons who assisted in the construction of the artwork. As he wrote for the first edition of *Parallax* in spring 1982: 'Content is to be discovered not in the work, but in our interaction *with* the work. All observations are participations.'[29] Curnow had his finger on the Euro-American pulse and took issue with the formalist modernism of Clement Greenberg in the 1960s. American art historian Rosalind Krauss published *Passages in Modern Sculpture* in 1977, in which she argued for similar phenomenological understandings between artworks and viewers.[30]

Chapter 1, 'A Place, a Question, a Challenge, a Call to Action', by Blair French offers a comprehensive survey of performance art of the 1970s, walking us through the performances of Jim Allen, Phil Dadson, Bruce Barber, Andrew Drummond, Gray Nicol, David Mealing and Nicholas Spill. This male-dominated period of performance art history in New Zealand is counterbalanced, however, by Natasha Conland's writing on Kimberley Gray (Chapter 2). The latter is an important analysis of Gray's archival material, now held at the E H McCormick Research Library, Auckland Art Gallery Toi o Tāmaki, where Conland curated the overview exhibition of performance art of the 1970s in Auckland, *Groundswell* (2018), which included Gray's performance art. As Conland notes, Gray's self-reflexive performance and installation engagement with ideas of time and place on this earth adds another dimension to an overview of performance art in the 1970s.

ALTERNATIVE NARRATIVES

As French notes in Chapter 1, Northern Irish artist and curator Ian Hunter, who arrived in New Zealand in late 1970 — he served as education officer and later curator of painting and sculpture at the National Art Gallery in Te Whanganui-a-Tara and co-founded the Artists Co-operative in the city in 1978 — has famously criticised New Zealand performance art of the 1970s for its lack of engagement with Māori artists and writers. Albeit in hindsight, in 2000 Hunter identified the period of the 1970s 'as the time of the long (white) silence' (a word-play on the Māori name for New Zealand, Aotearoa, which translates as 'the land of the long white cloud').

Hunter recorded a sense of 'personal loss and a professional failure' in not attempting 'a sustained dialogue or exchange with fellow Māori artists and writers'; he and others were 'too preoccupied with notions of legitimacy in the international art community' rather than the 'challenges and opportunities for cultural dialogue and exchange that awaited us at home'.[31] This major point of criticism for key artists of the period requires ongoing attention. It has fuelled one dominant narrative about performance artists of the 1970s as ambitiously intent on turning towards international trends, and as making prolific documentation to enable international outreach with less concern for political issues including Indigenous land rights. This book goes some way to counteracting such a narrative, asserting that these artists were, in fact, politically engaged.

An overly narrow reading of artworks of the time is one factor in reinforcing generalisations about the period. For example, Allen's 1974 *Contact* and his 1976 *Poetry for Chainsaws*, at the Experimental Art Foundation in Adelaide, carried anti-war meanings that have not been adequately contextualised. Furthermore, Allen's employment between 1952 and 1956 with the Art and Craft branch of the Department of Education in the Far

North of Aotearoa as a field officer, under Gordon Tovey's Northern Māori Project, has recently been discussed by curator and writer Charlotte Huddleston.[32]

Yet, it is also the case that some artists, such as Fiona Clark (who attended Elam from 1972 to 1975), made work that focused differently on current politics of gender and body image. As part of a panel discussion titled 'Out of Time', on the occasion of the *Groundswell* exhibition on 31 March 2019, Clark commented on the fact that her 1973 performance at the Pink Pussycat Club in Tāmaki Makaurau, exhibited in *Groundswell*, had been criticised at Elam as 'immature'.[33] She commented, 'I never took my clothes off and never participated in Jim Allen's works', and insisted, 'I kept my integrity': 'There were some women at Elam that wouldn't be involved, but some works did talk about gender.'[34]

I do not believe that Clark's comments downplay the significant contribution that Allen and others made to art education and post-object and performance art. But they do remind us that making generalisations about a decade of performance art is a mistake. One problem, which this book goes some way towards addressing, is that the history of performance art of this era was largely lost from institutional records, even by the 1980s. An alternative narrative we propose is that there was a porous division between visual art performance (sometimes esoterically conceptual) and other forms of performative art practice, including photography, sound and film.[35]

Contrasting Dadson's *Purposeless Work 1: Beach sweeping* or *Earthworks* (1971–72) with his From Scratch protests at nuclear testing in the Pacific or his sound work for the documentary *Te Matakite o Aotearoa, The Māori Land March* (1975) is one way of contextualising this 1970s division between performance art in its art-school-induced manifestations and other forms of politically inspired art practice (while always remembering that this division is untidy and generalised).

1970–85: RE-THINKING ART HISTORY

In re-thinking a history of New Zealand art between 1970 and 1985, Christina Barton has not only sought an alternative to that mainstream painting narrative (put forward, for example, by Michael Dunn's *New Zealand Painting: A concise history*, published in 2003), but also seeks 'an alternative, critical, socially inflected account of art practice' in this period.[36] With a focus on politically critical photographic and film practices in the 1970s, Barton proposed that films such as Geoff Steven's *Te Matakite o Aotearoa, The Māori Land March* (1975) — about the hīkoi led by Whina Cooper, with camerawork by Leon Narbey and sound by Phil Dadson — point to key links between experimental post-object art and a highly politicised non-mainstream deployment of camera and sound that closes the distance between filmmakers and participants.[37]

While Barton does not explicitly refer to performance art, she argues that films like *Te Matakite o Aotearoa* developed film and sound formats that refuse 'representation's objectifications' in favour of establishing 'different relations between artist and subject, art and its audiences'.[38] This is a common thread in discourses on performance art, such as in Amelia Jones's 1998 *Body Art/Performing the Subject*, which argues for a 'contingency of enactment' between the artist/self and audience/interpreter.[39] By Barton's account, 'The all-Pakeha crew travelled with the marchers, from their first steps up from the beach at Spirits Bay in the Far North, to their final entry into Wellington.' The hand-held camera 'was constantly on the move' registering 'rhythmic motions of bodies in

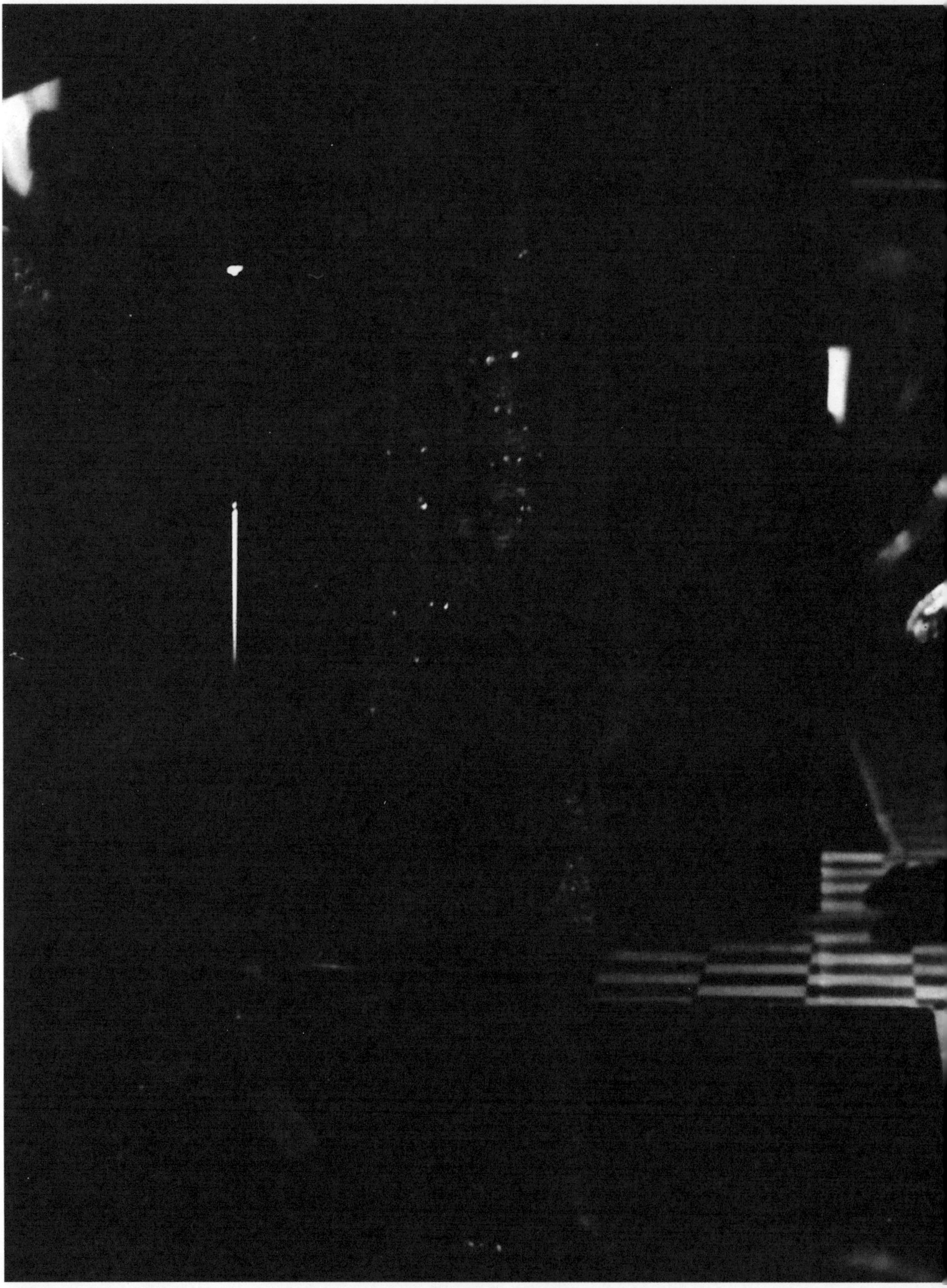

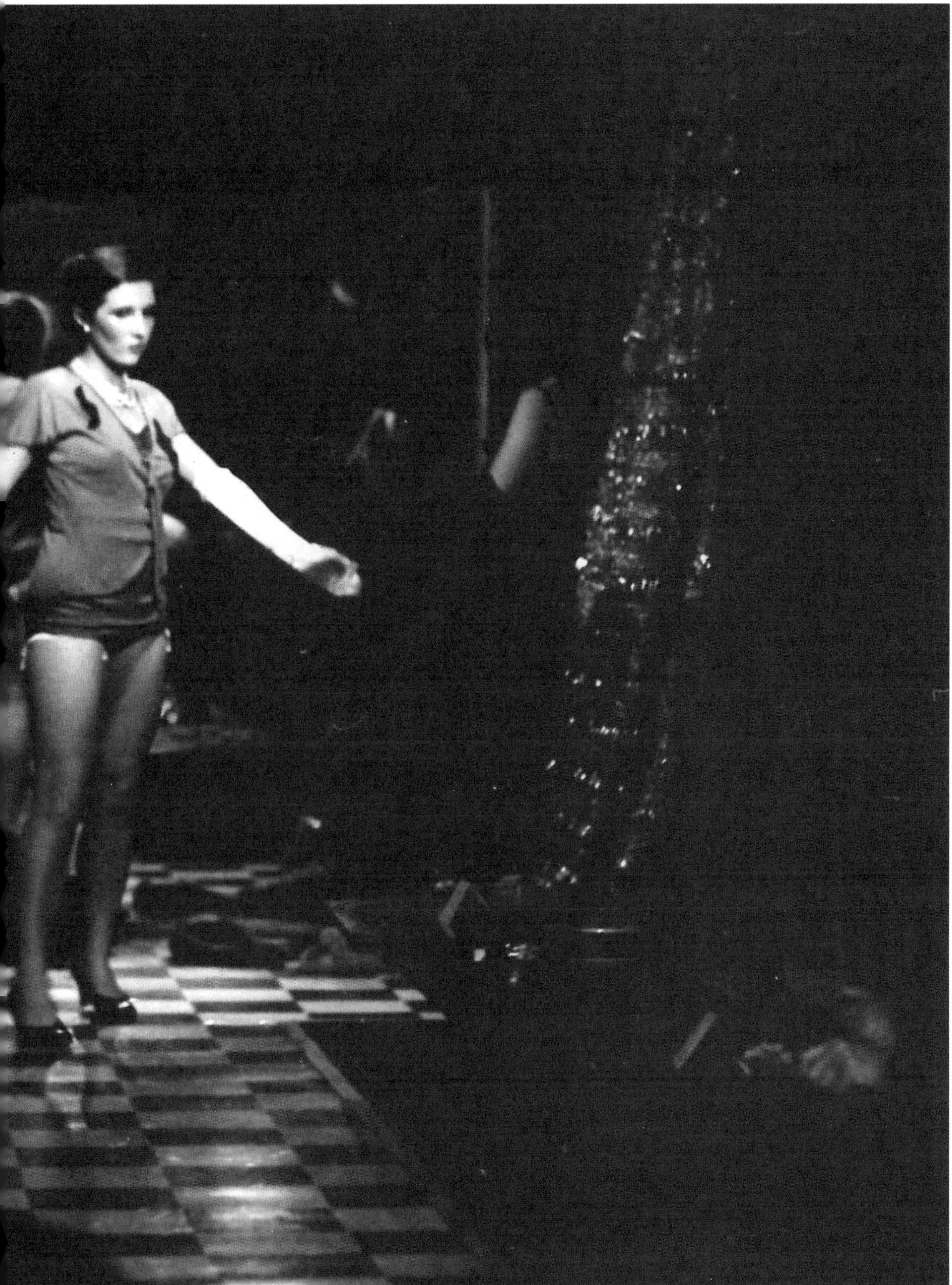

action'; Dadson's soundtrack featured 'the raw sounds of marchers' feet crunching over gravel', and marked the film as profoundly different from coverage by the mainstream media.[40] In arguing for contingency across art forms and activities, Barton's discussion conjures up a sense of walking and performing-as-film.

In a footnote, Barton also indicates her intention at the time to continue researching 'structural linkages' between the documentary *Te Matakite o Aotearoa* and these artists' 'artworks', including Dadson's *Earthworks* (1971–72).[41] Dadson's recorded performance event coincided with the autumn and spring equinoxes, on 23 or 24 September 1971 (depending on the longitude of location). For an instant in time at 1800 hours GMT, he aimed to bring together participants at fifteen diverse locations around the world. The New Zealand part in the event was recorded at 6 a.m. on 24 September on the central North Island volcanic plateau.

The resulting film, *Earthworks*, edited by Dadson in 1972, was filmed continuously onto a 10-minute roll of 16mm film by I. B. Heller and Leon Narbey. The film featured in Curnow's curated exhibition *Putting the Land on the Map* in 1989 at the Govett-Brewster Art Gallery, and is indicative of his interest in post-object art establishing New Zealand's relationship to the land, not just painting. Reviewing for *Art New Zealand* the same year, Allan Smith wrote: 'The . . . video provided some strangely poetic images of figures in black raincoats on a "darkling plain", chirruping and muttering into recording equipment and taking photographs.'[42]

Earthworks featured large in Conland's exhibition *Groundswell* and was the subject of a fifty-year anniversary project at ST PAUL St Gallery, *EQUINOX_1:03PM NZST_23-9-22*, which opened on the 2022 southward (vernal) equinox at 1.03 p.m. New Zealand Standard Time on 23 September.[43] The project attempted to listen for a radio signal broadcast fifty years ago, exploring Jones's theory of a contingency of enactment across immeasurable time and space. This was proposed through artistic actions such as Ziggy Lever's *Time Announcements* (2022), composed of intermittent sound recordings of announcements by fifteen participants worldwide commenting on time and weather conditions, and a Zoom autumn and spring equinox opening dialogue event at 1.03 p.m. on a huge orange mat titled *Conversation Mat*.[44]

Lever's sound performance echoed Curnow's poetic collage account of Barber's *Mt Eden Crater Performance*, and bears similarity to Smith's description of 'chirruping and muttering' in *Earthworks*. In these ways, *EQUINOX_1:03PM NZST_23-9-22* transposed the significance of *Earthworks* within current virtual Zoom interactions across the globe, influenced by the Covid-19 pandemic, and in relation to local time, gathered on a mat designed to induce conversation.

This sets the scene as a vast sweep across our fifty years of anthology: an alternative narrative of porous division between performance art 'proper' (albeit contentious in classification) and other forms of performative art practice that include: politically inspired walking-as-film in *Te Matakite o Aotearoa*, reaching for an instant in time across Earth's longitudes in *Earthworks*, and quantum contingency in time and dialogue in *Time Announcements* and *Conversation Mat*. These 'performances' refuse representation's objectifications in favour of an altogether different set of coordinates.

PREVIOUS: Fiona Clark in performance with Raewyn Turner as 'Ruby and Pearl' at the Pink Pussycat Club in Tāmaki Makaurau Auckland, 1973. *Courtesy Michael Lett Gallery and the artist*

1980S: A DECADE FOR PAINTING

As Paul Ardenne writes: 'In the early 1980s, the going advice was to be adept at painting if one wanted to have a career.'[45] The *New York Times* notes the 1980s as the biggest art boom in history;[46] in New Zealand, just as we had looked abroad for conceptual and performance art developments in the 1970s, we now looked with anticipation to the booming international markets of the 1980s. The financial stagnation that had characterised the 1970s was less apparent in the 1980s, despite the crippling after-effects of the 19 October 1987 Black Monday stock market crash.[47]

Art markets worldwide eluded predictions.[48] I was an undergraduate art student at Ilam School of Fine Arts at the University of Canterbury in Christchurch from 1982 to 1985, when I and other students marvelled at Julian Schnabel's plate painting, *Notre Dame* (1979), which sold in New York in 1983 for US$93,500. We all wanted a piece of this art market action, and gave little thought to performance art action.[49]

Robert Muldoon's National government was defeated in the snap election of July 1984, and David Lange's Labour government embarked on a programme of free-market reforms known as 'Rogernomics' (after Minister of Finance Roger Douglas). Financial markets were deregulated and the removal of tariff protection exposed local producers, including farmers. Despite these unstable times, the gallerist Sue Crockford returned to New Zealand from New York in 1985 and established Sue Crockford Gallery on Albert Street, Tāmaki Makaurau. Modelling her business approach on New York cult dealers[50] such as Castelli, Boone, Bischofberger, d'Offay, Maenz and Sperone, she opened with a group of eight established artists including Gretchen Albrecht, Richard Killeen and John Reynolds.

DOMINANT NARRATIVES IN QUESTION

After 1978–79 (Allen had moved to Sydney in 1976 and Barber to Canada the same year), the dominant narrative suggests there was a hiatus of more than a decade in experimental performance art practices, which were squashed by the burgeoning art market of the 1980s and its focus on saleable art commodities. Then, after the 1980s, as described by Ioana Gordon-Smith in Chapter 9, 'Urban Pasifika and Cold Islanders', the Pacific Sisters (formed in 1992) staged *Bottled Ocean* in 1994 at the Auckland City Art Gallery and *Motu Tangata* in Sāmoa in 1996. And there began a great increase in Māori and Moana performance art practices that had little reference to what had come before.

But the picture of New Zealand's art history, which has the 'radical period of experimentation of the 1970s dissolving into a story of painting, bravado and brush, despite what we know was happening socially', is not altogether true.[51] After all, 1980 was the year that Andrew Drummond performed *Filter Action* on the mudflats of Aramoana on Otago Harbour, north of Ōtepoti Dunedin, as Wynne-Jones and I discuss in Chapter 13 of this book. Drummond is one of a number of artists who performed in protest against plans by a consortium that included New Zealand-based Fletcher Challenge to build an aluminium smelter at Aramoana, which would have destroyed a wildlife reserve. And, as already mentioned, From Scratch performed their nuclear protest work *Pacific 3, 2, 1, Zero* for the 1982 Paris Art Biennale.

International performance art activity was also taking place under our noses. The year before I started art school I was at teachers' training college in Christchurch, and was in the front row of a demonstration that marched down Gloucester Street on 11 August to protest the Springbok tour of 1981. As it turns out, the march interrupted Curnow who, along with Marina Abramović and Ulay, was on his way to the first Australia New Zealand Artists Encounter (ANZART), for which Abramović and Ulay would present their performance *Witnessing* in the Great Hall of the Arts Centre on 27 August.[52]

Chapter 5, 'The Afterlives of Performance Art' by Christina Barton and Gregory Burke, which examines some of Peter Roche and Linda Buis's performances from 1979 to 1985, attests to this period as significant for performance art in its use of the camera in forms of active documentation, and performers and audiences submitting to forms of danger and vulnerability. This marks a shift in subject matter from the 1970s.

Burke was flatting with Roche when he performed *You Are Invited to Be Accepted* in their flat in Auckland in 1978. He recalls Roche's 48 hours of self-imposed exile and self-mutilation, during which he cut his arm so badly with a razor blade that he required stitches for the performance to continue, and implicated viewers in their ethical responsibilities as witnesses of his behaviour.[53] This was the era when the New Zealand rock and roll musician Chris Knox formed his first band, The Enemy, in Ōtepoti, and slashed his arm with broken glass to the song 'Iggy Told Me' at its second gig in late 1977.[54]

Adding to this picture of active performance art in Aotearoa during the 1980s, in Chapter 4, 'Body Politics', Melanie Oliver focuses on women artists in collaborative partnerships, such as Linda Buis and Peter Roche, Colleen Anstey and John Cousins, as well as Rosemary Johnson (1942–1982), Juliet Batten, Di ffrench (1946–1999), Mary-Louise Browne and Claire Fergusson. Oliver explores how these artists deployed performance as an art form to analyse interpersonal relationships and feminist ideas, which included engaging with politics around violence, gender, racism and inequality.[55]

PART TWO: 1992–2023
SETTING THE SCENE FROM THE 1990S

If, on 2 March 2014, you had journeyed down Tāmaki Makaurau's southern highway and turned off at Maungarei Mount Wellington, venturing as far as the suburb of Pakuranga and the front lawn of Te Tuhi Centre for the Arts, you would have come across a mystifying scene: an extended whānau group of Māori and Moana rowing arduously on stationary rowing machines. As described by Layne Waerea and Lana Lopesi in Chapter 10, 'Constellations of Subjectivity', artist Cora-Allan Wickliffe (now Lafaiki Twiss; Ngāpuhi, Tainui/Alofi, Liku) recruited participants to row a portion of the historical 7000-kilometre journey from Hawaiki to Aotearoa, made by early Indigenous tīpuna before the earliest settlement of Aotearoa. Quite a lot of rowing to do, then. Located on the eastern shore of the Tāmaki River, the Pakuranga area is part of the rohe of Ngāi Tai ki Tāmaki, who descend from the crew of the migratory waka *Tainui*, which visited the area around the year 1300.

As a counterbalance to Phil Dadson's *Purposeless Work 1: Beach sweeping* in 1971, discussed earlier, Lafaiki Twiss's conception for all that seemingly absurd stationary rowing follows a different kind of purposelessness. *Electric Waka* (2014) is one example, contextualised by Waerea and Lopesi, of how concepts such as whakapapa, gafa, mana, mana motuhake and mau are integral to the collective artistic practices of Māori and Moana performance artists. Also discussing the performances of Arapeta Ashton, Rosanna Raymond, Cat Ruka, Layne Waerea, Suzanne Tamaki and Leafā Wilson/Olga Krause, Waerea and Lopesi argue that Māori and Moana artists have interrelated ties to family, friends and wider community, creating intersections that are deeply informing and co-constitutive.

The metaphorical comparison of such 'constellations of subjectivity' and navigational wayfinding in Te Moana-nui-a-Kiwa relates to the constant mahi that Indigenous peoples are obliged to undertake on a daily basis in order to navigate modes of power exerted through colonialism and racism. Lafaiki Twiss's navigational wayfinding with her extended Māori and Moana whānau in Te Moana-nui-a-Kiwa is based on a hard-won whakapapa of Māori and Moana performance art practices since the early 1990s that has drawn on Indigenous knowledge, stories, ceremony, costume and dance to express Māori and Moana urban identities. By 1994, Pacific peoples comprised almost one-fifth of the national population; Tāmaki Makaurau is now home to the largest population of Pacific peoples in the world, arriving from throughout Te Moana-nui-a-Kiwa.

National Party leader Jim Bolger was prime minister from 1990 to 1997; he won a second term in office despite a major swing away from National in both seats and votes. New Zealand was experiencing an identity shift, from that of a British colony to occupying an Asia–Pacific or Pacific Rim regional framework. An emerging 'urban Pasifika'[56] context permeated performance art of the 1990s, as discussed by Ioana Gordon-Smith in Chapter 9. As Gordon-Smith argues, representation of Māori and Pacific New Zealand experiences was sorely lacking. The brown body was largely viewed through the lens of crime, cultural stereotypes and colonial fetishes.[57] But public attitudes were slowly changing in the 1990s: the majority of Pacific people in Aotearoa were Aotearoa-born and beginning to have more impact on public life.[58]

Often informed by migrant and diaspora experiences and their own Indigenous Pacific knowledge systems, the second half of the 1990s was a dynamic period of growth for Moana performance artists in Aotearoa. In 1996, Samoan author Albert Wendt published his ground-breaking work 'Tatauing the Post-Colonial Body', which became a key text for many Pacific performers. Wendt wrote of the Samoan concept of vā as an active space of relationship between two things or people.[59] For Samoan artist Ioane Ioane, for example, the vā frames performance as operating between perceptible and spiritual realms. Working between performance and sculpture, he creates spaces that are marked as sacred by way of performances. Following his seminal performance at Artspace in Quay Street, Ioane opened his 1999 multimedia installation *Fale Sā* (sacred place) at Auckland Art Gallery Toi o Tāmaki by running from the ocean (the Tāmaki Makaurau waterfront) to the gallery, flanked by performers playing conch shells and wind pipes.[60]

Fast-forwarding, the significance of the Pacific Sisters' 2018 retrospective *Fashion Activists* at Museum of New Zealand Te Papa Tongarewa cannot be underestimated and signalled a timely shift from the margins to the mainstream.[61] In 2017 Labour's Jacinda Ardern had become the second elected female prime minister of Aotearoa (after Helen Clark). By the time of her victory in the 2020 election, eleven members of Parliament identified as Pacific (9 per cent, compared to 3 per cent in 1996).[62] Smiling, Ardern was led by the hand into and among the opening performance of *Fashion Activists* by Ani O'Neill, as security guards looked on anxiously.

Aotearoa was now a very different place from when the Pacific Sisters held their 1994 exhibition *Bottled Ocean* at Auckland City Art Gallery. As discussed by Gordon-Smith in Chapter 9, this pan-ethnic (Māori and Pacific) collective was 'thrown out of the 1996 Festival of Pacific Arts and Culture (FESTPAC) in Sāmoa at the request of the Māori contingent, even though [they] had been officially invited by the festival director'.[63] The rejection was illustrative of the complex engagements between Māori and

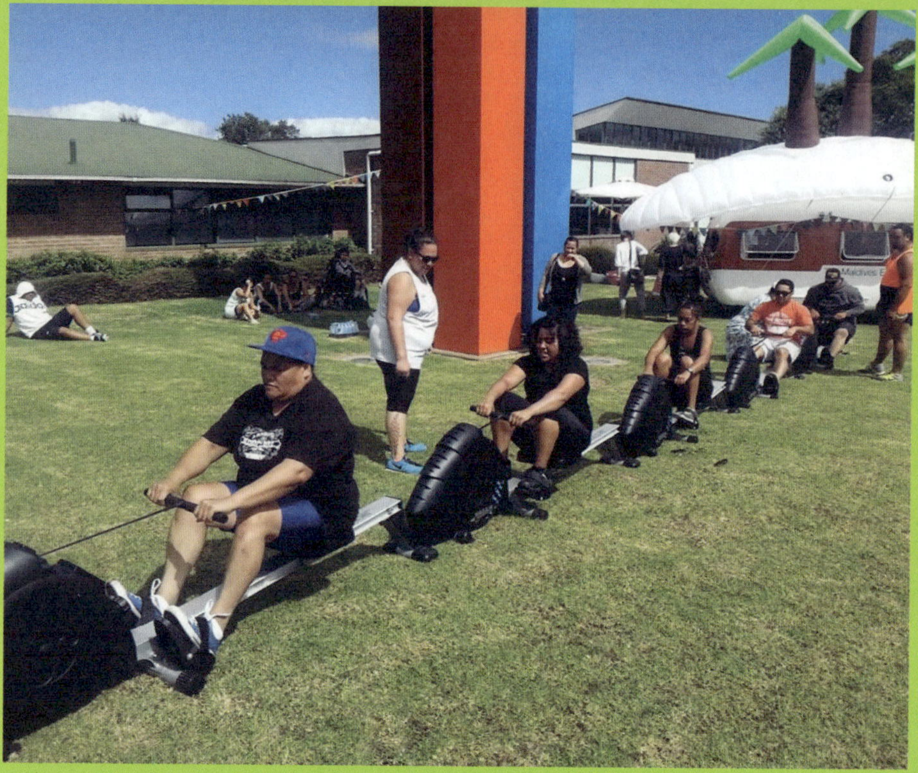

Cora-Allan Lafaiki Twiss (née Wickliffe), *Electric Waka*, 2014. Performed at Te Tuhi, Pakuranga, Tāmaki Makaurau Auckland, 8 March 2014. *Courtesy Te Tuhi. Photo by Amiria Puia-Taylor*

Moana identities, as well as a resistance to pan-disciplinary, contemporary and urban interpretations of Pacific culture.

Gordon-Smith traces these entanglements, noting milestone performances such as Lonnie Hutchinson's *Can You See Me?* (1997), in which the artist lay motionless in Queen Elizabeth Square in Tāmaki Makaurau, completely wrapped in brown packaging tape: a brown, unidentified and indeterminate body making a strong statement about New Zealand's race dynamics.[64]

LATE 1990S AND 2000S: TRACES OF PERFORMANCE THROUGH MEDIA

On 18 May 2000, Prime Minister Helen Clark (who was also Minister for Arts, Culture and Heritage) announced an extra $20 million budget for Creative New Zealand Toi Aotearoa (the Arts Council of New Zealand) to enable longer-term funding arrangements with major arts organisations over the following three years.[65] Together with this government funding increase, organisations such as Artspace Aotearoa and Tautai Contemporary Pacific Arts Trust (formalised as a charitable trust in 1995 by its founder, Samoan artist Fatu Feu'u) assisted many Māori and Pacific performance artists in the 2000s to realise projects, especially through Tautai's *Offstage*, an annual moving image and performance event that included artists such as Kalisolaite 'Uhila, John Vea, Darcell Apelu, Louisa Afoa, Tuāfale

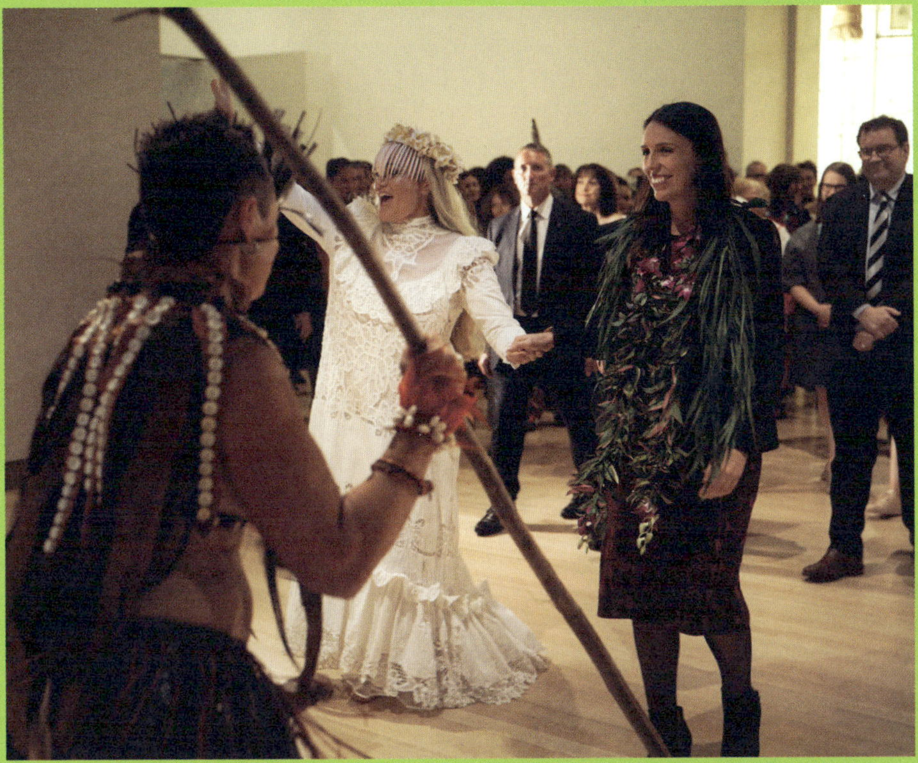

Pacific Sisters, 2018. The opening *Acti.VĀ.tion* of their retrospective exhibition *Pacific Sisters: Fashion Activists/He Toa Tāera*, Museum of New Zealand Te Papa Tongarewa. From left: Ema Lyon, Ani O'Neill, Prime Minister Jacinda Ardern. *Photo by Kerry Brown*

Tanoa'i aka Linda T, Natasha Matila-Smith, Faith Wilson, Olga Krause, Valasi Leota-Seiuli, Matavai Taulangau, Cora-Allan Wickliffe, Lonnie Hutchinson and Christopher Ulutupu.[66]

Coinciding with a rise in performance art activity in Aotearoa, Performance Studies international (PSi) was founded in 1997 to promote global awareness and research of performance art, and the influential Live Art Development Agency (LADA) was founded in London in 1999 by Lois Keidan and Catherine Ugwu. These were signs that performance art was establishing organisations and networks in concert with university research. I single out art historian Amelia Jones's 1998 *Body Art/Performing the Subject* as marking a critical moment for a re-evaluation of performance art from the 1960s to the 1990s. Her book opened the way for further critical debates and acknowledgement of performance art.[67]

When Jones and I worked together on the 2017 book *Animism in Art and Performance*, she emphasised — in relation to her curated 2013 exhibition at the Leonard and Ellen Bina Gallery in Montréal that included artworks by New Zealanders Alicia Frankovich, Paul Donald and myself — how photographic and sound media were deployed as a hinge between the live moment and its representation.[68] Jones commented on how performance-to-video 'puts pressure, precisely, on the hinge between the live body acting and the representationality of that acting' — activating what 'Roland Barthes called the "writerly" in relation to postmodern texts'; the idea that 'potential viewers . . . make meaning in relation to the performances'.[69] This harks back to Curnow's experimental and performative written account in 1973 of Barber's *Mt Eden Crater Performance* mentioned earlier.

From the 2000s was a more self-conscious effort by artists to perform for the camera and use the camera in different positions. As discussed by Wynne-Jones and Lopesi in Chapter 17, 'Cry for Attention', Jones has argued that these technologies of visual representation, while offering some confirmation of the body/self and its 'thereness', also expose a 'failure of representation to offer up the self as a coherent knowable entity'.[70] This push-and-pull between the body/self's representation and its failures is key to Campbell Patterson's performance-to-video works in which he pulls a camera about. *Chew* (2009), which was included in his solo Artspace Aotearoa exhibition in Tāmaki Makaurau titled *Floor Show* the same year, was set in his bathroom. Clad in pyjamas and a t-shirt, Patterson draped himself over the edge of the bath with his head on the tiled flooring, looking sideways at a camera some distance away on the floor. By means of a long piece of string, one end of which was attached to the camera and the other held in his mouth, he gradually pulled the camera towards himself across the floor using nothing but his mouth, by turning his head away from the camera. After each drag of the camera, he took up the slack string with his lips, tongue and teeth, effectively holding the bundle of string in his mouth cavity.

As they watched him repeatedly turn away from the camera and then turn back and collect the slack string in his mouth, viewers experienced the gradual and startling effect of Patterson's face getting closer and closer until, finally, the image deteriorated into darkness as the camera was pulled directly against his face. The camera's ability to record accurately is questioned through its uneasy and jolting passage across the bathroom floor, and Patterson's facial movements, similar to biting or chewing, in turn question the artist's role as coherent and rational.

Also using performance-to-video with an emphasis on the ways in which viewers experience bodily action mediated by the frame of the camera's view, Richard Maloy attempted to sculpt a bust self-portrait from a quantity of butter equal to his own weight. In *Yellow Grotto* (2008) at Sue Crockford Gallery, we witnessed Maloy's videoed and cropped body (only partially in view) engaged in an unsuccessful struggle to manipulate this fatty food substance that would normally be consumed. His continual failure to represent his own likeness was echoed by the relentless soundtrack of his labour.[71] It was as if we, the viewers, were invited to take part in the struggle to complete the artwork.

Activations of potential viewers is also the subject of Chapter 13, 'It's a Work' by myself and Wynne-Jones, as we explore how performance art is recorded for posterity as traces of performance in the aftermath of secret, private, one-on-one or unannounced performances, which evoke complex discussions about the significance of audiences as witnesses. This chapter ranges across performances from the 1980s, including Andrew Drummond's *Filter Action* (1980), Roche & Buis's *Night Piece* (1981), Daniel Malone's *Bad Omen* (1996–97), and later performance artworks in the 2000s by Sriwhana Spong, Alicia Frankovich and Kate Newby.

By highlighting possible occurrences of secret, private and unannounced performances, along with an array of possible traces (including writing or even talking about an event), we downplay the importance of having been there as witnesses of live performance, suggesting that we cannot easily distinguish live performance from its material trace. We argue that categories of live performance and documentation disappear when an ontology of trace is acknowledged.[72]

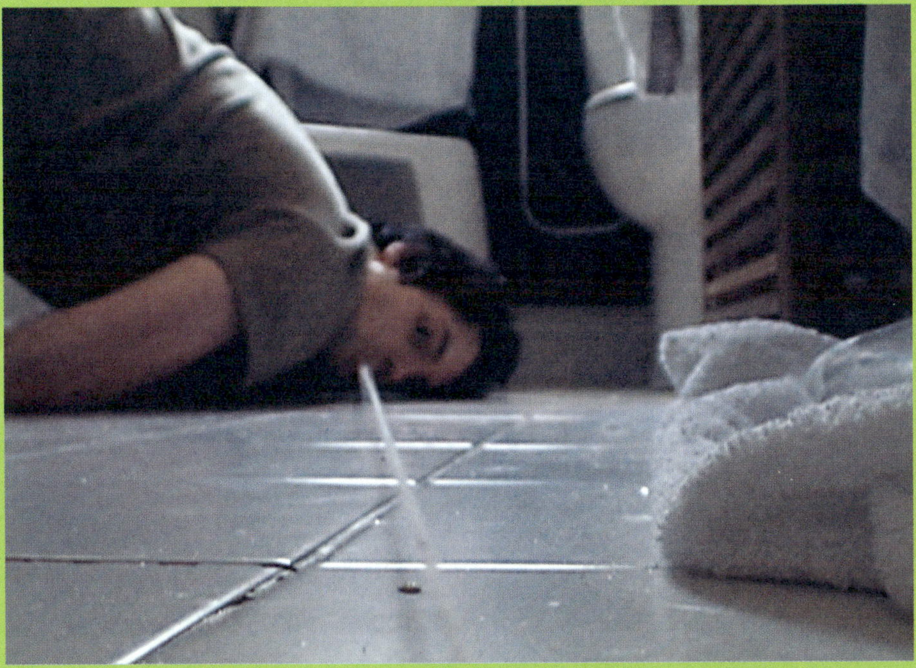

Campbell Patterson, *Chew*, documentation of performance, 2009. *Courtesy the artist*

GENEALOGIES OF PERFORMANCE

In the first decade of the new millennium, performance art in Aotearoa shifted towards modes of media representation such as photography, video and sound as often active agents. Research in this book suggests this shift has its basis in the experimental work of Linda Buis and Peter Roche (Chapter 5), Colleen Anstey and John Cousins, Rosemary Johnson, Di ffrench, Mary-Louise Browne and Claire Fergusson (Chapter 4).

Wynne-Jones and Lopesi in Chapter 17 position the post-internet and performances-to-video by Natasha Matila-Smith and Sione Tuívailala Monū within a broader history as productions of the self for posterity through orchestrated visual representations.[73] They argue for genealogies of performance that track back to Aotearoa artists Rosanna Raymond and Greg Semu, and suggest that post-internet art practice has a longer genealogy, stretching from Len Lye's technical innovations in the first half of the twentieth century to post-object practice of the 1970s, as exemplified in Allen's *Contact* (1974), to new media art experiments with a diverse range of hardware and software.

Chapter 8 by Layne Waerea, 'Mātauranga Māori and Whakapapa of Change in Performance Art of Aotearoa', explores this history with a specific focus on a Māori cultural continuum of ideas, philosophy and experience of the world that has helped shape performance art of Aotearoa. Waerea argues that performances created by Māori artists stem from origins distinct from prevailing Euro-American performance art categorisations. She borrows Māori artist and writer Robert Jahnke's term 'trans-customary', and applies it to contemporary performance art as she explores the tikanga surrounding performance as it has emerged from the traditions and customary practices of mātauranga Māori, and the role of oral narratives and performance traditions.

Mapping out these whakapapa of performance, Waerea weaves a transdisciplinary approach that combines aspects of performance art, theatre, dance, and sound and projected video installation. In discussing the performance practices of Rachael Rakena, Louise Pōtiki Bryant, Moana Nepia, Shannon Te Ao, Charles Koroneho and the collaborative work of Bianca Hyslop, Rowan Pierce and Tūī Matira Ransfield, the chapter focuses on notions such as te taiao and takiwā, and suggests the place of performance is transformed as if to a marae, where connections with tīpuna are passed across time and space.

THE 2010S AND BEYOND

In 2010 and 2011, there were several major earthquakes in Ōtautahi Christchurch. The most significant of these, on 22 February 2011, resulted in the deaths of 185 people and injuries to several thousand, and was ultimately responsible for the levelling of over 75 per cent of the central city. In Chapter 16, 'Performance Art in Post-quake Ōtautahi Christchurch', Audrey Baldwin and Khye Hitchcock kick off an assessment of performance from the 2010s. They describe how the post-disaster context gave rise to a network of community performances that created interactions and relationships between artists, viewers, collectives and communities, and demonstrated how performance art is worthwhile and even necessary in difficult times.

As if prefiguring an exploration into the dynamics of survival, Chapter 11 by myself and Ioana Gordon-Smith, 'Either For a Moment or For as Long as Possible', explores performances of endurance by artists Kalisolaite 'Uhila, Leafā Wilson, John Vea and Jeremy Leatinu'u. We focus on brown bodies that put themselves in the way of, or in relation to, institutions and viewers, and how notions of endurance and duration are linked as a forfeit of time. Closely aligned with this is Chapter 12, 'Three Types of Timepass' by Balamohan Shingade, who contrasts the concept of 'timepass' with the apparently active performances of marches, strikes or protests. Shingade explores the socio-political relevance of performances that use the inverse strategies of worklessness and withdrawal, refusals and retreats, passivity and purposelessness, and refers to works by Kalisolaite 'Uhila, Chris Braddock with Dialogue Group, Layne Waerea, Poata Alvie McKree and James Tapsell-Kururangi.

The ways in which performance art has engaged with notions of survival and passivity sometimes confound earlier observations about performance that had shifted towards modes of media representation in the 2000s. For example, Sean Curham's live performances, while documented through photography, often emphasise social interactions in the moment of their production. *Gentle Lying on the Bonnet of a Popular Car* (2016) explored the benefits of rest and casual one-on-one interaction in a public setting. Curham invited participants to lie on the bonnet of a car before making the viewers-turned-participants comfortable with cushions and blankets so they could relax for ten minutes. Adapting restorative yoga techniques, the artist constantly asked his participant for feedback and made small comfort adjustments for each individual.[74]

Many artists discussed in Chapters 9 to 14 have passed through the Art and Performance Research Group at AUT University (established in 2012), which has played a significant role in furthering rigorous tertiary pedagogy and culture for performance art.[75] Previously coordinated by performance artist John Vea and later by Ena Kosovac (with a participatory artistic practice in collaboration with a Rottweiler named Marlo), this research group has supported numerous artists undertaking master's and doctoral degrees and enabled the realisation of some major performance artworks by the likes of Brent Harris (Chapter 13), Layne Waerea (Chapters 10 and 12), Darcell Apelu (Chapter 9), Kalisolaite 'Uhila (Chapters 11 and 12), John Vea (Chapter 11) and Richard Orjis (Chapter 14).[76]

As noted, this book does not set out to secure any concise history of performance art for Aotearoa. This is particularly true of Ioana Gordon-Smith and Khye Hitchcock's musings on queer performance art in Chapter 14, 'Threads'. They gesture to an expansive, and even elusive, queer performance art history of Aotearoa. Beginning with Samoan fa'afafine artists Lindah Lepou and Yuki Kihara, they go on to discuss performance collectives such as FAFSWAG, which emerged in 2012, and end with recent performances such as Sung Hwan Bobby Park's *BTM Live*, performed as part of Auckland Pride 2023. This chapter covers a vast array of performance art in Aotearoa that has not been chronicled in this way before.

In Chapter 15, 'The Skin of Displaced Event in Aotearoa Performance Art', Lisa Samuels also counteracts any tendency towards normative readings of performance art and expectations about gender and genre. It focuses on the interior, exterior and in-between nature of 'art skin' in relation to a 2020 performance by Tāwhanga Nopera, and a 2016 moving-image installation, *Mercury*, curated by Elle Loui August, Elena Betros López, Juliet Carpenter and Nell Thomas. Samuels' reading of these performances challenges expectations about performance art as a category.

Turning to the contemporary and urgent concerns about the environment, in Chapter 18, 'Performing Environments with More-than-Human Whanaunga', Janine Randerson and Amanda Yates explore performance in the context of whanaungatanga and kaitiakitanga. Their chapter is a timely exploration of performance art that engages with the current ecological moment in the face of capitalist culture. They explore Indigenous approaches, including the HIWA kapa haka group, and artists Sarah Cameron Sunde, val smith and Forest Vicky Kapo, Jeremy Leatinu'u, Tru Paraha, Mark Harvey, Angela Tiatia and Alicia Frankovich.

CONCLUSION

Parts One and Two of this Introduction begin with Phil Dadson's *Purposeless Work 1: Beach sweeping* (1971) and Cora-Allan Lafaiki Twiss's *Electric Waka* (2014). Both works relate to place in terms of Aotearoa's diverse relations to profound political and cultural shifts over the fifty-year period of this anthology. They relate in moving ways to our islands' geography, attending to the liminal shorelines in relation to vast space and distance.

Like Allen Curnow's poetical odes to Karekare Beach, Dadson made a one-page document to accompany the photograph of *Purposeless Work 1*, with a handwritten poem at the top dated 31 March 1971, two days before the performance:

> brush the minds dust or level the surface configurations into a corner under a mat of imaginations making and emulate the imperceived excitation of vehicle earth & universe. This fragile skin continually in motion kaleidescoped at the whim of invisible tightropes recorded disinterestedly by pointers on instrument dials. In defiance of 'what's safe' clowns + daredevils are discoverers balancing with no-minded now-ness precision

Dadson's poem reveals his intense 'communion with the elements and the place',[77] the clowning 'no-minded now-ness precision' behind *Earthworks*, which was produced the same year. His performances mark a politicised and poetic response to the environment that adopts seemingly absurd and non-instrumental ways of 'putting the land on the map' in Aotearoa's art history.[78]

Unsurprisingly, the performance baton is taken in the 1990s by Māori and Moana artists working collectively in response to Anglo-European settler culture linked with urbanisation. Lafaiki Twiss's *Electric Waka* exemplifies whakapapa, not as linear genealogy but as a framework for understanding relationships between people, the natural world and the spiritual realm. Indigenous dynamics of mana motuhake and mana whenua (governorship and self-determination of natural resources) and Moana notions of mau (keeping, retaining and holding fast) enable the huge body of Māori and Moana performance art explored in this book to trace the patterns of mana-enhanced constellations across Moana-nui-a-Kiwa.[79] These Indigenous knowledges shape and perform our art history as never before.

NOTES

1 We use the terms 'Moana' and 'Pacific' to reference Pacific peoples. Pacific is a general term, but stems from colonial etymology. Moana is the Samoan term for the region and is sometimes used with reference to Samoan authors. An Indigenous term for the Great Ocean, it is found in several Indigenous Moana languages. Some argue that Moana is itself an imperfect term, particularly as a Polycentric word that minimises other Indigenous names for the region. See further discussion about this in Chapter 9 of this volume by Ioana Gordon-Smith.

2 This alternative history is different from some other mainstream anthologies. For example, Hamish Keith's 2007 *Big Picture: A history of New Zealand art from 1642* largely ignores performance art. Robert Leonard writes: 'Keith turns his back on the emerging complexity of New Zealand art after 1969 . . . He mentions post-object art, but trivialises it, and does little to show its relevance in the current moment.' Robert Leonard, 'Review of Hamish Keith "The Big Picture: A history of New Zealand art from 1642"', *Australian and New Zealand Journal of Art* 9, no. 1–2 (2008): 251–55. See https://robertleonard.org/hamish-keith-the-big-picture

3 Te Tiriti o Waitangi (the Treaty of Waitangi) is the 'founding document' of Aotearoa, signed by representatives of the British Crown and a number of Māori iwi on 6 February 1840. This upholding of mātauranga Māori pervades even our style: Māori terms are not italicised because they are not foreign words in Aotearoa, where te reo Māori is the founding Indigenous language.

4 Wystan Curnow, 'The Seventies: Have they reached their use-by date?', in *The Critic's Part: Wystan Curnow art writings 1971–2013*, edited by Christina Barton, Robert Leonard and Thomasin Sleigh (Wellington/Brisbane: Te Pātaka Toi Adam Art Gallery, Institute of Modern Art and Victoria University Press, 2014), 411.

5 Christina Barton, Tyler Cann and Mercedes Vicente, eds, *Points of Contact: Jim Allen, Len Lye, Hélio Oiticica*, exhibition catalogue (New Plymouth/Wellington: Govett-Brewster Art Gallery and Te Pātaka Toi Adam Art Gallery, 2012), 34.

6 Ibid. From Scratch gave their first public performance at the inaugural Sonic Circus festival at Victoria University of Wellington in 1974. Jim Allen suggests there was a previous performance at Elam. Phil Dadson recalls a previous semi-public From Scratch performance outdoors at the Old Government House, University of Auckland, as part of a university festival. Phil Dadson, email conversation with Christopher Braddock, 8 December 2023.

7 Barton et al., *Points of Contact*, 34.

8 Phil Dadson, email conversation with Christopher Braddock, 10 October 2023.

9 Ibid.

10 Toni Lochead performed other activities such as bailing the sea back with a bucket. See https://tonicara11.wordpress.com/2023/06/12/final-presentation-of-time-at-hand

11 Allen Curnow's poem 'The Loop in Lone Kauri Road' (1983–85) takes its name from the road where the Curnow family built their house. Andrew Clifford, 'Essays & Articles: The loop in Lone Kauri Road', University of Auckland Art Collection.

12 The poem was first published in book form in *Early Days Yet: New and collected poems 1941–1997* (Auckland: Auckland University Press, 1997). Peter Simpson, 'Contraries in Two Late Poems by Allen Curnow: "A Busy Port" and "Looking West, Late Afternoon, Low Water"', *Journal of New Zealand Literature* 37.2 (2019): 103–12.

13 Robert Leonard, 'Curnow's Leverage', in *The Critic's Part*, 1.

14 Wystan Curnow, 'Auckland: The first 100 years', *New Zealand Listener* (26 April 1971): 7.

15 The term is often applied to art of 1970s Aotearoa that explored an alliance between conceptual art, sculpture, installation, video and performance art, and which invested in transdisciplinary approaches, conscious of how time and space could be activated. Curnow gives post-object a wide berth as another name for new conceptual-art media (Curnow, 'The Seventies: Have they reached their use-by date?'). See also Christina Barton, 'Post-Object Art in New Zealand 1969–1979: Experiments in art and life' (Master's thesis, University of Auckland, 1987).

16 Curnow, 'Writing and the Post-Object', in *The Critic's Part*, 371; see also Leonard, 'Curnow's Leverage'.

17 Curnow, 'Author's Acknowledgment', in *The Critic's Part*.

18 Curnow, 'Writing and the Post-Object', 371; Leonard,

'Curnow's Leverage', 3.

19 Chris Nixon and John Yeabsley, 'Overseas Trade Policy: New Zealand, Britain and the EEC', *Te Ara — The Encyclopedia of New Zealand*, https://teara.govt.nz/en/overseas-trade-policy/page-4
20 *The Rainbow Warrior Affair*, TVNZ, 1986.
21 Natasha Conland, email conversation with Christopher Braddock, 9 December 2023.
22 SOUNZ: Centre for New Zealand Music, *Pacific 3, 2, 1, Zero*, https://sounz.org.nz/works/10955
23 'Ko Taku Toa Takitini | Finding Strength in the Collective', Auckland Art Gallery, 5 December 2020. www.aucklandartgallery.com/whats-on/exhibition/ko-taku-toa-takitini-finding-strength-in-the-collective
24 Jonathan Mane-Wheoki, 'Contemporary Māori Art — Ngā Toi Hōu: New developments in contemporary art: Interview with Māori artists and writers, 1973', *Te Ara — The Encyclopedia of New Zealand*, 2014, https://teara.govt.nz/en/video/45366/interview-with-maori-artists-and-writers-1973
25 Curnow, 'Writing and the Post-Object', 373.
26 Ibid., 378.
27 Leonard, 'Curnow's Leverage', 4.
28 Curnow, 'Writing and the Post-Object', 376.
29 Wystan Curnow, 'Postmodernism in Poetry and the Visual Arts', in *The Critic's Part*, 149; see also Christina Barton, 'Notes on Method', in *The Critics Part*, 14. Emphasis in the original.
30 Rosalind E. Krauss, *Passages in Modern Sculpture* (New York: The Viking Press, 1977), 201–03, 236–40, 295 n. 201. See also Yve-Alain Bois et al., *Art Since 1900: Modernism, anti-modernism and postmodernism* (New York: Thames and Hudson, 2004), 493.
31 Jennifer Hay, 'Trans-Marginal: New Zealand performance art 1970–1985', in *Intervention: Post object and performance art in New Zealand in 1970 and beyond*, edited by Jennifer Hay (Christchurch: Robert McDougall Art Gallery and Annex, 2002), 24; Victoria Wynne-Jones, 'Occasions & Situations for Seeing: Auckland's avant-garde 1971–1979', *Art New Zealand* 169 (Autumn 2019): 84.
32 Charlotte Huddleston, 'A Little Knowledge Let Loose on an Untrained Mind: Jim Allen as educator', *Reading Room: A Journal of Art and Culture* 6, 'Elective Proximities' (2013): 159.
33 See the collaboration between Artspace Aotearoa and Starkwhite Gallery, both in Tāmaki Makaurau, including the *For Pink Pussycat Club* exhibition that featured two photographs documenting Fiona Clark's 1973 performance at the Pink Pussycat Club. Starkwhite, 'Exhibitions: Fiona Clark | For Pink Pussycat Club as part of THE BILL 20.02.16–22.04.16', www.starkwhite.co.nz/exhibition/for-pink-pussycat-club-as-part-of-the-bill
34 Fiona Clark's comments were transcribed by Christopher Braddock at the 'Out of Time' panel discussion, Auckland Art Gallery Toi o Tāmaki, 31 March 2019.
35 As Natasha Conland points out, there is a growth in film and photo media works at this time, by the likes of Merata Mita (1942–2010), Barry Barclay (1944–2008), Phil Dadson and Leon Narbey, to meet the needs of our most political decade. Natasha Conland, email conversation with Christopher Braddock, 9 December 2023.
36 Christina Barton, 'Photographic Representation and Cross-Cultural Practice: The legacy of the 1970s' (unpublished paper, AAANZ Conference, Sydney, 2002), 1.
37 As Christina Barton notes, *Te Matakite o Aotearoa* 'was made under the aegis of the film company Steven and Dadson had formed in 1973, SeeHear Films, with funding from Nga Tamatoa, the Polynesian Panthers, the World Council of Churches, TV2 and the QEII Arts Council. Subsequently screened on TV2, it provided a coherent summary of the progress of the march and an insider's view that complemented the extensive daily, media coverage.' Ibid., 4.
38 Ibid., 2.
39 Amelia Jones, *Body Art/Performing the Subject* (Minneapolis: University of Minnesota Press, 1998), 9.
40 Barton, 'Photographic Representation and Cross-Cultural Practice', 4.
41 Ibid., 5 n. 2.
42 Allan Smith, 'Mapping Imperatives: Putting the land on the map at the Govett-Brewster Art Gallery', *Art New Zealand* 52 (Spring 1989): 78. Smith's quote was referenced by Jennifer Hay in her lead catalogue essay for *Intervention: Post object and performance art in New Zealand in 1970 and beyond* at the Robert McDougall Art Gallery & Annex, Christchurch, in 2000, on page 8. Note that the title of the video documentation is incorrect in the *Intervention* catalogue, where it states: *Dedicated To Peaceful Celebration of Planet Earth and Universe 18:00 Hours GMT 23/24 September 1971.*
43 *EQUINOX_1:03PM NZST_23-9-22* was curated by Chris Braddock, Eamon Edmundson-Wells and Ziggy Lever.
44 Chris Braddock with Balamohan Shingade, Layne Waerea and guests, *Conversation Mat*, 2022, cotton, wadding and scheduled activations, 3.08 x 9.8 metres.
45 Paul Ardenne, 'The Art Market in the 1980s', *International Journal of Political Economy* 25, no. 2 (1995): 125.
46 Peter C. T. Elsworth, 'The Art Boom: Is it over, or is this just a correction?', *New York Times*, 16 December 1990, www.nytimes.com/1990/12/16/business/the-art-boom-is-it-over-or-is-this-just-a-correction.html
47 Ardenne, 'The Art Market in the 1980s', 110.
48 Ibid.
49 A little later, in the 1990s, as Briar Williams notes, collector Jenny Gibbs bought Colin McCahon's painting *I Considered All the Acts of Oppression* from Webb's auction house for a record $503,000. Briar Williams, 'Controversy and Growth: The Auckland art scene in the 1990s', *BusinessDesk*, 5 June 2022, https://businessdesk.co.nz/article/the-life/controversy-and-growth-the-auckland-art-scene-in-the-1990s
50 Ardenne, 'The Art Market in the 1980s', 102.
51 Natasha Conland, *Art News* 198 (Winter 2023): 98.
52 Curnow, 'The Seventies', 414–15.
53 See *Night Piece* (2023), 'Part One', a documentary by Bridget Sutherland co-produced with Stuart Page. Faraway Films.
54 As reported by Curnow in the context of Roche's performance at Elam in 1979 titled *Get the Fuck Out*. Curnow, 'The Seventies', 412.
55 If anything, we detect a hiatus in performance art practices between 1985 and 1991, the year Interdigitate was founded by Phil Dadson (discussed by Andrew Clifford and Rachel Shearer in Chapter 6). The intense partnership between Peter Roche and Linda Buis had ended, and many of the women performance artists discussed by Melanie Oliver in Chapter 4 transferred lessons learned from performance into sculpture, photography and moving image artworks, especially with regards to deconstructing image and text.
56 Dan Taulapapa McMullin, 'The Acti.VA.tions of Rosanna Raymond', *Artlink*, 1 June 2017, www.artlink.com.au/articles/4603/the-activations-of-rosanna-raymond
57 Ioana Gordon-Smith, 'From the Margins to the Mainstream: Pacific Sisters at Te Papa', *The Pantograph Punch*, 18 April 2018, https://pantograph-punch.com/posts/pacific-sisters
58 Paul Spoonley, 'Ethnic and Religious Intolerance: Intolerance towards Pacific migrants', *Te Ara — The Encyclopedia of New Zealand*, https://teara.govt.nz/en/ethnic-and-religious-intolerance/page-4

59 Albert Wendt, 'Tatauing the Post-Colonial Body', *Span* 42–43 (April–October 1996): 15–29.

60 Caroline Vercoe, *John Ioane: Fale Sā*, exhibition catalogue (Auckland: Auckland Art Gallery Toi o Tāmaki, 1999). See also Caroline Vercoe, 'Art Niu Sila: Contemporary Pacific art in New Zealand', in *Pacific Art Niu Sila: The Pacific dimension of contemporary New Zealand arts*, edited by Sean Mallon and Pandora Fulimalo Pereira (Wellington: Te Papa Press, 2002), 191–207; Christopher Braddock, Ioana Gordon-Smith, Layne Waerea and Victoria Wynne-Jones, 'Aotearoa New Zealand Performance Art 1970–2020', in *The Routledge Companion to Performance Art*, edited by Jennie Klein, Natalie Loveless, Lucian O'Connor and Graciela Ovejero Postigo (Abingdon, UK: Routledge, forthcoming).

61 Gordon-Smith, 'From the Margins to the Mainstream'.

62 Spoonley, 'Ethnic and Religious Intolerance'.

63 Rosanna Raymond, 'A Walk Through My Eyelands,' *The Pantograph Punch*, 20 November 2020, www.pantograph-punch.com/posts/walk-through-my-eyelands

64 Ane Tonga, 'Lonnie Hutchinson: Black Out', Tautau Contemporary Pacific Arts Trust newsletter, December 2014. See also Ane Tonga, ed., *Declaration: A Pacific feminist agenda*, exhibition catalogue (Auckland: Auckland Art Gallery Toi o Tāmaki, 2022), 174–77.

65 www.beehive.govt.nz/release/government-announces-major-investment-arts-culture-and-heritage

66 It is also worth noting how artist-run spaces provided performance art opportunities in the late 1990s and the first decade of the 2000s for artists like Luke Willis Thompson, Simon Denny, Kate Newby and many more. In 1996 and 1997, three artist-run spaces opened: Fiat Lux and Rm3 in Tāmaki Makaurau, and The Honeymoon Suite in Ōtepoti. In 2000 Enjoy opened in Te Whanganui-a-Tara. Gambia Castle opened in 2007, and later Newcall, both in Tāmaki Makaurau. See Emma Bugden, 'A Brief History of Artist-Run Spaces in Aotearoa', https://citygallery.org.nz/blog/a-brief-history-of-artist-run-spaces-in-aotearoa

67 For further discussion, see Christopher Braddock, *Performing Contagious Bodies: Ritual participation in contemporary art* (London: Palgrave Macmillan, 2013), 17–18.

68 Amelia Jones and Christopher Braddock, 'Animacies and Performativity', in *Animism in Art and Performance*, edited by Christopher Braddock (London: Palgrave Macmillan, 2017), 177–90. These artworks included and discussed by Jones in the exhibition *Material Traces: Time and the Gesture* were: Christopher Braddock, *Above* (2007) and *Take Series* (2007); Alicia Frankovich, *The Opportune Spectator* (2013); and Paul Donald, *Would Work* (2011).

69 Ibid., 184.

70 Amelia Jones, *Self/Image: Technology, representation, and the contemporary subject* (London/New York: Routledge, 2006), xvii.

71 Braddock, *Performing Contagious Bodies*, 129–51. This artwork by Richard Maloy was exhibited in *Made Active*, Auckland Art Gallery Toi o Tāmaki, in 2012.

72 For further discussion about live performance and its documentation as trace, see Jones, *Self/Image*, 24, 128.

73 Philip Auslander, 'The Performativity of Performance Documentation', *PAJ: A Journal of Performance and Art* 28, no. 3 (September 2006): 3.

74 Victoria Wynne-Jones, *Choreographing intersubjectivity in performance art*, New World Choreographies (Cham: Palgrave Macmillan, 2021), 111–13, 235.

75 The Art and Performance Research Group is co-led by Chris Braddock, Janine Randerson and Layne Waerea. See https://artandperformance.wordpress.com

76 Other artists who contributed to the Art and Performance Research Group include Cora-Allan Lafaiki Twiss, Olivia Webb, Ziggy Lever, Louise Tu'u, Bobby Campbell Luke, Lance Pearce, Deborah Rundle, Amber Pearson, Josh Rutter, Ammon Ngakuru, Azadeh Emadi, Anthony Cribb, Ruth Myers, Ryder Jones, Elliot Collins, Julia Holderness, Narjis Mirza, Clare Fleming, Shelley Simpson, Emil Scheffmann Dryburgh, Sophie Sutherland, Liam Mooney and writer Abby Cunnane.

77 Phil Dadson, email conversation with Christopher Braddock, 10 October 2023.

78 As mentioned above, the name of Wystan Curnow's curated exhibition in 1989 at the Govett-Brewster Art Gallery.

79 For detailed discussion of these terms and their relationship to performance art, see Chapter 10 of this volume by Layne Waerea and Lana Lopesi.

REFERENCES

Allen, Jim and Wystan Curnow, eds. *New Art: Some recent New Zealand Sculpture and post-object art*. Auckland: Heinemann, 1976.

Ardenne, Paul. 'The Art Market in the 1980s'. *International Journal of Political Economy* 25, no. 2 (1995): 100–28.

Auckland Art Gallery. 'Ko Taku Toa Takitini | Finding Strength in the Collective'. 5 December 2020. www.aucklandartgallery.com/whats-on/exhibition/ko-taku-toa-takitini-finding-strength-in-the-collective

Auslander, Philip. 'The Performativity of Performance Documentation'. *PAJ: A Journal of Performance and Art* 28, no. 3 (September 2006): 1–10, 4–5.

Barber, Bruce, Blair French, Tony Green, Nicholas Spill and Jennifer Hay. *Intervention: Post object and performance art in New Zealand in 1970 and beyond*. Exhibition catalogue. Christchurch: Robert McDougall Art Gallery and Annex, 2002.

Barton, Christina. 'Photographic Representation and Cross-Cultural Practice: The legacy of the 1970s'. Unpublished paper. Art Association of Australia and New Zealand Conference, Sydney, 2002, 1.

——— 'Post-Object Art in New Zealand 1969–1979: Experiments in art and life'. Master's thesis, University of Auckland, 1987. http://hdl.handle.net/2292/17035

Barton, Christina, Tyler Cann and Mercedes Vicente, eds. *Points of Contact: Jim Allen, Len Lye, Hélio Oiticica*. Exhibition catalogue. New Plymouth and Wellington: Govett-Brewster Art Gallery and Te Pātaka Toi Adam Art Gallery, 2012.

Bois, Yve-Alain, Benjamin H. D. Buchloh, Hal Foster and Rosalind E. Krauss. *Art Since 1900: Modernism, anti-modernism and postmodernism*. New York: Thames & Hudson, 2004.

Braddock, Christopher. *Performing Contagious Bodies: Ritual Participation in contemporary art*. London: Palgrave Macmillan, 2013.

Braddock, Christopher, Ioana Gordon-Smith, Layne Waerea and Victoria Wynne-Jones. 'Aotearoa New Zealand Performance Art 1970–2020'. In *The Routledge Companion to Performance Art*, edited by Jennie Klein, Natalie Loveless, Lucian O'Connor and Graciela Ovejero Postigo. Abingdon, UK: Routledge, forthcoming.

Clifford, Andrew. 'Essays & Articles: The loop in Lone Kauri Road'. University of Auckland Art Collection. https://artcollection.auckland.ac.nz/essay/69339

Conland, Natasha. 'Peter Roche & Linda Buis'. *Art News* 198 (Winter 2023): 98.

Curnow, Wystan. 'Auckland: The first 100 years'. *New Zealand Listener* (26 April 1971): 7–8.

——— *The Critic's Part: Wystan Curnow art writings*

1971–2013, edited by Christina Barton, Robert Leonard and Thomasin Sleigh. Wellington/Brisbane: Te Pātaka Toi Adam Art Gallery, Institute of Modern Art and Victoria University Press, 2014.

Elsworth, Peter C. T. 'The Art Boom: Is it over, or is this just a correction?'. *New York Times*, 16 December 1990. www.nytimes.com/1990/12/16/business/the-art-boom-is-it-over-or-is-this-just-a-correction.html

Gordon-Smith, Ioana. 'From the Margins to the Mainstream: Pacific Sisters at Te Papa'. *The Pantograph Punch*, 18 April 2018. https://pantograph-punch.com/posts/pacific-sisters

Hay, Jennifer. 'Trans-Marginal: New Zealand performance art 1970–1985'. In *Intervention: Post object and performance art in New Zealand in 1970 and beyond*, edited by Jennifer Hay, 24. Christchurch: Robert McDougall Art Gallery and Annex, 2002.

Huaman, Elizabeth Sumida. 'How Indigenous Scholarship Changes the Field: Pluriversal appreciation, decolonial aspirations, and comparative indigenous education'. *Comparative Education Review* 66, no. 3 (August 2022): 391–416. https://doi.org/10.1086/720442

Huddleston, Charlotte. 'A Little Knowledge Let Loose on an Untrained Mind: Jim Allen as educator'. *Reading Room: A Journal of Art and Culture* 6, 'Elective Proximities' (2013): 158–66.

Jones, Amelia. *Body Art/Performing the Subject*. Minneapolis: University of Minnesota Press, 1998.

——— *Self/Image: Technology, representation, and the contemporary subject*. London/New York: Routledge, 2006.

Jones, Amelia and Christopher Braddock. 'Animacies and Performativity'. In *Animism in Art and Performance*, edited by Christopher Braddock, 177–90. London: Palgrave Macmillan, 2017.

Krauss, Rosalind E. *Passages in Modern Sculpture*. New York: The Viking Press, 1977.

Leonard, Robert. 'Review of Hamish Keith "The Big Picture": A history of New Zealand art from 1642'. *Australian and New Zealand Journal of Art* 9, no. 1–2 (2008): 251–55.

——— 'Curnow's Leverage'. In *The Critic's Part: Wystan Curnow art writings 1971–2013*, edited by Christina Barton, Robert Leonard and Thomasin Sleigh, 1. Wellington/Brisbane: Te Pātaka Toi Adam Art Gallery, Institute of Modern Art and Victoria University Press, 2014.

Mane-Wheoki, Jonathan. 'Contemporary Māori Art — Ngā Toi Hōu: New developments in contemporary art: Interview with Māori artists and writers, 1973'. *Te Ara — The Encyclopedia of New Zealand*, 2014. https://teara.govt.nz/en/video/45366/interview-with-maori-artists-and-writers-1973

McMullin, Dan Taulapapa. 'The Acti.VA.tions of Rosanna Raymond'. *Artlink*, 1 June 2017. www.artlink.com.au/articles/4603/the-activations-of-rosanna-raymond

Nixon, Chris and John Yeabsley. 'Overseas Trade Policy — New Zealand, Britain and the EEC'. *Te Ara — The Encyclopedia of New Zealand*, 2010. https://teara.govt.nz/en/overseas-trade-policy/page-4

Raymond, Rosanna. 'A Walk Through My Eyelands'. *The Pantograph Punch*, 20 November 2020. www.pantograph-punch.com/posts/walk-through-my-eyelands

Simpson, Peter. 'Contraries in Two Late Poems by Allen Curnow: "A Busy Port" and "Looking West, Late Afternoon, Low Water"'. *Journal of New Zealand Literature* 37.2 (2019): 103–12.

Smith, Allan. 'Mapping Imperatives: Putting the land on the map at the Govett-Brewster Art Gallery'. *Art New Zealand* 52 (Spring 1989): 78.

SOUNZ: Centre for New Zealand Music. *Pacific 3, 2, 1, Zero*. https://sounz.org.nz/works/10955

Spoonley, Paul. 'Ethnic and Religious Intolerance: Intolerance towards Pacific migrants'. *Te Ara — The Encyclopedia of New Zealand*. https://teara.govt.nz/en/ethnic-and-religious-intolerance/page-4

Starkwhite. 'Exhibitions: Fiona Clark | For Pink Pussycat Club as part of THE BILL 20.02.16–22.04.16'. www.starkwhite.co.nz/exhibition/for-pink-pussycat-club-as-part-of-the-bill

The Rainbow Warrior Affair. TVNZ, 1986.

Tonga, Ane, ed. *Declaration: A Pacific feminist agenda*. Exhibition catalogue. Auckland: Auckland Art Gallery Toi o Tāmaki, 2022.

——— 'Lonnie Hutchinson: Black out'. *Tautau Contemporary Pacific Arts Trust*, December 2014.

Vercoe, Caroline. 'Art Niu Sila: Contemporary Pacific art in New Zealand'. In *Pacific Art Niu Sila: The Pacific dimension of contemporary New Zealand arts*, edited by Sean Mallon and Pandora Fulimalo Pereira, 191–207. Wellington: Te Papa Press, 2002.

——— *John Ioane: Fale Sā*. Exhibition catalogue. Auckland: Auckland Art Gallery Toi o Tāmaki, 1999.

Wendt, Albert. 'Tatauing the Post-Colonial Body'. *Span* 42–43 (October 1996): 15–29.

Williams, Briar. 'Controversy and Growth: The Auckland art scene in the 1990s'. *BusinessDesk*, 5 June 2022. https://businessdesk.co.nz/article/the-life/controversy-and-growth-the-auckland-art-scene-in-the-1990s

Wynne-Jones, Victoria. *Choreographing Intersubjectivity in Performance Art*. New World Choreographies. Cham: Palgrave Macmillan, 2021.

——— 'Occasions & Situations for Seeing: Auckland's avant-garde 1971–1979'. *Art New Zealand* 169 (Autumn 2019): 80–85.

1

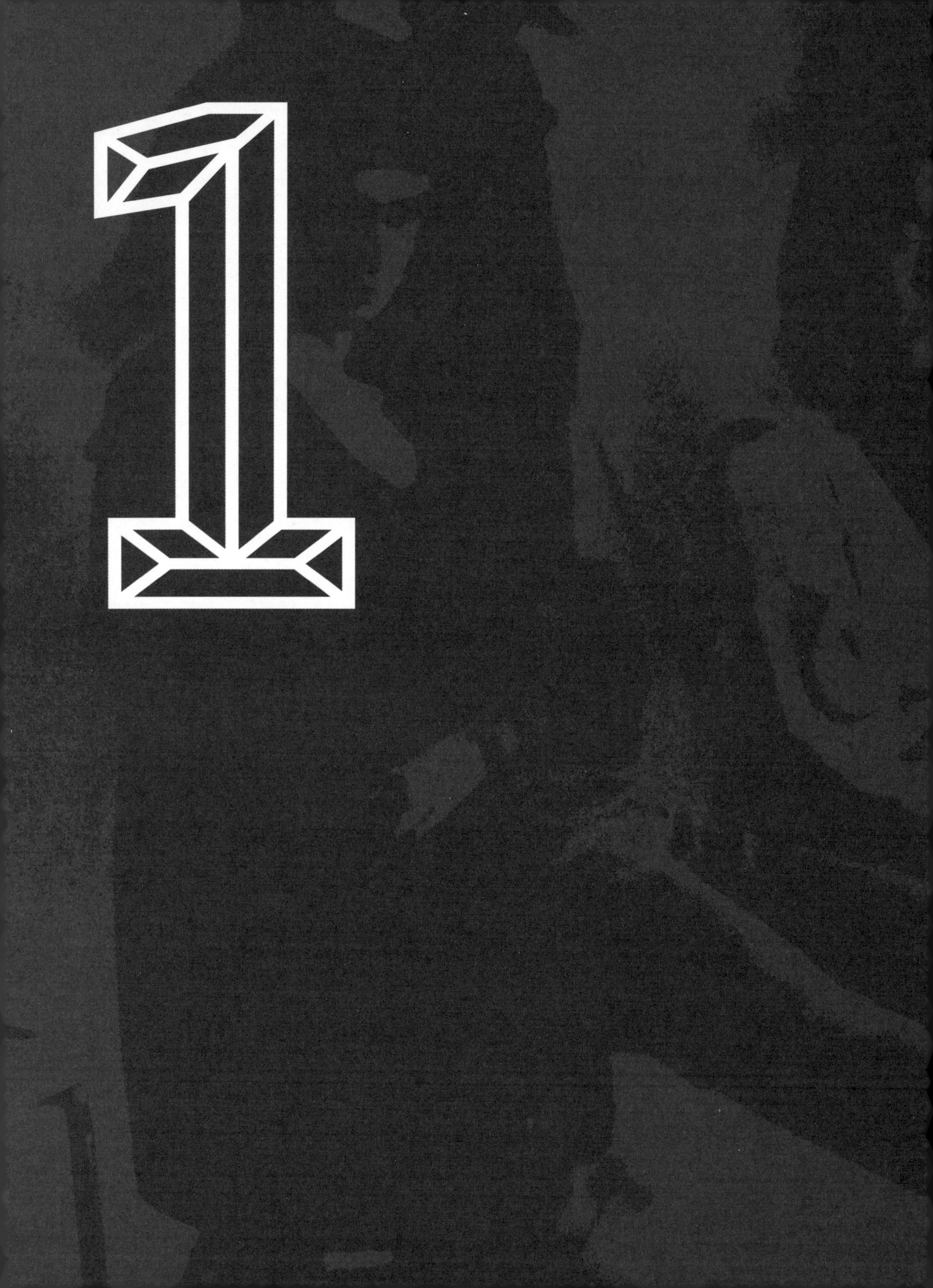

A PLACE, A QUESTION, A CHALLENGE, A CALL TO ACTION: PERFORMANCE IN THE 1970s

Blair French

On a midwinter's Sunday night in 1973, artist Bruce Barber performed his work *Bucket Action* at Kerikeri Memorial Hall for the first time (and later at Auckland City Art Gallery in 1974). The work began with Barber and an assistant[1] positioning ten galvanised iron buckets in two rows according to an instructional drawing prepared by the artist. The pair created parallel barriers by placing one long bamboo pole and two lengths of galvanised iron pipe on wooden trestles. On the floor they fixed lines of masking tape connecting the buckets in a zigzag pattern and traversing an area roughly 9 x 3.5 metres. They placed two dead fish on the floor.

With the performance area established and the audience gathered at its sides, the artist, clad in a wetsuit, picked up the two fish, placed them in the first bucket — the only one filled with water — then carried this along the first line of masking tape to the second bucket. As the work instructions detailed, 'Contents of Bucket A [were] then poured into Bucket B.'[2] A tape recorder played the phrase 'a fish out of water'. The assistant then placed a hood and the first bucket over the head of the artist.[3]

Deprived of visual orientation, the artist proceeded to feel his way along the masking tape pathway with the bucket of water and fish, navigating the barriers on the way. He tipped the water and fish into the next waiting bucket and took this with him, leaving the now empty one in its place. Barber repeated this action back and forth along the rows of buckets until the recorded phrase 'like water off a duck's back' marked the end of the performance.[4]

This exercise was both directed and necessarily improvisational — an experiment in performing basic tasks in a state of sensory deprivation.

Bucket Action is thoroughly documented in the 1976 book *New Art: Some recent New Zealand sculpture and post-object art* (1976), edited by artist Jim Allen and art critic Wystan Curnow. It includes the diagrammatic plan for the work in both handwritten and printed form, and the artist's descriptions of 'form', 'materials' and 'procedure'. Bryony Dalefield's photographic documentation of the work is represented through a page of gridded contact strips that convey something of the unfolding of the performance, as do seven larger photographs, and there is a transcript of a discussion between the artist and his colleagues, Allen, Kieran Lyons and psychologist Guy von Sturmer, as they reflect on the work soon after the Kerikeri performance.

This careful attention to substantive documentation is typical of performance art in the 1970s. Video (on occasion) and, more commonly, performance instructions, still photographs, participant and audience accounts and critical reviews provide the basis for art-historical analysis of performance art of the period. Artists, largely informed of international practices through documentation, created records that would assist both contemporaneous and historical contextualisation of their work. In recording an important moment in local art practice — self-consciously staking a claim for the 'new' as it was still playing out — *New Art* played a critical role in introducing subsequent generations to performance art in the 1970s.

When I first read about *Bucket Action* in *New Art* in the 1980s, the work appeared to me oddly deadpan and resolutely serious.[5] The discussion transcript conveyed something of the acute experience of the artist concentrating on tactility and sound to orient and guide himself through self-prescribed tasks, all the while cognisant of the other presences in the room — the 'passive participants' (audience) whom he came into contact with, literally, as he moved through the work. The shuffling of feet and hands feeling their way across the floor. An arm stretched out to test the position of a barrier. Water slopping and the faint smell of fish. The clanking buckets and creaking (and apparently ill-fitting) wetsuit. Fidgeting bodies,

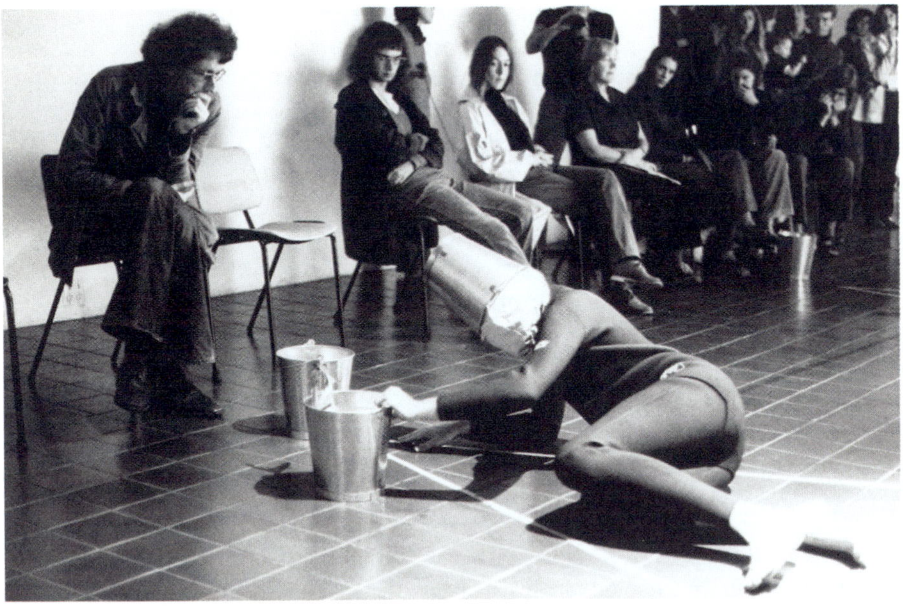

Bruce Barber, *Bucket Action Still*, documentation of performance, 1974, black and white photograph. *Chartwell Collection, Auckland Art Gallery Toi o Tāmaki, gift of Samuel Holloway and Michael Lett, 2023. Photo by Bryony Dalefield*

even tentative titters as Barber occasionally bumped into an audience member. All of this I could and still can only imagine and indeed fabricate — even when informed by footage and artist or audience accounts.[6]

Bucket Action was not necessarily the most significant work of performance art of the period, nor was it the first. It is, however, emblematic of practices that emerged from and in relation to the transformative context of the sculpture programme at Elam School of Fine Arts (Elam) at the University of Auckland under the leadership of Jim Allen from 1969 to 1976.[7]

POST-OBJECT ART

Although significant work was presented at different moments across the country, this chapter focuses largely on work in Tāmaki Makaurau Auckland, which orbited the sculpture department at Elam under Allen's leadership — a central focus also of the exhibition and performance programme *Groundswell: Avant-garde Auckland 1971–79* curated by Natasha Conland for Auckland Art Gallery Toi o Tāmaki (8 December 2018–31 March 2019).[8]

Here I consider aspects of the work of artist and musician Phil Dadson and, to a lesser extent, that of Allen, both of whom are considered in more detail in other chapters within this volume. A central figure in 1970s practice in Aotearoa New Zealand until his departure for Canada in 1976, Bruce Barber also features prominently in my discussion, and I note Andrew Drummond's early work, along with that of Peter Roche and Linda Buis. I examine work by Kimberley Gray and Gray Nicol, both closely associated with Elam, and also reference performance works by David Mealing and Nicholas Spill.[9]

This period in art history has been documented and discussed by significant writers, including Curnow and Tony Green, in contemporaneous publications such as *Spleen*, *Parallax*, *Auckland Art Gallery Quarterly*, the *New Zealand Listener* and *New Art*.

It has also been the focus of subsequent academic and curatorial reviews.[10] These include Christina Barton's 1987 master's thesis; the *Action Replay: Post-object art* exhibition series at Artspace Aotearoa, Govett-Brewster Art Gallery and Auckland Art Gallery Toi o Tāmaki 1998–99;[11] the exhibition *Intervention: Post object and performance art in New Zealand in 1970 and beyond* at the Robert McDougall Art Gallery and Annex, Ōtautahi Christchurch, in 2000, and its associated *Symposium 2000* conference;[12] and the more recent *Groundswell: Avant-garde Auckland 1971–79*.

Histories of the period generally refer to 'post-object' art, a dominant tendency within art of the time to move beyond or to elide a notion of art wedded to the production of an autonomous and unique material form. Modernism had traditionally privileged the art object independent from social context. The material products of modernism were autonomous, precious, tradeable. Internationally, through the 1960s this ontological bedrock of 'art' had been increasingly pressured from within by ephemeral and/or overtly spectator-orientated practices — by happenings, actions, minimalism and concept art — and externally by political and social movements that revealed the fallacies of both artistic autonomy and authentic, individuated artistic subjectivity.

Post-object art in Aotearoa was a localised manifestation of this move from commodity and representational imperatives to art practices that generated meaning in forms of relationship.[13] Sculptural objects were framed within installation and environment paradigms that highlighted the perceptual agency of the viewer, and in effect created performative situations for viewing. Performance art emerged both as an inquisitive practice of procedural activity in which performers were active respondents to the environments around them, and in relation to forms of social action such as gatherings and protests. Performance was often a strategic mobilisation of bodies (whether spontaneous or choreographed) in the public domain.[14]

THE AUCKLAND SCENE

In the late 1960s and early 1970s there was a radical proliferation of modes of art investigation and practice in Aotearoa, particularly in Tāmaki Makaurau.[15] Jim Allen recalled how work by Elam sculpture students during the latter part of the 1960s began to respond to increasingly open forms of interdisciplinary teaching and manifested a growing interest in propositional forms of spatial engagement and site-specificity.[16]

The creative energy in the Elam sculpture department accelerated following Allen's return in 1968 from his sabbatical sojourn in Europe, the United Kingdom and the United States. Allen led a number of key initiatives. First was the development of a contemporary art library at Elam.[17] Then came a visiting artist programme, initiated by Allen, which brought a range of artists working in conceptual and performance practices, such as Adrian Hall and Kieran Lyons, to Tāmaki Makaurau.[18]

There was the instigation of critical response and discussion sessions between staff and students that both fostered and demanded a culture of intellectual rigour, integrity and trust. And, finally, priority was given to creating opportunities for artists to present work publicly, as well as encouraging and supporting them to take their work overseas, initially to Australia for the Mildura Sculpture Triennials of 1973 and 1975.

Artworks from the department often borrowed from other artistic forms such as theatre, architecture, music, cinema and photography; they had strong associations with other academic disciplines, too, such as sociology, political science and psychology.

Sometimes curriculum-based and often with epistemological and pedagogical imperatives (albeit working with a much-expanded understanding of pedagogy within the institution), some of the work of this time can in retrospect sound prescriptive, over-determined, overly academic or 'research-based' (in present-day parlance).

Works often began with the advance delineation of their parameters, whether in terms of physical environment, structural plan, instruction to action, linguistic or numerical coordinates or permutations of relationships between set participants. A proposition — a question, a challenge or a call to action — was frequently posited within these parameters. Within the activity or action of the work itself, a testing of that proposition often took place via concurrent processes of pragmatic problem-solving, deduction and intuitive exploration. Many works were subjected to close retrospective analysis and reflection by artists, critics and participants and functioned as occasions for idea exploration and generation, amplified through this process and occasionally documented in texts.[19]

Elam and the University of Auckland were not the only important sites of activity in Tāmaki Makaurau at this time, however. Barry Lett Galleries played a critical role in supporting experimental practice that ran parallel to performance. Auckland City Art Gallery hosted the *Four Men in a Boat* projects, which included major performance works by Allen and Barber along with works by Phil Dadson and Kieran Lyons for the 1974 Auckland Festival, followed by the first set of solo-artist contemporary *Project Programme* exhibitions at Auckland City Art Gallery in 1975.[20]

There were numerous activities in public sites around the city and its environs, including Bledisloe Square, Whatipu Beach, Maungawhau Mount Eden, Epsom Showgrounds, Albert Park and, in the case of Elam student Matthew McLean's 1974 untitled night-time performance, amidst the throng of passers-by on Queen Street outside the St James Theatre.[21]

In Aotearoa, performance art practice emerged in the early 1970s within broader contexts of social and political activism. Although many works were interventionist, challenging or disruptive in form and action, it would be difficult to ascribe a driving ideological imperative. A number of outdoor works addressed environmental and ecological issues, and others contained an infusion of anti-war sentiment. However, with the exception of the work of David Mealing in particular (discussed below), overt engagement with urgent political imperatives of the time and the forms of social mobilisation that took place in response to them are difficult to ascertain in the work itself.

In the first half of the decade in particular, there was little explicit engagement with drives towards social change that were occurring at the time, such as Māori land rights and sovereignty movements, anti-racism and anti-apartheid campaigns, the feminist movement, protests against the Vietnam War or the anti-nuclear movement. Rather, the key linking element across works was a sense of inventive possibility identified within the making of performance itself anew in each action.

Notwithstanding the underpinning of a communal, reciprocal approach to education (fostered in part through Allen's experience of teaching during the 1950s in primary schools in Māori communities in the Far North) and a prevailing attitude of collective action as artists assisted each other, this sense of reflective remaking points also to an individualism underpinning the practice.[22]

Ian Hunter, an artist and curator/organiser from the period, is quoted by Jennifer Hay in her 2000 essay 'Trans-Marginal: New Zealand performance art 1970–1985', reflecting on the 1970s as the 'time of the long (white) silence'. In a letter to Hay in February 2000,

Hunter notes, 'I think that many of us in the 1970s were too preoccupied with notions of legitimacy in the international art community and failed to recognise or take up the real challenges and opportunities for cultural dialogue and exchange that awaited us at home.'[23]

With the work of Dadson a notable exception, the collective action or activities of the period do not necessarily correlate to a dominant collective ethos running through the work. From a present-day perspective, shaped by decades of subsequent social and culture change, the predominance of educated Pākehā men as 'authors' of much of this performance work evidences the gendered power dynamics not only of broader social structures but also of those specific institutional forms — in higher education and art — that produced and supported these practices.[24]

PURPOSELESS WORK

Phil Dadson had returned to Elam in 1970 to study in the sculpture department following a visit in 1968–69 to the United Kingdom, where he took part in an experimental music class with Cornelius Cardew that formed the basis of Cardew's improvisational Scratch Orchestra. On his return to Aotearoa, Dadson formed Scratch Orchestra (Antipodean Twig), and From Scratch in 1974. He created rhythmic, musical and spatial compositional structures (or scores) within which performers devised improvisational actions.[25] Scratch Orchestra (Antipodean Twig) on occasion involved more than fifty performers in a work.

In 1971 Dadson's Scratch Orchestra undertook three major activities. These included the first of the annual *Solar Plexus* winter solstice drumming performances, which ran from dawn to dusk in the Maungawhau crater in Tāmaki Makaurau; the multi-part works *Rearrangement for an Orchestra* (1971), where performers were confined within a tiny, cramped space; and *Blood and Bone* (1971), in which performers developed evolving sound actions within a set structure.

Dadson also created *Purposeless Work 1: Beach sweeping* (1971). He gave brooms to a group of participants and instructed them to sweep the shoreline on a West Auckland beach. The instructional 'score' was simple:

> Begin at one 'end' all together
> roughly span the sand's breadth
> brush towards the other 'end'
> Follow your nose
> at your own pace
> as a current
> there is no obligation to finish the distance . . .
> end instead
> when you have finished with sweeping . . .[26]

The work was purposeless in the sense that it was free of any determining intent. Structure and meaning were to be created in the process, with a nod to the relationship of labour to performance in the use of standard council worker brooms.

Dadson's *Car Performance* (1973) was shaped by a more complex score. The 'instruments' were cars, driven around the town of Kerikeri during the same festival at which Barber first performed *Bucket Action*. As Dadson said, 'It was very instruction based — sound making with cars. Everybody had a list of things that they followed:

people jumping out of cars, lifting up bonnets and hooting horns . . . it was slightly crazy.'[27]

Throughout the 1970s, and prior to his departure for Canada in 1976, Barber, like Dadson, produced an array of work across moving image, photographic, sculptural and installation activity, as more than fifteen significant performance artworks.[28] The years 1973 and 1974 (the period of his MFA degree) were particularly prolific. At Elam, Barber produced the performances *Dialogue, Youth in Asia, Lead Performance* and *Two Days* (incorporating *Box and Cox* along with the video works *Handgame* and *A Friend in Need is a Friend Indeed*).[29] He also undertook major outdoor performances (*Whatipu Beach Performance* and *Mt Eden Crater Performance*, both 1973) along with the work *Like a Bat Outta Hell* as part of the 1974 *Pavilion K* performance programme at Epsom Showgrounds.[30]

Often involving multiple participants with set functions, or personae acting within carefully proscribed spatial parameters, Barber's work of this time sought to interrogate conditions and limits of communicative acts, and to highlight unstable relationships between participant and audience, object and subject, embodied experience and cognition, seeing and being seen. *Whatipu Beach Performance* and *Mt Eden Crater Performance* both featured a pivotal 'blind master' figure experiencing a form of sensory deprivation — as in *Bucket Action* — whose actions or passage within the work provided its fulcrum. Barber used technologies of audio and video extensively to reflect upon technological shaping of perceptual experience along with repetition and the idea of journey — both spatial and temporal — accompanied by experiences of discomfort.[31]

Allen, Lyons, Kimberley Gray and Nicholas Spill also presented works at the Epsom Showgrounds in Tāmaki Makaurau. Gray studied in the sculpture department at Elam from 1970 to 1975 and made sculptural, installation and performance works. Christina Barton describes Gray as one of the first women to work with performance in any significant way in Aotearoa. In her 1993 essay 'Performance Art by Women in Aotearoa New Zealand 1974–1993', she describes Gray's *Draughts* from the *Pavilion K* programme:

> Gray paced out a path; marking her passage by stopping at intervals to check the direction of a candle flame which was subsequently extinguished by a draught of cold air from a fan she had located at the end of her journey. Her movements were marked with a trail of cloth she unravelled from around her body, which was revealed to the audience when the lights went on at the end of the performance. With simple gestures and a few readymade props, Gray used her movements to map a territory in both time and space, using the rhythms and structures of the piece to render literal abstract notions like respiration and circulation.[32]

As part of her MFA that same year, Gray made *As Good a Land . . .*, which involved flying in a small aircraft between Tāmaki Makaurau and Te Whanganui-a-Tara Wellington on a route that connected a series of scarecrows placed in the landscape. This work reflected aspects of others by Dadson and Andrew Drummond that were concerned with mapping land and space via different forms of motion and connection.[33]

Nicholas Spill produced a set of works at the showgrounds. *Artists Security Guard* required visitors to the pavilion to wear an ARTISTS SECURITY GUARD badge onsite, which they returned on departure. Spill came from a literary and dramatic background; he participated in and organised happenings but, as he described it, '[backed] into performance art and a conceptual frame of reference through the use of

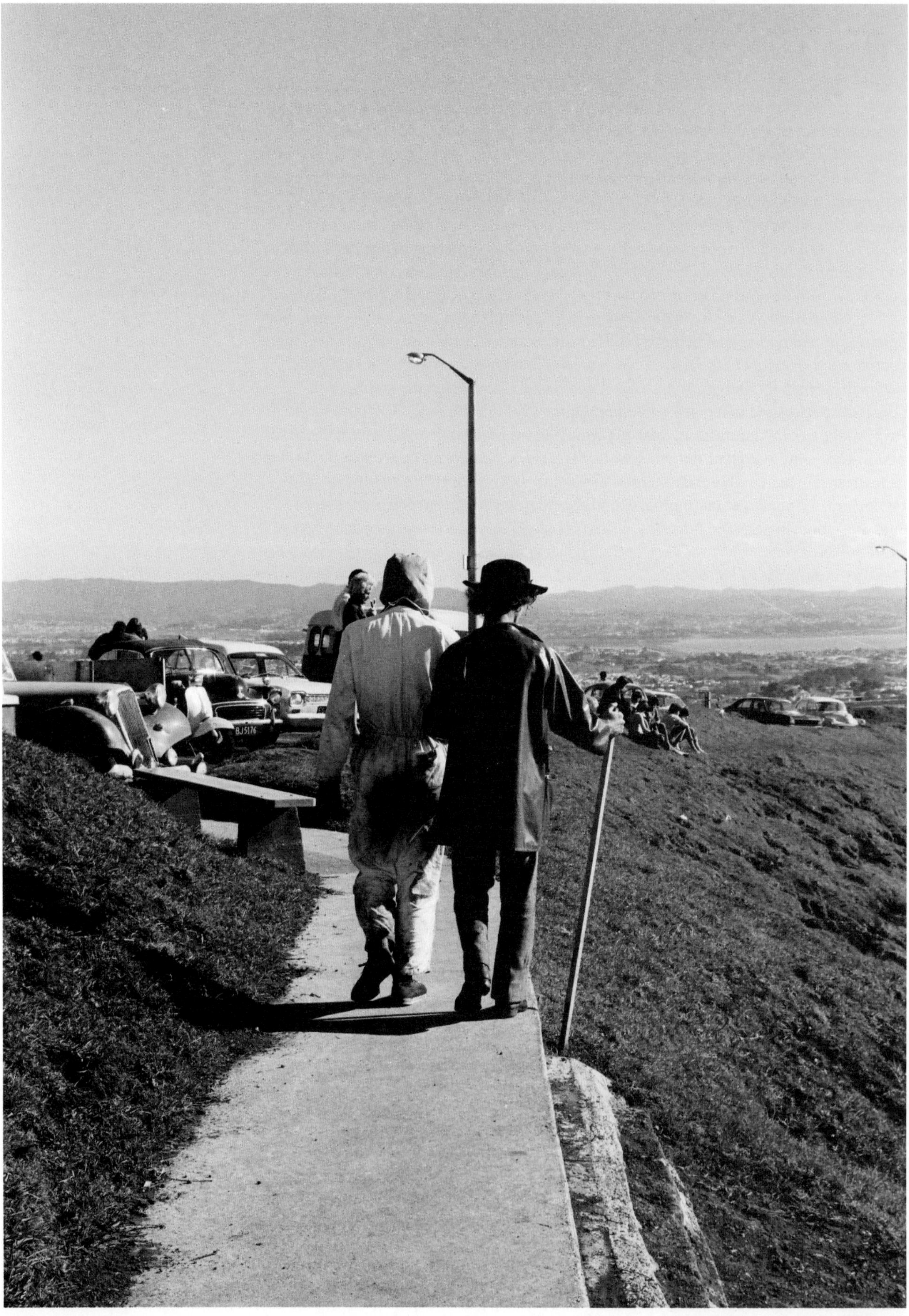
BJ5176

theatre and movement'.[34] His work often operated in a tensile space between language and images, and used puns and humour to undercut social convention — in particular assumptions around identity based in social and labour-determined roles — as well as representational structures.

Spill was a teacher, an exhibition officer at the National Art Gallery from 1976 to 1978, a curator and organiser of artists' events and a central figure in the propagation of Mail Art in Aotearoa. His performance on the steps of the National Art Gallery in Wellington, *Leaving the National Art Gallery Forever* (1978), along with his *Survival* work of the same year at Christchurch Society of the Arts, are early instances of institutional critique within the art of Aotearoa.

In 1976 Spill made two performances in a lecture room at Wellington Teachers' College at the invitation of artist Andrew Drummond. *Whipped Cream* and *Buttering Up an Old Friend* represented the raw emotions of anger and love respectively, and each gave action and embodiment to a form of wordplay. In the first, a male performer (not the artist) clad in a G-string poured cream into a large stainless-steel tray set on a sheet of black plastic on the floor, then proceeded to whip the cream with a bullwhip (borrowed rather remarkably from the National Museum), spraying cream over the plastic and the audience until the tray was emptied.

In the second, the artist, dressed in a tuxedo, methodically covered the naked body of a young woman lying on a white lace tablecloth with warm, soft butter. The apparent sexualisation of the work, with its gendered clothed/nude, active/passive, subject/object positions, was denied by Spill, who had initially intended a male participant, also dressed in a tuxedo, to be 'buttered up' in order to give emphasis to the formal structure of the action. When the participant failed to show on the night, the artist's wife agreed to take part in the work instead.[35]

Bruce Barber, *Mt Eden Crater Performance*, documentation of performance, 1973. *Courtesy the artist. Photo by Bryony Dalefield*

INSIDE THE INSTITUTION

Director Ernest Smith and exhibition officer John Maynard instigated *Project Programme*, which ran for almost three months at Auckland City Art Gallery in 1975. It featured installation, sculpture and performance within a programme that, in its changing activation of gallery spaces, was performative in structure in a manner now commonplace in public museums.

Bruce Barber's *Stocks and Bonds* was one of the first works in the programme and introduced 'extended duration' to the local performance vocabulary. For 48 hours, Barber was locked in a set of stocks located in a space between two galleries. A closed-circuit television feed allowed the public to view the artist even when the gallery was closed, and a public address system allowed Barber to harangue the audience both inside and outside the gallery. The figure of the artist was equated with that of an offender, confined and subjected to public scrutiny.

Gray Nicol, an Elam student between 1973 and 1977, a founding member of From Scratch and a notable video artist, also made a durational work for the *Project Programme*, in which his body was confined on public display for 24 hours on the outdoor forecourt of the gallery. Nicol lay under a 2-tonne slab of reinforced concrete that was suspended from a metal frame designed by the artist. Less redolent of overt social reference than *Stocks and Bonds*, and more static and sculptural in form, Nicol's *Concrete Suspension* was a concentrated study in corporeal resilience yet precariousness, with an almost meditative giving over to time (marked by the breathing body) beneath an industrial sculptural form.

David Mealing made a very different form of intervention within the museum setting for *Project Programme*, a work called *Jumble Sale/A Marketplace* (1975). Mealing had studied at Elam in the late 1960s and, after a period of travel in the mid-1970s, worked for a time teaching art in a prison. Working across installation, performance and film/video, he was constantly striving to collapse art/life distinctions in a practice that sought to use art as but one agent for social change.

Following earlier forms of socially engaged gestures and actions (in particular his 1973 work *Blood the River of Life: A collective art and life study* that brought to public display the everyday act of donating blood), for *Jumble Sale/A Marketplace* Mealing invited a number of community organisations to take part in a market within the museum space. The event provided an opportunity for those organisations to raise money, and not only brought a new set of visitors to the museum but also suggested a different purpose for visiting.

This form of social art practice — a recalibration of open spaces for gathering within an art institution in order to reconfigure its community use value — is now commonplace, but in Aotearoa in the mid-1970s it was a challenging proposition.[36] This was evidenced in media responses and canvased at length by Wystan Curnow in an essay for the *Auckland City Art Gallery Quarterly*, in which he claimed the work failed art audiences, jumble sale participants and the public alike in disguising its 'art' condition through its emphasis upon 'exchange'.[37]

In 1976 Jim Allen took up an artist residency at the Experimental Art Foundation (EAF) in Adelaide, a relatively new art organisation focused on the support of experimental and ephemeral practices. Here Allen produced a set of important works, including the performances *Poetry for Chainsaws*, *Newspaper Piece* and *On Planting a Native*.[38] Allen also continued to facilitate the work of others in the 1976 *Australian & New Zealand Post-Object Art: A survey* exhibition at the EAF. The exhibition included documentation of existing work by Mealing, Barber, Dadson and John Lethbridge; Mealing's *Bicycle-Lifecycle* and Barber's *The Whistler's Soliloquy*, with Billy Apple, were both created using performance instructions sent to Allen.

Allen himself also performed Kimberley Gray's *Sweater* according to her instructions: sitting spot-lit in a small space fenced with string, he crushed root ginger and scraped the residue into a pot of boiling water. The steam from the pot caused some residue to rise and stick to the ceiling. When Allen ran out of ginger, he turned off the spotlight and heat, wound up the string and exited the space.

The following year Allen became founding head of the School of Art at the newly formed Sydney College of the Arts. Over the next decade in this role he produced less artwork, but had a critical impact as an educator and in supporting an emerging local experimental art scene. Barber moved to Canada in 1976 for further study and built a career as an artist and academic at Nova Scotia College of Art and Design, while on occasion continuing to develop and present work in Aotearoa and Australia.[39]

Dadson remained based primarily in Tāmaki Makaurau. He took up a position at Elam in 1977 and developed a celebrated career in sound, performance and visual arts, both as a solo artist and through From Scratch. His *Triad* works of the late 1970s and early 1980s extended his earlier instructional pieces as he worked with increasingly structured parameters for performance (including music) in pieces that explored both the spatial environment and durational possibilities of a given action or score.

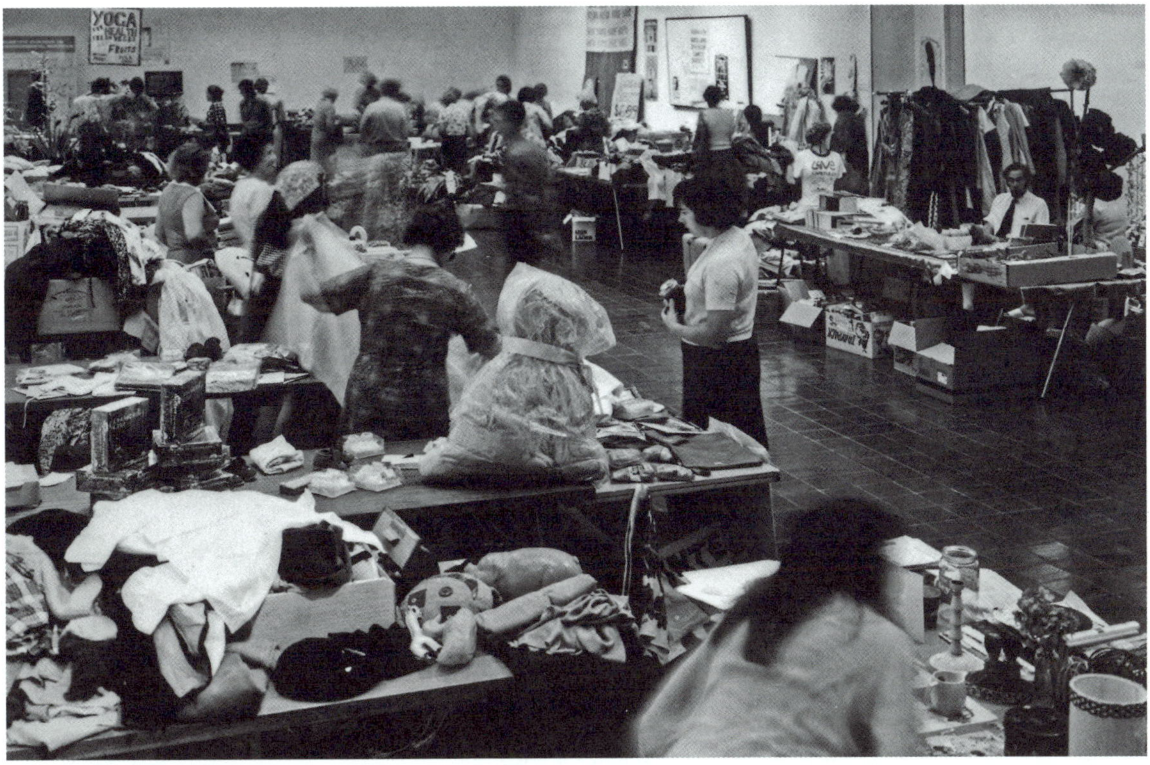

BODY/ENERGY

David Mealing, *Jumble Sale/A Marketplace*, 1975, black and white photograph. *Project Programme Archive, E H McCormick Research Library, Auckland Art Gallery Toi o Tāmaki*

Performance practices evolved significantly in the latter half of the 1970s. The exploration of both psychological and physical relationships became more overt and intense, and forms of ritual and the performance of elemental relationships of the body to the natural world became increasingly apparent. These works generally took place indoors in both institutional and non-institutional settings.

New performance-makers like Peter Roche and Linda Buis emerged in Tāmaki Makaurau, and work was increasingly presented in Te Whanganui-a-Tara through events organised by artists Nicholas Spill, Ian Hunter and Andrew Drummond in places such as the newly formed Artists Co-operative based in an old New Zealand Wool Board building on Lambton Quay, as well as through programmes in other cities, including Ōtautahi Christchurch and Te Papaioea Palmerston North.

Drummond returned to Aotearoa in 1976, having completed a fine arts degree in Ontario, Canada, and after a short period at the University of Edinburgh working with a group of post-Fluxus artists, including Joseph Beuys. Drummond took up a role as education officer at the National Art Gallery in Te Whanganui-a-Tara, organising artist events, and began to produce what would grow into one of the most substantial bodies of performance work in the art of Aotearoa. Ritual as a model for performance was central to his work. The artist appeared as a form of shamanistic figure — often dressed in a white boiler suit and white cap — in works focused on both representation and the

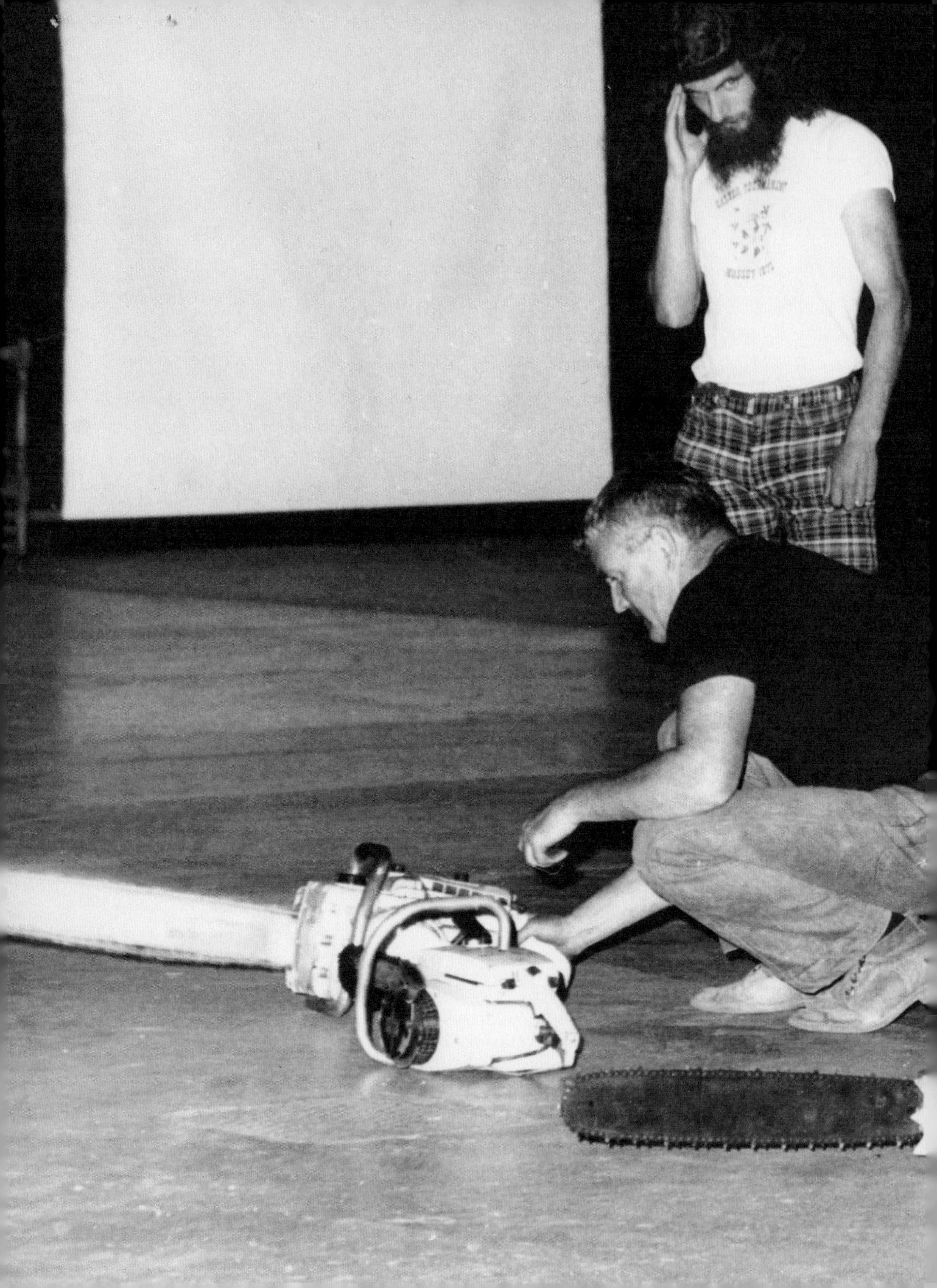

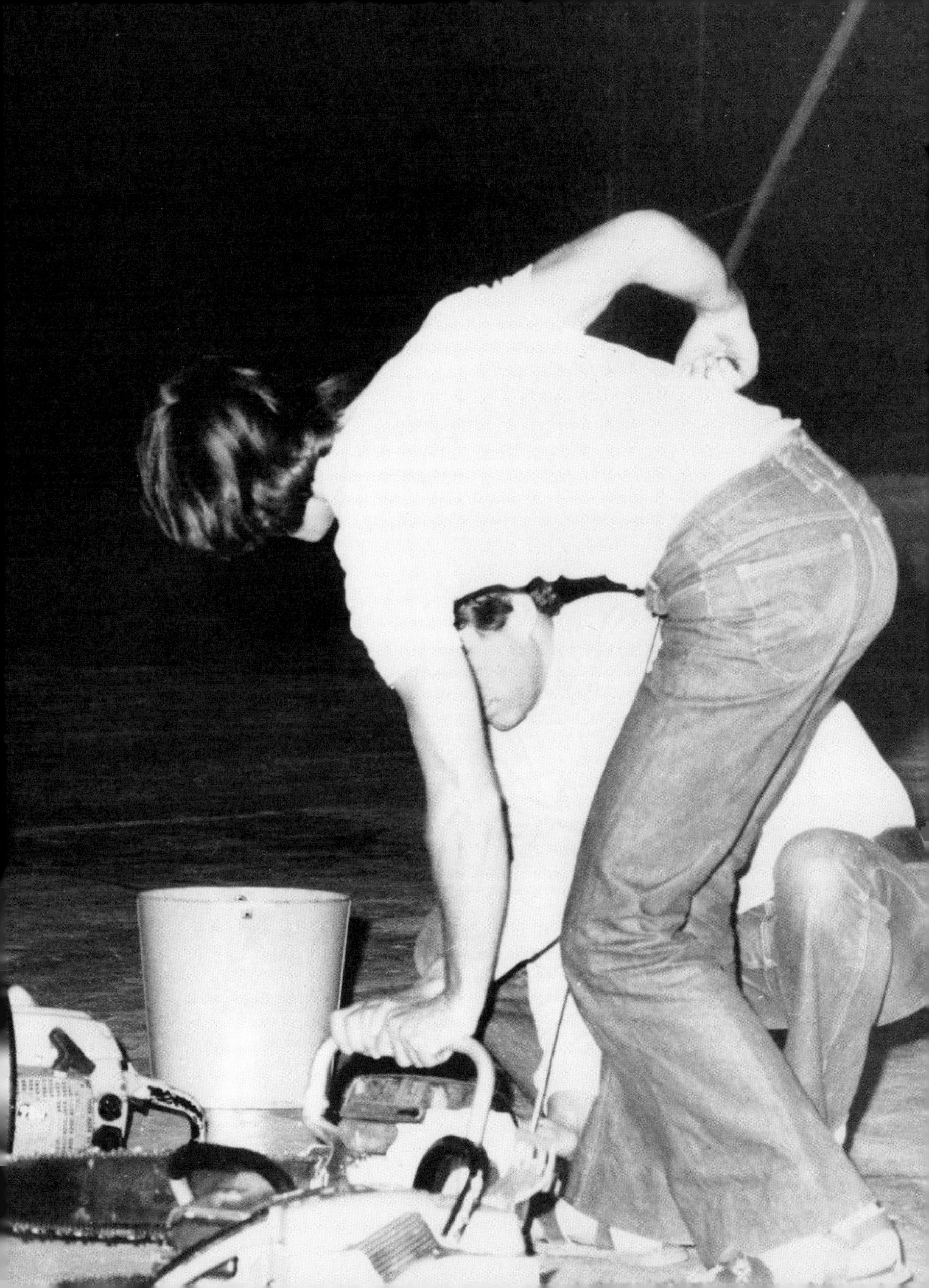

manifestation of bodily energy. Animal skins and bones featured frequently, and the works were generally documented in video and in photographs that were pasted onto card and annotated with handwritten notes by the artist describing the performance.

The first two performances made by Drummond on his return to Aotearoa also featured a cross — a symbol of sacrifice, pain and faith. In *Ritual for Summer Solstice*, performed at a private venue in Te Whanganui-a-Tara in late 1976, Drummond stretched himself onto a cross that lay on a slope, surrounded by a group of people who moved in a circle, chanting and clapping bones together. In *Onto Skin: A performance in 3 parts* (1977), performed first in Te Whanganui-a-Tara and then at Auckland City Art Gallery as part of the *New Zealand Young Contemporaries* exhibition, Drummond was strung out over a cross on the ground while an assistant poured latex over his back. Once set, the latex skin was peeled from the artist's body and laid over a structure of bones alongside which Drummond then curled up on an animal skin.

These elements of cross and latex were central to the later work *Crucifixion* (1978), in which a naked Drummond, wearing a gas mask and linked to a heart monitor, was bound to a St Andrew's Cross. A latex skin was made over his chest, peeled off and left in the gallery on the artist's departure.[40] A subsequent work, *Suspension/Ascension* (1979), performed first at Manawatu Art Gallery (using a metal cage) and then in Te Whanganui-a-Tara, also concluded with Drummond shedding a form of skin — in this case a wetsuit. Suspended by counter-weighted straps, the artist attempted to grasp an apple that hung just out of reach. When he finally succeeded, he collapsed exhausted to the ground, freed himself from the wetsuit and straps and sat naked, eating the apple, an image redolent with the symbolism of descent and the embrace of earthy pleasures.

In 1977 Drummond produced performances in venues in Ōtautahi, Te Papaioea, Te Whanganui-a-Tara and Mildura, Australia, including *Conversation Between Two Animals*, *Skin Print Event*, *A Ritual/Performance* and *Bones/Whirl/Skin*. He also began developing performances in the old Ngauranga Meatworks in Te Whanganui-a-Tara, which he then performed publicly at the Artists Co-operative on separate occasions over several months in 1978. These works became known collectively as *Ngauranga Set*. In the first of them, *Twenty Directions in an Enclosure*, Drummond made a set of random movements (determined by magnets and compasses) that were traced by flour that trailed from a bag suspended between his legs.[41]

For the second of the *Ngauranga Set* works, *Body/Skin Suspension Performance*, Drummond was bound and suspended beneath a stretched animal skin. Four candles burning under suspension points caused ropes to fail and the skin to drop over the artist. In *Onto Skin: A ritual for three skins*, Drummond threw liver and bags of flour at three animal skins that hung on a wall. And in the fourth work, *Like a Bull at a Gate*, the most overtly physical and, as conveyed in particular in the audio within the video documentation, relentless in its animalistic energy, Drummond charges again and again at a suspended animal skin and is repeatedly knocked back before eventually breaking through.

In 1980, when Drummond was Frances Hodgkins Fellow at the University of Otago in Ōtepoti Dunedin, he began an extensive body of work performing in and in direct relation to the Otago landscape. *Filter Action* and *Earth Vein* (both 1980) explored environmental and political issues performed in relationships between his body and the environment as mutually manifest sources of natural energy. *Filter Action* protested against a proposed aluminium smelter at the mouth of Otago Harbour that would have destroyed the settlements of Aramoana and Te Ngaru and threatened a local wildlife reserve.[42]

PREVIOUS: **Jim Allen, *Poetry for Chainsaws* at Experimental Art Foundation, Adelaide, 1976, black and white photograph. *Jim Allen Archive, E H McCormick Research Library, Auckland Art Gallery Toi o Tāmaki, gift of Jim Allen, 2012***

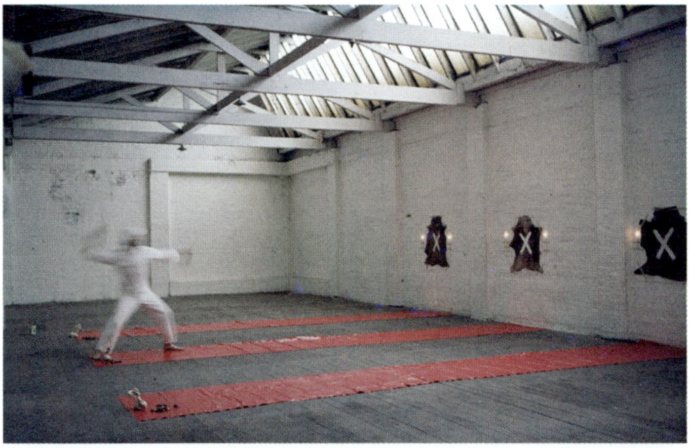

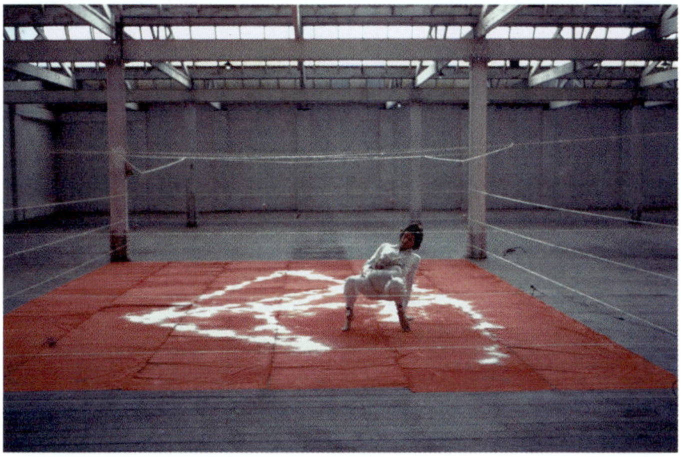

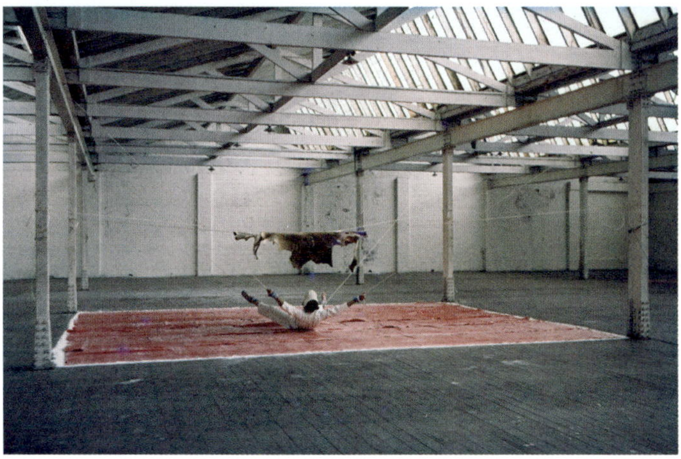

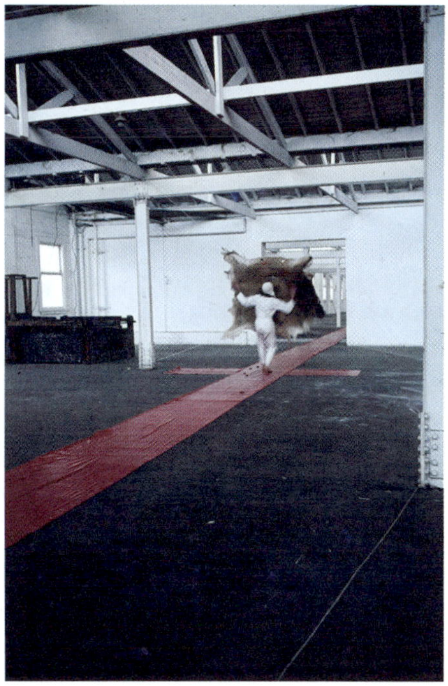

Andrew Drummond, *Ngauranga Set*, 1978. *Courtesy the artist. Photos by Nicholas Spill*

In 1997, as homage to the artist, Emma Bugden remade several Drummond performances, including *Filter Action*. At The Honeymoon Suite, an artist-run gallery in Ōtepoti, Bugden dressed in a Drummondesque white boiler suit and helmet. She offered the audience coloured milk that she had heated on a portable stove before washing and drying a sheep's kidney, sawing a hole in the floor of the gallery and 'burying' the kidney under the floorboards.[43]

Back in Tāmaki Makaurau, Peter Roche suspended himself from a wooden cross hanging in Albert Park for as long as he could endure (*Suspension Piece*, 1978).[44] At the time of his graduation from Elam in 1979, he had begun to attract attention for edgy, even potentially dangerous performances involving forms of 'self-wounding', described by curator Gregory Burke, in a collection of remembrances published online by City Gallery Wellington Te Whare Toi on Roche's death in 2020, as 'gruelling to encounter'.[45]

From 1979 until the mid-1980s, Roche produced an extensive body of performance works in partnership with Linda Buis. Treating performance art as a sculptural medium,[46] Roche & Buis created situations within which the relationship between two individuals, two minds and two bodies confined in space could be probed and tested. The audience were themselves often also drawn into this psychologically charged space. Burke, who photographed many of these works, best describes their tenor:

> While, on a few occasions, the artists placed themselves in dangerous situations, their focus was more the psyche than the physical body, in works that explored what it means to be in performance and 'in relation' — in relation to an audience, yes, but particularly in relation to another, in all its multiple dimensions. While the Roche/Buis works were less physically threatening than Roche's earlier performances, they were as demanding and no less psychologically charged.[47]

Roche & Buis were producing the most urgent performance work in Tāmaki Makaurau up until 1985 — work that was guided by complex planning and evolved in the moment.

ARTIST, AUDIENCE AND CRITIC

This chapter began with Bruce Barber's *Bucket Action* (1973), a conflation of material form, liveness, documentation, witness, participant, artist, audience and critic. The huge upsurge in performance art through the 1970s played a critical role in spotlighting the changing condition of each of these determinants of the 'artwork', and how the holding of each in relief by the others would come to recalibrate understanding of what might constitute a work of art (not just in performance) and its potential functionality within a changing social environment.

In concluding, it is important to note the role played by critic Wystan Curnow in Barber's *Mt Eden Crater Performance* of the same year, in which the 'live' participant writes both within and about that work.[48] Roche & Buis's work provided another framework for Curnow to operate as 'critic': to write from within as participant as well as in reflection upon and, as with the earlier works by Barber, to also incorporate the reflection of the artist. His 1983 text on three works by Roche & Buis — *Continuance in Action: Interferences* (1980), *Performance* (1981) and *Night Piece* (1981) — was written with Roche and art historian Tony Green.

A mix of reportage and reflections on the banality of daily activity that incorporates both description and analysis of the unfolding performances, the writing takes the reader back to the enigmatic, elusive yet somehow urgent energy of this period and to a fundamental impulse connecting much of the work described here, in order to make sense of the artist's relationship to an immediate physical, spatial, temporal and cultural environment. The final word in that text sits with the artist, as Roche describes standing with Buis above the site of *Night Piece* at the old gasworks in Freemans Bay in Tāmaki Makaurau, in midwinter, at the end of the performance: 'What a sight that was . . . We had described that space well.'[49]

By the late 1970s and early 1980s, performance from Aotearoa was increasingly finding an Australian audience through the Mildura Sculpture Triennials, the *Prime Export* programme involving seventeen artists from Aotearoa at Side/FX Gallery in Sydney, the 1979 Biennale of Sydney (within which Peter Roche presented an intense solo work of body art involving self-harm), and in 1981 at the first Australia New Zealand Artists Encounter (ANZART) event in Ōtautahi, initiated by Ian Hunter.[50] Performance continued to play a significant role in resetting the coordinates for an understanding of contemporary art as propositional, ephemeral, interventionist and at least potentially socially disruptive — coordinates that would be both overtly challenged and obliquely intensified by the booming recommodification of art by 1980s market models.

NOTES

1 Artist Kieran Lyons.

2 Jim Allen and Wystan Curnow, eds, 'Bruce Barber, 'Bucket Action' (Performance)', in *New Art: Some recent New Zealand sculpture and post-object art* (Auckland: Heinemann, 1976), n.p.

3 Ibid.

4 A video, just over an hour long, shot by Jim Allen documenting the Kerikeri performance of *Bucket Action* is held in Ngā Taonga Sound and Vision. Bruce Barber, 'Bucket Action. Bruce Barber', Ngā Taonga Sound and Vision, 1973.

5 I came across *New Art* in a second-hand bookshop in a regional town in the mid-1980s when I was an art history student. This first encounter with the book and the work it documented led eventually, some years later, to a period of concentrated research on post-object art in Aotearoa New Zealand, which I undertook in 1999–2000 under the auspices of an Australian Research Council Large Grant to Professor Terry Smith at the Power Institute, Foundation for Art and Visual Culture, University of Sydney. Much of this chapter is informed by that research.

6 *Bucket Action* was subsequently performed in 1974 by Barber within the larger project *Four Men in a Boat* at Auckland City Art Gallery.

7 The ongoing importance of *Bucket Action* was demonstrated by its re-performance by artist Hannah Valentine with Becky Richards in December 2018 as part of the *Groundswell: Avant-garde Auckland 1971–79* exhibition at Auckland Art Gallery Toi o Tāmaki.

8 Key responses to *Groundswell* include: John Hurrell, 'Seventies Auckland Avant-Garde', *EyeContact*, 3 February 2019; and Victoria Wynne-Jones, 'Occasions & Situations for Seeing: Auckland's avant-garde 1971–1979', *Art New Zealand* 169 (Autumn 2019): 80–85.

9 The work of Jim Allen, Phil Dadson, Andrew Drummond, Kimberly Gray and Peter Roche and Linda Buis is all further considered in other chapters within this volume. See Chapter 2, 'Kimberley Gray: A case study in the development towards performance, 1970–76' by Natasha Conland; Chapter 3, 'Getting It Straight: Contact, 1974 and 2010' by Jim Allen and James Charlton; Chapter 5, 'The Afterlives of Performance Art: The case of Peter Roche and Linda Buis' by Christina Barton and Gregory Burke; Chapter 6, 'Sound and Performance Cultures in Aotearoa' by Andrew Clifford and Rachel Shearer; and Chapter 13, 'It's a Work: Spectacular secrecy in private and unannounced performances' by Christopher Braddock and Victoria Wynne-Jones.

10 The E H McCormick Research Library at Auckland Art Gallery Toi o Tāmaki is a good source of such documentation, and its journal, *Reading Room: A journal of art and culture*, with eight issues published since 2007, is an important outlet for research into such archival material. In Tāmaki Makaurau the 'Open Drawer' files at Elam School of Fine Arta, established by Phil Dadson, historically played an important role in making artists' notes and ephemera as well as work documentation available to students and researchers.

11 Curated by Christina Barton, Wystan Curnow, John Hurrell and Robert Leonard.

12 Curated by Jennifer Hay, whose introductory essay in this catalogue, 'Trans-Marginal: New Zealand performance art 1970–1985', provides a comprehensive critical overview of this period, highlighting the presence and importance of work that took place outside of Tāmaki Makaurau, including in Ōtautahi Christchurch, Te Papaioea Palmerston North and Te Whanganui-a-Tara Wellington.

13 For a discussion on the parochial condition of the term 'post-object art', see Wynne-Jones, 'Occasions & Situations', 81.

14 Although performance is my specific focus here, it is important to acknowledge this wider post-object art context, and in particular the environments and installation works by artists as diverse as Jim Allen, who

created socially charged physical areas; Maree Horner, who created tensile, minimalist sculptural objects; and Leon Narbey, who worked with light and moving image to play with body and space.

15 Aspects of this section are drawn from my earlier essay, 'Jim Allen: From Elam to the Experimental Art Foundation', in Jennifer Hay, ed., *Intervention: Post Object and Performance Art in New Zealand in 1970 and Beyond*, exhibition catalogue (Christchurch: Robert McDougall Art Gallery and Annex, 2002), 35–46.

16 Interview with author, July 1999. For a more detailed discussion of aspects of (and background to) Allen's teaching philosophy and approach, see Wystan Curnow and Robert Leonard, 'Contact: Jim Allen Talks to Wystan Curnow & Robert Leonard', *Art New Zealand* 95 (Winter 2000): 48–55.

17 The loss of this library almost five decades later was the subject of both public protest and media scrutiny.

18 This fostering of international visitors extended to hosting eminent American art critic Lucy Lippard on a 1974 visit to Tāmaki Makaurau following the 1973 publication of her hugely influential book, *Six Years: The dematerialisation of the art object from 1966 to 1972*.

19 *Bucket Action*, along with a number of Bruce Barber's other 1973 and 1974 works also noted in this chapter, is exemplary in these regards.

20 Allen's major work, *Contact* (1974), presented in this programme along with its subsequent twenty-first-century re-enactment is discussed in Chapter 3 of this volume, 'Getting It Straight'.

21 Photographs of McLean's work by then fellow student Fiona Clark were exhibited in *Groundswell: Avant-garde Auckland 1971–79*.

22 Allen himself alludes to this, with particular regard to his own working position, in Pauline Barber, 'The Splinterview 4: Jim Allen', *Spleen* 4 (1976): n.p.

23 See Jennifer Hay, 'Trans-Marginal: New Zealand performance art 1970–1985', in Hay, *Intervention*, 24.

24 For example, prominent photographic artist Fiona Clark attended Elam from 1972 until 1975, first within the sculpture department working with installation, performance and Super 8 film. Some photographic stills relating to this work can be viewed online at https://fionaclark.com. Clark, however, moved into the Elam photography department in 1974. Photography provided a socially engaged means to represent and give a form of voice to communities marginalised within and by the predominantly conservative masculine culture of 1970s Aotearoa New Zealand. Her major early work from this period focused on trans and broader queer communities in downtown Tāmaki Makaurau.

25 Phil Dadson's immensely influential performative sound practice is discussed in more detail in Chapter 6 of this volume, 'Sound and Performance Cultures in Aotearoa'.

26 Andrew Clifford, 'A Quiet Revolution: Towards ecological Andegalitarian listening', in *Philip Dadson Polar Projects*, exhibition catalogue (Auckland: Gus Fisher Gallery, 2004), n.p.

27 Phil Dadson, interview with author, July 1999.

28 Barber also participated extensively in Scratch Orchestra works and was a founding member of From Scratch.

29 *Youth in Asia* was also performed at Auckland City Art Gallery in 1974 within the *Four Men in a Boat* project.

30 A single-channel video transferred from original Super 8 of *Whatipu Beach Performance* is accessible through circuit.org.nz. The *Five Evenings* programme was organised by Jim Allen and Bruce Barber.

31 *Like a Bat Outta Hell*, for example, was structured around three journeys. The first, made prior to the actual performance, resulted in video footage of train tracks from a moving train incorporated into the performance setting. In this setting a blindfolded male performer made an awkward and difficult journey along a tensioned wire attached to a wooden sleeper to which his feet were tied. (This form of physical restraint later appeared in the 1975 *Stocks and Bonds* work.) The third and repeating journey was made by a female performer moving along the wire to intercept the male performer.

32 Christina Barton, 'Performance Art by Women in Aotearoa New Zealand 1974–1993', in *Alter/Image: Feminism and representation in New Zealand art, 1973–1993*, edited by Deborah Lawler-Dormer and Christina Barton (Auckland/Wellington: Auckland City Art Gallery and City Gallery, 1993), 61.

33 Bruce Barber worked with Gray to videotape the work. In its use of a light aircraft *As Good a Land* . . . also prefigured two works by Te Whanganui-a-Tara-based Ian Hunter — *Lake Erie Salt Sculpture* (1976), in which Hunter chartered a light aircraft to drop twenty-five packets of salt in a two-mile pattern over the lake as a form of memorial to American artist Robert Smithson, and *Cook Strait Sculpture* (1977), in which Hunter dropped a bag of cooking oil and a bunch of tulips into Cook Strait as tokens of conciliation or reconnection with place.

34 Nicholas Spill, correspondence with author, February 2000.

35 Ibid.

36 Mealing's establishment of a live social situation looking to simultaneously collapse and hold art and life in the gaze of the other is a very different model of 'performance' from that otherwise discussed in this chapter. In subsequent performance and installation works — in the creation of discursively volatile situations within institutions that on occasion triggered public controversy — Mealing continued to use carefully framed public forms of action and gesture to confront entrenched cultural and institutional conservatism.

37 Wystan Curnow, 'Project Programme 1975', *Auckland City Art Gallery Quarterly* 62–63 (December 1976): 15–30. Republished in Christina Barton, Robert Leonard and Thomasin Sleigh, eds, *The Critic's Part: Wystan Curnow art writings 1971–2013* (Wellington/Brisbane: Te Pātaka Toi Adam Art Gallery, Institute of Modern Art and Victoria University Press, 2014), 68–81.

38 See Chapter 5 of this volume as well as Blair French, 'Jim Allen: From Elam to the Experimental Art Foundation', in *Intervention: Post object and performance art in New Zealand in 1970 and beyond*, edited by Jennifer Hay (Christchurch: Robert McDougall Art Gallery and Annex, 2002), 35–46.

39 Stephen Cleland and Blair French, eds, *Bruce Barber: Work 1970–2008* (Sydney/Manukau: Artspace Visual Arts Centre and Te Tuhi Cetre for the Arts, 2010).

40 Created at the Christchurch Society of Arts gallery for Christchurch Festival, *Crucifixion* was the subject of a public complaint regarding nudity in the documentation photographs left in the space. These were subsequently removed by the police and obscenity charges laid against Drummond, which he defended successfully.

41 This work was also performed at the 1978 Mildura Sculpture Triennial.

42 *Filter Action* is discussed in Chapter 13 of this volume, 'It's a Work: Spectacular secrecy in private and unannounced performances' by Christopher Braddock and Victoria Wynne-Jones. See also Christopher Braddock, Ioana Gordon-Smith, Layne Waerea and Victoria Wynne-Jones, 'Aotearoa New Zealand Performance Art 1970–2020', in *The Routledge Companion to Performance Art*, edited by Jennie Klein, Natalie Loveless, Lucian O'Connor and Graciela Ovejero (Abingdon, UK: Routledge, forthcoming). Drummond, whose work always had a clear

material and spatial definition, went on to make sculpture including installation and kinetic work.

43 Christina Barton, 'Post-Object and Conceptual Art: Revival of interest, 1990s to 2000s: "Filter Action"', *Te Ara — the Encyclopedia of New Zealand*, https://teara.govt.nz/en/photograph/43834/filter-action; Jonathan Nicol, '2 Cents: Filter Action', The Physics Room, 21 June 1997.

44 Like Drummond, Peter Roche would later go on to success as a sculptor in the area of large-scale kinetic and neon works.

45 Gregory Burke, 'Peter Roche: Committed', City Gallery Wellington Te Whare Toi, https://citygallery.org.nz/blog/peter-roche-committed

46 Ronald Brownson, ed., *A Documentation of Six Performances by Roche/Buis* (Auckland: Roche/Buis in association with the Queen Elizabeth Arts Council of New Zealand, 1983).

47 Burke, 'Peter Roche'.

48 Wystan Curnow, 'Mt Eden Crater Performance', in *New Art: Some recent New Zealand sculpture and post-object art*, edited by Jim Allen and Wystan Curnow (Auckland: Heinemann, 1976), n.p. Republished in Barton, Leonard and Sleigh, *The Critic's Part*, 49–53 .

49 Peter Roche, Wystan Curnow and Tony Green, 'Peter Roche/Linda Buis: A gathering concerning three performances', in *The Critic's Part*, 169. First published in *Parallax* 1, no. 2 (Summer 1983). See Chapter 13 of this volume for further discussion of Peter Roche and Linda Buis's *Night Piece* (1981).

50 Bruce Barber exhibited in the 1979 Biennale itself, restaging *E*, a performance first produced in Halifax, Canada, in 1978 with the assistance of Jim Allen and students from Sydney College of the Arts.

REFERENCES

Allen, Jim. *The Skin of Years: Interviews with Jim Allen by Phil Dadson and Tony Green.* Auckland: Clouds and Michael Lett, 2014.

Allen, Jim and Wystan Curnow, eds. 'Bruce Barber, "Bucket Action" (Performance)'. In *New Art: Some recent New Zealand sculpture and post-object art.* Auckland: Heinemann, 1976.

Barber, Bruce. 'Bucket Action. Bruce Barber'. Ngā Taonga Sound and Vision, 1973. www.ngataonga.org.nz/search-use-collection/search/F47212

Barber, Bruce, Blair French, Tony Green, Nicholas Spill and Jennifer Hay. *Intervention: Post object and performance art in New Zealand in 1970 and beyond.* Exhibition catalogue. Christchurch: Robert McDougall Art Gallery and Annex, 2002.

Barber, Pauline. 'The Splinterview 4: Jim Allen', *Spleen* 4 (1976): n. p.

Barton, Christina. 'Performance Art by Women in Aotearoa New Zealand 1974–1993'. In *Alter/Image: Feminism and representation in New Zealand Art, 1973–1993*, edited by Deborah Lawler-Dormer and Christina Barton. Auckland/Wellington: Auckland City Art Gallery and City Gallery, 1993.

——— 'Post-Object Art in New Zealand 1969–1979: Experiments in art and life'. Master's thesis, University of Auckland, 1987.

——— 'Post-Object and Conceptual Art: Revival of interest, 1990s to 2000s: "Filter Action"'. *Te Ara — the Encyclopedia of New Zealand.* https://teara.govt.nz/en/photograph/43834/filter-action

Barton, Christina, Wystan Curnow, John Hurrell and Robert Leonard (curators). *Action Replay: Post-object art.* Exhibition series. Auckland/New Plymouth: Artspace Aotearoa, Govett-Brewster Art Gallery, Auckland Art Gallery Toi o Tāmaki, 1998–99.

Braddock, Christopher, Ioana Gordon-Smith, Layne Waerea and Victoria Wynne-Jones. 'Aotearoa New Zealand Performance Art 1970–2020'. In *The Routledge Companion to Performance Art*, edited by Jennie Klein, Natalie Loveless, Lucian O'Connor and Graciela Ovejero Postigo. Abingdon, UK: Routledge, forthcoming.

Brennan, Stella, Robert Leonard and Hanna Scott, eds. *Action Replay: Post-script.* Auckland/New Plymouth: Artspace and Govett-Brewster Gallery, 2002.

Brownson, Ronald, ed. *A Documentation of Six Performances by Roche/Buis.* Auckland: Roche/Buis in association with the Queen Elizabeth Arts Council of New Zealand, 1983.

Burke, Gregory. 'Peter Roche: Committed | City Gallery Wellington'. City Gallery Wellington Te Whare Toi. https://citygallery.org.nz/blog/peter-roche-committed

Cleland, Stephen and Blair French, eds. *Bruce Barber: Work 1970–2008.* Sydney/Manukau: Artspace Visual Arts Centre and Te Tuhi Centre for the Arts, 2010.

Clifford, Andrew. 'A Quiet Revolution: Towards ecological and egalitarian listening'. In *Philip Dadson Polar Projects*, exhibition catalogue. Auckland: Gus Fisher Gallery, 2004.

Curnow, Wystan. 'Mt Eden Crater Performance'. In *New Art: Some recent New Zealand sculpture and post-object art*, edited by Jim Allen and Wystan Curnow. Auckland: Heinemann, 1976.

——— 'Project Programme 1975'. *Auckland City Art Gallery Quarterly* 62–63 (December 1976): 15–30.

——— *The Critic's Part: Wystan Curnow art writings 1971–2013*, edited by Christina Barton, Robert Leonard and Thomasin Sleigh. Wellington/Brisbane: Te Pātaka Toi Adam Art Gallery, Institute of Modern Art and Victoria University Press, 2014.

Curnow, Wystan and Robert Leonard. 'Contact: Jim Allen talks to Wystan Curnow & Robert Leonard'. *Art New Zealand* 95 (Winter 2000): 48–55.

Hay, Jennifer, John Finlay, Bruce Barber, Peter Leech and Pamela Hansford. *Andrew Drummond: Observation/action/reflection.* Exhibition catalogue. Christchurch: Christchurch Art Gallery Te Puna o Waiwhetū, 2010.

Hurrell, John. 'Seventies Auckland Avant-Garde'. *EyeContact*, 3 February 2019. https://eyecontactmagazine.com/2019/02/seventies-auckland-avant-garde

Nicol, Jonathan. '2 Cents: Filter Action'. The Physics Room, 21 June 1997. https://physicsroom.org.nz/archive/2cents/filter.htm

Wynne-Jones, Victoria. 'Occasions & Situations for Seeing: Auckland's avant-garde 1971–1979'. *Art New Zealand* 169 (Autumn 2019): 80–85.

2

KIMBERLEY GRAY: A CASE STUDY IN THE DEVELOPMENT TOWARDS PERFORMANCE, 1970–76

Natasha Conland

In the early 1970s, artist Kimberley Gray (1947–2017) was at the centre of a period of rapid and profound shifts in the definition of art. Reform was centred at the sculpture department of Elam School of Fine Arts at the University of Auckland, where artist Jim Allen's (1922–2023) teaching was radicalised towards open systems of enquiry. The tools for learning about the 'new art' were found as much in the city as the art school itself.

Gray's own journey was laboured with questioning, in isolation and alongside her peers, as she sought to understand the meaning and potential of these changes. Between 1971 and 1976 she exhibited fourteen works of performative sculpture, installations and performances in the manner of the new art, making her one of the most active practitioners in this short but dynamic period which ushered in change to art's fundamental categories. Despite this, today her work is largely unknown.[1]

The ephemeral nature of much of the art practice of this time, with its emphasis on happenings, performances, live video relay, sound, temporary assemblages and installations, makes this not entirely surprising, especially when coupled with the fact that, unlike her contemporaries, Gray made no 'permanent' works during her time in the sculpture department. However, given the extent and serious nature of her work, this does not entirely explain her almost full erasure.[2] Like many for whom this period had an intense impact both in art and life, Gray seemed to simply disappear from the art scene. In fact, she dedicated herself to teaching art and raising a child and, like many women of the subsequent decade who were engaged in a period of feminist enquiry, she significantly altered the way she worked and lived.

I had the opportunity to give Gray's work proper consideration in 2018 while preparing and curating an exhibition of experimental art practices at Auckland Art Gallery Toi o Tāmaki titled *Groundswell: Avant-garde Auckland 1971–79*. Although there had been previous exhibitions and publications on the emergence of what was known in Australia and New Zealand in the 1970s and 1980s as post-object art, the gallery's research library had since obtained two major artist archives with significant additional material relating to this period. The Jim Allen and Bruce Barber archives at the E H McCormick Research Library include exhibition ephemera and documentation that augment the gallery's own records, and which enabled me to give some substantive materialisation to a period that had been characterised by writer Wystan Curnow as the first truly contemporaneous moment for New Zealand art history — by which he meant that the art practices in Aotearoa were for the first time developing on par with international shifts.[3]

Arguably, the greatest of these in Western centres was the movement towards art's 'dematerialisation', as characterised by American art writer and critic Lucy Lippard in her reference work *Six Years: The dematerialization of the art object from 1966 to 1972*. Lippard had travelled to New Zealand in 1975 with artist Mel Bochner to support the exhibition *Some Recent American Art* at Auckland City Art Gallery (1974). Following the visit she wrote in the gallery *Quarterly* that she was 'rather condescendingly, amazed to discover' how well-informed New Zealand artists were about contemporary American art.[4] Lippard and Bochner went on to establish long-standing relationships with Jim Allen, Bruce Barber and local art students that were based on openness and like-mindedness.[5]

While the irony of trying to re-materialise a dematerialised art practice for exhibition was not lost on me, nor the greater weighting placed on the role of the archive, I was nonetheless determined to account for the period and its association with global art histories, while also understanding its differences. Understanding Kimberley Gray's artwork in relation to others became central to this research, as I became aware of the emphasis this small group of artists placed on the body's relationship with the earth.

The substantial focus of Gray's work was directed towards the perceptual orientation of our bodies on earth. This was also a thread of interest for other artists in Tāmaki Makaurau at the time, in particular Phil Dadson (1946–), but for Gray attention to the body-in-relation to its perceptual markers is quite conscious and consistent — and troubled. She combines scientific enquiry with notation, charting and mapping to observe and present the field outside normal human relativity.

Although I was able to elucidate three artworks by Gray for the exhibition, it was not until after *Groundswell* was finished, and our posthumous acquisition of her archive for the E H McCormick Research Library that I was able to read into the finer details of her work.

**

Gray was a contemporary of Dadson. Born in England in 1947, she moved to Tāmaki Makaurau Auckland in 1965 where she completed her schooling. Little is known about her relocation, but her archive and journals contain two geography assignments from 1968–69, which predate her time at art school. One is an essay on landforms and geomorphology, which asked students to assess the role that 'man' may play in modifying natural slopes; the other is an assignment in mapping landscape types. The latter received a rather poor grade and the marker's wry comment that 'psychedelic maps are not yet "in" in geography'.[6]

Gray's interest in observing and mapping landforms continued well into her degree in fine arts, which she began in 1970 — the year Bruce Barber and Maree Horner also entered Elam and Dadson returned from London, where he had been an early participant in the Scratch Orchestra.

This intake formed the first of Jim Allen's 1970s student cohorts, all of whom continued on to post-graduate study and achieved well under his new critical forums. Here open questions and exercises were offered without overt determination or reference to solutions.[7] Handouts for sculptural assignments sometimes had the appearance of concrete poetry, and the influence of this style is seen throughout Gray's early sketches and notations. One undated entry in her early journals has a small cartoon-style painting of the Earth personified, with an open mouth spitting out small human forms and the caption: 'All the world is saying "No".'

By the mid-1960s, awareness of damage to the environment was beginning to register, and campaigns like Save Manapouri (1969–72) gave form to these concerns — in this case the impact of building a power station that would raise the lake level by up to 30 metres. The later Maruia Declaration petition (1975) called for an end to the logging of native forest. The cultural scene began to introduce 'environmental evenings' and sit-ins contemporaneous with the early conservation movement.

Collected in Kimberley Gray's early references is an invitation to an 'environmental evening' at New Vision Gallery, Tāmaki Makaurau, on 3–12 June 1969, titled 'The Incredible Garden of Mysterious Earthly Delights'. Although it was largely an evening of experimental music and poetry, the cover image shows a man holding a small triangular structure over a textured globe.

Gray's journals from 1971, her second year of study and her first year in the sculpture department, are full of notes that record her close observations of sections of land (mostly in Grafton Gully on the perimeter of the art school). What is unusual about these is her attention, not just to the shape of the land (influenced by her geomorphology studies), but also to the light and its absorption, the movement of shadows, layers of

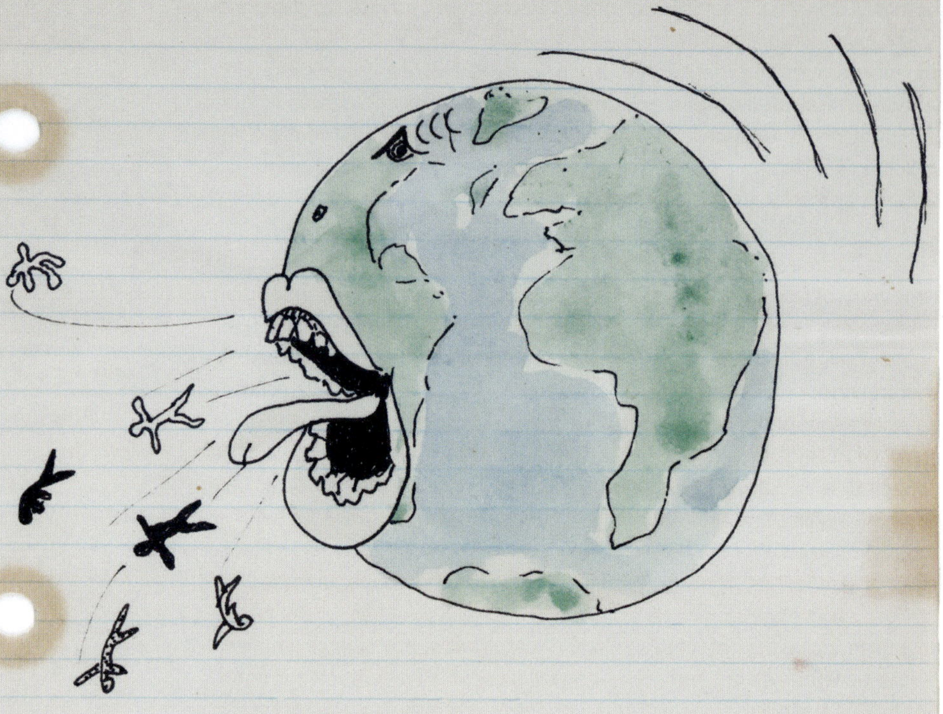

All the world is saying "No".

foliage, sounds, and notes her simultaneous attention. She described, in an almost scientific manner, to her own thoughts and sentiments, submerged in urban wilderness but proximate to the recently installed motorway. She created small sections within which to focus her attention and analysis in detail, recording time of day, orientation, slope and plant matter. She attempted to understand the visual signs of 'stillness' captured in these sections in comparison to the motorway activity.

Three works emerge from this period of observation and notation. The first Gray called *Digging Holes*, Grafton Gully, March 1971. Although she omitted this from her exhibition history in the 1970s, Gray reintroduced documentation of it in correspondence with Jim Allen in 2002. She dug holes around 1 x 2 metres deep in the sections of the gully she had been analysing. Gray writes that, initially, these works 'were part of an investigation of issues to do with displacement and human disturbance of the environment',[8] but her conceptual motivation shifted to an analysis of the process of shifting the landscape and the way light settled on the contours.

She comments: 'To understand its stillness I have moved closer into Section I into the shadows of its tree ferns. The stillness of this place seems to be evoked by visual sensations rather than sound.'[9] Gray seems to be asking, 'If I make subtle alterations to the environment, how does my awareness of its qualities change?' In the end her interests were in the analysis of the *kinetics* of light. With detailed diagrams of how light is interrupted and affected by the natural surrounds, she concludes, 'the pattern of light and shade alters kinetics. The nature of light projection depends upon the texture of ground surface.'[10]

In her second work from that year, *Tidal Time-Piece* (1971), Gray extends this enquiry into nature's time markers, from the passage of light to the passage of time as determined by tide. In many ways it is a simple concept: a line of weighted buoys, installed in three locations in the upper Waitematā Harbour, shift and are submerged with the changing tides. In her documentation we see a line of bright orange buoys that disappear gradually. To conduct the work, Gray developed detailed diagrams of the buoys' movement, maps and notation of tide times and measurements, which she referred to as a 'programme', indicating the performative nature of the piece. *Tidal Time-Piece* was fully documented with colour slide film, and Gray received assistance from her lecturers Jim Allen and Greer Twiss — indication of the serious intent of the project in which the buoys created a visual depiction of earth's shifting matter.

Her third work, *Time Wedge* (1971), was the participatory sculpture project made for the spring equinox. A large number of detailed preparatory drawings exist for this work, which was installed for just three days in the grounds at Elam. The plans and drawings show Gray working to find a suitable architectural form to house standing participants, an enclosed dark space in which to observe a beam of light channelled directly from the sun's position at noon at the equinox. Gray explored the geometry and physical resolution over some months in order to achieve the intended conditions, and settled on a triangular wedge form covered in heavy, dark material, from which a pipe extended towards the sky at the appropriate angle to capture the sun's rays. Inside, mirrors were set to reflect the light across the interior space. As the earth rotated, the narrow beam of light would shift.

Participants would register the enormity of the planetary system in action, 'the cosmos', and their single point of relationship with earth, and experience 'a physical sensation of earth moving'.[11] Gray explored the geometry and physical resolution for some months in order to achieve the right conditions. Photographer Max Oettli captured

Kimberley Gray, *Untitled Drawing*, 'All the world is saying "No"', c. 1972, ink on paper. *Kimberley Gray Archive, E H McCormick Research Library, Auckland Art Gallery Toi o Tāmaki, gift of Josephine Gray, 2019. Photo by Auckland Art Gallery Toi o Tāmaki*

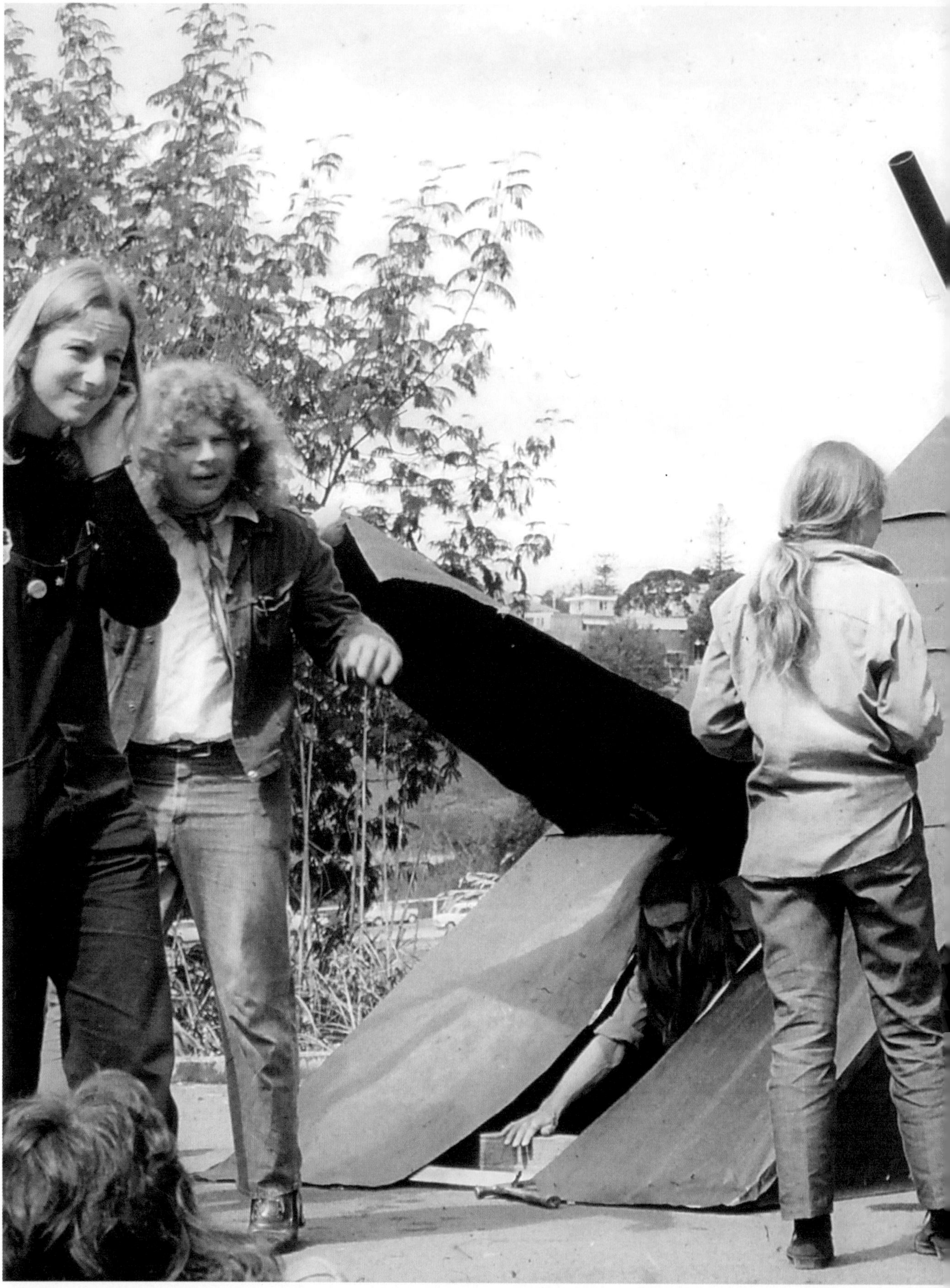

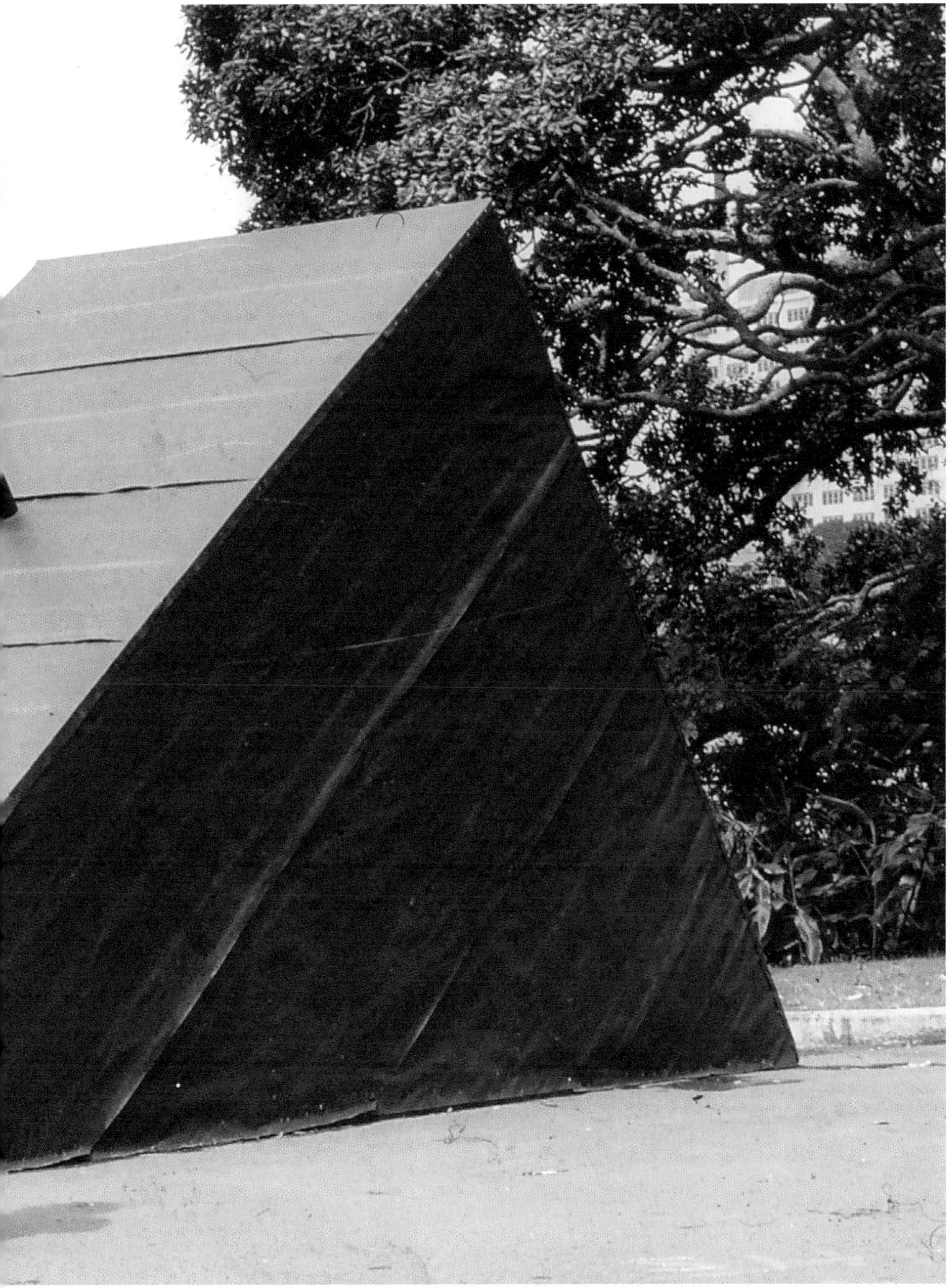

interior and exterior images of *Time Wedge*, which has the appearance of a student 'sit-in' structured around beams of shifting light.

PREVIOUS: Kimberley Gray, *Time Wedge*, 1971, black and white photograph. *Jim Allen Archive, E H McCormick Research Library, Auckland Art Gallery Toi o Tāmaki, gift of the artist, 2012. Photo by Max Oettli*

**

Early in her development of *Time Wedge*, Gray hints at the importance of plural experiences: art not for one, but 'success for all or none' — in other words, art solutions were better resolved in collaboration and through participation.[12] The 'all' she refers to is not just human multiplicity but our relationship with the universe itself. Her construction of a sculpture was turned into a tool for experiencing ourselves 'in relation' to others and the 'universe', after which its material form was dispensable. She is directing our senses outwards to the world and the effect of the environment on our bodies and selves. Reflecting on the work later, despite the awe experienced by viewers of *Time Wedge*, she cautioned herself: 'knocking people out just dulls their senses and boosts your own ego'.[13]

The following year Gray moved away from object-making and into participatory practice. Although her early interest in perception shares some similarities with the Light and Space artists who emerged in Southern California in the mid- to late 1960s, the medium of light was not the subject of her work. Nor was it her primary material, despite the fact that it may be the most visible. The real subject — and here we come closer to the concerns of American artist Robert Smithson (1938–1973) — is our location on a planet that is constantly in motion.

In 1972 Gray was a participating artist in *Influx*, a public art event for the Auckland Festival in Bledisloe Place in the central city. Conceptualised by students, it was nonetheless supported by Jim Allen's entrepreneurship and received financial and logistical support from Fletcher Construction. The temporary and public nature of *Influx* made it much like an early model of what we might now call a 'biennial' exhibition, with an ethos of new temporary artworks for the city by contemporary artists.[14]

The previous year's iteration, *Three Situations* — three large temporary sculptures in corresponding geometries (circle, square, triangle) and materials (plastic, wood, metal) by leading students Bruce Barber, David Brown and Maree Horner — was a more obvious extension of the sculpture department. *Three Situations* was ambitious in scale and production and involved temporary art situated in the city on a scale not seen before. *Influx* was an amorphous event with changing activities over the period 7–27 May. It was highly collaborative, and the authorial boundaries between the varying activities were difficult to determine, strongly participatory, performative and transient.

Gray proposed numerous ideas for audience encounters that would shift art's production of objects in urban space towards temporary encounters with the natural world, animals and agriculture. These included proposals for a 'spring grass' carpet (turf with springs underneath), a free fruit day, an arrangement of thirty-six chicken coops, a hot plate to alter the sound of rain, an 'earth day' with earth moved onto the location, a sugar-lump afternoon that would attract insects at night, and zoo-like cages for people with visiting animals.

There is humour and provocation within many of these initial ideas, which also responded to a localised debate at Elam about the role of art students at the university: they had been criticised for demanding special circumstances and framed as 'special animals'. However, these debates extended into serious enquiry for those who were attempting to define a new forum for art that could quite literally be in flux. Here in

Gray's notes they define a set of propositions that is timely for art's globally changing characteristics. A handwritten note by Gray describes the manifesto for *Influx* as follows:

> Evolving Complex (a flexible proposition) 1) that it be an evolving sequence of events 2) that it be based on the introduction of a 'force field' (an open situation) into the place 3) that the 'force field' comprise a sequence of ideas which will, with an element of spontaneity, be introduced, added to, subtracted from, reintroduced etc. according to the requirements of the participants in the place at the time[15]

With little surviving documentation, it is difficult to determine exactly what took place during the twenty days of *Influx*; that which does exist captures single moments or highly subjective recordings, often of incidental real-time occurrences.[16] For Gray, who, among other activities, ended up building an encounter on site with caged sheep, stacked hay sculptures, imported earth and trees, seeds and the daily documentation of rain patterns, *Influx* was an important catalyst for her transition towards an art practice that required active participation and states of change. In retrospect she wrote that 'the role of the public need not be limited to that of spectators nor receptacles for sensations, because we are not trying to entertain'.[17]

* *

Three years later, when asked to contribute to the *Project Programme* series of new art at Auckland City Art Gallery, Gray devised a seemingly abstract work, *Within Structures* (1975), in which she filled the entire Edmiston Gallery with a minimalist pyramid of haybales like a Robert Morris sculpture, twin light projections using empty slide carousels, and a spill of iron oxide. Entirely indeterminate and without contextual information, the work has remained an enigma. Seen in context, it was a clear case for art's open-ended formation, complete with empty frames of light in which visitors could perform.

This study and contestation of art that entertains rather than providing experimentation and research would occupy Gray for the following year. Alongside her exploration of philosophies that decentred intellectual/rational processes towards experiential/sensorial learning, the publication of Gene Youngblood's *Expanded Cinema* in 1970 was clearly an influence, not only for its exploration of the importance of video as art form, but also as a new form of communication, encounter and mediated interaction between people, highlighting the interconnected system within which individuals are immersed. Gray wrote: 'There is no permanent core self, only change within.'[18]

Following *Influx*, Gray produced three temporary and participatory installations that required viewers to take actions and perform meaning. The first was *Room 12*, exhibited in the fourteenth Universities Arts Festival and Air New Zealand Award in August 1972. The work consisted of a single room installation: a green lightbulb suspended from the ceiling, slightly off-centre, with shaving mirrors at ground level and a revolving chair.

Gray used compass points to position the light, chair and mirrors, although that was not made explicit. Participants were invited to enter, sit down and swivel on the chair. In contemplating the space and their location, they were asked to take a slip of paper, note their name and the time of their visit on it, and pin it to where they thought the chair should be placed. It was a confidently experimental work even among her peers at the time.

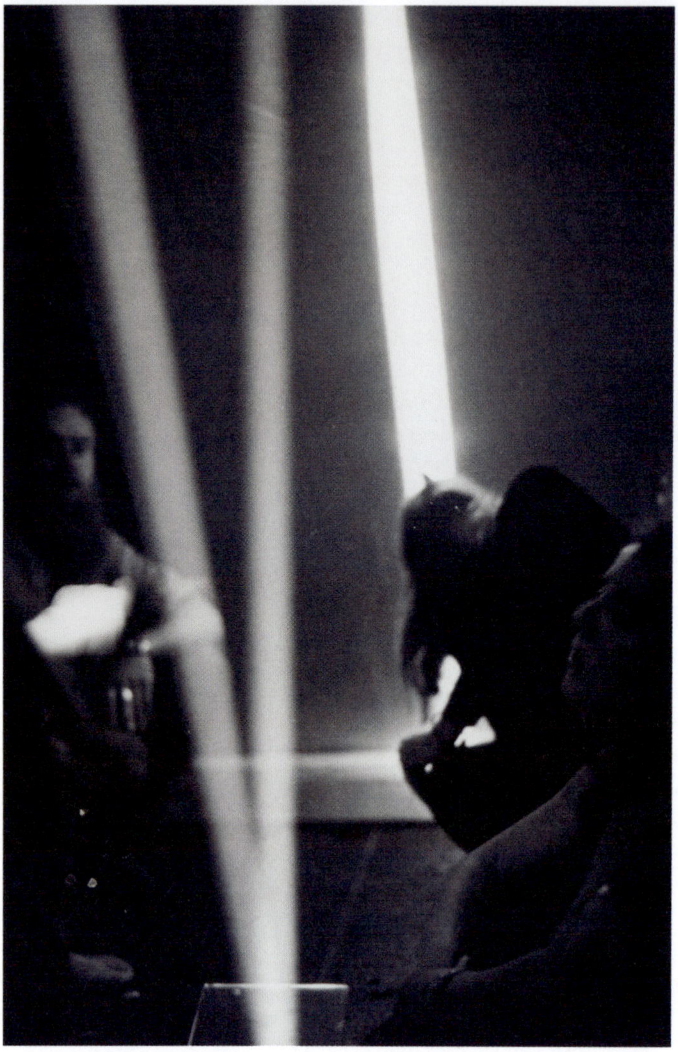

Kimberley Gray, *Time Wedge* (interior view), 1971, black and white photograph. *Jim Allen Archive, E H McCormick Research Library, Auckland Art Gallery Toi o Tāmaki, gift of Jim Allen, 2012. Photo by Max Oettli*

The second was *Pendente Lite* (1973), an installation she would reinstate for the Mildura Sculpture Triennial in 1975. *Pendente Lite* was equally sparse, this time with two 25-gallon (113-litre) tanks, one copper and one rubber. Both contained water. A lightbulb hung over the copper tank, on the bottom of which was the text 'ars est celare artem' ('it is art to conceal art', or 'true art conceals the means by which it is achieved'). The rubber tank contained the text 'amor sceleratus habendi' ('accursed love of possessing'), and a dripping hose disturbed the water's surface.

The seemingly open semantics of this work was an attempt by Gray to 'get herself out of the way' — in other words, to decentre the artist's position and place emphasis on the participant and their interpretative range, in this case 'reading' the association between these phrases and their material housing. By using the two well-known maxims in proximity but without defined association, Gray also intended to test the adequacy of words to define meaning, stressing the importance of the open-ended 'journey' of discovery.

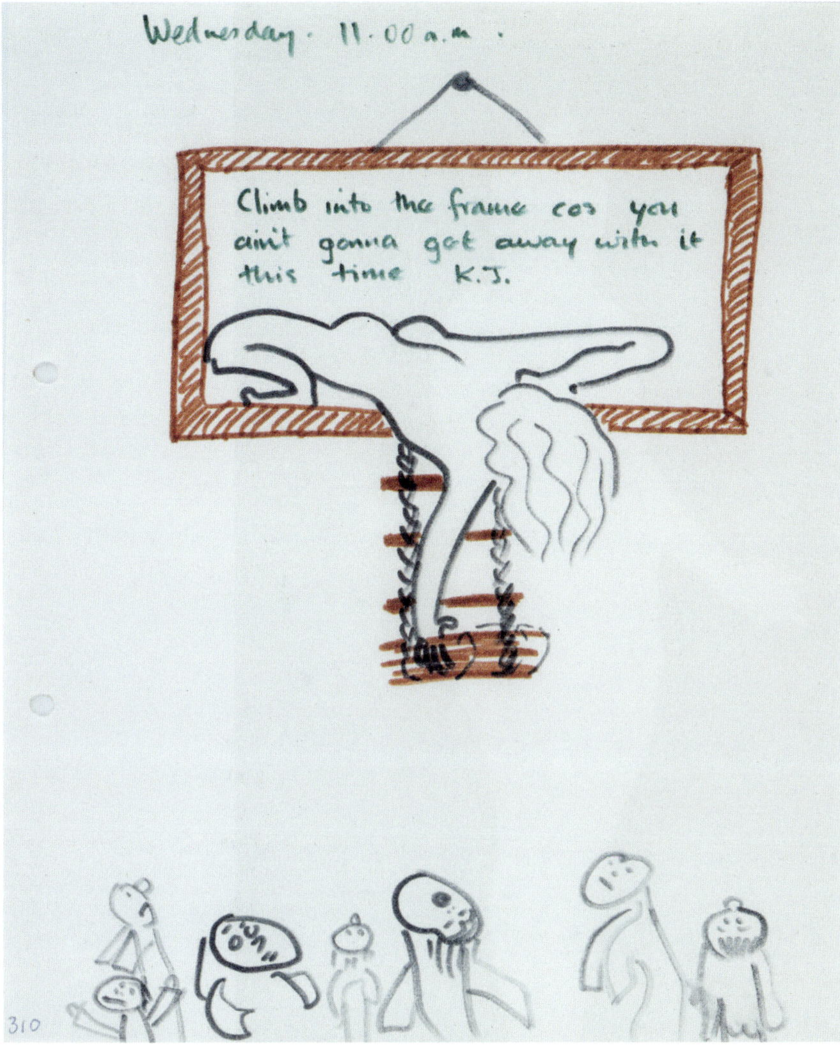

Kimberley Gray, *Untitled Drawing*, 'Climb into the frame . . .', c. 1973, ink on paper. *Kimberley Gray Archive, E H McCormick Research Library, Auckland Art Gallery Toi o Tāmaki, gift of Josephine Gray, 2019. Photo by Auckland Art Gallery Toi o Tāmaki*

Pendente Lite provoked much discussion among her peers at Elam and resulted in a period of intense enquiry for Gray. Her notes from her third year at Elam reveal a process of internalised critical appraisal: reflecting on Jack Burnham's *The Structure of Art* (1971) and the writings of anthropologist Claude Lévi-Strauss, she emerges with a deep suspicion of structuralist thinking. Conceptually and materially, this results in a critique of the 'frame' and systems that might provide barriers to the integration of art and life. She journeys through concepts of 'non-framing' in Eastern philosophy and the notion of Tao or uncontained flow.

* *

Ultimately this enquiry would be a catalyst for performance artwork that emerged in 1974, but ahead of this she made the third of the 'participatory' installations, titled *The Game*

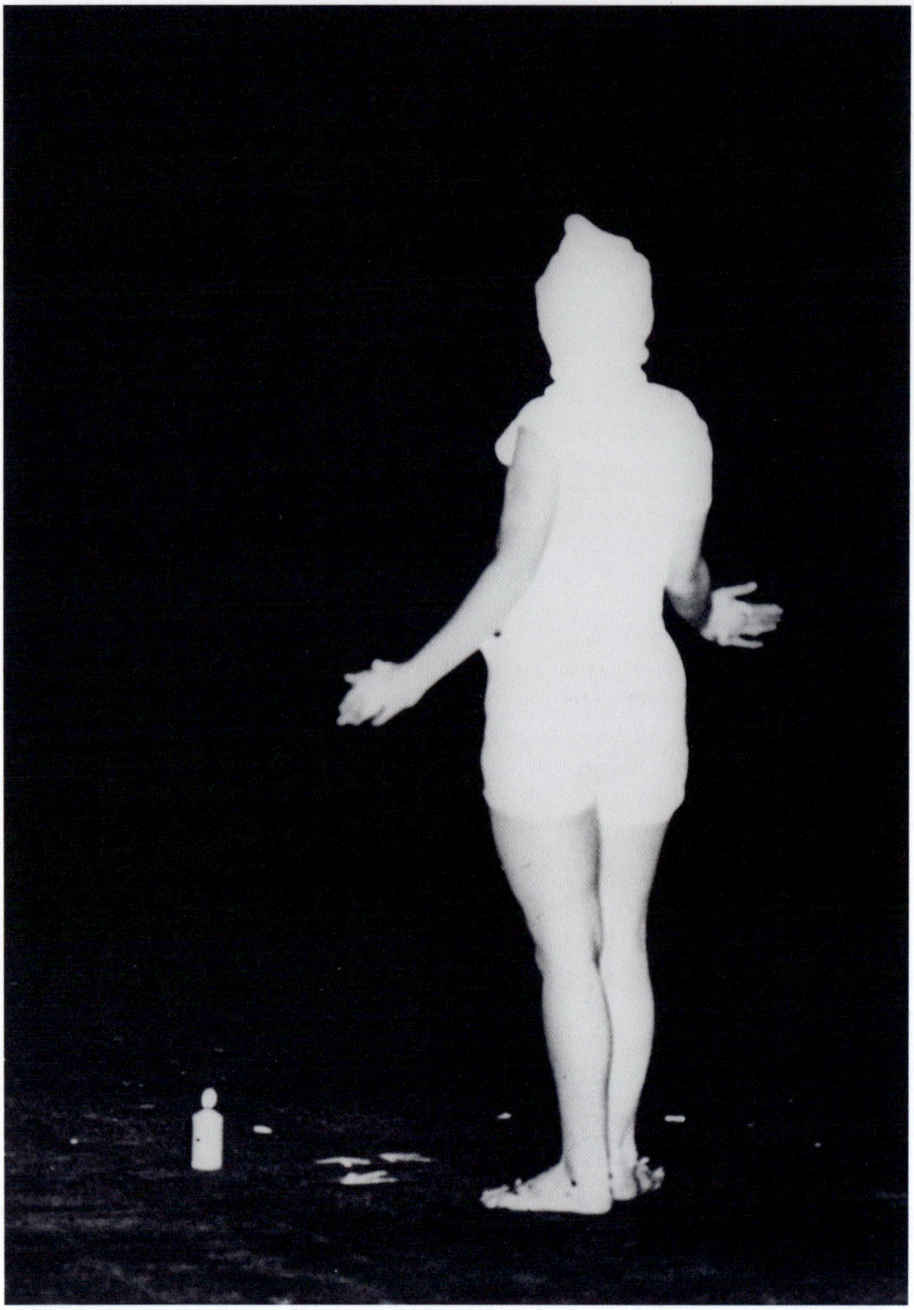

Kimberley Gray, *Draughts*, 1974, black and white photograph, performance documentation at *Pavilion K*, Epsom Showgrounds, Tāmaki Makaurau Auckland. *Jim Allen Archive, E H McCormick Research Library, Auckland Art Gallery Toi o Tāmaki, gift of the artist, 2012. Photo by Jim Allen*

Is Up — a clear reference to Youngblood's criticism of the role of games in entertainment culture. Gray herself removed this performative installation from her exhibition record after it was realised, despite the fact that it was at the time an important step in her attempts to realise the ungraspable and indefinable.

The Game Is Up had a fluid structure. Once again using the pre-existing format of a room, she erected four red lightbulbs and laid one on the floor. Four wooden stepladders were positioned, one beneath each bulb, and phrases printed on card in black Letraset were attached to the wall. The phrases read like incomplete parts of

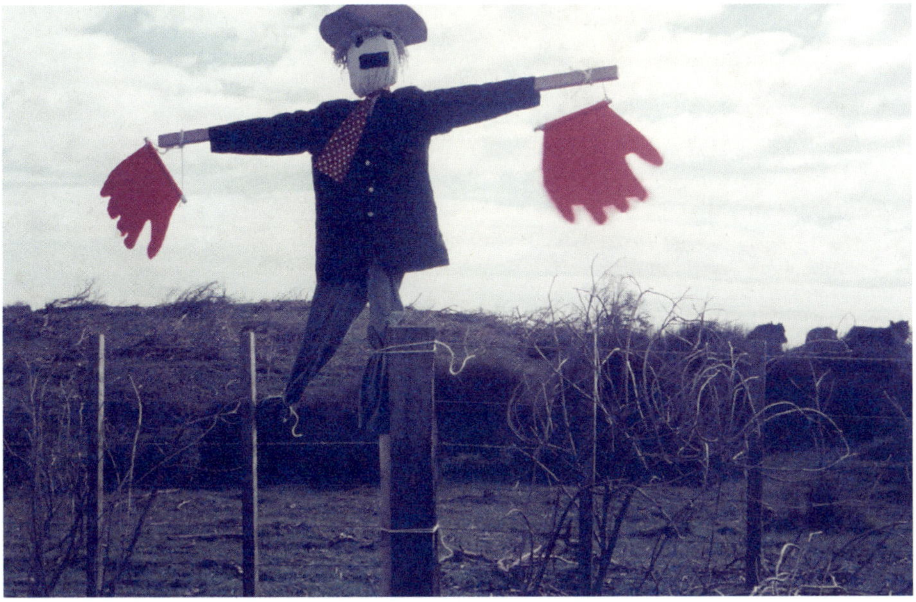

Kimberley Gray, *As Good a Land . . .*, 1974, site view of scarecrow installed, colour slide film. *Kimberley Gray Archive, E H McCormick Research Library, Auckland Art Gallery Toi o Tāmaki, gift of Josephine Gray, 2019*

a conversation and represented options or choices for participants. It seems some technical and structural issues with the components affected the experience of the work; however, its proposal was nonetheless interesting when considered in relation to contemporaneous work by Bruce Nauman, who also used rooms and language.

Given the amount of space devoted to problems of the frame in Gray's journal from 1973, it is interesting to reflect on Catherine Wood's definition of performance as 'a mode of working that draws attention to, and initiates transgressions of, art's defining frame'.[19] In this journal (noted as 'Wednesday 11.00 a.m.') she sketched a naked female body climbing out of a picture frame and down a suspended ladder. A cluster of figures (the audience) watches from below. In place of a picture, words inside the frame state: 'climb into the frame cos you ain't gonna get away with it this time K.J.'. The text reads like a restraining order, an echo of negative criticism, and a reminder of social and artistic boundaries.

Soon after this Gray undertook her first purely performance work with relatively few props and direct engagement of her own body. *Draughts* was realised for an event at the Epsom Showgrounds, organised by Allen and others and advertised simply as *Pavilion K*. It ran for five nights from 9 to 13 December 1974, and was a showcase of music, dance, installation and performance. Participants included Jack Body, The Feelers, Keir Volkerling, Richard Larter, Jim Allen, Nicholas Spill, John Lethbridge, Allan Thomas and John Cousins' Co-Active Play (CAP). Another student, Bruce Barber, also made a new work for the programme called *Like a Bat Outta Hell* (1974).

The photographic documents from *Draughts* show Gray wrapped in white bandages like a mummy, with a candle at her feet. It is austere and atmospheric. Jim Allen remembered her performance at *Pavilion K* as a 'very spectacular thing' because her presence was mysteriously positioned in relation to the audience. As the performance began, she whistled to the four points of the compass and recited an incantation while appearing fully wrapped in the white cloth of the bandage. When the incantation ceased the lights were cut and it became completely dark. When the lights came up again Gray had disappeared; in her place the white wrapping she had worn was streaming out from an industrial fan in the corner of the room and trailing across the floor.[20]

Gray represents the work somewhat differently, describing her body in the performance as an 'indicator' in the present, there to register elements of light and wind.[21] The work involved 'minimising the impositions on the space by including a vulnerable light source' susceptible to wind change, and marking the direction of the draught with coloured chalks on each day leading up to the performance. The presence of the body on the fifth day was there to register the otherwise invisible elements, leaving the bandaged remains in a trail of gusting wind as she disappeared from the space.

**

Gray had by now established a pattern of using tools such as mapping, graphing, notation and visual and aural records to record observations of her environment. But these alone do not explain the lyricism in the work. At this time she was reading substantial texts with a strong influence of Eastern thought. She stated in her notes that if she was going to release herself from 'the frame' — the mechanism that separates art from life, literally and figuratively — and develop a concept for a fluid structure for her work, she needed to travel East philosophically.

She turned to Russian philosopher Pyotr Demianovich Ouspensky, whose book *In Search of the Miraculous* (1949) summarised the teachings of mystic George Gurdjieff (1866–1949). Ouspensky, who had begun an exploration of Theosophy, journeyed to the East in search of higher knowledge. Following a meeting with Gurdjieff in 1915, he espoused his idea of 'the fourth way', a complex and metaphysical variation of Buddhist mindfulness that combined body, mind and emotions, described in scientific terminology. The relevance for Gray was Ouspensky's description of 'self-remembering', a technique that requires a division of attention, so that a person is attentive to what is going on not only in the exterior world but also in the interior.

This technique is very much in practice in her journals and notes, and in many ways explains her decision to enter into performance of the body, to amplify the senses and build awareness of the interior world within a primarily visual tradition. As was the case in many parts of the so-called Western world in this time, engagement with systems of belief that sat outside the conventions of knowledge aided the questioning of Western empiricism and revaluation of received cultural forms. Gray was not unique in her engagement with esoteric thought in this period, but her practice began to explore a counter-logical, de-structured position, which was radical even among her peers.

Similarly mystical in its relationship to the conventions of mapping and earthly terrain was *As Good a Land . . .* (1974), a performance project submitted for completion of her Master of Fine Arts at Elam. The work consisted of a line of scarecrows with enormous red hands, installed in the North Island of Aotearoa along a line that marked the shortest route on the map between Tāmaki Makaurau and Te Whanganui-a-Tara. Gray placed the scarecrows with the assistance of Allen and a white van on a trip that took them to remote locations in the central North Island, and enlisted participation from rural school children. She then hired a Piper aircraft to fly at low altitude down the island and, with the assistance of Bruce Barber, captured imagery of the scarecrows from the air in 16mm film and photographs.

It is hard to imagine an intention of the work other than a test and visualisation of the map's abstract framework on the land. In Gray's notes, however, it is clear the work has other motivations, in particular a kind of absurdist humour and word play. Alongside the formal deployment of the map's longitudinal line for the purpose of travel, Gray rearranges the expression 'as the crow flies', putting crows on the land and humans in the sky. The scarecrows are both substitute crows and a line of human-like figures.

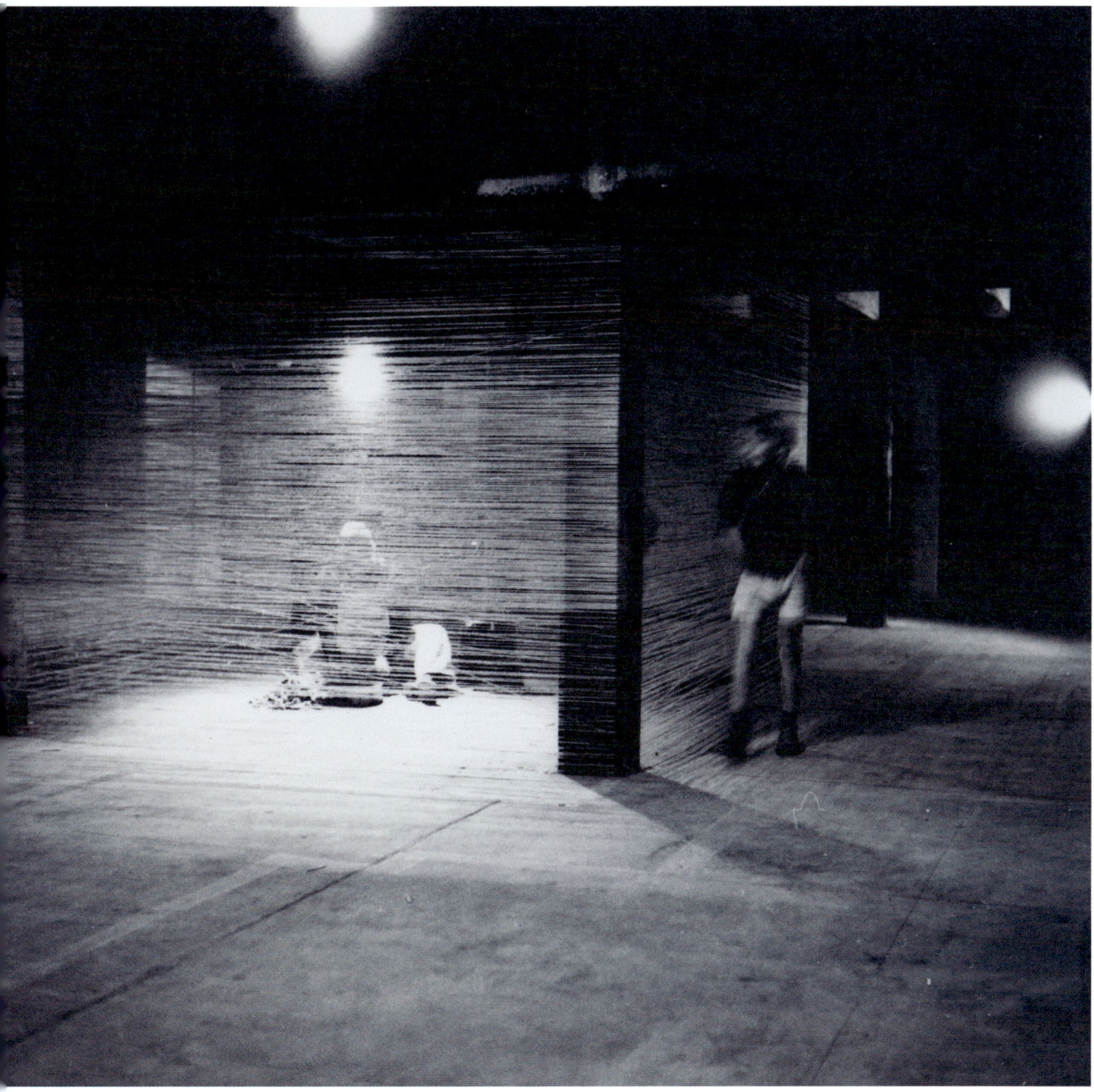

Kimberley Gray, *Sweater*, 1976, black and white photograph, performance documentation, Experimental Art Foundation, Adelaide, performed by Jim Allen. *Jim Allen Archive, E H McCormick Research Library, Auckland Art Gallery Toi o Tāmaki, gift of the artist, 2012*

For Gray, it was an absurdist, alternative route to mark an invisible line. Early in her development of the work she wrote: 'Diverging between the parallel flights of the crow and its spirit, the wingless travellers find their zone of credibility.'[22] She was certainly drawn to the structures that hold us in place on the earth, and points to the sometimes absurd mapping systems that orient the world through the lens of man.

**

In Gray's final performance work of this period, she emphasised the power of sensory cues. *Sweater* was realised for the 1976 Adelaide Festival of Arts, Australia, in the basement of the Experimental Art Foundation. The site was an old jam factory with the atmosphere of a bunker. Gray wove sisal thread around four concrete support pillars to create a room bounded by thread. The performance was made by Allen after Gray unexpectedly returned to Aotearoa. Photographs show him sitting on the floor in the centre of this threaded room, progressively smashing a sackful of root ginger with a mallet and putting the pulp into a pot of boiling water.

Sweater was Gray's response to the building's original use, creating an evocative exchange between there, here, now and its past, as well as an analogy of how smells and memories attach to clothing. Allen recalled the smell of ginger clinging to the thread, which in documentation creates a haze through which we view the activity.

Gray made one other performance during a teachers' conference in 1984, but *Sweater* was the last work she made for public exhibition. Although well supported by staff of the sculpture department at Elam, and Allen in particular,[23] there was no structure or example during this period for how a female artist could progress and sustain her highly ephemeral art practice while supporting herself financially. Although radical ephemerality and formlessness had been opened up in the Elam sculpture department in the 1970s, the mechanisms to support this practice were lagging, particularly for women.

It is also possible that the conviction with which Gray and her contemporaries addressed humanity's relationship with the earth, and its parallels with an international period of concern, faded out in the consumptive and economically buoyant period of the 1980s. While some artists continued to demonstrate engagement around key issues of environmental impact, such as nuclear testing in the Pacific, Gray's singular engagement with our sensorial, self-reflexive and persuasive understanding of our point in time and place on earth has faded from view. When examined in hindsight, however, it is clear that this deeply explorative period of work carried an ambition and depth of research that made it outstanding in its time, even by international standards.

Her concerns with perception and use of sculpture as a tool to bend light and reveal the atmosphere have contemporary resonance with such well-known figures as Olafur Eliasson. Deeply concerned with her immediate location on the planet, at a macro and micro level, Gray returned regularly to a small concrete poem she wrote across a pedestrian crossing in 1973, which expresses well the arc of her practice. Cognisant of her shift from the northern to the southern hemisphere as a young adult and what that meant conceptually and psychically, she wrote as if giving an impression of herself standing on the urban underlay: 'I jumped/ white to white/ on the crossing/ trying not to fall/ into the sky.'

NOTES

1 In 1976, Jim Allen and Wystan Curnow wrote and published *New Art: Some recent New Zealand sculpture and post-object art* (Auckland: Heinemann, 1976). They resisted any single terminology that had hovered around major changes in art's form in the late 1960s and 1970s internationally, including process art, performance art and so on.

2 Minor references to her work are included in the following: Anthony Green, 'The Spring Equinox at the School of Fine Arts', *Arts & Community* 7, no. 11 (1971): 7; Christina Barton, 'Post-Object Art in New Zealand 1969–1979: Experiments in art and life' (Master's thesis, University of Auckland, 1987); Deborah Lawler-Dormer and Christina Barton, eds, *Alter/Image: Feminism and Representation in New Zealand Art, 1973–1993* (Auckland/Wellington: Auckland City Art Gallery and City Gallery, 1993); *Action Replay: Post-script*, exhibition catalogue on the occasion of the *Action replay* series of exhibitions curated by Christina Barton, Wystan Curnow, John Hurrell and Robert Leonard (Auckland/New Plymouth: Artspace and Govett-Brewster Gallery, 2002), 18; and Curnow, *Putting the Land on the Map: Art and cartography in New Zealand since 1840*, exhibition catalogue published on the occasion of *Putting the Land on the Map* touring exhibition March 1989–November 1990 (New Plymouth: Govett-Brewster Art Gallery, 1989). However, Gray's work was not illustrated or included in retrospective exhibitions of the period until 2018 during *Groundswell: Avant-garde Auckland 1971–79*, Auckland Art Gallery Toi o Tāmaki.

3 Wystan Curnow, 'Making It New', *New Zealand Listener* (6 September 1975).

4 Lucy R. Lippard, 'Notes on Seeing Some Recent American Art in New Zealand', *Auckland City Art Gallery Quarterly* 59 (1975): 2.

5 Both the Jim Allen and Bruce Barber archives include ongoing correspondence with Lippard after her visit, and following Barber's relocation to North America, he would stay in touch. Equally during my interviews with the artists in *Groundswell* several recalled a period of reciprocity with Bochner, as he visited homes and studios.

6 Kimberley Gray, undated essay, Kimberley Gray Archive, E H McCormick Research Library, Auckland Art Gallery Toi o Tāmaki.

7 Recalling his time at Elam School of Fine Arts, Allen has said: 'I had to formulate my teaching philosophy from the ground up.' This meant 'unlearning' some of his academic training, reinforcing the use of new media, encouraging the breakdown of traditional artistic boundaries and, importantly, directing students outside the classroom. Jim Allen Archive, E H McCormick Research Library, Auckland Art Gallery Toi o Tāmaki.

8 Kimberley Gray, correspondence and documents sent to Jim Allen, 2002, Jim Allen Archive.

9 Kimberley Gray, unpublished artist notes, 1971, Kimberley Gray Archive.

10 Ibid.

11 Ibid.

12 Ibid.

13 Kimberley Gray, unpublished artist notes, 1973, Kimberley Gray Archive.

14 There was no art biennial or serial exhibition of contemporary art in Aotearoa at this time; however, the Mildura Sculpture Triennial occurred between 1961 and 1988, and included a large number of contemporary New Zealand artists. In many ways Mildura was the forerunner for the Biennale of Sydney, which had its first iteration in 1973, making it the third-oldest international biennial. In 1976 Auckland City Art Gallery launched the Pan Pacific Biennale, which was ultimately a one-off occurrence.

15 Kimberley Gray, unpublished artist notes, 1972, Kimberley Gray Archive.

16 There are several mentions of *Influx* in the Jim Allen and Bruce Barber archives through ephemera and some still documentation. Importantly there was also a review by Bruce Barber, 'Influx or Done Time in Bledisloe' in *Elam Seed* 5 (1972), and Adrian Hall's 'Influx and the Creative Continuum' in *Rhinocerotical* (1972). Barber makes the important point that the use of video recorder and monitors in *Influx* both documented and created real-time relay within the daily experience of the event. The Kim Gray archive also contains a 16mm film document from *Influx*, but its focus is largely on atmosphere and audience reaction, making it quite hard to determine content from this source.

17 Kimberley Gray, unpublished artist notes, 1974, Kimberley Gray Archive.

18 Ibid.

19 Catherine Wood, *Performance in Contemporary Art* (London: Tate Publishing, 2018), 10.

20 Jim Allen, conversation with the author, 2018.

21 Kimberley Gray, correspondence and documents sent to Jim Allen, 2002.

22 Kimberley Gray, unpublished artist notes, 1974, Kimberley Gray Archive.

23 Gray was twice the recipient of the Elam sculpture prize, 1972/1974.

REFERENCES

Barton, Christina. 'Post-Object Art in New Zealand 1969–1979: Experiments in art and life'. Master's thesis, University of Auckland, 1987.

Barton, Christina and Deborah Lawler-Dormer, eds. *Alter/Image: Feminism and representation in New Zealand Art, 1973–1993*. Wellington/Auckland: City Gallery Wellington and Auckland Art Gallery Toi o Tāmaki, 1993.

Brennan, Stella, Robert Leonard and Hanna Scott, eds. *Action Replay: Post-script*. Exhibition catalogue on the occasion of the *Action Replay* series of exhibitions curated by Christina Barton, Wystan Curnow, John Hurrell and Robert Leonard. Auckland/New Plymouth: Artspace and Govett-Brewster Gallery, 2002.

Curnow, Wystan. 'Making It New'. *New Zealand Listener* (6 September 1975).

——— 'Project Programme 1975, Nos. 1–6'. *Auckland City Art Gallery Quarterly* 62–63 (December 1976): 15–22.

——— *Putting the Land on the Map: Art and cartography in New Zealand since 1840*. Exhibition catalogue published on the occasion of *Putting the Land on the Map* touring exhibition March 1989–November 1990. New Plymouth: Govett-Brewster Art Gallery, 1989.

Curnow, Wystan and Jim Allen, eds. *New Art: Some recent New Zealand sculpture and post-object art*. Auckland: Heinemann, 1976.

Green, Anthony. 'The Spring Equinox at the School of Fine Arts'. *Arts & Community* 7, no. 11 (1971): 7.

Jim Allen Archive, E H McCormick Research Library, Auckland Art Gallery Toi o Tāmaki.

Kimberley Gray Archive, E H McCormick Research Library, Auckland Art Gallery Toi o Tāmaki.

Lippard, Lucy R. 'Notes on Seeing Some Recent American Art in New Zealand'. *Auckland City Art Gallery Quarterly* 59 (1975): 2–3.

Wood, Catherine. *Performance in Contemporary Art*. London: Tate Publishing, 2018.

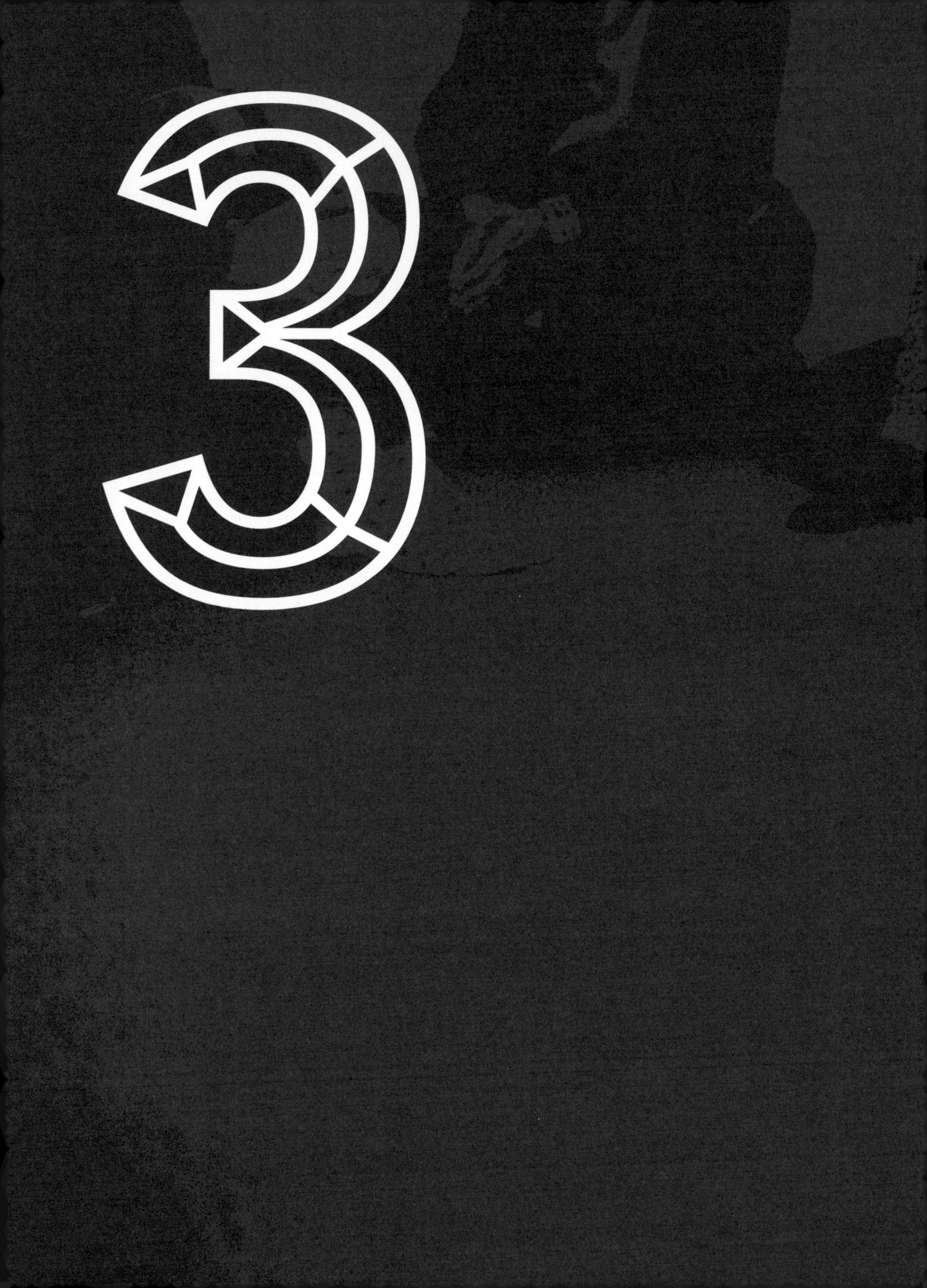

3

GETTING IT STRAIGHT: CONTACT, 1974 AND 2010

Jim Allen & James Charlton[1]

The 'corporate box' was full. Pressed up against the mezzanine handrail three or four deep, those who had made the pilgrimage to Ngāmotu New Plymouth on the west coast of Aotearoa New Zealand's North Island would have the 'god-view' of the re-enactment of *Contact* — Jim Allen's 1974 seminal post-object performance work. Staged by the Govett-Brewster Art Gallery as part of Tyler Cann and Mercedes Vicente's exhibition *Points of Contact: Jim Allen, Len Lye, Hélio Oiticica* (2010–11),[2] this was the first re-enactment of a work that had already come to assume a semi-mythical status for subsequent generations of artists — a reputation based largely on ephemera and sparse analogue documentation such as that found in Allen and Wystan Curnow's *New Art: Some recent New Zealand sculpture and post-object art.*[3]

What was it, one wonders, that the expectant crowd had come to New Plymouth to see? Surely they could not have come anticipating a repeat of the 'psychedelic'[4] arousal to which those who — arms crossed defensively — huddled within the roped-off entrance to Auckland City Art Gallery in 1974 bore witness: the 'delicious lubricant' of paint smeared with increasing eroticism across the spectatorial divide.[5] However, while ostensibly being the same work, the re-enactment was an altogether different event, one from which, perhaps inevitably, the zeitgeist of that earlier time had been estranged.

The original structure of *Contact* was described by Allen in 1974 as a cyclic live activity that moves 'progessively from "Computor Dance" to "Parangole Capes" and reaches a climax with "Body Articulation[/Imprint]"'.[6] Allen goes on to say: 'The "Computor Dance" situation is a parody on the computer and systems prevalent in our technological society. Communication is achieved only by means of a high-pitched electronic wail' emitted by infrared sensors. 'With the development of the "Cape" action a transformation is initiated.'[7] Bound in layers of fabric, the performers 'lie still for long periods. They explore the avenues of movement left to them, arching back and legs, inching the body and attempting to roll over' as they 'work their way to the centre of the space', where, 'using their teeth they proceed with the task of freeing each other'.[8] According to Allen, '"Body Articulation" is the antithesis of "Computor Dance" and the complete release of tensions generated by "Parangole Capes" . . . The whole occasion becomes a joyful happening accompanied by laughter and shouting as the players attack each other with buckets of colour.'[9]

Much like the objective stated by Allen and Curnow in *New Art* — 'our purpose here is to get some things straight'[10] — this chapter makes visible some connections to contemporary art practices that might otherwise remain unclear. 'Getting it straight', here, resonates with an authority of intent that can only be asserted over an artwork by the artist. This tone is, we hope, present in the text through Allen's voice as he takes the opportunity to reflect on the re-enactments of his work some fifty years on in the year of his 100th birthday. This voice (re)asserts questions about the importance of audiences and the nature of participation that seem to have been overlooked in the discourse around the performative nature of post-object art.

This chapter has been developed collaboratively out of conversations between us both (Jim and James) about Allen's work since 2010. Such extended conversations shun the interview model that would have contrived a formal relationship foreign to the shared understanding that has arisen over the years of interaction between us. This is not to say that we see eye to eye on all matters; rather that the whakapapa of ideas discussed here has been played out in conversations that are mutually formative. Such entanglement has its own way of straightening things out.

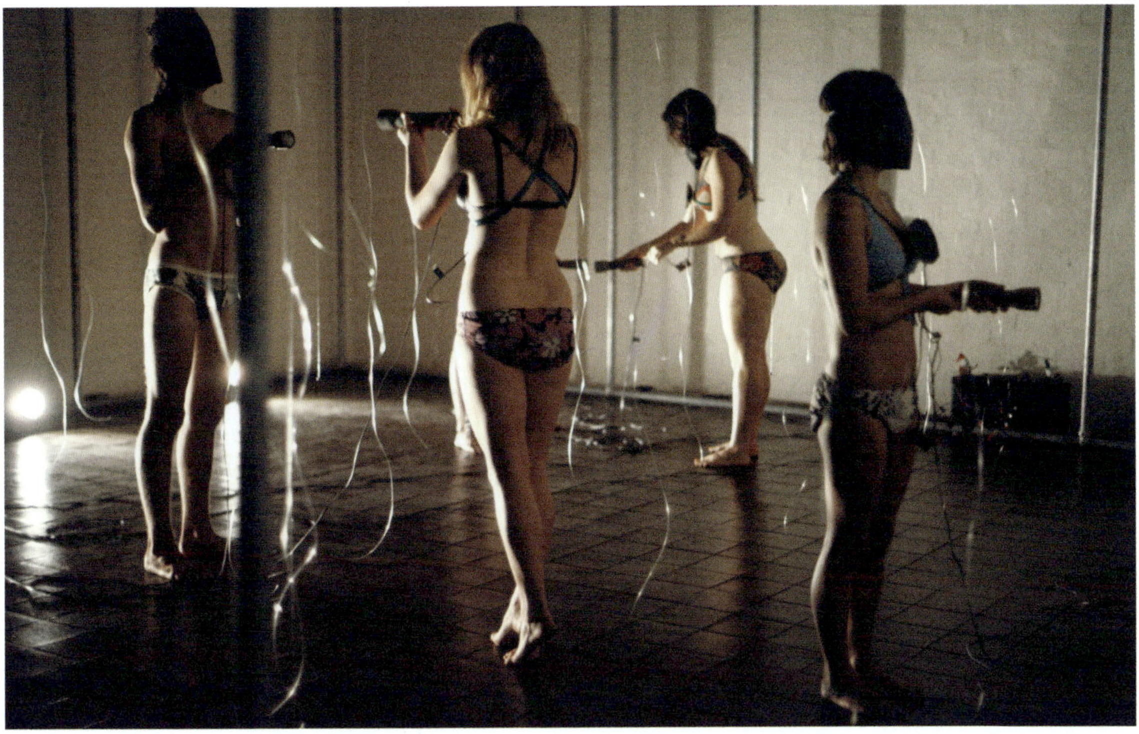

RE-ENACTMENTS

Jim Allen, *Contact (Computor Dance)*, 1974, colour photograph. *Jim Allen Archive, E H McCormick Research Library, Auckland Art Gallery Toi o Tāmaki, gift of Jim Allen, 2012. Photo by Bryony Dalefield*

As art critic Sven Lütticken chronicles, artists and art institutions in the early 2000s took an interest in re-enacting performance work.[11] As international institutions such as Whitechapel Art Gallery began staging re-enactments of works such as Carolee Schneemann's *Meat Joy* (1964) and Stuart Brisley's *Beneath Dignity* (1977),[12] it is not surprising that New Zealand curators cast their eyes back over Aotearoa New Zealand's own performance art history with comparable verve. In tracing connections between Allen and the Brazilian artist Hélio Oiticica, Cann and Vicente's 2010 *Points of Contact* is thus inevitably informed by the same questions about the nature of re-enactments that had been raised by northern hemisphere theorists: Can the present 'unpack, embody, or disentangle the past', or does it challenge the past, turning it into 'a site for invention and renewal'?[13]

Inasmuch as performance art resists the market 'by working with the one artistic medium that had not yet been commodified, namely, the human body',[14] re-enactments challenge the neoliberal marketplace through their propensity to destroy the possibility of 'presence'. The resulting paradox, Amelia Jones suggests, resides in 'the tension between our desire for the material (for the other's body; for "presence"; for the "true event") and the impossibility of ever fixing this in space and time'.[15] Such a hunger for past presences demands what Claire Bishop calls a 'mediating object'[16] — a representation in the form of re-enactment that has a tendency to 'lead inexorably to the marketplace',[17] resulting in 'art fair art': momentary spectacles in the performance of the present.[18]

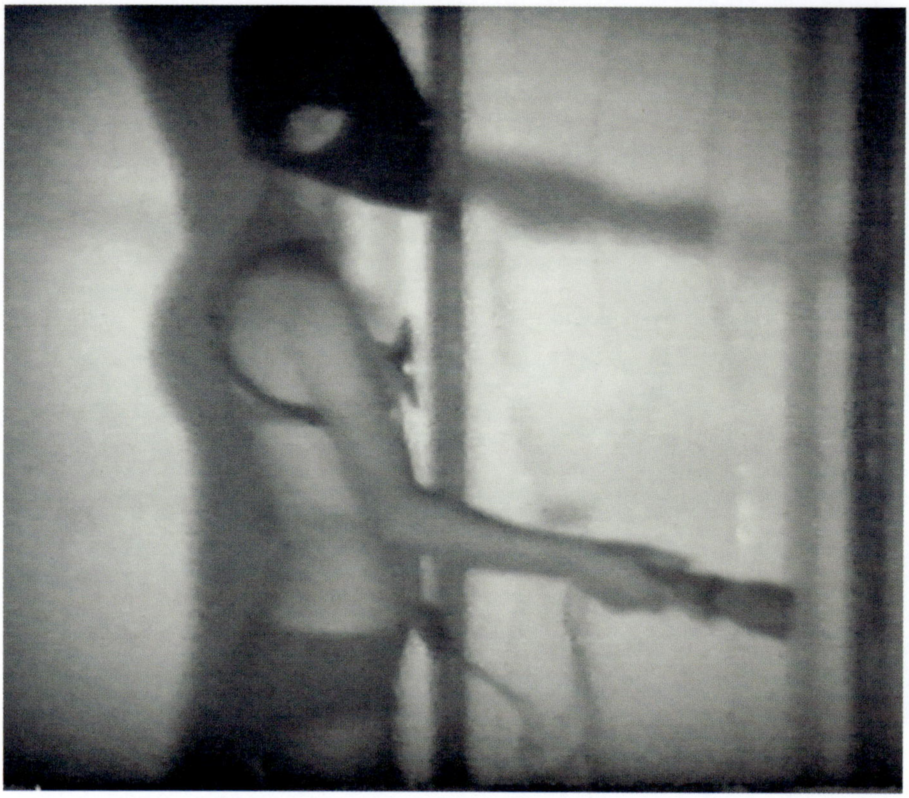

Jim Allen, *Contact (Computor Dance)* detail, 1974, black and white photograph. *Auckland Art Gallery Toi o Tāmaki, purchased 2013. Photo by Bryony Dalefield*

As might be inferred from our discussion of audiences, our focus here is not in questions of liveness or of spectacle — although consideration of Allen's work in this context is no doubt warranted. Rather, following Frazer Ward, we elect to re-enter Allen's work through the audiences and participants of the two performances, *Contact* 1974 and 2010, considering the positioning of each as it speaks to the nature of performance in post-object art as originally conceived by Allen. Ward's account of performances by Vito Acconci and Chris Burden makes it clear that minimalist dichotomies between interior/private and exterior/public served as a point of departure for key 1970s performance art by these artists.[19] Reflecting on minimalism's connection to post-object art in 2002, Curnow brings this point closer to home, clarifying the phenomenological basis of Ward's argument.[20]

Referring to an image of himself standing at the centre of Robert Morris' *Untitled* (1965), which had been included in the exhibition *Some Recent American Art* at Auckland City Art Gallery in 1974, Curnow notes how the '*work* and the *viewer* have exchanged places', decentring the artwork and blurring subject/object distinctions.[21] This kind of sculpture, he suggests, 'constructs a phenomenological viewer',[22] one who we suggest was annexed by post-object art rather than abandoned, as might be inferred from Ward.[23] The importance of Curnow's observation is that audiences-at-a-distance were called into question in favour of prioritising the audience-as-participant. Returning to the audiences and participants of *Contact*, then, it is important to set out the conditions surrounding the 1974 performance, as they are significantly different from those of later performances in a way that extends Curnow's framing of the 'phenomenological subject'.[24]

PEOPLE DON'T DO THESE THINGS IN FRONT OF OTHER PEOPLE

Contact (1974) was first performed at Auckland City Art Gallery as part of the exhibition *Four Men in a Boat*.[25] In contrast with contemporary turn-around times, the entire exhibition was relatively short, lasting only one week. *Contact* itself was performed on the first day of the exhibition, and videos of the performances played simultaneously on three black and white monitors for the remainder of the week. Although the event required significant planning and preparation on the part of the artists, there was relatively little publicity around it — an announcement in *Craccum*, the University of Auckland Students' Association magazine, is part of the sparse remaining evidence of advertising for the event.[26] The audience consisted largely of curious passers-by, with news of the exhibition spreading within the art community by word of mouth.[27] As Allen asserts, 'It just happened.' The audience was incidental and their enthusiastic response was something of a surprise!

By comparison, there was nothing left to chance about the audience for the 2010 re-enactment of *Contact*. It was attended by an altogether different crowd, one who knew what they were there for — to witness a spectacle of making present the past: a parody of presence which, as Jones has pointed out, is inextricably linked to documentation.[28] Websites were designed, adverts appeared in *Art New Zealand*, invitations were sent to selected mailing lists, catalogues were printed and ready for sale. The art machine of public and dealer galleries, along with funding bodies, was invested in this.[29]

This was a 'professional audience' and they mattered. But although the effect of the neoliberal marketplace on performance art is interesting to consider, this is not our purpose here.[30] What we want to get straight by making this comparison is not just that re-enactments are fraught with inherent contradictions of presence, but that the phenomenological subject of post-object art performances is, advancing Christina Barton writing on Curnow, '"inside" the work'.[31]

POST-OBJECT VIEWING

Curnow had become the 'house writer' of post-object art. Allen enthusiastically recollects Curnow's involvement, saying we 'got ourselves a writer', indicating how keenly aware the group was of the need for critical positioning of their work. Curnow was familiar with the work of his doctoral supervisor Morse Peckham, and in particular Peckham's concept of 'psychic insulation' as a means of disorienting the artist and audience in order to produce innovative experiences, which made him well equipped for the job.[32] But rather than seeking the privilege of distance — a god-view of performance art as critic and audience member — Curnow chose literally to immerse himself in the action; no longer audience but participant.

This positioning was perhaps most keenly evident in his text on Bruce Barber's *Mt Eden Crater Performance* (1974), written in situ as a participant in the work.[33] Significantly, as Barton clarifies, while Curnow was writing in the moment from inside the work, he understood that he was working *between* the artwork and the reader of his text, and that the phenomenological experience of being caught up in the artwork could not in any way be re-enacted.[34]

The phenomenological subject of post-object performance art was, then, not so

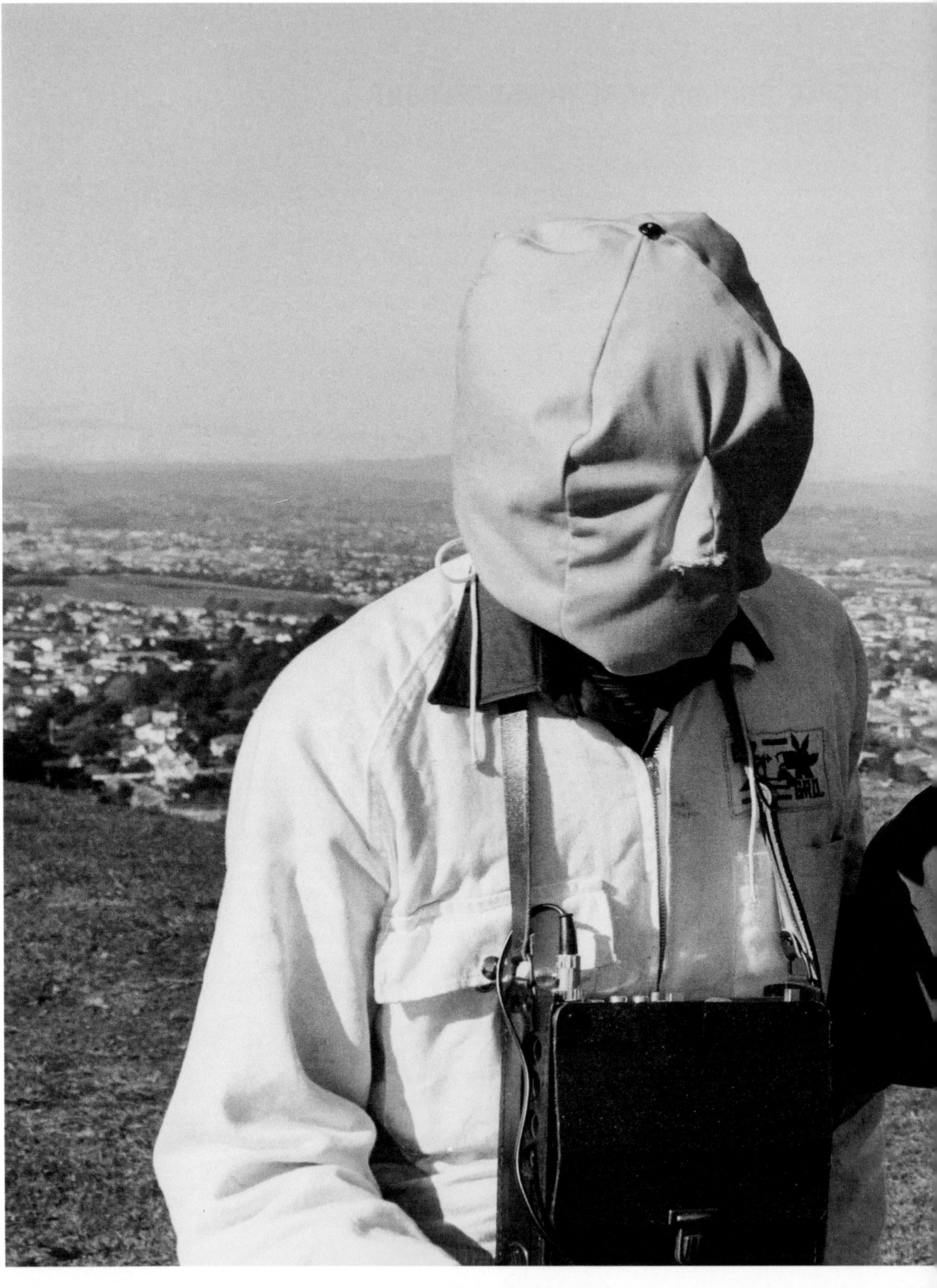

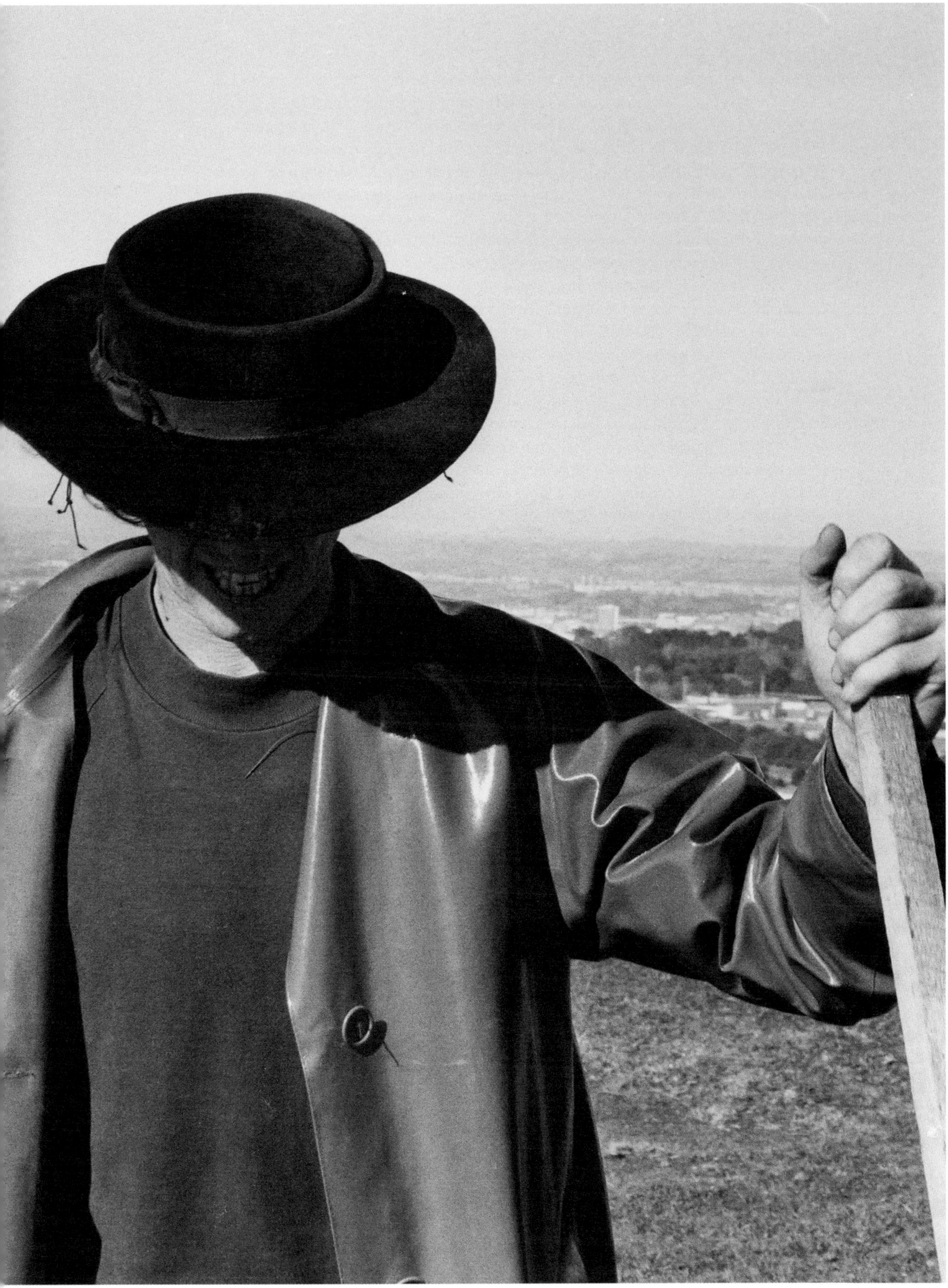

much the audience. Rather there was at best an ambivalence to the audience on the part of post-object artists. As Allen asserts, 'we really didn't care if there were any spectators or not', and certainly what might be called a 'professional audience' was of little interest.

This stance is echoed by Bruce Barber, another prominent figure in post-object art, who sought to exchange the terms 'performer' and 'audience' with the notion of 'active' and 'passive' participants, both considered as phenomenological subjects coexisting in the work.[35] Like the viewer of a minimalist artwork, Barber's subject is phenomenologically participatory: engaged in experiences of overload or deprivation through which their 'capacity for sensory and intellectual stimulation' might be enlarged.[36] Such psychedelic intent is evident in Barber's recurring persona of The Blind Master: the hooded character at the centre of *Mt Eden Crater Performance*,[37] just as it is evident in the masked and muted EZ-GRO employees in Kieran Lyons' *Spring from the Cross* (1975) as well as the blindfolded participants in part 1 of Allen's *Contact — Computor Dance*.

PREVIOUS: Bruce Barber, *Mt Eden Crater Performance*, The Blind Master detail, 1974. *Courtesy the artist. Photo by Kieran Lyons*

As such the performative undertaking of post-object art was to subject the artist, or the 'active participant', to mind-altering experiences by tasking them with something they had never done before.[38] Something totally new, an 'authentic' experience in which they were present for themselves: open to the experience of being active in the work without recourse to representation in a way that contested the need for an audience, even one reconceived as a 'phenomenological subject'.

Responding to a call for participants made by Allen to students at the School of Education,[39] the phenomenological subjects of *Contact* (1974) 'stumbled' into the work blind to the situations they were about to encounter.[40] Briefed in a pragmatic manner shortly before the performance, they were told the tasks they needed to undertake with minimal reference to *how* they should act. With limited awareness of contemporary art and having only met each other on the day of the performance, they were simply to be present in their psychedelic experience. In the sense that they were inexperienced, they were amateurs when compared to the professional performers recruited by Becca Wood for the 2010 re-enactment of the work.[41]

Although Allen briefed both groups in the same matter-of-fact tone, the trained dancers — who met for rehearsals in Tāmaki Makaurau Auckland several weeks before the 2010 performance — behaved 'professionally': they took it upon themselves to hold meetings, presumably to strategise and define roles within the given brief.[42]

As a result, the performers in the re-enactments of *Contact* were positioned very differently from those who participated in the earlier work. Rather than subjecting themselves to a psychedelic experience as understood through Barber, they were orchestrators of an experience for others: 'diva hokum', as claimed by Lydia Brawner in 2013.[43] As a 're-performer', Brawner — one of the professional performers engaged for Marina Abramović's Museum of Modern Art retrospective in New York City — brings insight into the inherent conflicts of re-enactment from the perspective of an active participant, pointing out that rather than peeking into their own minds, re-performers are engaged in the process of icon-making.[44]

It should be of little surprise, then, that things get bent out of shape when iconic works such as *Contact* are re-enacted and commitment to psychedelic transformation ceases to be the subject of the work, replaced by the icon figure of the artist, paradoxically made present though the absence of the phenomenal subject — one now transformed by professionalism into an iconic representation.

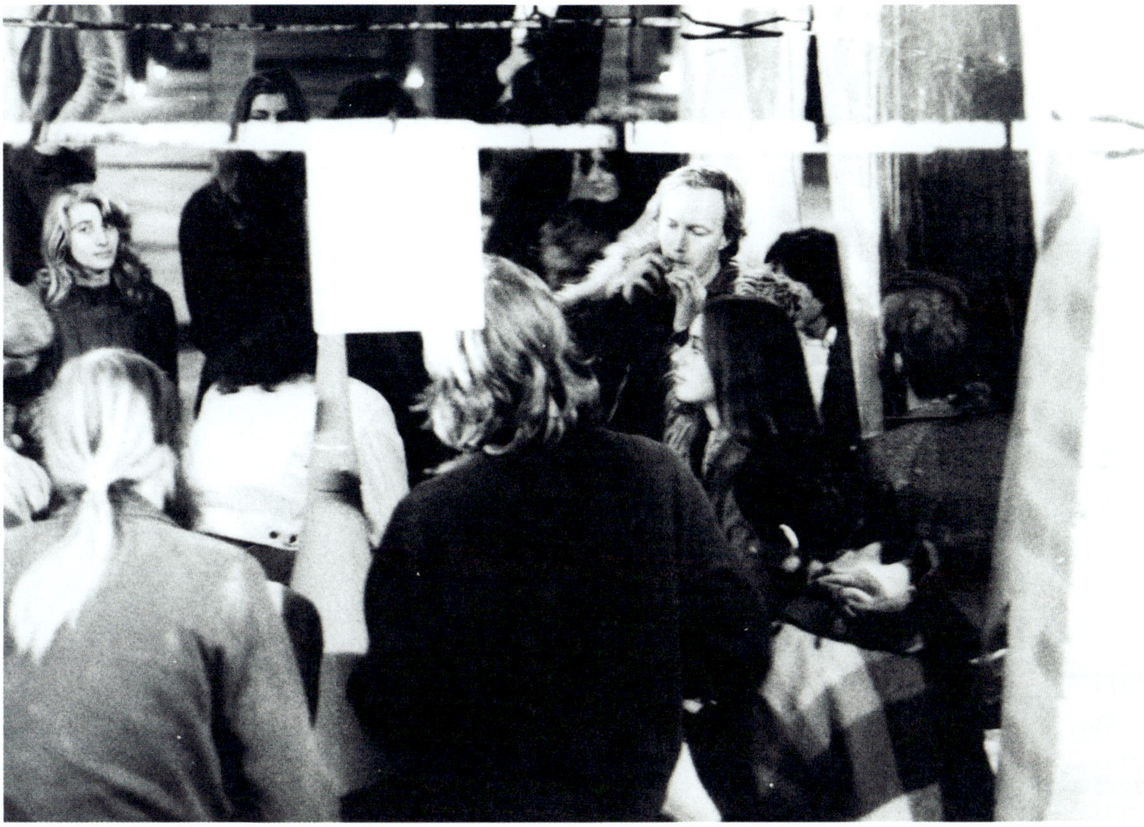

Jim Allen, *Elastic Sided Boot*, at Experimental Art Foundation, Adelaide, 1976. *Jim Allen Archive, E H McCormick Research Library, Auckland Art Gallery Toi o Tāmaki, gift of Jim Allen, 2012*

EVERYONE IS ON A DIFFERENT TRIP

> In art, models, metaphors, and images of possible forms of life can be freely generated, tried, and related to the actual forms of life. In art we can discover ourselves — perhaps even reinvent ourselves to the extent that we are truly plastic — almost without constraint.[45]

As noted by Allen in *The Skin of Years*, if post-object is at all useful as a term, it is as one that marks a 'shift away from consideration of the object to that of an idea-based work'.[46] While such a shift is, in Allen's practice, signalled by a move to performance works such as *Contact*, a broader interpretation — discussed here in terms of psychedelic intent — emphasises the phenomenological subject as the site of the work: a subject who is at the centre of the 'experiential turn' that Dorothea von Hantelmann asserts motivates many contemporary practices.[47]

Such practices, she suggests, mark 'a shift from what an artwork depicts and represents to the effects and experiences that it produces'.[48] In placing the emphasis on experience rather than on performance or object, von Hantelmann not only confirms the impetus for early post-object works discussed here, but also clarifies how, as events, post-object performances anticipated subsequent modes of practice.

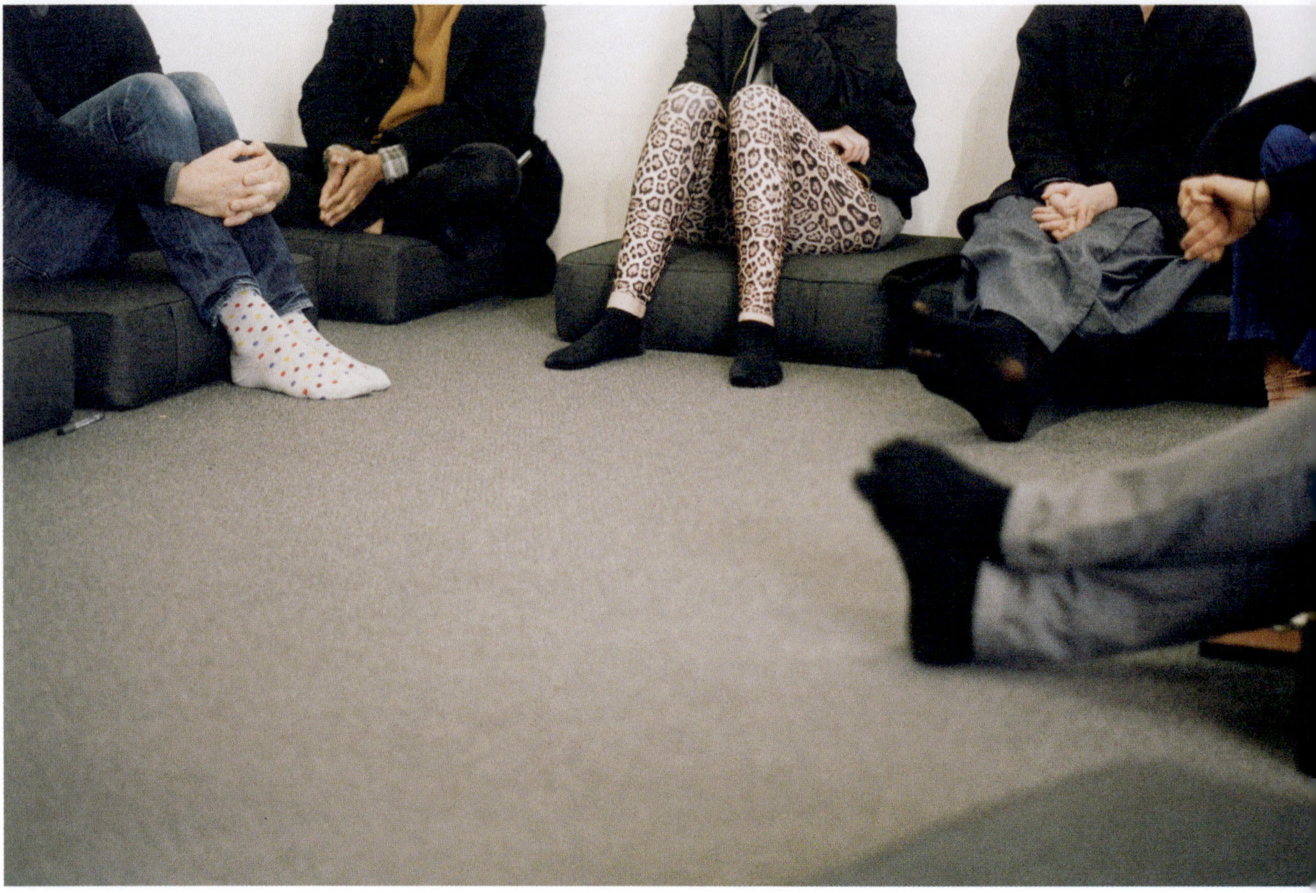

As Blair French acknowledges,[49] while the impulse to explore his own embodied experience was core to much of Allen's work, events such as *The Elastic Sided Boot* — a less well-known work presented in the basement of the Experimental Art Foundation (EAF), Adelaide, in 1976[50] — marks the clear emergence of the social as subject in Allen's work.[51]

If the briefing of the participant/performers in *Contact* (1974) was pragmatic, then the instructions provided for *The Elastic Sided Boot* were even less directive: performers — referred to as participants[52] — were left to invent ways to communicate with each other using sonic instruments that they themselves supplied.[53] The participants were crowded into an area of the basement defined by concrete pillars around which a double-sided strip of black and white photographic contact prints, taken by Allen the previous day, was stretched.

A section of the film strip held by the Auckland Art Gallery Toi o Tāmaki archives shows seemingly incidental street scenes busy with pedestrians, eyes steadfastly fixed ahead, walking purposefully past one another with little interaction or acknowledgement of the camera — a clear counter to the communication being attempted by participants.[54] Between each of the four 15-minute sessions, participants were invited to 'exchange a few pleasantries' and share food and drink supplied by the artists.[55] At its conclusion, evidence of the event, in the form of debris from the instruments and food, was left inside the cordoned-off area.[56]

Chris Braddock with dialogue group, *Invitation to Dialogue*, 2019. Performed at AUT ST PAUL St Gallery, Tāmaki Makaurau Auckland. *Courtesy ST PAUL St Gallery/Te Wai Ngutu Kākā Gallery and the artist. Participant and photographer Emily Parr*

In part a response to the general lack of interest, or even antipathy, shown at the time by the EAF community towards the work of New Zealand post-object artists, *The Elastic Sided Boot* extended an open invitation to be directly involved. The nature of this involvement was markedly different from that of the participant/performers of *Contact* in that its 'elastic' structure gave participants greater agency, imploring them to 'reflect sensitivity and care for [their] fellow man'.[57] Although documentation of the work shows two or three people standing around outside of the boundary of the work, there was no audience per se.[58]

There is no 'corporate box' here! No distance separates those involved from those observing. Even the ropes and stanchions that tentatively restrained the onlookers in *Contact* (1974) have been replaced by a paper-thin strip of film wrapped around pillars, embracing all as participants with/in the work. As subjects emancipated[59] by their endeavours to communicate, the participants in *The Elastic Sided Boot* were subjects of their own experience: active authors within communities empowered as social agents though their psychedelic experience within the work.

SHARED HALLUCINATIONS

What emerges in *The Elastic Sided Boot* is a participatory dynamic that is at once individual and collective. The very openness of the work invites participants into a 'dialogue' that resists observation as a privileged position, recognising, as quantum physicist David Bohm does, that 'the distinction between the observer and the observed cannot be maintained'.[60] As phenomenological subjects, participants are always entangled with each other inside the work.

Of course, in this 'age of entanglement' — an era in which quantum theory has helped prompt a much-needed revision of correlational assumptions — participatory practices have become commonplace in Aotearoa, as they have elsewhere.[61] Although there are many examples one might call on here,[62] Christopher Braddock's 2019 *Invitation to Dialogue*, presented as part of *How to Live Together* (an exhibition curated by Balamohan Shingade for ST PAUL St Gallery, AUT) is particularly useful, not least because of Braddock's interest in David Bohm's 'collective thought'.[63]

For Bohm, collective thought is a form of dialogue 'aimed at going into the whole thought process and changing the way the thought process occurs collectively'.[64] Whereas conventional thinking might be the purview of the individual, Bohm seeks a way of thinking together in which an individual's thoughts are at a tacit level coetaneous with the collective.

Perhaps in a similar way to Allen, Braddock extended an invitation to participate in an open dialogue built around Bohm's dialogic framework. Where Allen embraces participants with a strip of film, Braddock simply rolls out a grey carpet to denote the active space. Participants, signalling their inclusion by removing their shoes as they settle on an upholstered squab, endeavour to enter a dialogue: a stream of meaning-making among, through and between participants.

Echoing Allen's lack of concern for audiences, Braddock notes how audiences were a problem for *Invitation to Dialogue*: 'If someone entered the gallery during a dialogue session to "view" the artwork they had to either sit down with us or move on. Standing, looking, and listening to the dialogue was not an option.' As Braddock continues, 'There could be no viewer or passer-by.'[65] This stance aligns with Ward's earlier assertion, that in the abandonment of the audience by conceptual art there are no innocent bystanders in performance any more than there are in participatory works.[66]

In putting Bohm's ideas into practice, *Invitation to Dialogue* clarifies a shift that occurred between Allen's *Contact* and *The Elastic Sided Boot*. As Allen affirms, for an early post-object work such as *Contact*, we 'didn't give a stuff about the audience' as they were intent on the performers' psychedelic, mind-altering experience: 'The audience was an add-on' that might be done away with altogether, as it was two years later in *The Elastic Sided Boot*. In that later work, the audience-as-participants were co-opted into a dialogue; their thinking becoming part of the collective thought, articulated tacitly in the act of attempting to communicate via sonic instruments.

The psychedelic commitment of the work had not changed, however. Rather, the opportunity for individuals to discover themselves was, as Allen wrote while at EAF, extended into an opportunity for the collective self to reinvent itself.[67] Entangled in this way, thought becomes a shared hallucination from within which an individual's mind-altering actions are performed.

STRAIGHTENING UP

At this point, any expectation that this text might 'straighten things out' seems to have become ensnared in the psychedelic entanglement of performance and participation. But clearly, our purpose was never to draw lines of the shortest distance between the past and the present, between an act and its re-enactment, between performers/participants and audience, such as one might do from the 'corporate box': the optimised view constructed by re-enactments from where 'professional audiences' witness spectacles. Any straightening out of things has not been intent on distancing Allen's work from mind-altering practices.

Rather, by re/asserting the psychedelic intent of Allen's work and showing how it is entangled with the socially effective aspirations of post-object art,[68] we have sought to understand how re-enactments perform a *straightening* — a cleansing from mind-altering substances[69] — that is indicative of compliance. Such straightening affirms the competency of an individual to perform and leads to the construction of professionals — both performers/participants and audiences. Re-enactments are necessarily professional in that they seek to comply with that which is being enacted.

Conversely, unable to extract themselves from events, amateurs are seen to be entangled — undoubtedly a messy business compared to that of the professionals who, operating with detached efficiency, 'straighten things out'. The amateurs who turned up to perform and watch *Contact* (1974) were clearly entangled in the work. Engaged in doing something they had never done before, they participated in mind-altering experiences from which new models of the social might emerge. Entanglements of this nature are perhaps a better way to straighten things out. The last words, however, are perhaps best left to Jim Allen alone:

> Audiences are not very important, for they have no general purpose. I didn't care if there were any spectators or not — I was interested in experiencing what happened. I was looking for something outside of myself that maybe I could latch onto and turn into something. The audience was an add-on; that people got enthusiastic was a surprise.
> — Jim Allen, July 2022

NOTES

1 This chapter grew from conversations over the last thirteen years between Jim Allen (1922–2023) and James Charlton about re-enactments of Allen's performance art practice. Charlton assisted in the re-enactments of *Contact* at the Govett-Brewster Art Gallery in 2010 and at Artspace Auckland in 2011. Jim and James worked together on the chapter, finishing the final editing before Jim passed away on 9 June 2023 at the age of 100. Jim's statements are sometimes placed in quotation marks for emphasis.

2 Accompanied by an illustrated catalogue. See Christina Barton, Tyler Cann and Mercedes Vicente, eds, *Points of Contact: Jim Allen, Len Lye, Hélio Oiticica*, exhibition catalogue (New Plymouth/Wellington: Govett-Brewster Art Gallery and Te Pātaka Toi Adam Art Gallery, 2011).

3 In 1976 Jim Allen and Wystan Curnow wrote and published *New Art: Some recent New Zealand sculpture and post-object art* (Auckland: Heinemann, 1976).

4 While, in an art context, the term psychedelic is typically associated with an aesthetic of bright colours and highly distorted visuals linked to the use of hallucinogenic substances in 1960s counterculture, the use of the term here draws on a purer definition first used by Humphry Osmond (1957). Osmond 'proposed a new name for the class of drugs that would include their capacity to enrich the mind and enlarge the vision: *psychedelic*, a term coined from Greek roots indicating "manifesting the mind"' (M. Mangini, 'Treatment of Alcoholism Using Psychedelic Drugs: A review of the program of research', *Journal of Psychoactive Drugs* 30, no. 4 [1998]: 383). According to Osmond, psychedelics help 'us to explore and fathom our own nature' (Humphry Osmond, 'A Review of the Clinical Effects of Psychotomimetic Agents', *Annals of the New York Academy of Sciences* 66, no. 3 [1957]: 418–34). As such it bears comparison to Bruce Barber's desire to make artworks that overload the sensory system in order to expand intellectual capacity: to be mind-altering (Bruce Barber, 'Bruce Barber', in *New Art*, n.p.). This is not to infer that Barber and other post-object artists were using hallucinogenic substances as part of their work, although the term does seem to appropriately reflect the spirit of the times.

5 Guy von Sturmer, 'The Boundless Arena', in *New Art*, n.p.

6 'Computor Dance' is spelt with an 'o' in the 1976 *New Art* publication. We have followed the original spelling in this text. This original spelling was changed to 'Computer Dance' in the 2011 *Points of Contact* catalogue.

7 Jim Allen, 'Jim Allen: Contact', in *New Art*, n.p.

8 Ibid.

9 Ibid.

10 Jim Allen and Wystan Curnow, 'Introduction', in *New Art*, n.p.

11 Although Lütticken identifies the early 2000s as the point at which re-enactments became a 'mainstreamed' curatorial strategy, both he and Amelia Jones acknowledge the emergence of historical re-enactments in the 1960s, with Jones tracking the emergence of re-enactments via 1960s ephemera to the early 1990s. See Amelia Jones, 'Timeline of Ideas: Live art in (art) history, a primarily European-US-based trajectory of debates and exhibitions relating to performance documentation and re-enactments', in *Perform, Repeat, Record: Live art in history*, edited by Adrian Heathfield and Amelia Jones (Bristol: University of Chicago Press, 2012); Jennifer Allen et al., *Life, Once More: Forms of re-enactment in contemporary art*, edited by Sven Lütticken, exhibition catalogue (Rotterdam: Witte de With Center for Contemporary Art, 2005).

12 Rachel Withers, '"A Short History of Performance: Part One": Whitechapel Gallery', *Artforum* 41, no. 1 (September 2002): 214–15.

13 Cristina Baldacci, Clio Nicastro and Arianna Sforzini, eds, *Over and Over and Over Again: Re-enactment strategies in contemporary arts and theory* (Berlin: ICI Berlin Press, 2022), ix.

14 Allen et al., *Life, Once More*, ix.

15 Amelia Jones, '"The Artist is Present": Artistic re-enactments and the impossibility of presence', *TDR: The Drama Review* 55, no. 1 (2011): 19.

16 Claire Bishop, *Artificial Hells: Participatory art and the politics of spectatorship* (London: Verso, 2012).

17 Jones, 'The Artist Is Present', 36.

18 Jack Bankowsky, 'Tent Community: Art fair art', *Artforum* 44, no. 2 (2005): 228–32.

19 Frazer Ward, *No Innocent Bystanders: Performance art and audience* (Hanover: Dartmouth College Press, 2012), 40–41.

20 Wystan Curnow, 'Writing and the Post-Object', in *The Critic's Part: Wystan Curnow art writings 1971–2013*, edited by Christina Barton, Robert Leonard and Thomasin Sleigh (Wellington/Brisbane: Te Pātaka Toi Adam Art Gallery, Institute of Modern Art and Victoria University Press, 2014), 371–91.

21 Ibid., 385. Emphasis in original.

22 Ibid. See also Christina Barton, 'Notes on Method', in *The Critic's Part*, 14.

23 Ward makes an argument for the 'virtual abandonment of the audience' on behalf of performance art, noting that in Tehching Hsieh's works, *Tehching Hsieh 1986–1999/ Thirteen Year Plan* and *One Year Performance 1985–1986*, 'there were no bystanders at all, because there was nothing to stand by'. Ward, *No Innocent Bystanders*, 23. See Chapter 11 of this volume for further discussion of Hsieh's performances.

24 Curnow notes how many artists and critics in the late 1960s and early 1970s were reading Maurice Merleau-Ponty's essay 'Eye and Mind' (translated into English in 1960). Curnow, 'Writing and the Post-Object', 384.

25 The exhibition included Jim Allen, Bruce Barber, Phil Dadson and Kieran Lyons. *Contact* was performed on 15 April 1974 and took approximately three hours, after which video recordings of the 'activities' remained on exhibit.

26 A photograph of promotional text for the exhibition in *Craccum*, 12 March 1974, can be found in Jim Allen, *The Skin of Years: Interviews with Jim Allen by Phil Dadson and Tony Green* (Auckland: Clouds and Michael Lett, 2014), 148.

27 Few artists attended and even Elam School of Fine Arts students, it seemed, were too busy doing their own work.

28 Jones, 'The Artist Is Present'.

29 Michael Lett Gallery supported the development and reconstruction of several works for the exhibition.

30 For example, Jen Harvie's account of the role that state funding in the UK has played in the proliferation of participatory art projects that yield higher attendance rates might be applicable to Aotearoa, where the opportunity to participate in projects can be a criterion for awarding grants. Jen Harvie, *Fair Play: Art, performance and neoliberalism* (London: Palgrave Macmillan, 2013). See 'New Zealanders participate in the arts', Creative New Zealand Arts Council of New Zealand Toi Aotearoa, https://creativenz.govt.nz/funds-and-opportunities/guidelines/outcomes

31 Barton, 'Notes on Method', 14.

32 Thomasin Sleigh, 'Neither Here nor There: The writing of Wystan Curnow 1961–1984' (Master's thesis, Victoria University of Wellington, 2010), 34–35, https://doi.org/10.26686/wgtn.17011526.v1

33 Wystan Curnow, 'Wystan Curnow 25 June 1974', in

New Art, n.p. See Chapters 5 and 13 of this volume for further discussion of Curnow's writing on *Night Piece* (1981) by Linda Buis and Peter Roche for the publication *Parallax*.

34 Barton, 'Notes on Method'.

35 Barber, 'Bruce Barber'.

36 Ibid. Allen, Barber, Kieran Lyons and Guy von Sturmer further address the interconnection between the physical and intellectual aspects of Barber's work *Bucket Action*, noting the confusion caused by demand of actions undertaken. Bruce Barber et al., 'Bucket Action', in *New Art*, n.p.

37 As Curnow points out, The Blind Master is a recurring character in Barber's work: 'Since *Mt Eden Crater Performance*, the Blind Master has not been lost sight of. He's become, in his metamorphoses, Barber's epidermis [whose task] with a bucket of water and two dead fish required him to negotiate a tricky obstacle course . . . He was the blind-folded, sleeper-footed traveller in *Like a Bat Outta Hell* (1975), and the petty offender/artist who was locked in the stocks in Auckland City Gallery for forty-eight hours in *Stocks and Bonds*.' Curnow, 'Project Programme 1975', in *The Critic's Part*, 71. In each manifestation, the 'active participant' is subject to sensory, mind-altering deprivation as described by Barber.

38 Curnow's influence seems apparent here. As Thomasin Sleigh explains, Curnow drew extensively on Peckham's concept of psychic insulation as a means of disorienting the artist and audience in order to produce innovative experiences. Sleigh, 'Neither Here nor There', 34–35.

39 The decision to recruit students from the School of Education rather than Elam School of Fine Arts where Allen was teaching at the time indicates not only a desire to have an uninitiated audience but also, Allen suggests, because Elam students themselves were so caught up in their own psychedelic quests that very few even bothered to visit the gallery to see the *Four Men in a Boat* exhibition.

40 The documentation in *New Art* shows participants wearing an assortment of their own flower-patterned underwear. This was a last-minute response to Auckland Art Gallery's concerns about the performers being naked, as conceived by the artist, and must have been something of a surprise to the School of Education students. By comparison, the performers in the re-enactments were provided with to-size, black Calvin Klein underwear purchased from Farmers department store.

41 In a Facebook Messenger conversation with Charlton on 13 September 2022, Woods describes the performers as 'freelance dancers', most of whom had trained at Unitec's School of Creative Industries.

42 Rehearsals were held in the Creative Technologies Studio on the ground floor of Auckland University of Technology's WT Building on the corner of Rutland and Wakefield Streets. Allen was not present at the meetings.

43 Lydia Brawner takes ownership over this pejorative term coined by Holland Cotter, co-chief art critic of the *New York Times*, in his review of *Marina Abramovic: The artist is present* in 2010. Brawner's use of the term 'diva hokum' suggests forms of diva nonsense, or the antics of a diva, that 'becomes integral to the structure of the work, and a balancing act between the performance and its afterlife'. Lydia Brawner, 'The Artist Is Present: Performing the icon', *Women & Performance: A journal of feminist theory* 23, no. 2 (June 2013), https://doi.org/10.1080/074077 0X.2013.815522. See Holland Cotter, 'Performance Art Preserved, in the Flesh', *New York Times*, 11 March 2010, www.nytimes.com/2010/03/12/arts/design/12abromovic.html

44 Brawner, 'The Artist Is Present'.

45 Jim Allen, *Notes for EAF*, Jim Allen Archive, E H McCormick Research Library, Auckland Art Gallery Toi o Tāmaki, RC 2012/3/22/3.

46 Jim Allen, *The Skin of Years: Interviews with Jim Allen by Phil Dadson and Tony Green* (Auckland: Clouds and Michael Lett, 2014), 191.

47 Dorothea von Hantelmann, 'The Experiential Turn', in *Living Collections Catalogue*, Vol. 1, edited by Elizabeth Carpenter (Minneapolis: Walker Art Center, 2014), http://walkerart.org/collections/publications/performativity/experiential-turn

48 Ibid.

49 Blair French, 'Jim Allen: From Elam to the Experimental Art Foundation', in *Intervention: Post object and performance art in New Zealand in 1970 and beyond*, edited by Jennifer Hay (Christchurch: Robert McDougall Art Gallery and Annex, 2002), 35–46.

50 Allen was in residence at the EAF during a sabbatical leave from the University of Auckland in 1976. As well as presenting a number of solo performance works including *On Planting a Native* and *Newspaper Piece*, he arranged for work of other New Zealand post-object artists (Michael Bajko, Liz England, Kim Gray, John Lethbridge and David Mealing) to be shown alongside work by their Australian and Canadian post-object counterparts.

51 Although the social is perhaps evident in the work of other post-object artists such as Barber, prior to this the EAF's commitment to the social function of art clearly informed *The Elastic Sided Boot*.

52 Photograph of original instructions for *The Elastic Sided Boot* in Allen, *The Skin of Years*, 190.

53 The EAF community was asked to leave 'instruments' the previous day.

54 A notable exception to this selection of images is a police incident that Allen witnessed during his walk. This incident, in which a man confronted by police shot himself, left an impression on Allen such that the manner in which the space is demarcated takes on the quality of a crime-scene cordon.

55 Photograph of original instructions for *The Elastic Sided Boot* in Allen, *The Skin of Years*, 190.

56 Subsequently, in another cordoned-off area, a 'Lego man engaged in an endless repetitive operation', as well as looped footage from the performance, were projected. Allen, *The Skin of Years*, 190.

57 Photograph of original instructions for *The Elastic Sided Boot* in Allen, *The Skin of Years*, 190.

58 While the documentation shows a small number of people outside of the perimeter defining the work, these were EAF assistants supporting the project. (Based on an EAF catalogue held by E H McCormick Research Library, Auckland Art Gallery Toi o Tāmaki, these assistants likely included Steve Leishman, Steve Hayter and Ian Chance.)

59 With reference to Claire Bishop's trifold positioning of participants as active authors within communities. Claire Bishop, ed., *Participation*, Documents of Contemporary Art (London/Cambridge, MA: Whitechapel and MIT Press, 2006), 12.

60 David Bohm, *On Dialogue*, edited by Lee Nichol (London/New York: Routledge, 1996), 70.

61 Although the global tendency toward socially engaged and participatory practices is no doubt driven in part by institutional funding mechanisms that reward public engagement, in Aotearoa relational aesthetics are perhaps pre-empted by Moana epistemologies as suggested by Chloe Weavers. Chloe Weavers, 'Art as Experience: Collaborative and participatory practice in contemporary Pacific art' (Master's thesis, University of Auckland, 2011), https://researchspace.auckland.ac.nz/

handle/2292/6615. Numerous chapters in this volume address Moana approaches to performance art. See Chapters 6, 8–12, and 14–18.

62 For example, Letting Space's socially transformative projects (www.lettingspace.org.nz); Public Share's socially engaged projects (https://publicshare.co.nz); About Walking's walking projects (https://walkingabout.nz).

63 For a further discussion of Christopher Braddock's *Invitation to Dialogue* (2019), see Chapter 12 of this volume by Balamohan Shingade.

64 Bohm, *On Dialogue*, 9.

65 Chris Braddock, email exchange with James Charlton, 2023.

66 Ward, *No Innocent Bystanders.*

67 Jim Allen, *Notes for EAF*, Jim Allen Archive, Auckland Art Gallery Toi o Tāmaki, RC 2012/3/22/3.

68 Although motivation for this lies beyond the scope of this chapter, the influence of Roy Ascott's work on cybernetics is evident in Allen's notes on cybernetics and what he calls the 'Ascott Argument' in papers held in the Jim Allen Archive, Auckland Art Gallery Toi o Tāmaki, RC 2012/3/4/6.

69 The psychedelic inference here readily aligns straightness with being drug free — as in the colloquialism 'I'm going straight'. The compliant nature of straightening is of course equally applicable to the description of heterosexuals as straight. Straightening is normative in both uses of the term.

REFERENCES

Jim Allen Archive. E H McCormick Research Library, Auckland Art Gallery Toi o Tāmaki.

Allen, Jennifer, Sven Lütticken, Andrea Fraser, Peggy Phelan and Eran Schaerf. *Life, Once More: Forms of reenactment in contemporary art*. Exhibition catalogue. Rotterdam: Witte de With Center for Contemporary Art, 2005.

Allen, Jim. *The Skin of Years: Interviews with Jim Allen by Phil Dadson and Tony Green*. Auckland: Clouds and Michael Lett, 2014.

Allen, Jim and Wystan Curnow, eds. *New Art: Some recent New Zealand sculpture and post-object art*. Auckland: Heinemann, 1976.

Baldacci, Cristina, Clio Nicastro and Arianna Sforzini, eds. *Over and Over and Over Again: Reenactment strategies in contemporary arts and theory*. Berlin: ICI Berlin Press, 2022.

Bankowsky, Jack. 'Tent Community: Art fair art'. *Artforum* 44, no. 2 (2005): 228–32.

Barton, Christina, Tyler Cann and Mercedes Vicente, eds. *Points of Contact: Jim Allen, Len Lye, Hélio Oiticica*. Exhibition catalogue. New Plymouth/Wellington: Govett-Brewster Art Gallery and Te Pātaka Toi Adam Art Gallery, 2011.

Bishop, Claire. *Artificial Hells: Participatory art and the politics of spectatorship*. London: Verso, 2012.

———, ed. *Participation*. Documents of Contemporary Art. London/Cambridge, MA: Whitechapel and MIT Press, 2006.

Bohm, David. *On Dialogue*, edited by Lee Nichol. London/New York: Routledge, 1996.

Brawner, Lydia. 'The Artist Is Present: Performing the icon'. *Women & Performance: A journal of feminist theory* 23, no. 2 (17 June 2013). https://doi.org/10.1080/0740770X.2013.815522

Cotter, Holland. 'Performance Art Preserved, in the Flesh'. *New York Times*, 11 March 2010. www.nytimes.com/2010/03/12/arts/design/12abromovic.html

Curnow, Wystan. *The Critic's Part: Wystan Curnow art writings 1971–2013*, edited by Christina Barton, Robert Leonard and Thomasin Sleigh. Wellington/Brisbane: Te Pātaka Toi Adam Art Gallery, Institute of Modern Art and Victoria University Press, 2014.

French, Blair. 'Jim Allen: From Elam to the Experimental Art Foundation'. In *Intervention: Post object and performance art in New Zealand in 1970 and beyond*, edited by Jennifer Hay, 35–46. Christchurch: Robert McDougall Art Gallery and Annex, 2002.

Hantelmann, Dorothea von. 'The Experiential Turn'. In *Living Collections Catalogue*, Vol. 1, edited by Elizabeth Carpenter. Minneapolis: Walker Art Center, 2014. http://walkerart.org/collections/publications/performativity/experiential-turn

Harvie, Jen. *Fair Play: Art, performance and neoliberalism*. London: Palgrave Macmillan, 2013. https://doi.org/10.1057/9781137027290

Jones, Amelia. *Body Art/Performing the Subject*. Minneapolis: University of Minnesota Press, 1998.

——— '"The Artist is Present": Artistic re-enactments and the impossibility of presence'. *TDR: The Drama Review* 55, no. 1 (2011): 16–45.

——— 'Timeline of Ideas: Live art in (art) history, a primarily European-US-based trajectory of debates and exhibitions relating to performance documentation and re-enactments'. In *Perform, Repeat, Record: Live art in history*, edited by Adrian Heathfield and Amelia Jones. Bristol: University of Chicago Press, 2012.

Mangini, M. 'Treatment of Alcoholism Using Psychedelic Drugs: A review of the program of research'. *Journal of Psychoactive Drugs* 30, no. 4 (1998): 381–418. https://doi.org/10.1080/02791072.1998.10399714

Osmond, Humphry. 'A Review of the Clinical Effects of Psychotomimetic Agents'. *Annals of the New York Academy of Sciences* 66, no. 3 (1957): 418–34. https://doi.org/10.1111/j.1749-6632.1957.tb40738.x

Sleigh, Thomasin. 'Neither Here nor There: The writing of Wystan Curnow 1961–1984'. Master's thesis, Victoria University of Wellington, 2010. https://doi.org/10.26686/wgtn.17011526.v1

Stern, Nathaniel. *Interactive Art and Embodiment: The implicit body as performance*. Canterbury, UK: Gylphi Limited, 2013.

Ward, Frazer. *No Innocent Bystanders: Performance art and audience*. Hanover: Dartmouth College Press, 2012.

Weavers, Chloe. 'Art as Experience: Collaborative and participatory practice in contemporary Pacific art'. Master's thesis, University of Auckland, 2011. https://researchspace.auckland.ac.nz/handle/2292/6615

Withers, Rachel. '"A Short History of Performance: Part One": Whitechapel Gallery'. *Artforum* 41, no. 1 (September 2002): 214–15.

4

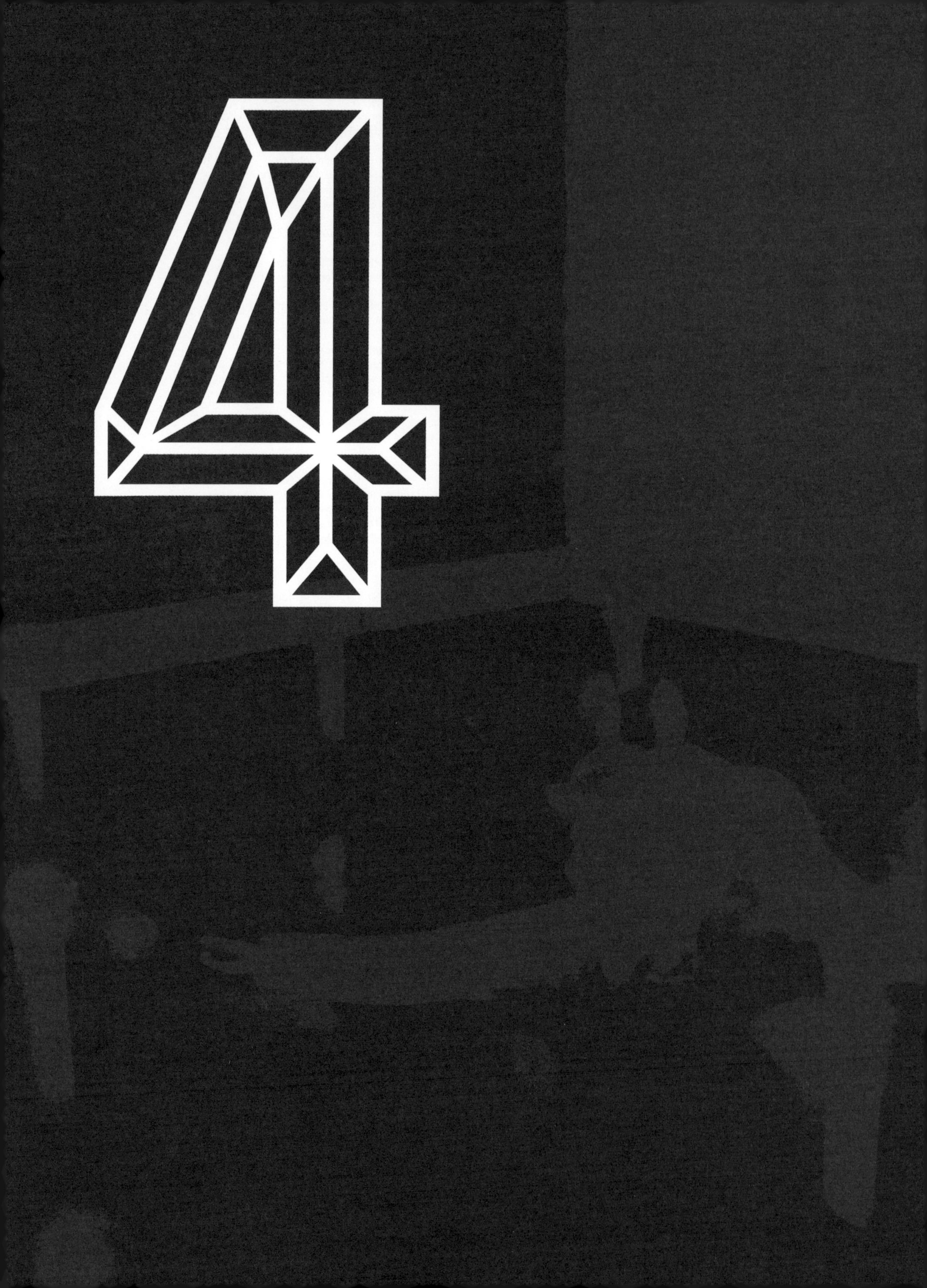

BODY POLITICS: WOMEN AND PERFORMANCE IN THE 1980s

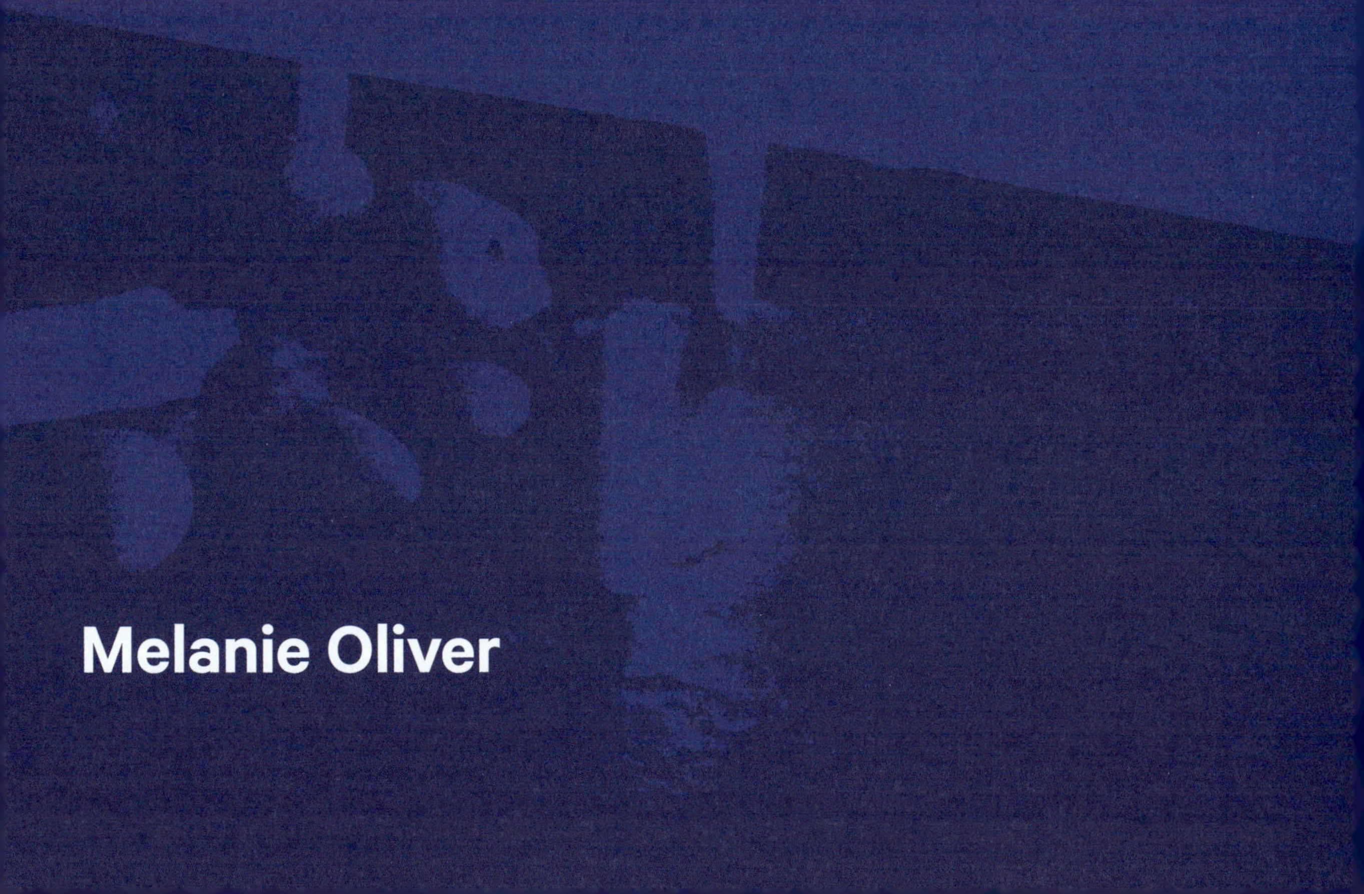

Melanie Oliver

In the early 1980s, performance art in Aotearoa New Zealand was dominated by women and infused with feminist ideas as well as broader socio-political concerns. Forerunners such as Kimberley Gray[1] and Colleen Anstey had explored concepts of time and interpersonal relationships; 1980s artists who considered themselves feminist, such as Juliet Batten, often worked with ritual or collaboration; others were operating from more theoretically informed gender politics or incorporated issues around environmentalism, racism and inequality. The works of Di ffrench and Mary-Louise Browne were experimental and complex, made in response to current issues and ideas.

Aotearoa artists were interdisciplinary in approach. They frequently used props, technology and projected imagery and audio. From the mid-1980s, many subsequently developed their work toward object-based practices. The later projects of these performance artists, whether sculpture, installation, photography or video art, can be seen as particularly dynamic, and the imprint of performance in their thinking and making is still evident today. This chapter traces a relatively small group of artists working in performance over a short period of time; however, the translation of ideas — through the artist's body and focus on process — has had a lingering influence for contemporary art in Aotearoa.

DEPARTING FROM THE 1970s

Time-based practices such as photography, installation and performance were significant media with which artists could critique the commodification of art, to subvert art's institutions in terms of structural biases — who and what could be exhibited — and to create dynamic audience relationships that connected with everyday lived experiences. Although the artists involved with post-object art of the 1970s were predominantly men (Jim Allen, Bruce Barber, Phil Dadson, Andrew Drummond and David Mealing, for example), collaborative partnerships were also common, such as between Linda Buis and Peter Roche or Colleen Anstey and John Cousins. Drawing on these individual and collaborative experiences, Anstey, ffrench, Browne and many other female artists went on to utilise performance as an interdisciplinary form that enabled artists to engage overtly political content in their artwork and to generate visceral immediacy for audiences.

The Women's Art Movement of the 1970s in Aotearoa, inspired by feminist politics in the United States and Britain, the 1960s protest era and the general discontent of women, led artists to address concerns around women's bodies, to reclaim marginalised or untold histories, and to challenge societal expectations and roles, such as the assumption that women would be homemakers or work in certain types of employment. Women artists were interested in a broad range of political issues, from the racism of the 1981 Springbok rugby tour to environmental causes and anti-nuclear protests, and some, like ffrench, brought multiple and intersecting concerns into their practice.

This chapter charts some of the themes and strategies of several female artists in the early 1980s who used performance as a way to analyse spatial, temporal and interpersonal relationships; feminist practices, ritual and collaborative works; and the politics around violence, gender, racism and inequality. The key venues for performance were artist-initiated galleries, alternative exhibition sites and symposiums, such as the Women's Gallery in Te Whanganui-a-Tara Wellington, *F1 New Zealand Sculpture Project* in Te Whanganui-a-Tara in 1982, and the *1984 Art in Dunedin* project.

In addition to these, the ANZART exhibitions in Ōtautahi Christchurch (1981), Hobart (1983) and Tāmaki Makaurau (1985) were key avenues for showcasing new work in a supportive environment, and enabled points of connection to both Australian artists and a broader international context. I have drawn from written and oral accounts and artists' recollections, so rather than serving as a full record of works that were presented during this time, the following is indicative of prominent practices and concerns only.

In the mid-1980s art critic Lita Barrie strongly objected to the lack of criticality in New Zealand women's art.[2] In response to feminist practices that she deemed too direct or didactic, such as the ritual work of Juliet Batten, Barrie claimed that most art by women was either essentialist, matrilineal, or ignored gender. Informed by French post-structural theory, she asserted that only artists who worked intuitively from their physical experience of connecting with the environment and reflecting signification of the body had the potential to be subversive. Her comments sparked controversy and debate in the arts community. As second-wave feminism in Aotearoa progressed over time, so too did the concerns, subjects and media of female artists. Both performance and the focus on feminism would wane in the late 1980s.

From the mid-1980s, the radical neoliberal economic reforms known as Rogernomics, made in response to 1970s inflation and unemployment, led to shifts in the social and cultural milieu of Aotearoa, and a number of artists returned to object-making in contemporary art.[3] Most of those discussed in this chapter went on to work in other media, such as photography, sculpture or installation. Their experience of making performance is discernible in their subsequent practices, however, as seen through the persistence of spontaneity, time-based processes, concerns around language as a structure and the situated body.

INTERRELATIONSHIPS

Linda Buis, working in partnership with Peter Roche from 1979 to 1985, contributed to performances that explored the artists' relationship to each other as well as endurance and institutional contexts.[4] For example, in *Liaison* (1980), the two artists stood facing each other for a considerable period of time, in front of their audience and at either end of a rectangular space. At the centre of the space was a pile of domestic mirrors. Suddenly, after considerable tension had been built through the suspense of action, the artists ran towards each other, screaming. The photographic documentation captures the pair careering past each other in full momentum.

Museum Piece (1980) also reflected on communication, or the lack of it, between the artists and members of the public. The duo described their task on a promotional postcard:

> We are walking for an indefinite period of time in a large circle around the base of the museum. We are moving in the same direction. We are documenting at twenty-minute intervals our positions relative to each other within the given space, activity, area. Moving within structure. Becoming separate. Homing in on each other.[5]

This work treated the built environment, the architecture of the museum, as a central monument to circumnavigate; their independent actions emphasised a relationship to each other as well as the potential dangers of the surrounding park.

Critic and witness Wystan Curnow described the works of Buis and Roche as 'unique and unrepeatable events'.[6] They often required bravery and had a certain physical or temporal pressure, though this was a 'different kind of fearful intensity' to Roche's solo projects, as critic John Hurrell reflected.[7] Their collaboration was founded on their relationship with each other as well as with the audience, who were made active too. Australian art historian Susan Best has written of performance works that are made by couples or duos as necessarily invoking intimacy, regardless of whether that is the focus of the work, allowing the audience to occupy the role of observer for interpersonal dynamics: 'in two-person works intimacy is the personal dimension that is simultaneously conjured and negated'.[8] Buis working with Roche can be seen to operate within this framework of scrutiny of communication and the complex negotiation of relationships.

Colleen Anstey performed in both solo and collaborative projects from the late 1970s. Initially taught in Ōtepoti Dunedin by Aotearoa's pioneer of modern dance Shona Dunlop MacTavish, Anstey brought her training in contemporary dance to her visual arts practice and to works made with composer and artist John Cousins. Anstey performed with Cousins in his three *Cube Studies* in Ōtautahi in 1975 and 1978. In 1979 she made her first solo performance work, *Watermelon Hours*, developed directly from movement, at the Canterbury Society of Arts and National Art Gallery in Te Whanganui-a-Tara.

In 1979–80 Anstey and Cousins travelled to Dartington College of Arts in Devon, England, to spend a month with American dance teacher and choreographer Mary Fulkerson. There, along with four other dance/performance artists, they developed an experimental form of working with movement, voice, storytelling and objects, to activate a precognitive state of movement. Anstey's second work, *I Left My Ship Behind* (1980), was made as a consequence of this experience. The dream-like work looking at childhood associations and motherhood featured two white helium balloons attached to a boat structure. This intuitive way of working was continued on their return to Aotearoa during 1980–82, when Anstey, Cousins, composer Chris Cree Brown and Bronwyn Officer performed the improvised works *In Real Time* in galleries across Aotearoa.

Anstey's solo works were conceptual explorations that often involved interrelationships between objects, light, sound, image and space alongside personal content. One such work was *Twenty Four Hours* (1982), a three-part performance at the *F1 New Zealand Sculpture Project*, held at a disused factory in Te Whanganui-a-Tara. In the first part, from the moment when the sun was directly overhead on the first day until the same moment the following day, Anstey plotted the path of light spilling into the room from a window, forming a string grid that left a trace of time passing.[9]

In the second part, once darkness had fallen in the evening, Anstey threw a schist stone, from the Shotover River in Central Otago, in through the window. The stone was then wrapped in a long bandage, anchored to the floor and put out the window again, where it remained suspended outside the building overnight. A cassette played a pre-recorded interview with a woman in her forties who was paralysed with multiple sclerosis, in which she described her planned suicide. In the morning the stone was retrieved and unwrapped to reveal a red circular stain in the centre. The use of Anstey's own body in the work must have enhanced the impact of this emotional narrative, and the careful charting of the shifting light stressed the swift passage of time, fragility or the vulnerability of life.

The following year, 1983, the Australia New Zealand Artists Encounter (ANZART) was held in Hobart at the old Post Office Mail Exchange building, and for this Anstey produced *Step*, a work focused on the nature of memory, learning and forgetting. Anstey had her feet and ankles encased in plaster to mid-calf three days before she left Ōtautahi and arrived in Tasmania on crutches. During the performance she removed the plaster; a

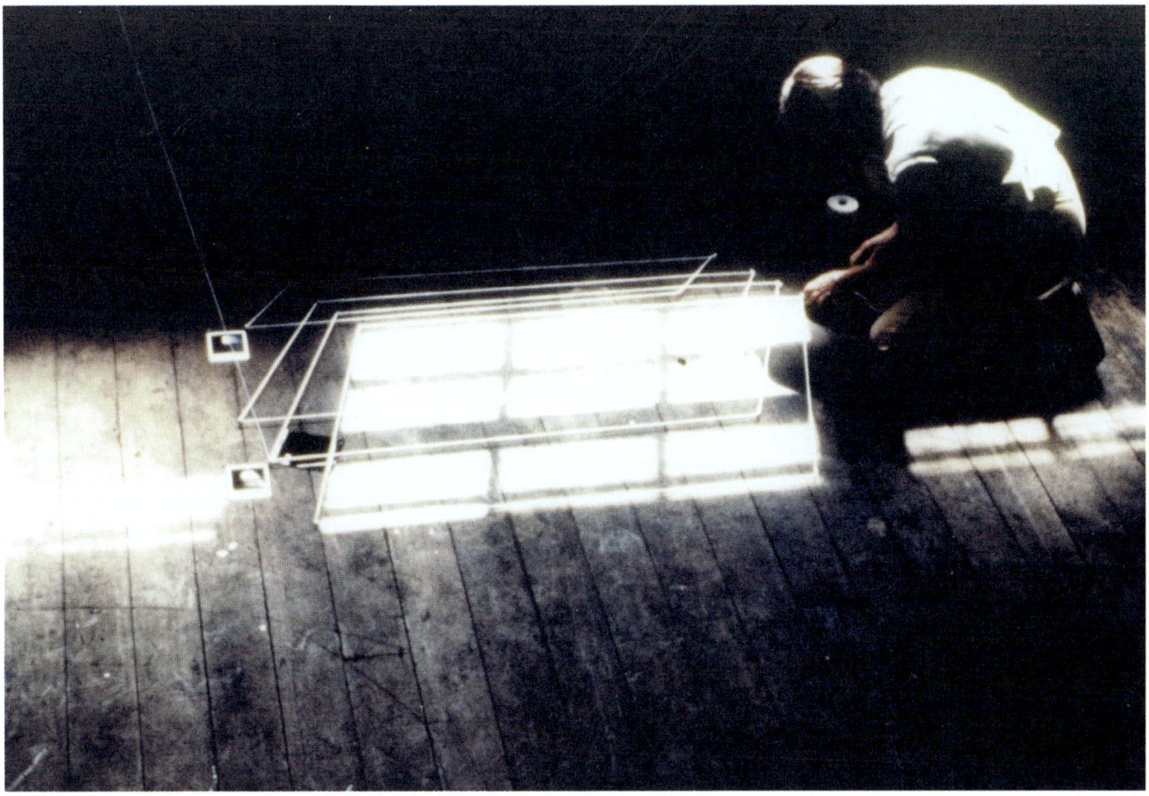

video was played of the application of the plaster, her movements through Customs and the initial stages of removal. Accompanying this was a cassette recording of somebody learning to play scales on a piano.

Anstey wore the glasses her mother had worn during the artist's childhood and had covered the lenses with photographs of her mother and grandmother as young women. The glasses were subsequently bound to the discarded plaster casts, smashed with a hammer and nailed to the floor. Contemporary technology, by now quite commonly used in performance settings, featured strongly in this work; Anstey would gradually move towards more sculptural installation and video in her practice.

For *1984 Art in Dunedin*, a project involving roughly sixty artists from around Aotearoa, held in the disused municipal chambers in Ōtepoti's Octagon, Anstey performed *Rain from the Moon*. A strong light shone from one end of a long space, obliterating a projected video of Anstey's hands dicing onions. This was gradually revealed by the growing shadow of the artist as she advanced towards the screen at the end of the room. Carrying on her back a stick and a cocoon, Anstey moved backwards at a deliberate and regular speed, pulling a length of tape over a Revox tape recorder so that it played the spoken phrase, 'A dollar — here's a dollar', which she had recorded at the pace of 3.75 inches (95 millimetres) per second.

In this evocative and immersive work, Anstey developed the functional relationships between media, light and sound and used her body as an instrument of change. She created the performance in response to interviews with a number of older

Colleen Anstey, *Twenty Four Hours*, 1982, documentation of the three-part performance at the *F1 New Zealand Sculpture Project*, Te Whanganui-a-Tara Wellington. *Courtesy the artist. Photo by John Cousins*

women, and although its full meaning was difficult for the audience to read, it was elegant and innovative in its use of technology to layer narratives.

Into the 1990s Anstey produced three collaborative works with dancer Bronwyn Judge, *Trilogy*, which addressed topics such as health and wellbeing, examined the limitations and possibilities of performance and explored the potential of the camera in relation to the performing body.

Across the performance practices of Gray, Buis and Anstey can be seen a range of approaches, from a focus on the individual body or self in relation to the surrounding environment, to the intimacy between two people and collaborative relationships, movement, technology and multimedia. These women built on their involvement with the post-object art scene of the 1970s to develop works relevant to their own lived experience. They used the given parameters of space, time, light, sound, ephemeral objects and the body as materials through which to explore phenomenological understandings of each other and our place within the world.

Each artist designed works that emphasised and negotiated the contingencies of their performing body to a thoughtfully constructed situation, sometimes using natural and artificial light as a means to deliver narrative components. They employed recording technologies in innovative and strategic ways, replaying and thereby rupturing the real time of the performance, or capturing the moment of performance as documentation for the future. They deployed temporality and liveness to connect to everyday life and to the living, breathing audience, with themes related to healing, endurance and the fragility of our bodies.

FEMINISM, RITUAL AND COLLABORATION

Curator and writer Kyla McFarlane highlighted the importance of temporality as both subject and metaphor for durational practices in Australia between 1975 and 1985.

> The selected bodies of work by a relatively small number of artists . . . reflect prevalent debates and modes of practice — the dematerialisation of the art object, the role of film theory, and the adoption of diaristic and durational modes of practice, including performance, photography and film.[10]

This concern with diaristic and durational modes of practice can be similarly applied to Aotearoa, where burgeoning feminist theory and practice led to new approaches to art-making. In her analysis of the period through the exhibition and catalogue *Intervention*, curator Jennifer Hay pointed out that feminism encouraged women to focus on the process rather than the object.[11] However, Hay further claims that there was more transdisciplinary work, particularly in Aotearoa. She charts the significant practitioners of the time, noting:

> Rather than employing specifically body art motifs as seen in the work of Australian, European and American women artists, the tendency was to instead cross-reference disciplines in order to establish and support a feminist and political consciousness.[12]

Women used performance as a means of investigation, in collaboration with men, as solo artists, and increasingly as part of the organised feminist spaces like the Women's Gallery, a collective in central Te Whanganui-a-Tara Wellington from 1980 to 1984 that used various art forms to address the concerns of women's everyday realities. Art historian Kirsty Baker suggested the gallery provided a space for experimentation both politically and creatively, because it was removed from the patriarchal structures of existing art galleries and cultural spaces.[13]

Talking about feminism in Aotearoa is complicated in that the movement is generally associated with middle-class, Pākehā, heteronormative women and fails to acknowledge other groups, ideas and politics, such as kaupapa mana wāhine, or queer and intersectional understandings of gender. Yet there were aspects of performance that connected strongly to feminist issues of the time, especially given the centrality of the body to performance; bodies as a contested site of politics; and the growing understanding of gender as performed and not a fixed or stable quality. As with the post-object artists of the 1970s, there was a strategic emphasis on the dematerialisation of the art object, and a disruption of art market and gallery conventions through production of performance instead of, for example, painting or sculpture.

Performance art was common at the Women's Gallery, although performances were generally not called that at the time. Exhibitions, such as *Women and Violence* (1980), focused on topical issues, and there was an emphasis on creativity and the collective production of interdisciplinary works rather than uniquely identifiable works. For example, Women's Gallery participant, author Keri Hulme (Kāi Tahu, Kāti Māmoe), performed readings and presented installations of objects as well.

One key artist who presented performance works at the Women's Gallery was Rosemary Johnson (1942–1982). Primarily a sculptor, when faced with a terminal illness Johnson shifted to making performance works for the two years prior to her untimely death. She began to reflect on concepts of despair, belief and spiritual renewal. In 1981 for *Ring of Light*, as part of the *Spirituality* exhibition, Johnson performed tentative pieces in and around an installation of stones and recycled materials, including tape, candles, wool and wood.[14] The strong sense of ritual to her works was perhaps heightened by her deteriorating health as she mediated the idea of spiritual renewal through belief.

Also interested in ritual and healing, Auckland-based Juliet Batten's works are best described as collaborative projects rather than performance, though they are prominent examples of a woman working in a performative mode. *The Menstrual Maze* (1983), facilitated by Batten at the old Greer's Factory in Auckland, was a collaborative art environment in which people were invited to participate in a ritual journey celebrating menstruation, or to experience the maze as an exhibition.[15] For the former, women who were menstruating were asked to wear a red band of wool; performers or 'sentinels' dressed in black facilitated a journey through the space. The first part of the maze, intended to represent the vagina, was lined with red cloth and coiled black tubes that recalled the cramps that occur during menstruation. This was followed by a lighter passage of white gauze fabric, which clung to those walking through, and where messages were pinned to the wall or tucked away in envelopes.

Ranging from negative associations to joyous reflections, the messages were memories of menstruation, and participants were invited to contribute their own. While Barrie criticised works like this for being essentialist (founded on the idea that gender differences are inherent, innate and unchanging, rather than socially constructed and relative), the treatment of the usually taboo subject matter as mystical and in need of ritual was of its time, and was an enriching process for many who were involved.[16]

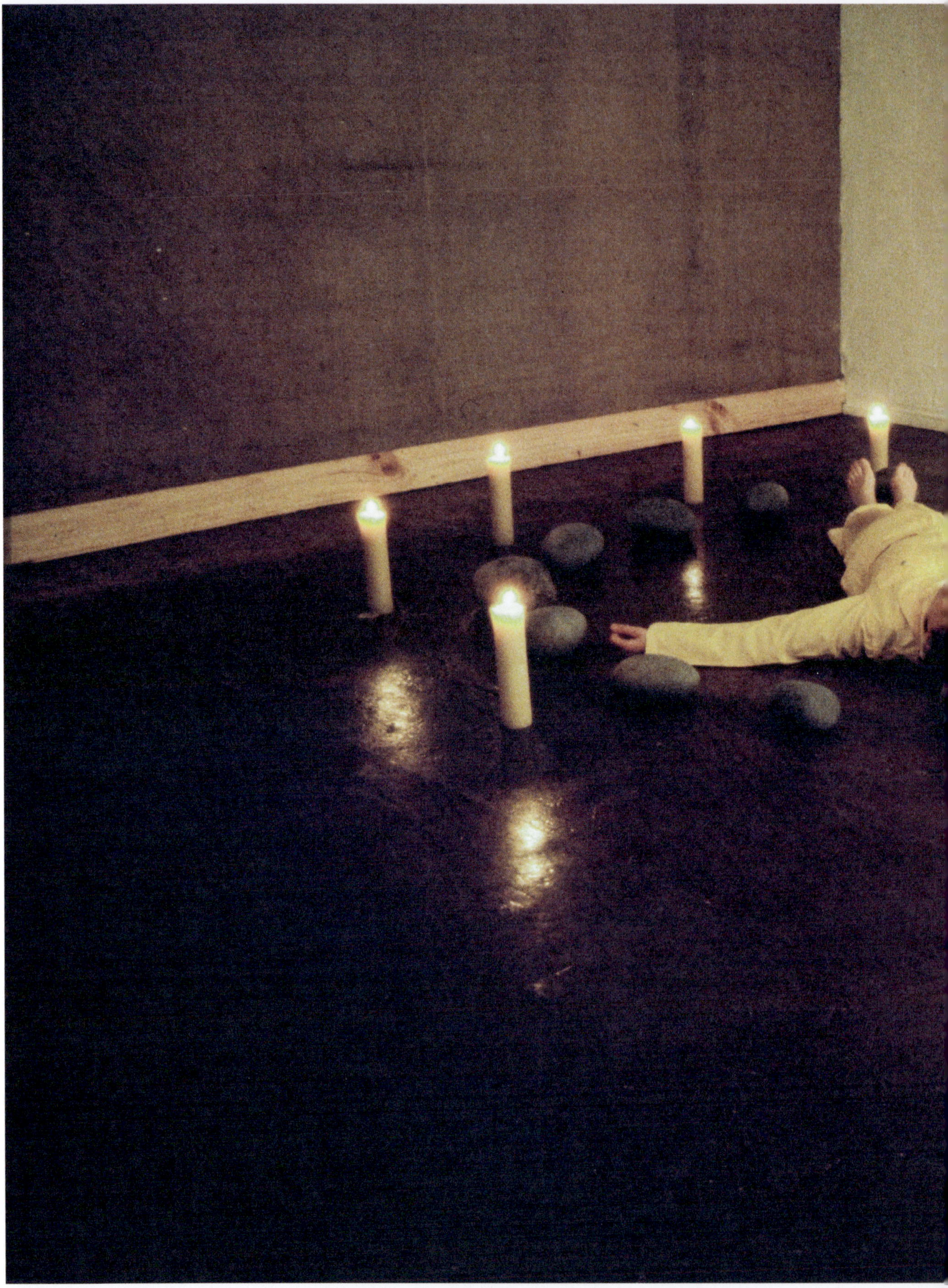

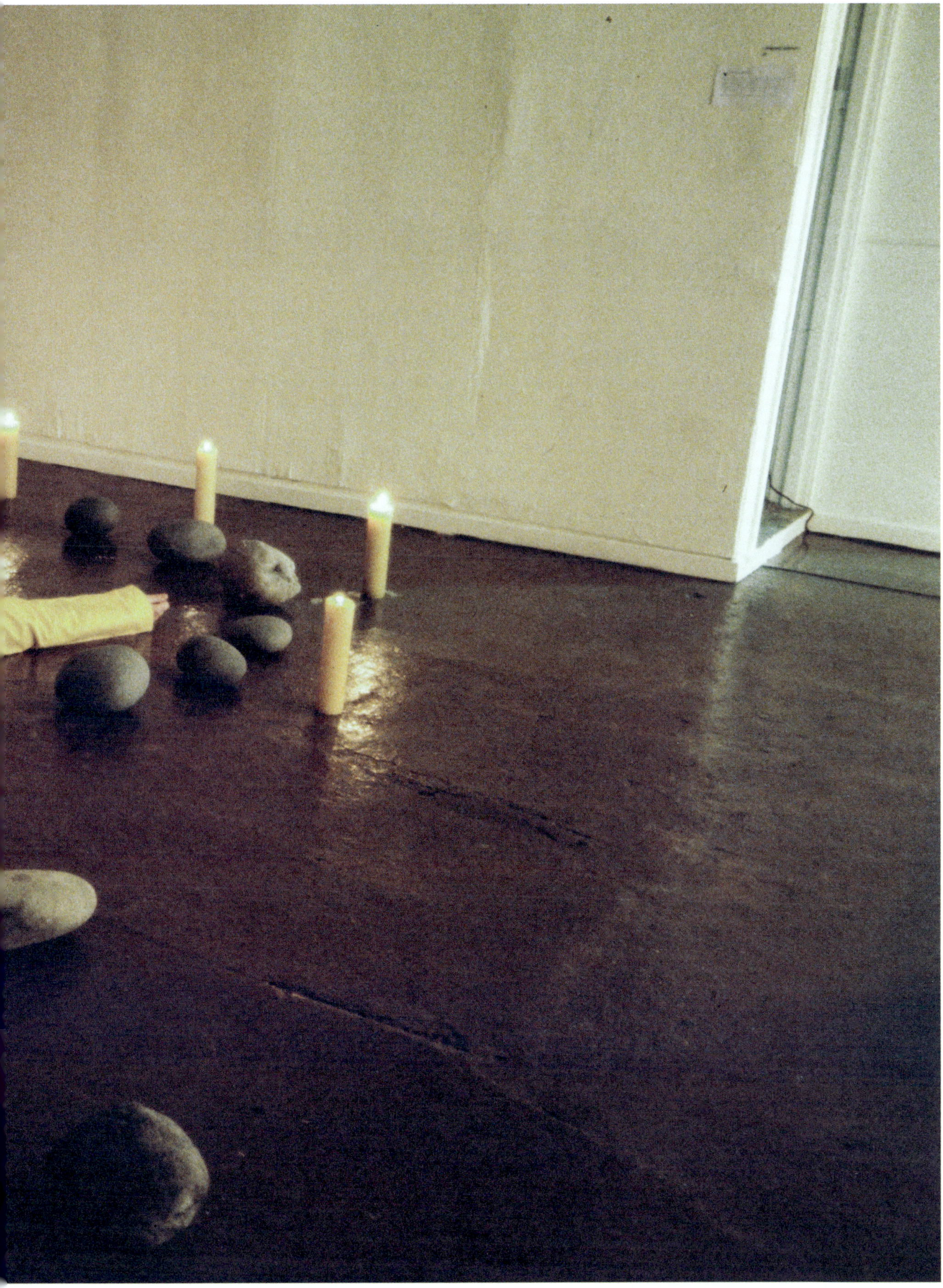

In 1984 Batten created *Ongoing Rituals* at Outreach Gallery in Tāmaki Makaurau, which she dedicated to the women who have disappeared over the ages. The audience became an integral part of the ritual. Candles were lit and placed at intervals, and baskets containing a range of objects — seashells, herbs, small cakes and stones — were covered with white gauze and placed in the centre of the space. A black box containing written messages was opened ceremoniously and the contents read aloud. At the end, each spectator was given a bantam egg wrapped in gauze.

Another large-scale collaborative event was the *100 Women Project* at Te Henga Bethells Beach in 1985 as part of ANZART. It involved women collectively making mounds of sand along the beach, according to a plan laid out by Batten.

In 1986 Priscilla Pitts curated the exhibition *Women and Culture* for Outreach Gallery, Tāmaki Makaurau, to challenge the dichotomy of women and nature as compared to men and culture. Batten contributed *Unearthing*, a performance and installation to highlight women's hidden histories (such as the story of Ettie Rout and her promotion of contraceptives for soldiers in the First World War) and appeared to shift away from the collaborative rituals towards storytelling.[17] Batten filled a large boxed area in the gallery space with hundreds of kilograms of soil, which was then covered with turf to simulate a piece of land, which was then staked out with white string like an archaeological dig. Each day 'artefacts' were uncovered (including a condom, knitting needles, broken zips and fragments of Plunket and recipe books) related to many aspects of women's stories through four time layers, including Māori women in the deepest layer.

This range of works presented by women involved with consciousness-raising in the early 1980s reveals several key trends: from the use of the artist's body as a politically engaged site to the importance of rituals and healing, spirituality and collaborative experiences. Themes such as birth control, motherhood, the right to have control of one's body, terminal illness and the health system, and issues around gender and sexuality were at the core of many works, and were delivered powerfully through the performing body and audience participation.

A specific materiality was involved too, and bandages, candles, textiles and earth frequently demonstrated a reparative impulse. Although works were not always identified as performance art and could be seen as part of an interdisciplinary practice, the aims of feminist artists working at this time aligned with and utilised performance to explore and express their experience through and of the body.

PREVIOUS: Rosemary Johnson, *Ring of Light*, 1981, performance documentation, *Spirituality* exhibition, Women's Gallery, Te Whanganui-a-Tara Wellington. *Courtesy Rosemary Johnson Collection, Robert and Barbara Stewart Library and Archives, Christchurch Art Gallery Te Puna o Waiwhetū. Photo by Claire Fergusson*

GENDER AND POLITICS

In the early 1980s, Mary-Louise Browne produced conceptual performance works and installations, before progressing into witty and poetic language-based sculptures and prints. As a student at Elam School of Fine Arts, Browne became interested in performance because of its temporal nature, a response to the overtly commercial implications of objects, and through the influence of intermedia lecturer Phil Dadson. At the time there were very few women in the sculpture department of Elam. Browne's work was political or, as she describes it, 'gender political'.[18]

Her installations had performance origins and attributes. For example, in *Rebus* (1980), an installation for the artists' space 100m² in Tāmaki Makaurau, Browne installed texts such as 'a few small words' and 'TITLED' on the walls and left them as remnants.

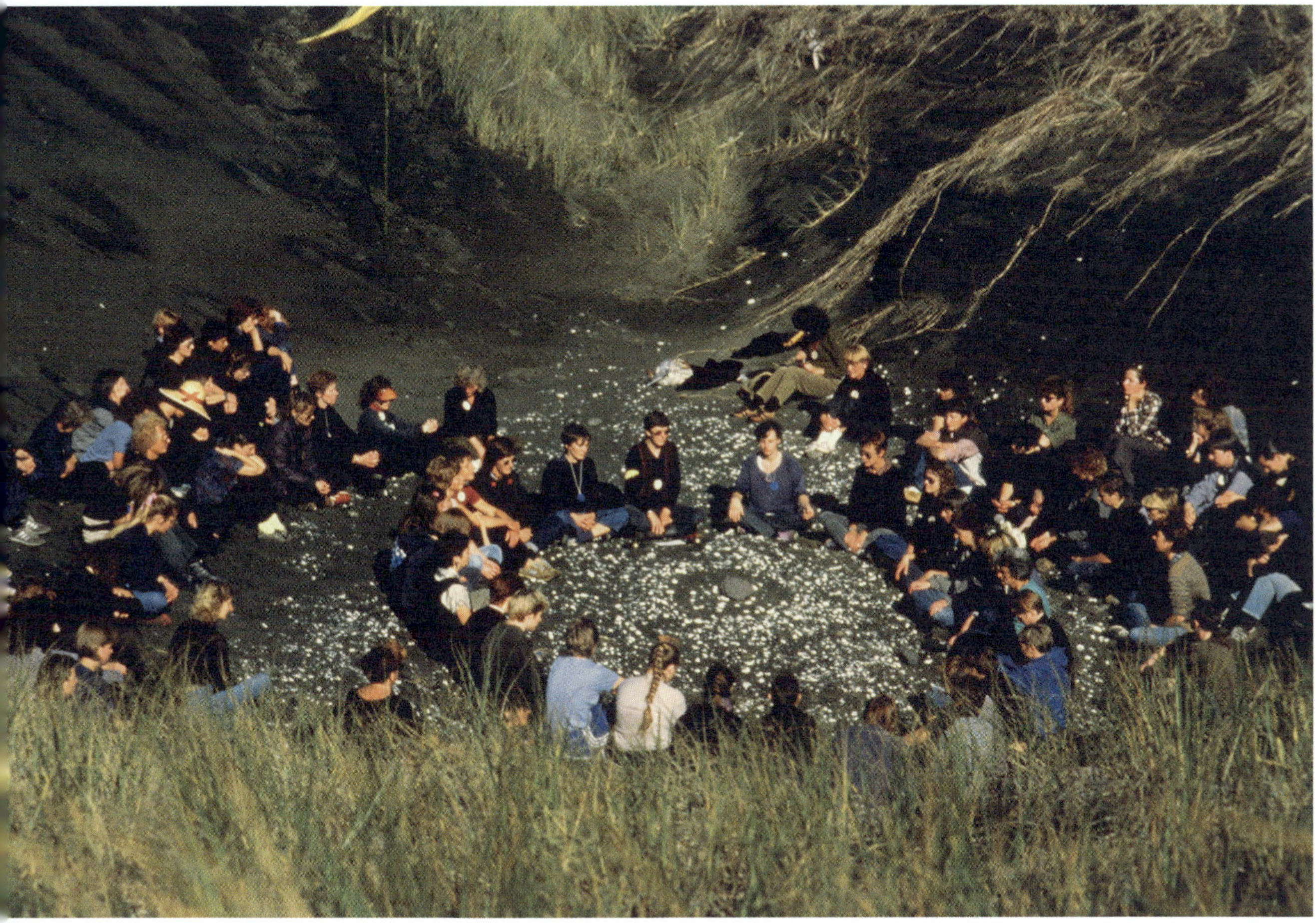

With Ngaire Mules, an artist interested in the relationship of video to performance, Browne performed *Beyond the Pale* (1980) at 100m² and then again in Melbourne as part of the first Australian Sculpture Triennial in 1981, at the Drama Theatre, La Trobe University. Described by the artists as a performance towards an installation, the work featured an area of sand with a paddling pool, a maypole at the centre and two large, white muslin bags oozing red liquid that dripped into amplified pans. Their synchronised performance described a lunar cycle and gradually became frenetic, engaging feminist concerns around menstruation and our human relationship to the environment.[19]

From 1980 to 1981 Browne spent time in San Francisco, where she saw performance works that incorporated dance and simple movements of the body, experiences that affirmed and influenced her subsequent works. In 1981 Browne performed *Howlback* in two iterations, first at 100m² and then during *Women and the Environment* at the Women's Gallery. This work examined menstruation and energy cycles, and the artist performed a series of actions in relation to specific forms, materials, colours and sounds, including a circle of sand and red oxide and a punch bag filled with salt water.

Four tape recorders relayed the sound the artist made when running a finger around the rim of a crystal glass. Throughout, Browne chalked numbers, letters and strokes systematically on the floor in white. Such works were not always easily understood by audience members but were challenging and powerful, and were described by one critic as intense and extremely valuable.[20]

Juliet Batten, *100 Women Project*, 1985, Te Henga Beach, for ANZART in Tāmaki Makaurau Auckland. *Courtesy the artist*

Browne performed *Time and Motion (The Dignity of Labour/The Tyranny of Work)* with Frank Stark in Te Whanganui-a-Tara as a part of *F1 New Zealand Sculpture Project* (1982), and *Working Conditions* for ANZART 1983 in Hobart. For these she used an orange marker pen to outline her silhouette repeatedly on the wall, working from the corners of the room towards the centre. A programmable rhythm generator strapped to her chest produced a loud ticking sound, the tempo of which increased at intervals. Part way through the performance Browne tied on an apron so her silhouettes became gendered. She positioned them to appear as if they were holding hands, thereby questioning gender roles and the division of labour: the expectation that women will cook, clean and raise children while men go to work. Across these performances Browne alluded to ideas of feminism and Marxism, constructing complex works that could be read in multiple ways.

Di ffrench (1946–1999) was another key producer of performance art in the early 1980s. Across her exhibition history we see her work shifting from performance to photographic slide presentation and performance installation, although her works disrupted these finite descriptions. ffrench asserted herself as a multimedia artist and favoured the term 'performance sculpture'. She viewed performance as a way to connect various sculptural elements and provoke audience responses, and her role as activating the materials and concepts rather than performing per se, and used her body to advance the political content of the work.[21] ffrench, who identified as a feminist, applied a critique of the male gaze and binary patriarchal orders, though her works were often created to prompt discussion on urgent socio-political issues. This was increasingly apparent in her work over the years, and she often accompanied her works with text handouts to describe her specific intent.

The use of 35mm slide-show imagery became a core part of several works, such as *Fractures* (1981), performed with Rosemary Johnson and Bridie Lonie at the Women's Gallery. Here ffrench explored her identity as a woman and an artist. Clad in a cocktail dress, stilettos and full makeup, she placed floral arrangements in crystal vases on several plinths, then overlaid paint directly from the tube onto the glass of three text collages (made from Walter Foster's *How to Paint* booklets). She then discarded the feminine dress, shoes and makeup, pulled on a blue boiler suit — the marker of a serious artist — and smashed the crystal vases.[22]

One of her key works, *Gut Reaction* (1981), a 35mm slide presentation and performance at University of Canterbury in Ōtautahi, concerned violence and popular protest. ffrench devised it in the aftermath of the death of Bobby Sands, a member of the Irish Republican Army who died while on hunger strike in prison in Ireland. Three videos played images of ffrench's abdomen on a loop for the duration of the performance as she hurled missiles (rocks, concrete and asphalt) at a target on the wall to the sound of semi-automatic gunfire. She declared:

> Increasing levels of awareness towards violent issues in our society are now decisively with us in the 80s. Directly observed in the essence of actual time or indirectly transmitted through various media . . . Public protest is one form of individual or collective *opinion.* Other more reflexive actions usually follow a *gut reaction* to a given situation.[23]

ffrench's powerful ANZART performance *Fontanel* (1981), at the Christchurch Arts Centre, was concerned with life and death polarities. *Fontanel* included associations with birth and death through the breaking out of the womb and then the breaking open of

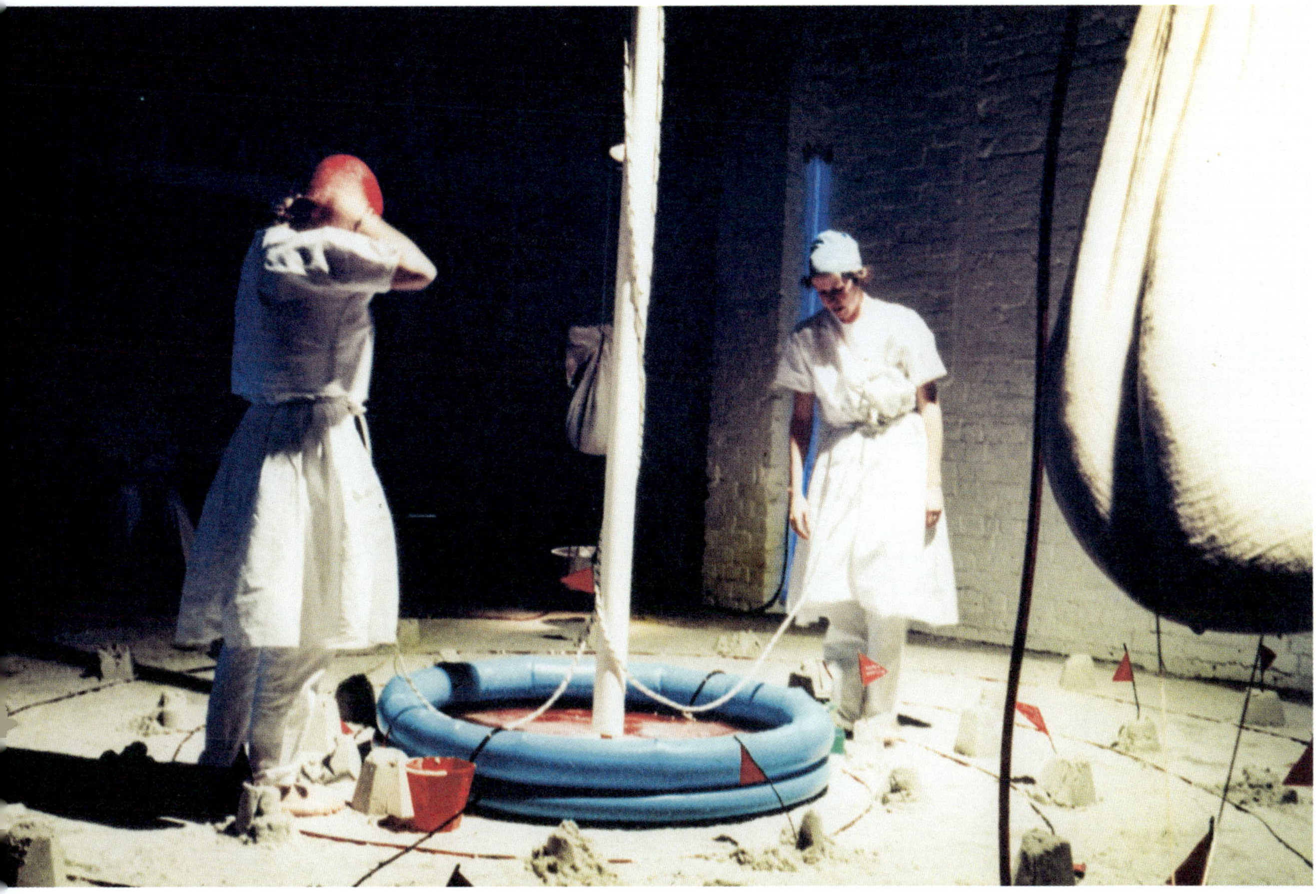

vessels of containment, a reference to a death haiku from Japanese poet and lay-priest of Buddhism Kobayashi Issa. It spoke strongly of the political turmoil in Uganda during the 1970s, the police brutality under the dictatorship of Ugandan military officer and politician Idi Amin who served as the third president of Uganda from 1971 to 1979, and what ffrench saw as the increasing brutality of the world. Hay described the work:

Mary-Louise Browne and Ngaire Mules, *Beyond the Pale*, 1980, 100m², Tāmaki Makaurau Auckland. *Courtesy the artist*

> A room in the Christchurch Arts Centre was lit with five candles and the floor was covered with black builder's paper on which a circle of seven skull-sized, rock-like ovoid forms were placed. A slide projector, situated above the installation, was turned on and the candles then blown out. Working to a precise beat (pulse and breath), ffrench projected 36 slides of black Africans in 'reverse' (photographic negative) within the ring of forms, followed by its mirror image (the photographic positive) . . .
>
> After the completion of the slides, ffrench walked into the area and sprayed the paper with toxic white lacquer. The next sequence of *Fontanel* evoked a curious sense of violence and unveiling . . . Leaving the image of the last slide on, ffrench, armed with a steel machete, struck each vessel across the fontanel, at which they crumbled, spilling ash over the 'white lacquer, over the projected sepia portrait taking up the colour — becoming a landscape merging like a ghost'.[24]

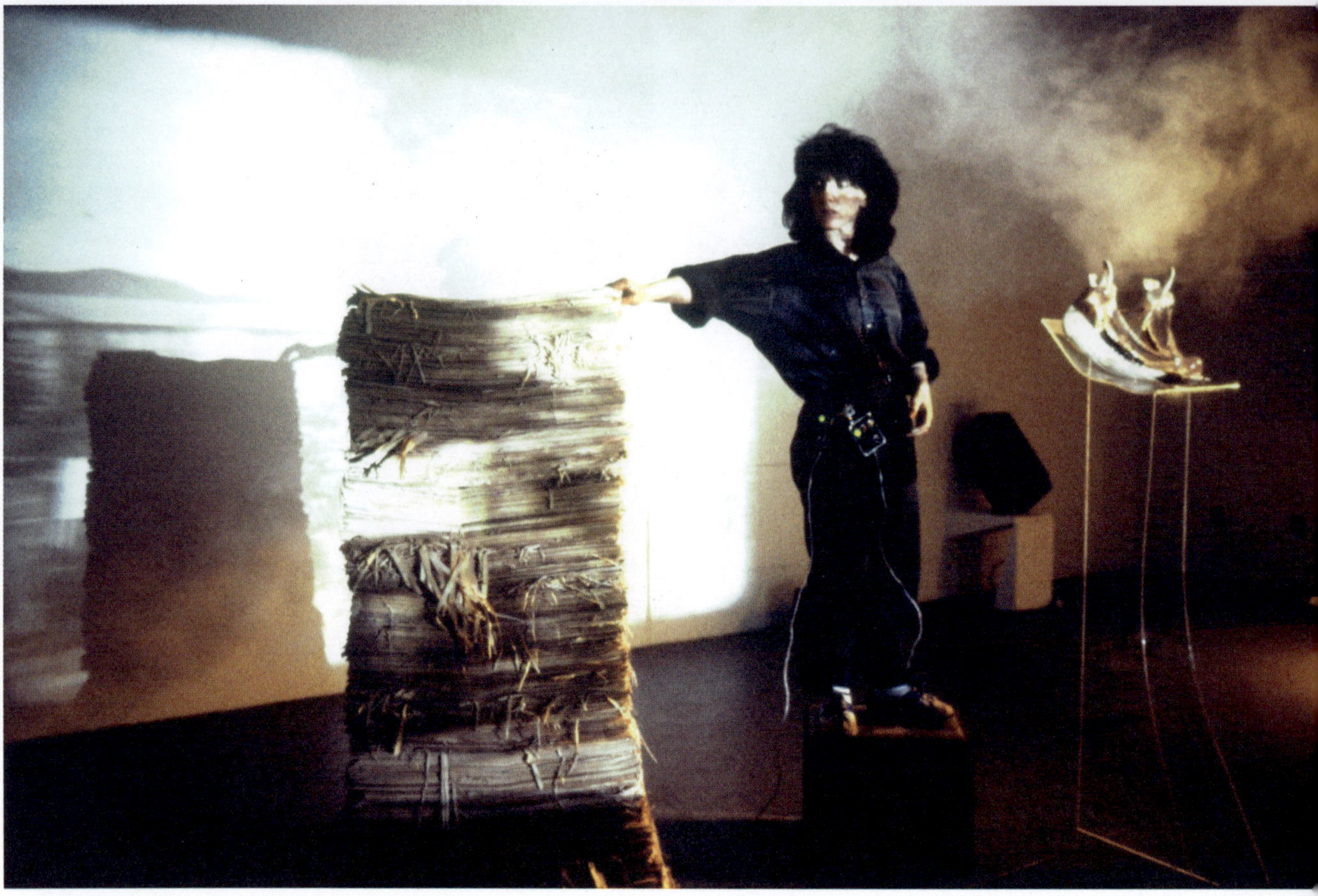

LEFT: Di ffrench, *The Opinion*, 1984, documentation of performance at Auckland Art Gallery. *From Di ffrench papers r.5308, Hocken Collections, Uare Taoka o Hākena*

BELOW: Claire Fergusson, *Y–Z (New York–New Zealand)*, 1981, documentation of performance featuring pāua-shell eyes with kiwi head beak mask, Aotearoa soil, tea service, two gallery attendants, two fairies performed by Rose Collins and Kate Collins, projected slides of Aotearoa and the audience, ANZART, Ōtautahi Christchurch. *Courtesy the artist*

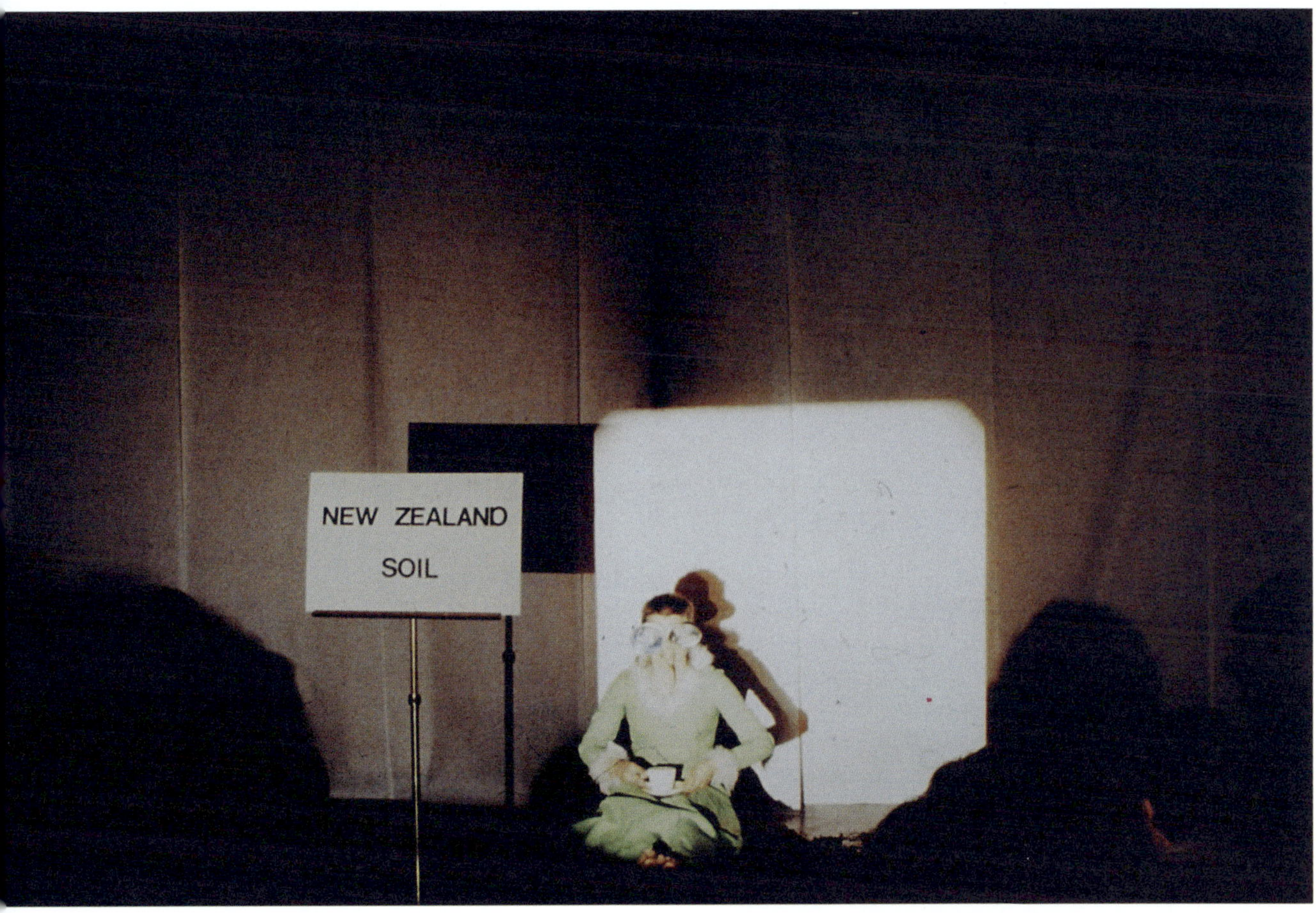

The violence was both visually arresting and confrontational. ffrench explained the work was about cruelty and our innate capacity to be cruel to one another.

Another work that prompted a strong response was *Asters*, performed for the 1983 ANZART in Hobart, Tasmania. According to art critic John Hurrell, who was present at the performance, ffrench, dressed in mechanic's overalls, began by hanging a bow on the wall and spraying a large black clay egg full of ashes with acrid-smelling white paint.

There were also tender images projected as slides, and video of a naked man with cascades of silvery pink aster petals falling over him. Though Hurrell criticised the work for the lack of movement when the projection was playing, the ritualised action, references to weapons, penetration, birth and death together created a complex layering of meaning.[25]

ffrench's work *The Opinion* (1984) for Auckland Art Gallery Toi o Tāmaki further galvanised perspectives on her work. This piece dealt with the theme of the public exchange of ideas and was presented as a performance and static installation. ffrench positioned herself behind a lectern on top of a plinth of stacked newspapers, where she screwed up pieces of paper. A newsreel of a 1951 Labour Party rally was projected through the objects, accompanied by the sound of the incoming tide. A text was handed out to the audience.

As Cheryll Sotheran writes, ffrench suggested that ideas expressed in Aotearoa at the time were characterised by 'mechanical repetition, banality and an inability to be original, being rather dependent on "overseas opinion"'. Sotheran asserted that ffrench's performances postulated a 'willingness on the part of the public (the viewers) to be confused by smokescreens of untruth'. While Sotheran reviewed the work as 'meticulous, striking, provocative', she also found it slightly confusing, and her attempts to find meaning through the experience of the performance were out of step with the written description of the content.[26]

In 1985 ffrench, aware of the focus performance placed on her own body rather than on the issues she wanted to address, made a decision to transfer her energies to photography. The body was central to her practice, however, regardless of medium. She wrote: 'I feel that some performance works can be extended into photographic areas. But not all performances, only those which suggest the possibility of extension into new work.'[27] As mentioned earlier, this trajectory from performance to another medium was common across makers of this period.

INTERNATIONAL CONNECTIONS

As described, key venues for performance in the early 1980s were the *F1 New Zealand Sculpture Project*, held at a disused factory space in Wellington in 1982, and the *1984 Art in Dunedin* project. The environment at these artist-initiated projects encouraged and supported experimental works, and the short duration of the exhibitions was well suited to performance art. The other significant sites for performance art were the ANZART exhibitions.

Although the Hobart ANZART (1983) had a less consistent curatorial approach, international content and context were critical for artists of Aotearoa, and these exchanges were fruitful as a platform to share new work, develop conceptual frameworks and build a supportive community of New Zealand practitioners. In addition to ANZART, artists travelled overseas and returned with new ways of working or thinking about their practice, and international visitors brought an expanded sense of what performance could be.

Auckland-born and New York-based artist Claire Fergusson began making performance work in 1978 with *Morris Louis Performance* at Franklin Furnace in New York, a work that involved pouring paint over her naked body as if she were a Morris Louis painting. Fergusson wrote:

> My performance was about the relationship between 'painting as an historical form' and 'being a person making those paintings'. It was a literal visual layering of these two aspects. The process of painting that is usually separated in many ways — painter from painting, execution from exhibition, and audience from artist — was brought together so that the whole process took place at one time.[28]

Having left Aotearoa at the age of ten, in 1981 Fergusson returned and toured the country, presenting lectures and her performance works at a range of venues. Wystan Curnow wrote about several of these and favoured the work *Date Day*, where Fergusson projected onto her naked body a series of photographs of her clothed self that had been taken each day for a year. In the performance she described her responses to the outfits and the memories and associations they provoked, reinforcing the shifting nature of the self and the dissonance between body and image.

Fergusson's work *My Grandmother* was shown at Real Pictures Gallery in Tāmaki Makaurau and also involved the projection of photographs, this time images of herself and her grandmother projected onto each of their bodies, wherein the youthful granddaughter was overlaid on the elder woman while the younger woman aged with the images of her grandmother.

Y–Z (1981), a work developed specifically for ANZART in Ōtautahi and delivered also in Whakatū Nelson, focused on Fergusson's personal observations of differences between New York and Aotearoa. The performance explored the land of Aotearoa and the artist's relationship to it through actions and dialogue. First, a pile of soil was wheeled in by two gallery attendants and dumped in the middle of the space. Fergusson spread the dirt across the floor by rolling back and forth in it, saying 'the wide sea the ocean rolling and coming onto the shore'. Images of ocean and sky were projected as a backdrop alongside depictions of demonstrations against the 1981 Springbok tour.

Then, resting on the pile of soil, Fergusson put on a kiwi mask complete with beak and pāua shells for eyes while an image of Queen Elizabeth II was projected onto and behind the artist. The gallery attendants served everybody tea, Fergusson stood up, mixed soil into the teapot, poured it over herself, then buried her body in the soil. Two young children (termed 'fairies' by the artist)[29] laid fern fronds on top while the gallery attendants smeared mud on the walls behind them. Finally, Fergusson jumped up from the soil and cried, 'If you feel sincere, stand up and cheer!' The audience rose and applauded. Participation was key for Fergusson: she intended the audience to be part of the artwork.

As an artist participating in the New York performance art scene Fergusson would have sparked curiosity, but there was also some disconnection and she was not always warmly received by local audiences. Whereas Fergusson was used to being part of a large community of performance artists, those working in Aotearoa were operating in a more cohesive environment, a smaller ecosystem of institutions, participants and audiences, where there was perhaps more fluidity across disciplines and a less focused interrogation of the artist's body as artwork.

Fergusson was part of the feminist movement in the United States in the 1970s, and her work also employs ideas from this context, particularly around women's bodies and institutional sexism. Her performance at the Women's Gallery in Te Whanganui-a-Tara met with a more supportive response in terms of these ideas but less understanding of the specific performance art criticism she was accustomed to.

END OF AN ERA

By the mid-1980s performance was no longer the favoured medium for the majority of the artists discussed here. The radical energy of the feminist movements had largely been spent, and there was a turn towards post-structural theory and postmodern practice, especially an analysis of language and text. There was a noticeable desire to focus less on the artist's body, and a need to return to exhibitable and saleable objects. Performativity became part of the creative process rather than the outcome, and artists used lessons learned from performance in sculpture, photography and moving image. In response to the changing demands of a transformed economic, social and political landscape, as well as countercultural retort from hippie to punk, artists repurposed technologies that had been so vital to performance to address fresh concerns and ways for art to circulate and be consumed.

NOTES

1 For detailed discussion of Kimberley Gray, see Chapter 2 by Natasha Conland.

2 Lita Barrie, 'Remissions: Toward a deconstruction of phallic univocality', *Antic* 1 (June 1986): 87–104; Lita Barrie, 'Further Toward a Deconstruction of Phallic Univocality: Deferrals', *Antic* 2 (March 1987): 18–47.

3 The introduction of neoliberal economic policies in Aotearoa were named Rogernomics after Roger Douglas, the minister of finance 1984–88 in the Fourth Labour Government of New Zealand (26 July 1984 to 2 November 1990).

4 For detailed discussion of Peter Roche and Linda Buis's performances between 1979 and 1985, see Chapter 5 by Christina Barton and Gregory Burke.

5 See Museum of New Zealand Te Papa Tongarewa, 'Museum Piece', https://collections.tepapa.govt.nz/object/194093

6 Wystan Curnow, 'Peter Roche: Committed', City Gallery Wellington, 4 October 2020, https://citygallery.org.nz/blog/peter-roche-committed

7 John Hurrell, 'Peter Roche: Committed', City Gallery Wellington, 4 October 2020, https://citygallery.org.nz/blog/peter-roche-committed

8 Susan Best, *It's Not Personal: Post 60s body art and performance* (London: Bloomsbury Academic, 2021), 75.

9 This is an interesting but perhaps unintended connection to the performance artwork of Kimberley Gray. There is no evidence they were aware of each other. See Chapter 2 of this volume by Natasha Conland.

10 Kyla McFarlane, ed., *A Different Temporality: Aspects of Australian feminist art practice 1975–1985*, exhibition catalogue (Melbourne: Monash University Museum of Art, 2011), 7.

11 Jennifer Hay, 'Trans-Marginal: New Zealand performance art 1970–1985', in *Intervention: Post object and performance art in New Zealand in 1970 and beyond* (Christchurch: Robert McDougall Art Gallery & Annex, 2000), 6.

12 Ibid., 21.

13 Kirsty Baker, 'Inhabiting the Threshold: The Women's Gallery as liminal space in New Zealand's feminist art history' (Master's thesis, Victoria University of Wellington, 2016), ii. http://researcharchive.vuw.ac.nz/handle/10063/5129

14 Bridie Lonie, 'Rosemary Johnson 1942–82', *Spiral* 5 (1982): 33.

15 Bronwen Nicholson, 'In a Feminist Sense. Review of "The Menstrual Maze"', *Broadsheet* 112 (1983): 46.

16 Ibid.

17 Sandra Coney, 'Strength in Cohesion', *New Zealand Listener* 114 (13 December 1986): 63.

18 Mary-Louise Browne, 'The Thingness of Things: An interview with Mary-Louise Browne', interview by Emma Bugden, 21 July 2016, https://smallborebooks.com/2016/07/21/the-thingness-of-things-we-interview-mary-louise-browne

19 Ngaire Mules and Mary-Louise Browne, 'Beyond the Pale, Part II', *Spiral* 5 (1982): 36.

20 Margaret Leniston, 'Art Review', *Spiral* 5 (1982): 38.

21 Bridie Lonie, 'Five Photographers: Di Ffrench', *Art New Zealand* 43 (Winter 1987): 65.

22 Jennifer Hay, 'Textures of Light', in *Di Ffrench: Light and illusion*, exhibition catalogue (Christchurch: Robert McDougall Art Gallery & Annex, 2000), 24.

23 Di ffrench, *Gut reaction*, Xerox handout to accompany performance, University of Canterbury, 1981, cited in Marian Evans, Bridie Lonie and Tilly Lloyd, eds, *A Women's Picture Book: 25 women artists of Aotearoa*. (Wellington: Government Printer, 1988), 111. Emphasis in the original.

24 Hay, 'Textures of Light', 26. The last phrase is from ffrench in Evans, Lonie and Lloyd, *A Women's Picture Book*, 114.

25 John Hurrell, 'The New Zealand Presence in Tasmania', *Art New Zealand* 28 (Spring 1983): 21.
26 Cheryll Sotheran, 'Exhibitions: Auckland', *Art New Zealand* 33 (Summer 1984): 15.
27 Di ffrench, notes accompanying *The Same Leaves*, Women's Gallery, Wellington, October 1981, cited in Rob Garrett, 'Horizontal Vertigo: The photographic works of Di Ffrench, 1984–98', in *Di Ffrench: Light and illusion*, exhibition catalogue (Christchurch: Robert McDougall Art Gallery & Annex, 2000), 9.
28 Claire Fergusson quoted in Wystan Curnow, 'Claire Fergusson: Performance and photography', *Art New Zealand* 21 (Spring 1981): 34–35.
29 Claire Fergusson, email conversations with the author and editors, August 2023.

REFERENCES

Baker, Kirsty. 'Inhabiting the Threshold: The Women's Gallery as liminal space in New Zealand's feminist art history'. Master's thesis, Victoria University of Wellington, 2016. http://researcharchive.vuw.ac.nz/handle/10063/5129

Barrie, Lita. 'Further Toward a Deconstruction of Phallic Univocality: Deferrals'. *Antic* 2 (March 1987): 18–47.

——— 'Remissions: Toward a deconstruction of phallic univocality'. *Antic* 1 (June 1986): 87–104.

Barton, Christina. 'Performance Art by Women in Aotearoa New Zealand 1974–1993'. In *Alter/Image: Feminism and representation in New Zealand art 1973–1993*, edited by Christina Barton and Deborah Lawler-Dormer, 61–63. City Gallery Wellington and Auckland Art Gallery Toi o Tāmaki, 1993.

Best, Susan. *It's Not Personal: Post 60s body art and performance*. London: Bloomsbury Academic, 2021.

Browne, Mary-Louise. 'The Thingness of Things: An interview with Mary-Louise Browne'. Interview by Emma Bugden, 21 July 2016. https://smallborebooks.com/2016/07/21/the-thingness-of-things-we-interview-mary-louise-browne

Coney, Sandra. 'Strength in Cohesion'. *New Zealand Listener* 114 (13 December 1986): 63.

Curnow, Wystan. 'Claire Fergusson: Performance and photography'. *Art New Zealand* 21 (Spring 1981): 34–35.

——— 'Peter Roche: Committed'. City Gallery Wellington, 4 October 2020. https://citygallery.org.nz/blog/peter-roche-committed

Evans, Marian, Bridie Lonie, and Tilly Lloyd, eds. *A Women's Picture Book: 25 women artists of Aotearoa*. Wellington: Government Printer, 1988.

Garrett, Rob. 'Horizontal Vertigo: The photographic works of Di Ffrench, 1984–98'. In *Di Ffrench: Light and illusion*. Exhibition catalogue, 9–19. Christchurch: Robert McDougall Art Gallery & Annex, 2000.

Hay, Jennifer. 'Textures of Light'. In *Di Ffrench: Light and Illusion*. Exhibition catalogue, 21–30. Christchurch: Robert McDougall Art Gallery & Annex, 2000.

——— 'Trans-Marginal: New Zealand performance art 1970–1985'. in *Intervention: Post object and performance art in New Zealand in 1970 and beyond*, 5–25. Christchurch: Robert McDougall Art Gallery & Annex, 2000.

Hurrell, John. 'Peter Roche: Committed'. City Gallery Wellington, 4 October 2020. https://citygallery.org.nz/blog/peter-roche-committed

——— 'The New Zealand Presence in Tasmania'. *Art New Zealand* 28 (Spring 1983): 21–23.

Leniston, Margaret. 'Art Review'. *Spiral* 5 (1982): 38.

Lonie, Bridie. 'Five Photographers: Di Ffrench'. *Art New Zealand* 43 (Winter 1987): 65–67.

——— 'Rosemary Johnson 1942–82'. *Spiral* 5 (1982): 33.

McFarlane, Kyla, ed. *A Different Temporality: Aspects of Australian feminist art practice 1975–1985*. Exhibition catalogue. Melbourne: Monash University Museum of Art, 2011.

Mules, Ngaire and Mary-Louise Browne. 'Beyond the Pale, Part II'. *Spiral* 5 (1982): 36.

Museum of New Zealand Te Papa Tongarewa. 'Museum Piece'. https://collections.tepapa.govt.nz/object/194093

Nicholson, Bronwen. 'In a Feminist Sense: Review of "The Menstrual Maze"'. *Broadsheet* 112 (1983): 46.

Small Bore Books. 'The Thingness of Things: An interview with Mary Louise-Browne', 2016. https://smallborebooks.com/2016/07/21/the-thingness-of-things-we-interview-mary-louise-browne

Sotheran, Cheryll. 'Auckland', *Art New Zealand* 33 (Summer 1984–85): 15.

5

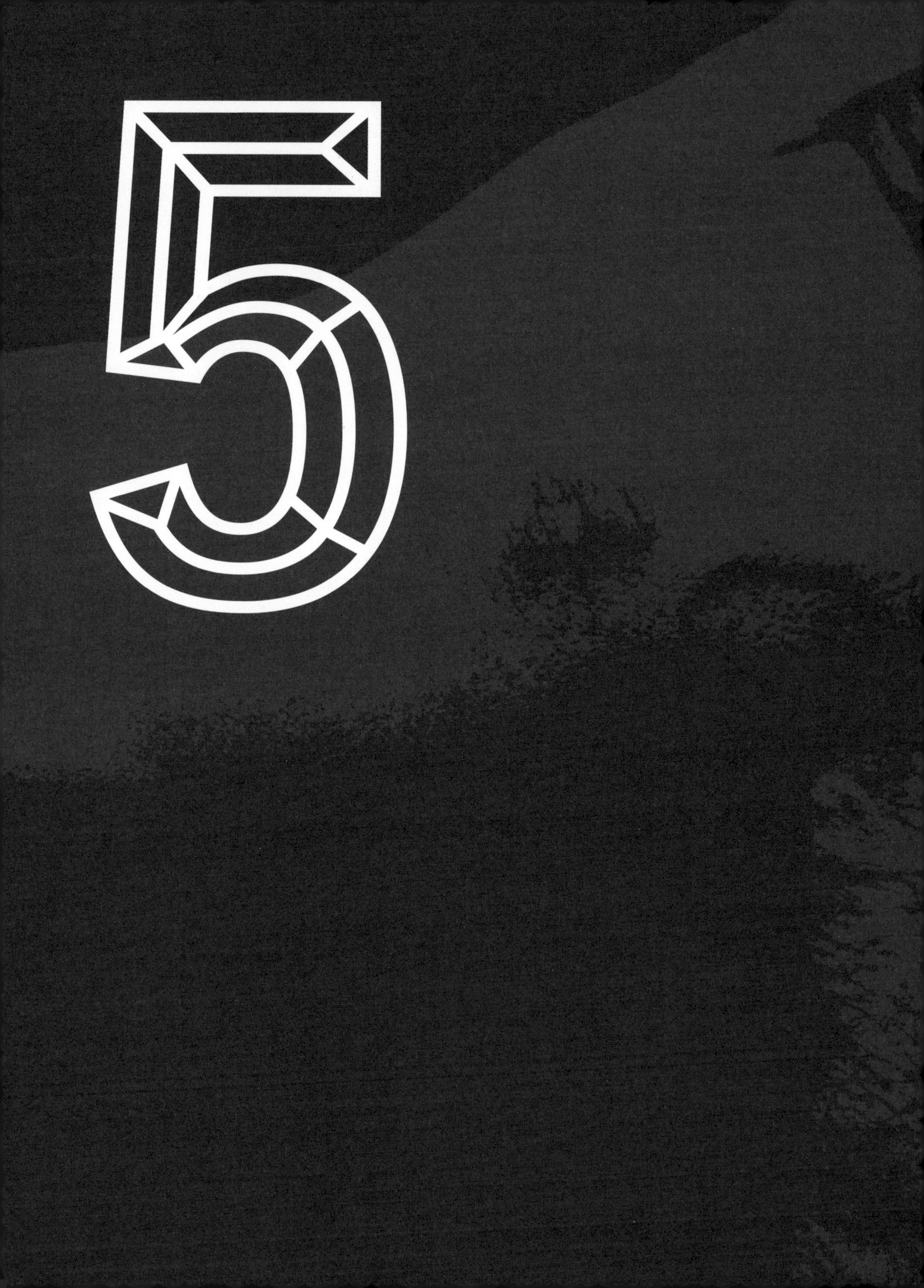

THE AFTERLIVES OF PERFORMANCE ART: THE CASE OF PETER ROCHE AND LINDA BUIS

Christina Barton
& Gregory Burke

It follows that, in the museum also, we are responsible not only for an act of preservation but also of re-creation.
— Guy Brett[1]

In 2023 at Te Pātaka Toi Adam Art Gallery we presented the exhibition *In Relation: Performance works by Peter Roche & Linda Buis 1979–1985*, which documented twenty-five performances that artist couple Peter Roche (1957–2022) and Linda Buis (1954–2014) executed in the early 1980s in a wide array of art and non-art spaces in Aotearoa New Zealand and Australia.[2] Using the surviving archive of photographs, film and video footage, drawings, texts, artist publications and published and unpublished commentary, we re-examined the artists' demanding durational live performances, which challenged both the artists and their audiences, physically and psychologically.

Our first aim in undertaking this project was to salvage a little-known chapter in Aotearoa's performance art history in order to ensure it found its place in the annals of this art form. A second, related aspiration was to properly understand the trajectory of Roche & Buis's work, executed over an intense six-year period that mirrored the duration of their personal relationship. We wanted to understand the arc of their practice, to see how it took shape, evolved and transformed.

Aided by the relatively short span of their collaboration, we were able to delineate and track an oeuvre to provide what all art historians strive to deliver: a narrative. Our exhibition charted how the artists quickly shifted away from confrontation and physical violence towards a tense balancing act between risk and tension on the one hand and a kind of concentrated attention on the other. Their live performances together ended when the pair came to the point where they did not want to repeat or further expose themselves, turning instead to making drawings, sculptural assemblages and installations that served as surrogates for the energies they had previously given vent to via their bodies.

Tying the whole together, we posited the self-described concept of 'vulnerability' as a key state the artists set out to explore: a physical and psychological condition felt by the artists and generated through their work, which they also wanted their audience to experience.[3]

The strength of the exhibition did not lie primarily in the quality of our archival research, however, nor in the historical narrative we created. It lay, in the end, in the calibre of the photographic and textual documentation made by the artists themselves and one of their exemplary witnesses, critic Wystan Curnow. Roche & Buis took great care to document their work, collaborating with friends and fellow artists to produce still photographs that recorded each event, and writing and exchanging notes afterwards that described and assessed their performances.

What they chose to keep as the visual record of their work and what they said in its wake are all we have left. This is the conundrum of performance art — in this case rendered even more poignant by the fact that both artists died in their sixties without setting down their recollections of what they did.

Our argument in the exhibition and in this chapter, where we take the opportunity to reflect, is that Roche & Buis's photographs and films not only document what happened in the moment but also enable us to engage anew: to see, imagine, speculate and propose as active participants in the production of meaning. We believe that this opportunity is particular to performance art, in its disinvestment in the idea of art as a singular object created by an artist for aesthetic contemplation by a viewer. If the performance itself is unrepeatable, conditioned as it is by context and occasion, its surviving documentation lives on.

Seldom treated as precious, recommissioned in different formats, merged with text and dispersed in printed matter, this material demands a different kind of attention. Although we relied on the photographs to tell us about Roche & Buis's performances, we also used them as active agents, believing that they can still *perform* in the wake of performance.

For this publication, we chart and appraise key aspects of Roche & Buis's performance works and offer insights into our exhibition project, which we recognise retrospectively was our effort to address the ontological and methodological challenges of revisiting live, situation-specific performance art. By laying out the lineaments of Roche & Buis's practice and exploring the constitutive role of the exhibition as its own phenomenological event, we hope to contribute to a critical history of art in Aotearoa.

BEING THERE

Having connected with Peter Roche at Elam School of Fine Arts at the University of Auckland in June 1978, I [Gregory] was enlisted to document on video his first live action event, *Meat Lift*, which involved dropping a butchered sheep's carcass from a plane into Auckland's Waitematā Harbour.[4] In the following years I witnessed most of Roche & Buis's performances, many of which I was charged with photographing.

These were the socially and politically turbulent years of the authoritarian Muldoon era that followed the bold, independent and progressive policies of the Kirk government. In response to the Muldoon regime, growing numbers of people mobilised to protest its policies, particularly those of welcoming both nuclear-armed American warships and sporting ties with South Africa, the climax of the latter being the violent anti-Springbok tour protests of 1981. The punk movement was on the rise, defined in part by scepticism toward the idealism of the hippie era earlier in the decade. The tone at Elam had changed also, with the experimental practices Jim Allen had earlier championed as head of sculpture receding in favour of a return to traditional media.

At the same time, postmodern sensibilities, coupled with an engagement with intermedia practices involving some deployment of the performative, were emerging in the work of various students and members of the wider Tāmaki Makaurau Auckland art community. I am thinking, for example, of the photography of Megan Jenkinson, Marie Shannon and Christine Webster; the films of Ronald Brownson and Alison McLean; the text works of Mary-Louise Browne; the alternative theatre of the Humanimals; and the sonic and filmic output of Fetus Productions. It was within this broader context that the work of Roche & Buis was often received; and although their works repudiated both theatrical and traditional art media, they had a diverse audience with notable art world figures such as Philip Clairmont and Peter Peryer attending their performances.

It was a time when criticism and theory, including feminist theory, became increasingly influential, with publications such as *Parallax* and *Splash* in New Zealand and *Art + Text* in Australia; and it was a time when the local discourse, which had previously been regional and mainly male, was opening to an international dialogue. By 1979 the Sydney Biennale was expanding its international reach and including New Zealand artists in its mix, and the series of Australia New Zealand Artists Encounter (ANZART) exchanges was inaugurated in Ōtautahi Christchurch.

Roche & Buis participated in the latter in 1981 as well as in subsequent iterations in Tasmania (1983), Portsmouth (1984) and Tāmaki Makaurau (1985). Although these

ANZART events foregrounded performance work, they were also notably cross-disciplinary and included artists pushing at the boundaries of various media. In this context, while Roche & Buis adhered to a pure idea of performance — as a focus on body and self in unrehearsed real-time situations — from the outset they also incorporated film, video, photography and text as elements in their work.

Although Roche was aware of the experimental practices Jim Allen fostered in the early 1970s, it is notable that he studied painting at Elam and only moved to the sculpture department after staging *Meat Lift* in 1978. Principal references at this point, from material in Elam Library, were the installations and live actions of Joseph Beuys, and Allan Kaprow's durational events known in the 1960s as 'happenings'. By early 1979 Roche's interest had shifted to the confrontational performances of Gina Pane and Marina Abramović, which involved endurance and self-inflicted harm, and, not least, to the transgressive performance, photographic and video works of Vito Acconci. In his performance works Acconci defied socially inscribed boundaries between public and private, often performing for the viewer via photographic stills or video, including live closed-circuit video — media also deployed by Roche & Buis in their performances.

In January of that year Roche realised the durational work *You Are Invited to Be Accepted*, the first in a series of performances that tested his physical and psychological limits as well as the tolerance and complicity of viewers. The only photos of that performance show Roche with a bandaged arm, at a point of exhaustion, sitting beneath a pinned-up photo of his new partner Linda Buis, taken by her father Simon Buis, a noted documentary photographer and charismatic member of Tāmaki Makaurau's art community. Roche had endured forty-eight hours of self-imposed exile, deprivation and self-mutilation, having shut himself in an empty room with only a camera and tripod, a full-length mirror, typewriter and paper, a razor blade and various stimulants, including wine and cigarettes. With the typewriter, he recorded his increasingly sleep-deprived and psychologically altered state before cutting his arm badly with the blade, a wound that had to be stitched before the performance continued.

Roche had invited guests to visit him in a private space in his home and, if willing, to take his photograph using a camera set up in the space. Each guest was unwittingly given their own specific time to attend, which meant they would not only be a sole witness in the given moment, but also a tacit participant in the performance with a corresponding and heightened responsibility for what transpired. The option of taking Roche's photograph more overtly engaged the guest in questions of their complicity in reinforcing Roche's self-harming behaviour.

Over the following six months, in solo performances involving bodily mutilation and laceration, Roche continued to probe the psychological interaction between body, performer, audience and self.

In October 1979 Buis became an active performer for *Oh Shit No, On the Contrary*. The work had two versions. The first involved Roche with a microphone and stand in front of an audience. A looped film sequence of Buis's face being slapped repeatedly was projected next to him, and large headshots of Roche, taken by Buis, were pinned to an adjacent wall. One couldn't see Roche's hand slapping Buis's face, but one sensed it from her distressed reaction. Buis herself sat at a table, at intervals operating a tape deck that played segments of herself verbally berating Roche. Together, the far-from-endearing photographs of Roche, which he described as 'psychological mutilation',[5] the intentionally disturbing footage of Buis being slapped, and the audio of her unrelenting attack on Roche, made for a challenging situation for both Roche and the audience.

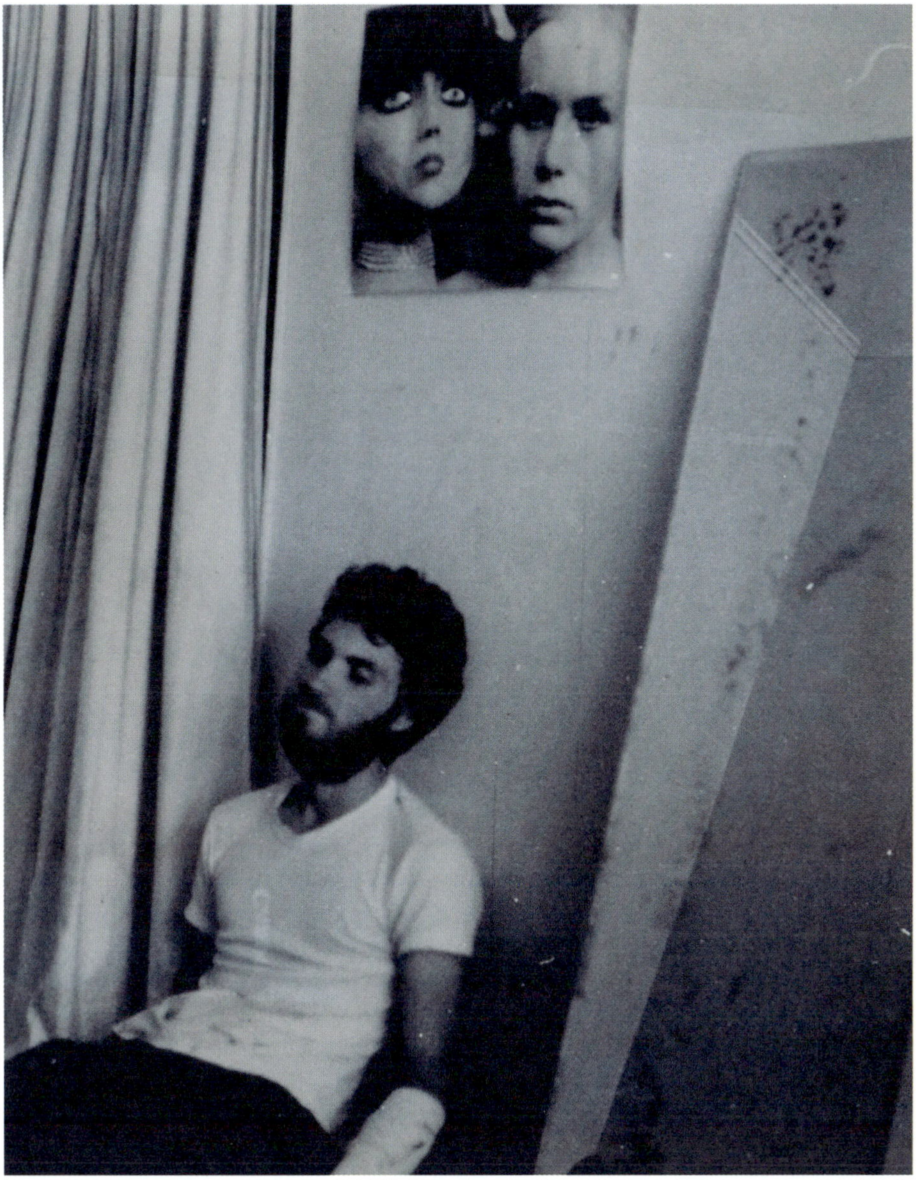

Peter Roche, *You Are Invited to Be Accepted*, performance, January 1979, black and white photograph, Peter Roche and unknown photographer. *Courtesy Peter Roche Estate and Te Pātaka Toi Adam Art Gallery*

Confronted by such material, all Roche could do was pace before the audience, at times going to the microphone where he tried to muster words to defend himself. In notes made after the performance he wrote that he felt the attack on his character was too 'one sided', although he did note that after half an hour 'it began to work in [his] favour' by instilling a level of sympathy in the audience.[6] Despite the violence he had enacted against Buis, it appeared she had the upper hand.

Two weeks later the piece was performed again with the addition of a second film loop, depicting Roche & Buis sensuously if somewhat arduously tonguing each other, and a second audiotape of Buis flattering Roche and expressing strong emotional support for him.

On this occasion, Buis moved between two decks and alternated the playback of the tapes according to Roche's actions and responses. With greater emotional range, sympathies were able to be shifted and Roche's vulnerability more fully and variously manipulated.

Although attention was focused primarily on Roche, his physical actions and psychological responses were predicated on Buis's decisions of when to change the audio and his assessment of where he stood in relation to his audience. Importantly, although the performance clearly inferred a consideration of gender relations, possibilities for interpretation were not predetermined. As Roche noted, 'it is a truly live and vital situation that I am attempting to work with'.[7]

Roche titled the two films *Offence/Defence*, in tandem with Buis's alternating audiotapes, indicating that they were not simply documents but rather key installational components of a situation he had structured to perform in. Intentionally provocative, it is hard to conceive that the film of Buis being slapped could be produced in the current context of heightened awareness of domestic abuse. It is important to realise, though, that with these films and audiotapes, Roche & Buis took on personae and performed them in real time, like the approach Acconci took in many works in the 1960s, and not too dissimilar to the tactics of Cindy Sherman when she began performing personae for camera from the late 1970s. That Roche contrived a shameful persona is borne out from notes he made prior to the first performance, where he says that having 'never consciously inflicted pain on another', slapping Buis 'was a considerable shock to the system'.[8]

On the other hand, Buis's persona, that of the passive recipient of Roche's blows, is challenged by her feisty and articulate presence in the audiotapes. By engaging such contradiction, as well as exploiting their vulnerability and the lack of predictability inherent in an unscripted situation, Roche & Buis drew attention to psychological ambiguities that issue from evolving power relations — between each other, and between the performers and their audience.

Following the singular force of Buis's participation, the artists continued to explore subtleties of interaction engaged by their performance as equal partners in a series of works that form a remarkable chapter in the history of performance art in Aotearoa. They broke from the dominant mode of performance in New Zealand, which focused on the solo artist, most often male. Consciously deciding to work together as a couple in life and art, they chose to treat their bodies, the dynamics of their relationship, and their actions executed for and in response to their audiences, as the basis for a sustained negotiation of what it meant to be 'in relation', both physically and psychologically. Unafraid to distinguish themselves as a man and a woman, alone and as a pair, and as they interacted with others, they saw themselves as 'prototypes' who could test what it felt like to be subjects in their moment.[9]

Roche & Buis formally announced their partnership in March 1980 with an evening of performances held at Real Pictures, a photography gallery in Tāmaki Makaurau. As part of the event they presented two previous collaborations performed for camera: the looped Super 8 film *Liaison Assertive Cooperative* (1980) and a sequence of photos from *Street Piece* (1980). The film documents a performer in the distance walking toward the camera, becoming more prominent in the frame as if confronting the viewer. On reaching the camera the performer turns it to face the second performer, who then repeats the action of walking toward the camera before turning it to face the other, who is back in their starting position.

The actions are repeated and looped to convey endless repetition and non-hierarchical cooperation. By directing the camera, each performer asserts themselves, but in so doing they also deflect attention from themselves to the other performer. This

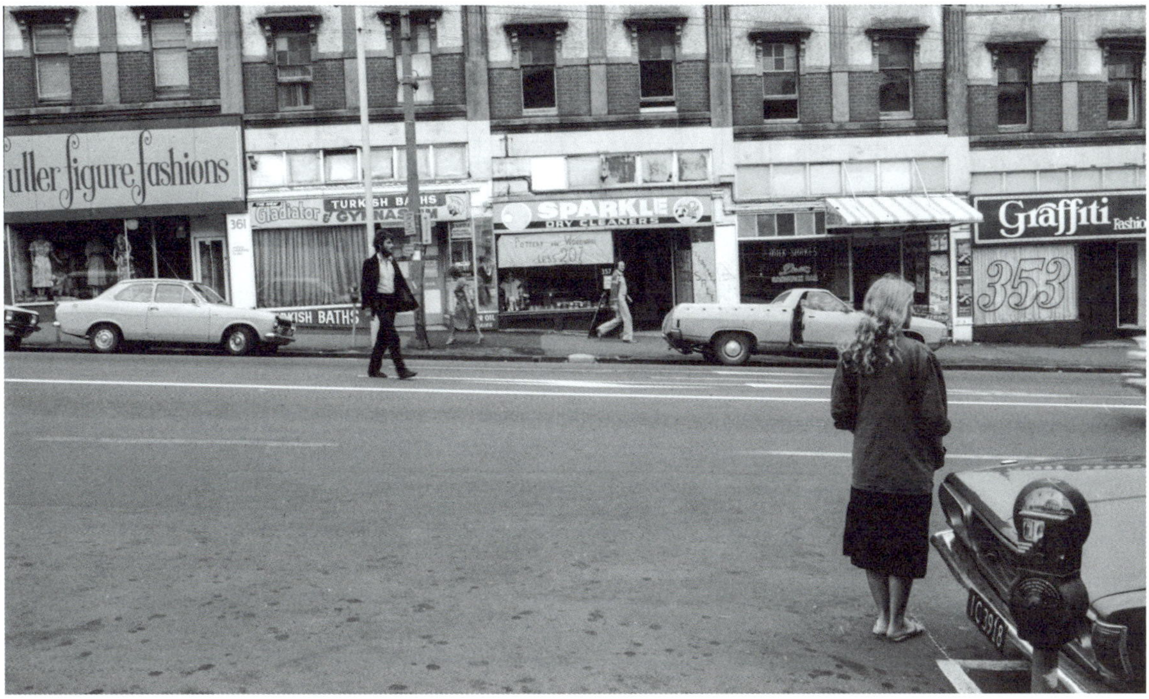

Peter Roche and Linda Buis, *Street Piece*, February 1980, performance on Queen Street, Tāmaki Makaurau Auckland, digital print from original negative. *Courtesy Peter Roche Estate and Linda Buis Estate. Photo by Gregory Burke*

process of decentring themselves to focus instead on the dynamics and conditions of their relationship as individuals continued throughout subsequent performances.

Their format of performing collaboratively but separately within a predetermined structure is also evident in *Street Piece*, in which the artists crisscrossed Queen Street, Auckland's busy main street, walking from top to bottom. They focused on their interaction or liaison as performers, separate from but always aware of each other, at times close, at others distant, their movements to some extent determined by traffic.

They were documented on film by the third participant, the unseen photographer who recorded their passage and their encounters with pedestrians and drivers, who also became active if unwitting participants, caught on film as they too traversed the street. Importantly, this performance was experienced by an art audience as a poster that artists distributed, which reproduced some of the photos alongside a text that read, 'We are crossing a street continuously. Moving diagonally. Moving in similar directions.'

For the first performance in *Liaison*, the artists stood adjacent to one another in the entrance; arriving audience members were forced to brush their bodies against those of the performers and sidle sideways into the gallery. For their second performance, Roche & Buis stood motionless in front of the audience on either side of the space, as if sizing each other up. After a lengthy period and without warning, they rushed at each other, screaming, crossing paths in the centre of the space where they had hung a vertical array of mirrors and where the photographer had positioned a camera and tripod. Whereas Roche had looked single-minded, assertive and tense in the lead up, Buis appeared more open, relaxed and self-controlled.

This contrasting of male/female roles was heightened for the third performance, in which the artists came together again in the centre facing each other in uncomfortable proximity. Roche asserted himself and intimidated Buis by repeatedly burping in her face. She stood her ground as if in disdain. Finally, in response to her counter provocation, he slapped her face. At once she moved swiftly to the back wall where she crouched down in

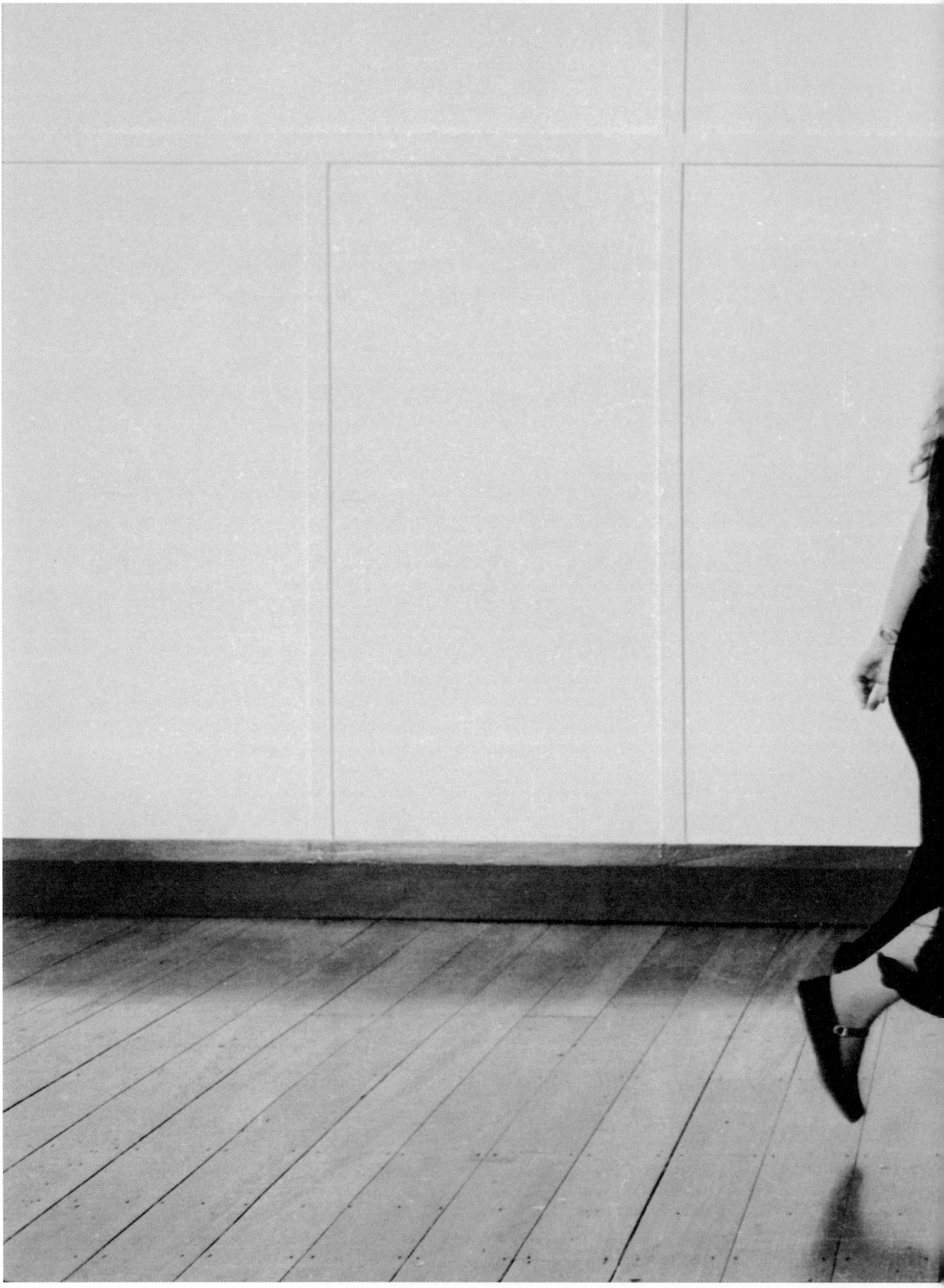

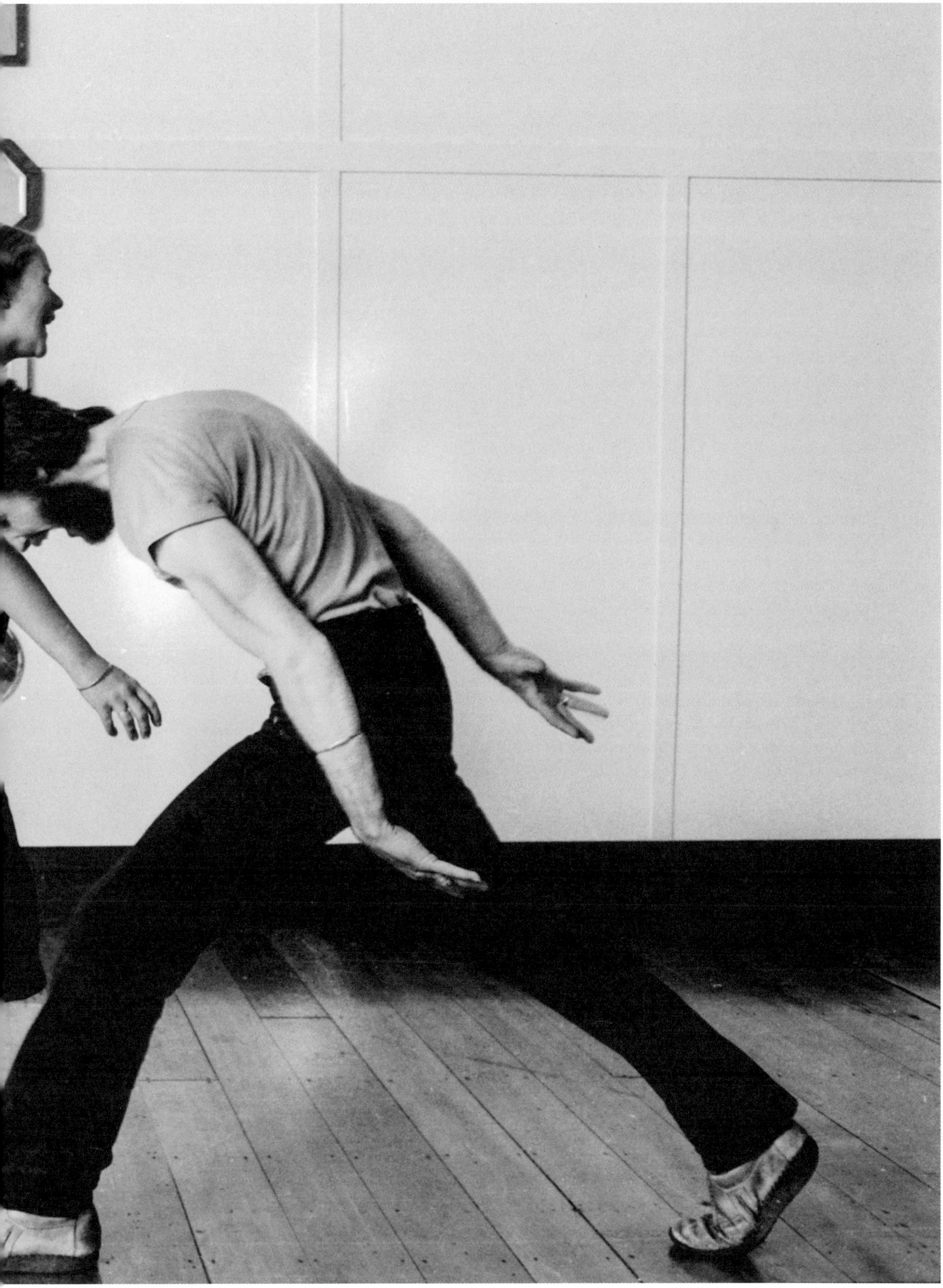

front of the mirrors, wailed for a prolonged time then cut her arm, drawing blood, thereby ending the performance.

Later, Curnow noted in his diary that Buis's howls were a 'magnificent screaming' that came to 'resemble the belching male speech'.[10] This focus on non-verbal cues and actions — from forcing the audience to physically negotiate their access to the room, to bodily gestures and noises serving to communicate and convey reactions — vacillated between interaction and confrontation, and tested the limits of the artists' and their audience's physical and psychological comfort zones.

The evening's three performances bear some similarity to early performance works by the duo Marina Abramović and Ulay. Most obvious is Abramović/Ulay's *Imponderabilia* (1977) where they too stood on either side in a doorway, albeit naked, forcing visitors to choose who to face as they passed. The major difference of intention was that the Abramović/Ulay piece was singular and extended in duration whereas, as Curnow has noted, Roche & Buis's relatively short interaction merely cued the evening's focus on the idea of liaison and the associated issues to be addressed.[11]

Comparisons can also be drawn between the evening's subsequent performances and *Relation in Space* (1976) and *Light/Dark* (1977), also by Abramović/Ulay. In the first, the naked performers rush toward and physically collide with each other at speed, the exceptionally violent action repeated over an extended period and with Abramović coming off worse for wear. In the second, Abramović and Ulay slap each other's faces repeatedly with increasing force. Roche & Buis's performances did not involve physical contact, save for the final moment, which was subdued by comparison to the blows Abramović/Ulay inflicted on each other. Rather, their focus was an interaction mostly delineated by sociological rather than physical factors.

Over the course of their work together, Abramović/Ulay's interest in interacting involved a weaving together of the physical and the transcendent to achieve a level of unity with each other as spiritual co-dependents. In 1983 Thomas McEvilley noted their interests in Buddhism and Theosophy and went so far as to describe them as 'Tantric collaborators'.[12] By comparison, Roche & Buis were interested in the relationship between self and the social environment and theorists such as social psychologist Erving Goffman and Gestalt therapist Fritz Perls. They highlighted their independence within their performative situations, their co-dependency defined more by their individuality, by asserting that their states of consciousness, while influenced by each other, were separate and socially inscribed.

In all their performances, Roche & Buis continued to work with the dynamics and conditions of their relationship, frequently testing viewers' expectations in situations structured carefully by the artists. Examples include their next work, *Continuance in Action: Interferences* (1980), for which viewers arrived at Barry Lett Galleries to find Buis in the front room standing on one foot with the other propped against the wall. Out of sight of Buis, Roche had adopted a similar pose in the larger back room. They held their positions for an uncomfortable amount of time, thereby shifting attention onto and unsettling an audience who were unsure whether to greet or interact with them.

In a later work in the same space, *Performance* (June 1982), Roche & Buis stood in a doorway for the duration, Buis facing viewers as they arrived and Roche facing the opposite way towards the back gallery, where rows of chairs were set out, suggesting viewers should enter and sit. Invitations that indicated different start times ensured a steady flow of viewers. As each person approached to enter the gallery, Roche would seemingly engage them by asking 'How are you?', but before they had a chance to

PREVIOUS: Peter Roche and Linda Buis, *Liaison*, 17 March 1980, part two of a three-part performance at Real Pictures, Tāmaki Makaurau Auckland, digital print from original negative. *Courtesy Peter Roche Estate and Linda Buis Estate. Photo by Gregory Burke*

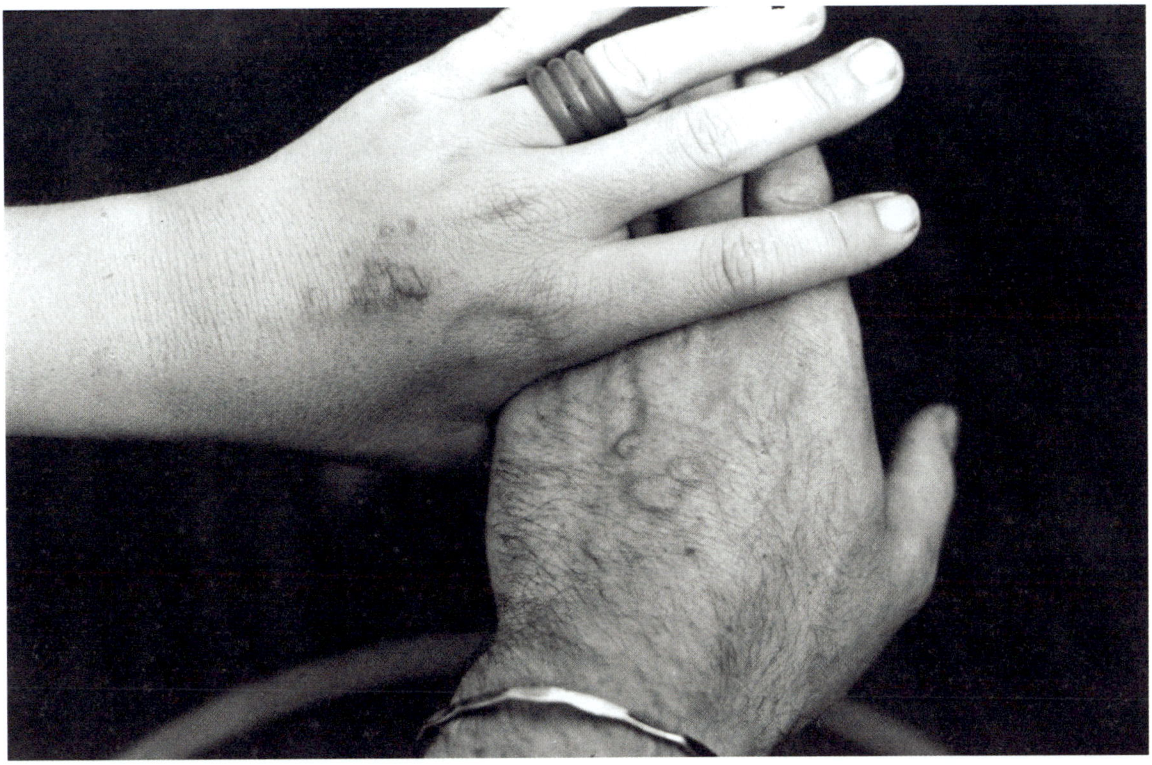

Peter Roche and Linda Buis, *Hands Piece*, 1981, one of nine black and white photographs. *Peter Roche Archive, courtesy Peter Roche Estate and Linda Buis Estate*

respond, Buis would answer as she saw fit, leaving the visitor perplexed as to their role. Once inside the door, visitors were lit by two spotlights, triggering the recognition that they were the focus for those seated and thus active performers in the work.

This performance was a rare instance of Roche & Buis utilising verbal communication. Another was the last in the three-part performance *Continuance in Action: Interferences*. Starting about 5 metres apart and both with hand-held microphones, the performers closed in on one another, establishing an offensive/defensive polarity, Roche yelling 'Turn around!' and Buis replying defiantly 'Go back!'. As Roche noted, 'At the point of exhaustion, we were standing face to face . . . breathing into each other's mouths.'[13] They started the evening separate and out of sight of one another, and concluded feeling each other's breath — but not touching.

Significantly, after *Liaison* they rarely connected physically in their work or engaged in physical harm. A possible exception was *Hands Piece* (1981), performed privately for camera and realised as nine photographs, which show what we assume to be the backs of Roche & Buis's hands, side by side, to document the healing process of minor scars they shared. Each pairing shows their hands in different states, sometimes open, at others tightened into fists. That the scarification was designed to bring them together through the infliction of pain is only inferred. Here signification is relayed via bodies that mix tenderness and intimacy with toughness.

Many performances relied on Roche & Buis's awareness of but separation from each other, including *Museum Piece* (1980), which they performed in isolation for the duration and without an audience. Circumnavigating the Auckland War Memorial Museum after midnight, each photographed the building's exterior at 20-minute intervals, their camera flashes signalling their location and proximity to each other — and to others who may have posed a threat, given the museum's park setting was a lonely and unsafe place at night. A poster and artist book were their means to disseminate the work, which presented the paired exterior views each had captured of the museum with an accompanying text that concluded, 'Moving within structure. Becoming separate. Homing in on each other.'

While psychological vulnerabilities as performers were drawn on in previous works, *Museum Piece* was the first to engage a potentially hazardous situation. More works involving physical precarity followed, such as *Performance* (1981), notable for its 10 p.m. start time and its setting, which not only included the Tāmaki Makaurau artist-run space 100m² but also the length of the street in which the venue was located. For the most part the audience remained in 100m², its floor drenched in water and its only initial light source a lit candle placed in a corner behind an inward-facing triangular mirror. Once again subverting audience expectations, Roche & Buis entered the space only briefly, at lengthy intervals and separately, each lighting more candles according to their own system.

As Roche subsequently wrote, the space was transformed into 'a kind of thoroughfare, a shelter, a bus terminal'.[14] For the most part, the artists walked up and down several blocks of the street outside, encountering each other infrequently. Roche later noted that predatory male advances had been directed at Buis. The dark street courted danger, and the artists' connection, conditioned by their awareness of their own and each other's physical vulnerability, intensified the further they moved apart.

Night Piece (1980) raised the level of danger to an unprecedented and unequalled degree. Once again the performance took place at night, around 8 p.m., in a former gasworks left in a derelict condition amid overgrown scrub and putrefying rubbish and with 'No Trespassing' signs signalling the threat of apprehension. Using a ladder they brought with them, Buis made the decision to climb to the top of a crumbling wall they estimated to be 60 feet (18 metres) high and then crawled edgily but deliberately along its length. The risk was palpable.

On the ground, Roche lit candles at intervals along the base of the wall, thereby enabling Buis to mark her progress via a small mirror she carried, until she reached the end and climbed down the now repositioned ladder. Curnow is the only person known to have attended the performance; he and Roche were silently aware of each other. In his writing on the performance, Curnow conveyed his own sense of the danger posed by both the site and the artists' actions.[15]

Curnow's attendance at this and many performances and the detailed notes he and the artists wrote and shared were decisively generative in the artists' evolving practice. This body of writing forms an extraordinary critical corpus. Curnow published several of his reflections in journals, including *Parallax*, the *New Zealand Listener* and the Australian journal *Art Network*; Roche & Buis often released their notes, adjacent to images of specific performances, as follow-up artist books in which they analysed their thoughts on the success or failings of the performance and used these as mental notes linking one performance to the previous and next.

Although their live performances were time bound, the artists overtly challenged conventional boundaries between performance and documentation, extending the work both spatially and temporally. For example, the afterlife of *Street Piece* demonstrates the several layers of documentation they deployed. First circulated as a poster with an array of images and a text that doubled as both pre- and post-script, the photographs were then recycled into the *Liaison* performance as the poster for the performance and as printed photographs on the wall adjacent to the Real Pictures' entrance. These images returned as distant echoes in *Continuance in Action: Interferences*, where documentation of *Liaison*, including images of *Street Piece*, was pinned to the wall. A single photograph from the series also featured in their *Six Performances* photo-book, self-published in 1983.

For *Performance* (1982) at RKS Art, they placed two artist books on a table in the space to provide cues for the viewers' live encounter with the artists, who sat facing each other washed in light, some distance apart, raising their arms repeatedly in gestures of greeting. In contrast to the live situation, the two artist books, titled respectively 'I am extending my hand' and 'Please take it', documented their outstretched hands directed towards the camera and thus towards the viewer/reader rather than in profile facing each other across the space. This dual presentation shifted the reading between a closed and open interpretation of the performance.

Photographs of this performance were subsequently included in 1983 in an exhibition at RKS Art surveying their recent work, where one enlarged image of each of six performances was presented adjacent to smaller framed prints of the respective performance, skirting distinctions between document and artwork. In addition, during the run of the exhibition the artists performed a new work in the space, ensuring that the exhibited images contextualised and mediated its reception.

On occasion the artists also used video feeds to mediate a performance in real time, as with *Closed Circuit* (1980), which punned on the medium and their actions. While the artists paced back and forth beside walls at right angles to each other for a duration of six hours, their actions were relayed live to the viewer via a tower of five monitors in the doorway that impeded the viewer's entry. In effect, the monitors concealed more than they revealed. Here, the artists tested the terms of live performance. By restricting access and conditioning the viewer's experience via the mediation of the camera, the act of seeing was rendered inadequate to the full complexity of what was happening.

Roche & Buis's use of text and camera as structuring elements in the execution and reception of their work was coupled with an exacting and sometimes fraught consideration of the physical, functional and societal contexts in which they performed. Whether amid static exhibits in the hallowed spaces of public galleries or in disquieting non-art situations, a comparison between the authenticity of their work and its context was paramount to its reception. Cycling through public and commercial galleries, alternative art spaces, other institutional spaces — such as a disused synagogue — and public spaces, such as on the street and private property, their performances frequently foregrounded and put pressure on both physical and socially defined preconditions of a given site and its limitations. This entailed testing themselves and their audiences by allowing situations to unfold that were confronting, unpleasant and even dangerous.

They used the intimacy of their personal relationship to tap and expose modes of interaction that breached the autonomy of the individual subject, proving their own and our vulnerability. In devising these situations within such a multiplicity of spaces and contexts, Roche & Buis not only upended the art world's conventional hierarchies of space but also tested and thereby destabilised boundaries between public and private, artist and audience, and more specifically between art space and life space. Like their treatment of the division of performance and documentation as permeable, they challenged prevailing orthodoxies and worked to delineate expanded possibilities and contexts for contemporary art.

Roche & Buis worked on the brink of Aotearoa's opening up to a more mobile global art world. Though most of their actions were executed in Tāmaki Makaurau, they also undertook performances at various international forums for contemporary practice that were beginning to bring like-minded artists together across the Tasman (in the ANZART events in Christchurch, Hobart and Auckland) and from further afield (Melbourne's Sculpture Triennial, ANZART in Portsmouth). It is symptomatic of the era, however, that their time spent living in the Netherlands and the United Kingdom in 1984 found them working at the fringes, often alone and without the support they enjoyed at home.

There is something poignant about the small box labelled 'Little Studio' that contains notes and drawings for imagined and unrealised works that could only take this form as they struggled to make ends meet, with no access to a studio and few entrées to the local scenes where they spent time. This speaks volumes about the power dynamics that structured the uneven relations between the so-called 'centres' and 'peripheries' of the art world in the 1980s.

Roche & Buis began working together at the cusp of seismic change in the intellectual climate, when artists everywhere began to appreciate that images were not merely objective records of external facts but constructed meaning as a particular order of sign within a structured system. Implicitly they seemed to grasp this shift, preferring to mediate the reception of their work by the careful deployment of photographs, as documents of unwitnessed actions, as mobile and multiple devices that can be circulated, and as temporal tools to connect present events with past actions. A history of postmodernism in Aotearoa has yet to be written. If it were to be undertaken, Roche & Buis's practice would function as an emblematic pivot, serving to pinpoint the moment when live action began to perform its meanings for the camera.

HERE/AFTER

In Relation: Performance works by Peter Roche & Linda Buis 1979–1985 presented its curators with challenges and opportunities. The exhibition brought together many of the surviving images and documents the artists left behind. This was our chance to review their archive, make it public, and use it to reconstruct their oeuvre. It helped enormously to have Gregory's first-hand experience, and to be able to speak to Wystan Curnow, who had attended thirteen of their performances.

But humans are fallible and memory is notoriously faulty. So much was missing from the recollections of these eye-witnesses. To fill the gaps, we painstakingly interrogated images and texts to build a fuller account of each work, taking note of the nature of each venue, the duration of each piece, what the artists wore, how they occupied the space, and what they and Curnow said in their handwritten, typed or published notes in the wake of each work.

A key instance of the practical challenge of reconstituting their work was the effort required to understand Roche's first performance in which Buis was an active presence: *Oh Shit No, On the Contrary* (1979). Aided immeasurably by filmmaker Bridget Sutherland, who had digitised audiotapes, Super 8 film and photographic negatives in an early research phase associated with her planned documentary on Peter Roche, we had access to the performance's discrete elements. We also had typescripts of the two essays Roche had written about the performance and a sparse selection of images documenting the live action. But Gregory was unsure if the photographs documenting the performances were his, and Curnow's notes have him in attendance at just one venue. It was only in assessing these items that we realised there were not one but two

RIGHT: Peter Roche and Linda Buis, *Liaison Assertive Cooperative*, 1980, Super 8 film transferred to digital video, silent, duration 2 minutes 0.8 seconds looped, installed as part of *In Relation: Performance works by Peter Roche & Linda Buis 1979–1985*, Te Pātaka Toi Adam Art Gallery, Te Whanganui-a-Tara Wellington, 2023. *Courtesy Peter Roche Estate and Linda Buis Estate, Bridget Sutherland and Te Pātaka Toi Adam Art Gallery. Photo by Ted Whitaker*

BELOW RIGHT: Peter Roche and Linda Buis, *Performance*, October 1982, RKS Art, Auckland, digital prints from original negatives (photos by Gregory Burke), installed as part of *In Relation: Performance works by Peter Roche & Linda Buis 1979–1985*, Te Pātaka Toi Adam Art Gallery, Te Whanganui-a-Tara Wellington, 2023. *Courtesy Gregory Burke, Peter Roche Estate and Linda Buis Estate and Te Pātaka Toi Adam Art Gallery. Photo by Ted Whitaker*

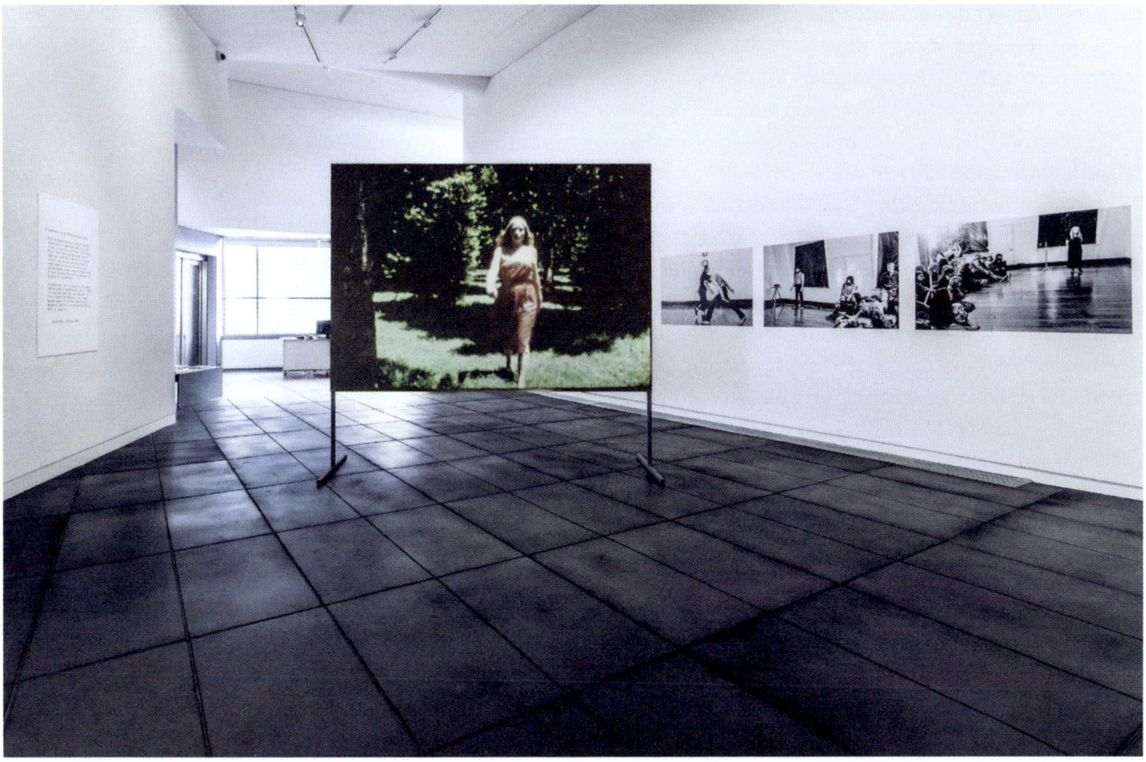

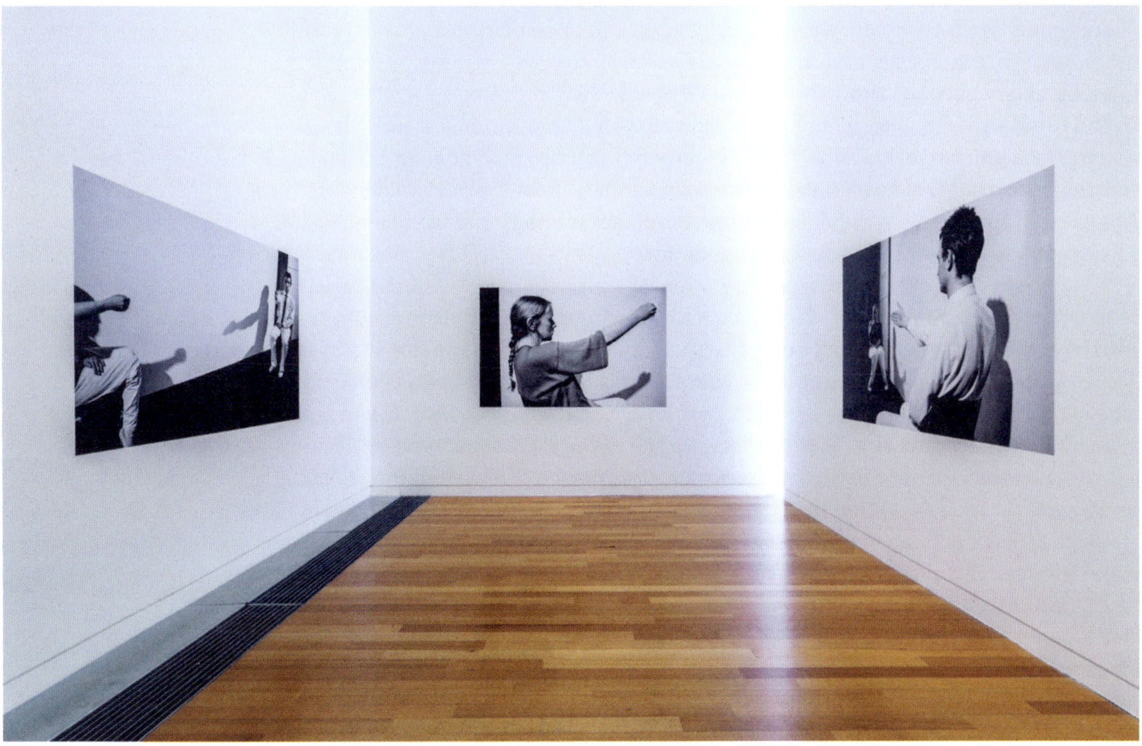

performances, and that a second audiotape and film were made in response to the first iteration presented at the Grafton Art Centre on 14 October. From these investigations we were able to describe the evolution of the piece and show how Roche's assessment of the failings of the first led to the revised second version, which juxtaposed new and existing audiotapes and films as part of an evening of performances at the Little Maidment Theatre at the University of Auckland on 27 October.

Despite this sleuthing, we were confronted by the inevitable challenge of reconstructing live art. Between what the artists said and what the audience saw, a wealth of detail evaded definition: what did each space bring to the occasions? How did the recordings sound? And what was it really like to hear what was said and to witness Roche's reactions? The nuances of the individual and collective emotional and psychological labour exerted in real time could never be fully recaptured. Even if the piece were to be re-enacted, everything about it would be different.

So, what did this realisation mean for our exhibition, where a new audience encountered the work in the muted setting of a curated show? Rather than admit defeat at the intractability of time or pretend that our archival work was adequate to the moment, we made the materiality of the surviving documents a feature and, at the same time but with opposite outcomes, we manipulated freshly digitised images to construct new, real encounters that at least partially evoked Roche & Buis's tactics as performers. Working with an understanding that any exhibition is an experiential event, situating real bodies and active minds in time and space, we set out to engage viewers as embodied subjects, enabling them to encounter the works in ways that hinted at the psychological and physical charge of the originals.

In the case of *Oh Shit No, On the Contrary*, we decided to show the two videos on box monitors at head height on either side of a temporary wall around which visitors could circumnavigate. Viewers were forced into uncomfortable proximity with either Buis's face being slapped or the couple kissing vigorously, the wall creating a sharp boundary between alternate actions. While watching these tapes, visitors were invited to wear wireless headphones that allowed them to move freely around the space listening to a remixed audio file that merged Buis's two monologues praising and denigrating Roche. This opened the viewer to the ambiguity of the performance. To have Buis's voice in one's ears while watching the too-personal imagery made one question how words and images were meant to go together.

Listening to both the cruel putdowns and the simpering compliments, head to head with the two protagonists, one felt caught within their tight orbit, physically bound into the action by the exhibition's equipment, unsure with whom to identify: the male perpetrator of physical violence or his female persecutor. Even the action of placing the headphones over one's ears felt like a gesture of complicity, while a decision to take them off effectively read as a failure of nerve to see the performance through. Though this presentation was not true to either original performance, it reworked the surviving components in such a way that the audience was required to interact, thus activating one of Roche & Buis's primary motivators: to turn passive viewers into active, and sometimes vulnerable, participants.

We used such strategies at several junctures in the exhibition. For example, as they entered the building visitors were greeted by a large screen onto which we projected *Liaison Assertive Cooperative* (1980), the short looped film showing each performer walking in a straight line through an avenue of trees in a sunny park, seemingly towards the viewer/camera/each other. This was a conscious ploy on our part to engage our audience, a literalisation of the exhibition's title: 'In Relation'. Even though Roche & Buis made this film alone and only screened it once at Real Pictures as part of an evening of performances collectively titled *Liaison*, we used this work as punctum for the whole project.

We read the film as key to the coordinates of the couple's practice, where they treated each other as their constituent opposite in a play of connection and misalliance, using the camera as a structuring mechanism: the pivot around which the short film turned. Although it was the first work visitors encountered, it was also the last people saw as they exited the space. We hoped that viewers would look again before they left, realising that this endless loop of missed encounters was in fact a fitting metaphor for the curatorial enterprise, which could only fail in its efforts to revivify Roche & Buis as live actors.

A second key factor determining our curatorial rationale was the fact that Roche & Buis chose to document their performances with still photographs taken by themselves or by others closely associated with them. A still photograph can capture only a moment in a live action; it cannot show how the piece unravels in time. We took their decision as a conscious and meaningful one, which allowed us to treat the photographic records as more than mere documentation. The artists would have spent time and effort selecting the images that would serve as stand-ins for their performances, elevating specific photographs to the status of definitive statements.

Following their lead, we chose to enlarge certain images and used the architecture of the Adam Art Gallery to frame and focus viewers' attention. One obvious instance was the placement, at the centre of the long feature wall in the gallery's foyer, of the photograph taken at the exact moment when Roche & Buis crossed paths in the second *Liaison* performance. Another was the selection of three photographs of the October 1982 performance at RKS Art, in which the artists sat on two chairs at some remove from each other with their eyes closed, lifting their arms in gestures of greeting for the duration of the work.

These were enlarged to almost life size and placed on three sides at the end of a long narrow gallery, with a striking profile view of Buis centred at the far end of the lengthy view-shaft, between photographs of the two performers shown from different perspectives. With her calm self-absorption and gently raised arm, Buis's composure anchored the room. We wanted her there, a strong female presence, reaching out to her partner without any hint of insistence. In a post #MeToo moment, it was important to use the images the artists had selected but to re-think them in light of a changing socio-sexual context.[16]

For me [Christina] as an art historian coming to their work after the fact, a key insight gleaned from our work putting together the exhibition was the way in which Roche & Buis's photo-documentation performed its own meanings separate from the live moment. Looking closely at the left-hand image in this framing triptych, in which Roche appears with his arm thrust out, pointing slightly towards the audience opposite Buis's arm, which is cropped from the rest of her body, I noticed that her upheld arm ended with her fingers curling gently inward in stark contrast to Roche's firm gesture. Yet the shadow of her arm caught serendipitously by the camera showed what looked like a clenched fist. While Roche seemed to be seeking connection, even approval from his audience, Buis appears utterly self-possessed.

Here, one might argue that the performance does not end when the live action stops; it is carried over and can take on a different agency through the independent performance of the photograph as it is actively read by an audience. Perhaps this is because a third party took the photograph, catching something latent that could not be read in the moment by either of the performers. The point here is that these images were not consciously 'authored' by the artists, even though they are credited to them. They are instead products of an exchange, an interaction, a process of interpretation carried out collectively and caught by the camera. In the slippage between live event and photographic record, between performers and photographers, a space opens for new and various readings.[17]

Roche & Buis understood implicitly that their photographic documentation could be put to work, adapted for different circumstances, shown in different formats, multiplied and circulated. They utilised images from one performance to announce another; combined photographs with texts on posters, invitation cards and flyers that displaced and extended the work spatially and temporally; and integrated photo-sequences of past performances to frame and give context to new ones. In two cases, long after their partnership had ended Roche even rethought this documentation for gallery presentation, in a sense licensing our decisions to scale up and sequence images in order to activate the exhibition and pace the audience's movement through the space.[18]

One of these, *Museum Piece* (1980/1993) — the only work in the exhibition held in a museum collection — is Roche's critical response to an invitation to make a work for a permanent collection.[19] He monumentalised a secretive action, up-scaling and framing fourteen prints developed from the negatives shot by each artist as they walked around Auckland War Memorial Museum in the dead of night, and hung these shaky action shots, of a building caught in the glare of the camera's flash, high on the wall above seven ticking clocks, the hands of which were set at 20-minute intervals. By this means he reflexively inserted their renegade gesture into the very system they had so assiduously avoided, thus concretising for posterity the disruptive potential their 1980s works proposed.

In putting together our exhibition we took the artists' lead, fully exploiting the rich performative potential of their photographic documentation to engage our audience and activate the Adam Art Gallery's spaces. Dislodged from claims of authorship and the reifications of objecthood, their photographic documentation served us well as a relevant record of a vital project and as a productive means to access the psychological and physical charge of their interactions. We see their performances as a vivid response to the times.

Spanning the realpolitik of the 1970s and the artifice of the 1980s, Roche & Buis provide a bridge that refuses the compartmentalisations of art history. They show us how actions and images can together produce meanings that are at once real *and* constructed, evading both modernism's expressive myths (which include investment in the singular [male] genius), and the disillusionment of the postmodern, to which so much of the commentary of the 1980s subscribed. By exploring the contingent relations between subjects, audiences, contexts and meanings, they contributed to the transformations in art-making that have set the terms of what we now call 'the contemporary'.

NOTES

1 Guy Brett, 'Life Strategies: Overview and selection. Buenos Aires–London–Rio de Janeiro–Santiago de Chile, 1960–1980', in *Out of Actions: Between performance and the object 1949–1979*, edited by Paul Schimmel (Los Angeles: Thames and Hudson and Museum of Contemporary Art, 1998), 225.

2 Christina Barton and Gregory Burke, *In Relation: Performance works by Peter Roche & Linda Buis 1979–1985*, exhibition guide (Wellington: Te Pātaka Toi Adam Art Gallery, 2023).

3 The concept of 'vulnerability' was first expressed by Peter Roche in an unpublished essay titled 'Polarity', which summarised his account of *Offence/Defence* and *Oh Shit No, On the Contrary*, dated September 1979. Photocopy of typescript, collection of Christina Barton.

4 While we have written this essay together, the occasional first-person interpolations are intentional. In this instance, Gregory Burke is recounting his association with the artists.

5 Peter Roche, 'Self-Preservation', unpublished essay, 1979. Photocopied typescript, collection of Christina Barton.

6 Ibid.

7 Ibid.

8 Roche, 'Polarity', unpublished essay, Post-Object Archive, previously Elam School of Fine Arts Library, now University of Auckland Library, September 1979.

9 Peter Roche & Linda Buis, 'A Statement on Our Working Relationship', in *Six Performances: Roche/Buis*, artist book, Auckland, October 1982, n.p.

10 Wystan Curnow, notebook entry for *Liaison* performance, Notebook no. 12, 1979/80, collection of Wystan Curnow.

11 Ibid.

12 Thomas McEvilley, 'Marina Abramović/Ulay, Ulay/Marina Abramović', *Artforum* 22, no. 1 (1983): 52.

13 Peter Roche, Tony Green and Wystan Curnow, 'Peter Roche/Linda Buis: A gathering concerning three performances', edited by Wystan Curnow, *Parallax: A Journal of Postmodern Literature and Art* 2 (Summer 1983): 173–87.

14 Ibid., 175.

15 Ibid., 181–87. See Chapter 13 of this book for further discussion of *Night Piece* (1980).

16 It is worthwhile noting that Roche & Buis also selected this image as the sole representative of the RKS Art performance in the publication *Six Performances: Roche/Buis*, 1982.

17 This idea, of the viewer making their own meaning, is allegorised in the exhibition by the pairing of two sets of photographs (by Gregory Burke and Ronald Brownson) of the same performance (at Space in January 1983) that were markedly different responses to the same situation.

18 *Museum Piece* (1980) and *Night Piece* (1980) were both reworked years after the pair had ended their partnership. The former is discussed in our text; the latter was re-presented as a grid of digital photographs and texts for the exhibition *Terrain Vague: A short history of creative trespass*, curated by Allan McDonald for Snowwhite Gallery, Unitec, Auckland, 2006.

19 *Museum Piece* was commissioned for the Museum of New Zealand Te Papa Tongarewa in 1993. This was during Christina Barton's short tenure as Curator Contemporary New Zealand Art (1992–1994).

REFERENCES

Barton, Christina and Gregory Burke. *In Relation: Performance works by Peter Roche & Linda Buis 1979–1985*. Exhibition guide. Wellington: Te Pātaka Toi Adam Art Gallery, 2023.

Curnow, Wystan. Notebooks. Collection of Wystan Curnow, 1985–1979.

McEvilley, Thomas. 'Marina Abramović/Ulay, Ulay/Marina Abramović'. *Artforum* 22, no. 1 (1983): 52–55.

Roche, Peter. 'Polarity'. Unpublished essay. Post-Object Archive, previously Elam School of Fine Arts Library, now University of Auckland Library, September 1979.

Roche, Peter. 'Self-Preservation'. Post-Object Archive, previously Elam School of Fine Arts Library, now University of Auckland, October 1979.

Roche, Peter and Linda Buis. *Six Performances*, edited by Ronald Brownson. Auckland: Roche & Buis in association with the Queen Elizabeth Arts Council of New Zealand, 1983.

Roche, Peter, Tony Green and Wystan Curnow. 'Peter Roche/Linda Buis: A gathering concerning three performances', edited by Wystan Curnow. *Parallax: A Journal of Postmodern Literature and Art* 2 (Summer 1983): 173–87.

Schimmel, Paul, ed. *Out of Actions: Between performance and the object 1949–1979*. Los Angeles: Thames and Hudson and the Museum of Contemporary Art, 1998.

6

SOUND AND PERFORMANCE CULTURES IN AOTEAROA

Rachel Shearer
& Andrew Clifford

Not all performance art is primarily concerned with sound, except that it is usually present, even if only as an incidental by-product.[1] Conversely, not all sound practice is specifically concerned with performance dynamics, even if performance is embedded in the production of sound. In this chapter we consider the overlapping cultures of performance and sound practices from Aotearoa New Zealand, and examine live performance strategies as well as the use of sound to produce art.

We note that bodily actions that are part of a sound performance may be more than just those required to play conventional instruments. They may deconstruct classical approaches to instrumental performance, including the relationship between audience and performer. In doing so, these practices may fall within (or between) the worlds of experimental music, theatre, dance or performance art. We focus primarily on those with a degree of proximity to the last.

In surveying key examples of performance and sound practice from the late 1960s, we take a whakapapa approach that acknowledges influential connections and lines of ancestry. This approach is not chronological but moves between different timeframes as a way of suggesting those lines of ancestry. We explore overlapping themes: sound that enables political or social activities; sound that is created through the performative activation and exploration of materials; making space for sound; sound that is generated by or activates the body of the performer or audience; and sound that activates the landscape.

SOCIAL AND POLITICAL PERFORMANCES

I kahuria te kupu e te whē: The word was clothed by sound[2]

The Reverend Māori Marsden is a respected tohunga from Te Tai Tokerau the Far North of Aotearoa. In the traditional higher learning institution of that area, Te Wānanga o Tai Tokerau, he learned the following version of the creation story. Within it he describes a sequence where consciousness manifests as sound. Just before time and space as we know it dawns — in a process from i te kore (out of nothingness), ki te pō (into the night) and ki te ao mārama (into the world of light)[3] — the thinking mind known as Te Hinengaro emerges from Te Mahara, primordial memory.

In this process, Te Whakaaro (thought) gives way to Te Whē (sound), described by Marsden as clothing 'the word' to create knowledge, Te Wānanga.[4] From Te Wānanga emerges Te Ao Mārama — the world of light, time, space and materiality as we know it. Sound emerges in this sequence of becoming as the voice of unfolding universal consciousness.

While the details may differ between iwi, this creation story recognises the importance of the voice and spoken word in te ao Māori (the Māori world), expressed in the rich oral traditions of whaikōrero (oratory), waiata (song), mōteatea (traditional chant, sung poetry) and the many other genres that make up Māori oral traditions. Equally significant is the performance of those words.

Shannon Te Ao's (Ngāti Tūwharetoa, Ngāti Wairangi, Te Pāpaka o Māui) performance-to-video works are rich with interwoven references to traditions and histories of both te ao Māori and te ao Pākehā and their combined colonial affects. In considering sound in his performance works, the inclusion of specific genres of Māori oral literature are recognisable motifs. There is a politic inherent to including these Māori oral literatures and indeed te reo itself. The Māori language is the pou on which the culture and traditions of te ao Māori are communicated between generations. In the colonial drive to first eradicate and then assimilate Māori during the late nineteenth and early twentieth centuries, this pou — te reo Māori — was systematically severed. The act of reclaiming it has been hard won and is ongoing.

Te Ao's *Follow the Party of the Whale* (2012) imagines the Parihaka prisoners, unjustly sent to Ōtepoti Dunedin by the Crown for protesting peacefully against European settlement on land confiscated from Māori. The pacifist Parihaka community was led by the Taranaki prophets Te Whiti-o-Rongomai and Tohu Kākahi. Discussing this work with writer Megan Dunn, Te Ao questions the role of performance art in relation to activism: 'Is performance art futile in relation to actual political change? Alongside the history of Te Whiti and Tohu, the Parihaka movement and Māori activists today, sometimes our practice is a bit dumb.'[5]

Dumb — voiceless rather than stupid — is the operative word here. Barefoot and wrapped in a woollen blanket, Te Ao gulps and spurts from his mouth 50 litres of soda water, a reference to the Parihaka prisoners' internal drowning by tuberculosis.[6] In contrast, subsequent works by Te Ao notably utilise sound and Māori traditions of language to tell his stories through performance. For *two shoots that stretch far out* (2013–14), a work that won the prestigious 2016 Walters Prize, five filmed sequences show Te Ao reciting the English translation of 'He Waiata Mo Te Moe Punarua' (A Song about Two Wives) to a group of introduced animal species. In this pre-colonial composition, Matahira of Ngāti Porou iwi describes her raw grief in response to her husband transferring his affections to a new wife. The simplicity of the scene belies the complex storytelling, which involves translation, colonisation, communication with the more-than-human, the Greek myths of Hermes and Leda, shapeshifting, sexuality and loss.[7]

With minimal props, the sound of Te Ao's recitation translates and transports the grief of Matahira through cultures and time. Te Ao talks of trying to extend his storytelling to a state of temporal, experiential and spatialised performance, acknowledging existence in a continuum of past, present and future.[8] His engagement with specific cultural technologies of sound continued in works such as *With the sun aglow, I have my pensive moods* (2017), for which he worked with translation and notions of duration to slow down his voice and introduce synthesised treatments, such as a vocoder, to abstract or translate his mōteatea into a communication of wordless soundscape elements.[9]

FESTIVALS AND COLLECTIVES — SONIC CIRCUS

Fringe avant-garde activities often thrive when there is collective support to spur each other on. Sound and music practices often involve group activities and festival environments, which provide a gathering point or platform to bring together and create visibility for otherwise underground activities. In Aotearoa, these have included Off the Deep End, Australia New Zealand Artists Encounter (ANZART), Sound/Watch, Rotate Your State/Soliton, Interdigitate, Lines of Flight, Alt.music and Sonic Circus.[10]

Sonic Circus was first organised by composer Jack Body in 1974 for the New Zealand Broadcasting Corporation and initially held at Victoria University of Wellington. It brought together artists from across the country and from various backgrounds: art, theatre and different fields of music. A 'dream room' was created, and included paintings by Edward Bullmore accompanied by recordings by Annea Lockwood, John Cousins and

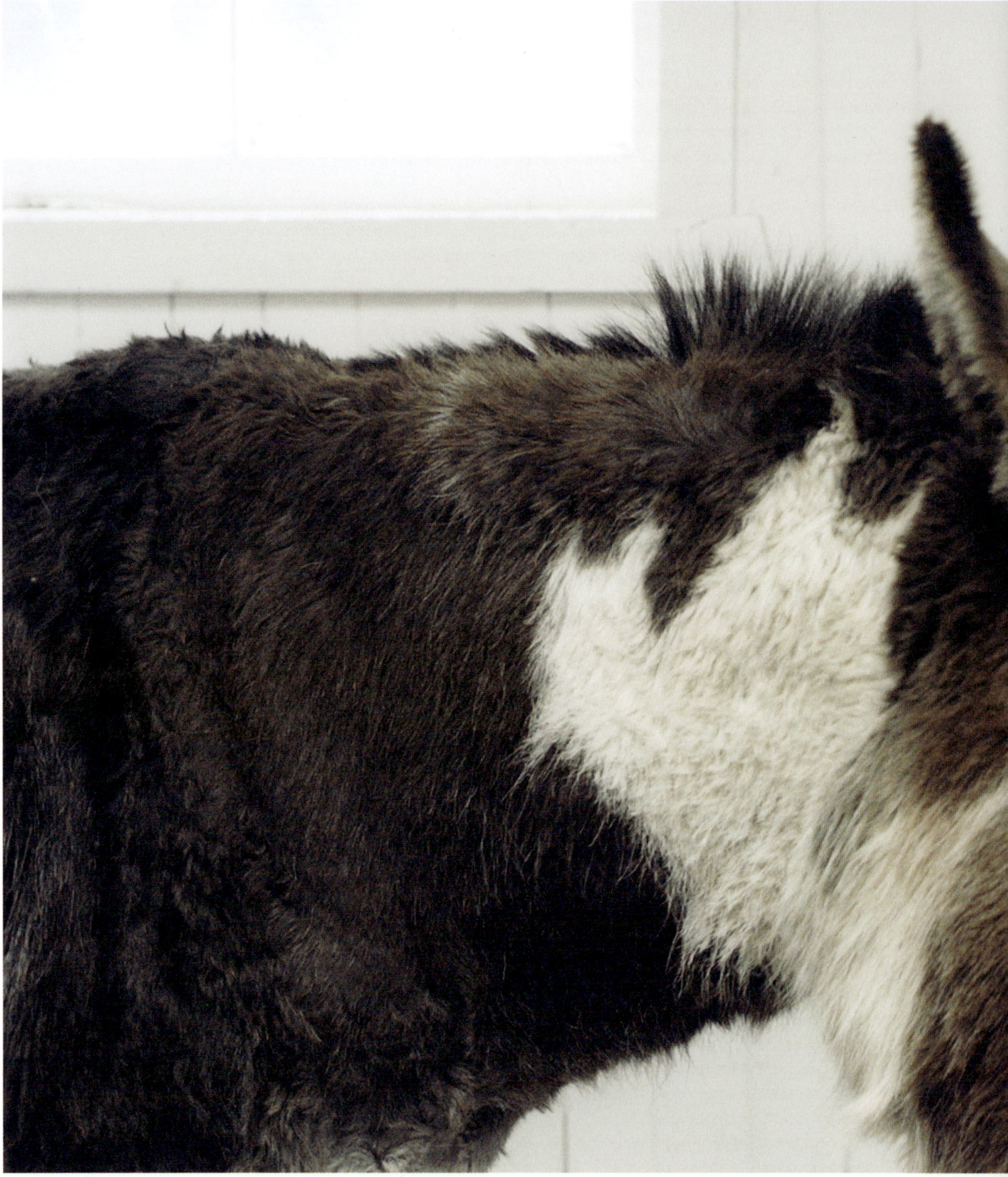

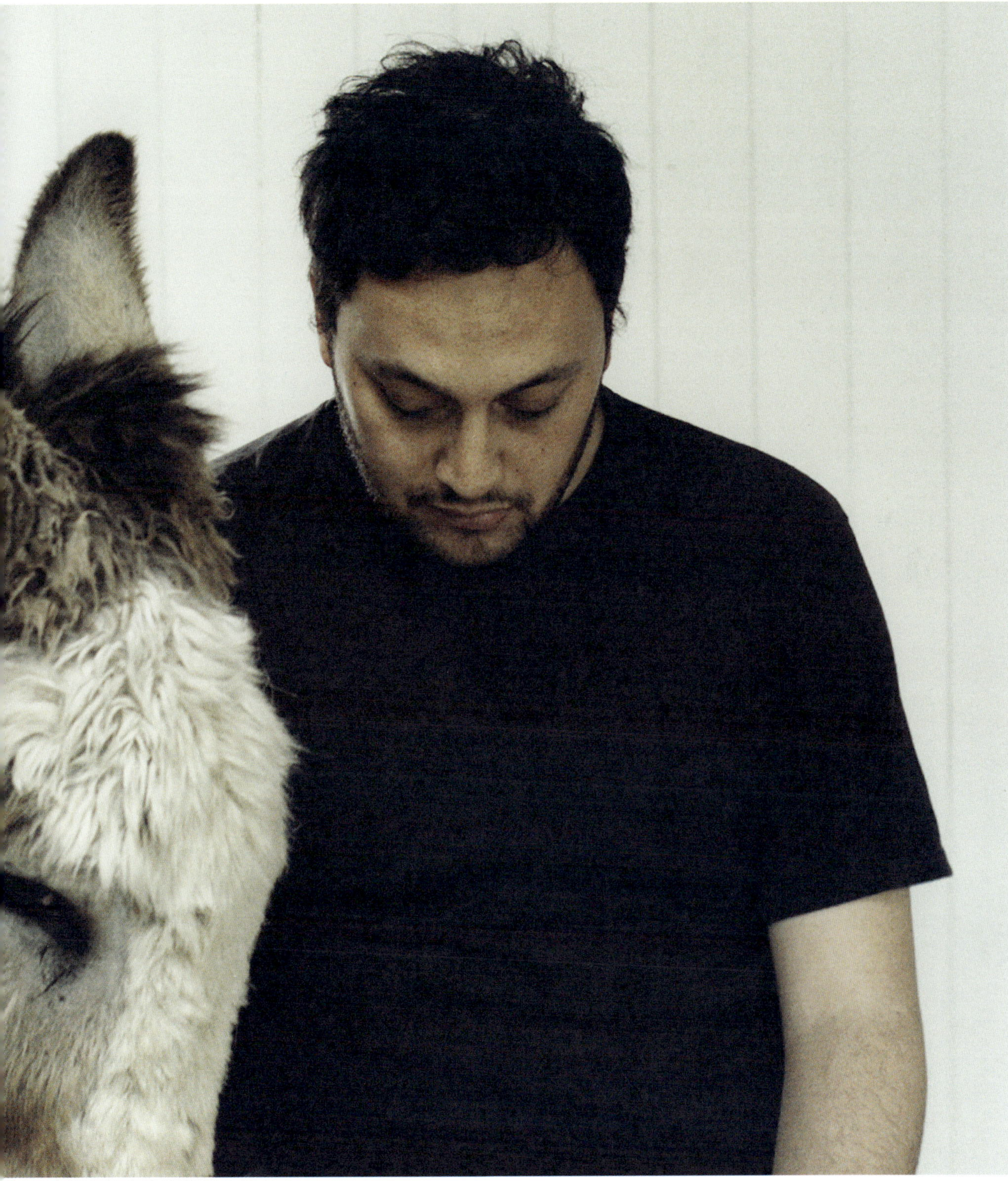

Body. Victoria University's electronic music studio was turned into a live installation by composer Ross Harris, who enabled visitors to contribute sound through a microphone fed through synthesisers and other processors.

This first event also featured inaugural performances by From Scratch (discussed shortly) and the John Cousins project Co-Active Play (CAP), the latter also including Gary Wilby and Eric Biddington (joined at later events by Colleen Anstey and others). CAP's performance involved enigmatic activities with found objects and electronics, following undisclosed rules that the audience were advised to 'observe with a flexible imagination — using our activities as raw material for your own phantasy'.[11]

Sculptor and performance artist Jim Allen was present for the first Sonic Circus, and is listed in the programme as participating at the following year's sequel, Sonic2, presenting *Poetry for Chainsaws* and *Tea Tree and Microphones*. The former involved the artist reading poetry with chainsaw accompaniment, while the latter is described in the programme as an installation of live microphones placed in pieces of tea tree and making small sounds in the university's garden.[12] Other presenters in 1975 included theatre group Red Mole, poet Ian Wedde, potter Anneke Boren and painter Juliet Peter.

PREVIOUS: Shannon Te Ao (Ngāti Tūwharetoa, Ngāti Wairangi, Te Pāpaka o Māui), *two shoots that stretch far out*, 2013–14. Single channel video, colour and sound, duration 13 minutes 46 seconds. Cinematography by Iain Frengley. *Courtesy the artist*

FROM SCRATCH ORCHESTRA TO FROM SCRATCH

While studying at Elam School of Fine Arts, University of Auckland, Phil Dadson took time out from 1968 to 1969 to travel to London, where he became part of experimental composer Cornelius Cardew's foundation group for a scratch orchestra, a Fluxus-influenced collective of artists, musicians and non-musicians. On his return to Tāmaki Makaurau Auckland, Dadson established an Aotearoa splinter (or 'twig') group of the Scratch Orchestra (UK), which became an important part of life at Elam in the early 1970s and received endorsement from head of sculpture Jim Allen.

Underpinning all of the activities of both Scratch Orchestras was an egalitarian approach in which the groups' many participants — and they were open to anyone — made equal contributions with no leader or soloists, using all manner of instruments and sound-makers, bought, found or home-made. This culminated in a large-scale presentation over several nights in 1972 of Cardew's *The Great Learning*, based on Confucian texts.

The Scratch Orchestra later went into hiatus, and the next phase was From Scratch, which developed more structured and sophisticated sculptural instruments, choreography and numerically based rhythms. The original members, who appeared at Sonic Circus, were Dadson, Bruce Barber, Geoff Chapple and Gray Nicol. The egalitarian approach remained and was evident in their intricate 'hocketed' phrasing, in which sounds from each performer were combined to create a single rhythmic/melodic phrase — a common phenomenon found in nature such as cicadas chirping and frogs chorusing.

From Scratch's best-known and most overtly political work is *Pacific 3, 2, 1, Zero*, devised for and performed at the 12th Paris Biennale in 1982, then released on LP by Flying Nun in 1985, and later turned into an award-winning performance film in collaboration with director Gregor Nicholas in 1993. The work is a protest against French nuclear testing and waste dumping in the Polynesian Pacific.

As with many From Scratch works, the presentation of the performance is based on a 'ground plan', which provides a visual score-plot and layout for each instrument's placement, and creates zones within which certain activities take place, as well as acting

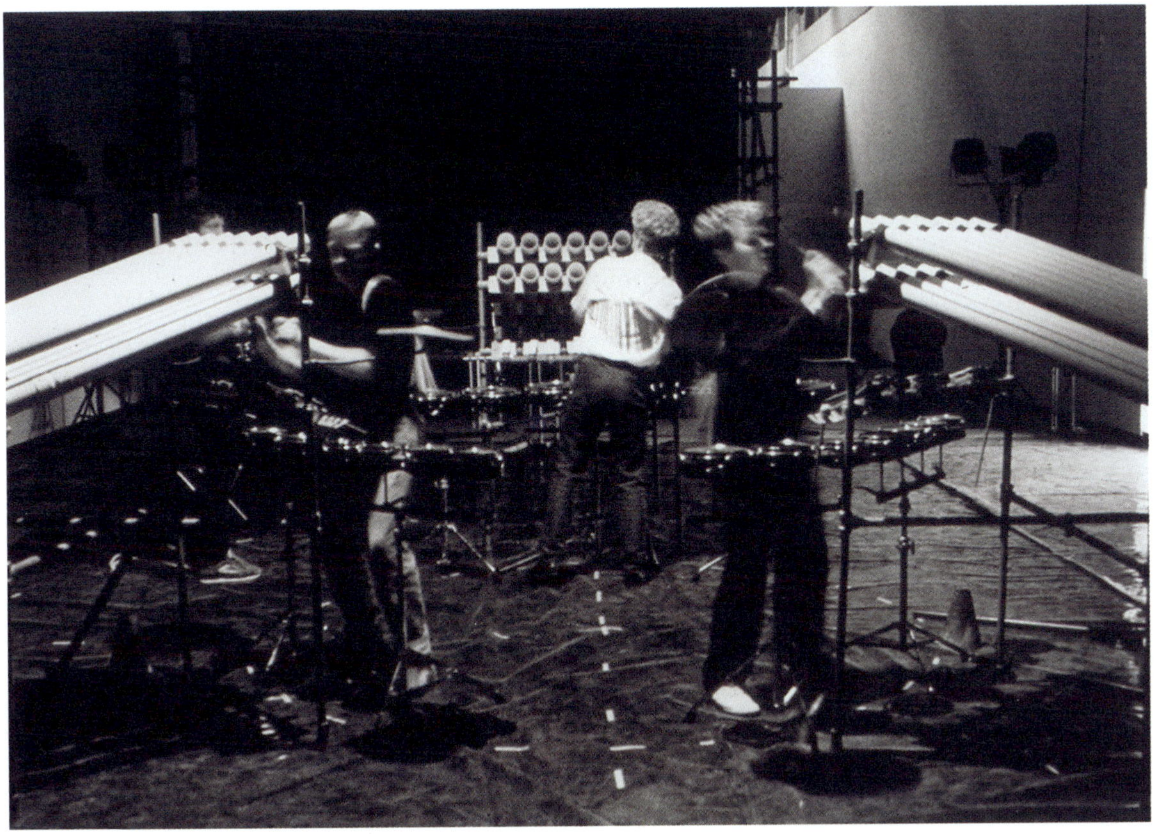

From Scratch, *Pacific 3, 2, 1, Zero*, 1986. Rehearsal image, Shed 11-National Art Gallery. Performers Don McGlashan, Wayne Laird and Phil Dadson. *Courtesy Phil Dadson. Photo by Luit Bieringa*

as a graphic in its own right. In this case, the placement of their distinctive PVC pipe percussion racks echoed the symbol for nuclear disarmament. Unusually for the group, whose work to this point had primarily been instrumental, *Pacific 3, 2, 1, Zero* included vocal chants of lament and protest:

> The syllables heard in the first vocal section are taken from the names of individual islands within Micronesia, Melanesia and Polynesia. These are mirrored and inverted in the same way as the rhythms in the music are. In a later vocal section the names of contaminated islands testing sites: Mururoa (France), Fangataʻufa (France), Christmas Island (UK/USA), Johnston Island (USA), Enewetak (USA), Bikini (USA) are sung, then shouted and drummed on tins to sound both lament and warning.[13]

PERFORMATIVE COUNTERCULTURE

As counterculture movements became more prominent in Aotearoa in the 1960s and 1970s, performance and spectacle became an important part of the storytelling that underpins making a statement and asserting new ideas. The boundaries between protest actions (both moving hīkoi and static occupations), theatre, happenings, performance art and music performance became less defined, and strategies from each discipline became useful in different contexts — an important influence on performance culture of this period.

Composer Jenny McLeod established a pedigree of working with sound, not just music, through her studies in Europe with classical music avant-garde heavyweights Olivier Messiaen, Karlheinz Stockhausen and Pierre Boulez. Her large-scale performance *Earth and Sky* (1968) was as much a happening as it was a sophisticated fusion of theatre, literature, musical traditions and sound sources. It has been described as '[embracing] the movement's spirit of enquiry, love of spectacle and sense of scale'.[14] McLeod created a music-theatre extravaganza based on missionary and writer Richard Taylor's translations of Māori creation poetry. It was a hugely ambitious work of 'music theatre in three acts' for multiple choirs, taped narration, brass, woodwind, percussion orchestras, pianos and organ.[15] As Denis Smalley recounts in his 1970 review of the recorded work:

> **In *Earth and Sky*, movement, shape, colour and light grow out of sound in natural response. The sound itself weaves and pushes through the taped narrative, with choruses and instrumentalists projecting the narrative into movement.**[16]

This work also came at a time of social change: the counterculture movements included a Māori renaissance. In the work, a booming English voice recites the Māori creation whakapapa 'from the nothing, the begetting, the abundance'. In scouring information on this work, we found no indication of Māori involved in consultation, production or responding to it. Awareness of consultation and intellectual property have moved on since this work was performed in front of Queen Elizabeth II in 1972. The digital platform SOUNZ: Centre for New Zealand Music Toi te Arapūoru states that 'its success made a contribution to New Zealand's burgeoning biculturalism'[17] (and no doubt it did raise Pākehā awareness of Māori cultural forms), but there remains a question of what Māori thought of this cultural interpretation and appropriation at the time.

Counterculture and alternative lifestyles increasingly became part of popular culture in the 1970s. Music-theatre-performance group BLERTA, an 'anarchic multimedia collective of men, women and children travelling in a psychedelic house bus', started in 1971.[18] In a similar vein, the travelling Māori rock-theatre group Mahana presented psychedelic rock opera performances for each iteration of the Nambassa Festival, held in 1978, 1979 and 1981. Nambassa was a hub for counterculture and hippie ideals and included workshops and education activities alongside entertainment programmes. Mahana featured Māori and Pākehā musicians and performed music with Māori narrative content and costumes.

Also at Nambassa in 1979 were The Plague, whose origins were quite distinct from the hippie eco culture that permeated much of the festival. Formed in 1978, they were influenced by the London punk movement, a new wave of counterculture that, in Aotearoa, emerged under the shadow of Robert Muldoon's National government. Youth took up instruments they could barely play and The Plague launched themselves as Tāmaki Makaurau's first theatrical/political punk band, led by poet/performer Richard von Sturmer, who contributed lyrics to other post-punk bands of the period, including Blam Blam Blam.[19] Parodying the dominant hippie culture of Nambassa, the group's front people performed naked in stark, single-colour body paint; the backing band (including future members of the Blams) wore white clothing. Performer Sarah Fort wore yellow. Renamed Serum Delirium, Fort later became part of the media collective/band Fetus Productions.

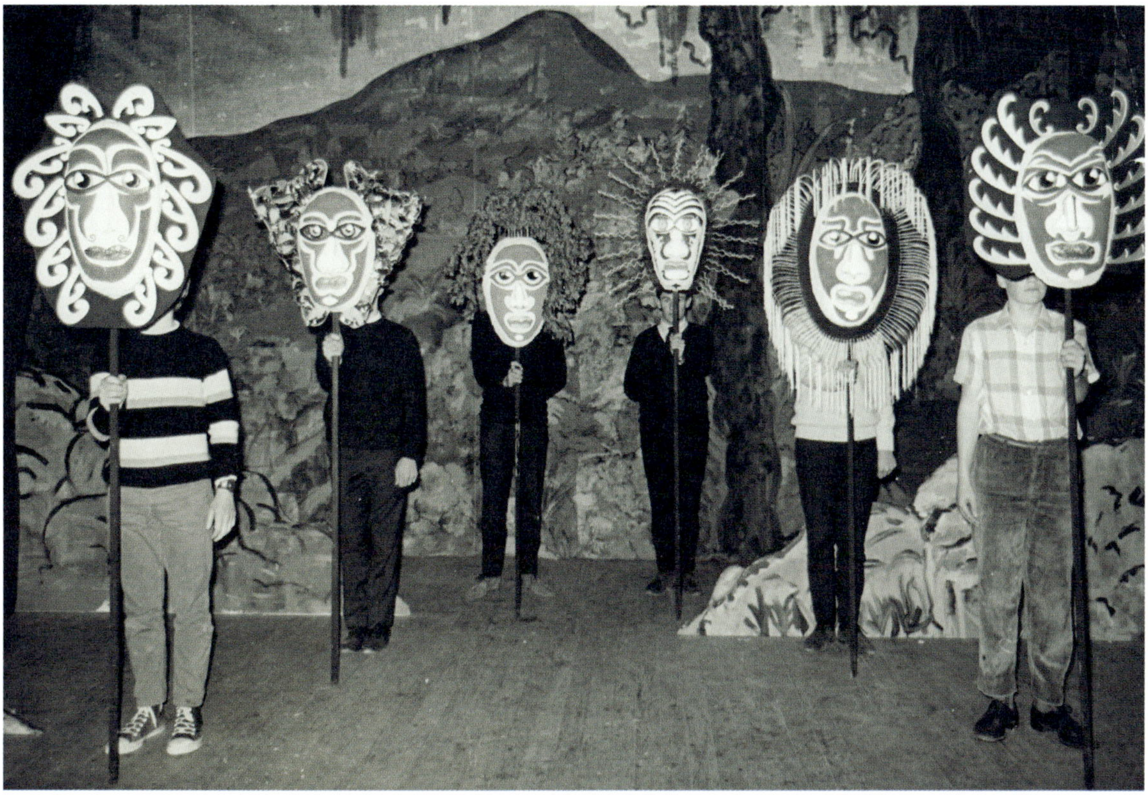

Jenny McLeod, *Earth and Sky*, 1968, Whakaoriori Masterton. *Alexander Turnbull Library, PAColl-5204-2-001. Photo by Wairarapa Times-Age*

FETUS PRODUCTIONS

Punk and post-punk had a close association with the art scene. Many bands were formed by artists and were inspired by punk's Dada-like shock tactics and spirit of experimentalism, including stage costumes, artwork and the conceptualisation of their music. Other local examples of the era include the Suburban Reptiles, Gordons and future experimental filmmaker and performer Brent Hayward. Fetus Productions initially began with former members of The Features — Jed Town, Karel van Bergen and artist-musician James Pinker — with the addition of Fort and artist (and future fashion designer) Mike Brookfield.

From their punk origins they moved into experimenting with electronic tools, using tape recorders, synthesisers and eventually samplers to create industrial music that incorporated found sounds and video footage. Their stage performances were intended to conjure strong reactions. Live performances incorporated tapes and film projections which Town hoped would produce a 'multi-sensational effect'.[20] Films of car crashes, plastic surgery and mutilations, many collected by Town on Super 8 from medical libraries, were contrasted with filmed sunsets, all projected onto screens. Consistent with the earlier punk ethos, the intention was to present a raw realism as a contrast to the sleepy white-picket-fence veneer of the conservative mainstream.

Fetus Productions retained a strand of pop sensibility woven into their electronic approach. Others would follow their path in exploring the possibilities of electronic and industrial sound and multimedia live performances. In Ōtautahi Christchurch, the group Tinnitus began to organise media events that were part ritual and part festival. This continued to evolve after they relocated to Tāmaki Makaurau, notably with the Rotate Your State events launched at the music venue the Gluepot. The events were an attempt to shift the dynamics of pub-based music performances into a more socially constructed high-tech lounge space with installations, videos and food stalls, and less primary focus on the bar and stage.[21]

Tinnitus evolved into Pitch Black, a techno-dub-video duo of Mike Hodgson and Paddy Free, and Rotate Your State evolved into Soliton (1997, 1998, 1999 and 2003), which began as a series of nightclub-based live music/dance/performance/art/film/multimedia events that were decidedly not in art venues. Much like Andy Warhol's Factory happenings, they were as much for the social interaction of a party or club as for the presentation of artwork.[22]

As with Soliton, the live use of technology was an important ingredient of Interdigitate (1991–2007), notably the ability to combine sound and image in interactive ways. Interdigitate was founded by Phil Dadson as part of Elam's Intermedia programme, and was later run by the Moving Image Centre. For Soliton '99, dancers Becca Wood, Kelly Moynihan and Tasha Alpe activated sound and video using MIDI switches installed across the floor. The earliest iterations of Interdigitate took place at the Aotea Centre in Tāmaki Makaurau and focused on ways to activate the venue's multi-panel video wall of thirty-six monitors.

Interdigitate's inaugural work was Dadson's *Footstep Hocket*, a recorded sound performance for the thirty-six-monitor format that set the scene for subsequent live performances. In 1992, Sean Kerr and James McCarthy reprised their work *Bang On*, a percussion-and-video piece that had been performed earlier that year for the Soundwatch '92 festival as a two-channel presentation, now enlarged with various-sized configurations across the thirty-six-monitor array.[23] For the 1995 Interdigitate, Lisa Reihana produced a thirty-six-channel video interpretation of the Pacific Sisters' *Ina and Tuna*, a performance presented in different iterations that combined storytelling, music, costumes and performance.[24]

MAKING SPACE FOR SOUND

Many marginal practices, such as performance, thrive best when given a context to work within. As already discussed, festivals and recurring events frequently provide a critical mass and a platform for new work. Often sitting somewhere between experimental music, theatre and art, these events are just as likely to take place in a gallery, a music venue context or some other sort of borrowed space such as a shop, home or hall. Across the six decades that this survey addresses, examples include the *Project Programmes* series at Auckland Art Gallery Toi o Tāmaki from 1975 to 1978, the *Static Mansion* performance series in Ōtautahi, and Auckland Art Gallery's *In Audio* sound performance series from 2003 to 2006, as well as the weekly Vitamin-S improvisation nights that have taken place almost continuously since 2002.

Vitamin-S began at Tāmaki Makaurau's Odeon café, but since 2006 has mostly taken place at the music venue The Wine Cellar.[25] Every week artists are selected at random to perform in trios. Many come from different areas of the music world, and some have a background in dance, theatre or art. Artists who span these different worlds, including Dadson, James McCarthy, Matthew Brennan, Ivan Mršić, Colin Woods and John Radford, have often been participants in what has evolved into a loose collective that also performs in the larger ensemble 10 Acre Bloc, which has presented renditions of Cornelius Cardew's *The Great Learning*.

Although there have been some substantial sound-based projects and performance programmes in galleries and other venues, ongoing support for experimental and cross-disciplinary practices has been intermittent.[26] But there have been some dedicated spaces established to nurture these practices, around which a scene is able to grow. Alongside underground music venues such as The Space and Pyramid Club in Te Whanganui-a-Tara Wellington, of note are The Auricle (2013–17) in Ōtautahi, the Moving Image Centre (1993–2011) and the Audio Foundation (est. 2004, gallery and venue opened 2011) in Tāmakai Makaurau, the latter still operating.[27] These last three venues hosted both exhibition programmes and live events, resulting in a crossover between modes of sound and performance practice.

Observing the awkward fit within established institutions for diverse and interdisciplinary practices, including sound performance, the Uniform collective, established in 2013 in Tāmaki Makaurau, chose to work more independently. Core members Elizabeth Dawson (aka Beth Ducklingmonster), Tina Pihema (Ngāti Whātua), Kiran Dass, Hannah Lacey and Sjionel Timu (Ngāti Porou, Ngāti Kahungunu) place importance on working together to create their No Venues community performance 'events' that occupy unconventional urban or domestic spaces.[28] These events mix music, films and parties alongside self-publishing visual outputs, including posters, comics and zines. Dawson states: 'The queer punk community I identify with exists in the meeting of radical feminism (with roots in the 1990s Riot Grrl movement), Indigenous allyship, sexuality and gender fluidity.'[29]

NEW SOUNDS, NEW MATERIALS

Many of Aotearoa's early explorations in contemporary sound performance grew from international experiences. The move from conventional instruments to electronic sources was led by composer Douglas Lilburn, who took a sabbatical in 1963 to visit international studios before returning to set up Aotearoa's first electronic studio at Victoria University. The link between composition and live instruments was severed at this point: a composer could develop sounds alone with machines, assemble them, collage-like, onto tape, and present the completed work to an audience from a reel-to-reel tape machine, which now occupied the stage at electronic music events.

Like Lilburn, Annea Lockwood also ventured abroad, leaving in 1961 to explore the new possibilities of working with sound and to study music at the Royal College of Art in London. During a summer school in Darmstadt, where the likes of Karlheinz Stockhausen and Pierre Boulez were lecturing, as had John Cage the previous year, she witnessed La Monte Young perform his work *Furniture Music*, in which he pushes a chair around the room.[30] In contrast to the controlled organisation of the then dominant approaches of electronic music and serialism, Young's performance embraced the possibilities of sound, chance and the changing dynamics of materials such as wood.

Lockwood's notable early performance series was her *Piano Transplants*, each of which was a proposition that allowed for sound to manifest in a non-compositional way in which time is emphasised by the materials and the environment. The first and most

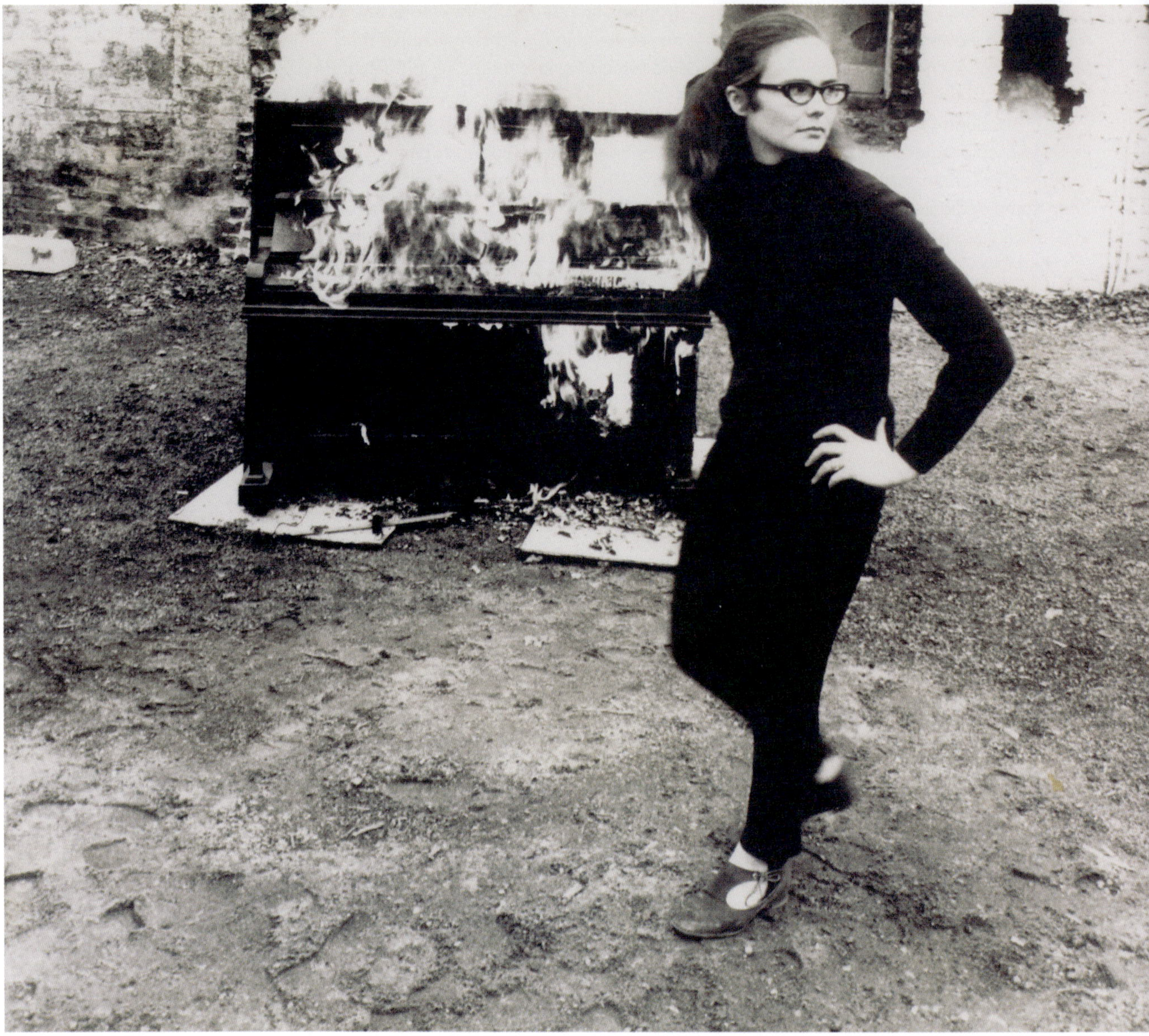

Annea Lockwood, *Piano Burning*, 1968, Chelsea Embankment, London. *Courtesy the artist. Photo by Geoff Adams*

memorable of these was *Piano Burning* (1968), in which an (unrepairable) upright piano was amplified and carefully set alight to burn slowly, activating the elements of the piano's structure and materials as they transformed and broke down, from the outer laminates and varnish to the inner harp and the popping of strings.

Another in this series was *Piano Drowning* (1972), in which a piano was left to sink slowly in a body of water. In *Piano Garden* (1969–70), pianos were partially buried and left to deteriorate in a slow-moving event that largely defied human perception or control. *Southern Exposure* (1982) required a piano, attached to a ship's anchor, to be left on a beach at the high-tide mark until it disappeared.[31]

Lockwood also began to work with amplified glass as a material, from small microscope slides to 6-foot (2-metre) panes, some hung from scaffolding and others bowed with glass tubes or rods. *Glass Concert* performances (1967–70) started in full darkness and required audiences to focus on the unfamiliar sounds and consider their origins before the lights were slowly brought up to reveal the materials and playing methods, which could then be better appreciated for the remainder of the performance. These works anticipated Lockwood's later interest in meditative and trance states for listening.

In 1969 Lockwood connected with another expatriate artist and Royal College of Art graduate, Billy Apple, then living in New York, who had become an acquaintance of Cage and the local Fluxus scene, including Nam June Paik and Charlotte Moorman. Apple had also been working with glass as a found everyday material, and the pair agreed to collaborate on a work for Zeez Arts in London in 1970. *Glass Transformation* advertised for participants to throw glass into the gallery, which was then swept into seven boxes for a closing performance, which was recorded.

The following year Lockwood had the resulting 128 kilograms of glass crushed and hand-sieved by a milling company, and recorded this process, too. The audio was then presented in complete darkness in a New York loft gallery in 1972, and in subsequent exhibitions and presentations.[32] The culmination is not only an apparent subtraction of the material form of the glass from the surrounding streets, like Apple's cleaning performances of the same period, but also its physical and conceptual transformation throughout the process, from physical presentation to audio.

Apple continued to work periodically in performance and with composers and musicians throughout his career. Several projects utilised the translation of information into musical notation by composer Jonathan Besser, including nautical and weather data and a soundtrack for the ascending and descending of stairs. On one occasion at Lopdell House Gallery in Tāmaki Makaurau, in 1998, Wystan Curnow read a text while Besser performed associated notes derived from the golden ratio; and at the public gallery Te Uru in 2015, jazz musician Nathan Haines led a group through a rendition of an Apple–Besser score.

ROTACTION/DRONE

James McCarthy, a From Scratch member and one of Dadson's Intermedia students at Elam, also established his own percussion ensemble. Rotaction first performed at the 1989 Sound/Watch festival. It used a variety of elaborate, sculptural invented instruments, including internally lit sun-drums, aka Sputniks, which required considered movement to play, as well as movement between instrument stations.[33] In one Rotaction performance, at Artspace Aotearoa, wire instrument strings were installed by bow and arrow.

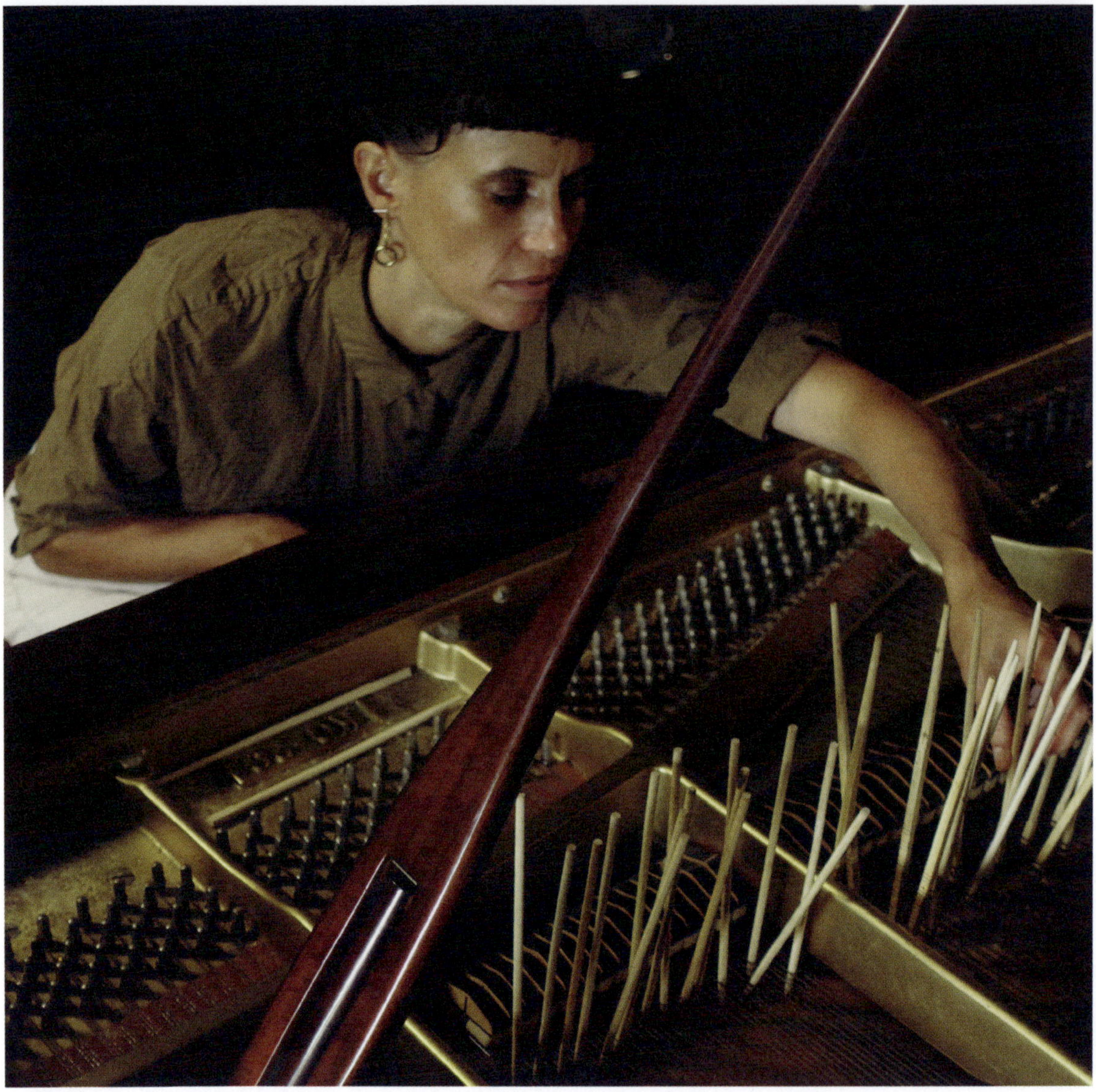

Hermione Johnson during a performance at the Audio Foundation, Tāmaki Makaurau Auckland, 2021. *Courtesy the artist. Photo by Andrew McLeod*

In later solo performances, McCarthy climbed walls and attached instrument wires to form large linear drawings that were then played like a stringed instrument, combining the materiality of instrument design with architecture and bodily technique. For his 2006 performance *Ascent* at the Govett-Brewster Art Gallery, he used a climbing harness and crampons to manoeuvre across the 'instrument' and activate the drawing by playing sounds on the wires.

Formed in 1986, Drone (aka DRONEnsemble) also made use of invented instruments and performance. The group featured two of Dadson's students, Daniel Newnham and Darryl Hocking, as well as Rosemary Whitehead, with occasional guests including McCarthy and Gareth Farr. Their approach was more industrial and focused on amplification, and included *Spinner,* a rotating clothesline-like structure with mounted speakers and oil drums, as well as more mobile self-amplified percussion devices. Also using traditional instruments, they crossed over with the experimental rock scene.

PERFORMING BODIES AND EXTENDED INSTRUMENTS

Exploring relationships between the body and sound as a typically autobiographical statement, John Cousins' performance *Membrane* was presented at the Edinburgh Festival in 1984. For this 7-hour performance, Cousins was connected to a series of tubes that provided him with fresh water that he then expelled as urine, which dripped through pitched pipes onto drums, directly connecting the artist to the instrument as part of a cyclical filtering system of transformation.[34]

Guitarist Greg Malcolm may play one of popular music's most ubiquitous instruments, but his technique is certainly not conventional. Rather than efficiently reproducing notes, one of his guitars has been customised to emphasise sounds that are not usually highlighted, with an extra pick-up installed on the 'wrong' side of the bridge and other modifications to amplify body noise and harmonics or vibrations, much in the way John Cage modified pianos to create new tonal possibilities.[35]

As if challenging the bodily limits of what a single player can do and control, Malcolm often plays several guitars at once: one on the floor is played with his feet as a rhythmic bass accompaniment, and another generates drones through the use of a fan or e-bow against the strings. Springs are attached to the guitar's head, rubber bands are attached to the guitar or over Malcolm's face, or are launched at the audience so they can fire them back at the instrument, and a repertoire of string manipulation methods includes scraping, banging and choking to expand the possibilities for 'proper' guitar playing, all further complicating the way sound is created.[36]

In 2004 Malcolm performed on an Ōtautahi tram in collaboration with percussionist Chris O'Connor (a later member of From Scratch) as part of the performance series *Trambience.*[37] Chimes were distributed to passengers/audience and gongs and bells were hung from the rails, creating a soundscape that swayed with the tram's motion while O'Connor played a small drum kit and Malcolm played his guitar in a variety of ways, including triggering electromagnetic noises using a camera flash.

When does extreme musicianship and virtuosity become performance art? For performers like Malcolm and saxophonist Jeff Henderson, it can be the limits of control and endurance rather than techniques of precision that create a synergy between body, instrument, architecture and audience. Intense overblowing can overwhelm an instrument's usual ability to reproduce prescribed notes, opening up new possibilities for tonalities (and atonalities), as well as creating enough volume to incorporate a room's acoustic qualities into the sound being created. This use of the acoustics of an architectural space is much like Alastair Galbraith's collaborations with American artist Matthew De Gennaro in the late 1990s, in which piano wires were stretched across gallery spaces then activated like a giant bowed instrument as the performers walked and stroked the length of the wire. The resonance of the walls was a significant factor, placing both performer and audience inside the instrument.

Classically trained pianist Hermione Johnson draws a huge range of moods, timbres and genres from the piano. A long-time free improviser and composer, at times she attacks the piano keys with frenetic physicality; at others she gently draws resonant

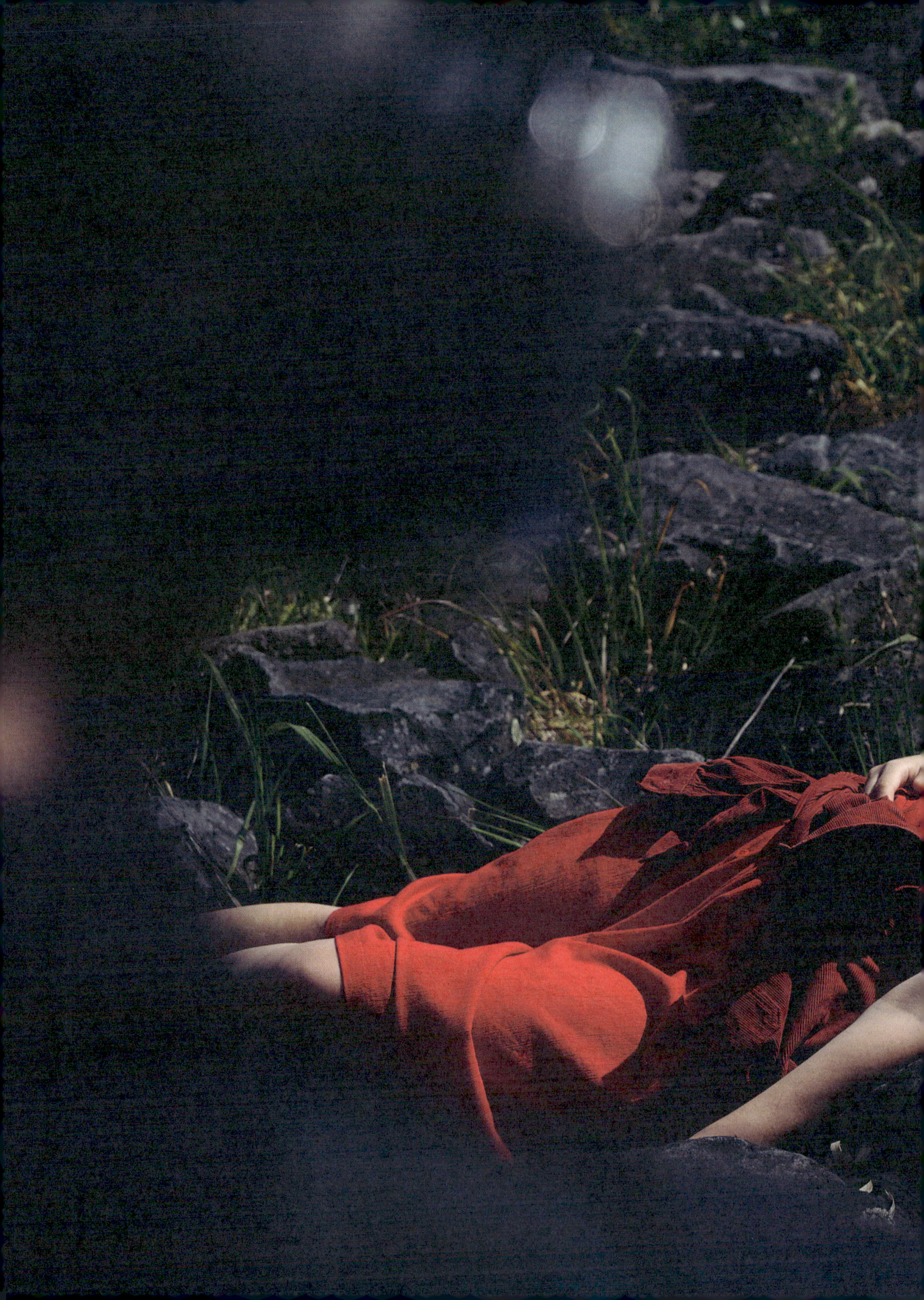

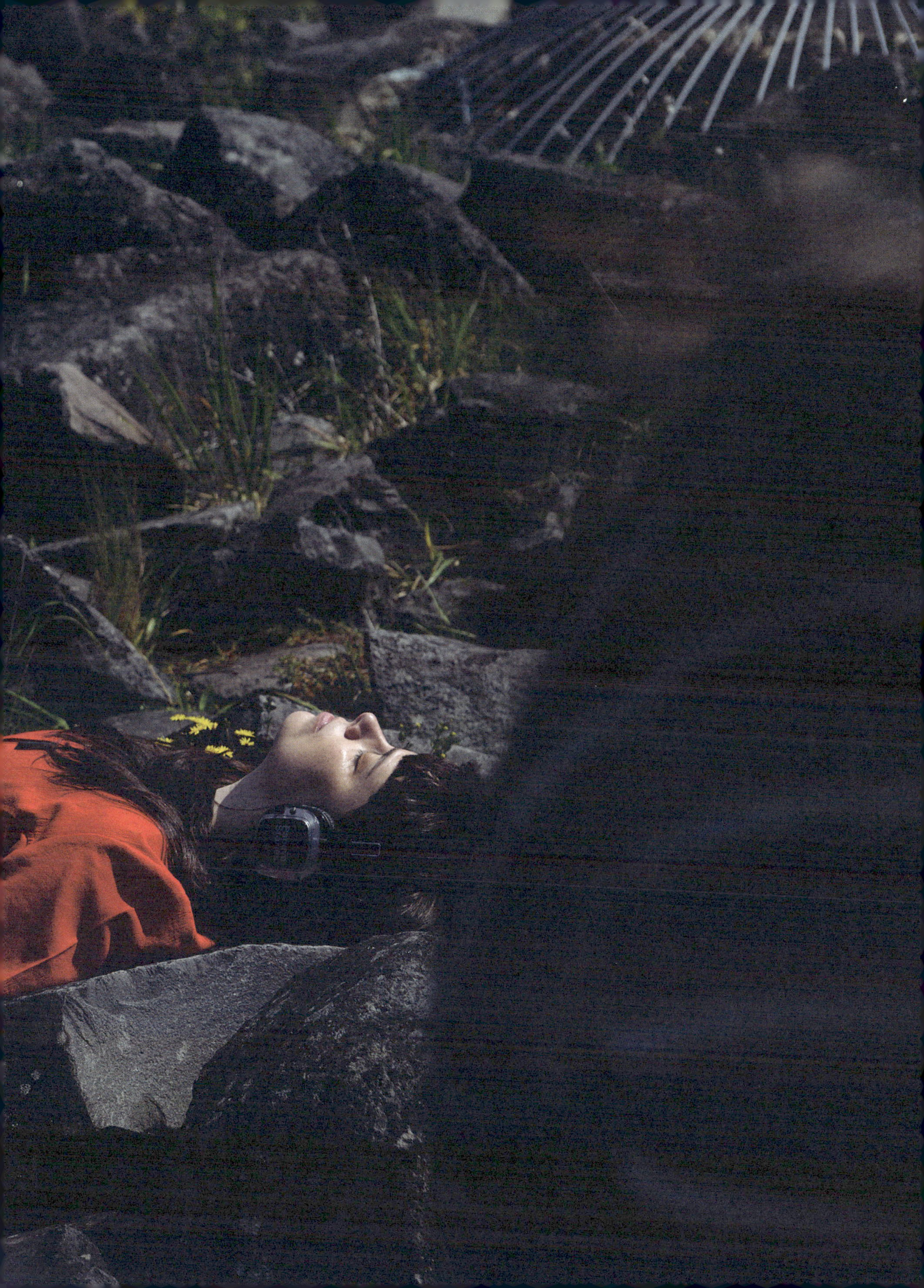

tones via chopsticks lodged in the piano strings. A prolific performer and collaborator, one piano recital of note was an activation of the 2013 exhibition *Michael Parekowhai et al* at Michael Lett Gallery. Through her improvised response to the et al. Samuel Holloway score nested within the work *Upright Piano*, she made the exhibition and the gallery space resonate with sound accompanied by a naturally occurring thunderstorm.[38]

PREVIOUS: Becca Wood, *Unearthing Frequencies — Stone Stories*, 2022, Tāmaki Makaurau Auckland. Performer: Kate Bartlett. *Courtesy the artist. Photo by Sam Hartnett*

SOUND THAT ACTIVATES THE LANDSCAPE

Aotearoa's iconic landscapes have often played a prominent role across all of our cultural fields, as a backdrop, a reference and as a material. Of particular note is *Solar Plexus*, an annual solstice outdoor dawn-to-dusk drumming and performance event in the crater of Maungawhau in central Tāmaki Makaurau. Initiated by Dadson in 1970, *Solar Plexus* ran for more than twenty-five years and created a forum within which many other performances took place.[39]

Slippage and layering between signs, signifiers and simulacra is an important strategy in John Lyall's overlapping practice of installation, drawing, photographic and performance works, in particular the mediation of and packaging of the landscape and 'nature' through technology. His large-scale installations and performances reference iconic settings such as the Pink and White Terraces near Lake Tarawera, a popular nineteenth-century tourist destination until they were buried in the 1886 Tarawera eruption. These 'hyper-feral'[40] landscapes and ecologies, sometimes constructed and activated as a noisy live performance, involve romantic touristic depictions such as waterfalls, typically built from construction and junk materials.

Lyall's group, People Who Hit Things, participated in the 1989 Sound/Watch festival in Tāmaki Makaurau. He was one of the New Zealand performers for the 1993 Tokyo iteration of the SoundCulture festival, and at the 1999 Tāmaki Makaurau SoundCulture event he presented a performance of his 'cyber opera', *Requiem for Electronic Moa*. Based on the story of a device built to simulate the (imagined) sound of the mating call of a moa, it evolved into a story of unrequited love for the electronic moa. Later works by Lyall included stuffed animals, particularly birds and big cats, some with their own electronic voice chips and often purchased from souvenir shops and made to perform with accompaniment from a variety of boomboxes deployed and moved around the space.

Becca Wood's recent projects, described as choreoauratic performances, use sound and participation to create an embodied experience and understanding of the landscape and its histories. Her project *The Public Stand*, delivered in 2020 as part of Te Uru's *About Walking* performance series, combined real-time movement in space, sensory experience and audio information through digital technology. Presented at the Avondale Racecourse, it directed participants to move together around the racecourse, following instructions and listening to a prepared recording on headphones.

As well as a collage of soundtrack material, the audio delivered instructions and narration along with testimonies from local community members about their different experiences of the site, often timed to coincide with the participant's progress around the track and to synchronise with live performance actions also taking place. The recordings, both recent and more distantly remembered or imagined, were like ghosts, simultaneously indicating previous events and occupations in the space while also creating an absence through shifts in time-space, all encountered together with the embodied experience of walking the racetrack with other participants and performers.[41] In her own notes, Wood describes the performance of walking, or hīkoi te whenua, as navigating our own life maps and being positioned in the land in relation to our whakapapa.[42]

Unearthing Frequencies — Stone Stories (2022), a subsequent project by Wood produced in collaboration with Molly Mullen and Tamati Patuwai, focused on the Stonefields suburban development in a former Tāmaki Makaurau quarry beside the volcanic cone Maungarei. Using similar strategies of headphone soundtracks, narration and testimony, it focused on the deeper geological time-space of the site while moving through and pondering the future of the ongoing development. Extending the sensory connection to the site's deep time, participants were encouraged to hold, carry, walk on, listen to and place stones while contemplating their stories. Performers were encountered along the way, activating spaces and stories.

In one encounter a performer removed stones from their mouth, recalling the tradition of waha kōhatu in which placing stones in one's mouth is used as a multisensory memory aid for reciting oral histories.[43] Patuwai accompanied the group as a representative of local iwi Ngāti Whātua Ōrākei (who carry many of the stories of that area) and sometimes joined the performed vignettes, blurring the distinction between participant and performer.

As performer, filmmaker and artist Pīta Turei would affirm, the simple act of storytelling and sharing waiata, combined with specific timing and locations, can be a powerful way to connect people and places, weaving together an awareness of earlier events and a stronger cognisance of the spaces we occupy through history and observation of our environment.

CONCLUSION

Sound is an extension of the material world, an inherently relational medium vibrating and agitating spaces between and in bodies and things. Through the performance of sound, different vibrations, connections and histories are physically activated. Documentation of performances, printed or digital exhibition and event ephemera, and oral histories of performances, either experienced or participated in, all provide the basis of the material selected here. In looking beyond the confines of the art gallery, we note that expressions of sound in performance as art can be located in a range of overlapping contexts.

While looking to acknowledge some influential connections and lines of ancestry in this field of practice, the authors acknowledge that there are many possible omissions from the untidy edges of performance art and sound; where different forms of practice merge, where you had to 'be there', where geography or unwitting bias are factors. The idea of performance art itself emerges from Western art concepts and the inevitable transposition of culture through colonial histories. The works considered here are transformations, charted through crafted ephemeral experiences and acoustic activations, releasing chains of associations and actions, and reflecting combinations of inherited cultural understandings and practices specific to or emerging from Aotearoa.

NOTES

1 For discussion of the problematics of defining sound art as a distinct practice, see Caleb Kelly, *Sound Full: Sound in contemporary Australian and New Zealand art*, in Sound Full/Among the Machines, exhibition publication (Dunedin: Dunedin Public Art Gallery, 2013): 11–12.
2 Te Ahukaramū Charles Royal, '"Let the World Speak": Towards Indigenous Epistemology', Monograph Two (Porirua: Mauriora ki te Ao/Living Universe Ltd, 2009), 8. https://researchspace.auckland.ac.nz/handle/2292/16689
3 Michael P. Shirres, *Te Tangata: The human person* (Auckland: Accent Publications, 1997), 16.
4 Māori Marsden, *The Woven Universe: Selected writings of Rev. Māori Marsden*, edited by Te Ahukaramū Charles Royal (Ōtaki: Te Wānanga o Raukawa; Estate of Rev. Māori Marsden, 2003), 58.
5 Shannon Te Ao, 'Off the Dome: An interview with Shannon Te Ao', interview by Megan Dunn, 12 August 2017, https://pantograph-punch.com/posts/interview-shannon-te-ao
6 Martin Patrick, 'Exploring Posthuman Masquerade and Becoming', in *Animism in Art and Performance*, edited by Christopher Braddock (Cham, Switzerland: Palgrave Macmillan, 2017), 213–31.
7 See Anthony Byrt, *This Model World: Travels to the edge of contemporary art* (Auckland: Auckland University Press, 2016); Patrick, 'Exploring Posthuman Masquerade and Becoming'; Matariki Williams, 'The Singing Word: On Shannon Te Ao's "My Life as a Tunnel"', *The Pantograph Punch*, 22 June 2018, https://pantograph-punch.com/posts/singing-word; Christopher Braddock, 'Entangled Animisms: Whakaaro and dialogue in the artwork of Shannon Te Ao', *Performance Research* 24, no. 6 (On Animism) (18 August 2019): 69–78, https://doi.org/10.1080/13528165.2019.1686584.
8 See Braddock, 'Entangled Animisms'.
9 Andrew Clifford, 'With the sun aglow, I have my pensive moods'. *Contemporary HUM*, 4 December 2017, https://contemporaryhum.com/writing/with-the-sun-aglow-i-have-my-pensive-moods
10 See Andrew Clifford, 'Sound/Art Festivals', in Bruce Russell, *Erewhon Calling: Experimental sound in New Zealand* (Auckland: Audio Foundation and CMR, 2012); Russell, 'Lines of Flight: "The most perfectly autonomous sector of the field of cultural production"', in *Home, Land and Sea: Situating music in Aotearoa New Zealand*, edited by Glenda Keam and Tony Mitchell (Auckland: Pearson, 2011), 265–79.
11 Gary Wilby, Eric Biddington and John Cousins, 'Artist Statement', in *The Sonic Circus Festival Programme*, The Sonic Circus, 1974 This programme is part of the author Andrew Clifford's personal archive.
12 The first performance of *Poetry for Chainsaws* is commonly said to have taken place in Adelaide in 1976, so perhaps the 1975 Sonic2 presentation in Wellington did not go ahead. It certainly existed as an idea if it was in the 1975 programme, so the work was not entirely developed in Adelaide.
13 SOUNZ, *Pacific 3, 2, 1, Zero*, https://sounz.org.nz/works/10955
14 Nick Bollinger, 'Ten Musical Moments from the New Zealand Counterculture', *AudioCulture Iwi Waiata*, 1 September 2022, www.audioculture.co.nz/articles/ten-musical-moments-from-the-new-zealand-counterculture
15 Elizabeth Kerr, 'Jenny McLeod at 80: "To me I'm always me . . ."', *Five Lines* (blog), 9 November 2021, www.fivelines.nz/articles/jenny-mcleod-at-80-to-me-im-always-me
16 Denis Smalley, 'Record Reviews: Earth and sky (1968)', *Salient* 33, no. 10 (8 July 1970): 13.
17 SOUNZ, 'Jenny McLeod Composer Biography', https://sounz.org.nz/works/10955
18 Nick Bollinger, *Jumping Sundays: The rise and fall of the counterculture in Aotearoa New Zealand* (Auckland: Auckland University Press, 2022), 203.
19 Blam Blam Blam included Don McGlashan, also a member of From Scratch and later a member of performance/music group The Front Lawn. See Matthew Bannister, *33⅓: Songs from The Front Lawn* (Bloomsbury Academic, 2023).
20 Matthew Goody, *Needles and Plastic: Flying Nun Records, 1981–1988* (Auckland: Auckland University Press, 2022).
21 Clifford, 'Sound/Art Festivals'.
22 Wendy Vaigro, 'Soliton '99', *Art New Zealand* 94 (Autumn 2000): 36–39.
23 Keith Hill, 'Interdigitate', *Art New Zealand* 65 (Summer 1992–93): 70–71.
24 Wendy Vaigro, 'High Performance Optics: Interdigitate 95', *Art New Zealand* 76 (Spring 1995): 52–54.
25 Paul Buckton et al., 'Vitamin S: Get in, get wet — a format for improv', in Bruce Russell, *Erewhon Calling*, 84–87.
26 See Su Ballard, 'All Night Silence: Live experimental sound in New Zealand public art galleries', in Russell, *Erewhon Calling*, 54–59.
27 The Moving Image Centre was more broadly focused on new media practice, but took leadership of Interdigitate in its later years and also hosted a number of performance events that included sound.
28 Uniform Collective, 'What Is Uniform', https://whatisuniform.tumblr.com
29 Elizabeth Barbara Dawson, 'Hanging Out for Real: Enacting improvisations with audio-visual materials to create installational amplifications in social city sites I inhabit' (Master's thesis, Auckland University of Technology, 2022), https://hdl.handle.net/10292/15725
30 Ron Hanson, 'Listening Like Breathing: Environmental immersion in the work of Annea Lockwood', *Contemporary HUM*, 9 December 2020. https://contemporaryhum.com/writing/listening-like-breathing
31 *Piano Burning* was first presented in London in 1968; *Piano Garden* in Ingatestone, Essex, in 1969–70; *Piano Drowning* in Amarillo, Texas in 1972; and *Southern Exposure* was first realised at Bathers Beach, Freemantle, in 2005.
32 Everson Museum of Art, 1976; Maidment Little Theatre, 1979; Artspace Aotearoa, 1998; Te Uru, 2015; Te Pātaka Toi Adam Art Gallery, 2021.
33 Clifford and Dadson, 'Sonic Invention: Experimental sound-making', in *Home, Land and Sea: Situating music in Aotearoa New Zealand*, 245–64 256–57.
34 Ibid., 254–55.
35 Ibid., 252.
36 Jonathan Bywater, 'Music Not Done Properly: The swinging sounds of Greg Malcolm'. *Music in New Zealand* 32 (Autumn 1996): 38–39.
37 Joyce, 'City Loops,' in Russell, *Erewhon Calling*, 178–83.
38 et al. Samuel Holloway's 2013 *Upright Piano* was also later activated by Hermione Johnson as part of *Shout Whisper Wail! The 2017 Chartwell Show*, Auckland Art Gallery Toi o Tāmaki.
39 It is difficult to pinpoint the exact end date of Solar Plexus as it continued to run under its own momentum for a number of years without Dadson's involvement.
40 Nigel Clark, *John Lyall: Towards an hyper-feral art, Aotearoa: Picketing the sublime; given both a blue displacement and an illuminating vessel*, exhibition catalogue (Auckland: Auckland: Auckland Art Gallery Toi o Tāmaki, 1997), https://find.slv.vic.gov.au/discovery/fulldisplay/alma997938923607636/61SLV_INST:SLV.
41 Molly Mullen gives a personal account of participating in

this event in 'To gather together, but a/part', in Houghton, Laing and Wood, eds., *About Walking*, 48–51.

42 Becca Wood, 'About About Walking', in Christina Houghton, Melissa Laing and Becca Wood, eds, *About Walking: 15 months of artist walks in Tāmaki Auckland* (Auckland: Te Uru Waitākere Contemporary Gallery, 2021), 19.

43 Rachel Trow and Morgan Godfery, 'Whose Land Is It Anyway: Inside the fraught battle for mana whenua recognition in Auckland', *Metro*, 9 January 2023. www.metromag.co.nz/society/whose-land-is-it-anyway.

REFERENCES

Bannister, Matthew. *33⅓: Songs from The Front Lawn*. Bloomsbury Academic, 2023.

Bollinger, Nick. *Jumping Sundays: The rise and fall of the counterculture in Aotearoa New Zealand*. Auckland: Auckland University Press, 2022.

——— 'Ten Musical Moments from the New Zealand Counterculture'. *AudioCulture Iwi Waiata*, 1 September 2022. www.audioculture.co.nz/articles/ten-musical-moments-from-the-new-zealand-counterculture

Braddock, Christopher. 'Entangled Animisms: Whakaaro and dialogue in the artwork of Shannon Te Ao'. *Performance Research* 24, no. 6, 'On Animism' (August 2019): 69–78. https://doi.org/10.1080/13528165.2019.1686584

Byrt, Anthony. *This Model World: Travels to the edge of contemporary art*. Auckland: Auckland University Press, 2016.

Bywater, Jonathan. 'Music Not Done Properly: The swinging sounds of Greg Malcolm'. *Music in New Zealand* 32 (Autumn 1996): 38–39.

Clark, Nigel. *John Lyall: Towards an hyper-feral art, Aotearoa: Picketing the sublime; given both a blue displacement and an illuminating vessel*. Exhibition catalogue. Auckland: Auckland Art Gallery Toi o Tāmaki, 1997. https://find.slv.vic.gov.au/discovery/fulldisplay/alma997938923607636/61SLV_INST:SLV

Clifford, Andrew. 'Exhibitions and Infrastructure'. *Te Ara — the Encyclopedia of New Zealand*, 2014. https://teara.govt.nz/en/media-art/page-4

——— 'With the sun aglow, I have my pensive moods'. *Contemporary HUM*, 4 December 2017. https://contemporaryhum.com/writing/with-the-sun-aglow-i-have-my-pensive-moods

Clifford, Andrew and Philip Dadson. 'Sonic Invention: Experimental sound-making'. In *Home, Land and Sea: Situating music in Aotearoa New Zealand*, edited by Glenda Keam and Tony Mitchell, 245–64. Auckland: Pearson, 2011.

Clifford, Andrew and Roger Horrocks. *Fetus Reproductions: Fetus productions, 1981–2002*, edited by Stella Brennan and Hanna Scott. Exhibition catalogue. Auckland: Artspace Aotearoa, 2002.

Dawson, Elizabeth Barbara. 'Hanging Out for Real: Enacting improvisations with audio-visual materials to create installational amplifications in social city sites I inhabit'. Master's thesis, Auckland University of Technology, 2022. https://hdl.handle.net/10292/15725

Goody, Matthew. *Needles and Plastic: Flying Nun Records, 1981–1988*. Auckland: Auckland University Press, 2022.

Hanson, Ron. 'Listening Like Breathing: Environmental immersion in the work of Annea Lockwood'. *Contemporary HUM*, 9 December 2020. https://contemporaryhum.com/writing/listening-like-breathing

Hill, Keith. 'Interdigitate'. *Art New Zealand* 65 (Summer 1992–93): 70–71.

Houghton, Christina, Melissa Laing and Becca Wood, eds. *About Walking: 15 months of artist walks in Tāmaki Auckland*. Auckland: Te Uru Waitākere Contemporary Gallery, 2021.

Huddleston, Charlotte, ed. *Mostly Harmless: A performance series*. Exhibition catalogue. New Plymouth: Govett-Brewster Art Gallery, 2006.

Kelly, Caleb and Susan Ballard, eds. *Sound Full: Sound in contemporary Australian and New Zealand art*. Exhibition publication. Dunedin: Dunedin Public Art Gallery, 2013.

Kerr, Elizabeth. 'Jenny McLeod at 80: "To me I'm always me . . ."'. *Five Lines* (blog), 9 November 2021. www.fivelines.nz/articles/jenny-mcleod-at-80-to-me-im-always-me

Marsden, Māori. *The Woven Universe: Selected writings of Rev. Māori Marsden*, edited by Te Ahukaramū Charles Royal. Ōtaki: Te Wānanga o Raukawa; Estate of Rev. Māori Marsden, 2003.

Patrick, Martin. 'Exploring Posthuman Masquerade and Becoming'. In *Animism in Art and Performance*, edited by Christopher Braddock, 213–31. Cham, Switzerland: Palgrave Macmillan, 2017.

Royal, Te Ahukaramū Charles. '"Let the World Speak": Towards indigenous epistemology'. Monograph Two. Porirua: Mauriora ki te Ao/Living Universe Ltd, 2009. https://researchspace.auckland.ac.nz/handle/2292/16689

Russell, Bruce, ed. *Erewhon Calling: Experimental sound in New Zealand*. Auckland: Audio Foundation and CMR, 2012. https://sounz.org.nz/resources/822

——— 'Lines of Flight: "The most perfectly autonomous sector of the field of cultural production"'. In *Home, Land and Sea: Situating music in Aotearoa New Zealand*, edited by Glenda Keam and Tony Mitchell, 265–79. Auckland: Pearson, 2011.

Shirres, Michael P. *Te Tangata: The human person*. Auckland: Accent Publications, 1997.

Smalley, Denis. 'Record Reviews: Earth and sky (1968)'. *Salient* 33, no. 10 (8 July 1970): 13.

SOUNZ (Centre for New Zealand Music Trust). 'Jenny McLeod Composer Biography'. https://sounz.org.nz/works/10955

——— *Pacific 3, 2, 1, Zero*. https://sounz.org.nz/works/10955

Te Ao, Shannon. 'Off the Dome: An interview with Shannon Te Ao'. Interview by Megan Dunn, 12 August 2017. https://pantograph-punch.com/posts/interview-shannon-te-ao

Trow, Rachel and Morgan Godfery. 'Whose Land Is It Anyway: Inside the fraught battle for mana whenua recognition in Auckland'. *Metro*, 9 January 2023. www.metromag.co.nz/society/whose-land-is-it-anyway

Uniform Collective. 'What Is Uniform'. https://whatisuniform.tumblr.com

Vaigro, Wendy. 'High Performance Optics: Interdigitate 95'. *Art New Zealand* 76 (Spring 1995): 52–54.

——— 'Soliton '99'. *Art New Zealand* 94 (Autumn 2000): 36–39.

Wilby, Gary, Eric Biddington and John Cousins. 'Artist Statement'. In *The Sonic Circus Festival Programme*, The Sonic Circus, 1974.

Williams, Matariki. 'The Singing Word: On Shannon Te Ao's "My Life as a Tunnel"'. *The Pantograph Punch*, 22 June 2018. https://pantograph-punch.com/posts/singing-word

7

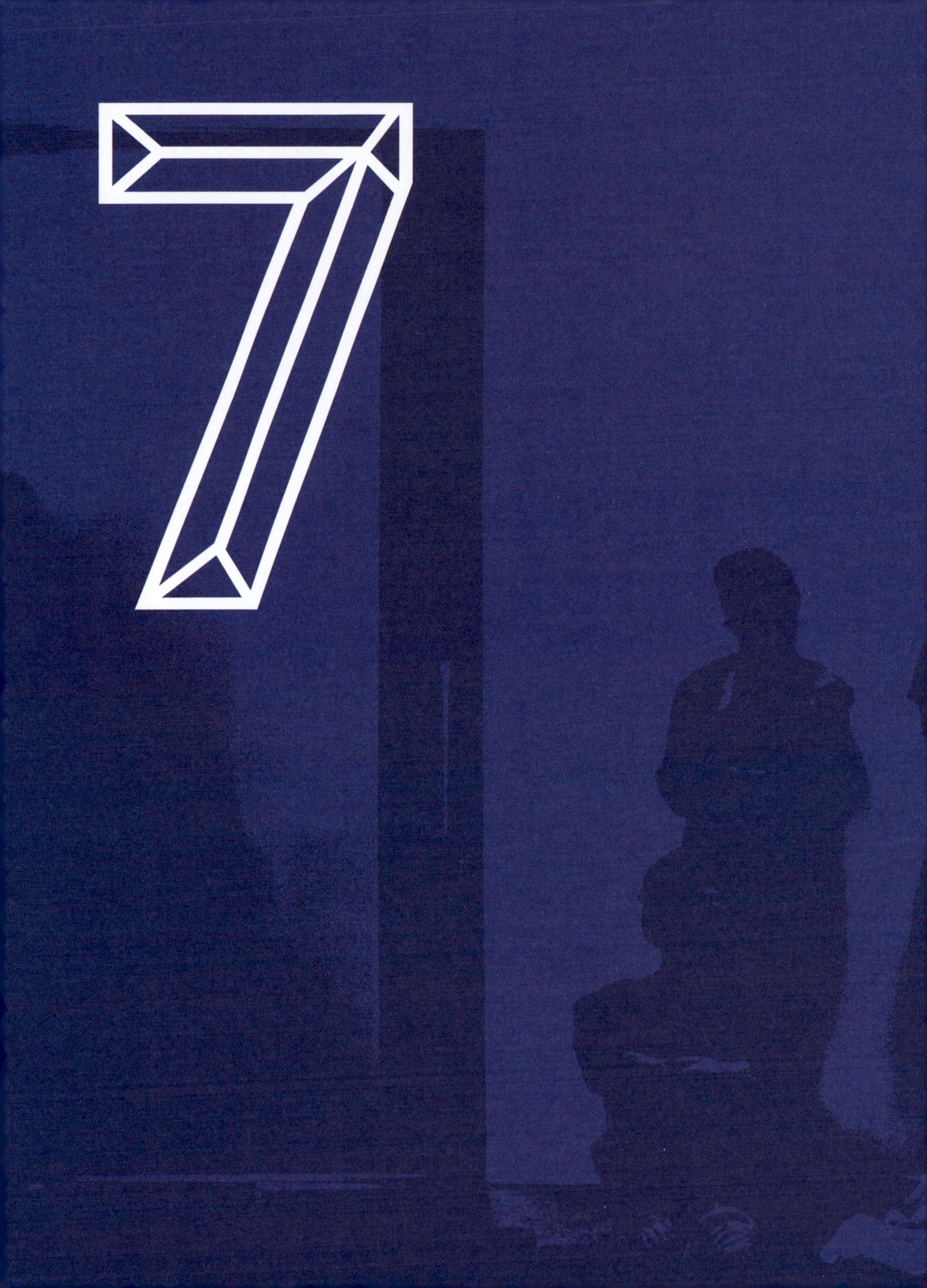

CURATING PERFORMANCE/ CURATORIAL PERFORMATIVITY: A SELECTED HISTORY OF CURATING PERFORMANCE ART IN AOTEAROA 1970–2020

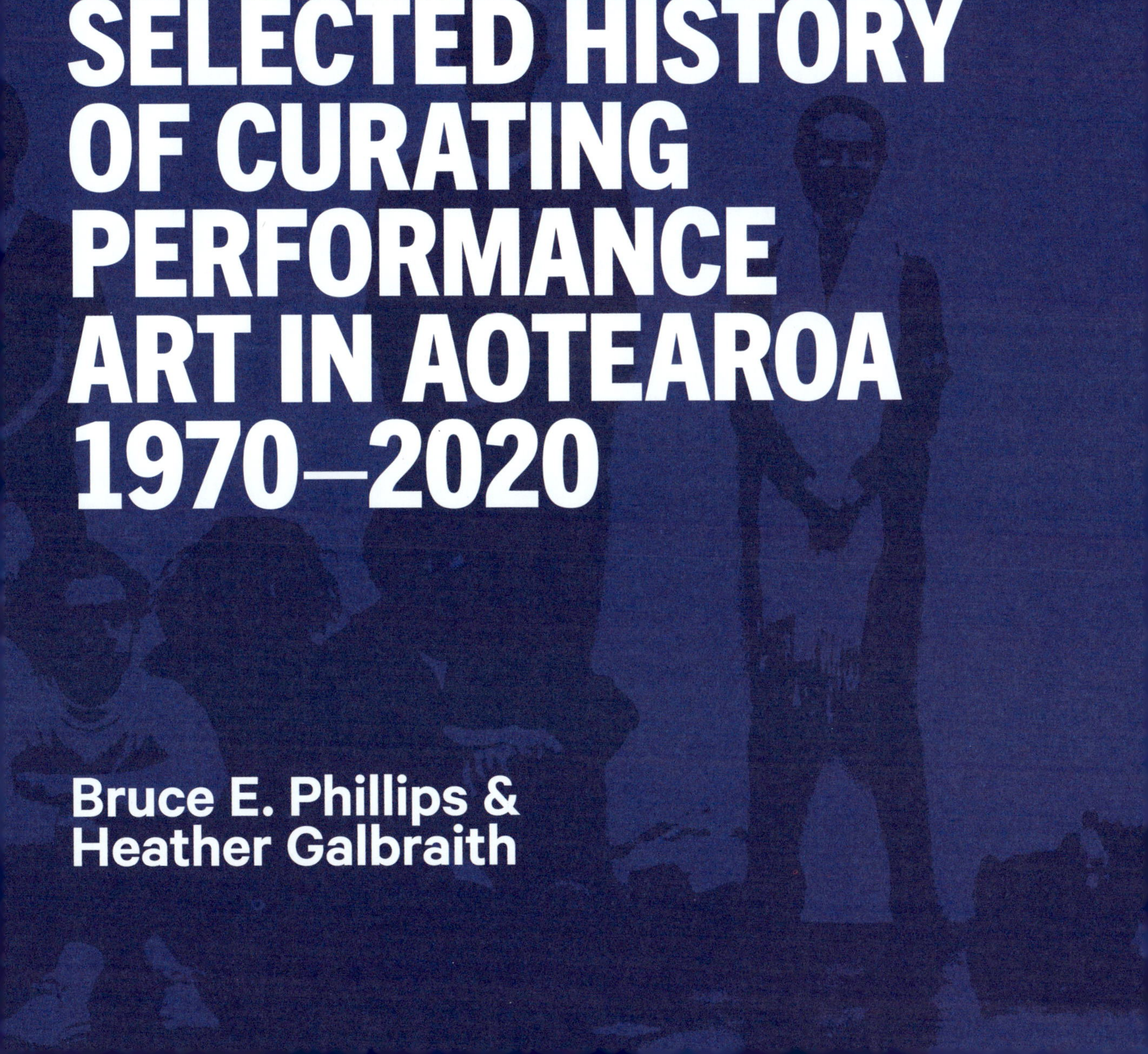

Bruce E. Phillips &
Heather Galbraith

Performance art's continued relevance and potency stems in part from its inherent transdisciplinary nature, regardless of whether it manifests as a solo bodily action, sound, material trace, social exchange, video documentation, cultural ritual, a process of research or collaboration. However, this rich disciplinary ambiguity can present a significant challenge for curators and institutional infrastructures. To give the expanded understanding of performance its due emphasis, curators are required to navigate the hurdle of getting artists and audiences together within institutions of visual art.

This challenge can sometimes lead curators to rely on 'default' event-based conventions or, conversely, to introduce novel curatorial approaches that could risk impinging upon artistic agency. But the challenge also presents many possibilities, especially when disciplinary definitions are relaxed and when exhibition forms and institutional processes are made more malleable.

The examples of exhibition-making practice discussed in this chapter suggest that curators and other exhibition-making practitioners[1] in Aotearoa have employed forms of curatorial performativity to overcome, engage or indulge these tensions and possibilities of exhibiting performance art in its expanded sense. This discussion draws on patterns of curatorial and exhibition-making practice identified through a recent survey of performance-focused and performance-inclusive group exhibitions across fifty years (1970–2020) in forty-seven of Aotearoa's publicly funded art organisations.[2] In attending to this history we have aimed to reflect on and explore the vitality that performance art gives us, and to consider how institutionally supported curatorial practice has taken on performative modalities to support this diverse art form.

Due to the limitations of this research, the exhibition examples discussed are predominantly those supported by galleries and museums, with the exception of a few entities such as Letting Space, The Performance Arcade, One Day Sculpture and Tautai Contemporary Pacific Arts Trust, whose projects have existed outside gallery-based structures or are supported through hybrid partnerships and funding models.

This research focuses specifically on group exhibitions/events that have taken place in Aotearoa. Group exhibitions are, of course, not the only means through which curators and exhibition-makers in Aotearoa have supported performance art. The examples discussed suggest that performative modes of curating are not only implemented by individual curators and exhibition-makers, but are also pursued through group or collective effort — be that the programming strategy of a gallery or the collective drive of a community. Many of the projects discussed also display an awareness that exhibitions can operate beyond gallery walls in extended timeframes and display practices.

It is also important to acknowledge that there was significant performance activity initiated by artists within this time period, including numerous collaborative endeavours and artist-curated projects not covered in this chapter.[3] This was particularly prominent in the 1970s and early 1980s when existing infrastructures, commitment and competencies within established galleries and exhibition spaces were less well developed or resourced. The archival histories of these projects are patchy and rely heavily on documentation and archival image deposits from a modest number of sources. The exhibition *Intervention* at the Robert McDougall Art Annex in 2000 dug into archives and collections to corral artist testimonies and other materials. Jennifer Hay's essay 'Trans-Marginal: New Zealand performance art 1970–1985'[4] provides a strong overview of the projects and artist-led initiatives in Ōtautahi Christchurch, Te Whanganui-a-Tara

Wellington and Tāmaki Makaurau Auckland, as well as the importance of trans-Tasman engagements that embraced performative interdisciplinarity.[5]

These structures and the interplay between different forms, and fostering of spaces where self-determination can be enabled, feel structurally and conceptually aligned with many of the more contemporary examples we see initiated later at artist-led/focused organisations such as Artspace Aotearoa, Blue Oyster Art Project Space, Enjoy Contemporary Art Space and Tautai Trust. The remit of this chapter sits with initiatives staged in Aotearoa, but a rich chapter could also be written in relation to offshore projects or the interplay between Aotearoa and international practitioners and platforms.

'Curatorial performativity' is used within this discussion to describe the way curators and other exhibition-making practitioners utilised collaborative, spatial, discursive and expanded formats to comprise the meaning-making function of an exhibition.[6] The term 'performativity' has been used within curatorial discourse for at least twenty years. The theoretical origins of performativity have been attributed to the work of linguist John L. Austin, in particular his 1955 theory on 'performative utterances', which proposes that speaking does not merely communicate information but is a type of action within social relations.[7] In the 1980s, political theorist Judith Butler expanded this line of enquiry in relation to the social construction of gender, describing gender as a 'stylized repetition of acts'.[8] Butler's extension of performativity from post-structuralist linguistics to gender was influential in opening up its application to deconstructing the truth claims that underpin other social conventions such as art.[9]

Most applicable to this discussion is the work of Katharina Schlieben who, in 2002, applied this theoretical lineage of performativity to the curatorial and institutional practices as a means of considering how the 'stage-setting processes' of exhibition-making are important to the production of meaning.[10]

The relevance of this perspective, Schlieben proposes, is also in line with shifts in artistic practice that, at least in the context of the late 1990s and early 2000s, were preoccupied with deconstructing the processes and social dimensions of art production rather than the autonomous art object.[11] Examples of performative curating have, therefore, been attributed to exhibitions where there is critical consideration of its collaborative, spatial, discursive and expanded formats.[12] Emphasis in such areas has been described as leading to curatorial approaches and exhibition forms that allow for iterative encounters, time-compressed or extended durations, open-ended collaborations and the use of a variety of venues and locations.[13]

In the intervening years since Schlieben's text, the use of the term 'performative' has shifted from emphasising the importance of transparency and self-reflexivity to take on the opposite association — what has become termed 'performative allyship' and 'performative activism', where socio-political agents, be they politicians, corporations or citizens, perform speech that does not correlate with their actions.[14] The ideology of the curatorial and the profession of curating has also been accused of this type of doublespeak, where curators might proclaim certain political virtues only to face criticisms that suggest the contrary, leading to protests, resignations, boycotts and more.

Rather than smooth over this tension between the philosophical roots of the performative and its contrary contemporary use, our discussion here aims to engage both perspectives: that embracing the post-structuralist understanding of performativity is a relevant lens for understanding curatorial practices in Aotearoa that have supported performance art; and that this form of curatorial practice requires scrutiny for any disjuncture between speech and action.

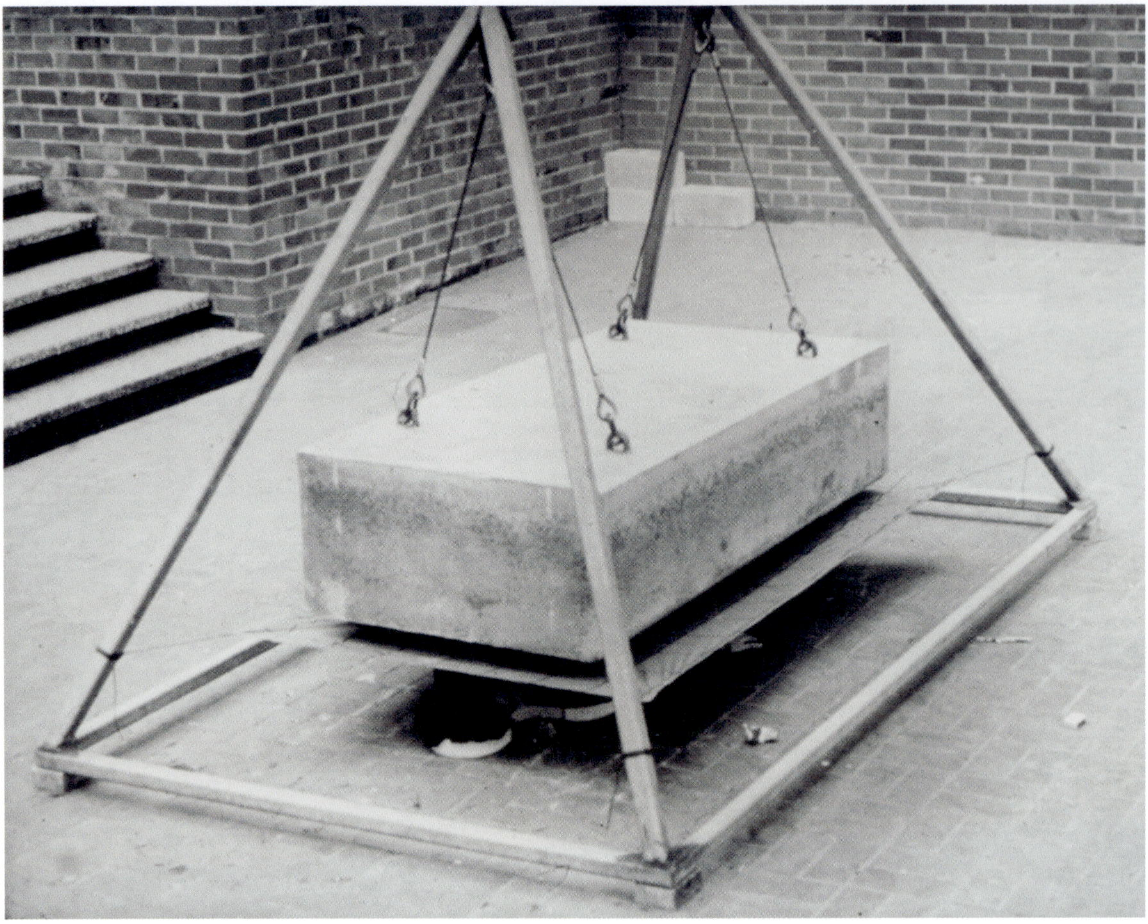

Gray Nicol, *Untitled [Project Programme 7]*, 1975, black and white photograph. *Project Programme Archive, E H McCormick Research Library, Auckland Art Gallery Toi o Tāmaki. Photo by Auckland Art Gallery Toi o Tāmaki*

ORGANISATIONAL AND COLLECTIVE PERFORMATIVITY

One early example of performative traits supported by an organisation can be found in Auckland City Art Gallery *Project Programme* (1975–78) initiated by curator John Maynard and Jim Allen.[15] This four-year-long series included works such as Gray Nicol's *Project 7* (1975) in which the artist spent 24 hours shackled to the ground under a 2-tonne concrete block in front of the gallery — an action that elicited a range of responses from passers-by.[16] Bruce Barber's *Stocks and Bonds* (1975) similarly drew public attention, but from inside the gallery.[17] In this work Barber assumed the role of an 'offender', enduring 48 hours of fasting with his arms and legs locked in medieval-style wooden stocks, monitored by CCTV and being questioned by gallery visitors.[18]

For *Jumble Sale/A Marketplace* (1975), David Mealing hosted a market in the gallery in collaboration with at least fifty-two charities and groups servicing social needs.[19] On a more intimate scale was Andrew Drummond's *Tattoo Tapes* (1978), a video of tattoo artist Roger Ingerton incising an elaborate back tattoo on a man named Murray Hagen. The work was accompanied by a transcript of Drummond interviewing both men about the cultural and personal significance of tattoos.[20]

Overall, the *Project Programme* offered an emerging generation of artists the opportunity to experiment in their respective practices while also testing the relationship between Auckland City Art Gallery and the city's social environment. The support of these actions, experiences and content was undoubtedly uncommon for a municipal gallery in Aotearoa at this time, but arguably would be equally challenging to replicate today.

For all these aspects of performativity, however, it must be observed that, in the published materials, there is an apparent lack of transparency and self-reflexivity concerning gender and ethnic diversity in selected artists, and also a lack of discussion concerning representations of masculinity throughout the majority of the series.

Echoes of Maynard's curatorial approach[21] and Auckland City Art Gallery's organisational support can be found decades later in events, series and exhibitions from the mid-1990s onwards, most notably at Artspace Aotearoa. The marked difference, however, is that in contrast to Maynard's programming, Artspace's exhibitions for the most part considered the diversity of selected artists and/or a critical understanding of gender dynamics as an explicit curatorial rationale.

One of the most enduring examples generated by Artspace's early programme was Letting Space. This project was originally conceived and organised by Mark Amery, Sophie Jerram and Judy Millar in 1994–95 as a series of works responding to the economic decline sustained from the 1987 stock market crash and the way it affected Tāmaki Makaurau's urban environment. Letting Space was later developed by Amery and Jerram into an independent organisation of the same name, in 2010, following the ripple effects of the 2008 global financial crisis on the city of Te Whanganui-a-Tara. In both instances, the remit of Letting Space created opportunities for works that responded to the many vacant commercial properties as a result of economic recession, to 'place art in the domain of commerce'[22] and, in its latter evolution, to broker the apparent gap between business interests, artists and communities as a type of social enterprise.

The performative characteristics of Letting Space are evident in its mid-1990s infancy as an offsite project held in various inner-city locations and durations over seven months. This series included a performance by the art band Wendyhouse and street performances by Tessa Laird, alongside a range of other works in shop windows and office spaces.

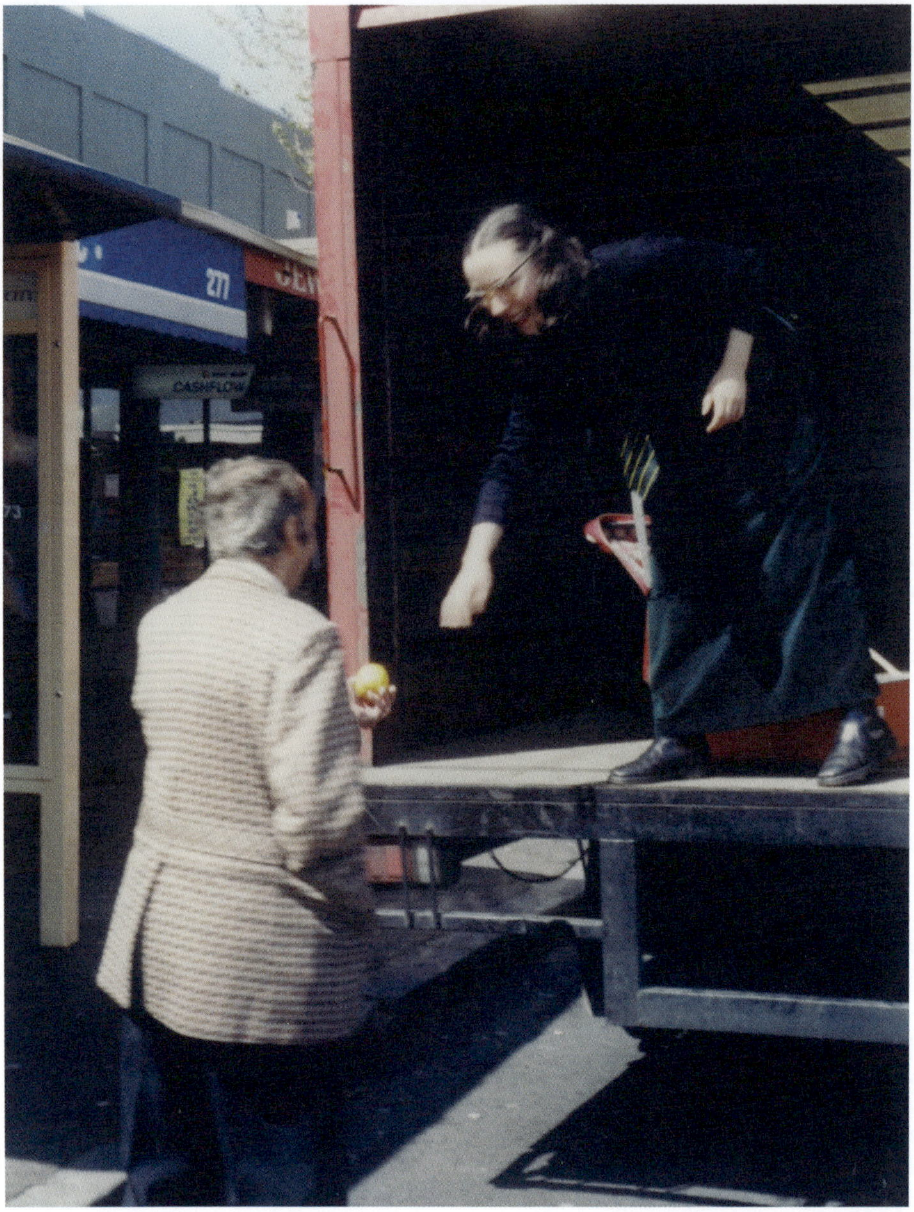

Tessa Laird, *Science Shows/Springs Upon Us (and pins us there, there)*, documentation of performance for Letting Space at Moa-Hunter Books, 279 Ponsonby Road, Tāmaki Makaurau Auckland, 15–29 October 1994. *Courtesy the artist*

A year later Laird curated a series of her own for Artspace titled *Oestrogen Rising* (1996). Promoted as a 'feminist separatist event' and 'art for chicks', this one-day event was exclusive to female-identifying performers and audiences and claimed to 'battl[e] technophobia' and other forms of gender discrimination that can impact art production.[23] *Oestrogen Rising*'s programme promised stunt wrestling by Joyce Campbell and Larissa Lofley, audience makeovers by Booby Tuesday with polaroid portraits taken by Ann Shelton, contributions from the likes of the Pacific Sisters, Allie Eagle and Judy Darragh as well as talks, poetry, comedy, singing and video works.[24]

By embracing the short duration of a day, Laird, Artspace, artists and participants were able to sustain a level of social energy that would arguably be difficult to maintain if drawn out over the course of a standard exhibition cycle counted in weeks or months. In this example, the advantages of performative curating can be seen as emboldening the political stance of curators and galleries in full knowledge that business as usual would commence the day after.

Artspace's 1996 programme also featured *RELAY: Sound and performance*, a series of two-hour evening performance events involving at least thirty-five artists, curated and organised by a group of twelve artists, which aimed to promote performance art with a sound/sonic bias, provide opportunities to practices underrepresented in other venues of this time, and experiment with the context and conventions of connecting audiences and artists.[25] *RELAY* consisted of five parts, each with a different thematic and curatorial approach ranging from a type of open-mic format of 60-second performances to performances in a blackout environment that removed the reliance on visual content/experiences.[26]

From the early 2000s through to the late 2010s, programmed annual and biannual performance-specific exhibitions, performance series and showcase-style events began to emerge. These occurred most notably at Blue Oyster Art Project Space in Ōtepoti (2001, 2006–16)[27] and Enjoy Contemporary Art Space in Te Whanganui-a-Tara (2001–13),[28] and from 2009 were joined by Tautai Contemporary Pacific Arts Trust with *Offstage*, an annual moving image and performance event run in partnership with various galleries and venues. In 2010 the Engine Room gallery held *Performance Week*, an idea later continued by the artist-run initiative play_station, which staged two iterations of *PAWA* (*Performance Art Week Aotearoa*) (2017, 2018) followed by a commitment to regular performance events (2019–21).

The Audio Foundation, dedicated to sound, experimental music and performance art,[29] was established in 2003, and in 2011 The Performance Arcade first took place in Tāmaki Makaurau and Te Whanganui-a-Tara. This later became an annual offsite performance-dedicated exhibition on Te Whanganui-a-Tara's waterfront promenade. These organisations have all made a significant contribution to supporting performance practice in Aotearoa, and have also contributed to replicating exhibition and event formats as pragmatic devices to unite audiences and artists — though some iterations have been self-critical of this tendency.

SPATIAL PERFORMATIVITY

Other collective curatorial and exhibition-making approaches that have critically engaged the pragmatics uniting artists and audiences include those that have experimented with spatial design. The 2006 Govett-Brewster Art Gallery exhibition/performance series *Mostly Harmless: A performance series*, curated by Charlotte Huddleston, is one such example. The exhibition layout, designed by Brian James, comprised mobile AV units equipped with tube monitors, DVD players and headphones that enabled visitors to view performance documentation and works made for film and video. The role of the moving image in performance art was embraced in its many forms, including international examples such as Vito Acconci's *Theme Song* (1973) and Chris Burden's *Shoot* (1971).

These stations were periodically wheeled to the side of the gallery space to make space for live performances, remnants of which — such as the piano-wire drawing of Taranaki Maunga and violin bows left over from James McCarthey's *Ascent* (2006)

— lingered in the space. McCarthy scaled the gallery walls in crampons, the spikes penetrating the gib board as if it were made of ice. His lifeline was a length of piano wire connected via a harness and tensioned by a ratchet winch, which he stroked with a bow, resulting in a sound that changed pitch as he climbed. Another performance remnant that graced the gallery space in *Mostly Harmless* were the tattered fragments from Jim Allen's *News*, a re-enactment of his 1976 work in which he repeatedly read and scrunched up a broadsheet newspaper until it was rendered unreadable and lay discarded on the ground.

The Performance Arcade, directed by Sam Trubridge, has pushed this spatial approach to a more elaborate scale. Using shipping containers as an architectural unit, the arcade's design changes in each iteration to accommodate proposed works, audience engagement and particularities of the Te Whanganui-a-Tara waterfront space. This approach evolved from its inaugural 2011 installations in Te Whanganui-a-Tara and Tāmaki Makaurau as a side-by-side row of containers, each containing a single performance work, to the 2018 design, which resembled a multi-part village complex complete with multiple levels and zones including a bar, music stage and a writing residency space.

Single containers were also configured for a variety of works, from video installations to interactive sculpture, and the small spaces accommodate quieter or more intimate performances. Naturally this unique spatial approach has led to artists responding to its conceptual significance, resulting in works such as Kalisolaite 'Uhila's work *Stowaway* (2012), in which he hid behind a wall of wooden pallets for twenty-four hours in reaction to stories of illegal migration to Aotearoa.

The Performance Arcade's curatorial ethos has also operated beyond the container construction. In 2021 it expanded to include *What If the City Was a Theatre?*, a month-long season of performances throughout Te Whanganui-a-Tara that spanned dance, performance art, drag performances and music performances and featured 300 individual performances from twenty-five collaborators. Although interrupted by weather and a global pandemic, this season led to one of the most performance-saturated events the city had seen.

Recognising the importance of spatial design need not require the level of construction demonstrated in The Performance Arcade. This is emphasised by Ioana Gordon-Smith in her curation of the performance series *More Than We Know* (2013), held at and in response to the architecture and social history of the Gus Fisher Gallery, located in the Kenneth Myers Centre, University of Auckland, a neo-Romanesque-style building purpose-built in the 1930s as the country's first public radio facility, and later home to Television New Zealand and finally the art gallery and a dance school. Acknowledging that 'some rules are baked into a given space,'[30] Gordon-Smith's framing of the series addressed social and physical parameters of the building as a site for performance. Her conceptual approach to spatial performativity recognised the aesthetic lineage of the building's design as a symbolic relic of empire,[31] coupled with that of public broadcasting and tertiary education as the performances through which social norms and ideologies are enculturated.

One response to this physical and social architecture of power was Kalisolaite 'Uhila's opening-night performance of *Uiaki fono* (2013), in which he stood precariously upon the building's castle-like parapet, calling out in Tongan to the surrounding glass-walled high-rise buildings, home to the city's financial and legal district, while gallery guests lingered in the street below. The action, explained by Rangituhia Hollis and Gordon-Smith in their catalogue essays, invokes the *uiaki fono* role of Tongan tradition — a type of town crier who relays messages from the king or village authorities.[32]

Other performance art responses to the material and social architecture of the Kenneth Myers Centre included Jeremy Leatinu'u's (Tainui, Samoan) recorded actions

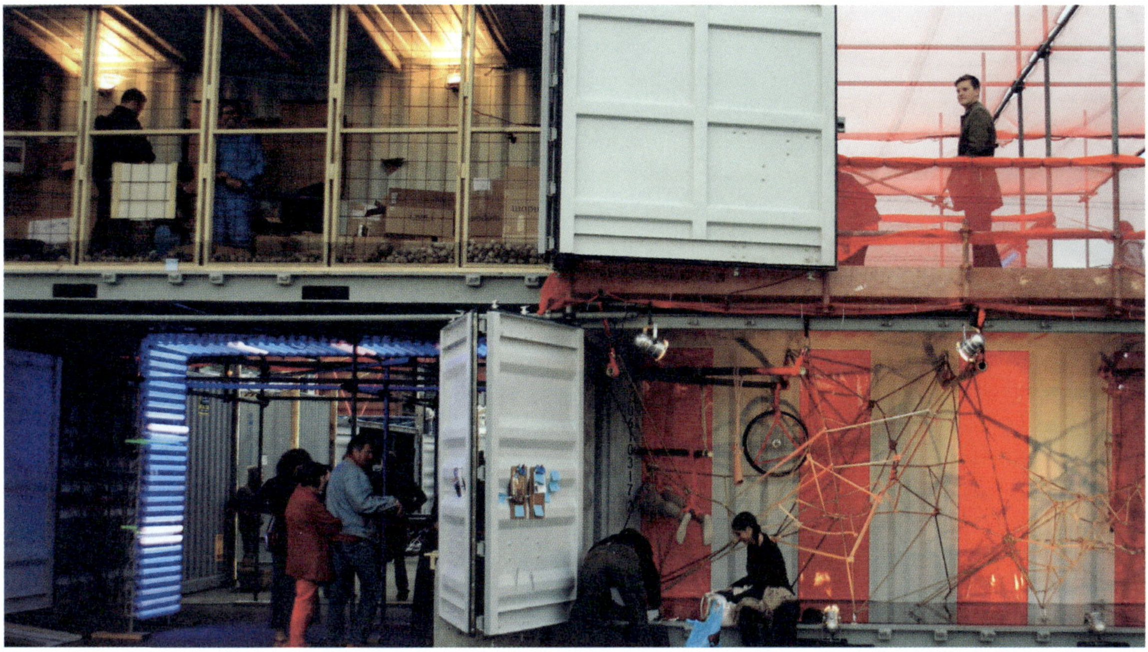

testing the percussive potential of the building's bricks and mortar with his hands, and Nastashia Simeona Apelu, who guarded the building's entrance by whirling and cracking a whip, an action that linked sound with physical harm.[33]

The Performance Arcade, Te Whanganui-a-Tara Wellington, 2014. Works pictured: *Carriage* by Mick Douglas (above left) and *Pharmakos* by Touch Compass with Suzanne Cowan (below right). *Courtesy Sam Trubridge and The Performance Arcade. Photo by Sam Trubridge*

DISCURSIVE LEVELS OF PERFORMATIVITY

In shifting focus to the discursive dimension of the performative, we can consider how exchanges between curators, gallery staff, artists and the public can take place on a granular scale. Application of the discursive here is intended to be inclusive of all manner of verbal and nonverbal forms of communication, from body language to writing and even to forms of care and hosting such as welcoming, cooking, cleaning and transportation. In this sense the discursive, as an element of the performative, could be considered to comprise the intimate levels of speech acts that inform the meaning-making mechanics of curating in support of performance art practitioners and/or audiences, particularly in collective forms of production.

A prime example of this level of interaction is *TEZA* (*Transitional Economic Zone of Aotearoa*) an offsite Letting Space project curated by Mark Amery and Sophie Jerram together with co-producer Helen Kirlew Smith, which has taken place in two locations: New Brighton in Ōtautahi in 2013 and Porirua in 2015. *TEZA* was conceived to initiate temporary exchanges between visiting artists and communities that might have lasting impact in a specific location. Visiting artists' engagement with local communities sought to create 'common ground between outsider and resident, new immigrant and established family, whilst recognising mana whenua and local knowledge' through various open-call invitations, public discussions and collaborative art projects.[34]

Other contributions supported within *TEZA*'s discursive framework included performances, such as Phil Dadson's *The Bicycle Choir* (2013) in which the public were invited to join him to reclaim the quake-damaged streets of Ōtautahi by creating a pedal-powered group and replacing the ubiquitous car 'vroom' with a polyvocal siren. Mark Harvey (Ngāti Raukawa ki te Tonga) produced *Productive Promises* (2013), a type of volunteer army who performed helpful actions, from removing rubbish to writing to local politicians, and more marginally productive actions such as 'Thank You protests', at the request of local residents. In Porirua Harvey took a similar approach in *Volunteer Refinery* (2015), in which he provided consultation to local community volunteer groups to help improve 'ecological productivity'. Also in Porirua, the Pasifika–Māori artist collective Kava Club held *Chop Suey Hui* (2015), a recurring programme of performances, discussions and presentations by Porirua-based artists.[35]

The 2014 Artspace exhibition *to and fro* similarly supported a freedom of performance practice. Curator Khye Hitchcock devised a framework that incorporated an initial three-day period of discussion and workshops between a group of nine artists, who then undertook a rota of residencies over six weeks. It was an opportunity for artists to have the freedom to create ad hoc and hold planned and unplanned performances.[36] Taking advantage of this free-flowing environment was Hana Pera Aoake with their work *Intended Consequences* (2014), in which they acted out a series of instructions written in pencil on the gallery wall that described common social behaviours that one might observe at a gallery opening; and indeed, these performances were no doubt already being enacted by their audience.[37]

There were also more clearly defined event-based performances, such as Darcell Apelu's *New Zealand Axemen's Association: Women's sub committee — president* (2014). Utilising her athletic expertise as a champion wood-chopper, Apelu decimated a log with an axe and sent chips of wood flying around the gallery.[38]

How to Live Together (2019) at AUT's ST PAUL St Gallery, curated by Balamohan Shingade, similarly created a porous framework that encouraged the artists to provide input into the curatorial framework. Shingade invited artists to contribute to a rhythmical mode of scheduling that enabled various contributions of different audiences, times, scales and locations both inside and outside the gallery.[39] Building on Shingade's dialogic framework, Chris Braddock initiated *Invitation to Dialogue* (2019), a weekly discussion group. Part installation, part performance art and collaborative design,[40] this temporary community of participants sought to establish commonality through non-hierarchical communication. In *Living with My Grandmother for One Year* (2019), James Tapsell-Kururangi (Ngāti Whakaue, Ngāti Mākino, Ngāti Pikiao, Te Whānau-a-Rakairoa, Ngāti Raukawa) took the opportunity to live in Rotorua in the home of his recently deceased grandmother, with the intention of reconnecting with her life and memory. After first engaging in a discussion with ST PAUL St Gallery staff and beginning a friendship with Tapsell-Kururangi, gallery visitors were invited to visit the home.[41]

PERFORMATIVITY OF THE EXPANDED FIELD

Many of the exhibitions discussed so far have also been produced with the awareness that an exhibition can operate beyond the gallery walls and the timeframes of conventional display practices. The understanding of the exhibition as an expanded field, encompassing everything from events and publications to alternative schools and radio broadcasts, has been well ensconced within contemporary curatorial discourse and practices. In Aotearoa, the explicit engagement with an expanded field of exhibition-making is often accompanied by or devised specifically for either sculpture and performance, or practices that are hard to distinguish between these disciplines. In such examples, curatorial projects explicitly attempt to reimagine how, where and when performance art might be engaged.

One example is One Day Sculpture (2008–09), which was born of Massey University's Litmus Research Initiative and later led by curators David Cross and Claire Doherty, along with seventeen other curators from around the country. One Day Sculpture was an ambitious collaborative project that involved twelve of Aotearoa's leading art organisations. Staged over twelve months across six locations, it commissioned twenty-one new works, each existing for a total duration of 24 hours.[42] This dispersed programme was intended to stretch the limits of place-based and event-based exhibitionary formats, in comparison to biennial-style mega-exhibitions and public sculpture exemplars such as Skulptur Projekte Münster.[43]

Despite its name emphasising 'sculpture', this expanded format created a time-critical and site-responsive context that naturally lent itself to commissioning performances as sculpture, and sculptures as performances — so much so that the series could have been titled 'One Day Performance'. In fact, to promote the concept of One Day Sculpture, Cross and Doherty restaged Roman Ondák's *Good Feelings in Good Times* (2003), in which a group of roving performers formed polite queues across Wellington city.

In terms of the commissions, there were many that engaged a performance art register. James Luna staged the day-long *Urban (Almost) Rituals* (2009), drawing on customary knowledge and life experiences as a Luiseño Native American with performance vignettes by local artists in Soundings Theatre in Te Papa. Bedwyr Williams parodied the quintessential *en plein air* painter in *Le 'Welsh' Man's 24hour* (2009), complete with beret, easel, palette and brush, in a comedic race against time to execute twenty-four landscape paintings at various locations across Wellington. Also racing throughout the city was a relay of runners ringing antique decommissioned ships' bells that were arranged along the forecast sea-level-rise mark, in Amy Howden-Chapman's *The Flood, My Chanting* (2008).[44] In *Intermission* (2009), staged in Ōpunake's historic Everybody's Theatre, Javier Téllez arranged for a lion to face off with a recording of the MGM production logo.

Beyond One Day Sculpture's expanded ambition and support of performance/sculptural practices, it arguably also imposed strict limitations on artists via Doherty's curatorial statement, which defined what would be accepted as a 'one day sculpture'.[45] The statement led to some charged conversations among the local suite of curators, artists and the curatorial directors, but resulted in a series that had both overarching coherence and considerable diversity in form, scale, weighting towards the role of the object, the role of the body/performer and the dynamics of context-specific investigations and responses.[46]

While One Day Sculpture is one of the most comprehensive projects to push the limits of the expanded field in Aotearoa's exhibition history, several smaller but no less significant curatorial projects predate and precede it. **The Picnic** (2000) is one such example. This collaborative project, organised by Caro McCaw and Blue Oyster, invited online and onsite audiences to visit a website or one of five locations throughout the country during their lunch break, to encounter and participate in a virtual exhibition.[47] Another relevant Blue Oyster exhibition was *Mobile* (2004), curated by Tessa Giblin, which consisted of intimate one-on-one performances accessed by dialling certain phone numbers.[48]

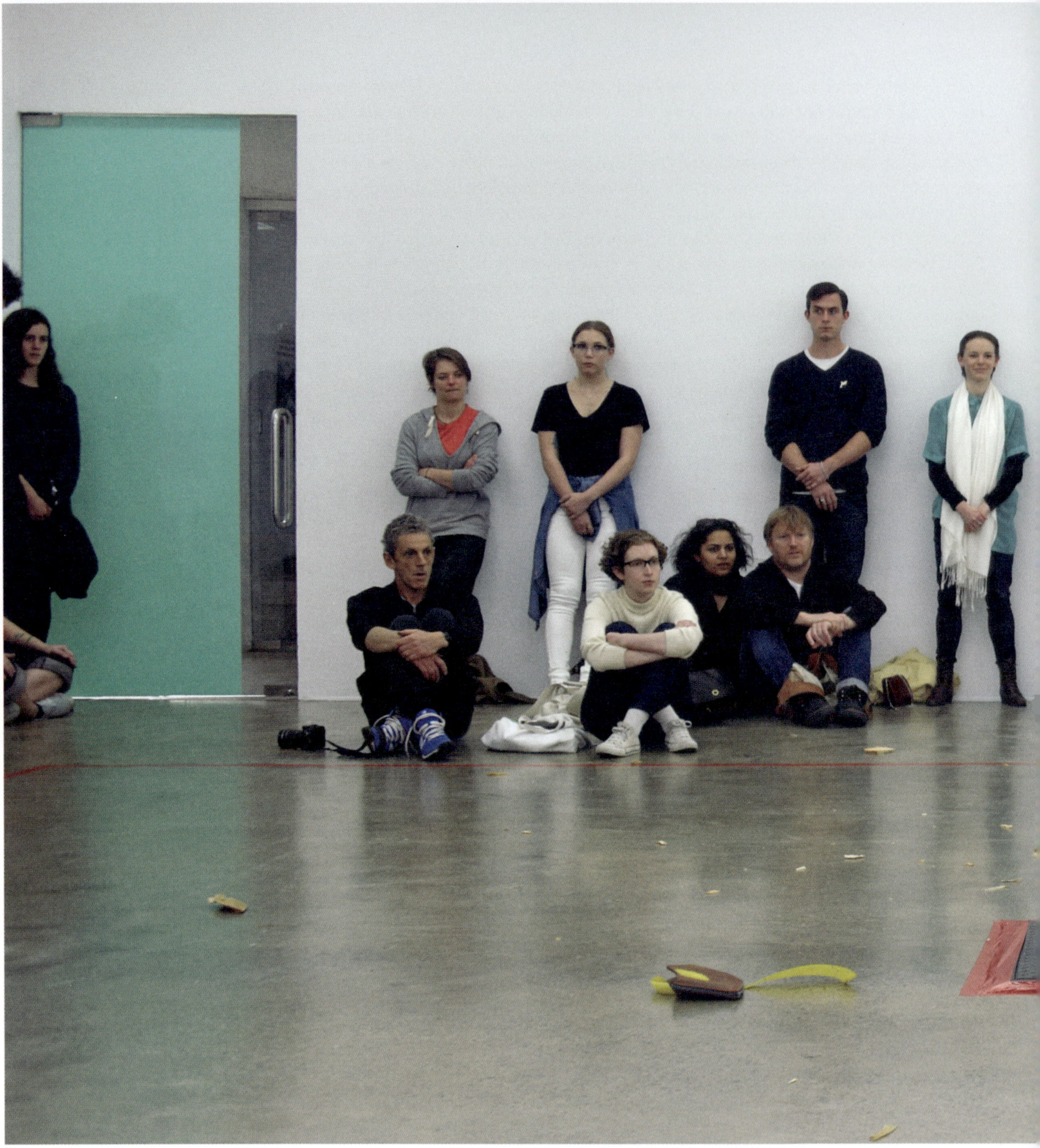

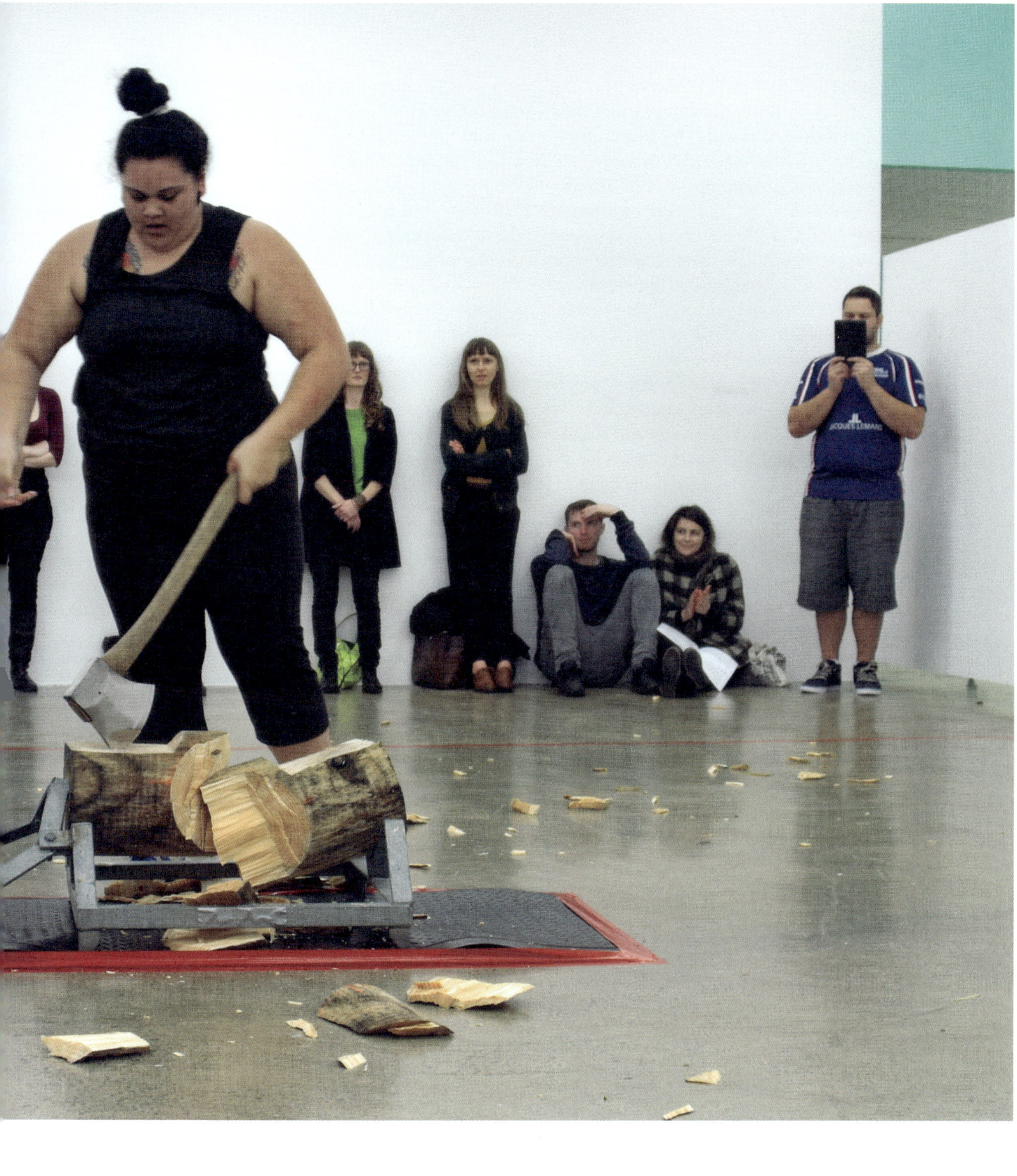

PREVIOUS: Darcell Apelu, *New Zealand Axemen's Association: Women's sub committee — president*, 2 August 2014, documentation of performance. *Courtesy Artspace Auckland. Photo by Peter Jennings*

Te Pātaka Toi Adam Art Gallery's *The Commons Project: Performance series in public/private space* (2011), curated by Laura Preston, involved performances that took place in a number of quasi-public locations/venues as a means to seek out or re-establish the 'commons' in the cityscape of Te Whanganui-a-Tara.[49] Harnessing the power of the commons was also a strategy in the 2020 *Artspace Queer Pavilion*, curated by Richard Orjis. Located in and around the Albert Park band rotunda in Tāmaki Makaurau (the site of Gay Day, Aotearoa's first public gay liberation/pride event), the *Artspace Queer Pavilion* sought to establish a 'drifting structure for art, performance and conversation'.[50]

Of course, we could include the influence of recurring exhibitions and programmes such as *Telecom Prospect/Prospect*,[51] the Auckland Triennial and SCAPE Public Art, for their propensity to operate in multiple locations, formats and durations. Yet the degree to which such biennial-style exhibitions engage the expanded field to support performance practices is hard to pry apart from their other function of creating a large-scale art spectacle. As has been debated since the rise of so-called 'biennialisation', such events arguably add to city or government agendas of commodifying place, adding to gentrification, providing a gravy train circuit for 'star curators', playing into the hand of the art market, and setting homogenised standards of practice to be replicated the world over.

That said, such a totalising critique in Aotearoa's small art system risks overlooking notable examples of performance practices that might not have occurred without the support or occasion of the exhibitions mentioned. *Telecom Prospect 2004*, for instance, enabled the second-only installation of Maddie Leach's rectangular ice rink on which visitors were invited to perform their skating abilities by negotiating the rink's purposely disruptive rectangular design. The 4th Auckland Triennial (2010) provided Tāmaki Makaurau audiences with the opportunity to experience works by performance artists Tino Sehgal and Shigeyuki Kihara. *SCAPE 7* (2013) took on the quake-wounded social and built environment of Ōtautahi with *Level Playing Field* — a type of sports tournament created by David Cross in which teams of players aimed to destabilise their competitors as they ran across an unstable inflatable structure.

Four of the twelve *SCAPE 7* projects had strong performance aspects: Maddie Leach and Jem Noble's *I Was Using Six Watts When You Received Me*, Zina Swanson's *Can Anybody Hear Me* and Phil Dadson's *Bodytok Quintet: The human instrument archive.*

RE-PRESENTATION AND RE-ENACTMENTS

Although this chapter has focused on the curatorial performativities that have evolved to support the creation of new performance works, another thread of re-presentation and re-enactment has also been instrumental in this history. This small but important thread of curating and exhibition-making is worth mentioning in terms of the way visibility and deeper discourse around performative practices (particularly of the post-object period of the 1970s and 1980s) developed. Three group exhibitions staged by major institutions are prominent: *Action Replay* (1998), *Intervention* (2000), and *Groundswell: Avant-garde Auckland 1971–79* (2018).[52]

Additionally, we note the focused concentration on works by influential artist/teacher Jim Allen, and how re-consideration of the *Contact* series[53] and live re-presentation of the works *Poetry for Chainsaws* and *News* (among others) have enabled multiple audiences to access these works, and been a catalyst for acquisitions bringing pieces of these projects into public collections.[54]

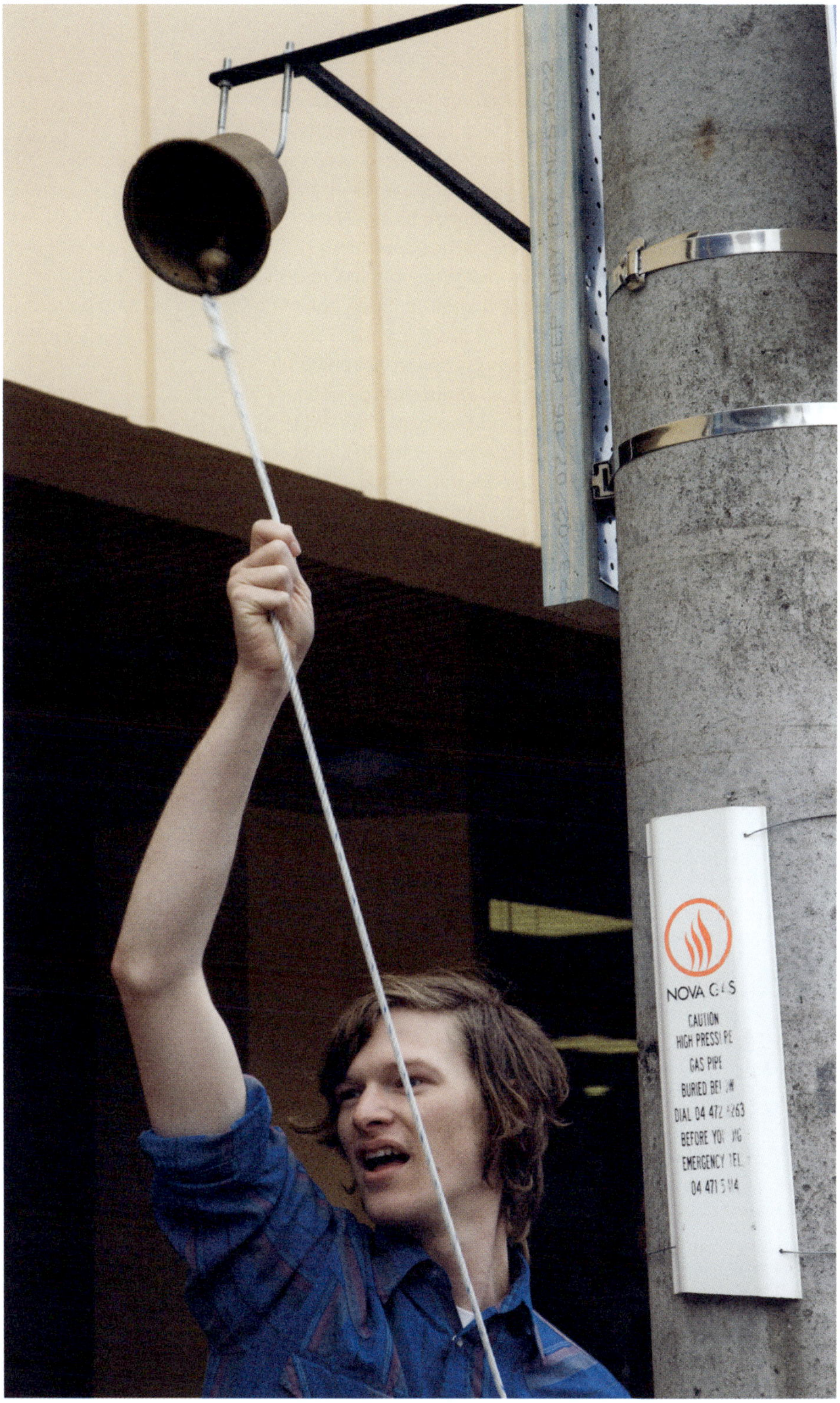

Amy Howden-Chapman, *The Flood, My Chanting*, 2008, performance curated by Heather Galbraith for One Day Sculpture, commissioned by City Gallery Wellington. *Courtesy Toi Rauwhārangi College of Creative Arts, Massey University. Photo by Steve Rowe*

CONCLUSION

The curatorial approaches noted within this selected history offer critical reflection on how curatorial and exhibition-making strategies, processes and collaborations have sought to foster and support performance art practices in Aotearoa over a fifty-year period. With such an expanse of time it is only possible to consider a sample of projects, and our attention has been on performance-focused and performance-inclusive group exhibitions in forty-seven of Aotearoa's publicly funded art organisations. We acknowledge the many innovative projects that have been instigated and delivered outside these parameters, and have sought to nod to specific artist-led projects and gallerist-supported projects where appropriate.

Contemporary performance art and the criticalities and context-specific awareness within programming and audience engagement strategies have become considerably more nuanced and comfortable with fluidity and flexibility. The curatorial commitment to the potency of performance art practices, by responding in kind through performative modes of curating and exhibition-making, has created an enduring field of practice over the last fifty years in Aotearoa — exploring the dynamics of body, space, time, and the socio-political, cultural and ecological connections and tensions of our age.

NOTES

1 Our definition of 'exhibition-making practitioners' is inclusive of all manner of workers, facilitators, organisers or contributors such as but not limited to: artists, curators, gallery staff, designers, preparators, writers and communities and/or their representatives.

2 Auckland Art Gallery Toi o Tāmaki; Te Pātaka Toi Adam Art Gallery; Aratoi Wairarapa Museum of Art and History; Artspace Aotearoa; Ashburton Art Gallery and Heritage Centre; Audio Foundation; Blue Oyster Art Project Space; Christchurch Art Gallery Te Puna o Waiwhetū; Circuit Artist Film and Video Aotearoa New Zealand; City Gallery Wellington Te Whare Toi; COCA, Centre of Contemporary Art Toi Moroki; Corbans Estate Art Centre; Dunedin Public Art Gallery; Enjoy Contemporary Art Space; Fresh Gallery Ōtara; Govett-Brewster Art Gallery, Len Lye Centre; Gus Fisher Gallery; Hastings City Art Gallery; He Waka Tuia Art + Museum; Ilam Campus Gallery; Letting Space; Litmus Research Initiative Massey University; Malcolm Smith Gallery; Māngere Arts Centre Ngā Tohu o Uenuku; MTG Hawke's Bay Tai Ahuriri; Ngā Taonga Sound & Vision; Papakura Art Gallery; Pātaka Art + Museum; Ramp Gallery; RM Gallery & Project Space; Rotorua Museum Te Whare Taonga o Te Arawa; AUT ST PAUL St Gallery; Tauranga Art Gallery Toi Tauranga; Tautai Contemporary Pacific Arts Trust; Te Manawa Museum of Art, Science and Heritage; Museum of New Zealand Te Papa Tongarewa; Te Tuhi; Te Uru Waitākere Contemporary Gallery; The Dowse Art Museum; The Engine Room; The Performance Arcade; The Physics Room; The Sarjeant Gallery Te Whare o Rehua Whanganui; The Suter Art Gallery Te Aratoi o Whakatū; Toi Pōneke Arts Centre; Waikato Museum Te Whare Taonga o Waikato.

3 These include projects such as: *Earthworks* (September 1971) and the resulting video work *'Earthworks' Represents a Temporary Instant in the Continuum of Universal Ebb and Flow* (1972); the establishment of the Wellington Artists Co-op by Ian Hunter (1978–80); Australia New Zealand Artists Encounter (ANZART) projects (1981–85), for which Ian Hunter was also a key driver; and the *F1 New Zealand Sculpture Project* (1982) including Ian Hunter with David Mealing, Stuart Griffiths, Barbara Strathdee, Mary-Louise Browne and Vivian Lynn, which was a five-week festival of installation, performance, seminars and video held at the Teal Lemonade Factory in Wellington. See Jennifer Hay, 'Trans-Marginal: New Zealand performance art 1970–1985', in *Intervention: Post object and performance art in New Zealand in 1970 and beyond* (Christchurch: Robert McDougall Art Gallery & Annex, 2000). There was also *Platforms* at Canterbury Society of Arts curated by Martin Mendelsberg, Rosemary Johnson and Neil Dawson, where Andrew Drummond's *Crucifixion* performance was staged — and led to the first performance to hit the headlines in Aotearoa.

4 Jennifer Hay, 'Trans-Marginal'.

5 Such as ANZART 1981–85, *Platforms* at the Canterbury Society of Arts, curated by Martin Mendelsberg, Rosemary Ford and Neil Dawson (where Andrew Drummond's *Crucifixion* performance was staged, leading to the first performance to hit the headlines in Aotearoa), and the Experimental Art Foundation (EAF), Adelaide, including many highly influential works by Jim Allen.

6 Claire Doherty, 'Performative Curating', in *Sculptural Projects Münster 07*, edited by Brigitte Franzen, Kasper König and Carina Plath, exhibition catalogue (Cologne: Verlag der Buchhandlung Walther König, 2007), 413–14; Katharina Schlieben, 'Curating Per-Form: Reflections on the Concept of the Performative' (Munich: Kunstverein München, 2002).

7 J. L. Austin, *How to Do Things with Words*, edited by J. O. Urmson and Marina Sbisà, 2nd edn (Cambridge, MA: Harvard University Press, 1975).

8 Judith Butler, 'Performative Acts and Gender Constitution: An essay in phenomenology and feminist

theory', *Theatre Journal* 40, no. 4 (1988): 519. https://doi.org/10.2307/3207893
9 Schlieben, 'Curating Per-Form', 1.
10 Ibid., 2.
11 Ibid..
12 Doherty, 'Performative Curating'; Schlieben, 'Curating Per-Form'.
13 Ibid.
14 Cerise L. Glenn, 'Activism or 'Slacktivism?': Digital media and organizing for social change', *Communication Teacher* 29, no. 2 (April 2015): 81–85. https://doi.org/10.1080/17404622.2014.1003310; Amber Kelly and Jessica Powell, 'Accomplices in the Academy in the Age of Black Lives Matter', *Journal of Critical Thought and Praxis* 6, no. 2 (April 2017): 42. www.iastatedigitalpress.com/jctp/article/id/551
15 Hay, 'Trans-Marginal', 12; Gray Nicol, 'From Project Programme No. 7: Gray Nicol', *Auckland City Art Gallery Quarterly* 64 (May 1977): 11–13.
16 Hay, 'Trans-Marginal', 12; Nicol, 'From Project Programme No. 7'.
17 Wystan Curnow, 'Project Programme 1975, nos. 1–6', *Auckland City Art Gallery Quarterly* 62–63 (December 1976): 15–22; Hay, 'Trans-Marginal', 12–13.
18 Bruce Barber, *On the Stocks: A catalogue complement/supplement to the performance 'STOCKS AND BONDS'* (Auckland: Auckland Art Gallery Toi o Tāmaki, 1975); Hay, 'Trans-Marginal'.
19 Curnow, 'Project Programme 1975, Nos. 1-6.'; David Mealing, *Jumble Sale/A Marketplace: Project Programme 1975 Auckland City Art Gallery* (Auckland: Auckland Art Gallery Toi o Tāmaki, 1975).
20 Andrew Drummond, *Tattoo Tapes* (Auckland: Auckland Art Gallery Toi o Tāmaki, 1978).
21 We note here that John Maynard was called an exhibition officer at this time as no curators existed.
22 Mark Amery, 'On the Bone', *Quote Unquote* 20 (January 1995), 6.
23 Tessa Laird, *Oestrogen Rising*, exhibition ephemera (Auckland: Artspace Aotearoa, 1996). While *Oestrogen Rising* was promoted as a 'feminist separatist' event, Laird recalls that this was, in the 1990s, understood with some degree of irony, and the event included a drag performance by Booby Tuesday. Email conversation with Tessa Laird, 20 February 2024.
24 Ibid.
25 *RELAY: Sound and Performance*, exhibition ephemera, photographs and meeting minutes (Auckland: Artspace Aotearoa, 1996). Publicity material found in the Artspace archive provides no reliable list of these 35 artists or those who curated/organised *RELAY*. The names mentioned in the publicity material are: Marcel Bear, Danny Butt, David Carman, Frances Chan, Marc Chesterman, Jasmine Cufford, Sean Curham, Phil Dadson, Cushla Donaldson, Mike Dunn, Tabatha Forbes, Bryce Galloway, Ross George, Tony Green, Peter Haeder, Michael Hodgson, John Kennedy, Sean Kerr, Peter Kirk, Tessa Laird, Kitt McGregor, Michael Morley, Julian Oliver, Leonie Oliver, Damian Sawyfr, Suzanne Styche, Guy Tradgold, Steve Veale, Megan Verelle, Clinton Williams and Greg Wood, as well as pseudonyms/collectives: STELARC, Gate, The Project and Sandoz Lab Technicians.
26 *RELAY: Sound and Performance.*
27 Biannual from 2006 to 2012 and annual from 2013 to 2016.
28 Descriptions of Enjoy's annual performance-specific programming (2001–10 and 2012–13) differed over time. For instance, they were originally titled 'Enjoy Performance Series', and later were contextualised in more subtle ways in relation to performance specificity. However, the annual occurrence indicates a deliberate programming strategy to reserve a space for performance practice within the annual programme, comparable to the *Blue Oyster Performance Series* and *Offstage*.
29 See Chapter 6 of this book for detailed discussion about sound art and sound venues in relation to performance art.
30 Ioana Gordon-Smith, 'Performing on the Border: A series of site-specific responses', in *More Than We Know* (Auckland: Tautai Contemporary Pacific Arts Trust, 2013), 15.
31 The design could be analysed as an infatuation with the supremacy of the ancient Roman empire recast through the values and aspirations of New Zealand's colonial modernity.
32 Gordon-Smith, 'Performing on the Border', 22; Rangituhia Hollis, 'The Other Side of Speaking', in *More Than We Know*, 8–10.
33 Gordon-Smith, 'Performing on the Border', 18.
34 Letting Space, 'The TEZA Concept', *TEZA 2015* (blog), 2015, https://teza.org.nz/the-teza-concept
35 Lana Lopesi, 'Response #2: Lana Lopesi — who is it for?', *TEZA 2015* (blog), 23 November 2015, https://teza.org.nz/2015/11/23/response-2-lana-lopesi
36 Victoria Wynne-Jones, 'In Response to the Exhibition: to and fro', Artspace Aotearoa/Rūma Pānui | Reading room, December 2014, https://artspace-aotearoa.nz/reading-room/in-response-to-the-exhibition-to-and-fro-organised-by-amelia-hitchcock-at-artspace-julyaugust-2014
37 Ibid.
38 Ibid.
39 Balamohan Shingade, 'How to Live Together', ST PAUL St Gallery — AUT — Past Exhibitions, 2019; 'How to Live Together | Exhibition Guide', ST PAUL St Gallery AUT, 2019, https://stpaulst.aut.ac.nz/exhibitions/past-exhibitions/2019/how-to-live-together
40 Christopher Braddock, 'Invitation to Dialogue', 2019.
41 Balamohan Shingade, 'On TK Returning to Rotorua', *Drain* 17, no. 1 (Social/Affects) (2021), http://drainmag.com/on-tk-returning-to-rotorua
42 David Cross and Claire Doherty, 'One Day Sculpture: A curatorial overview', in *One Day Sculpture*, edited by David Cross and Claire Doherty (Bielefeld: Kerber Verlag, 2009), 7–16.
43 Ibid., 8.
44 The artist has since updated the title of this work to *You Can't Unring a Bell/The Flood, My Chanting*. See www.amyhowdenchapman.com/node/23
45 Cross and Doherty, 'One Day Sculpture', 8; Claire Doherty, 'Curatorial Statement'.
46 Cross and Doherty, 'One Day Sculpture', 8.
47 *'Past Exhibition: *The Picnic*'*, Blue Oyster Art Project Space.
48 'Mobile: Curated by Tessa Giblin', Blue Oyster Art Project Space, 2004.
49 Laura Preston, 'The Commons Project: Performance series in public/private space', Te Pātaka Toi Adam Art Gallery, 2011, https://www.adamartgallery.org.nz/past-exhibitions/the-commons-project
50 Artspace Aotearoa/Kaupapa Toi | Programme, 'Queer Pavilion 2020', https://artspace-aotearoa.nz/exhibitions/queer-pavilion
51 Titled *Telecom Prospect* in 2001 and 2004, then just *Prospect* in 2007 and 2012.
52 *Action Replay*, a series of five exhibitions critically re-evaluating a lost chapter in New Zealand art history, post-object art of the 1970s. Staged at Artspace, Govett-Brewster Art Gallery and Auckland Art Gallery in 1998 and curated by Christina Barton, Wystan Curnow, John

Hurrell and Robert Leonard; *Groundswell*, curated by Natasha Conland at Auckland Art Gallery Toi o Tāmaki.

53 See Chapter 3 of this volume, by Jim Allen and James Charlton, which focuses on the re-enactments of Allen's *Contact* from 1974.

54 Including projects and publications mounted by Leonhard Emmerling, Christina Barton, and acquisitions of reconstructions of sculptural works by the Museum of New Zealand Te Papa Tongarewa, and photographic documentation and archival material acquired by Auckland Art Gallery Toi o Tāmaki. The re-staging of Jim Allen's work supported by curator Charlotte Huddelston and gallerist Michael Lett is also a notable omission worthy of further discussion.

REFERENCES

Amery, Mark. 'On the Bone'. *Quote Unquote* 20 (January 1995).

Artspace Aotearoa/Kaupapa Toi | Programme. 'Queer Pavilion 2020'. https://artspace-aotearoa.nz/exhibitions/queer-pavilion

Austin, J. L. *How to Do Things with Words*, edited by J. O. Urmson and Marina Sbisà, 2nd edn. Cambridge, MA: Harvard University Press, 1975.

Balzer, David. *Curationism: How curating took over the art world and everything else*. Toronto: Coach House Books, 2014.

Barber, Bruce. *On the Stocks: A catalogue complement/supplement to the performance 'STOCKS AND BONDS'*. Auckland: Auckland Art Gallery Toi o Tamaki, 1975. https://cdn.aucklandunlimited.com/artgallery/assets/media/1975-project-programme-2-bruce-barber-catalogue.pdf

Bell, Andrea. 'Passionate Instincts'. In *A Year of Conscious Practice*. Dunedin/Christchurch: The Physics Room and Blue Oyster Art Project Space, 2016. https://ayearofconsciouspractice.com/texts/passionate-instincts

Blue Oyster Art Project Space. 'Mobile: Curated by Tessa Giblin'. 2004. https://web.archive.org/web/20220208080500/http://www.blueoyster.org.nz/exhibitions/curated-by-tessa-giblin

Braddock, Christopher. 'Invitation to Dialogue'. 2019. www.christopherbraddock.com/artworks/invitation-to-dialogue

Butler, Judith. 'Performative Acts and Gender Constitution: An essay in phenomenology and feminist theory'. *Theatre Journal* 40, no. 4 (1988): 519–31. https://doi.org/10.2307/3207893

Butt, Danny. 'The Curatorial as a Liveable Subject Position: Hospitality and differential consciousness'. In *A Year of Conscious Practice*. Dunedin/Christchurch: The Physics Room and Blue Oyster Art Project Space, 2016. https://ayearofconsciouspractice.com/texts/curatorial-hospitality-and-differential-consciousness

Charlesworth, J. J. 'Curating Doubt'. In *Issues in Curating Contemporary Art and Performance*, edited by Judith Rugg and Michele Sedgwick, 91–99. Bristol: Intellect Books, 2007.

Cross, David and Claire Doherty. 'One Day Sculpture: A curatorial overview'. In *One Day Sculpture*, edited by David Cross and Claire Doherty, 7–16. Bielefeld: Kerber Verlag, 2009.

Curnow, Wystan. 'Project Programme 1975, nos. 1–6'. *Auckland City Art Gallery Quarterly* 62–63 (December 1976): 15–22.

Doherty, Claire. 'Performative Curating'. In *Sculptural Projects Münster 07*, edited by Brigitte Franzen, Kasper König and Carina Plath, 413–14. Cologne: Verlag der Buchhandlung Walther König, 2007.

——— 'Curatorial Statement'. ONE DAY SCULPTURE, 2008. https://ndhadeliver.natlib.govt.nz/webarchive/20090211193009/http://www.onedaysculpture.org.nz/ODS_programme_cstatement.html

Drummond, Andrew. *Tattoo Tapes*. Auckland Art Gallery Toi o Tamaki, 1978. www.aucklandartgallery.com/page/project-programme-14-andrew-drummond?q=%2Fpage%2Fproject-programme-14-andrew-drummond

D'Souza, Aruna. *Whitewalling: Art, race & protest in 3 acts*. New York: Badlands Unlimited, 2018.

Esche, Charles. 'Coda: The curatorial'. In *The Curatorial: A philosophy of curating*, edited by Jean-Paul Martinon, 241–44. London, New York: Bloomsbury Academic, 2013.

Gentles, Tim. 'The (Old) New Spirit of Curating and Myths of Nomadism'. In *A Year of Conscious Practice*. Dunedin and Christchurch: The Physics Room and Blue Oyster Art Project Space, 2016. https://ayearofconsciouspractice.com/texts/curatorial-hospitality-and-differential-consciousness

Glenn, Cerise L. 'Activism or 'Slacktivism?': Digital media and organizing for social change'. *Communication Teacher* 29, no. 2 (April 2015): 81–85. https://doi.org/10.1080/17404622.2014.1003310

Gordon-Smith, Ioana. 'Performing on the Border: A series of site-specific responses'. In *More Than We Know*, 15–24. Auckland: Tautai Contemporary Pacific Arts Trust, 2013. https://issuu.com/tautaipacificartstrust/docs/more_than_we_know

Hay, Jennifer. 'Trans-Marginal: New Zealand performance art 1970–1985'. In *Intervention: Post object and performance art in New Zealand in 1970 and beyond*, 5–25. Christchurch: Robert McDougall Art Gallery & Annex, 2000. https://christchurchartgallery.org.nz/media/uploads/2016_09/Intervention2.pdf

Hollis, Rangituhia. 'The Other Side of Speaking'. In *More Than We Know*, 3–12. Auckland: Tautai Contemporary Pacific Arts Trust, 2013. https://issuu.com/tautaipacificartstrust/docs/more_than_we_know

Jones, Amelia. *Body Art/Performing the Subject*. Minneapolis: University of Minnesota Press, 1998.

——— '"Presence" in Absentia: Experiencing performance as documentation'. *Art Journal* 56, no. 4 (1997): 11–18. https://doi.org/10.2307/777715

Kelly, Amber and Jessica Powell. 'Accomplices in the Academy in the Age of Black Lives Matter'. *Journal of Critical Thought and Praxis* 6, no. 2 (April 2017). www.iastatedigitalpress.com/jctp/article/id/551

Krieger, William. 'Martin Kippenberger: MOMAS-Museum of Modern Art Syros'. In *The Artist as Curator: An anthology*, edited by Elena Filipovic, 247–58. Milan/London: Mousse Publishing and Koenig Books, 2017.

Laird, Tessa. *Oestrogen Rising*. Exhibition ephemera. Auckland: Artspace Aotearoa, 1996.

Letting Space. 'The TEZA Concept'. *TEZA 2015* (blog), 2015. https://teza.org.nz/the-teza-concept

Lopesi, Lana. 'Response #2: Lana Lopesi — who is it for?'. *TEZA 2015* (blog), 23 November 2015. https://teza.org.nz/2015/11/23/response-2-lana-lopesi

Martinon, Jean-Paul. *Curating As Ethics (Thinking Theory)*. Minneapolis: University of Minnesota Press, 2020.

Mealing, David. *Jumble Sale/A Marketplace: Project Programme 1975 Auckland City Art Gallery*. Auckland: Auckland Art Gallery Toi o Tāmaki, 1975. www.aucklandartgallery.com/page/project-programme-6-david-mealing?q=%2Fpage%2Fproject-programme-6-david-mealing

Moon, Je Yun. 'Curatorial Research as the Practice of Commoning'. In *Institution as Praxis — New Curatorial Directions for Collaborative Research*, edited by Bill

Balaskas and Carolina Rito, 32–42. Berlin: Sternberg Press, 2020.
Nicol, Gray. 'From Project Programme No. 7: Gray Nicol'. *Auckland City Art Gallery Quarterly* 64 (May 1977): 11–13.
O'Neill, Paul. *The Culture of Curating and the Curating of Culture(s)*. Cambridge, MA; London: The MIT Press, 2016.
'*Past Exhibition: *The Picnic**'. Blue Oyster Art Project Space. https://blueoyster.org.nz/exhibitions/the-picnic
Phillips, Bruce E. 'A Contextual Tightrope'. *EyeContact*, 23 March 2018. https://bruceephillips.com/writing/performancearcade
Preston, Laura. 'The Commons Project: Performance series in public/private space'. Te Pātaka Toi Adam Art Gallery, 2011. www.adamartgallery.org.nz/past-exhibitions/the-commons-project
Reilly, Maura. *Curatorial Activism: Towards an ethics of curating*. London: Thames & Hudson, 2018.
RELAY: Sound and Performance. Exhibition ephemera. Auckland: Artspace Aotearoa, 1996.
Rendell, Jane. 'Space, Place and Site in Critical Spatial Arts Practice'. In *The Practice of Public Art*, edited by Cameron Cartiere and Shelly Willis, 33–55. New York: Routledge, 2008.
Rogoff, Irit. 'The Expanded Field'. In *The Curatorial: A philosophy of curating*, edited by Jean-Paul Martinon, 41–48. London/New York: Bloomsbury Academic, 2013.
Schlieben, Katharina. 'Curating Per-Form: Reflections on the concept of the performative'. Munich: Kunstverein München, 2002. Web archived link: http://web.archive.org/web/20070810031230/http:/www.kunstverein-muenchen.de/03_ueberlegungen_considerations/en_performative_curating.pdf. Original link accessed 9 July 2009.
Sheikh, Simon. 'Exhibition-Making and Political Imaginary: On modalities and potentialities of curatorial practice'. PhD thesis, Lund University, 2012. http://lup.lub.lu.se/record/2520477
——— 'Towards the Exhibition as Research'. In *Curating Research*, edited by Paul O'Neill and Mick Wilson. London/Amsterdam: Open Editions and de Appel Arts Centre, 2015.
Shingade, Balamohan. 'How to Live Together'. ST PAUL St Gallery — AUT — Past Exhibitions, 2019. https://stpaulst.aut.ac.nz/exhibitions/past-exhibitions/2019/how-to-live-together
——— 'A Resource for How to Live Together'. ST PAUL St Gallery AUT, 2019. https://stpaulst.aut.ac.nz/__data/assets/pdf_file/0014/331601/Resource.pdf
——— 'How to Live Together | Exhibition Guide'. ST PAUL St Gallery AUT, 2019. https://stpaulst.aut.ac.nz/__data/assets/pdf_file/0004/298903/Exhibition-Guide-v1.2.pdf
——— 'On TK Returning to Rotorua'. *Drain* 17, no. 1, 'Social/Affects' (2021). http://drainmag.com/on-tk-returning-to-rotorua
Simon, Joshua.'The Way Things Are Organized: The mesoscopic, the metastable, "The Curatorial"'. In *Curating After the Global: Roadmaps for the present*, edited by Paul O'Neill, Simon Sheikh, Lucy Steeds and Mick Wilson, 157–72. New York: MIT Press, 2019.
Smith, Terry. 'Mapping the Contexts of Contemporary Curating: The visual arts exhibitionary complex'. *Journal of Curatorial Studies* 6, no. 2 (October 2017): 170–80. https://doi.org/10.1386/jcs.6.2.170_1
——— *Thinking Contemporary Curating*, edited by Kate Fowle. New York: Independent Curators International, 2012.
Velázquez, Yaiza María Hernández. 'Imagining Curatorial Practice after 1972'. In *Curating After the Global: Roadmaps for the present*, 255–74. New York: MIT Press, 2019.
Vidokle, Anton. 'Art Without Artists?'. *e-flux Journal* 16 (May 2010). www.e-flux.com/journal/16/61285/art-without-artists
Wynne-Jones, Victoria. 'In Response to the Exhibition: To and fro'. Artspace Aotearoa/Rūma Pānui | Reading room, December 2014. https://artspace-aotearoa.nz/reading-room/in-response-to-the-exhibition-to-and-fro-organised-by-amelia-hitchcock-at-artspace-julyaugust-2014
Žerovc, Beti. *When Attitudes Become the Norm: The contemporary curator and institutional art*. Iza Editions. Berlin: AC Books, 2017.

8

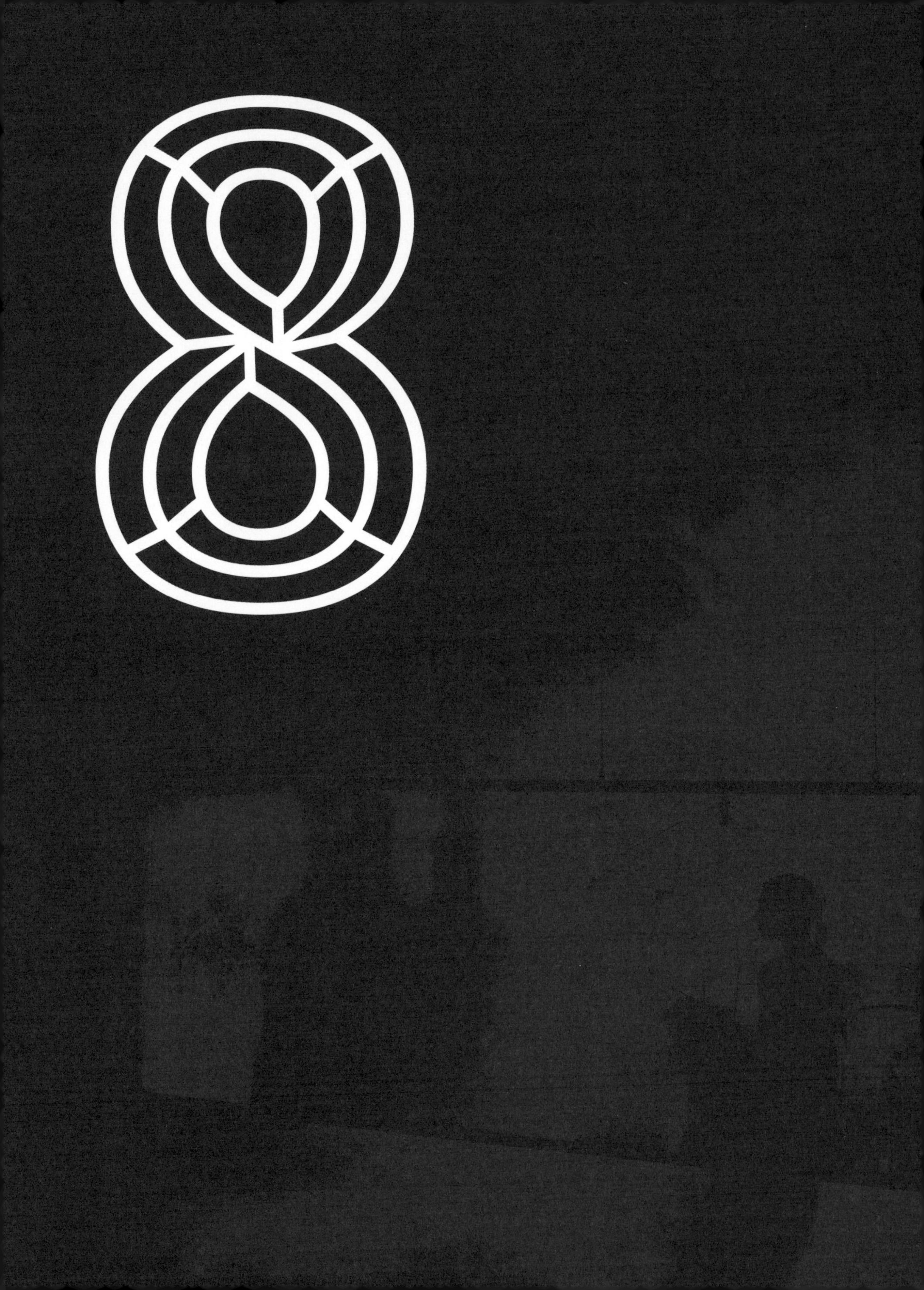

MĀTAURANGA MĀORI AND WHAKAPAPA OF CHANGE IN PERFORMANCE ART OF AOTEAROA

Layne Waerea[1]

This chapter operates on two levels in relationship to a history of Māori performance and its extended connection to contemporary performance art. First, I argue that performances created by Māori artists acknowledge origins distinct from the prevailing Euro-American performance art categorisations. I recognise that the role of Māori performance and the ways in which performance is sometimes linked with protest have arisen from 'a Māori cultural continuum of ideas, philosophy and experience of the world that is Māori'.[2]

This leads me to consider the ways in which the role of Māori cultural traditions and tikanga surrounding performance have been explored and adapted through contemporary Māori performance. I discuss performance artists, such as Rachael Rakena, who draw inspiration from the whakapapa or lineage of kapa haka dance performance and storytelling within a te ao Māori worldview.

Second, in attempting to map out these whakapapa of performance, I encounter a strongly transdisciplinary approach that combines aspects of performance art, theatre and dance, as well as sound and projected video installation. At times, this challenges distinctions between the performing arts and the genre of (visual arts) performance art. Many Māori performance artists are represented in other chapters of this volume, but this chapter prioritises these transdisciplinary attitudes. For example, dancer and choreographer Moana Nepia's performances and installations, which deploy video projections, explore iwi-centric interpretations of Te Kore — a key element of creation narratives within te ao Māori — both as a 'void' or 'darkness' and as a space of creative potentiality.

It is characteristic of this kōrero to consider the nature of traditional performance and its transformation into contemporary art while also exploring the nature of transdisciplinary performance. The artists featured in this chapter include Rachael Rakena, Louise Pōtiki Bryant, Moana Nepia, Shannon Te Ao, Charles Koroneho, and the collaborative work of Bianca Hyslop, Rowan Pierce and Tūī Matira Ransfield. In each case, I prioritise a discussion of what it means to perform as Māori in relation to Indigenous knowledge and notions such as te taiao and takiwā. In addressing these, I explore how performance art has been a vehicle for redefining the parameters of how customary practices of mātauranga Māori, or Māori knowledge, may be interpreted.

MĀTAURANGA MĀORI

Mātauranga Māori can be described as 'the explanation of human behaviour that is based upon traditional concepts handed down through the generations'.[3] Prominent Māori leader, anthropologist and artist Hirini Moko Mead believes a Māori art form 'must be seen to have arisen out of a Māori cultural continuum'.[4] Responding to this idea of continuous cultural whakapapa, Te Ahukaramū Charles Royal extends earlier definitions of mātauranga Māori by imagining this continuum as ever-evolving and singles out 'the creative potential paradigm', in which new creative potential in te ao Māori requires looking at and learning from the past 'to be inspired for new thinking to be born'.[5]

Integral to mātauranga Māori is the role of oral narrative and performance traditions, which often involve exploration of whakapapa: a key process for Māori artists in determining how creative potential builds on the past but also adapts to the present. Those oral and performing narratives for the artists featured in this chapter include haka, pūrākau, and the forces of ancestral presence in Te Kore as the primordial void. Additionally, I explore waiata and mōteatea, and observe the rituals of 'pure', a healing process aimed at releasing individuals from dangerous spells or restoring their health.

These customary practices are crucial for Māori who seek to create and convey meaning about themselves, represent their own worldview, and establish their place within the world. The practices help to shape a current and contemporary identity and belonging for Māori people, and inform and are present in the artworks in this chapter. In many of the examples that follow, the place of performance — be it gallery, theatre, warehouse or transformed through video — becomes a marae, a sacred meeting place where we encounter tīpuna.

A WHAKAPAPA OF CHANGE

Exploring the role of kaupapa Māori and mātauranga Māori within the contexts of the art world and academia necessarily involves discussions of whakapapa, a key process for Māori in determining how creative potential builds on the past but also adapts to the present. Ngāti Porou statesman and politician Apirana Ngata described whakapapa as a layering of one element upon another: new layers of interpretation are laid over original ideas to shape wisdom as a cumulative and layered concept. This alternative genealogical paradigm privileges a Māori worldview over Western frameworks.[6] Further, as argued by artist Moana Nepia, whakapapa can be used to analyse various forms of art, providing sensory avenues for knowledge creation and understanding, particularly in the context of performance, performance art, video and installation art.[7]

In considering a whakapapa of change that has evolved in contemporary Māori performance art practices, it is worth considering *A Whakapapa of Tradition* (2016) by art historian Ngarino Ellis (Ngāpuhi, Ngāti Porou), who discusses the role of tradition in Māori culture with a focus on transformations in Māori art and architecture from 1830 to 1930 in Aotearoa New Zealand.[8] Ellis describes how the prevailing art forms of waka taua, pātaka and whare rangatira were substituted with whare karakia, whare whakairo and wharekai over this time, and considers the reasons and mechanisms behind these profound shifts, with particular emphasis on the Iwirākau school of carving, located in the Waiapu Valley on the east coast of the North Island.

The concept of 'tradition' in Māori culture is closely linked to tikanga, which signifies what is just, fair, right or correct. Tikanga plays a significant role in Māori society, guiding moral behaviour and environmental practices such as the protection of and responsibility for natural resources.[9] Hirini Moko Mead, in his book *Tikanga Māori*, describes tikanga as a ritually correct set of beliefs and practices established over time that provides a framework for behaviour and understanding, and ensures predictability in various activities.[10] He refers to Mason Durie, who highlights the dynamic nature of tikanga, emphasising that it is shaped by consensus, tribal precedent and evolving circumstances.[11]

In the context of Māori art, there has been limited exploration of what tradition truly means. Ellis suggests that terms such as 'traditional' and 'contemporary' need to be treated with care when writing about Māori art, and argues that tradition evolves over time through a combination of innovation and repetition.[12] She refers to artist Robert Jahnke's (Ngāti Porou) description of tradition as 'customary', and his use of the term 'trans-customary', designed to create space for artists drawing on tradition while addressing current issues such as land rights or the environment.

Jahnke adopts this term to avoid an artificial dichotomy between the terms 'traditional' and 'contemporary' because, he argues, traditional art might also be created today, and the use of the term 'contemporary Māori art' participates in a sometimes elitist and hierarchical endeavour in being deemed more innovative.[13]

Ellis and Jahnke refer to the artwork of Cliff Whiting (Te Whānau-ā-Apanui) in the context of thinking through the term 'trans-customary'. Whiting's involvement in the South Pacific Festival of the Arts, held in Rotorua in March 1976, has been discussed by art historian Christina Barton, who notes that the festival was the first context in which Whiting's 7.6-metre-long mural *Te Wehenga a Rangi raua ko Papa* (1969–74) was presented. As Barton points out, Whiting believed his depiction of the pūrākau about the beginning of Māoridom with the separation of Rangi and Papa within Māori cosmology was 'the first major expression of a traditional story in new materials and forms'. The mural combined native timbers and fibres with synthetic board and acrylic paint. She notes: 'Whiting importantly saw this not as Western art made by Māori but an adaptation and development of Māori art.'[14]

Te Wehenga a Rangi raua ko Papa was presented as part of Ngā Puna Waihanga, a gathering of Māori arts practitioners that began in 1973 with the inaugural hui of the Māori Artists and Writers Society, convened by poet Hone Tūwhare (Ngāpuhi) at Tūkākī wharenui at Te Kaha in the Eastern Bay of Plenty.[15] With prominent Māori artist Para Matchitt as president, this annual hui explored often ground-breaking work of Māori visual, performing and literary artists within an inclusive, affirming cultural environment.[16]

More than anything, these discussions about relationships between traditional and contemporary or trans-customary arts and design hinge on the perceived problems associated with change. In discussing the historical experience of Māori peoples in the early nineteenth century, Ellis refers to Mason Durie's conviction that, although there have been consistent core beliefs about reality and life, the expression of Māori culture has been subject to change, making change the norm.

Hirini Moko Mead further highlights the deliberate and purposeful changes in Māori architecture and art, emphasising the significant role played by Māori artists in introducing new technologies and inventive combinations of traditional art elements, and the positive reception of these. This tradition of innovative problem-solving has been a defining feature of Māori art over time. Upon their arrival in Aotearoa from the Pacific, early Māori creatively addressed practical challenges such as food storage in a colder climate (resulting in the pātaka), and symbolic issues such as the visual representation of land guardianship (resulting in pou rāhui).[17]

With reference to American cultural critic James Clifford, Ellis emphasises that cultural forms are inherently dynamic and subject to constant and sometimes radical change, requiring communities to adapt and draw from their past while persuading both insiders and outsiders to acknowledge communal developments. As Ellis concludes, a primary concern was the survival and preservation of Māori culture amid changing times.

**

Perhaps Jahnke's term 'trans-customary' can be applied here to performance art. From the 1990s there are clear examples of Māori artists developing traditional design into the arenas of digital installation and performance. For example, Lisa Reihana produced a thirty-six-channel video interpretation of the Pacific Sisters' *Ina and Tuna* in 1995 for *Interdigitate 95* as part of *FILMFEAST 95* at the Aotea Centre's Herald Theatre in Tāmaki Makaurau Auckland, a programme founded by artist Phil Dadson as part of the Elam School of Fine Arts Intermedia programme (1991–2007). Reihana wove digital imagery of a coiling eel and a rainstorm throughout a stacked wall of thirty-six video screens.

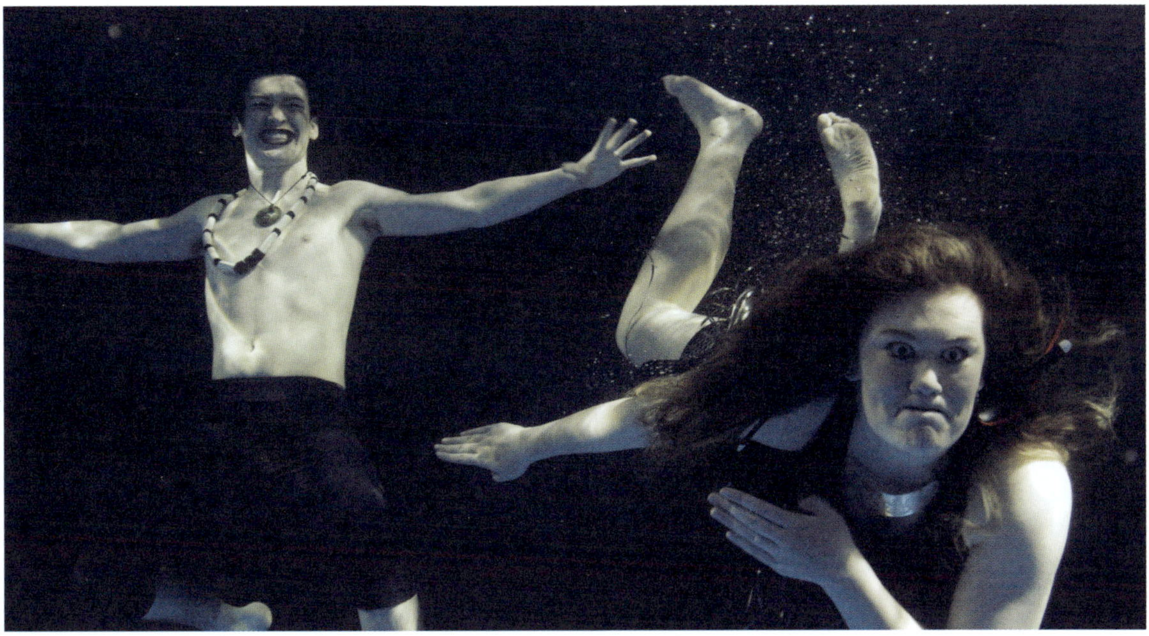

As Wendy Vaigro describes, 'Lisa Reihana's videowall programming demanded a complicated synchronising of two tapes to join the eel's head and body', combined with a 'tropical rainstorm, flickering lights patterning the screens [and] tapa patterns [as] pure optical patterns, inviting the stare'.[18] Vaigro's account in *Art New Zealand* described how the Pacific Sisters (Ani O'Neill, Rosanna Brown and Fiona Wall) performed a Cook Islands version of the traditional Pacific legend *Ina and Tuna*, which tells the story of the origins of the coconut palm, in front of the thirty-six-channel video wall.

Reihana's early digital artwork combined with Pacific Sisters' performances operated as iterations that combined elements of traditional costumes, storytelling and music in extremely contemporary or trans-customary ways.[19] Royal's extension of earlier definitions of mātauranga Māori as a continuum is made manifest in their transdisciplinary combination of theatre, performance and digital video installation.

Rachael Rakena (Ngāi Tahu, Ngāpuhi, Pākehā), *Ko te wai he wai ora*, 2021, film still, sixteen-channel film. Collaborating creatives: Paulette Tamati-Elliffe (Kāi Te Pahi, Kāi Te Ruahikihiki [Ōtākou], Te Ātiawa, Ngāti Mutunga) and whānau, Komene Cassidy (Ngāpuhi, Ngāi Takoto), Rachael Rakena, Michael Bridgman (Tonga, Pākehā), Laughton Kora (Ngāi Tūhoe, Ngāti Pūkeko, Ngāti Awa), Iain Frengley, Ross Hemera (Waitaha, Ngāti Māmoe, Ngāi Tahu), Mara TK (Ngāi Tahu, Ngāti Kahungunu, Tainui), Amber Bridgman (Kāi Tahu, Kāti Mamoe, Waitaha, Rabuvai) and He Waka Kōtuia. *Courtesy the artists*

KO TE WAI HE WAI ORA

Conceived and directed by Rachael Rakena (Kai Tahu, Ngāpuhi), *Ko te wai he wai ora* (2021) is a performance relayed to a video installation consisting of sixteen large, connected screens, which offer a watery panoramic occasionally adorned with a wall pattern reminiscent of fragmented koru spiral stems. Collaboratively produced by a group of ten individuals led by Rakena, *Ko te wai he wai ora* is a profound contemplation of the deterioration of water bodies and wetlands and provokes reflection on the urgent need for change.[20]

Rakena creates an immersive and collaborative fusion of performance and video art influenced by Māori tikanga and values. With a heritage that combines Māori and Pākehā roots, she draws inspiration from the historical narratives of both her tribal affiliations and her European ancestry. Her work has been installed in various locations throughout Aotearoa, from marae to art galleries, and revolves around the idea of a space that exists between fluidity, immersion and continuity within a Māori framework.

Rakena's practice is influenced by the whakapapa of kapa haka performance and pūrākau. As noted by Royal, as a precursor to the modern day kapa haka — where 'kapa' means to stand in a row and 'haka' means to dance — whare tapere performances were conducted by troupes of men and women who visited neighbouring iwi or hapū to dance, perform songs and tell stories to their audience.[21] Perhaps Rakena's collaboratively produced project reflects these whare tapere performances in a spirit of whānau participation that plays out across her digital screens.

Water is a consistent feature in Rakena's work, symbolising the tribal space of Ngāi Tahu and serving as a metaphorical and protective medium for her reinterpretation and reimagining of Ngāi Tahu culture.[22] At the beginning of *Ko te wai he wai ora*, an awe-inspiring aerial perspective unveils a sprawling riverscape, the flow of water resembling a sinuous taniwha.

After experiencing the artwork on the 'Big Wall' of the mezzanine of Dunedin Public Art Gallery, poet and art writer David Eggleton described how this captivating imagery unfolded gracefully across the screens, accompanied by a mournful electronic soundtrack and eliciting a sense of sorrowful reflection.[23] Farmland emerges beyond the river's willow trees, suggesting the influence of agricultural run-off and the way once-thriving wetlands have been supplanted by industrial-scale dairy farming.[24]

Next, the video transports viewers into the depths of dark water, where the narrative unfurls and a burst of vibrant kapa haka performance of a pātere abruptly replaces the previous soundtrack. The water becomes animated with submerged human figures in customary costume, looming and gesturing, their legs and hands propelling them through the wai. Their faces convey a palpable sense of urgency, as if they are swimming for their lives in a spirit of kapa haka defiance and a deep connection to the land. This artistic protest vigorously proclaims the precarious balance of the environment, and acts as a resounding political voice that amplifies the pressing necessity for change.[25]

Ko te wai he wai ora was part of the larger group exhibition *Paemanu: Tauraka Toi — A Landing Place*, held at Dunedin Public Art Gallery from 2021 to 2022. Its forty-eight exhibiting artists all had local iwi/Ngāi Tahu whakapapa or had contributed under Ngāi Tahu guidance. Ōtepoti Dunedin was home to the tangata whenua Ōtākou Kāi Tahu before they were gradually excluded from the area after the arrival of British settlers. References to this early history of interaction and subsequent marginalisation, together with an ongoing call-out to Māoritanga's holistic relationship with the environment, underpinned this exhibition, and is especially important at a time when Indigenous thinking is beginning to offer alternative ways to heal the planet.[26]

TA TAKI O TE UA

Ngāi Tahu artist and choreographer Louise Pōtiki Bryant's work also featured in *Paemanu: Tauraka Toi — A Landing Place*. Her collaboration with Ariana Tikao (Ngāi Tahu) and Paddy Free, *Ta Taki o te Ua/The Sound of Rain* (2021/2022), also focused on environmental degradation and the broader impact of climate change in Te Waipounamu the South Island of Aotearoa.

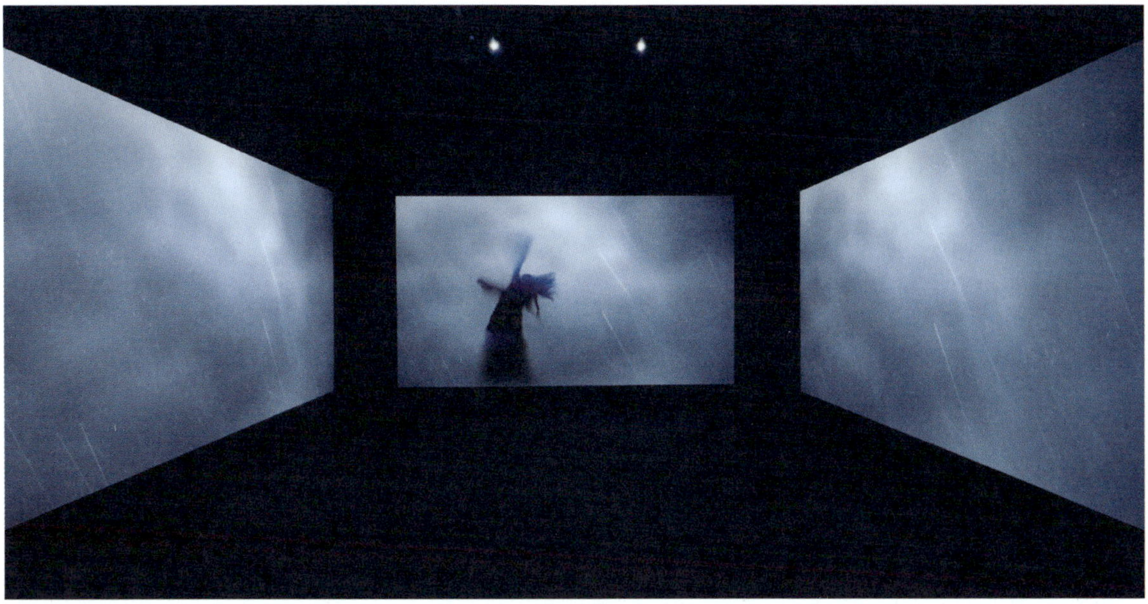

Louise Pōtiki Bryant (Ngāi Tahu, Kāti Māmoe, Waitaha), *Ta Taki o te Ua/The Sound of Rain*, installation view, 2021/2022. Collaborators: Ariana Tikao (Ngāi Tahu, waiata and taoka puoro composition and performance) and Paddy Free (composer and director of photography). *Courtesy the artist*

The three-channel installation is structured into three parts, each focused on a different aspect of the water cycle: mist, drought and storm. Three interconnected video works combine various artistic elements such as dance, waiata, taoka puoro, animation, video and soundscape. Drawing on performative and Indigenous knowledge, the videos reference te taiao and the impacts of climate change within the takiwā of Ngāi Tahu.

One of the video works, 'Waikohu/Mist', serves as an artistic expression of the balanced water cycle, and pays tribute to the emergence of freshwater following the separation of Ranginui (the Sky Father) and Papatūānuku (the Earth Mother). The other two videos, 'Pakapaka/Drought' and 'Āwhā/Storm', explore the anticipated rise in the frequency and intensity of droughts, storms and floods and draw attention to the detrimental effects of climate change within areas of Ngāi Tahu's takiwā. Various iwi deploy this form of pūrākau about the origins of time through atua Māori.

Like Whiting's mural *Te Wehenga a Rangi raua ko Papa*, the pūrākau is an ancient form of transmitting ideas and creating shared meaning and thus identity. Pūrākau can be iwi-specific and therefore similar in substance but different in form. Pōtiki Bryant uses pūrākau both as research for her artistic practice and as storytelling content for her artwork. In this regard, contemporary scholars have examined the ways in which pūrākau can be employed both as a research method and as a tool for decolonisation.[27]

**

Both Moana Nepia (Ngāti Porou) and Shannon Te Ao (Ngāti Tūwharetoa, Ngāti Wairangi, Te Papaka o Māui) use the pūrākau of the primordial concept of Te Kore. Nepia's performance and video installation *Maungauika Trilogy* (2011) and Te Ao's performance work *Follow the Party of the Whale* (2013) revisit two historical sites — Maungauika North Head on the Waitematā Harbour in Tāmaki Makaurau Auckland and Parihaka in the Taranaki region — as they trace thoughts and actions to their respective sources through performance.

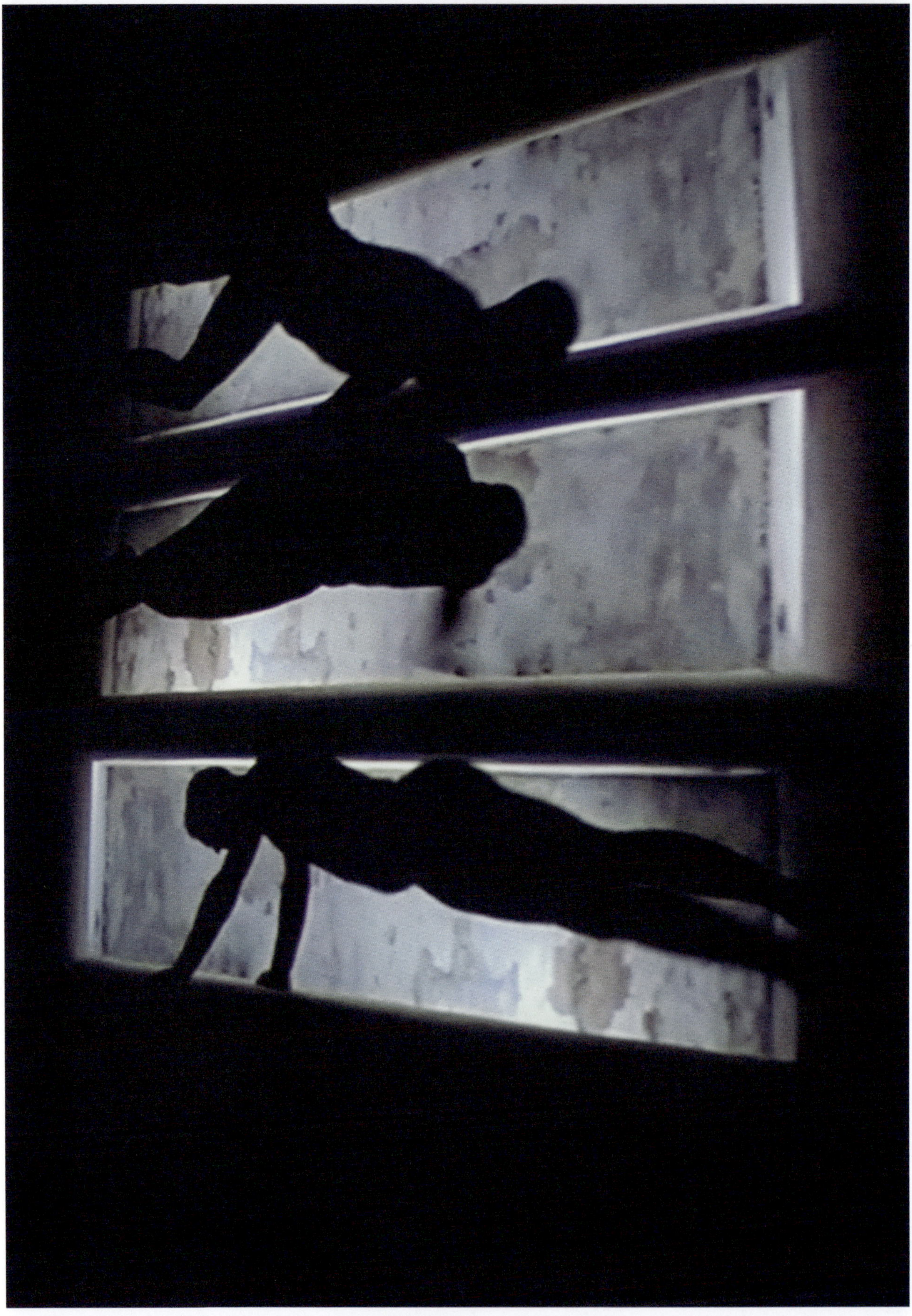

MAUNGAUIKA TRILOGY AND FOLLOW THE PARTY OF THE WHALE

Moana Nepia (Ngāti Porou), *Maungauika Trilogy*, 2010, film still, single-channel video. *Courtesy the artist*

Nepia's silent video installation *Maungauika Trilogy* is an interpretation of the Māori philosophy known as Te Kore, a 'nothingness' that is understood as filled with potential — an incubation space and nurturing void that fosters the emergence of life.[28]

Nepia transformed City Gallery Wellington into a crypt-like environment symbolising the transitional realm between life and death. Visitors entered via a tunnel that revealed a dimly lit expanse, on the walls of which shadowy figures were projected, moving slowly and deliberately, straddling the boundary between night and day. Nepia recorded the performance in abandoned military tunnels beneath Maungauika, a claustrophobic subterranean setting that provided an evocative backdrop to delve into the Māori primordial concept of Te Kore, and to explore whether the rich potential of 'the nothingness' could be considered a kaupapa or foundation for the art-making creative process.

The concept of Te Kore, expressing the limits of imagination and serving as the source of all things, holds a crucial place in Māori perspectives on creativity. In this context, Te Kore is usually conceptualised as a realm of nothingness or void in relation to Te Po (a multi-layered realm of night), in which the primordial parents Ranginui and Papatūānuku were locked in an eternal embrace. Following the separation of Rangi and Papa by their son Tāne-nui-ā-Rangi, Te Ao Mārama (the realm of illumination, contemporary knowledge and mankind) evolved.[29]

Although many Māori tribal traditions depict Te Kore as the primordial void, some also incorporate Te Kore within Te Ao Mārama, considering it as an ancestral presence within the realm of human existence. This perspective does not dismiss portrayals of Te Kore as an absolute void or annihilation; instead, it embraces concepts of hope, renewal, balance and the potential for new things to emerge — qualities essential for endurance.[30] Māori philosopher Carl Mika, commenting on Robert Jahnke's *Whenua kore* (2019), writes:

> Te Kore is not simply a deceased relative, an ancient ancestor who happened to leave a legacy of light. It lives on independently and fundamentally as a ground that founds the existence of all things — the orientation of rock, plant, human, mountain, and even corona viruses, towards and within the world. Specifically for the human, each entity is embedded, and has its own way of being, in-the-world. Te Kore demands contemplation and open-ended conversation, infusing everything and structuring the parameters of thought, and thus speech.[31]

In this sense, Te Kore is conceived not only as a primordial source but also as part of what constitutes us, part of our contemporary existence and experience of the world as Māori. *Maungauika Trilogy* therefore is not an absolute void or nothingness, but rather a space pregnant with possibilities, a space of creative potential linking past to present; bodies and thoughts to ancestral bodies, practices and traditions of thought.

Shannon Te Ao's performance-to-video *Follow the Party of the Whale* (2013) contends with the darkness of revisiting the historical site of the November 1881 invasion of the pan- tribal Indigenous community Parihaka by over 1500 colonial soldiers and militia.[32] Te Ao performs in the 'empty' or 'void' space of the invasion.[33] Like Nepia, Te Ao describes Te Kore not only as a point of nothingness but also as a point of departure or potential. As he has said:

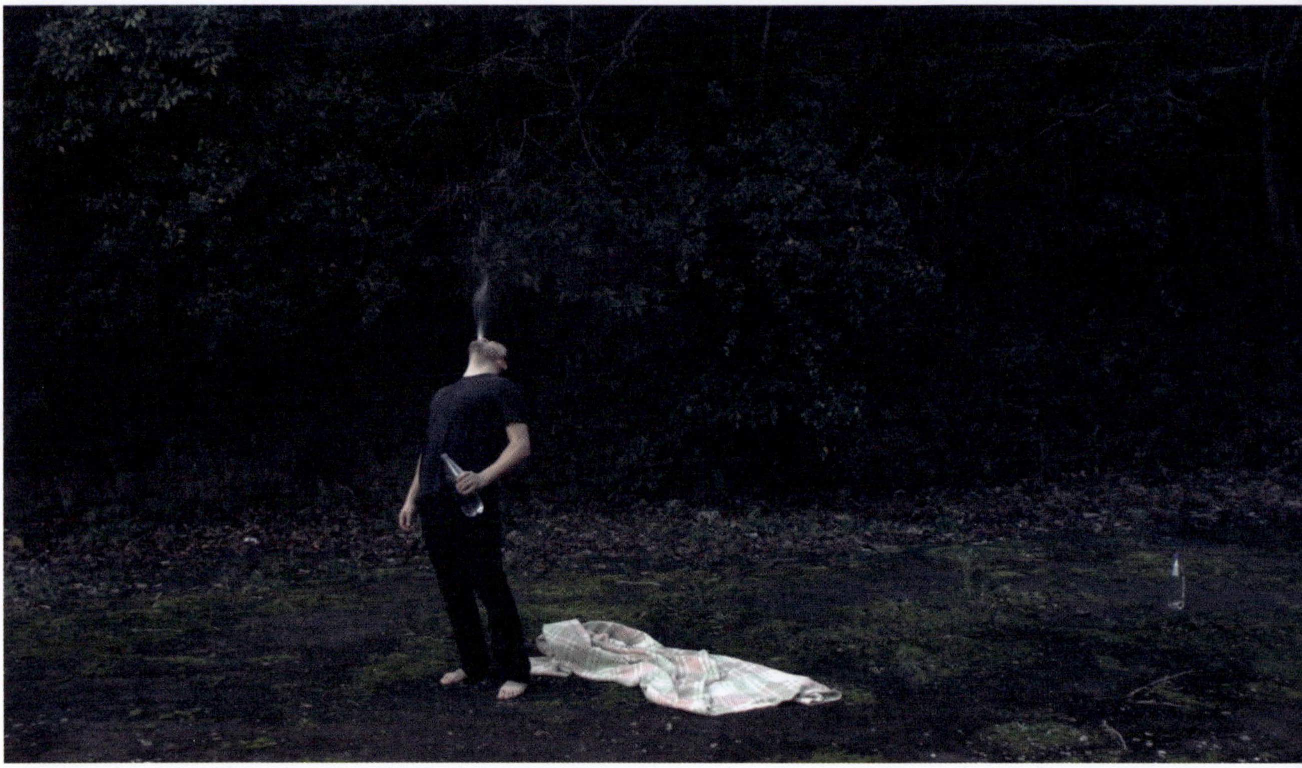

> Within Māori ideology, Te Kore may describe a point of nothingness — a void. Similarly Te Kore may propose a primary point of departure, a social paradox — without reference or resource — of fundamental autonomy and interminable potentiality. Te Kore and its variant 'Te Korekore' suggest that *what we see is not all there is.* This state, or state of being, exists beyond the realm of everyday experience and is commonly linked to narratives of creation, exploration and uncertainty, and through these mana, tapu and mauri.[34]

Shannon Te Ao (Ngāti Tūwharetoa, Ngāti Wairangi, Te Papaka o Māui), *Follow the Party of the Whale*, 2013. Two-channel video, colour and sound, duration 12 minutes 51 seconds. Cinematography by Iain Frengley. *Courtesy the artist*

Martin Patrick describes how, prior to the invasion, the rule of law was suspended by the passing of the Maori Prisoners' Trials Act, which enabled Parihaka prisoners to be incarcerated without legal recourse. Many died of tuberculosis during their imprisonment.[35] Signifying the ghastly death by internal drowning that results from tuberculosis, in his performance Te Ao swigs 50 litres of soda water, spurting mouthful after mouthful into the air as if spouting like a whale.

Te Ao's gurgling oratory performance could be interpreted as a form of waiata or, more specifically, a mōteatea, a song of lament for the Parihaka prisoners. Christopher Braddock has noted how Te Ao is acutely aware that the orality of Māori culture keeps connections alive with tīpuna as taonga passed across time and space. Writing about Te Ao's use of waiata, Braddock references '[Carl] Mika's experience of whakaaro [as] poignant: "when I move through a term I move through its influence, and the influence of other things", which, for Māori, includes distant ancestors'.[36]

As with *Maungauika Trilogy*, Te Kore in this context is a creative space of potential, somehow reaching back in order to connect and redeem ancestral bodies. As Patrick writes: 'Te Ao's work connects into a larger continuum of past and present, particularly if one acknowledges Indigenous notions of time, and the Māori adage ka mua, ka muri (one walks backwards into the future).'[37]

Moana Nepia's *Maungauika Trilogy* and Shannon Te Ao's *Follow the Party of the Whale*, contemporary affirmations in performance, dance and video installation, may be understood as Māori assertions of tino rangatiratanga, the principle of self-determination, chieftainship and sovereignty. This includes resisting assimilationist practices and institutionalised forms of cultural oppression, rewriting history from Māori perspectives, and centralising kaupapa Māori and mātauranga Māori within academic contexts.

PURE

The capacity of dance performance to offer insight into our lives is foregrounded in *Pure* (2013), a performance work developed in collaboration with Te Toki Haruru research platform created in 1997 by Charles Koroneho (Ngāpuhi, Te Mahurehure, Te Parawhau, Ngāti Hau). In te reo Māori, pure means a ritual and action that consists of 'loosening' from dangerous elements and 'binding' to beneficent ones.

In *Pure*, Koroneho explores mourning and loss of whānau, re-committing to aspects of family, whānau, place and culture, and reflecting on the transformation wrought by relocation to Canada. This work offers a ritualised space in which those watching are also invited to reflect.

Situated in a location defined by transitions, the performance progresses through a sequence of ritual presentations, portraying Koroneho's body as resonating on the threshold between various realms — bridging the physical and spiritual, the present and the past, and the material and the virtual. Koroneho understands these performances as 'tests' of the endurance and focused energy needed to bring about change.[38]

In this context the theatre becomes a marae, a sacred tribal meeting place, accenting and embellishing the role of the theatre as a site where we meet tīpuna *and* a machine for transformation. As dancer and choreographer Carol Brown writes:

> The border between the darkened auditorium and the stage, a fourth wall has historically marked a limit. But if contemporary Māori performance like Charles's invites us to think of the theatre as a marae then it is also a place to dwell. This role of theatre, its ritual potential, aligns with Charles's and other Māori choreographers' work. But rather than being organised around acts of disappearance, around what is missing, what cannot be shown or witnessed in an absence/presence duality, we are invited to be with the ancestors in a place of belonging.[39]

PŌHUTU

In a 2019 collaborative installation of *Pōhutu* by Bianca Hyslop (Te Arawa, Ngāti Whakaue), Rowan Pierce and Tūī Matira Ransfield (Te Arawa, Tainui, Mataatua, Arai-te-uru, Tākitimu, Manuka, Kurahaupō) titled *Te Mauri o Pōhutu* (the essence or life-force of Pōhutu) at Toi Pōneke Arts Centre in Te Aro, Te Whanganui-a-Tara Wellington,[40] a grey metal loudspeaker attached to the wall jumps to life with a karanga composed by Ransfield. A suspended Perspex screen transforms into a whiteboard, a canvas for projections, and a vessel emitting steam reminiscent of Rotorua's thermal landscapes.

Pōhutu commences with a slow-moving figure adorned in a sheer red tulle gown, clutching what seems to be a glass-like mere. The mere sparkles as the figure advances then vanishes in an instant. The performance is a tense dance, accompanied by music that oscillates between classical notes and the faint echoes of waiata. In a different way to the work of Shannon Te Ao discussed above, this waiata is reminiscent of mōteatea as songs of lament that include pātere, waiata wawata, oriori and more. Reviewer Tenga Rangitauira writes, 'They're songs of sadness, of farewell, of loss and grieving. Full of poetry and imagery, simile and metaphor, they're the most emotional of the waiata in our kapa haka.'[41]

The dancers adapt their movements to the evolving music, transitioning from graceful glides to movements reminiscent of kapa haka. Like the music, which at times is inaudible, their actions seem unfulfilled and evoke visible tension. Reviewer Matariki Williams wrote that this 'visceral, arresting and immersive' work, integrating video, voice, music, lighting design, dance and drawing,[42] 'bubbles and beats with tension and relief'.[43] Her response was attuned as much to underlying cultural and intellectual traditions of thought informing the work as to the sensual physicality and design of the performance.

From its inception, research and workshop development as part of Atamira Dance Company's 2018 Hou season, *Pōhutu* grounded its interpretation of psychological condition through connection to the beating heart of Papatūānuku and the restlessness of her unborn child, Rūaumoko, turning within her. Whakarewarewa, the ancestral home of Tūhourangi people to whom Hyslop and her grandmother belong, is understood as a place where the earth is always performing.

Through its causative prefix whaka, 'to make' or 'being made', and the verb rewarewa, 'to move in a body', 'to melt, float or dissolve', Whakarewarewa also describes the convergence of temporal, thermostatic, chemical and experiential transformations specific to that place, and 'taking place' as preconditions for social interaction and performance. From the inside out, Papatūānuku is always 're-making' and 're-forming herself', and is a dynamic source of sustenance and wellbeing.[44]

Responding to *Pōhutu*, reviewer Sinead Overbye likened one of the videos projected on the Perspex screen — of hands seeking coins underwater in *Penny Diving* (2019) — to 'searching for something in the depths'; and 'the penny we find' to the 'mātauranga the artists are craving to reclaim'.[45] Overbye suggested the hands of an older woman and a child, reaching towards one another in a second video, *Ngā ringa kūia mau ringa moko* (2020), depicted a reaching for knowledge: '[W]e want what the kuia's hand offers us. We want all her knowledge and her expertise.'[46] Here, the gallery and installation elements perform through their capacity to tautoko the main kaupapa, or ancestral grounding, and the swimming together of bodies and ideas.

Simultaneously rooted in personal experience, family history and deeply felt connections to place, *Pōhutu* reaches beyond the specifics of its origins: storytelling and performance language. Through its poetic responses to pathological disorientation, the loss of memory, dignity and personal identity, and to the fractious and explosive potential of Rūaumoko, the Māori deity of seismic, volcanic and geothermal activity, we are reminded of our own mortality, the fragility of our environment and the strength needed to confront challenges to cultural identity and mental, physical and social wellbeing.

Charles Koroneho (Ngāpuhi, Te Mahurehure, Te Parawhau, Ngāti Hau), *Pure*, 2013, solo performance. *Courtesy the artist. Photo by Brad Gledhill and Elizabeth Thipphawong*

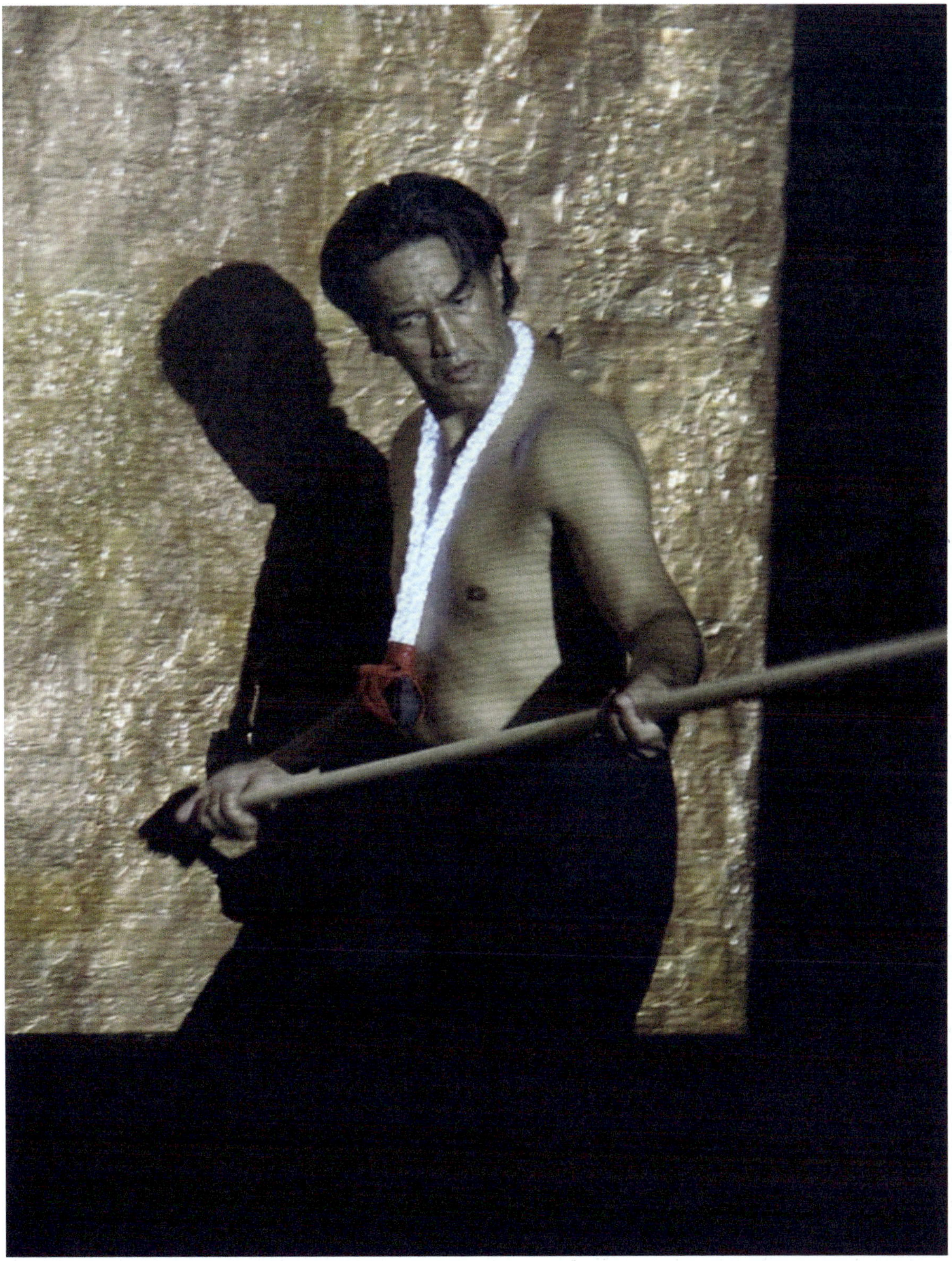

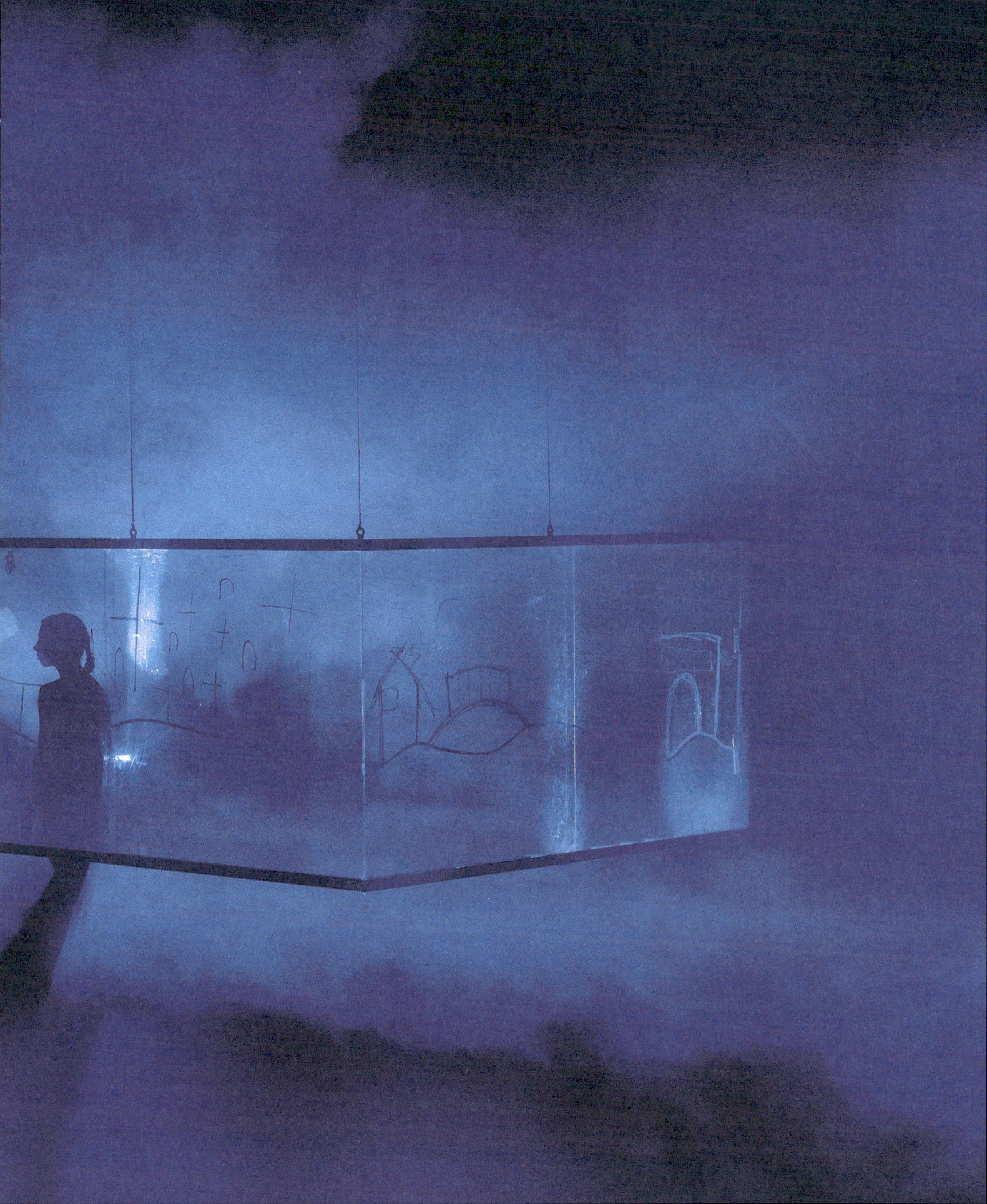

PREVIOUS: Bianca Hyslop, Rowan Pierce and Tūī Matira Ranapiri Ransfield (Te Arawa, Tainui, Mataatua, Arai-te-uru, Tākitimu, Manuka, Kurahaupō), *Te Mauri o Pōhutu*, 2021. *Courtesy Rowan Pierce. Photo by Jinki Cambronero*

CONCLUSION

As noted by Ngarino Ellis, Hirini Moko Mead argued that Māori customs and traditions cannot remain static. Mead advocated for a continued respect for traditions while also seeking change, and argued that these customs connect Māori to their ancestors, their knowledge and their wisdom and need to be nurtured and evolved for future generations.[47] I have argued that a tradition of innovative problem-solving has been a defining feature of Māori art over time and, in that spirit, have adopted Jahnke's term 'trans-customary' and applied it here to performance art.

Discussing the trans-customary and transdisciplinary performance practices of Rachael Rakena, Louise Pōtiki Bryant, Moana Nepia, Shannon Te Ao, Charles Koroneho, and the collaborative work of Bianca Hyslop, Rowan Pierce and Tūī Matira Ransfield, I have explored what it means to perform as Māori in relation to mātauranga Māori and concepts such as te taiao and takiwā. I have argued that forms of contemporary and trans-customary performance help to shape identity and a sense of belonging for Māori people. The places and spaces of performance are transformed such that they become sacred meeting spaces akin to a marae, where Māori meet their ancestors in a place of profound belonging.

NOTES

1 I acknowledge the input of dancer and choreographer Moana Nepia who began co-authoring this chapter but could not continue for health reasons.

2 Te Ahukaramū Charles Royal, 'Te Whare Tapere: Towards a model for Māori performance art' (unpublished doctoral dissertation, Victoria University of Wellington, 1998), 16.

3 Whatarangi Winiata, Te Wānanga-o-Raukawa 1997, 246.

4 Sidney Moko Mead, *Māori Art on the World Scene* (Wellington: Āhua Design and Illustration Ltd/Mātau Associates, 1997), 231.

5 Te Ahukaramū Charles Royal, 'The Creative Potential Paradigm Emerging in Iwi/Māori Communities' (keynote address delivered to *Tranzform: Te Tīnihanga*, a conference of the Library and Information Association of New Zealand, 10 September 2007), 4.

6 Apirana Ngata, 'The Terminology of Whakapapa', *Journal of the Polynesian Society* 128 (2019): 19–42.

7 Moana Nepia, 'Te Kore: Exploring the Māori concept of void' (PhD thesis, Auckland University of Technology, 2012).

8 Ngarino Ellis and Natalie S. Robertson, *A Whakapapa of Tradition: 100 years of Ngāti Porou carving, 1830–1930* (Auckland: Auckland University Press, 2016).

9 Ibid., 11.

10 Ibid., 13. See Hirini Moko Mead, *Tikanga Māori: Living by Māori values* (Wellington: Huia, 2003).

11 Ellis and Robertson, *A Whakapapa of Tradition*, 13.

12 Ibid., 15.

13 Ibid., 13. Ellis comments on Robert Jahnke adopting this term. See Robert Jahnke, 'Māori Art: Fact or fiction', in *Māori: Art and culture*, edited by Dorota Starzecka (London: British Museum Press, 1998), 159.

14 Christina Barton, 'Together/Apart: Regional networks in a global age. Imagining the Pacific in New Zealand, 1976', *Reading Room: A Journal of Art and Culture* 6, 'Elective Proximities' (2013): 79.

15 See www.aucklandartgallery.com/whats-on/exhibition/ko-taku-toa-takitini-finding-strength-in-the-collective

16 Jonathan Mane-Wheoki, 'Contemporary Māori Art — Ngā Toi Hōu: Ngā Whanaketanga Hou', *Te Ara — the Encyclopedia of New Zealand*, 2014. https://teara.govt.nz/en/video/45366/interview-with-maori-artists-and-writers-1973. See Barton, 'Together/Apart', 79 and 85 n. 43.

17 As cited in Ellis and Robertson, *A Whakapapa of Tradition*, 16.

18 Wendy Vaigro, 'High Performance Optics: INTERDIGITATE 95', *Art New Zealand* 76 (Spring 1995): 52.

19 See Chapter 9 of this volume by Ioana Gordon-Smith who discusses the Pacific Sisters' first rendition of the story of *Ina and Tuna* in 1994 with the exhibition *Bottled Ocean* at the Auckland City Art Gallery.

20 Collaborating creatives include: Paulette Tamati-Elliffe (Kāi Te Pahi, Kāi Te Ruahikihiki (Ōtākou), Te Ātiawa, Ngāti Mutunga) and whānau, Komene Cassidy (Ngāpuhi, Ngāi Takoto), Rachael Rakena (Kāi Tahu, Ngāpuhi), Michael Bridgman (Tonga, Ngāti Pākehā), Laughton Kora (Ngāi Tūhoe, Ngāti Pūkeko, Ngāti Awa), Iain Frengley (Ngāti Pākehā), Ross Hemera (Waitaha, Ngāti Māmoe, Ngāi Tahu), Mara TK (Ngāi Tahu, Ngāti Kahungunu, Tainui), Amber Bridgman (Kāi Tahu, Kāti Mamoe, Waitaha, Rabuvai) and He Waka Kōtuia.

21 Royal, 'Te Whare Tapere'. As Royal notes, the ongoing significance of modern-day kapa haka is most evident in the biennial Te Matatini kapa haka competitions, which stand as a remarkable cultural phenomenon in Aotearoa. Engaging participants from across New Zealand and Australia at local, regional and national tiers, these competitions have become a significant contemporary platform and play a crucial role in nurturing Māori and iwi identity, as well as championing specific Māori causes.

22 See www.bartleyandcompany.art/artists/rachael-rakena

23 Ibid.

24 David Eggleton, 'Mauri and the Spirit of Art in Te Wai Pounamu', 2022, www.circuit.org.nz/writing-and-podcast/a-restoration-of-mauri

25 Ibid.
26 Ibid.
27 J. Lee, 'Decolonising Māori Narratives: Pūrākau as a method', *MAI Review* 2 (2009).
28 See 'Moana Nepia: Maungauika Trilogy', City Gallery Wellington, 16 April–15 May 2011. https://citygallery.org.nz/exhibitions/moana-nepia-maungauika-trilogy
29 Te Ahukaramū Charles Royal, as cited in Nepia, 'Te Kore'.
30 Moana Nepia, cited in 'Te Kore as Potentiality', www.natekore2018.com/kauhau-kai-mahi/moana-nepia
31 Cark Mika, 'Print archive: The void and its parody: Thinking alongside Robert Jahnke's Whenua kore', *The Artpaper*, 2021, www.the-art-paper.com/journal/in-print-the-void-and-its-parody-thinking-alongside-robert-jahnkes-whenua-kore
32 For further discussion of *Follow the Party of the Whale* (2013), see Chapter 6 of this volume by Andrew Clifford and Rachel Shearer.
33 Martin Patrick, 'Exploring Posthuman Masquerade and Becoming', in *Animism in Art and Performance*, edited by Christopher Braddock (Cham, Switzerland: Palgrave Macmillan, 2017), 213–31.
34 Shannon Te Ao, 'Part Tree, Part Canoe' (Master's exegesis, Massey University, 2015), 15 (emphasis in the original). Also referenced by Patrick, 'Exploring Posthuman Masquerade and Becoming'.
35 Patrick, 'Exploring Posthuman Masquerade and Becoming', 226–27.
36 Christopher Braddock, 'Entangled Animisms: Whakaaro & dialogue in the artwork of Shannon Te Ao', *Performance Research Journal* 24, no. 6, 'On Animism' (2019): 69–78, 75. See Carl Te Hira Mika, 'The Thing's Revelation: Some thoughts on Māori philosophical research', *Waikato Journal of Education* 20, no. 2 (2015): 61–68, 65.
37 Patrick, 'Exploring Posthuman Masquerade and Becoming', 227.
38 Charles Koroneho, as cited in Carol Brown, 'Dancing Between Whenua, Land and Matariki, Stars: On learning how not to be imperial' (paper presented at Mission Inn & the Culver Center of the Arts Riverside, California, 2013), https://researchspace.auckland.ac.nz/bitstream/handle/2292/38608/CORD_16Nov2013.pdf?sequence=2&isAllowed=y
39 Brown, 'Dancing Between Whenua, Land and Matariki, Stars', 5.
40 Bianca Hyslop, Rowan Pierce and Tūī Matira Ransfield, *Te Mauri o Pōhutu*, Toi o Poneke, 5–26 June 2019, https://toiponeke.nz/events/2021temauriopohutu
41 Tenga Rangitauira, 'Mōteatea: A window into the world of our ancestors', *E-Tangata*, 2022, https://e-tangata.co.nz/arts/moteatea-a-window-into-the-world-of-our-ancestors
42 www.pohutu.live/he-whakaaro-the-work
43 Matariki Williams, 'The Menace of Memory: A review of Pōhutu', *The Pantograph Punch*, 7 June 2019.
44 Australian Performing Arts Market, 'Pōhutu', 2019, https://apam.org.au/artist/bianca-hyslop-rowan-pierce
45 Sinead Overbye, 'Finding Each Other in the Dark', *The Pantograph Punch*, 19 June 2019, www.pantograph-punch.com/posts/finding-each-other-in-the-dark
46 Ibid.
47 Ellis and Robertson, *A Whakapapa of Tradition*, 14.

REFERENCES

Australian Performing Arts Market. 'Pōhutu', 2019. https://apam.org.au/artist/bianca-hyslop-rowan-pierce

Bartley & Company Art. www.bartleyandcompany.art/artists/rachael-rakena

Barton, Christina. 'Together/Apart: Regional networks in a global age. Imagining the Pacific in New Zealand, 1976'. *Reading Room: A Journal of Art and Culture* 6, 'Elective Proximities' (2013): 79.

Braddock, Christopher. 'Entangled Animisms: Whakaaro & dialogue in the artwork of Shannon Te Ao'. *Performance Research Journal* 24, no. 6, 'On Animism' (2019): 69–78.

Carol Brown. 'Dancing Between Whenua, Land and Matariki, Stars: On learning how not to be imperial'. Paper presented at Mission Inn & the Culver Center of the Arts Riverside, California, 2013. https://researchspace.auckland.ac.nz/handle/2292/38608

Eggleton, David. 'Mauri and the Spirit of Art in Te Wai Pounamu'. 2022. www.circuit.org.nz/writing-and-podcast/a-restoration-of-mauri

Ellis, Ngarino and Natalie Robertson. *A Whakapapa of Tradition: 100 years of Ngāti Porou carving, 1830–1930*. Auckland: Auckland University Press, 2016.

Jahnke, Robert. 'Māori Art: Fact or fiction'. In *Māori: Art and culture*, edited by Dorota Starzecka. London: British Museum Press, 1998.

Lee, Jenny. 'Decolonising Māori Narratives: Pūrākau as a method'. *MAI Review* 2 (2009). www.review.mai.ac.nz

Mead, Sidney Moko. *Māori Art on the World Scene.* Wellington: Āhua Design and Illustration Ltd/Mātau Associates, 1997.

Mead, Hirini Moko. *Tikanga Māori: Living by Māori values.* Wellington: Huia, 2003.

Mika, Carl. 'Print archive: The void and its parody: Thinking alongside Robert Jahnke's Whenua kore'. *The Artpaper*, 2021. www.the-art-paper.com/journal/in-print-the-void-and-its-parody-thinking-alongside-robert-jahnkes-whenua-kore

Nepia, Moana. 'Te Kore: Exploring the Māori concept of void'. PhD thesis, Auckland University of Technology, 2012. https://openrepository.aut.ac.nz/items/f6c5cae2-171b-4aa5-9796-282e838d0954

Ngata, Apirana T. 'The Terminology of Whakapapa'. *Journal of the Polynesian Society* 128 (2019): 19–42.

Overbye, Sinead. 'Finding Each Other in the Dark'. *The Pantograph Punch*, 19 June 2019. www.pantograph-punch.com/posts/finding-each-other-in-the-dark

Patrick, Martin. 'Exploring Posthuman Masquerade and Becoming'. In *Animism in Art and Performance*, edited by Christopher Braddock. Cham, Switzerland: Palgrave Macmillan, 2017.

Rangitauira, Tenga. 'Mōteatea: A window into the world of our ancestors'. *E-Tangata*, 2022. https://e-tangata.co.nz/arts/moteatea-a-window-into-the-world-of-our-ancestors

Royal, Te Ahukaramū Charles. 'Te Whare Tapere: Towards a model for Māori performance art'. Unpublished doctoral dissertation, Victoria University of Wellington, 1998.

——— 'The Creative Potential Paradigm Emerging in Iwi/Māori Communities'. Keynote address delivered to *Tranzform: Te Tīnihanga*, a conference of the Library and Information Association of New Zealand, 10 September 2007.

——— 'Whare Tapere'. 2020. www.charles-royal.nz/whare-tapere

Te Ao, Shannon. 'Part Tree, Part Canoe'. Master's exegesis, Massey University, 2015.

Vaigro, Wendy. 'High Performance Optics: INTERDIGITATE 95'. *Art New Zealand* 76 (Spring 1995): 52.

Williams, Matariki. 'The Menace of Memory: A review of Pōhutu'. *The Pantograph Punch*, 7 June 2019.

9

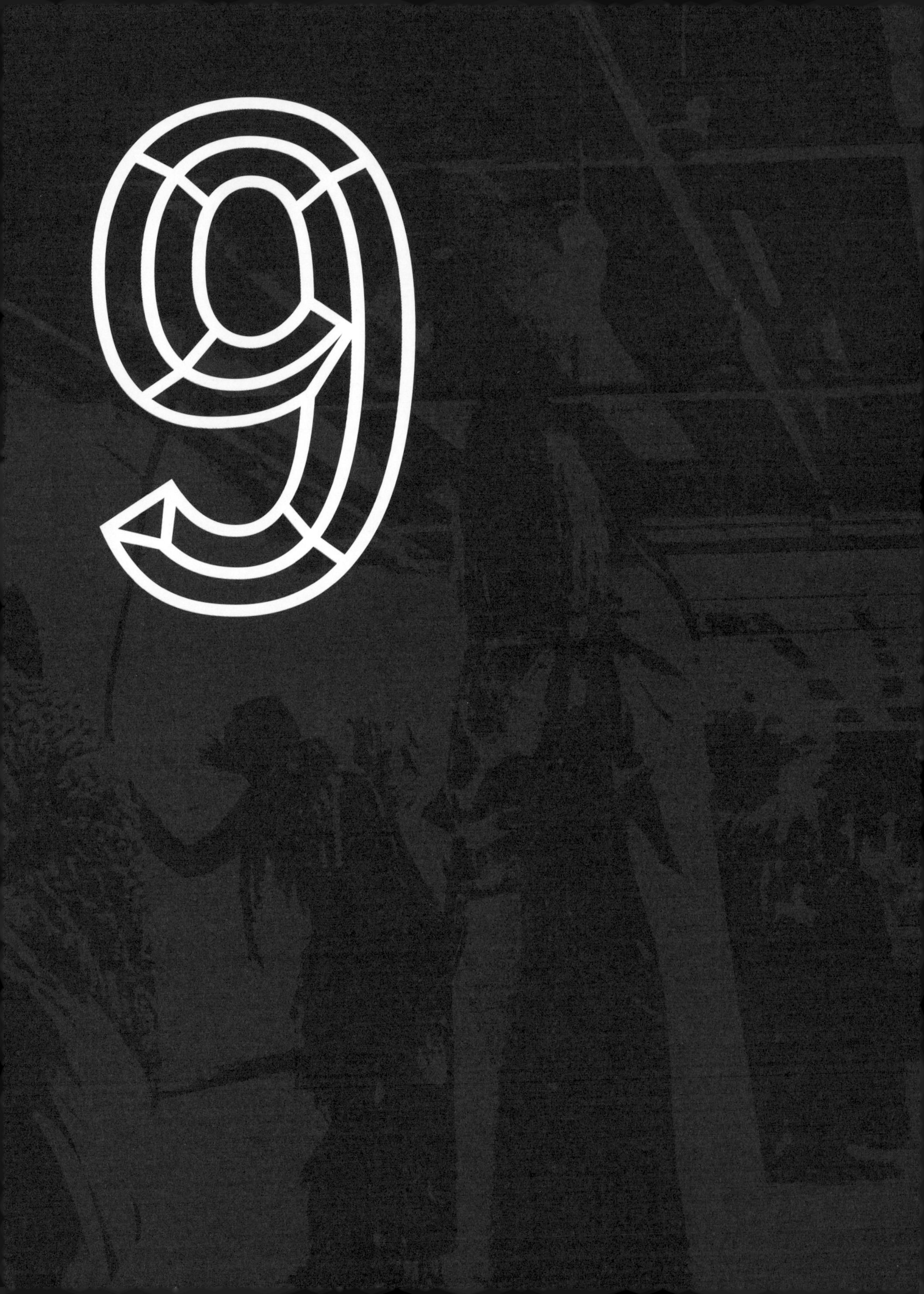

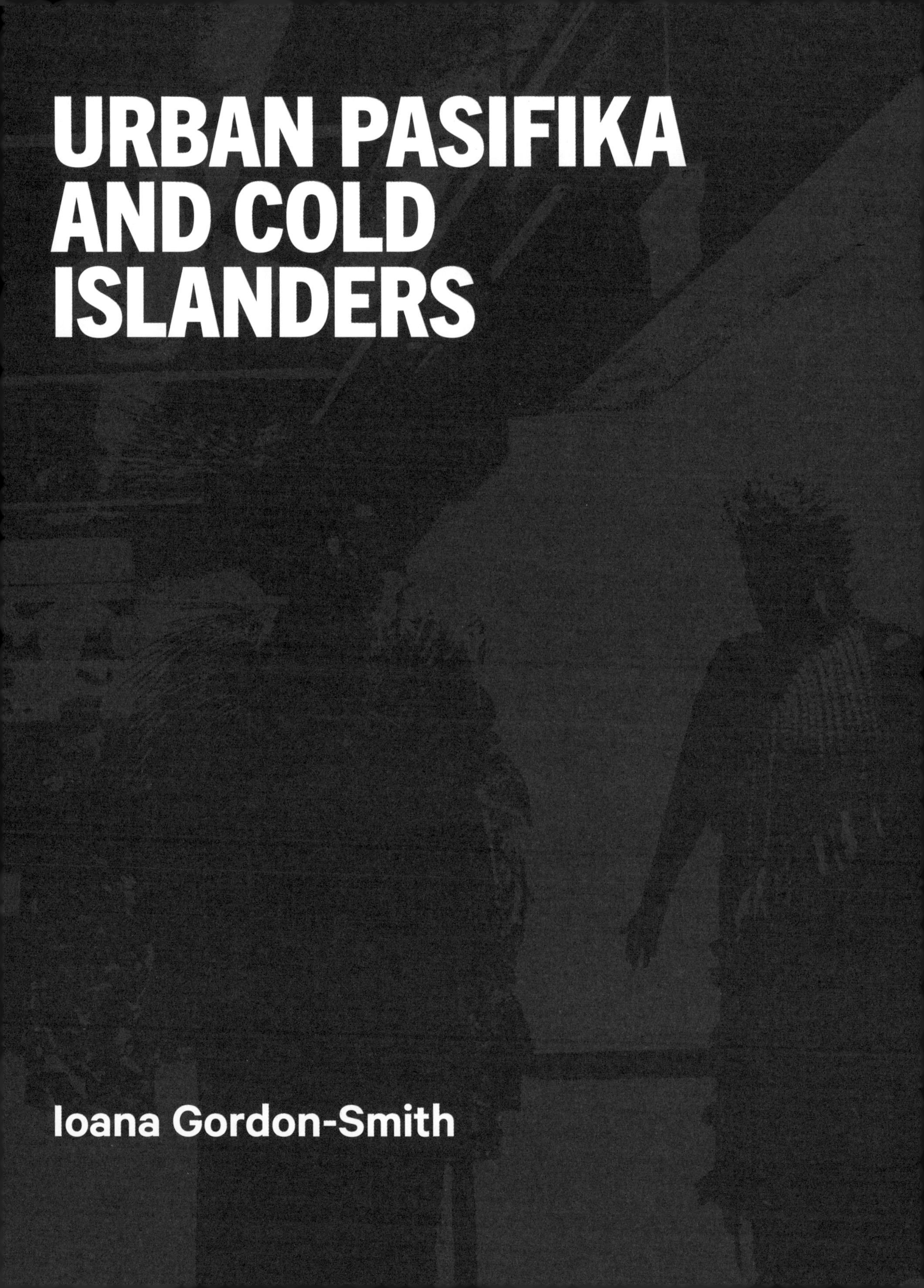

URBAN PASIFIKA AND COLD ISLANDERS

Ioana Gordon-Smith

We follow the ancient way of working from the environment. We get our inspiration from our immediate urban/media environment. We don't stare at coconut trees — we stare at motorways.[1]
— Rosanna Raymond

From a small migrant community in the 1940s, Aotearoa's Moana population has grown significantly over the decades.[2] The first major wave of Moana migration is often traced to the 1950s. Labour shortages coupled with expanding manufacturing, service and processing industries created a need for migrant workers from the Moana. Tens of thousands of Samoans and Tongans migrated to New Zealand in the 1960s and early 1970s by way of work visas; Cook Islanders, Niueans and Tokelauans could enter as citizens of the country's Moana outposts.

Although migration fuelled the initial increase of Moana peoples in New Zealand, the rise in the country's Moana population now results mostly from natural birth rates. Today, more than half of Moana peoples living in New Zealand were born here.[3] Moana scholar Damon Salesa notes that while the generational shifts between Moana peoples who migrated to New Zealand and those born here are not universal, some trends can be discerned. Aotearoa-born Islanders are more likely to speak English as their first language, less likely to identify as religious, and more likely to claim more than one ancestry.[4] As Stats NZ has noted, 'Today's Moana population is mostly New Zealand-born, predominantly young, and highly urbanised. It is also a diverse population made up of many different ethnic groups.'[5]

The rise of Moana peoples living and often raised in New Zealand necessitated new terminology. 'Pasifika' was coined by government agencies to describe Moana peoples living in New Zealand as well as their descendants. Described as a 'term of convenience' by New Zealand's Ministry of Education, the term 'Pasifika' is broad in two instances: first in being a pan-Moana term that covers multiple island groups, and second in covering both New Zealand-born and Island-born Moana peoples. Although the Ministry of Education admits that any definition of 'Pasifika' will always be a work in progress, its main denotative function is to signal a new ethnicity defined by the twin conditions of Island heritage and the New Zealand context.

Just as this duality required new language, so too did it necessitate the expression of a newly emerging diaspora experience. Although artistic creatives were embracing the multiplicity of Western and Moana influences, claiming both identities often produced a doubled invisibility. These new experiences found little representation or embrace within Pākehā mainstream culture. As artist Rosanna Raymond writes of Pasifika:

> These were invisible bodies, faceless, nameless, often only reflected in data counting the unemployed, the incarcerated and the hospitalised. These bodies bore little resemblance to the Dusky Maidens and the Noble Savages that most Europeans associated them with. Now wearing jeans, sweatshirts, workers' overalls, gumboots, steel caps, high heels, they assimilated into life in Aotearoa. We had no reflection of ourselves as an urban community living in New Zealand besides what had been constructed for us by organised religion, mainstream media and the colonial past.[6]

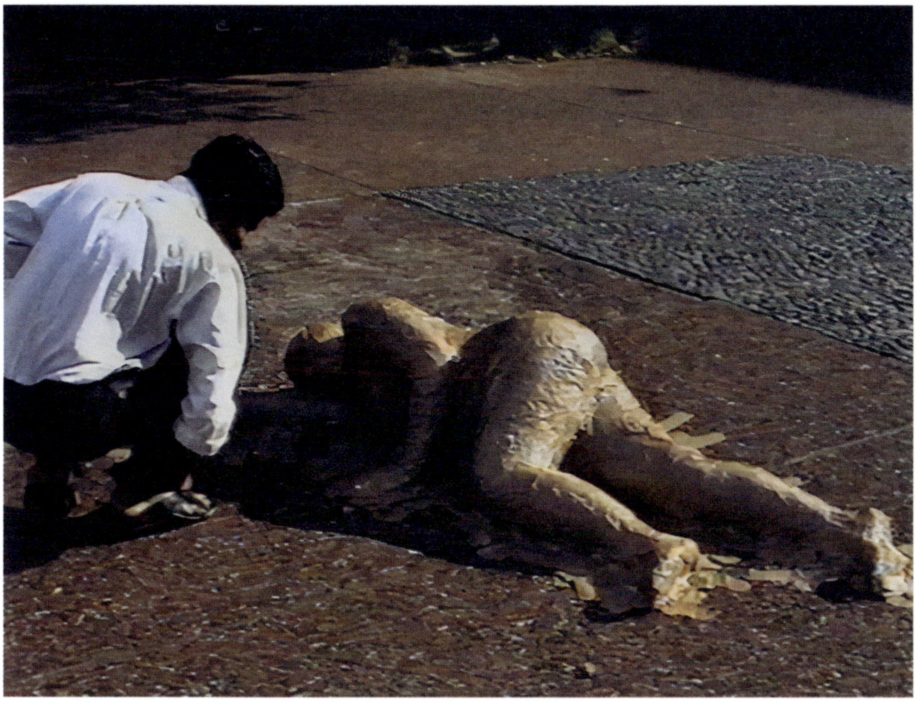

Lonnie Hutchinson (Ngāi Tahu, Ngāti Kuri ki Ngāi Tahu), *Can You See Me?*, 1997. *Auckland Art Gallery Toi o Tāmaki, purchased 2022*

However, what is equally significant is the way in which Pasifika were also side-lined within a conservative cultural context. Raymond continues, explaining:

> We often sat outside our own Pacific Island community, not feeling comfortable in the churches; our lack of language and anger at the acculturation of past generations made an uneasy pact with our elders.[7]

Several Moana artists were turning to performance to bring attention to this state of relative invisibility. In Lonnie Hutchinson's (Ngāi Tahu, Ngāti Kuri ki Ngāi Tahu) 1997 *Can You See Me?*, the artist lay motionless in various public spaces in Tāmaki Makaurau Auckland. The work was first performed at Cream, an early outdoor performance space at Unitec, before being performed in its most confrontational of public sites, the Queen Elizabeth II square in Tāmaki Makaurau's CBD.[8] For each performance the artist covered herself completely in brown packaging tape. All personal identifiers were removed, and the body was signified to the viewer only as a female form. The work confronted and sought to elicit a reaction to the unidentified body, presented as both brown and yet racially indeterminate, performing the identity reduction that was already apparent in New Zealand's race dynamics.

The exploration, contestation and production of new identities was occurring across Moana art in Aotearoa and spanned a wide spectrum of disciplines in both rural towns and city centres. Moana arts practice exists nationwide, but the concentration of Moana migration in urban centres such as Porirua, Ōtara and Māngere has often fuelled concentrations of arts within these sites. In the mid-1990s urban areas were humming with Moana creativity across the gamut of creative practice, particularly in music, theatre and fashion. Moana musicians, for instance, were often sampling across cultural influences, urban contexts and the global popularity of R&B and hip-hop to create localised sounds.

Tāmaki Makaurau was a particularly sweltering epicentre, but the music scene was equally active in Ōtautahi Christchurch with the work of Pacific Underground and in Te Whanganui-a-Tara Wellington with the Upper Hutt Posse. The music was eclectic both in its influences and its output; Upper Hutt Posse created bilingual tracks, OMC and Sisters Underground were creating global hits, a new record company named Urban Pasifika was established, and the local gig scene across Auckland, Wellington and Christchurch was popping off. The recombination of urban and Moana influences to describe diasporic identity also featured across poetry, writing, fashion design, photography, visual arts, activism and of course performance art.

COINING 'URBAN PASIFIKA'

One of the first artist collectives to embrace and promote this growing movement was the Pacific Sisters. The Pacific Sisters first emerged on the arts scene in 1992 with three members: Selina Haami (née Forsyth), Suzanne Tamaki and Nephi Tupaea.[9] Over the years, the Sisters' membership has evolved continuously as new collaborators come into and leave the fold. In their 2018 survey exhibition *Fashion Activists*, exhibiting members included Lisa Reihana, Rosanna Raymond, Ani O'Neill, Suzanne Tamaki, Selina Haami, Nephi Tupaea, Henry Ah-Foo Taripo, Feeonaa Wall and Jaunnie 'Ilolahia. On the Honolulu Triennial website the list of past and present members is even fuller and includes Rosanna Raymond, Ani O'Neill, Jaunnie 'Ilolahia, Favaux Valepo, Jeanine Clarkin, Henry Ah-Foo Taripo, Feeonaa Wall, Bethany Edmunds, Selina Haami, Ema Lyon, Sofia Tekela-Smith, Karlos Quartez, Greg Semu, Lisa Reihana, Darryl Thompson (DLT), Katharine Losi, Te Miringa Hohaia and Maaka Pepene.[10]

The Pacific Sisters collective is both pan-disciplinary and pan-ethnic. Comprising visual artists, models and fashion and jewellery designers, the Sisters spans a number of different island backgrounds across the Moana and is inclusive of Māori too. The makeup of the Sisters reflects the new forms of coalition happening in New Zealand, and often in urban centres, where Moana peoples from across different ancestries collided with a generation of Māori who grew up outside of their rohe in the wake of a Māori 'urban drift' that followed the Second World War.[11]

This regional idea of a Māori and Moana identity is particular to Aotearoa's Pasifika context. A pan-Pacific identity is often developed in diaspora. As Patrick Saulmatino Thomsen, Lana Lopesi and Kevin Lujan Lee note, regional terms and grouping, including Pasifika but also 'Pacific' and 'Moana', are arguably diasporic concepts. Within their ancestral homelands, people often identify by their specific island or village; but in diaspora, regional identities can offer a means of 'panethnic collectives built on panethnic solidarity'.[12]

The fashion scene has been a central part of the Sisters' collaborative pan-disciplinary practice. When they first formed, Haami was a costume designer at Mercury Theatre, while Tamaki and Tupaea were making jewellery. One of the first collaborations between the Sisters occurred when Haami and Tamaki staged a fashion show, *Te Hou Wairua Wahine*, for which Rosanna Raymond was MC and Ani O'Neill a model. The collaborations that emerged from this 'do-it-yourself' gig scene of urban Auckland are indicative of the way in which the Sisters worked. As Raymond has noted, nightclubs, warehouse parties, film sets and fashion shoots were all places where creatives could meet, fuelling future projects.[13]

Their works often combine both culturally specific materials, such as tapa, with found materials, such as raffia or video tape reels. The blend of Western and Pacific influences is evident in both forms and material choices; the clothing and adornments feature distinctly Pacific materials, such as shells and tapa, while also creating fashion from sheer fabric. The combination of materials and the finished designs have at times come under criticism from various Pacific people. In this context, working collaboratively between Sisters, across media and projects, was vital in the battle against criticism. As Raymond remarks:

> By working on projects together, we are trying to rewrite our own cultural history. We aren't trying to be Pasifika necessarily, we are urbanites trying to find our identity within a white settler, marginalised Pacific Island community. Art is a way we can articulate our stories.[14]

The Sisters' fashion became a prompt for large-scale multimedia productions. One of their first forays into galleries and museums came in 1994 with the exhibition *Bottled Ocean*. For the opening of the exhibition's Auckland City Art Gallery presentation, the Sisters performed the story of Ina and Tuna. Ani O'Neill played Ina, wearing a blue plastic raffia skirt to evoke water, while Rosanna Raymond appeared as Tuna, wearing tapa with a coconut-shell puppet.[15] Through their costuming and performance, Raymond and O'Neill conveyed the story of how Ina, a young girl, falls in love with the shapeshifter Tuna. Moving between human and eel forms, Tuna could meet with Ina secretly and return to the water without being noticed. However, sensing that death would eventuate from the secret liaison, Tuna instructs Ina to cut off his head and plant it.

This story, particular to Mangaia, explains the origin of the coconut. It is from Tuna's buried head that the coconut tree is said to grow. Various versions of this 'Ina and Tuna' story can be found across different Pacific cultures, and it was this shared experience that first drew the Sisters to the story.[16] It is a pan-Pacific story, and a fitting narrative for a collective with members from diverse cultural backgrounds. Over future performances, the Sisters changed costuming and means of dancing and storytelling to amend the version. The story also became the focus of a new, thirty-six-channel video installation produced by Lisa Reihana and presented in Interdigitate, a new-media and performance art festival, in 1995.[17]

The Pacific Sisters were invited to perform at the 7th Festival of Pacific Art in Sāmoa in 1996. Held every four years by a different hosting island nation, the festival is a mega event where makers and artists from different islands and disciplines gather. The 1996 iteration was the first time Pacific Islanders were included in the New Zealand contingent, but as participants within wider pan-Moana and Māori collectives. Expert weaver Misa Emma Kesha, for example, travelled as part of the Dunedin Multicultural Weavers Association, and the Pacific Sisters themselves included Māori artist Lisa Reihana.

The Sisters intended to present *Motu Tangata*, a large-scale fashion extravaganza. However, as Raymond notes, the Sisters 'were thrown out of the 1996 Festival of Pacific Arts and Culture (FESTPAC) in Sāmoa at the request of the Māori contingent, even though we had been officially invited by the festival director'.[18] The rejection illustrates the invisibility of the place of Pacific peoples at the time within the discourses of New Zealand identity. Already in Sāmoa, the Sisters instead presented an offsite show, still titled *Motu Tangata*, which showcased the work of twelve fashion designers of Pacific heritage from Aotearoa.[19] A home-style recording, *Motu Tangata* (1996), directed by Clifton May, captures this presentation of a New Zealand-born Urban Pasifika in Sāmoa.[20]

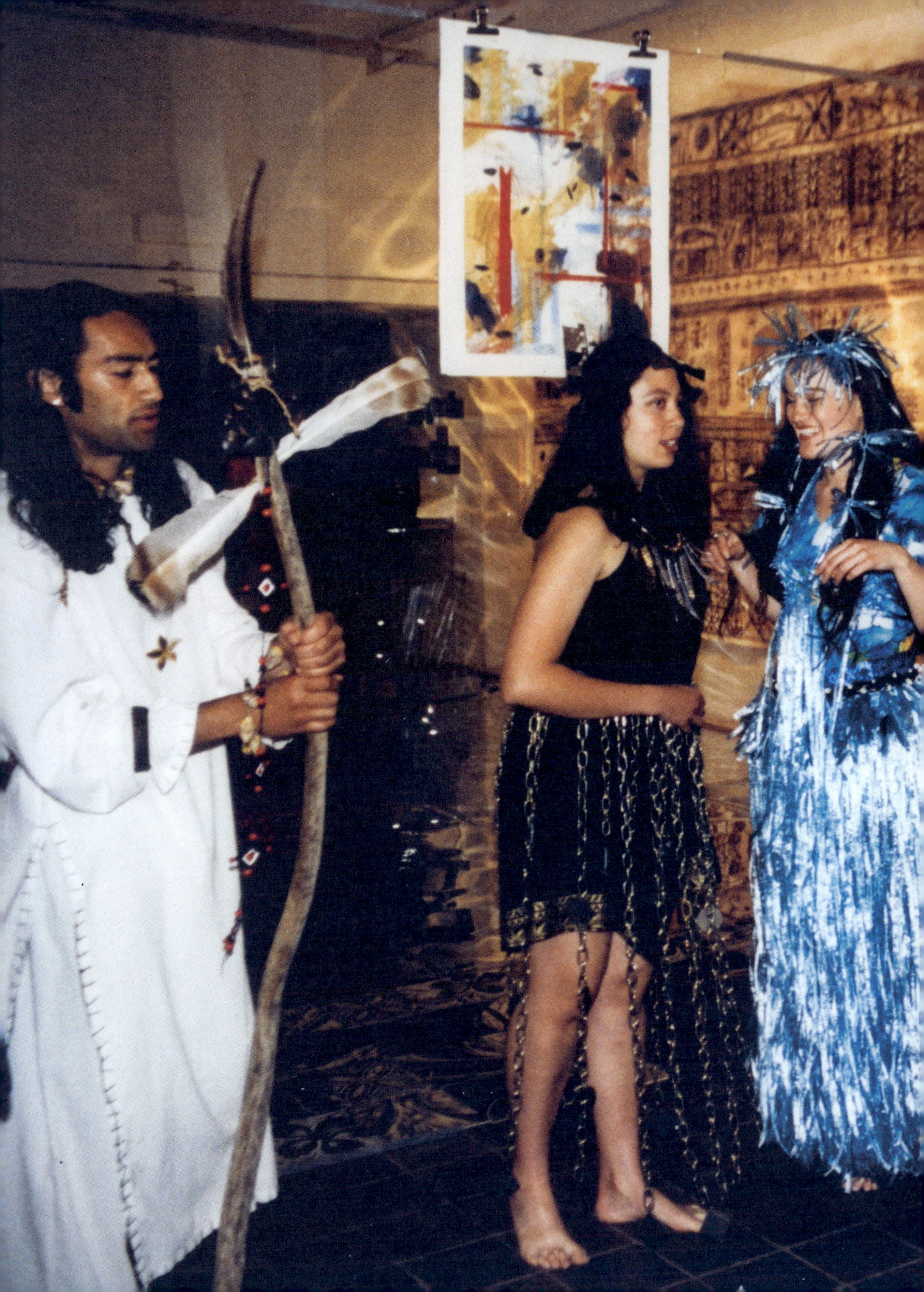

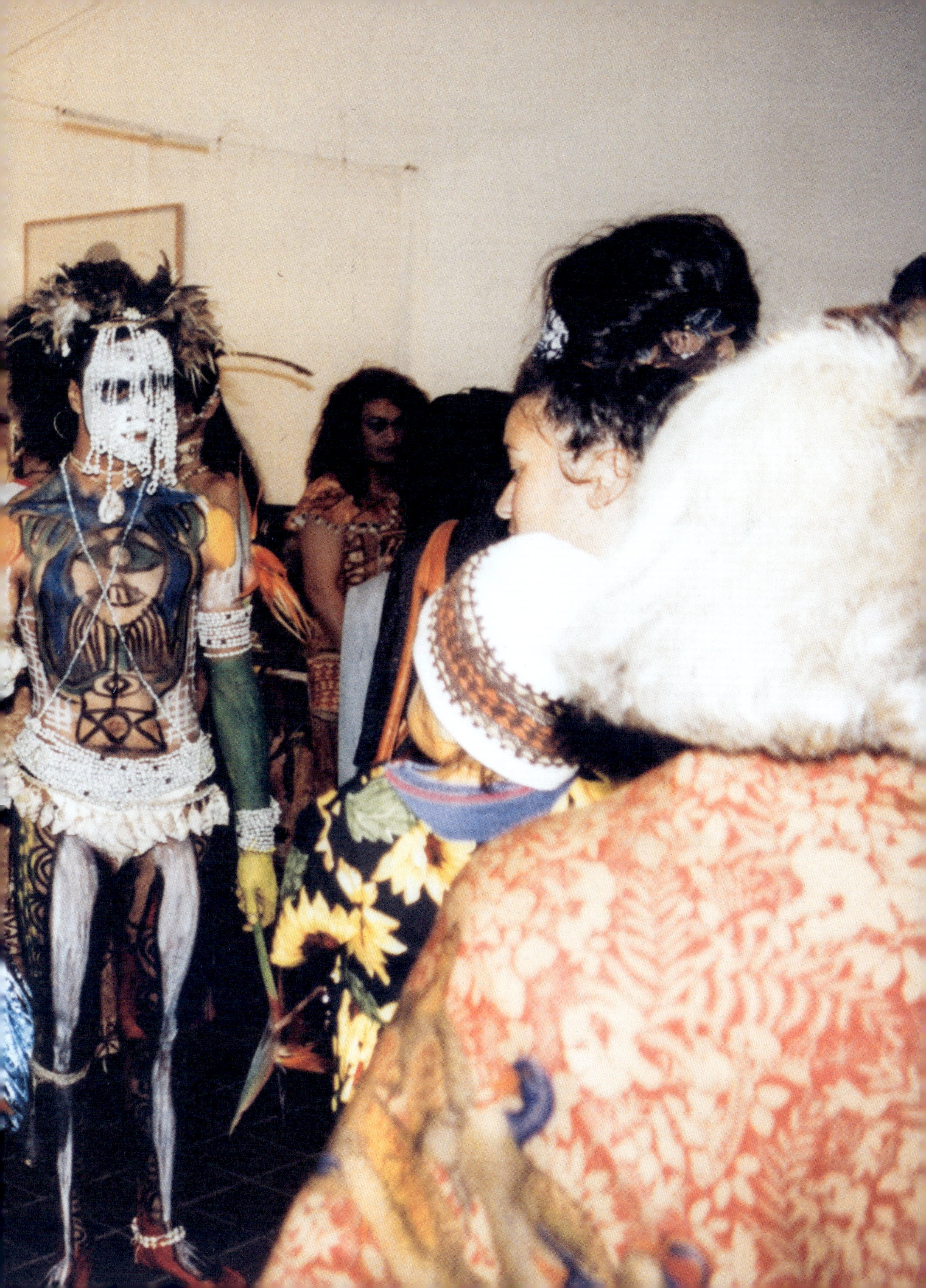

Urban Pasifika, then, came to stand for the need for a visible presence and cultural expression for a 1990s generation of artists, as curator Nina Tonga describes it, 'for whom the Pacific existed as a kind of here, there and elsewhere'.[21] And due in large part to the momentum of the Pacific Sisters, the Urban Pasifika movement has become largely associated with Tāmaki Makaurau and, to a lesser extent, Te Whanganui-a-Tara and Ōtautahi, in a moment of 1990s creative explosion.

PREVIOUS: The Pacific Sisters at the opening of *Bottled Ocean*, 1994, Auckland Art Gallery Toi o Tāmaki. From left: Karlos Quartez, Feeonaa Clifton (née Wall), Ani O'Neill, Teokotai Paitai. *E H McCormick Research Library, Auckland Art Gallery Toi o Tāmaki. Photo by Auckland Art Gallery Toi o Tāmaki*

CHANGING PRACTICES

The convergence of Pasifika from many generations and island heritages has been explored in performance as a source of both intense collectivity and potential tension. In the 1990s and early 2000s, Michel Tuffery produced a series of larger-than-life animal-form sculptures. Constructed from food cans, the sculptures drew attention to the impact of colonial contact on Samoan food practices and ecologies. *Pisupo Lua Afe (Corned Beef 2000)* (1994), for instance, featured flattened corned beef cans sculpted into the form of a bull; the fish shape of *Asiasi [Yellowfin] II* (2000) is made primarily from fish cans.

Both works compare the live food source with its commercial and mass-produced counterpart. The bull sculptures were also employed in a series of high-energy performances that introduced new layers of meaning to the works. *Povi Tau Vaga (The Challenge)* was a performance collaboration between Michel Tuffery and Futunan/New Caledonian artist Patrice Kaikilekofe, first performed in Wellington in 1994 and again for the Asia Pacific Triennial in Brisbane in 1999.

As sculptures, Tuffery's works offer a clear and uncompromising critique of the impact of colonial and global trade on Moana food practices. However, when activated through performance, the large bulls evoke a more equivocal reading. As art historian Caroline Vercoe documents, Tuffery describes these works as the performance and enactment of a challenge.[22] The entire performance plays out as a type of 'mock battle'. Two large bulls and two smaller bulls — all made from corned beef tins — were taken out onto the street and joined by more than ninety dancers and performers. Replete with firecrackers and props that doubled as potential weapons, the performance was staged as a type of battle as the performers and cattle cavorted towards each other.

Tuffery explains that this battle was indicative of the tensions between 'displaced Polynesians, and Polynesians actually growing up in the city' as well as Polynesians who have immigrated to Australia or New Zealand.[23] The performers themselves comprised a mix of cultural heritage as well as a mix of connections with the Brisbane location: performers from Futuna were there temporarily for the exhibition; the local Samoan performers were Moana diaspora living in Australia; and the First Nations performers were indigenous to Australia.

This conflation of Indigenous and Pacific groups with different levels of connection to *Povi Tau Vaga (The Challenge)* as it played out at the Asia Pacific Triennial both represents and performs the difference *within* Indigenous peoples who coexist in the urban melting pots of Island cultures. Tuffery explains:

> You know there's some of us who do live in cities but we've adapted in a different way and taken on different attitudes, and then you've got the ones who were born in the Islands and they've got their own attitudes . . . Sometimes they actually clash. And this is what this whole performance piece is about.[24]

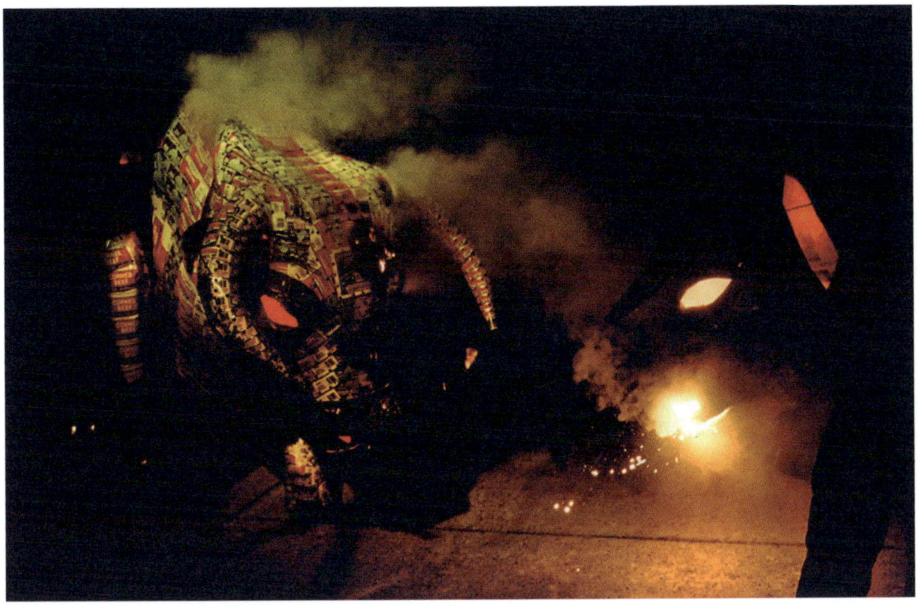

Povi tau vaga (The challenge), collaboration performance artwork by Michel Tuffery (Aotearoa, Sāmoa, Cook Island, Ma'ohi Tahitian) and Patrice Kaikilekofe (Futuna, New Caledonia) at the Queensland Art Gallery's Third Asia Pacific Triennial of Contemporary Art (APT3), 1999. *Courtesy the artist Michel Tuffery*

The urban here becomes the literal stage for the performance of tensions, whether restricted to the performance itself or indicative of Tuffery's perception of real tensions that exist. In this context, as much as it might be a space for galvanising, the urban is a battleground.

OPERATING SYSTEMS

The diasporic city context continued to inform performance art practices. In 2012 Auckland Art Gallery Toi o Tāmaki staged a survey of Moana art titled *Home AKL*. AKL, an abbreviation for Auckland, was premised on both the urban city as home to a concentration of Moana peoples and the strategic marketing of Auckland as a Pacific city.[25] One of the artists in the exhibition was Siliga David Setoga, a Samoan Niuean New Zealand artist whose practice spans graphic design, installation and performance art. Setoga gained early success with his t-shirt line Popohardwear. Popohardwear repurposes commercial logos as vehicles for sardonic cultural commentary.

As curator Nina Tonga notes, however, Popohardwear 'is not based around simple reversals but the creation of a complex politics of identity and representation where economics, suburbia, and urban life converge'.[26] Indeed, Popohardwear maps out the many urban influences that Moana diaspora face. The designs variously subvert derogatory terms, proudly display Moana colloquialisms, question the adoption of Americanisms, critique the commercial exploitation of Moana peoples, and even challenge pillars of Moana culture.

The urban context as a site of converging influences and identities plays a big role in Setoga's performances. Raised in central Tāmaki, Setoga's urban world was Pākehā while fa'a Sāmoa prevailed in his family home.[27] Setoga has described this as contributing to 'feeling neither here nor there and always wondering, questioning and searching for a place of belonging'.[28]

An early, untitled performance indicates the constant shapeshifting performed by urban Pasifika. The entire work occurs behind an ironing board. Setoga, dressed in his white casual lavalava and singlet, first irons a typical uniform for a factory worker: a white boiler suit. He then irons an 'ie faitaga,[29] a white shirt, a red tie and a white blazer — typical church garb for a pastor's son. Donning these, Setoga adopts the persona of the faithful churchgoer. The swapping of identity between the Pākehā world and the fa'a Sāmoa world is expressed succinctly through the change of clothes.

A white boiler suit became something of a performance uniform for Setoga, and he was often seen wearing one at exhibition openings or events. The uniform doubles as both homage to Moana workers and a critique of the socio-economic status of Moana peoples in Aotearoa. In *Marching* (2011), Setoga, dressed in white boiler suit and white gumboots, marched through Grey Lynn Park. Marching was often performed at the end of church events that Setoga attended throughout his youth. However, as more Moana peoples moved out to West and South Auckland in search of affordable housing, Moana histories in the CBD have been slowly erased from memory. In this performance, Setoga performed the past and present, reinserting into the central city the image of both an invisible Moana history and the present invisible Moana labour.

Marching points to the long Moana histories of urban occupation. However, the work also points to a sustained invisibility of Moana within the workforce. This lack of socio-economic progress is a constant refrain and concern in Setoga's practice. While critical of the commercial exploitation and racism which inform that reality, Setoga has never been one to shy away from the limitations of fa'a Sāmoa for diaspora success either. Fa'a Sāmoa, often translated as 'the Samoan way', describes a set of practices and values that are central to a sense of Samoan identity and fosters the maintenance of cultural identity even in diaspora. Across many of his performances, Setoga critically questions the compatibility of an intractable fa'a Sāmoa 'operating system' within the New Zealand 'operating system'.[30] He explains:

> We've taken a system that works in Sāmoa and directly transplanted it here. It's not working here. After all this time in this country, we still haven't climbed out of our lower socio-economic rut. The only thing we've got from coming to this country is a bigger, flasher church. Samoans came here for a better life. We haven't fulfilled what we've come here for.[31]

It is important to note that Setoga here is critiquing not fa'a Sāmoa specifically, but rather its lack of adaptation within New Zealand. A critique of an unadjusted fa'a Sāmoa was put forward in a 2017 performance by Setoga, *O le moa e soso i le matatuai e tele ana pegu* (*The chicken closest to the scraper will reap the rewards*). The artist sits on a bench and scrapes the flesh from coconuts. By his feet are several chickens. As Setoga notes:

> Chickens are naturally inquisitive. In Sāmoa where they are free range, they don't see boundaries but rather find a way through those boundaries, hopping through fences, under gates to forage and find food.[32]

The chickens in *O le moa e soso i le matatuai e tele ana pegu* unknowingly perform the dilemma of whether to risk approaching the artist scraping flakes of coconut flesh at the expense of their own safety or to shy away from the body of the artist. The work

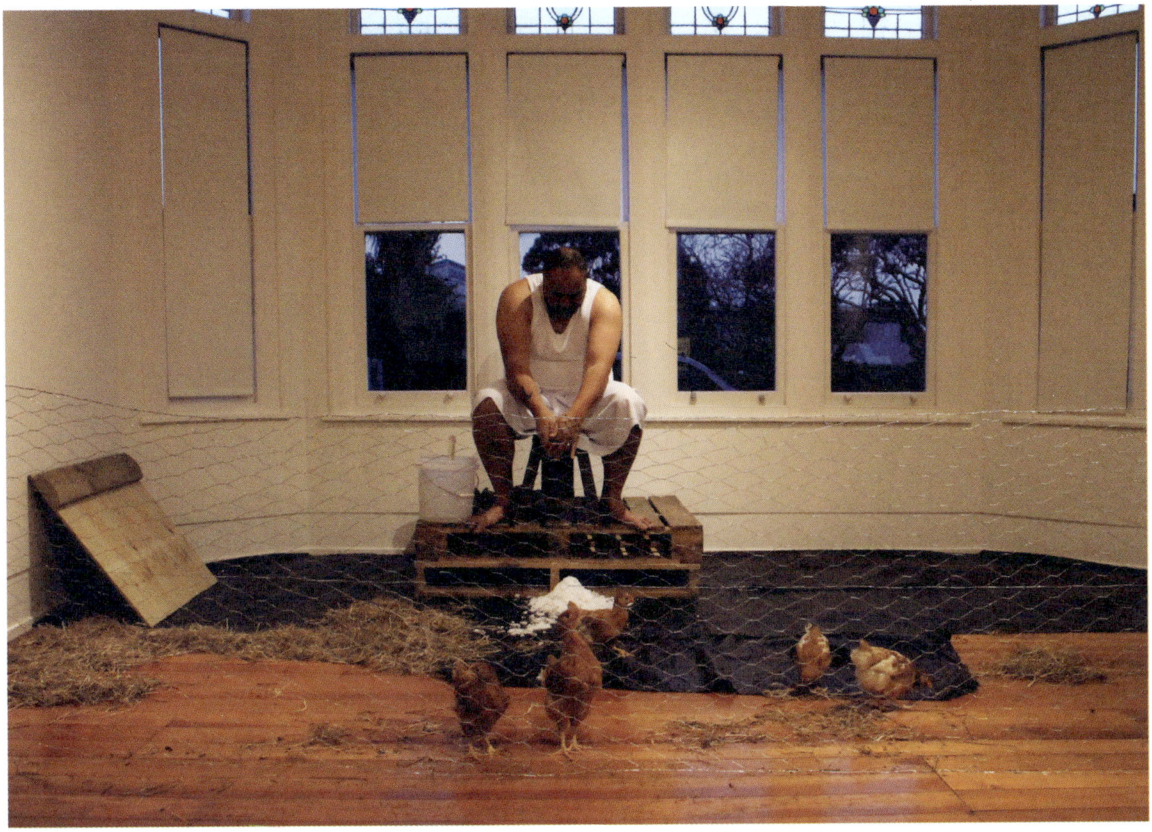

Siliga Setoga, *O le moa e soso i le matatuai e tele ana pegu*, 2017. In *Body Surface* at Corban Estate Arts Centre with Ioane Ioane, Jeremy Leatinu'u and Siliga David Setoga. *Courtesy Homestead Galleries, Corban Estate Arts Centre*

metaphorically performs the risks that diaspora Moana peoples must weigh up in pursuing their own success. Specifically, the risks here refer to going against certain behaviours enshrined within fa'a Sāmoa. As Setoga explains:

> We are a part of a generation that is debilitated by the notion of failure so much so that 'having a go' is less important than carrying the tag 'epic fail'. Shame is a bag we choose to carry. In the communal body I was raised in, if one could not carry their shame and did not show remorse for an act that brought disrepute to the Aiga, Village or Church then you were arrogant, lacked humility, which usually resulted in being excluded, banished from the Village or excommunicated from Church. Shame in this case is a tool of control. This shouldn't be the excuse for not 'having a go' but rather the risk we have to negotiate in order to rise above all our fears for the rewards we deserve.[33]

Setoga's willingness to question the unmediated import of fa'a Sāmoa into an urban New Zealand context is itself a bold risk. Though critical, his approach centres Moana peoples living in New Zealand. While pointing to the shapeshifting that urban Pasifika deal with daily, his performances ultimately question whether it might not be the 'operating systems' that need to shapeshift.

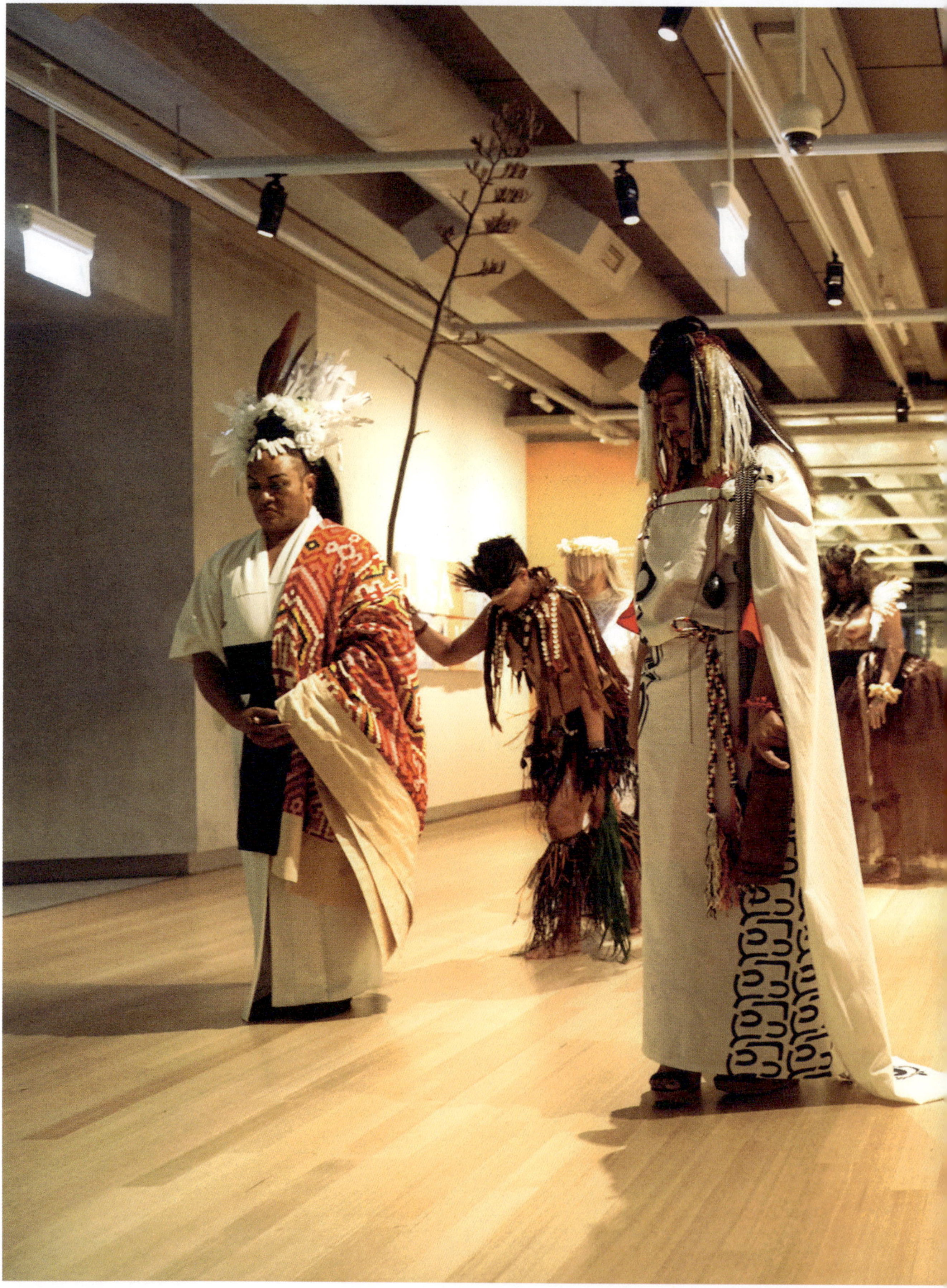

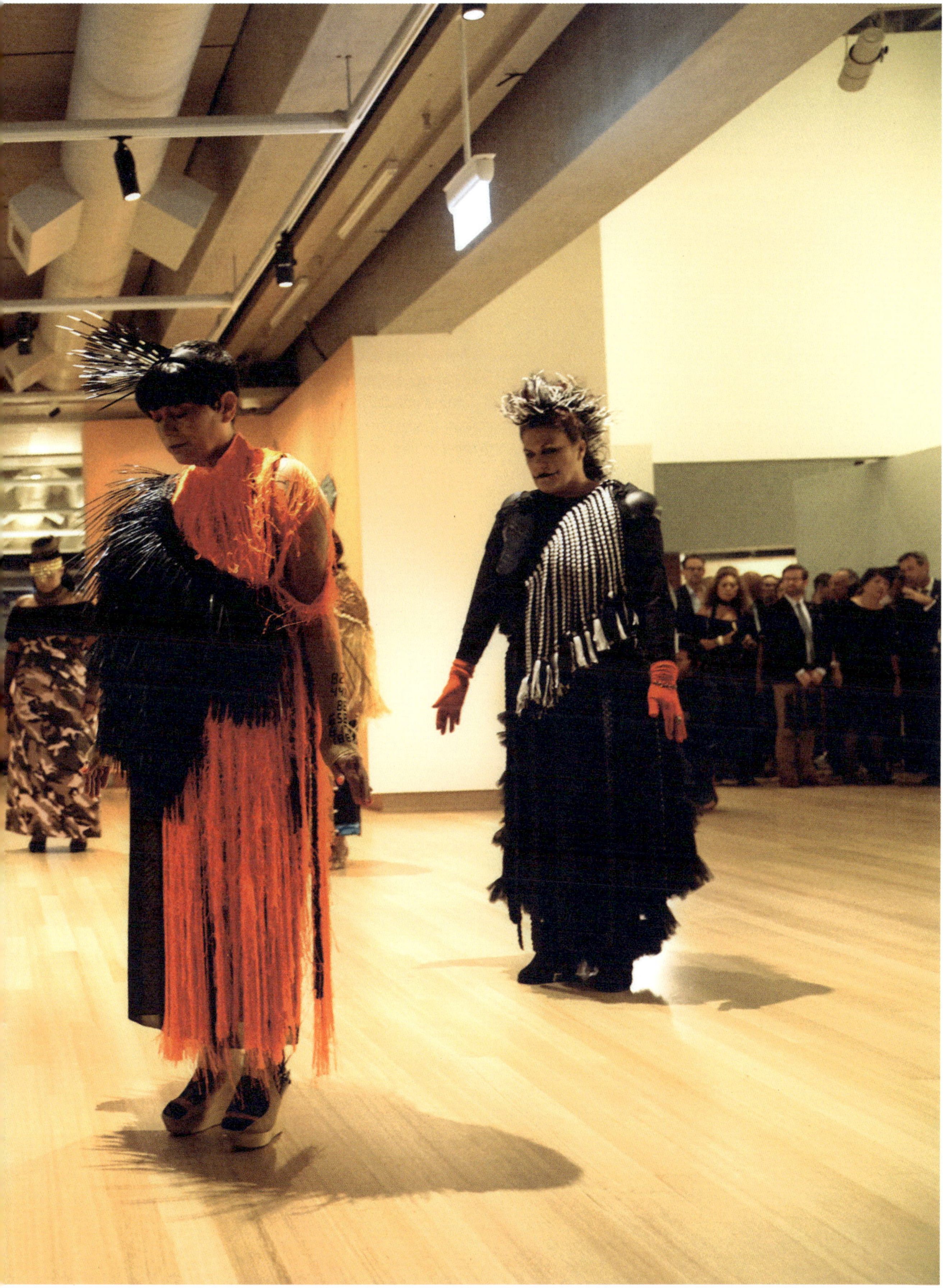

COLD ISLANDERS

In 2017 Leafā Wilson curated the exhibition *Cold Islanders: Art on the Pacific spectrum* for Waikato Museum, coining a new term to describe a second and third generation of New Zealand-Moana artists.

> The islands, you think of warmth, being sweaty and running around with a nice lavalava and a T-shirt on. Here in Aotearoa, we're doing the same thing except it's freezing, so it's always in my head, what has this made us into? It's not a negative, not a positive. It's just that we are different.[34]

The concept of 'Cold Islanders' was also developed in Wilson's thesis 'Cold Islanders' (2020), where she notes that while those raised by Island-born parents may not face intense issues of cultural distance, there is 'a sense of cultural insecurity' that lingers for those who have been raised in New Zealand. Finding current language insufficient to describe this ongoing reality, Wilson came up with the term 'Cold Islanders', which, as she writes, 'states succinctly the way I feel in this world':

> Not born in the nurturing heat of our island homes, but in a place that experiences frost and snow; to be cold in the sense that to be 'left out in the cold' is to feel a sense of exclusion. To be a CI is to contend with self-hood continually and piecing bits of cultures that belong partially to one's parents and grandparents, or also to European Aotearoa/New Zealand.[35]

Within the exhibition, three video performance works speak to the negotiating of one's cultural identity and attachments within New Zealand's settler-colonial context. In Darcell Apelu's *Response Series — Individualistic, Musu, Reaction to Insults* and *Social Drinks* (2013) — the artist's face fills the frame. Spot-lit against a black backdrop, the artist performs a series of reactions to social stereotypes imposed on Moana peoples. For the video *Individualistic*, she applies foundation that is shades lighter than her natural complexion; in *Musu* she stares back at the viewer; in *Reaction to Insults* she draws the concentric circles of a bull's-eye target on her face with red lipstick; and in *Social Drinks* she sips slowly from a can of Coca-Cola.

Christopher Braddock recalls the first presentation of Apelu's *Response Series* at AUT's ST PAUL St Gallery in 2013, in which the artist handed out the performances of *Musu* and *Reaction to Insults* to the gathered audience as videos playing on several tablets.[36] This juxtaposition of both the artist as a person in real life in front of the audience, and again as a video recording of her dead-on stare at the camera, heightens the audience's live act of viewing and the *Response Series* as a pre-recorded reaction. Unable to react to the current moment of viewing, the recorded performances respond to the entrenched and generalised gaze turned upon Pacific people. As the artist performs an awareness of being viewed while fixed in the moment of a pre-recording, the performance creates a glitch or rupture in the timescale of social dynamics that Pacific peoples and unidentified viewers span; while a viewer can at any moment select how to read the performance, the artist is immortalised in the moment of pre-emption.

Louisa Afoa's *Pink Flamingo* (2016), part of the ongoing series 'A Pool Is Not the Ocean', was also part of the *Cold Islanders* exhibition. Through this series of works,

PREVIOUS: Pacific Sisters, 2018. The opening *Acti.VĀ.tion* of their retrospective exhibition *Pacific Sisters: Fashion Activists/He Toa Tāera*. Museum of New Zealand Te Papa Tongarewa. From left: Henry Ah-Foo Taripo, Ema Lyon, Ani O'Neill, Feeonaa Clifton (née Wall), Rosanna Raymond, Jaunnie 'Ilolahia, Lisa Reihana, Selina Haami (née Forsyth, obscured), Suzanne Tamaki. *Photo by Kerry Brown*

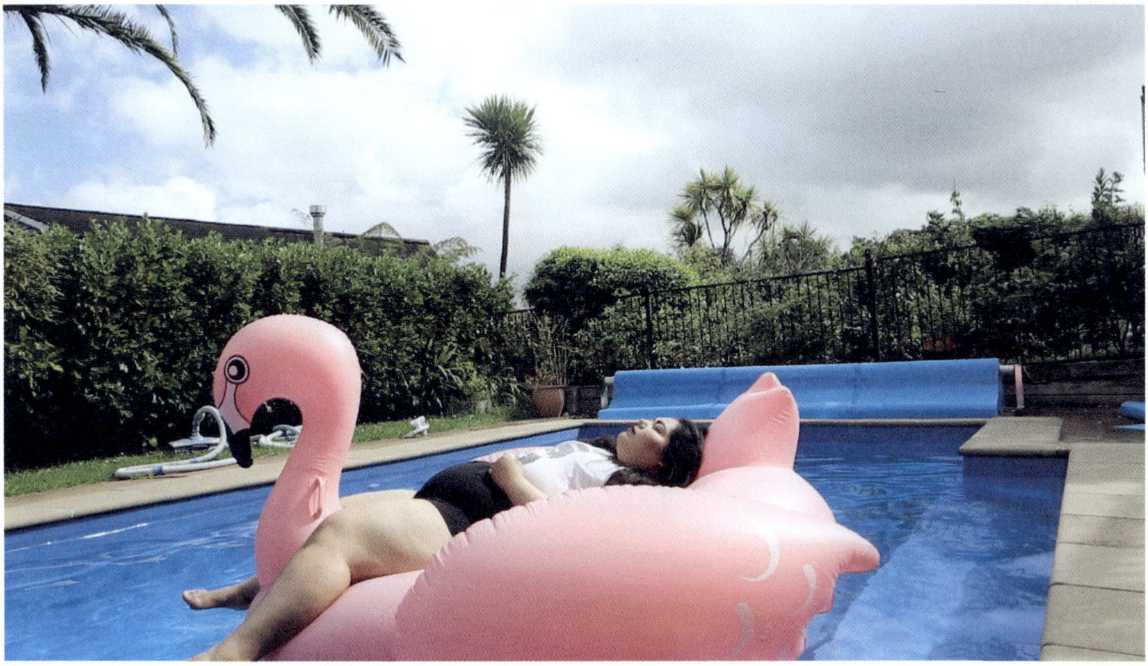

Louisa Afoa, *Pink Flamingo I*, 'A Pool Is Not the Ocean', 2017, video still. Single-channel video, colour, sound. *Courtesy the artist*

Afoa employs the pool as shorthand for a wealthy, suburban and often Pākehā context.[37] While the ocean has often been theorised as the home of Moana peoples,[38] a pool, the work's title tells us, is not the ocean. The comparison between the ocean and the pool designates the latter as a foreign space, or perhaps a space that renders the artist's body foreign. While the artist's body is non-deviant within the ocean, in the pool the body politics of size and colour are marked out as signifiers of difference.

Negotiating multifaceted identity, cultural connections and a sense of belonging as a Moana person in New Zealand is a consistent refrain across the performance videos in *Cold Islanders*. Melanie Rands and Ahilapalapa Rands' *Across the Sea* is a collaborative work in which the methods of learning the hula art form are adapted to geographical distances and the impacts of colonisation on cultural transmission.

In the single-channel video performance, Ahilapalapa Rands performs a hula for the camera. Her knowledge of this specific hula derives from written instructions. As Wilson notes, 'The Rands' choreographic notes come from their grandmother/great grandmother who transcribed the instructions.'[39] The video work alludes to the difficulty and required persistence of learning physical movement from text. Here, the embrace of all potential learning tools — including the less customary form of writing — is put forward as a necessary adaption for those in diaspora.

Across the performance works in *Cold Islanders* we see the use of performance art to negotiate the space between diaspora, ancestral connections and racial stereotypes. Instead of seeking to resolve the distance between ancestral and adopted homelands, the performances here unearth the negotiations, translations, encounters and confrontations that emerge in the space between. Indeed, the various works by the Pacific Sisters, Michel Tuffery, Siliga Setoga, Leafā Wilson and the works shown in the exhibition *Cold Islanders* suggest the ongoing relevance of diaspora as a concern across Moana performance art in New Zealand.

What emerged from the Pacific Sisters' coining of the term 'urban Pasifika' is the failure of pre-existing terminology to capture and convey the heady mix of influences and the negotiation happening between them that were found in urban centres, from the ongoing cultural attachments to the influence of New Zealand Pākehā contexts as well as global popular culture, through to the ways in which Moana and Indigenous peoples relate to each other. As the works discussed here suggest, the formation of identity and the various relations Moana artists hold are constantly in flux and being renegotiated from site to site. Though the urban is by no means the only site where Moana artists, performance and subjectivities are re-negotiated and reformed, its significance persists as a site where influences co-mingle. Forever moving between communities, operating systems and expectations of identity, Moana performance art speaks consistently of the need to find new terms and expressions when the current available ones do not fit.

NOTES

1 Robert Leonard and Caroline Vercoe, 'Pacific Sisters: Doing it for themselves', *Art and Asia Pacific* 14 (1997): 42–45.

2 The term 'Moana' is used throughout this chapter to refer to the region most known as the Pacific. The Moana is an Indigenous term for the Great Ocean found in several Indigenous Moana languages. It is used here in recognition of and as an alternative to the colonial etymology of terms such as Pacific and Oceania. While the Moana is itself an imperfect term — particularly as a Polycentric term that minimises other Indigenous terms for the region — its use here signals the subjective position of the co-author as a Samoan (for which Moana is the Samoan term for the region).

3 'Demographics of New Zealand's Pacific Population' (Wellington: Statistics New Zealand and Ministry of Pacific Island Affairs, 2010), 8. www.stats.govt.nz/reports/demographics-of-new-zealands-pacific-population

4 Damon Salesa, *Island Time: New Zealand's Pacific futures* (Wellington: Bridget Williams Books, 2017), 15.

5 'Demographicsof New Zealand's Pacific Population'.

6 Rosanna Raymond, 'A Walk Through My Eyelands', *The Pantograph Punch*, 20 November 2020, www.pantograph-punch.com/posts/walk-through-my-eyelands

7 Ibid.

8 Ane Tonga, 'Lonnie Hutchinson: Black Out', Tautau Contemporary Pacific Arts Trust newsletter, December 2014. See also Ane Tonga, ed., *Declaration: A Pacific feminist agenda*, exhibition catalogue (Auckland: Auckland Art Gallery Toi o Tāmaki, 2022), 174–77.

9 Ioana Gordon-Smith, 'From the Margins to the Mainstream: Pacific Sisters at Te Papa', *The Pantograph Punch*, 18 April 2018, https://pantograph-punch.com/posts/pacific-sisters

10 Hawai'i Contemporary, 'Hawai'i Triennial 2022: Pacific Sisters', https://hawaiicontemporary.org/artist-pacific-sisters

11 'During the World War II era, 75 percent of Māori lived in historic, generally rural, tribal areas. By the 1970s, 80 percent of Māori had migrated to the nation's urban centers due to the expanding manufacturing sector and the centralization of industry in the cities.' Elizabeth M. DeLoughrey, 'Adrift and Unmoored: Globalization and urban indigeneity', in *Routes and Roots: Navigating Caribbean and Pacific Island literatures* (Honolulu: University of Hawai'i Press, 2007), 199. Citing M. H. Durie, *Te Mana, Te Kāwanatanga: The politics of Maori self-determination* (Oxford/New York: Oxford University Press, 1998), 95.

12 Patrick Saulmatino Thomsen, Lana Lopesi and Kevin Lujan Lee, 'Contemporary Moana Mobilities: Settler-colonial citizenship, upward mobility, and transnational Pacific identities', *The Contemporary Pacific* 34, no. 2 (2022): 342.

13 Ginny Fisher, 'Shining a Light on the Pacific Sisters' Artistic Legacy', *New Zealand Herald*, 7 March 2018, www.nzherald.co.nz/viva/culture/shining-a-light-on-the-pacific-sisters-artistic-legacy/D2LSUBUEOMXQUOT5KWG6BWI4MU

14 Rosanna Raymond quoted in Fisher, 'Shining a Light'.

15 Gordon-Smith, 'From the Margins to the Mainstream'.

16 Ibid.

17 Ibid.

18 Raymond, 'A Walk'.

19 Doris de Pont, 'Stories: Pacific Sisters,' New Zealand Fashion Museum, April 2019, http://www.nzfashionmuseum.org.nz/pacific-sisters

20 'Pacific Sisters Present "Fresh Flashbacks"', Auckland Art Gallery Toi o Tāmaki, 14 July 2019. www.aucklandartgallery.com/whats-on/event/pacific-sisters-present-fresh-flashbacks

21 Nina Tonga, 'Staring at Motorways: Urban Pacific art — a genealogy of sorts', abstract, in *Indigenous Modernisms: Histories of the contemporary.* Multiple Modernisms: Twentieth-Century Artistic Modernisms in Global Perspective (Wellington: Museum of New Zealand Te Papa Tongarewa, 2014).

22 Caroline Vercoe, 'Art Niu Sila: Contemporary Pacific art in New Zealand', in *Pacific Art Niu Sila: The Pacific dimension of contemporary New Zealand arts*, edited by Sean Mallon and Pandora Fulimalo Pereira (Wellington: Te Papa Press, 2002), 199.

23 Michel Tuffery, 'APT3/Michel Tuffery: Povi Tau Vaga (The Challenge)', YouTube video, 5:09, 9 October 2018. Queensland Art Gallery, www.youtube.com/watch?v=1YPtAKzGO2o

24 Michel Tuffery quoted in Vercoe, 'Art Niu Sila', 199.

25 For more on Auckland's adoption of a Pacific brand see Lana Lopesi, 'So, You Want to Be the "Largest Polynesian City in the World"?', *The Pantograph Punch*, 6 April 2018, https://pantograph-punch.com/posts/largest-polynesian-city

26 Nina Tonga, 'siliga david setoga: "i'm got to be good for you"', Tautau Contemporary Pacific Arts Trust, June 2011, 1.

27 Fa'a Sāmoa loosely translates as the Samoan way, or in the manner of Sāmoa.

28 Siliga David Setoga, 'Siliga David Setoga', profile, *The Big Idea*, https://web.archive.org/web/20221213045348/https://thebigidea.nz/profile/siliga-david-setoga

29 An 'ie faitaga is a wrapped fabric worn at the waist by men that is usually black, reaches the shin and has pockets. Often described as a formal lavalava, it is a type

of dress usually worn at church or on special occasions, and is increasingly becoming a uniform option within schools.

30 Operating system is a term Setoga uses in talanoa with Chikako Yamauchi in Chikako Yamauchi, 'Talking Story about Art and Life: Narratives of contemporary Oceanic artists and their work' (Master's thesis, University of Canterbury, 2014).

31 Setoga in Yamauchi, 'Talking Story about Art and Life', 190.

32 Ioane Ioane, Jeremy Leatinu'u and Siliga David Setoga, 'Body Surface', exhibition handout (Corban Estate Arts Centre, 2017), 6.

33 Ibid.

34 Leafâ Wilson in Sela Jane Hopgood, 'NZ-born Pacific Artists Challenge Stereotypes in Hamilton', *RNZ*, 25 August 2017, www.rnz.co.nz/international/pacific-news/338011/nz-born-pacific-artists-challenge-stereotypes-in-hamilton

35 Olga Hedwig Janice Wilson, 'Cold Islanders: Moana Pasifika/Oceania identified artists creating and occupying respectful stances of strength and confidence in Aotearoa' (Master's thesis, Auckland University of Technology, 2021), 6.

36 Christopher Braddock, 'Animism, Animacy and Participation in the Performances of Darcell Apelu', in *Animism in Art and Performance*, edited by Christopher Braddock (Cham, Switzerland: Palgrave Macmillan, 2017), 193, 206.

37 These works were performed and filmed on Auckland's North Shore, an area often perceived as wealthy and Pākehā. They mark the artist's move to the neighbourhood from Papakura, a more demographically mixed suburb.

38 Epeli Hau'ofa and Albert Wendt have been particularly influential in popularising an Ocean-based regional framework.

39 Leafâ Wilson, *The Cold Islanders: Art on the Pacific spectrum*, exhibition catalogue (Hamilton: Waikato Museum, Te Whare Taonga o Waikato, 2017), 14.

REFERENCES

Auckland Art Gallery Toi o Tāmaki. 'Pacific Sisters Present "Fresh Flashbacks"'. 14 July 2019. www.aucklandartgallery.com/whats-on/event/pacific-sisters-present-fresh-flashbacks

Braddock, Christopher. 'Animism, Animacy and Participation in the Performances of Darcell Apelu'. In *Animism in Art and Performance*, edited by Christopher Braddock, 191–211. Cham, Switzerland: Palgrave Macmillan, 2017.

de Pont, Doris. 'Stories: Pacific Sisters'. New Zealand Fashion Museum, April 2019. www.nzfashionmuseum.org.nz/pacific-sisters

DeLoughrey, Elizabeth M. 'Adrift and Unmoored: Globalization and urban indigeneity'. In *Routes and Roots: Navigating Caribbean and Pacific Island literatures*, 196–228. Honolulu: University of Hawai'i Press, 2007.

'Demographics of New Zealand's Pacific Population'. Wellington: Statistics New Zealand and Ministry of Pacific Island Affairs, 2010. www.stats.govt.nz/reports/demographics-of-new-zealands-pacific-population

Durie, M. H. *Te Mana, Te Kāwanatanga: The politics of Maori self-determination*. Oxford/New York: Oxford University Press, 1998.

Fisher, Ginny. 'Shining a Light on the Pacific Sisters' Artistic Legacy'. *New Zealand Herald*, 7 March 2018. www.nzherald.co.nz/viva/culture/shining-a-light-on-the-pacific-sisters-artistic-legacy/D2LSUBUEOMXQUOT5KWG6BWI4MU

Gordon-Smith, Ioana. 'From the Margins to the Mainstream: Pacific Sisters at Te Papa'. *The Pantograph Punch*, 18 April 2018. https://pantograph-punch.com/posts/pacific-sisters

Hawai'i Contemporary. 'Hawai'i Triennial 2022: Pacific Sisters'. https://hawaiicontemporary.org/artist-pacific-sisters

Hopgood, Sela Jane. 'NZ-Born Pacific Artists Challenge Stereotypes in Hamilton'. *RNZ*, 25 August 2017. www.rnz.co.nz/international/pacific-news/338011/nz-born-pacific-artists-challenge-stereotypes-in-hamilton

Leonard, Robert and Caroline Vercoe. 'Pacific Sisters: Doing it for themselves'. *Art and Asia Pacific* 14 (1997): 42–45. Republished: https://robertleonard.org/pacific-sisters-doing-it-for-themselves

Lopesi, Lana. 'So, You Want to Be the "Largest Polynesian City in the World"?'. *The Pantograph Punch*, 6 April 2018. https://pantograph-punch.com/posts/largest-polynesian-city

Raymond, Rosanna. 'A Walk Through My Eyelands'. *The Pantograph Punch*, 20 November 2020. www.pantograph-punch.com/posts/walk-through-my-eyelands

Salesa, Damon. *Island Time: New Zealand's Pacific futures*. Wellington: Bridget Williams Books, 2017.

Setoga, Siliga David. 'Siliga David Setoga'. *The Big Idea*. https://web.archive.org/web/20221213045348/https://thebigidea.nz/profile/siliga-david-setoga

Thomsen, Patrick Saulmatino, Lana Lopesi and Kevin Lujan Lee. 'Contemporary Moana Mobilities: Settler-colonial citizenship, upward mobility, and transnational Pacific identities'. *The Contemporary Pacific* 34, no. 2 (2022): 327–52.

Tonga, Ane. 'Lonnie Hutchinson: Black Out'. Tautau Contemporary Pacific Arts Trust newsletter, December 2014.

——— *Declaration: A Pacific feminist agenda*. Exhibition catalogue. Auckland Art Gallery Toi o Tāmaki, 2022.

Tonga, Nina. 'Siliga David Setoga: "I'm Got to Be Good for You"'. Tautau Contemporary Pacific Arts Trust newsletter, June 2011.

——— 'Staring at Motorways: Urban Pacific art — a genealogy of sorts'. In *Indigenous Modernisms: Histories of the contemporary*. Wellington: Museum of New Zealand Te Papa Tongarewa, 2014. https://multiplemodernisms.maa.cam.ac.uk/contemporary-modernism-december-2014-wellington-new-zealand

Tuffery, Michel. 'APT3/Michel Tuffery: Povi Tau Vaga (The Challenge)'. Queensland Art Gallery, 9 October 2018. www.youtube.com/watch?v=1YPtAKzGO2o

Vercoe, Caroline. 'Art Niu Sila: Contemporary Pacific art in New Zealand'. In *Pacific Art Niu Sila: The Pacific dimension of contemporary New Zealand arts*, edited by Sean Mallon and Pandora Fulimalo Pereira, 191–207. Wellington: Te Papa Press, 2002.

Wilson, Leafâ. *The Cold Islanders: Art on the Pacific spectrum*. Exhibition catalogue. Hamilton: Waikato Museum, Te Whare Taonga o Waikato, 2017.

Wilson, Olga Hedwig Janice. 'Cold Islanders: Moana Pasifika/Oceania identified artists creating and occupying respectful stances of strength and confidence in Aotearoa'. Master's thesis, Auckland University of Technology, 2021. https://hdl.handle.net/10292/14116

Yamauchi, Chikako. 'Talking Story About Art and Life: Narratives of contemporary Oceanic artists and their work'. Master's thesis, University of Canterbury, 2014. http://hdl.handle.net/10092/9354

10

CONSTELLATIONS OF SUBJECTIVITY: ENGAGING THE EMERGENT, ADAPTIVE AND FLUID NATURE OF LIVED SOCIAL DIFFERENCE IN MĀORI AND MOANA PERFORMANCE ART

Lana Lopesi &
Layne Waerea

A line of rowing machines sat on the lawn outside Te Tuhi Centre for the Arts in Tāmaki Makaurau Auckland. Artist Cora-Allan Wickliffe (now Lafaiki Twiss; Ngāpuhi, Tainui/Alofi, Liku), assembled a group of Māori and Moana participants recruited through an open call. She invited them to row a portion of the historical and symbolic 7000-kilometre journey from Hawaiki to Aotearoa made by Indigenous tīpuna in the century before the earliest settlement of Māori people in Aotearoa.

As she states: 'Through the act of rowing I am interested in moving into the future by maintaining a connection with the past oceanic mobility of Indigenous Pacific people.'[1] As Māori and Moana descendants performed the past *into* the future, entanglements between the participants and the artist's own genealogical subjectivities intersected with all of their subjectivities as Indigenous people in the contemporary settler-colonial context of Aotearoa New Zealand.

This work, *Electric Waka* (2014), is one example of how concepts such as whakapapa, gafa, mana, mana motuhake and mau are integral to the individual or collective artistic practices of Māori and Moana performance artists. The lives of artists are interrelated with their roles as family members, friends and members of the public: these are, we argue, mutually informing and co-constitutive. As discussed in this chapter, these cultural concepts enable performance art, which draws from the constant and fluid state of negotiating multiple subjectivities, be they artistic, cultural and/or legal.

In this chapter we borrow the phrase 'constellations of subjectivity' from New Zealand academics Danielle Johnson, Meg Parsons and Karen Fisher[2] to consider how a selection of Māori and Moana performance artists hold, practise and adapt their multiplicities, drawing from cultural concepts and beyond. As we reference constellations of subjectivity, we note the navigational metaphor as a hidden resonance here between the idea of constellations in the formation of subjectivity, and navigational wayfinding in Te Moana-nui-a-Kiwa the Pacific Ocean — which, in turn, relates in poignant ways to the oceanic mobility of the participants in *Electric Waka*.

Subjectivity, as we use it, describes the way that one's lived subject position impacts one's perceptions and interpretations of the world.[3] For Māori and Moana artists in Aotearoa, their Indigenous subject position exists in relation to modes of power exerted through settler colonialism and racialisation. These subjectivities, made in relation to modes of power, converge with subject positions drawn from their own Indigenous culture to create 'constellations of subjectivity'. Subjectivity in constellation follows the notion that one experiences oneself as a subject in relation to other subjects by constantly drawing closer to or further away from these.[4] In this sense, the concept of subjectivities (rather than identity) is used to convey the emergent, adaptive and fluid nature of lived social difference.[5]

For many performance artists from the Moana, multiple subjectivities converge, intersect or sit in constellation with their practice. In the most obvious sense, it is the intersection of their subjectivity as an artist within the field or discipline of contemporary art, with their Indigenous subjectivity as Māori, Samoan or Niuean, for example, that is immediately observable.

Beyond these identifiers, artists also exist within complex webs of whakapapa and gafa that further complicate and acknowledge a layered texture to their own subjectivities. They might also belong to other professional worlds as lawyers, educators or activists. Each of these examples of subjectivity combines to create different assemblages of subjectivity that take form depending on context and where a particular subjectivity becomes dominant or recedes.

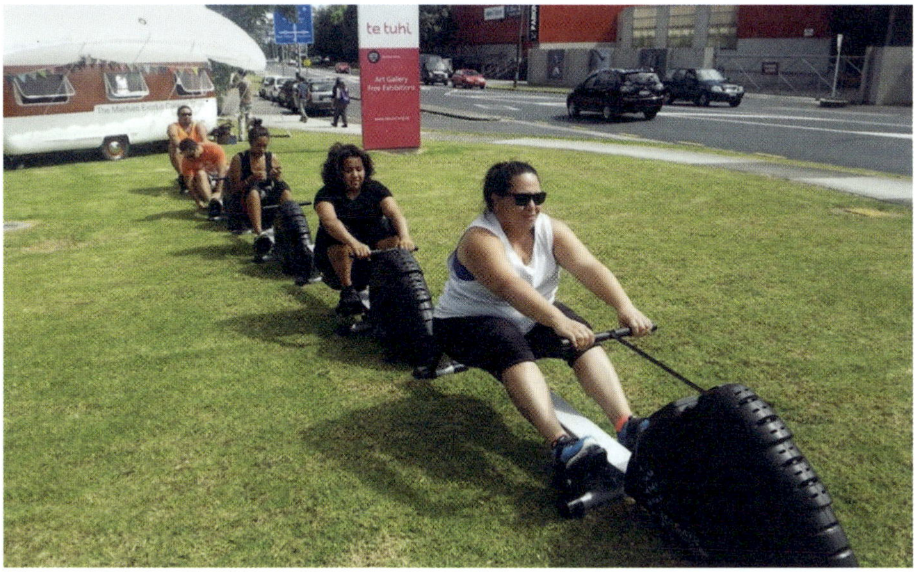

Cora-Allan Lafaiki Twiss (née Wickliffe), *Electric Waka*, 2014. Performed at Te Tuhi, Pakuranga, Tāmaki Makaurau Auckland. *Courtesy Te Tuhi. Photo by Amiria Puia-Taylor*

The artists featured in this chapter include Cora-Allan Lafaiki Twiss, Arapeta Ashton, Rosanna Raymond, Cat Ruka, Layne Waerea, Suzanne Tamaki and Leafā Wilson/Olga Krause. We argue that their artworks reveal how their lived artistic experiences reflect and are informed by these intersections; intersections that are not fixed but remain emergent and responsive to the different and multiple subjectivities at play. These constellations of subjectivity provide important sources of agency for Māori and Moana performance artists; opportunities to explore the rich layers — inherited and ongoing — and to hold space, acknowledge the connection to the past and take on new meaning.

WHAKAPAPA

The genealogical subjectivities drawn on in *Electric Waka* can be understood through Māori and Moana conceptions of genealogy such as whakapapa and gafa. In *Tikanga Māori: Living by Māori values*, theorist Hirini Moko Mead emphasises that whakapapa is not only a linear genealogy but also a source of identity and belonging for Māori people, one that provides a framework for understanding relationships between people, the natural world and the spiritual realm.[6] In this light, the complex webs of whakapapa that Māori and Moana performance artists belong to are an essential part of their layered subjectivities and influence their artistic practice. Lafaiki Twiss's *Electric Waka* signifies these entanglements or constellations of layered subjectivities as participants symbolically, and with great physical effort, navigate their way through complex whakapapa.

Perhaps similar in motivation to *Electric Waka*, the 2018 exhibition *Acts of Passage* at Te Tuhi Centre for the Arts in Tāmaki Makaurau Auckland explored the therapeutic effects on the body of small rituals and cleansing gestures. The participating artists drew on their diverse knowledge systems to connect humans with nature, myth and ancient cultural values. Arapeta Ashton's *Te au o te moana* (2017) was a single-channel video that documented a performance which took place in the artist's hometown of Whangateau Harbour in Aotearoa.

During the performance, Ashton, partially submerged in the ocean's current, wore a pākē (Māori rain cape), woven by the artist, to channel the tide. Although the title translates as 'the current of the ocean', the performance explores the tidal movements of the ocean, in memory of and physical connection to the artist's ancestors who journeyed across Te Moana-nui-a-Kiwa from their ancestral home of Hawaiki.[7] The rhythmic tidal washing of the body here, as with the earlier rowing strokes of *Electric Waka*, offers another way to connect to and remember whakapapa.

GAFA

The Samoan word gafa means lineage and genealogy. Within Samoan cosmogonies, genealogy plays a significant role in one's subjectivity. As Leali'ifano Albert Refiti has noted, Samoan subjectivity is often described as lacking a fixed self or sense of individualism. Rather, one's attachment to gafa plays a more significant role than individual desires. Refiti describes the Samoan person as 'dividual or distributed as a fractal Self, stretched along many lines and alliances'.[8] From this perspective, Samoan subjectivity is entangled with one's own gafa or genealogical ties as a constellation of subjectivity.

Samoan artist Rosanna Raymond uses the concept of gafa in her performance art practice. For two decades Raymond has sought to reinvigorate Moana measina (treasures) held in museums, through performance or activation that connects the measina to Raymond's own body, which, as a vessel, reconnects the measina to their own gafa. One example of this is the *Pasifika Styles* exhibition (2006–08) curated by Raymond and Amiria Salmond for the Museum of Archaeology and Anthropology at the University of Cambridge, United Kingdom. The exhibition was among the first within the Moana art context to bring contemporary artists into museological space to collapse the rift between art and artefact, dead and living, to emphasise instead the living and genealogical constellations within which everyone and every thing exists.

This connection to genealogy goes both ways. Raymond writes: 'Their gafa or genealogy not only exists through the hands that created them, but also inhabits the very substances they are made from, and thus, they connect us to our cosmological genealogical origins.'[9] Thus, genealogy here is not exclusively the domain of humans, but rather connects humans to the inanimate, to the more-than-human, highlighting the interconnectedness of all things.

MANA

Another element of Māori and Moana constellations of subjectivity is mana. Mana as a traditional concept in a Māori worldview has been translated as power, authority, prestige, and 'a special and non-ordinary presence or essence that can flow in the world — in persons, in places and events'.[10] There is no single source or acknowledgement of mana; it is understood instead in terms of degrees of mana and multiple energies and presences in the natural world, and is inextricably linked to concepts of tapu (sacred restrictions) and mauri (life force) — relationships that ultimately allow the mana to flow in the natural world.[11]

Refiti glosses mana from a Samoan perspective simply as power, but goes on to articulate its divine nature: 'Mana is the elevated and invisible seat of power and prestige emanating from the ancestor gods.' Acknowledging its unseen quality, Refiti notes that mana can take place 'both within persons and objects of special qualities, which allows the person or object to emanate an ideal condition'. In that way it is a cosmic or supernatural force that is 'knowable only indirectly, through its efficacy and through its manifestation in things'. [12]

Composer and researcher Te Ahukaramū Charles Royal offers a modern nuance of mana that centres on the features and qualities of mana, in which 'mana is some kind of quality, energy or consciousness in the world which can be harnessed and expressed in human activities through acts of generosity and wisdom'.[13] One does not speak of one's own mana; it is evident in one's creativity, insight and knowledge and the relationships fostered in one's communities.

MANA WĀHINE

Cat Ruka (Ngāpuhi, Waitaha, Ngāi Te Rangi) is a versatile artist, having worked as a performer, choreographer, educator, mentor and artistic director. In her work *Playing Savage* (2009), Ruka explores the concept of temporal sovereignty and how alternative notions of Indigenous Oceania sovereignty and self-determination can challenge the historical stereotypes of Māori women who have been subject to the 'affective regimes of colonialism'.[14] Through the performance of *Playing Savage*, Ruka takes up the colonial disciplining of Māori women's bodies, and uses her own body, clad in traditional Māori attire, to challenge the viewer's perceptions of Māori women. Angela Lynn Robinson gives an account of the performance:

> Ruka coolly sits on a large chair, bare-breasted, wearing a traditional Māori piupiu, or flax skirt. Her body, positioned in the trite Pacific Islander woman stance of the mythical Pania of the Reef and aggrandized in the artwork of French post-impressionist Paul Gauguin, is out of place in the elaborate décor and furnishings of a British colonial drawing room.[15]

In the programme notes, Ruka describes *Playing Savage* as a performative ritual aimed at subverting the ideas, symbols and images associated with Māori women.[16]

Playing Savage uses performance to confront the viewer's perceptions of Māori women and their bodies, taking up a challenge presented by Ngāhuia Te Awekotuku in emphasising the importance of self-determination for Māori women and celebrating their strength and creativity. In her book *Mana Wāhine Māori* (1991), Te Awekotuku, a Māori lesbian, academic and art historian, discusses the reassertion and celebration of Māori women, from traditional roles to the emergence of new ones in the future. She emphasises the importance of self-determination for 'ourselves as Māori women', prioritising pro-action and the rediscovery of essential strength and harmony between genders.[17]

Te Awekotuku describes the Māori women's art world as a powerful force that carries a range of emotions and experiences. As someone who navigates multiple worlds, she concludes in her chapter 'Māori and Feminist: My view' that she has been challenged personally 'to consider the colliding urgencies' in her life. She writes: 'I move within many worlds, yet share the confidence and security of my community of tribal women, and a branching global network of lesbian sisters . . . I claim *all* my cultures, all my conflicts. They make me what I am; they will shape what I am becoming.'[18] In this context, Ruka's performance and Te Awekotuku's text highlight the resilience and agency of Māori women in the face of historical and ongoing colonialism. Ruka's powerful performance involving

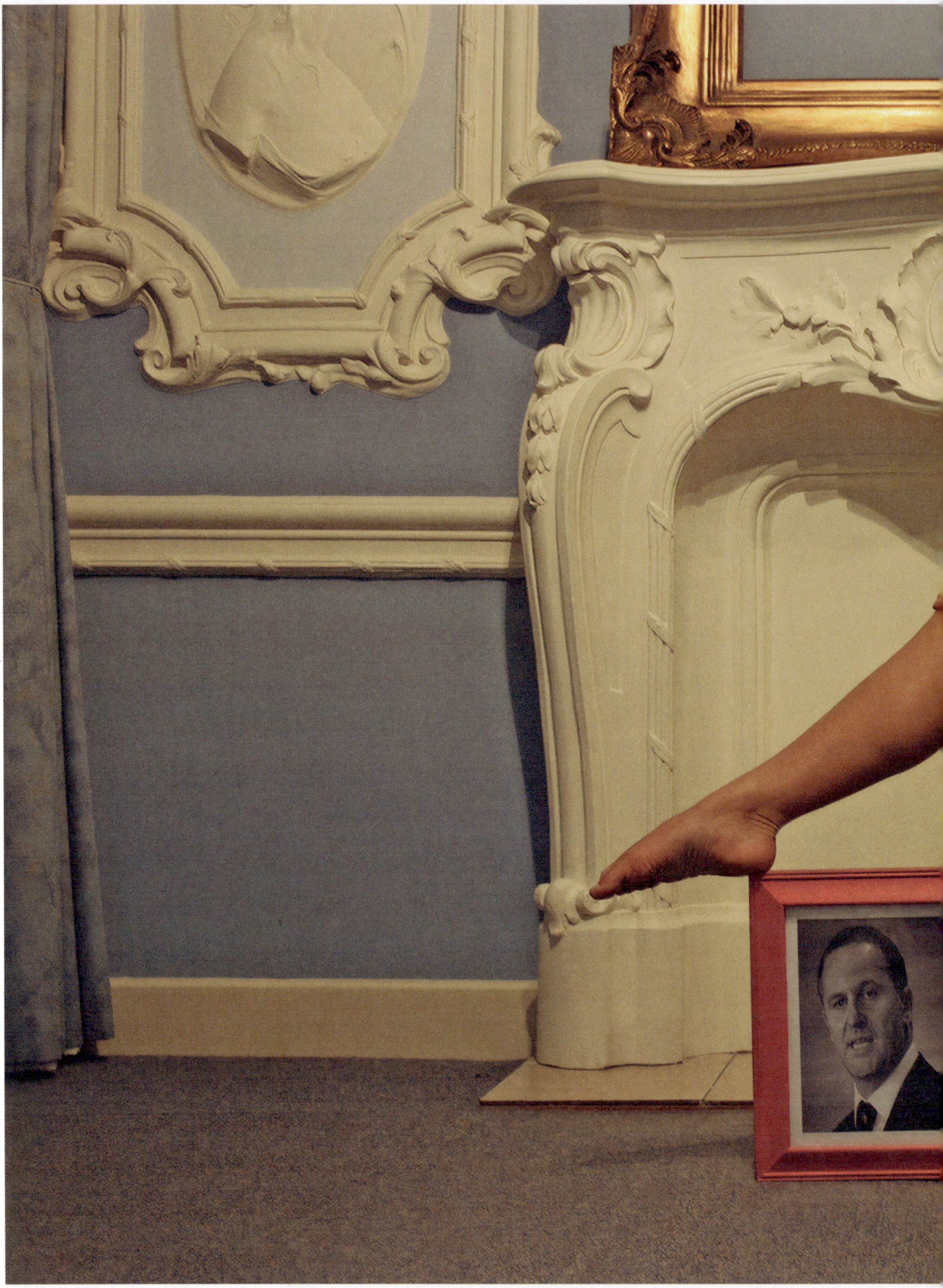

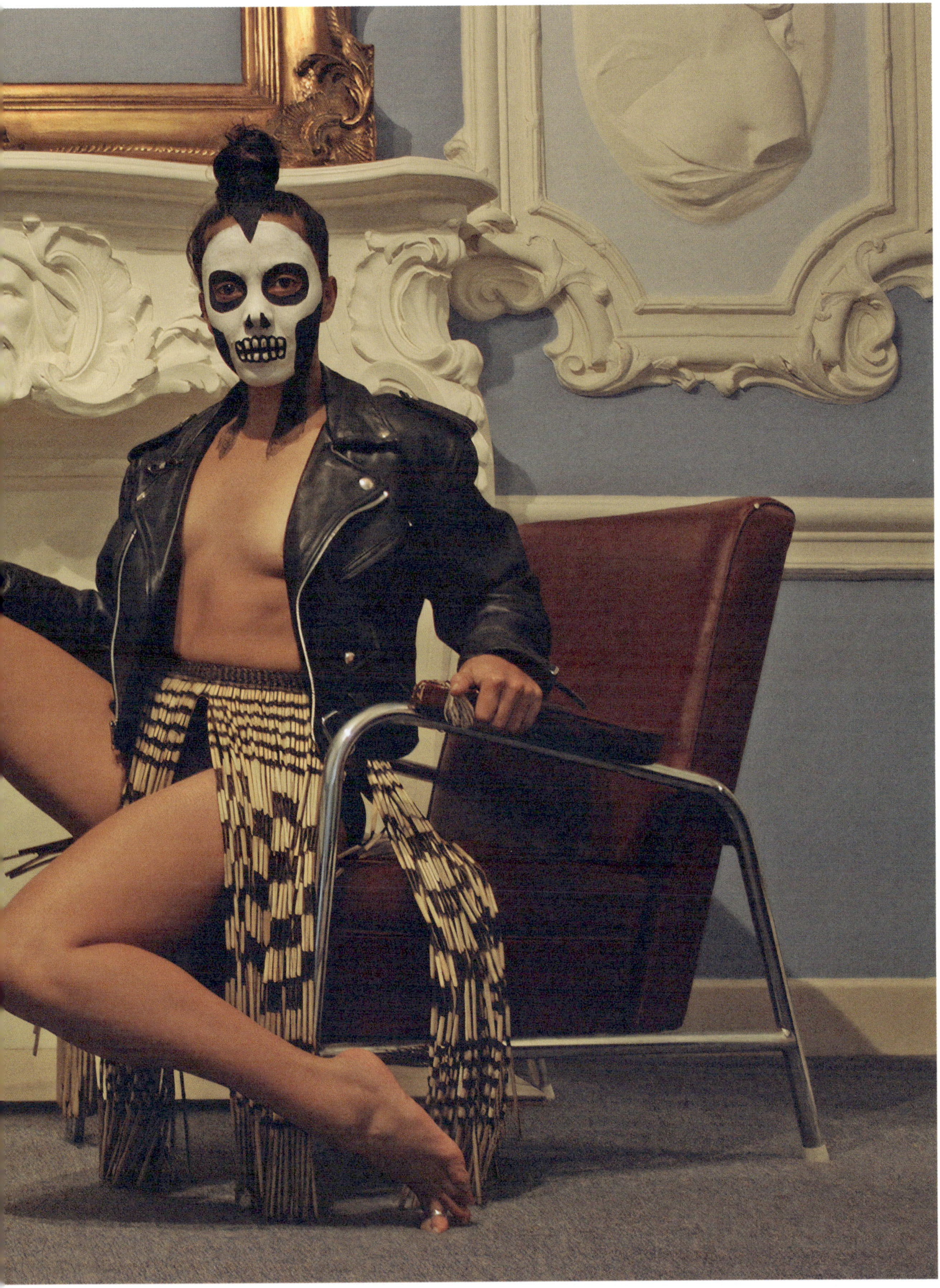

costume, pose and assertive body placement asserts mana wāhine subjectivities, made in relation to modes of colonial power to create constellations of subjectivity.

PREVIOUS: Cat Ruka (Ngāpuhi, Waitaha, Ngāi Te Rangi), *Playing Savage*, 2009, documentation of performance. *Courtesy the artist*

MĀORI ACTIVISM: MANA MOTUHAKE

Academic and author Ranginui Walker wrote that the notion of Māori activism can trace its beginnings to the signing of Te Tiriti o Waitangi in 1840 and the subsequent misinterpretation of what was being agreed to between Māori tribal chiefs and representatives of the British Crown. Te Tiriti o Waitangi is Aotearoa's founding document and was first signed on 6 February 1840 as an agreement, in Māori and English, made between the British Crown and about 540 Māori rangatira (chiefs).

Walker writes that tribal chiefs were 'misled into signing away their sovereignty in a document that has never been ratified or recognised as a treaty of international law'.[19] Within twenty years of the signing, continued efforts by the governor under the British Crown to extend British sovereignty at the expense of Māori culminated in the New Zealand Land Wars of the 1860s.

Māori activism and the dynamics of mana motuhake and mana whenua were two founding principles of the Māori King movement that emerged in 1858. Mana motuhake embraced and encompassed the different layers of authority of tribal groups to determine their own cultural, spiritual, political and economic destiny; and mana whenua ensured the exercise of this same authority over land. The history of Māori activism since this time has evolved in different forms and scale, and includes Māori political parties, legal intervention in the courts and the Waitangi Tribunal, and large-scale public protest as seen in the Māori Land March or hīkoi of 1975, in which 5000 people walked over 1000 kilometres from the northern districts of the North Island of Aotearoa to Parliament in Wellington to deliver a petition signed by 60,000, which demanded the end of land alienation by the New Zealand government.[20]

With this as a historical, political and legal backdrop, some Māori performance artists have taken up the challenge of their predecessors, where visual and performative protest inspires and engages the artist's multiple subjectivities for the purposes of the artwork.

Artist and social provocateur Suzanne Tamaki (Te Arawa, Ngāti Maniapoto, Tūhoe) works across various artistic mediums such as fashion, performance, photography and moving image. Her visual narratives acknowledge and respond to the cultural, legal and political landscape of Aotearoa, exploring the complexities of Indigenous feminisms, Indigenous land 'ownership' and te reo language retention in the South Pacific and challenging the colonial perspective.

The group show *Māori Moving Image Ki Te Tuhi* (2021) features five Māori artists who use the Japanese social entertainment of karaoke to explore oral histories, waiata and protest performance. The project call-out was simple: '*Pāua ball* is spinning and the mic is ready for you! Five Māori artists have made karaoke videos for five Māori songs, inviting you to sing your heart out in this bespoke karaoke booth.'[21] Tamaki's video *Owner* (2021), number four on the karaoke playlist, features the same-titled song written and performed by Māori recording artist and television presenter Ria Hall. Hall's (protest) song was written 'out of a desire to challenge Western philosophies around the notion of "ownership"' of natural resources, challenging and reminding us of our duty instead to look after, nourish and protect our land, waters and forests.[22]

Layered behind the sub-titled lyrics, Tamaki's video shows the artist riding a bicycle — a hīkoi on wheels — in the middle of a busy Newtown road in Te Whanganui-a-Tara Wellington. Taking up public space, Tamaki cycles past familiar landmarks as she follows the road along the waterfront, an area of reclaimed land, before arriving at her destination: the gates of Parliament grounds. The Tino Rangatiratanga flag features prominently, both as an acknowledgement of the continuing call for sovereignty and self-determination for Māori and as appropriate cycling fashion, the artist being well-known for having converted the decommissioned Museum of New Zealand Te Papa Tongarewa's forecourt flags into articles of clothing.

Artist and curator Ane Tonga writes that Tamaki's works critically examine Western notions of nationhood, using her lived experience either as an individual Māori artist and designer or as a member of the collectives the Pacific Sisters and the SaVAge Art K'lub to fashion works like *Owner* that continue as forms of social and cultural protest.[23]

Another artist exploring the critically contested notion of mana motuhake and how it relates to governorship and self-determination of our natural resources is Layne Waerea (Ngāti Wāhiao, Ngāti Kahungunu, Pākehā). In *MAORI LANE* (2012), Waerea darts in and out of traffic on Tāmaki Makaurau's busy Symonds Street, chalking a new route with road markings that read 'MAORI LANE', in order to provoke conversations with passers-by. Waerea has practised and lectured in law, and her performances explore what she calls 'socio-legal artistic performance' with reference to the principles of Te Tiriti o Waitangi (partnership, participation and protection), and how the people of Aotearoa (both tangata whenua and tangata tiriti, Māori and Pākehā) can respect and manage current and future natural resources.[24]

Her works are often located in the public sphere: Waerea has offered free water on Tāmaki Makaurau's Queen Street and 'sold' free air online. Her performance interventions are both complicit in and critical of the everyday social and legal rules that govern public behaviour.[25] Waerea's performances balance humour with a history of acts of resistance and activism that continue to challenge social and legal practices concerning ownership of our natural resources — land, water and air — and what this can mean in Aotearoa.

MAU

An equivalent to mana motuhake, the Samoan notion of mau means to keep, retain, hold fast, stick firmly, and was the name of Sāmoa's independence movement. The Mau movement started in Savai'i as the Mau a Pule movement — pule referring to the leadership or rule over a place. The Mau's fight for self-determination and sovereignty from New Zealand, which at the time was colonial administrator of Sāmoa, resulted in the decolonisation of the archipelago. The Mau movement has since been cemented as a symbol of colonial resistance. For Moana artists in the New Zealand diaspora, who are guests or settlers on Māori land, mau becomes an embodied method or process of resistance that can also be extended into artistic practice.

At the Talanoa Mau symposium in 2020, Salā Lemi Ponifasio, founding director of performance group MAU, described mau as sovereignty. As Lana Lopesi wrote in her doctoral thesis, 'Ponifasio's use of mau in this 2020 arts context, however, is not about a particular kind of universal or agreed-upon sovereignty but rather sovereignty over one's own ideas, one's own thinking and one's own positionality.'[26] Mau can be likened to Métis art critic David Garneau's notion of 'creative sovereignty', which describes the sovereignty

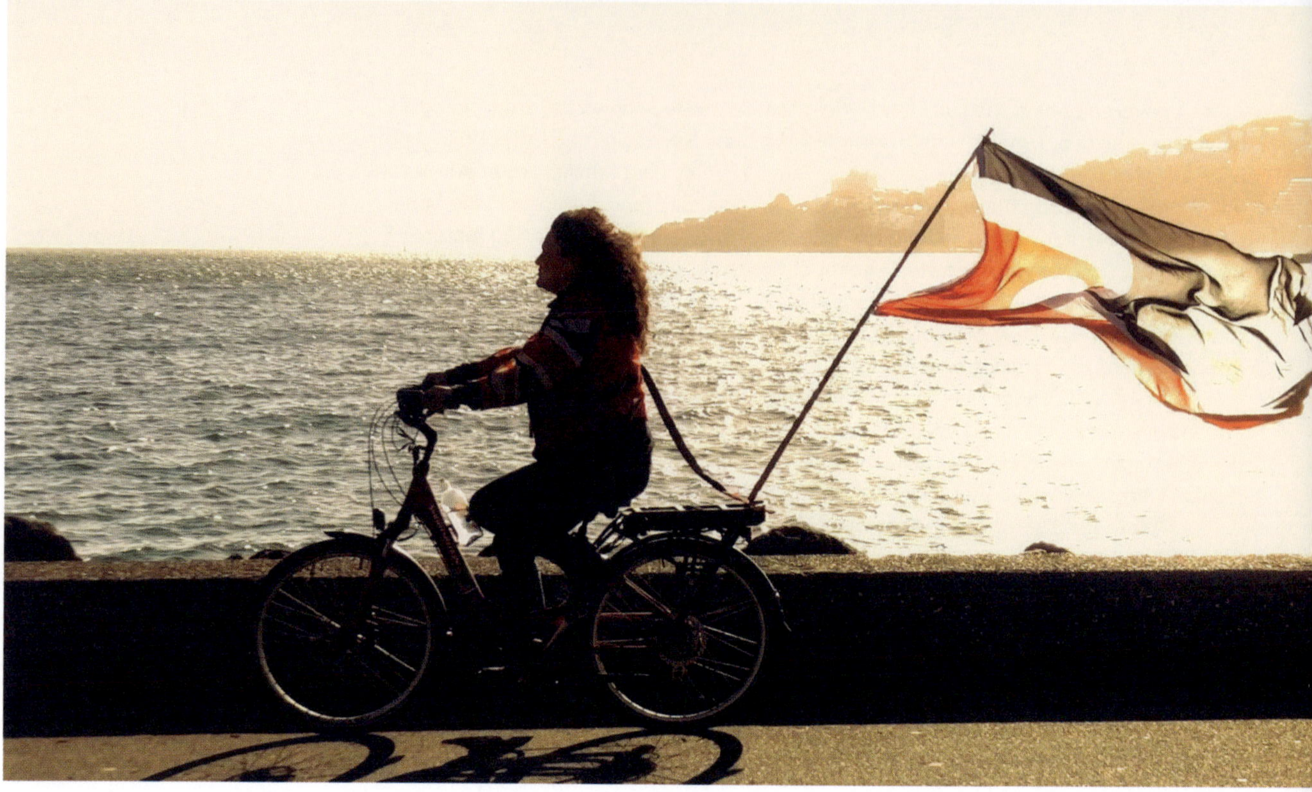

LEFT: Suzanne Tamaki (Te Arawa, Ngāti Maniapoto, Tūhoe), *Owner* (still), 2021. Single-channel karaoke video, duration 3 minutes 24 seconds. Written and performed by Ria Hall (Ngāi Te Rangi, Ngāti Ranginui). Videography by Elise Lanigan. *Courtesy the artist, Loop Publishing/ Kobalt and Loop Recordings Aot(ear)oa*

BELOW: Layne Waerea (Ngāti Wāhiao, Ngāti Kahungunu), *MAORI LANE*, 2011, documentation of performance. *Courtesy the artist. Photo by Layne Waerea*

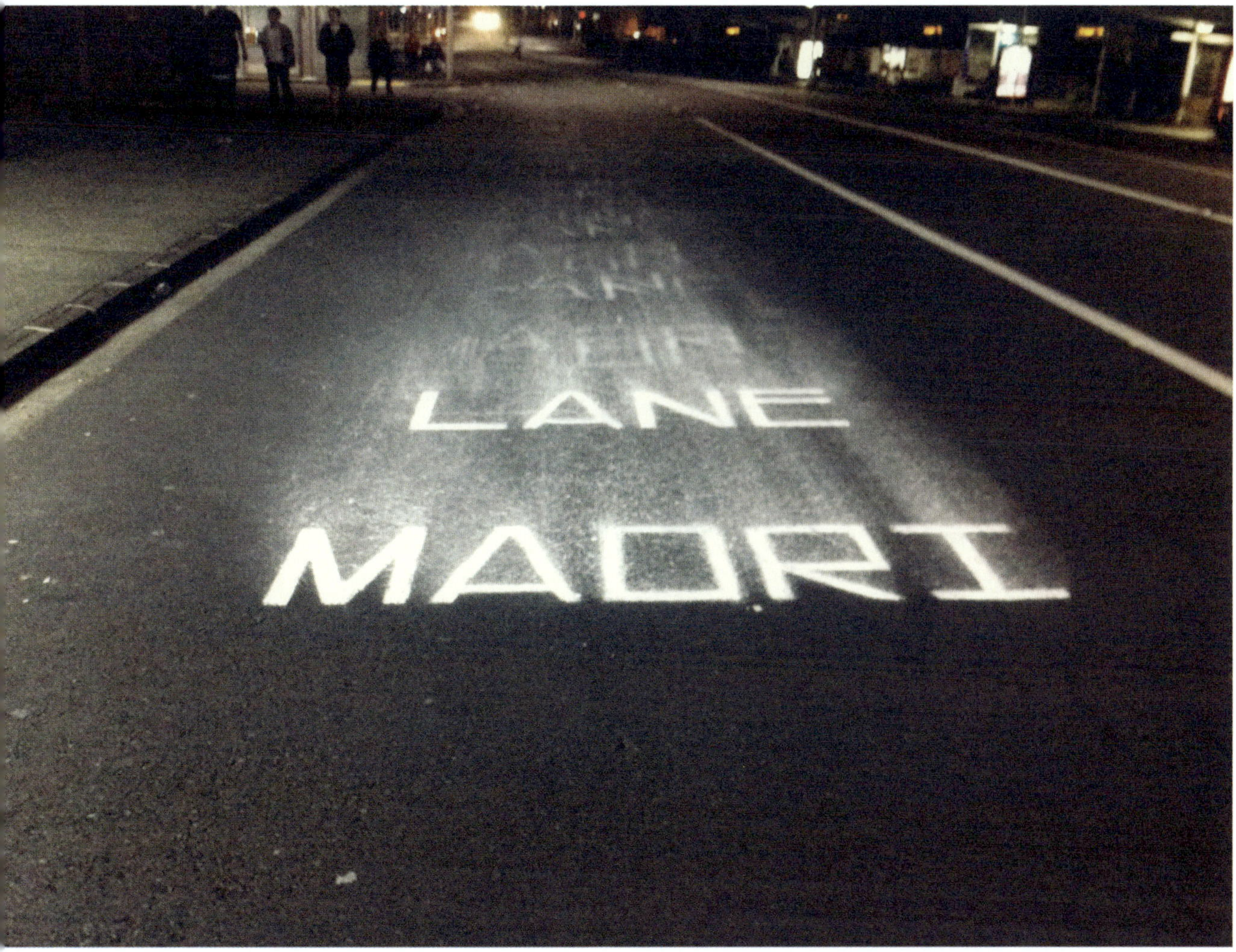

artists have in their own practices that enables them to determine their own articulations of the world free from external pressures, including pressures from within Moana art communities about what constitutes Moana art.[27]

Leafā Wilson/Olga Krause is a multidisciplinary artist and curator of Samoan and German heritage. In her performance work *Unprotected #1: This ain't no disco* (2017), the artist built and inhabited a structure within ST PAUL St Gallery in Tāmaki Makaurau.[28] A tent-like form made of orange fabric was suspended by rope from the roof. Inside it was a foil floor and a small lamp. The structure represented a holding ground in the gallery in which the artist could be protected from the conventions of Western art. In the performance Wilson/Krause pierced her skin, bleeding onto a white dress as she danced with disco lights.[29]

Wilson/Krause's work spoke directly to the structural inequities that often exist within arts institutions. Of the work she writes: 'Tired of everything. Tired of the white cube culture wars, tired of fighting for causes, tired of art.'[30] This reference to the intellectual battlefield of the gallery is emphasised in the artwork's title, which is drawn from the Talking Heads' lyrics in 'Life During Wartime' (1979).

In her refusal to conform to an easy-to-read Moana subjectivity, Wilson/Krause enacts creative sovereignty, offering a Moana subjectivity that emerges from her own specific constellation of subject positions. These include her Samoan and German ancestry, her role at the time as an institutional curator, and her position as a Moana artist within the gallery space. Experiencing her own subjectivity in relation to the 'super politicised' space of the art gallery, as she describes it, she enacts a Moana subjectivity of refusal. In an interview about the work, she commented:

> The white space performances for me differ greatly from works in public spaces because the gallery is the Mt Everest that we all wish to conquer. But in my mind, it was and always will be my right, the right of any artist of any gender, colour, creed (to a degree . . .) to use up some space. To be the Rosa Parks of the galleries.[31]

Wilson/Krause draws out the idea, found in all the artworks discussed here, that part of the constellations of Māori and Moana subjectivities is made in relation to the subject position of indigeneity. This subject comes to the fore as the Indigenous artists make work in relation to a colonial space, whether an art gallery, a museum, in front of a colonial statue or in a 'Māori lane'. In highlighting the intersections built into the constellation of Moana and Māori subjectivity, each of these artists pushes against simplistic expectations of identity, making space for alternative and complex Māori and Moana subjectivities to emerge.

In advocating for complex Samoan identities, Uesifili Unasa notes that today these are 'no longer one thing or another' but are necessarily coalitional and multi-layered: it is, he says, 'becoming increasingly problematic to determine what is Samoan or non-Samoan'.[32] Rather, he calls for constellations of Samoan subjectivities that highlight multiplicity. These can be understood through Tui Atua's idea of a 'cultural blend', which supports unapologetic selves and gives equal time and respect to different cultural references, allowing each element to sit alongside others 'without apology'.[33] This concept of 'cultural blend' enables different people to work with and find a synthesis of sometimes conflicting or contradictory cultural references.

The quest for tradition and authenticity can be a burden for Indigenous peoples in the twenty-first century. Cultural practices are often 'sanctioned by their brand

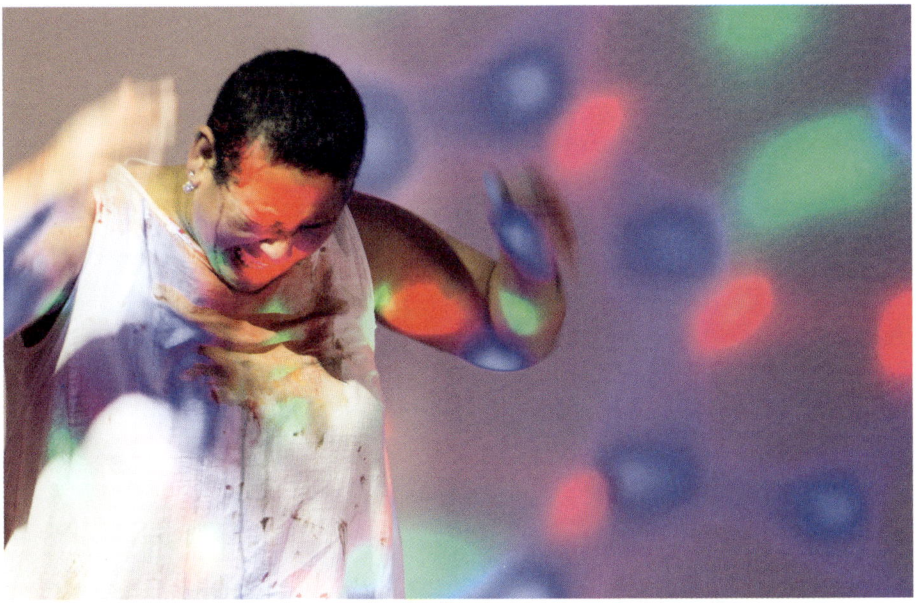

Leafā Wilson/Olga Krause, *Unprotected #2: This ain't no disco*, 2017, documentation of performance, from *Still, Like Air, I'll Rise*, The Physics Room, Ōtautahi Christchurch. *Still, Like Air, I'll Rise* was developed by AUT ST PAUL St Gallery and curated by Abby Cunnane and Charlotte Huddleston. First shown at AUT ST PAUL St Gallery, 24 February–31 March 2016. *Photo by Charlie Rose Creative*

of "tradition"'; anything that is ulterior to visions of tradition is dismissed.[34] Yet the simplistic idea that there is only one way to be Māori or Moana relegates Indigenous peoples to a past, frozen in time. Not only was this never the case, but it also foreclosed the inherent multiplicity found within Māori and wider Moana subjectivities in the present, as well as in the past.

As has been argued many times before, quests for authenticity are by and large an outcome of colonisation that operates by freezing Indigenous peoples in so-called primitive pasts and discounting their participation in the present.[35] In contemporary societies where heterogeneous lived realities such as class, gender and sexuality alter how people who belong to single Indigenous groups experience their shared Indigenous identity, as seen in the performance artworks discussed throughout this chapter, there is no room for such reductive thinking.

Acknowledging and then accepting multiplicity with Māori and Moana performance art is important because it works towards undoing introduced notions of competition and scarcity that can occur in settler-colonial contexts. Within these contexts, it can mean that only so-called authentic notions of identity prevail, while everything else is dismissed. Maintaining multiplicity is a way to enhance the mana of the constellations of subjectivity found across the Moana. This regenerative approach enables us to move away from a 'damage-centred'[36] way of thinking and towards one that is generous, productive and empowered.

As Samoan novelist Albert Wendt noted, although sources of mana have been destroyed through colonisation, there is still the possibility for artists to explore their 'own mana unfettered by accepted conventions'.[37] As a proposition for empowerment, however, these intersecting constellations of subjectivity — Indigenous and socio-cultural — offer and generate agency for Māori[38] and Moana artists, subverting a marginal negotiation to foster instead generative spaces that acknowledge and draw from this constant.

The concept of subjectivity in constellation reveals the emergent, adaptive and fluid nature of lived social differences for Māori and Moana performance artists in Aotearoa. Their Indigenous subject positions intersect with modes of power exerted through settler colonialism and racialisation through the colonial apparatus of the gallery and the discipline of art history, as well as with their own complex webs of whakapapa and gafa, to create unique assemblages of subjectivity. These constellations of subjectivity provide important sources of agency for the artists to explore their rich layers of inherited and ongoing connections, and to take on new meaning and subjectivities.

The featured artists' lived experiences reflect and are informed by these intersections, highlighting the dynamic and responsive nature of their subjectivities in different contexts. By acknowledging and embracing their constellations of subjectivity, Māori and Moana performance artists hold space and honour their connection to the past while opening up opportunities for new forms of expression and meaning-making.

NOTES

1 Cora-Allan Lafaiki Twiss, quoted in Te Tuhi, 'Cora-Allan Wickliffe: *Electric Waka*', 2014, https://tetuhi.art/exhibition/cora-allan-wickliffe-electric-waka
2 Danielle Emma Johnson, Karen Fisher and Meg Parsons, 'Diversifying Indigenous Vulnerability and Adaptation: An intersectional reading of Māori women's experiences of health, wellbeing, and climate change', *Sustainability* 14, no. 9 (May 2022).
3 Marjo Lindroth, 'Paradoxes of Power: Indigenous peoples in the permanent forum', *Cooperation and Conflict* 46, no. 4 (2011): 547.
4 Jane E. Goodman, Matt Tomlinson and Justin B. Richland, 'Citational Practices: Knowledge, personhood, and subjectivity', *Annual Review of Anthropology* 43 (2014): 455.
5 Johnson, Fisher and Parsons, 'Diversifying Indigenous Vulnerability and Adaptation'.
6 Hirini Moko Mead, *Tikanga Māori: Living by Māori values* (Wellington: Huia, 2003).
7 Te Tuhi, 'Acts of Passage', 2018, https://tetuhi.art/exhibition/acts-of-passage
8 Albert Refiti, 'Mavae and Tofiga: Spatial exposition of the Samoan cosmogony and architecture' (PhD thesis, Auckland University of Technology, 2015), 109.
9 Rosanna Raymond, 'Conser.VĀ.tion|Acti.VĀ.tion Museums, the Body and Indigenous Moana Art Practice' (Master's thesis, Auckland University of Technology, 2021), 58.
10 Te Ahukaramū Charles Royal, 'A Modern View of Mana', keynote address delivered to the joint conference of the Australasian Psychological Society and the New Zealand Psychological Society, Skycity Auckland Convention Centre, 2006. See transcript in Jhanitra Gavala and New Zealand Psychological Society, 'A Modern View of Mana', *Bulletin* 107 (November 2006): 10.
11 Mana is often discussed in connection with tapu. Te Ahukaramū Charles Royal states: 'Tapu refers to the state that an object or person is in having come into possession of mana. In order to remain in possession of this mana, one needs to fulfil certain conditions and adhere to certain practices (tikanga and kawa). This entire process, however, is predicated upon the presence of mauri within the object or person itself who becomes the receptacle (taunga) of this mana. The presence of mauri within a physical object or person is necessary before mana can come into it.' Gavala and New Zealand Psychological Society, 'A Modern View of Mana', 11.
12 Refiti, 'Mavae and Tofiga,' 41, 81, 82.
13 Gavala and New Zealand Psychological Society, 'A Modern View of Mana', 12.
14 Angela Lynn Robinson, 'Indigenous Performance in Oceania: Affect, sociality, and sovereignty' (PhD thesis, UCLA, 2019).
15 Ibid., 124.
16 Kristian Larsen and Cat Ruka, 'Playing Savage', *YELLINGMOUTH* (blog), 17 April 2010, https://yellingmouth.blogspot.com/2009/09/improvisational-performance-that-uses.html
17 Ngahuia Te Awekotuku, *Mana Wāhine Māori: Selected writings on Māori Women's art, culture and politics* (Auckland: New Women's Press, 1991), 10.
18 Ibid., 20–21.
19 Ranginui J. Walker, 'The Genesis of Maori Activism', *The Journal of the Polynesian Society* 93, no. 3 (1984): 280.
20 Ibid.
21 Te Tuhi, 'Māori Moving Image Ki Te Tuhi', 2022, https://tetuhi.art/exhibition/maori-moving-image-ki-te-tuhi
22 Ria Hall, 'OWNER Was Written . . .,' Facebook post, 4 March 2020, www.facebook.com/riahallNZ/videos/ria-hall-owner-live/494358944591768
23 Ane Tonga, ed., *Declaration: A Pacific feminist agenda*, exhibition catalogue (Auckland: Auckland Art Gallery Toi o Tāmaki, 2022), 168–70.
24 Layne Melissa Waerea, 'Free Social Injunctions: Art interventions as agency in the production of socio-legal subjectivities not yet imagined or realised' (PhD thesis, Auckland University of Technology, 2016).
25 Waerea, 'Free Social Injunctions'. See also Christopher Braddock, 'Layne Waerea's Public Laughter', *Australasian Drama Studies* 69 (2016): 60–81.
26 Lana Lopesi, 'Moana Cosmopolitan Imaginaries: Toward an emerging theory of moana art' (PhD thesis, Auckland University of Technology, 2021), 139.
27 David Garneau, 'Can I Get a Witness? Indigenous art criticism', in *Sovereign Words: Indigenous art, curation and criticism*, edited by Katya García-Antón (Amsterdam/Oslo: Valiz and Office For Contemporary Art Norway, 2019).
28 For a further discussion of Leafā Wilson/Olga Krause's lifework performance, from a different perspective of endurance, see Chapter 11 of this volume by Christopher Braddock and Ioana Gordon-Smith.
29 Leafā Wilson's artwork *Unprotected #1: This ain't no disco* (2016), as discussed in this passage, included stains of her blood on her dress and body within a performance carried out at Auckland University of Technology's (AUT) ST PAUL St Gallery in 2016. The editors wish to acknowledge that appropriate discussions have taken place at AUT about issues of tikanga surrounding the artist's blood in this performance.
30 ST PAUL St Gallery, AUT, 'Still, Like Air, I'll Rise', 2017.
31 Wilson/Krause in Lana Lopesi, 'Waking Giants: The politics of existing', *The Pantograph Punch*, 30 March 2017, https://pantograph-punch.com/posts/waking-giants-politics-of-existing
32 Uesifili Unasa, 'The Borderlands: Relocating Samoan identity', in *Su'esu'e Manogi = in Search of Fragrance: Tui Atua Tupua Tamasese Ta'isi Efi and the Samoan*

Indigenous Reference, edited by Tamasailau M. Suaalii-Sauni et al. (Wellington: Huia, 2018), 354.

33 Tui Atua Tamasese Ta'isi Efi, *Su'esu'e Manogi = in Search of Fragrance: Tui Atua Tupua Tamasese Ta'isi Efi and the Samoan indigenous reference*, edited by Tamasailau M. Suaalii-Sauni et al. (Wellington: Huia, 2018), 9.

34 Unasa, 'The Borderlands', 355.

35 See Lopesi, 'Moana Cosmopolitan Imaginaries'; Lana Lopesi, 'Su'ifefiloi: A Samoan methodology for transdisciplinary theorising in cosmopolitan worlds', *The Journal of New Zealand Studies*, no. NS33 (December 2021): 127–39.

36 Eve Tuck, 'Suspending Damage: A letter to communities', *Harvard Educational Review* 79, no. 3 (October 2009): 409–28.

37 Albert Wendt, *Lali: A Pacific anthology*, edited by Albert Wendt (Auckland: Longman, 1980), xvi. See also Carl Franklin Ka'ailā'au Pao, 'Ā Kua', in *Atua: Sacred gods from Polynesia*, edited by Michael Gunn (Canberra: National Gallery of Australia, 2014), 167.

38 Johnson, Fisher and Parsons, 'Diversifying Indigenous Vulnerability and Adaptation'.

REFERENCES

Awekotuku, Ngahuia Te. *Mana Wāhine Māori: Selected writings on Māori women's art, culture and politics*. Auckland: New Women's Press, 1991.

Braddock, Christopher. 'Layne Waerea's Public Laughter'. *Australasian Drama Studies* 69 (2016): 60–81.

Efi, Tui Atua Tamasese Ta'isi. *Su'esu'e Manogi = in Search of Fragrance: Tui Atua Tupua Tamasese Ta'isi Efi and the Samoan indigenous reference*, edited by Tamasailau M. Suaalii-Sauni, I'uogafa Tuagalu, Tofilau Nina Kirifi-Alai and Naomi Fuamatu. Wellington: Huia, 2018.

Garneau, David. 'Can I Get a Witness? Indigenous art criticism'. In *Sovereign Words: Indigenous art, curation and criticism*, edited by Katya García-Antón. Amsterdam/Oslo: Valiz and Office for Contemporary Art Norway, 2019.

Gavala, Jhanitra and New Zealand Psychological Society. 'A Modern View of Mana'. *Bulletin* 107 (November 2006): 8–13. www.psychology.org.nz/journal-archive/Bulletin-Nov06-JC-KeynoteCRoyalsmall.pdf

Goodman, Jane E., Matt Tomlinson and Justin B. Richland. 'Citational Practices: Knowledge, personhood, and subjectivity'. *Annual Review of Anthropology* 43 (2014): 449–63.

Gordon, Lewis R. 'Disciplinary Decadence and the Decolonisation of Knowledge'. *Africa Development* 39, no. 1 (January 2014): 81–92.

——— 'Disciplining as a Human Science'. *QUADERNA: A Multilingual and Transdisciplinary Journal* 3 (2015). https://quaderna.org/3/disciplining-as-a-human-science

Gordon-Smith, Ioana. 'Close Encounter: Meeting with the Queen'. *Art New Zealand* 154 (Winter 2015): 87–91.

Hall, Ria. 'OWNER Was Written . . .'. Facebook post, 4 March 2020. www.facebook.com/riahallNZ/videos/ria-hall-owner-live/494358944591768

Hollis, Rangituhia. 'The Other Side of Speaking'. *Puehu: Cultural dust* (blog), 2013. https://puehu.tumblr.com/post/46894545042/the-other-side-of-speaking

Houkamau, Carla A. 'Māori Identity and Economic Wellbeing'. In *Routledge Handbook of Indigenous Wellbeing*, edited by Christopher Fleming and Matthew Manning. London: Routledge, 2019.

Johnson, Danielle Emma, Karen Fisher and Meg Parsons. 'Diversifying Indigenous Vulnerability and Adaptation: An intersectional reading of Māori women's experiences of health, wellbeing, and climate change'. *Sustainability* 14, no. 9 (May 2022). https://doi.org/10.3390/su14095452

Larsen, Kristian and Cat Ruka. 'Playing Savage'. *YELLINGMOUTH* (blog), 17 April 2010. https://yellingmouth.blogspot.com/2009/09/improvisational-performance-that-uses.html

Lindroth, Marjo. 'Paradoxes of Power: Indigenous peoples in the permanent forum'. *Cooperation and Conflict* 46, no. 4 (2011): 543–62.

Lopesi, Lana. 'Moana Cosmopolitan Imaginaries: Toward an emerging theory of Moana art'. PhD thesis, Auckland University of Technology, 2021. https://hdl.handle.net/10292/14298

——— 'Su'ifefiloi: A Samoan methodology for transdisciplinary theorising in cosmopolitan worlds'. *Journal of New Zealand Studies*, no. NS33 (December 2021): 127–39. https://doi.org/10.26686/jnzs.iNS33.7387

——— 'Waking Giants: The politics of existing'. *The Pantograph Punch*, 30 March 2017. https://pantograph-punch.com/posts/waking-giants-politics-of-existing

Mead, Hirini Moko. *Tikanga Māori: Living by Māori values*. Wellington: Huia, 2003.

Meijl, Toon. 'Culture versus Class: Towards an understanding of Māori poverty'. *Race & Class* 62 (May 2020): 78–96. https://doi.org/10.1177/0306396820923482

Pao, Carl Franklin Ka'ailā'au. 'Ā Kua'. In *Atua: Sacred gods from Polynesia*, edited by Michael Gunn, 167. Canberra: National Gallery of Australia, 2014.

Pihama, Leonie. 'Mana Wahine: Decolonising gender in Aotearoa'. *Australian Feminist Studies* 35, no. 106 (October 2020): 351–65.

Raymond, Rosanna. 'Conser.VĀ.tion | Acti.VĀ.tion Museums, the Body and Indigenous Moana Art Practice'. Master's thesis, Auckland University of Technology, 2021. https://hdl.handle.net/10292/14325

Refiti, Albert. 'Mavae and Tofiga: Spatial exposition of the Samoan cosmogony and architecture'. PhD thesis, Auckland University of Technology, 2015. https://hdl.handle.net/10292/9248

Robinson, Angela Lynn. 'Indigenous Performance in Oceania: Affect, sociality, and sovereignty'. PhD thesis, UCLA, 2019. https://escholarship.org/uc/item/5xv520v9

Royal, Te Ahukaramū Charles. 'A Modern View of Mana'. Keynote address delivered to the joint conference of the Australasian Psychological Society and the New Zealand Psychological Society, Auckland, Skycity Auckland Convention Centre, 2006.

ST PAUL St Gallery, AUT. 'Still, Like Air, I'll Rise'. 2017. https://stpaulst.aut.ac.nz/all-exhibitions/still-like-air-ill-rise

Te Tuhi. 'Acts of Passage'. 2018. https://tetuhi.art/exhibition/acts-of-passage

——— 'Cora-Allan Wickliffe: *Electric Waka*'. 2014. https://tetuhi.art/exhibition/cora-allan-wickliffe-electric-waka

——— 'Māori Moving Image Ki Te Tuhi'. 2022. https://tetuhi.art/exhibition/maori-moving-image-ki-te-tuhi

Tonga, Ane, ed. *Declaration: A pacific feminist agenda*. Exhibition catalogue. Auckland: Auckland Art Gallery Toi o Tāmaki, 2022.

Tuck, Eve. 'Suspending Damage: A letter to communities'. *Harvard Educational Review* 79, no. 3 (October 2009): 409–28.

Unasa, Uesifili. 'The Borderlands: Relocating Samoan identity'. In *Su'esu'e Manogi = In Search of Fragrance: Tui Atua Tupua Tamasese Ta'isi Efi and the Samoan indigenous reference*, edited by Tamasailau M. Suaalii-Sauni, I'uogafa Tuagalu, Tofilau Nina Kirifi-Alai and Naomi Fuamatu, 353–64. Wellington: Huia, 2018.

Waerea, Layne Melissa. 'Free Social Injunctions: Art interventions as agency in the production of socio-legal subjectivities not yet imagined or realised'. PhD thesis, Auckland University of Technology, 2016.

Walker, Ranginui J. 'The Genesis of Maori Activism'. *Journal of the Polynesian Society* 93, no. 3 (1984): 267–81.

Wendt, Albert. *Lali: A Pacific anthology*, edited by Albert Wendt. Auckland: Longman, 1980.

11

EITHER FOR A MOMENT OR FOR AS LONG AS POSSIBLE

Christopher Braddock
& Ioana Gordon-Smith

Throughout histories and writings on performance art, endurance has often been sensationalised, made into an act of suffering and resilience that creates a spectacle for passive audiences. Art historian Jennie Klein notes that 'endurance performance' is most often understood as involving 'the artist using her or his body to the point of privation, discomfort, corporeal danger, or even pain for long periods of time, ranging from several hours/days to a year or longer'.[2]

Sandra Ruiz's focus on Puerto Rican artists and the effects of colonialism chimes with Klein's emphasis on privation as well as duration. Ruiz explores endurance in performance as bodily endurance against US colonialism through different measures of time. She writes about the body as 'an aesthetic site in corporeal suffering' that can 'counter the demands of . . . colonial time, through variations of time itself'.[3] Ruiz explores the way artist Ryan Rivera 'manipulates time as a way to address the limited space allotted for Brown bodies in everyday places and locations of art'.[4]

Within this discussion about definitions of endurance in performance art, Lara Shalson has veered away from an understanding uniquely concerning forms of hardship, pain, solitude and exhaustion.[5] Asking what it might be to intentionally *perform* endurance in art practices, as well as political acts beyond the realm of art, Shalson suggests a guiding structure that often involves the following-through of an intentional physical plan 'whose outcome cannot be determined in advance':

> The artist designs and then endures an unfolding of events that can never be fixed from the start. This indeterminacy arises from another essential element of endurance: namely, that it is always performed *in relation* to forces that are beyond the performer's control.[6]

Our chapter will weave through these various definitions of performing endurance. The artworks discussed (by Kalisolaite 'Uhila, Leafā Wilson, John Vea and Jeremy Leatinu'u) explore endurance as it appears within everyday life: the endurance of capitalist demands for productivity, enduring colonial structures across public spaces and art institutions, and the endurance demanded within a racialised, capitalist society. These performances reframe and refuse the demands of endurance. Primarily through the performance work of Kalisolaite 'Uhila and Leafā Wilson, we also explore art institutions as co-performers to performance as 'life'. We argue for the ways in which art institutions and their staff become subsumed in complex acts of endurance of the everyday.

AGAINST PRODUCTIVITY

Mo'ui Tukuhausia (2012, 2014) is arguably Kalisolaite 'Uhila's best-known performance work. First staged in the Tāmaki Makaurau Auckland suburb of Pakuranga as part of the Te Tuhi art gallery group exhibition *What do you mean, we?*, the work consisted of 'Uhila living as homeless around Pakuranga for two weeks. Art historian Nina Tonga translates the title — *Mo'ui Tukuhausia* — as 'a life exposed to the dew, left out in the cold, or at the mercy of the elements'.[7] The performance was triggered in part as an attempt by the artist to acquire a personal, lived understanding of homelessness.[8] Contextualised within the exhibition's wider premise — to consider how art might reveal deeply entrenched neuroses — the work also acquired a quality of social commentary and drew out collective assumptions about homelessness.

Mo'ui Tukuhausia was re-performed two years later as one of four works nominated for the 2014 Walters Prize at Auckland Art Gallery Toi o Tāmaki. This time, the performance spanned the full three-month duration of the Walters Prize exhibition and took place over winter. As an occupation of public spaces rather than a performance of specific actions, much of the performance occured 'off-stage', so to speak. Bruce Phillips, curator of *What do you mean, we?,* noted of *Mo'ui Tukuhausia*: 'There may not be anything to see, as such, because the expectations of a conventional viewer experience are put to the side in favour of the artist engaging with the given public context.'[9]

There may not have been much recognisable 'art' on view, but art historian Gregory Minissale notes that Auckland Art Gallery Toi o Tāmaki was infiltrated with unforeseen food packages, gifts, paper wrappers, blankets and graffiti that appeared 'on the gallery walls where visitors left their own messages of support, critique or art'.[10] Minissale recalled: 'The glass walkway where visitors look down on the amphitheatre [was] peopled by 'Uhila's destitute companions [which] reversed the panopticon and put the gallery visitors on show.'[11] In this way, Minissale continues, '*Mo'ui Tukuhausia* ("life put aside") also cuts through the exhibition system like a knife.'[12]

These encounters between artist, visitors and destitute companions thus felt like happenstance: by-products of 'Uhila's performance rather than predetermined moments for presentation. Stephen Cleland, coordinating curator for the Walters Prize in 2014 (and responsible for the planning and realisation of *Mo'ui Tukuhausia*), notes how 'Uhila also wanted to resist forms of predictable photographic documentation: 'The performance involves a kind of active withdrawal that is distinct from the mindset entered into by an artist who is performing for the camera. Accordingly, 'Uhila developed strategies so he could not be easily documented.'[13] One of these strategies was to have no set timeframe for 'performing' the artwork, either in Auckland Art Gallery Toi o Tāmaki or around the city.[14] Cleland continues:

> 'Uhila retained full autonomy over where he performed and lived, which sets entirely different parameters for the work than a performance by Tino Sehgal, for example, which is typically choregraphed for a specific gallery and unfolds within that space during the full hours of public access.[15]

Artist Janet Lilo's documentation of *Mo'ui Tukuhausia* offers a sense of this kind of happenstance. Lilo's photograph of the artist's phone charger depicts one of many traces of 'Uhila around the gallery that spoke of him going about his performance without concern for how visible — or indeed, invisible — he was. In addition to the phone charger, at times viewers might see a shopping trolley loaded with materials for survival, a bike parked in various places in and around the gallery, or a folded blanket or sleeping bag tucked neatly away. All of these were objects of practical purpose, and glimpses of them conjured a sense of accidentally witnessing, a happenstance view, and indicated a commitment to the challenge of living as if homeless.

The presence of the phone charger also indicated a level of accessibility that was not shared by all who visited the gallery. For a performance so elusive, it was strange to think that contact with the artist might be just a text away. It served as a visual reminder of an informal and personal network that 'Uhila, and by extension *Mo'ui Tukuhausia*, were part of, and which did not include the general public.

For others, an arguably more intimate witnessing of 'Uhila's performance was taking place, and paradoxically a few moments were recorded on Facebook, Instagram

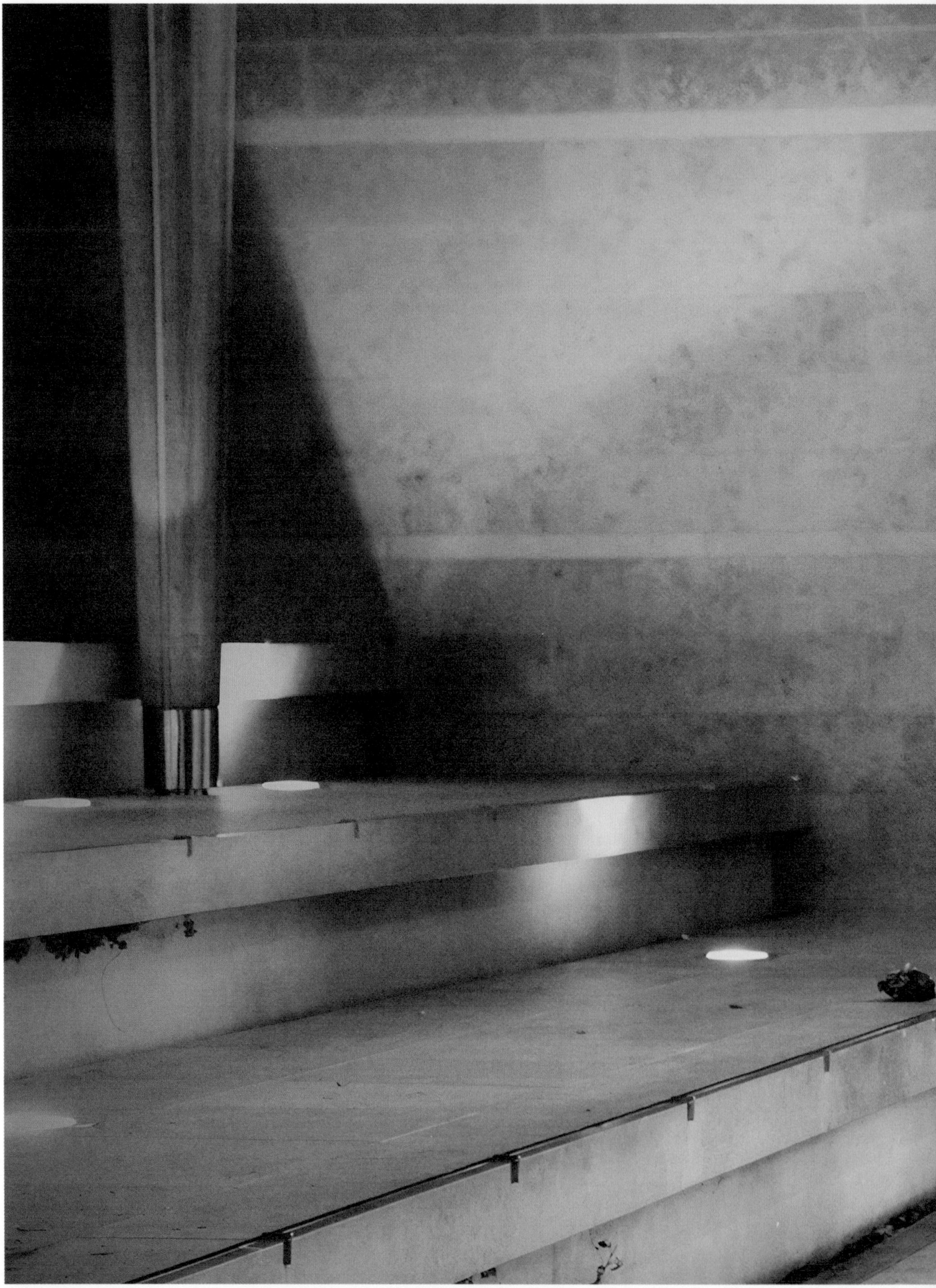

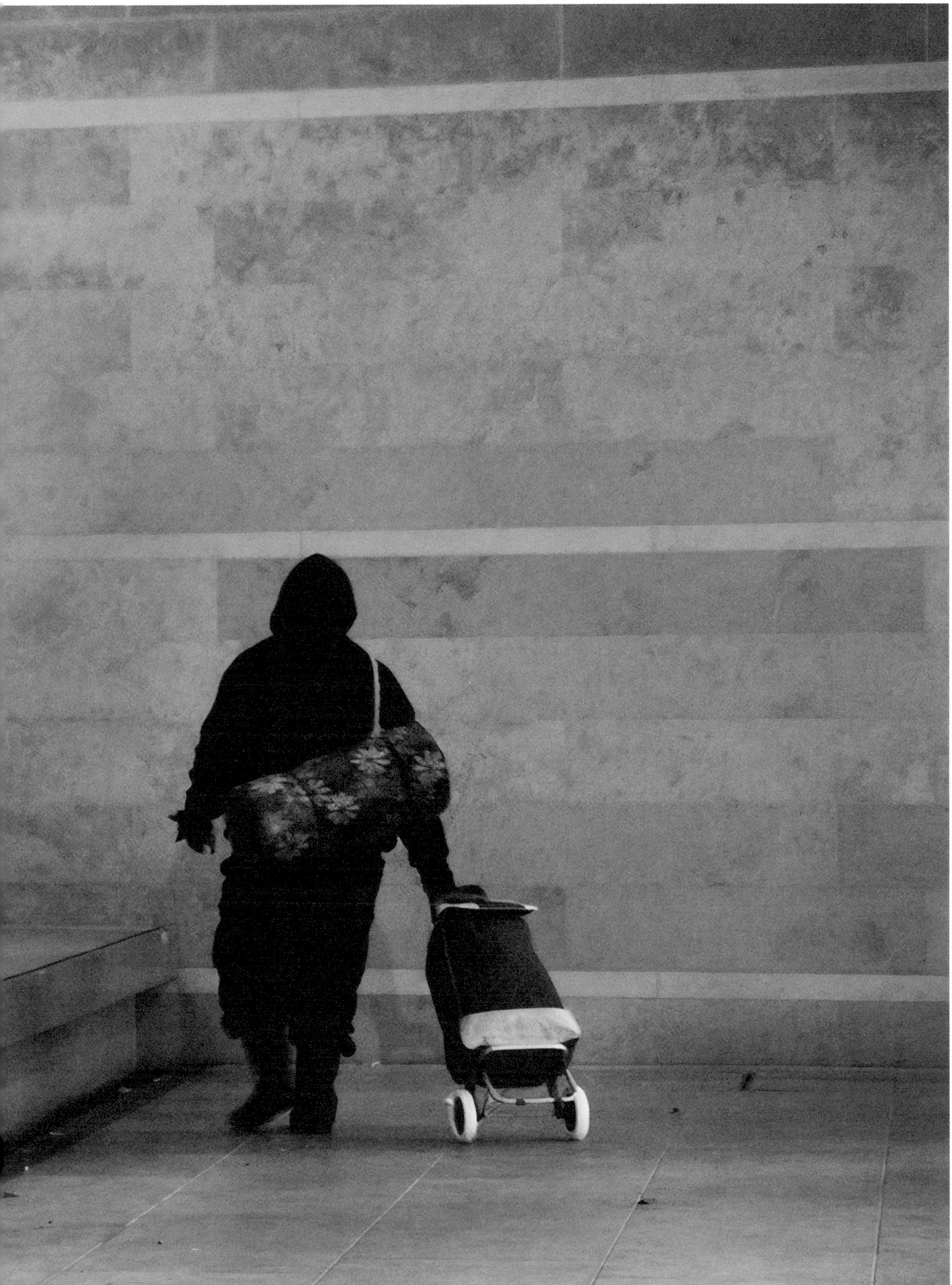

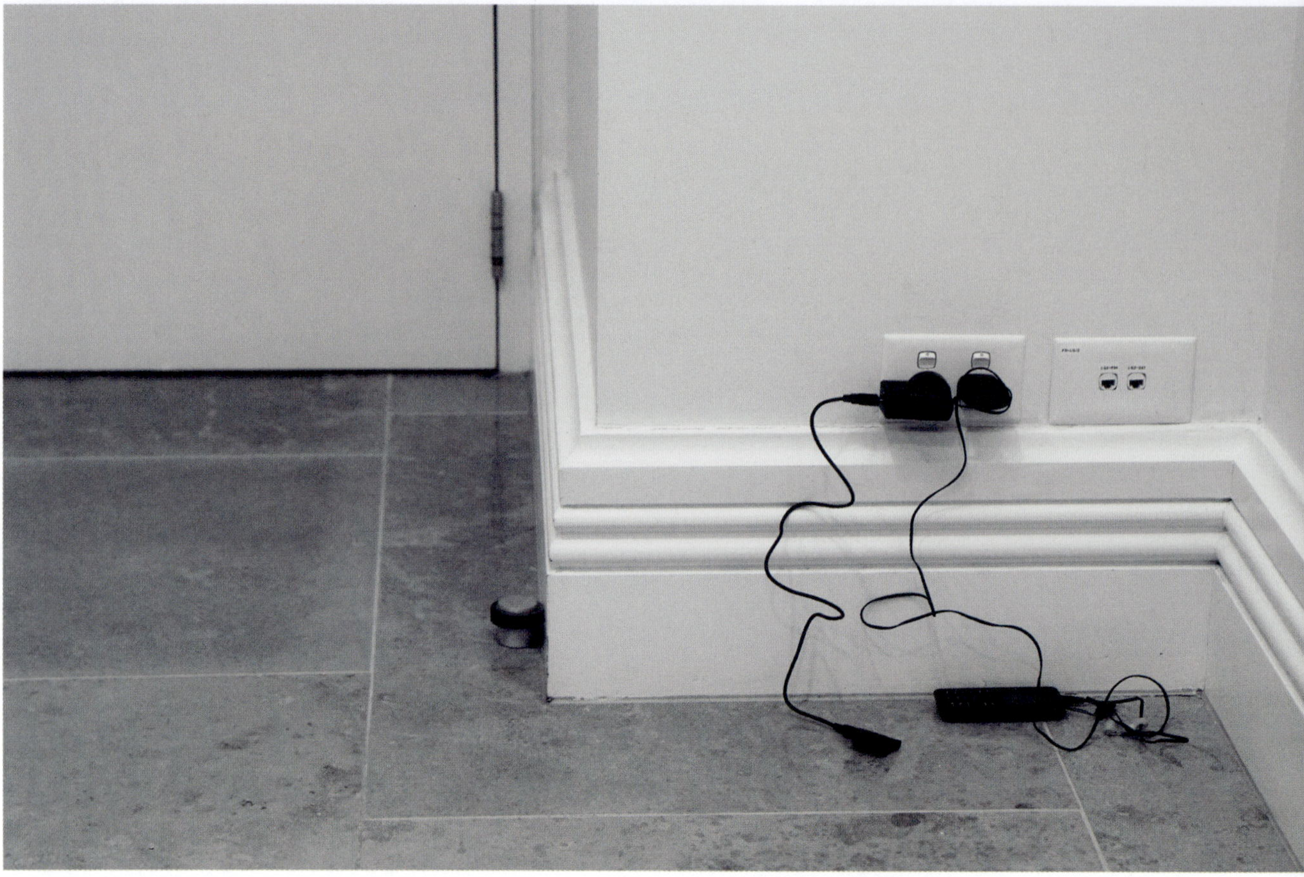

and email. One image captured 'Uhila outside an Auckland dealer gallery with his bike; another showed him having lunch at a local Japanese eatery with two others; yet another captured the artist having lunch in South Auckland. As Tāmaki Makaurau-based artist Natasha Matila-Smith wrote:

> I've seen 'Uhila several times recently — once when he was in the Symonds St Starbucks, another he was walking down Karangahape Rd. He basically stays within a certain radius of the Auckland Art Gallery — so, if one really wanted to see him, it wouldn't be that difficult.[16]

It is tempting to consider these encounters as somehow 'outside' of the work, as if they disqualify the perceived authenticity of the performance.[17] Curator and 2014 Walters Prize juror[18] Anna-Marie White has noted of *Mo'ui Tukuhausia*:

> There has been a lot of speculation about this work and the perceived notions of authenticity that accompany it. Many people seem to believe that in order to have any integrity this work needs to mimic the conditions of homelessness as much as possible.[19]

Some of these attitudes were articulated in guest books and visitor responses in the 2012 performance. Phillips notes that responses included comments such as, 'He should smell

PREVIOUS & ABOVE:
Kalisolaite 'Uhila, *Mo'ui Tukuhausia*, 2014, from the Walters Prize exhibition at Auckland Art Gallery Toi o Tāmaki, July–October 2014. *Photos by Janet Lilo*

like urine and faeces. This guy smells too clean, I am not yet convinced', and 'Homeless people don't wear balaclavas'.[20] The comments suggest visitors to the gallery were searching for a 'projected' sense of authenticity to homelessness.

Living for three months in the Tāmaki Makaurau CBD in the middle of winter, 'Uhila faced a number of issues, including hostility from the existing and potentially territorial homeless community in the area, aggression from local residents, malnourishment and the risk of hypothermia. Added to this list, then, was hostility from gallery visitors. As a result of his refusal to be productive, in many senses of the word, 'Uhila's performances opened themselves to a distinct lack of control. This kind of happenstance extends to re-assessing the very nature of the 'homeless' endeavour.

The various traces of 'Uhila's performance that challenged viewers' assumptions of an authentic homeless existence also suggested the artist was interested less in the 'performance' of homelessness and more in its lived duration, without concern for others' perception or predetermined sensationalism.[21]

Returning to Ruiz's exploration of endurance in performance as bodily endurance against colonialism through different measures of time, 'Uhila's actions put his brown body in the way of public expectations of both homelessness and standard 'working' hours. It is ironic that the city's most established public art gallery bent over backwards to host his performance, to provide the best possible professional art institutional support and to support the 'homeless' artist even outside working hours. But what is striking here is that the institution was forced (as Shalson argues for performance artists of endurance) to perform in relation to forces beyond its own control. In other words, the institution was subjected to performing endurance as co-performer in its everyday life.

In this way we observe differences between 'Uhila's homeless existence and an artist such as Tehching Hsieh (discussed shortly) who also lived homeless, by virtue of the art gallery that hosted 'Uhila. 'Uhila was endorsed by the independent jury that chose him for the 2014 Walters Prize, in effect requiring Auckland Art Gallery Toi o Tāmaki to host the complex set of relations that would follow.[22]

ARTWORKS AS LIFEWORKS INSTITUTIONALISED

Adrian Heathfield has described modes of performance art that subvert the 'prevailing social organization of time and its attendant cultural expressions', including industrialised and capitalised notions of 'clock' time that must be accounted for and measured.[23] In particular, he points to the emergence of durational or endurance performances that employ seemingly futile actions as a refusal to 'use' time to produce consumer goods, services or affective labour. Comparison could be made between 'Uhila's *Mo'ui Tukuhausia* and Hsieh's *One Year Performance 1981–1982 (Outdoor Piece)*, in which he spent an entire year in New York City between 26 September 1981 and 26 September 1982 with only a backpack and a sleeping bag, never entering a building or subway or seeking shelter.[24]

Heathfield coined the term 'lifeworks' with regard to Hsieh's performances, which he describes as 'unparalleled . . . in their absolute conception and enactment of art and life as simultaneous processes'.[25] *One Year Performance 1981–1982 (Outdoor Piece)* was by and large unmediated by institutional life such as a public gallery. As Heathfield argues, Hsieh's work has more to do with the order of temporality as duration and the 'practice of living' than anything else.[26]

By contrast, the practices of living embodied in ‘Uhila’s *Mo‘ui Tukuhausia* had a pervasive demand on the staff and spaces of Auckland Art Gallery. As curator, Cleland needed to get his head and heart around peoples’ understanding of homelessness, including the differences between rough sleeping, couch surfing and sleeping in cars. ‘Uhila was sleeping rough, and the city became integral to the artwork in its staging. In preparation for the exhibition, Cleland talked to Diane Robertson, then CEO of Auckland City Mission, to get a better understanding of homelessness. As a consequence, the gallery donated money to the City Mission, and established a food station near the gallery’s reception area where the public could leave food parcels for the City Mission to support the homeless.[27]

Although ‘Uhila signed a waiver that the gallery could not be held responsible for his health for the duration of the exhibition, staff still felt an uneasy sense of obligation regarding where their responsibilities lay. For example, Cleland notes that if ‘Uhila texted him saying ‘I’m hungry’, he would respond, ‘Let’s meet up and I’ll buy you dinner.’ ‘I’m not just a curator but a person and I had sleepless nights worrying about him.’ He wondered whether his actions violated the rules of the performance, but in the end decided they did not: ‘His complete dependence on others for sustenance — including me — was not a professional but a personal imperative.’[28]

It was never simply a question of preserving and nurturing the relationship between curator and artist, however: over 100 gallery staff had to be involved in different ways. A critical mass of internal departments, many of which do not typically engage directly with artists, needed to understand why the artwork should happen, for its existence required their direct involvement. The work crossed the threshold between back of house and front of house, and extended beyond the hours that a gallery is open, in particular implicating the gallery’s 24-hour security team. Both curator and gallery encountered ethical problems about when responsibility begins and ends.

For example, ‘Uhila’s lived manifestation of the work forced the gallery to alter its rules concerning moving along rough sleepers who congregated around the building. Not only might the artist be living among them; he also relied on allies within that community for his own safety. According to Cleland, ‘The gallery’s relaxed tolerance of rough sleepers . . . was challenging, as neither the gallery nor the artist could control who would be among them. In some isolated incidents security staff were placed in vulnerable situations because of that community.’[29]

Auckland Art Gallery also had an exhibition programme to uphold. Questions arose about the broad scope of the artwork and whether ‘Uhila was occupying the gallery for enough time. Cleland was experienced in negotiating performance artworks that have instructions, such as Bruce Barber’s scores, which operate like a schematic that conceptualises the work.[30] The only score for *Mo‘ui Tukuhausia* seemed to be the artist sleeping rough. As Cleland notes:

> He had an extraordinary way of maintaining agency, in navigating the tenuous space between private and public. At times I was concerned that I hadn’t seen him for a few days, and it might be perceived that he wasn’t ‘turning up’. But then colleagues would testify to having seen him in the building for extended periods. The scale of the gallery and staff meant that the institution could tenuously track the artwork’s development as well as checking on ‘Uhila himself.[31]

Cleland notes how concerns about the visibility of the exhibition programme lent this artwork profound meaning with regard to the visibility of homelessness. He notes the way 'Uhila

> developed a poetics of disappearance; had a fascination with disappearance. He could withdraw from the world and become almost invisible. He was skilled at entering the building and not being seen, perhaps playing on the possibility that many of us have trained ourselves not to *see* the homeless.[32]

As understanding of the artwork developed over time, the institution encountered other problems. 'Uhila's activities extended beyond his designated exhibition space: he left things around the gallery in spaces that were not 'his' in such a way that staff needed to discern the difference between 'rubbish' and matter deriving from the performance. Furthermore, as noted by Minissale above, 'Uhila's improvisational writing, impressed directly onto the walls of the gallery space, was bolstered by messages of support from the public. Cleland recalls, 'The gallery's registrars were alarmed that the public was writing on the walls without invitation, and asked if the penned messages of support should be erased.'[33]

ENDURING THE ART WORLD

The works discussed in this chapter share a concern with endurance as a pervasive demand on both artists and art institutions within everyday life.[34] Performance art that encompasses such demands provides a means of invigorating an awareness of political and racialised asymmetries within the workplace and public sites.[35]

The work of multidisciplinary artist and curator Leafā Wilson also extends these concerns to the gallery and museum context. Wilson's performance works at times focus on the phenomenological experience of being present in a time and place, and at others consider the overlooked labour of migrants and workers of colour.[36] As broad as Wilson's practice has been, many of her performances operate under the umbrella of a lifelong performance work, *Olga Krause — Deutsche Kuenstlerin*, in which the artist uses her German name, the one found on her birth certificate: Olga Hedwig Janice Krause.

The performance artwork *Olga Krause — Deutsche Kuenstlerin* is impossible to witness in its entirety. Formally, it is found within room sheets, press releases and catalogue biographies, where the work is attributed to Olga Krause. The artist's use of her German name creates a dilemma for institutions and its conventions: she has at various times been credited as 'Leafā Wilson & Olga Krause', 'Leafā Wilson aka Olga Hedwig Krause', 'Leafā Wilson/Olga Krause', 'Leafā Wilson aka Olga Krause', and 'Leafā Wilson (Olga Krause)'.[37]

The various stylings indicate the difficulty in reconciling the ethnic connotations of a German name with the artist's brown body. Underpinning *Olga Krause — Deutsche Kuenstlerin* is knowledge that a German name carries the expectation and privilege of a Caucasian artist, an assumption reiterated in 'Deutsche Kuenstlerin', meaning 'German artist'. The work thus sets up a subversive critique of the Western art world's racial assumptions and asymmetries. As the artist explains, *Olga Krause — Deutsche Kuenstlerin*

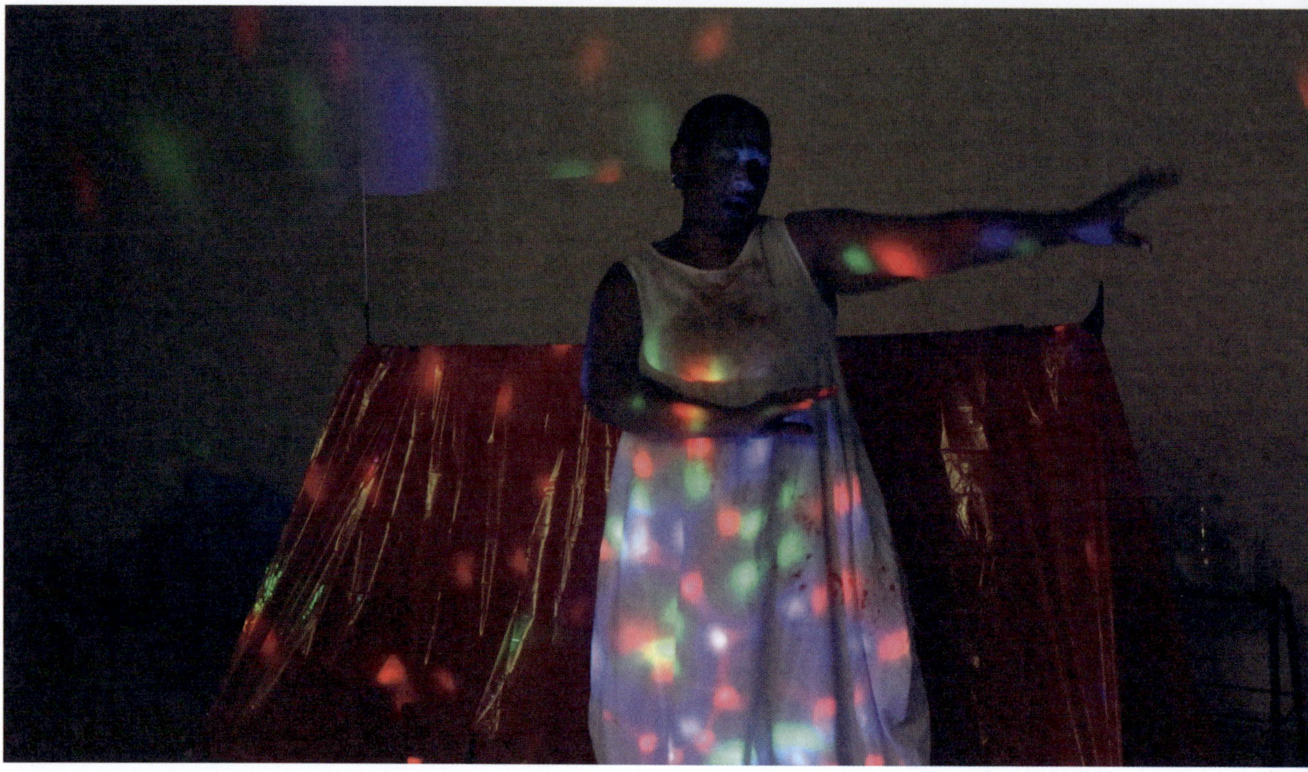

> is [a] lifelong durational performance art work. It is strategy. It is a working professional name. It is a name by which I have survived as a person of colour in the Western whiteness that makes up the majority of art institutions in Aotearoa.[38]

Leafā Wilson/Olga Krause, *Unprotected #1: This ain't no disco*, 2017, documentation of performance, from *Still, Like Air, I'll Rise*, AUT ST PAUL, Tāmaki Makaurau Auckland. *Courtesy ST PAUL St Gallery/Te Wai Ngutu Kākā Gallery. Photo by Alex Schipper*

As noted, the work operates for the most part within the formal, textual conventions of the art world. At times, Wilson/Krause's specific individual performances and her lifelong performance *Olga Krause — Deutsche Kuenstlerin* coincide to amplify an institutional critique. Her work *Unprotected #1: This ain't no disco* (2017), for example, directly addressed the constant endurance brown bodies undertake within mainstream white cube gallery spaces. In this work, the artist danced for as long as she could endure under coloured disco lights, as Talking Heads' 'Life During Wartime' played on loop.

Wilson/Krause began in a pristine white dress. In the course of the performance she pricked her chest and legs, drawing blood. Dribbles of Fanta and beans that the artist consumed mixed with blood on the dress.[39] At the end of her dancing, Wilson/Krause retreated to a makeshift orange tent, removed her dress, lit candles, and exited the tent for good.

The joyful colours and sounds of disco music provided a foil to the racialised inequalities that *Unprotected #1: This ain't no disco* performed. If *Olga Krause — Deutsche Kuenstlerin* can function as a lifework, it is because the racial inequality that it exposes is itself a lifelong endurance.

EVERYDAY LABOUR

Wilson's performance works have made visible the labour of workers of colour. Notions of labour are, of course, inscribed in particular ways on the brown body. Migrants have historically been a key source of labour in New Zealand, and opportunities for work spurred the waves of Moana migration from the 1950s.[40]

The endurance demanded of labourers has been explored in the artwork of John Vea, who often works closely with Moana communities to learn and share experiences and stories of working in Aotearoa. He describes these casual interactions and informal conversations as 'talanoa'.[41] Talanoa education scholar Timote Vaioleti writes that the term means 'talking about nothing in particular, and interacting without a rigid framework'.[42] Vea employs talanoa as a specific counter to dominant and impersonal modes of data collection and analysis 'Multiple exchanges through story-telling and networks of collaborators result in artistic research that could not have been pre-planned or foreseen.'[43]

Vaioleti argues for talanoa as a research methodology understood as 'a personal encounter where people story their issues, their realities and aspirations'.[44] Through talanoa, people are able to become the agents of their stories rather than objects for research. For Vea, talanoa offers a set of relational ethics that guide his way of operating as a performance artist engaged with social encounters.[45]

Vea's *Finish this week off and that's it!* was first made in 2009 in response to a friend's redundancy — a grim reality faced by many workers after the 2007–08 global financial crisis.[46] The five-channel video presented portraits of the artist holding a 40-kilogram rock for as long as possible. The five channels mirror the five working days of the week, and gradually, each figure disappears from the frame until only the rock remains as a trace of the artist's endurance.

In 2014 Vea remade the video work for an exhibition at Artspace Aotearoa in Tāmaki Makaurau. For this version he incorporated more recent talanoa he had shared with workers about the reality of living on the minimum wage. Vea filmed each frame over the course of a week, during which time he restricted his food budget to $2.40 a day (at that time it was one definition of poverty in Aotearoa). The five frames measured not only the endurance and five-day week of an average worker, but also the effects of insufficient nourishment on the artist's body.

Finish this week off and that's it! can be read as a surrogate performance of endurance that Vea makes to draw attention to the realities faced by numerous labourers in Aotearoa. In his 2018 work *you kids should only experience this for a moment — don't be here for life like me,* Vea forces viewers into the same surrogate position. Drawing on first-hand accounts of working at the PepsiCo Bluebird potato chip factory in Tāmaki Makaurau, this installation re-created aspects of the factory experience.[47] Walking through a curtain made of PVC plastic strips, visitors to the exhibition were faced with a pair of suspended video projections that showed two men (Vea and artist Matavai Taulangau, who also sustains a living through factory jobs) gazing listlessly at an installation of plaster potato forms lying between them on a length of mechanised rollers. Their performed actions demonstrate boredom and fatigue, in imitation of a worker whose job is simply to scrutinise potatoes for quality control as they pass on a conveyer belt.[48]

The labour re-performed in this installation is mundane, repetitive and endless; employed in a job comprised primarily of watching, the performers expend not a deliberate type of labour but instead their own currency of time. They reference the ways in which time is ordered, regulated and commandeered by a capitalist system, most overtly apparent within a Fordist factory setting: a forfeit of time in return for wages. In this installation, components are synchronised with a clock to mirror the time of an actual day in the potato chip factory. Every two hours, the video projections turn off and a monitor turns on to signal the start of break time; at the end of the allocated break, the projections recommence. A clock on the wall keeps track of this regulated time.

This synchronisation establishes an odd type of aesthetic reception. As we watch the work, our watching of art mirrors the performers 'watching': we watch watching. The act of watching becomes closely linked with the act of giving up time. In these ways, Vea draws distinctions between the types of ways that time can be spent — between looking at potatoes and looking at art. In many ways what we see is simply the forfeit of time. As the plaster potatoes churn endlessly on top of the mechanised rollers, their dust slips between the cracks as if through the artist's painfully slow hourglass. In *you kids should only experience this for a moment — don't be here for life like me*, endurance is thus closely related to the word 'duration'. Duration, however, is recontextualised as a phenomenon that has been capitalised.

WAITING AGAINST COLONIALISM

Artist Jeremy Leatinu'u (Tainui, Samoan) uses his body to resist or depart peacefully from the social conventions expected in public spaces.[49] As with all the artists discussed in this chapter, endurance and duration are linked as a forfeit of time, often counteracting time as commandeered by capitalist and colonial systems of power. For *Queen Victoria* (2013), Leatinu'u travels to four major cities in Aotearoa — Tāmaki Makaurau, Te Whanganui-a-Tara Wellington, Ōtautahi Christchurch and Ōtepoti Dunedin — in order to spend 'time with the Queen'.[50] We see Leatinu'u filmed from behind, sitting astride a tall ladder as 'plinth', elevated yet always just lower than the statue of Queen Victoria that is before him. When installed, four flat-screen monitors make a grid of the performance videos, with only distant traffic noise interrupting the simple, quiet gesture 'that nonetheless represents a mild transgression of "proper" place; an act that forces a meeting between statue and artist on more equal terms'.[51]

Leatinu'u's performances often utilise silence and passivity to draw attention to the transgression of his body being in a particular place. What we find important about *Queen Victoria* are the social conventions embedded in the civic memorials themselves: raised in the four major cities of Aotearoa, they are placed so the monarch has an elevated position and purview over her domain. In using a portable ladder to establish an equal, though temporary, perch alongside the figure of the queen, Leatinu'u protests and silently contemplates the status of their relationship. The 'DIY' nature of the work, Leatinu'u's portable ladder and makeshift perch, enable the disallowed act of waiting, face to face, on an equal footing with the queen.

Leatinu'u's best-known work is perhaps *Public Observations II* (2010), in which the artist sits silently on the concrete floor in the middle of the bustling Ōtara market in Tāmaki Makaurau, his body an obstacle to the people around him. The camera is placed at the performer's eye level so we can observe the feet of the passers-by who are forced to step around him.

The significance of eye contact, or a lack thereof, is notable across both these works. In *Public Observations II*, the direct eye relation is between the artist and camera/

viewer; his relationship to the passers-by is one of avoidance rather than a meeting of eyes. In *Queen Victoria* the viewer becomes the outside observer, witness to the meetings between statues and the artist.

In discussing the role of silence in *Public Observations II* with curator Bruce Phillips, Leatinu'u notes:

> I think that being silent is an important part of the performance. When a person speaks all attention is focused on what they are saying, but when a person is silent attention is directed to their body, where they are positioned, the amount of space they are taking up and the disruptions they may be creating.[52]

Silence enables the role of the body and the bodily relations to take primacy. Without narrative and conversation, the positioning of his body, his gaze and his relations with others or the viewer are revealed as both strategic and deliberate, rupturing our expectation of the social dynamics that could be anticipated in a public context.

Leatinu'u's silent, still and waiting body is reminiscent of Lara Shalson's exploration of how performances of endurance address structures of power by redefining agency in relation to objecthood.[53] As Shalson writes, 'objecthood' often describes a passive and sometimes silent performer 'whose capacity to be acted upon precedes any ability to act of one's own volition, and whose dependence upon others exceeds any capacity to make oneself known'.[54]

A state of objecthood relates to Shalson's argument, mentioned earlier, that a key factor of performing endurance involves artists' bodies 'performed *in relation* to forces that are beyond the performer's control'.[55] She insists this dependency upon others is not contrary to a condition of subjecthood but a precondition of it, which we all share.[56]

Arguably, the most innovative chapter of Shalson's book *Performing Endurance* explores non-art contexts of political protest during the US civil rights movement in the 1960s, in particular the Greensboro Lunch Counter Sit-In. On 1 February 1960, four black college students sat down at the 'whites only' lunch counter in the Woolworth's 'five and dime' store in Greensboro, North Carolina, and ordered a cup of coffee.[57] They were not served, but remained seated until the store closed, and returned the next day with twenty-seven other students. By day four the number of protesters had reached 300, overflowing to nearby Kress department store. Some white supporters joined their number, refusing to be served until their black colleagues had been served before them.[58]

Various forms of violence occurred. A white man poured a glass of Coke over the head of a coloured student and by day five some arrests had ensued, including of a white male opponent for setting a protester's coat on fire.[59] Shalson notes that within two months, sit-ins had occurred in nearly eighty communities.[60] Five months later, the lunch counter at Woolworth's in Greensboro was integrated and, as Shalson reports, 'Within a year, the Congress on Racial Equality reported that 138 communities throughout the South had integrated at least some of their facilities.'[61]

In relation to a state of objecthood, she writes how 'remarkably, in the sit-ins the recipients of violence had "authorship" of the scene even though *they did not fully control it*'.[62] Shalson compares these dynamics to the work of performance artists Yoko Ono and Marina Abramović, just as we might compare them with Leatinu'u's performances of silence and passivity as he confronts issues of colonisation and determination.[63] She writes: 'Like sit-ins, these actions put bodies *in the way* — especially those bodies that prevailing systems neglect.'[64]

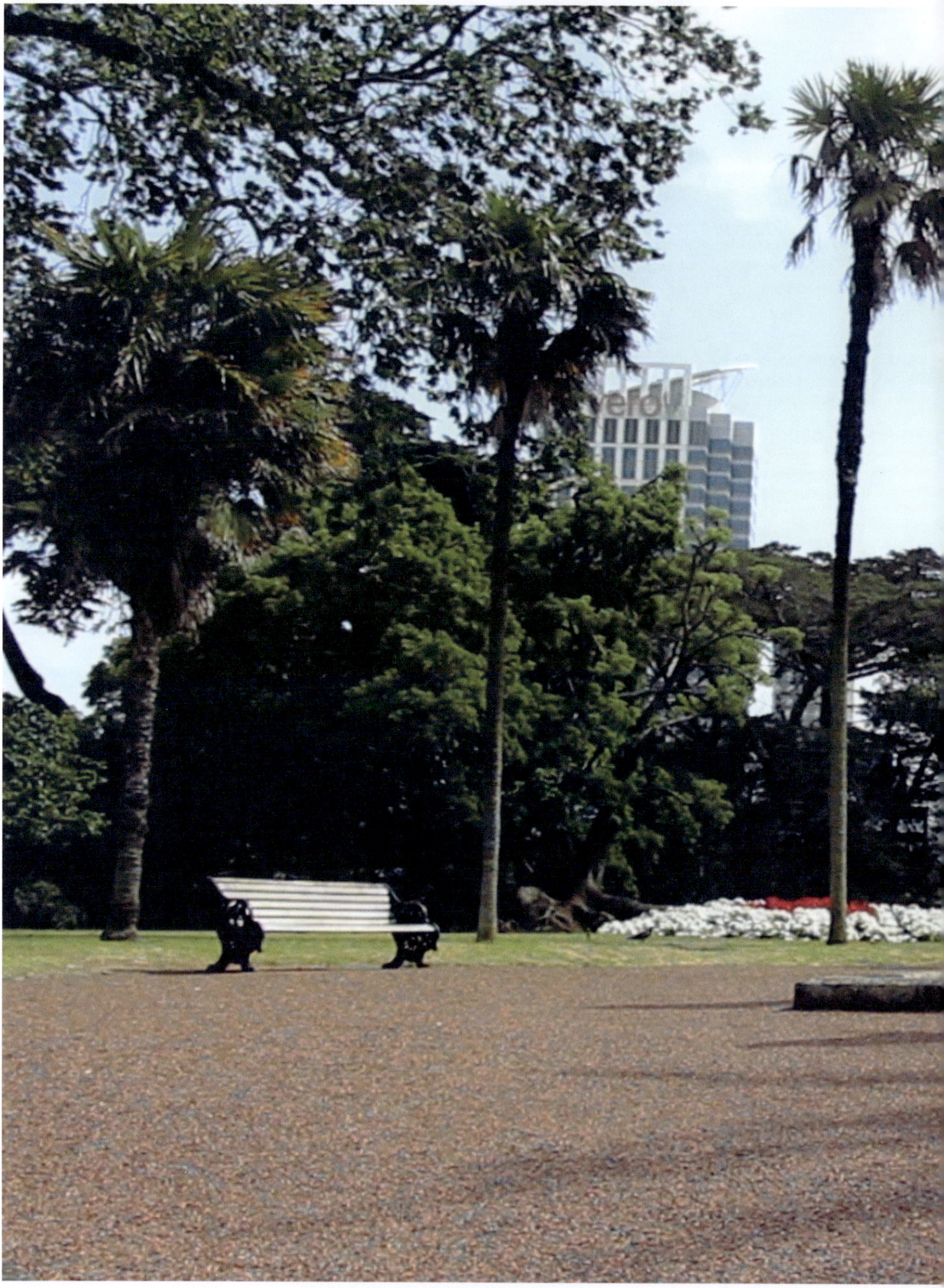

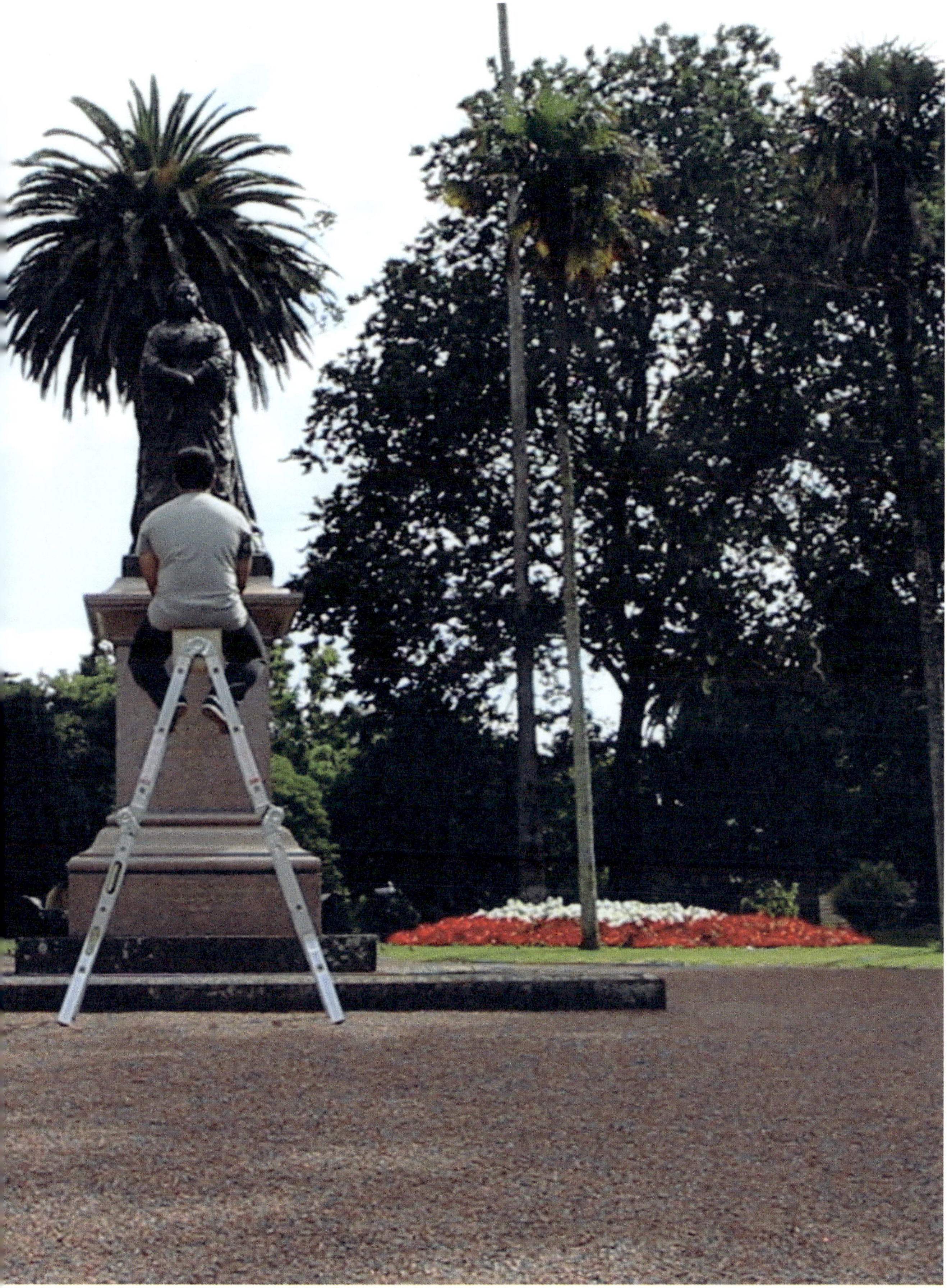

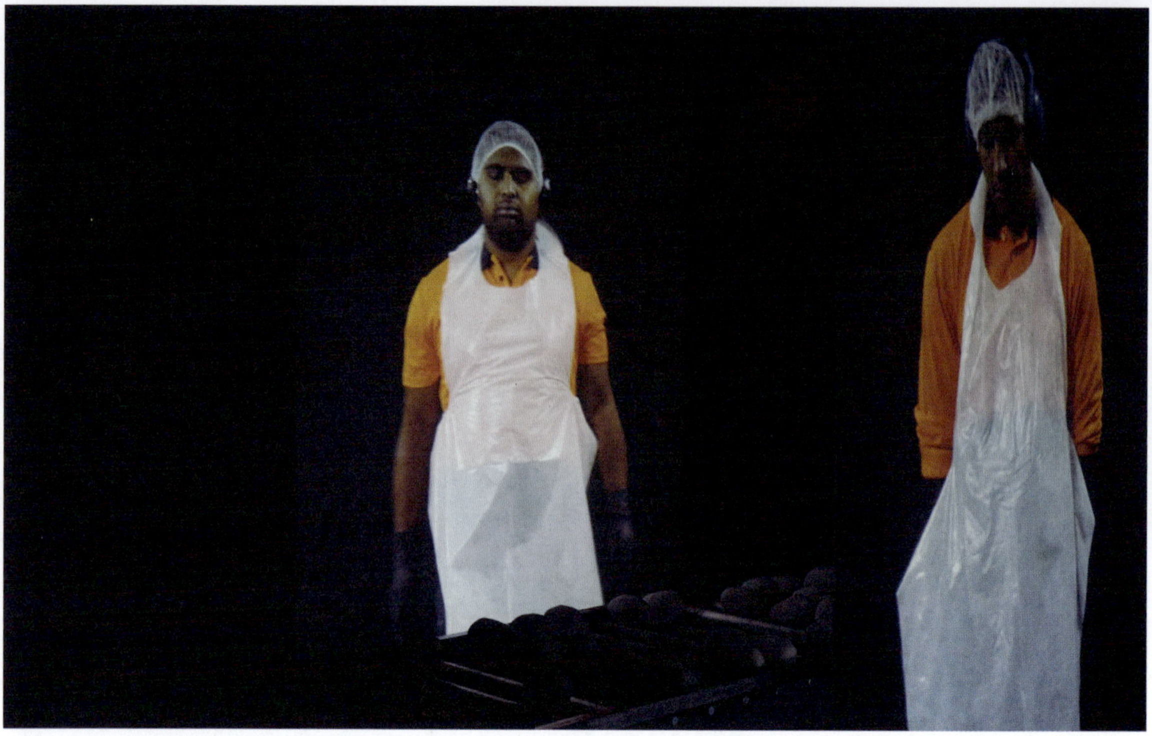

John Vea, *you kids should only experience this for a moment — don't be here for life like me*, 2018 (installation view), commissioned by Te Tuhi, Pakuranga, Tāmaki Makaurau Auckland. *Courtesy Te Tuhi. Photo by Sam Hartnett*

In refusing to narrate his encounters with Queen Victoria or his stance in the busy Ōtāra market in *Public Observations II*, Leatinu'u 'rewrites the rules of racist and misogynist encounters through a willingness to endure them in a new way: via object-hood'.[65] Perhaps like the Greensboro Lunch Counter Sit-In, his performance 'is a confrontation of artful quietude that breaks the pattern of oppressively violent structures'.[66] The same could be argued for Kalisolaite 'Uhila living homeless in his performances of *Mo'ui Tukuhausia*. As curator of the 2012 version Bruce Phillips said of the second version of this work: 'Two years on and Kalisolaite's original iteration of the work still strikes me as being profound for its ability to fracture the veneer of social niceties through such a passive action.'[67]

Andrew Russeth's article 'Art About Waiting — and What It Takes to Endure' contextualises Tehching Hsieh's performances with the 'performance' of waiting during the Covid-19 lockdowns: 'Part of the reason waiting is such a powerful artistic practice is because the act itself is so intensely human, how it often involves the artist losing control — of time, of agency — or intentionally giving it up.' Such artworks, he continues, require us to re-evaluate slowdowns, delays and closures and 'invite reflection both about institutional commitments, as well as about what we owe one another'.[68]

Returning once again to Sandra Ruiz's exploration of endurance performance and its propensity to counter the demands of capital and colonial time, Jeremy Leatinu'u's silent, waiting body recalls the 'work' of Kalisolaite 'Uhila, John Vea and Leafā Wilson in their occupation of institutional and public spaces in Aotearoa. To borrow the words of Ruiz as she quotes Adrian Heathfield, each artist is concerned with how 'to disturb or suspend narrative resolutions and consolidated identities'.[69] All practise a forfeiture of time in order to return it to us with different agency, and invite us to re-evaluate what we owe one another, either for a moment or for as long as possible.

NOTES

1 This chapter offers the perspectives of Chris Braddock (as Pākehā artist and writer) and Ioana Gordon-Smith (as Samoan/Pākehā curator), who are in different ways interested in the power dynamics of performance art as a medium and the power dynamics of endurance as demanded by everyday life.

2 Jennie Klein, 'Endurance Performance', in *Reading Contemporary Performance: Theatricality across genres*, edited by Meiling Cheng and Gabrielle H. Cody. (Abingdon, UK: Routledge, 2015), 22.

3 Sandra Ruiz, *Ricanness: Enduring time in anticolonial performance* (New York: New York University Press, 2019), 11. http://ebookcentral.proquest.com/lib/aut/detail.action?docID=5784038

4 Ibid., 153.

5 Lara Shalson, *Performing Endurance: Art and politics since 1960* (Cambridge, UK: Cambridge University Press, 2018), 3.

6 Ibid., 10, 12. Shalson's emphasis.

7 Nina Tonga, 'Roaming All Levels', *Off the Wall* 6 (August 2014): 2. https://tetuhi.art/wp-content/uploads/2020/06/Te-Papa_Roaming-all-levels.pdf

8 Bruce E. Phillips, 'A Voice for the Voiceless', in *The Walters Prize 2014*, edited by Clare McIntosh, exhibition catalogue (Auckland: Auckland Art Gallery Toi o Tāmaki, 2014), 73. https://issuu.com/aucklandartgallery/docs/wp_catalogue_single-page

9 Ibid., 73.

10 Gregory Minissale, 'Problem Spaces in the Walters Prize', *Reading Room: A Journal of Art and Culture* 7, 'Risk' (2015): 141.

11 Ibid., 145.

12 Ibid.

13 Stephen Cleland in conversation with Chris Braddock, 15 March 2023 in Tāmaki Makaurau Auckland.

14 Thinking about timeframes in *Mo'ui Tukuhausia*, see Nina Tonga's discussion of the Tongan concept of *tu'a* that is defined as 'time behind or beyond' and 'connotes a physical, social and temporal periphery' that means 'Uhila exists 'in the "shadows of time", outside the daily routines and rituals that marked the passing of the day', Tonga, 'Roaming All Levels', 2–3.

15 Stephen Cleland in conversation with Chris Braddock, 15 March 2023.

16 This quote was originally part of Natasha Matila-Smith's review of the 2014 Walters Prize published as 'Something Is Wrong with This Picture' on *EyeContact*, but was removed at the request of the author. We use this reference with permission of the author.

17 Regarding performance art practices that engage the flows of everyday life, performance art scholar Lara Shalson resists separating what might be perceived as 'inside' and 'outside' the artwork. She insists, for example, on not dividing the gallery's open and closing hours in Marina Abramović's *The House with the Ocean View* (2002), during which Abramović lived in Sean Kelly Gallery, New York, for twelve days and nights. Shalson's point is that it would be a mistake to consider the performance during the open hours of the gallery as the performance 'event' and the performance during the closing hours of the gallery as Abramović's 'everyday life'. She writes: 'Both periods make up the piece, and both periods were part of Abramović's life during this time.' Shalson, *Performing Endurance*, 30 n. 90.

18 Finalists for the Walters Prize are chosen by an independent jury of four.

19 Anna-Marie White in conversation with Kate Brettkelly-Chalmers, *Ocula*, 18 January 2014, https://ocula.com/magazine/conversations/anna-marie-white

20 'Kalisolaite 'Uhila: Life set aside', interview by Bruce E. Phillips, 2015. Originally published in Bruce E. Phillips, 'Kalisolaite 'Uhila: Life set aside', *Le Roy* 3, 'The Soft Issue' (2015).

21 Another performance work by Kalisolaite 'Uhila that refused sensationalism was *Maumau Taimi* (2016) — which loosely translates to 'wasting time' — for which 'Uhila sat on a bench in the window gallery of AUT ST PAUL St Gallery for a standard 8-hour working day. See Chapter 12 in this volume by Balamohan Shingade for a full discussion of this artwork.

22 See Victoria Wynne-Jones' discussion of *Mo'ui Tukuhausia* from the perspective of intersubjective relations that include the infrastructure of the art gallery: Victoria Wynne-Jones, *Choreographing Intersubjectivity in Performance Art* (Cham, Switzerland: Palgrave Macmillan, 2021), 216–19.

23 Adrian Heathfield and Tehching Hsieh, *Out of Now: The lifeworks of Tehching Hsieh* (London/Cambridge, MA: Live Art Development Agency and MIT Press, 2009), 20.

24 Taiwanese artist Tehching Hsieh immigrated to New York without permission in 1974. He carried out five one-year and one thirteen-year-long performances. Shalson, *Performing Endurance*, 111.

25 Heathfield and Hsieh, *Out of Now*, 11.

26 Ibid., 17. As Adrian Heathfield notes with respect to Tehching Hsieh's performances, 'durational aesthetics give access to other temporalities: to times that will not submit to Western culture's linear, progressive meta-narratives, its orders of commodification; to the times of excluded or marginalized identities and lives; to times as they are felt in diverse bodies'. Heathfield and Hsieh, *Out of Now*, 23.

27 Auckland City Mission responds to poverty concerning housing, food and mental health. See www.aucklandcitymission.org.nz

28 Stephen Cleland, in conversation with Chris Braddock, 15 March 2023.

29 Ibid.

30 See Chapter 1 of this volume, where Blair French discusses Bruce Barber's performance work *Bucket Action* (1973) and the use of scores.

31 Stephen Cleland in conversation with Chris Braddock, 15 March 2023.

32 Ibid.

33 Ibid.

34 Campbell Patterson's performance video series *Lifting My Mother for as Long as I Can* (2006–11) offers another take on endurance as an everyday reality. First performed in 2006, the video documents the artist picking up his mother in both arms. While lifting in itself focuses on the arduous physical endurance, the artist's choice of his mother as the 'object' of his labours introduces an ambiguous relationality into the work. See: The Dowse Art Museum, 'Lifting My Mother for as Long as I Can', 2012, https://dowse.org.nz/exhibitions-and-events/exhibitions/2012/lifting-my-mother-for-as-long-as-i-can. See also: Christopher Braddock, Ioana Gordon-Smith, Layne Waerea and Victoria Wynne-Jones, 'Aotearoa New Zealand Performance Art 1970–2020', in *The Routledge Companion to Performance Art*, edited by Jennie Klein, Natalie Loveless, Lucian O'Connor and Graciela Ovejero Postigo (Abingdon, UK: Routledge, forthcoming). Gabriel White's *Scenic Journey* (2022) also engages with ideas of repeated and cyclical endurance. In this performance-to-video, White strenuously and repeatedly pushes a large JJ's Waste Bin up a steep incline only to let it roll back down with each iteration. The video only shows White's Sisyphean effort halfway up the incline, thus further confounding any sense of closure. See www.circuit.org.nz/work/scenic-journey

PREVIOUS: Jeremy Leatinu'u (Tainui, Samoan), *Queen Victoria*, 2013, documentation of performance, Albert Park, Tāmaki Makaurau Auckland. *Videography and image courtesy the artist*

35 Other performances of endurance mobilise sites such as the ocean as part of a wider planetary context, such as Angela Tiatia's (NZ/Samoan) *Lick* (2015) and *Holding On* (2015). See Chapter 18 by Janine Randerson and Amanda Yates in this volume for discussion about Tiatia's artwork.

36 For instance, *Me and My Salu Lima* (2017) and *Back to It* (2011) involve the artist cleaning to consider the value and visibility of Moana labour.

37 AUT ST PAUL St Gallery, 'Still, Like Air, I'll Rise', 2017; 'Artspace Aotearoa — OFFSTAGE 8', Artspace Aotearoa/ Kaupapa Toi | Programme, 2017; Louise Rutledge, 'Editorial,' To Find a Place | Enjoy Contemporary Art Space, 2018, https://enjoy.org.nz/publishing/the-occasional-journal/to-find-a-place/editorial; 'Patch: Bungaswehr, OBJECT | PART OF ART COLLECTION, Collections Online,' Museum of New Zealand Te Papa Tongarewa, 2020; 'Causing Something to Start,' Manatū Taonga Ministry for Culture and Heritage, 2022.

38 Leafā Wilson and Olga Krause, 'On Being an Art Anakema', *The Pantograph Punch*, 12 March 2021, www.pantograph-punch.com/posts/on-being-an-art-anakema

39 Leafā Wilson's artwork *Unprotected #1: This ain't no disco* (2016), as discussed in this passage, included stains of her blood on her dress and body within a performance carried out at Auckland University of Technology's (AUT) ST PAUL St Gallery in 2016. The editors wish to acknowledge that appropriate discussions have taken place at AUT about issues of tikanga surrounding the artist's blood in this performance.

40 'Moana' is used throughout this chapter to refer to the region most known as the Pacific. The Moana is an Indigenous term for the Great Ocean found in several Indigenous Moana languages. It is used here in recognition of and as an alternative to the colonial etymology of terms such as Pacific and Oceania. While the Moana is itself an imperfect term — particularly as a Polycentric term that minimises other Indigenous names for the region — its use here signals the subjective position of the co-author as a Samoan (Moana is the Samoan term for the region).

41 Ioana Gordon-Smith, 'Planting Objects | Yielding Stories', 2015, https://ioanagordonsmith.com/2015/10/26/planting-objects-yielding-stories

42 Timote Masima Vaioleti, 'Talanoa Research Methodology: A developing position on Pacific research', *Waikato Journal of Education* 12 (2006): 23.

43 John Vea and Chris Braddock, 'Moana Nui Social Art Practices in Aotearoa', *DAT Journal of Design, Art, and Technology* 3, no. 2 (2018): 291–324, 295.

44 Vaioleti, 'Talanoa Research Methodology', 21.

45 Vea and Braddock, 'Moana Nui Social Art Practices in Aotearoa', 300. See also John Vea, 'Exploring Pacific Talanoa Research Methods in Visual Arts Installation and Performance Art Practices' (PhD thesis, Auckland University of Technology, 2021).

46 Gordon-Smith, 'Planting Objects | Yielding Stories'.

47 Potato chips are also known as crisps.

48 For a detailed account of *you kids should only experience this for a moment — don't be here for life like me* (2018) see Vea, 'Exploring Pacific Talanoa Research Methods', 90–100. This emphasis on duration is reminiscent of Karen Gonzalez Rice's characterisation of endurance art as durational performances that 'blur the border between art and life, and urge the body of the artist (and, by a proxy of sorts, the body of the spectator) into situations that resemble or require situations of meaningful distress, in which the ordeal is not (merely) a plea for attention or a cry for help, but a strategy that "metonymically enacts survival through the Practice of self-discipline".' Dominic Johnson, 'Chickens, Saints, and Corpses: Endurance art in the United States', *Art Journal* 77, no. 2 (April 2018): 103–05. https://doi.org/10.1080/00043249.2018.14955 38. Quoting from Karen Gonzalez Rice, *Long Suffering: American endurance art as prophetic witness* (Ann Arbor: University of Michigan Press, 2016), 2.

49 Ioana Gordon-Smith, 'Close Encounter: Meeting with the Queen', *Art New Zealand* 154 (Winter 2015): 87.

50 Rangituhia Hollis, 'The Other Side of Speaking', *Puehu: Cultural Dust* (blog), 2013, https://puehu.tumblr.com/post/46894545042/the-other-side-of-speaking

51 Gordon-Smith, 'Close Encounter'.

52 Bruce E. Phillips and Jeremy Leatinu'u, 'The Power of Presence: A conversation with Jeremy Leatinu'u', *Puehu: Cultural Dust* (blog), 20 July 2014, https://puehu.tumblr.com/post/93298800802/the-power-of-presence-a-conversation-with-jeremy

53 Nik Wakefield, 'Performing Endurance: Art and politics since 1960 by Lara Shalson (review),' *TDR: The Drama Review* 64, no. 2 (Summer 2020): 178.

54 Ibid., 19.

55 Shalson's emphasis.

56 Ibid., 18–19.

57 Ibid., 80–81. Shalson contextualises her discussion of racism and colonialism through the work of Homi Bhabha and Frantz Fanon.

58 Ibid., 84–85.

59 Ibid., 86.

60 Ibid.

61 Ibid.

62 Ibid., 89. Shalson's emphasis.

63 See Heike Roms' review of Lara Shalson's *Performing Endurance*: Roms, 'Performing endurance: art and politics since 1960', *Contemporary Theatre Review* 29, no. 4 (October 2019): 482–83. Roms writes about Shalson's reading of Yoko Ono's *Cut Piece* (1964) and Marina Abramović's *Rhythm 0* (1974) as works that 'made audience members endure their own objecthood by experiencing themselves as bodies that are acted upon as they act upon an other' (Roms, 'Performing Endurance', 483).

64 Shalson, *Performing Endurance*, 185.

65 Wakefield, 'Performing Endurance (review)', 178.

66 Ibid.

67 Phillips, 'Curator's Response'.

68 Andrew Russeth, 'Art About Waiting — and What It Takes to Endure', *New York Times*, 17 September 2020, www.nytimes.com/2020/09/17/t-magazine/Tehching-Hsieh-endurance-art.html

69 Ruiz, *Ricanness*, 11. Quoting Heathfield and Hsieh, *Out of Now*, 22.

REFERENCES

'Artspace Aotearoa — OFFSTAGE 8'. Artspace Aotearoa/ Kaupapa Toi | Programme, 2017. https://artspace-aotearoa.nz/exhibitions/offstage8

Braddock, Christopher, Ioana Gordon-Smith, Layne Waerea and Victoria Wynne-Jones. 'Aotearoa New Zealand Performance Art 1970–2020'. In *The Routledge Companion to Performance Art*, edited by Jennie Klein, Natalie Loveless, Lucian O'Connor and Graciela Ovejero Postigo. Abingdon, UK: Routledge, forthcoming.

Gordon-Smith, Ioana. 'Close Encounter: Meeting with the Queen'. *Art New Zealand* 154 (Winter 2015): 87.

——— 'Planting Objects | Yielding Stories'. 2015. https://ioanagordonsmith.com/2015/10/26/planting-objects-yielding-stories

Heathfield, Adrian and Tehching Hsieh. *Out of Now: The lifeworks of Tehching Hsieh*. London/Cambridge, MA: Live Art Development Agency and MIT Press, 2009.

Hollis, Rangituhia. 'The Other Side of Speaking'. *Puehu: Cultural Dust* (blog), 2013. https://puehu.tumblr.com/post/46894545042/the-other-side-of-speaking

Johnson, Dominic. 'Chickens, Saints, and Corpses: Endurance art in the United States'. *Art Journal* 77, no. 2 (April 2018): 103–05. https://doi.org/10.1080/00043249.2018.1495538

Klein, Jennie. 'Endurance Performancem'. In *Reading Contemporary Performance: Theatricality across genres*, edited by Meiling Cheng and Gabrielle H. Cody, 22–24. Abingdon, UK: Routledge, 2015.

Krause, Olga and Leafā Wilson. 'On Being an Art Anakema'. *The Pantograph Punch*, 12 March 2021. www.pantograph-punch.com/posts/on-being-an-art-anakema

Manatū Taonga Ministry for Culture and Heritage. 'Causing Something to Start'. 2022. https://mch.govt.nz/causing-something-start

Minissale, Gregory. 'Problem Spaces in the Walters Prize'. *Reading Room: A Journal of Art and Culture* 7, 'Risk' (2015): 126–47.

Museum of New Zealand Te Papa Tongarewa. 'Patch: Bungaswehr, Object | Part of Art Collection'. 2020. https://collections.tepapa.govt.nz/object/1874468

Phillips, Bruce E. 'A Voice for the Voiceless'. In *The Walters Prize 2014*, edited by Clare McIntosh, 71–74. Exhibition catalogue. Auckland: Auckland Art Gallery Toi o Tāmaki, 2014. https://issuu.com/aucklandartgallery/docs/wp_catalogue_single-page

——— 'Curator's Response: Kalisolaite 'Uhila's Mo'ui Tukuhausia'. *OUTPOST: Blogs from Staff and Friends of Auckland Art Gallery Toi o Tāmaki* (blog), 21 August 2014. http://aucklandartgallery.blogspot.com/2014/08/curators-response-kalisolaite-uhilas.html

——— 'Kalisolaite 'Uhila: Life set aside'. *Le Roy* 3, 'The Soft Issue' (2015).

Phillips, Bruce E. and Jeremy Leatinu'u. 'The Power of Presence: A conversation with Jeremy Leatinu'u'. *Puehu: Cultural Dust* (blog), 30 July 2014. https://puehu.tumblr.com/post/93298800802/the-power-of-presence-a-conversation-with-jeremy

Rice, Karen Gonzalez. *Long Suffering: American endurance art as prophetic witness*. Ann Arbor: University of Michigan Press, 2016.

Roms, Heike. 'Performing Endurance: Art and politics since 1960'. *Contemporary Theatre Review* 29, no. 4 (October 2019): 482–83. https://doi.org/10.1080/10486801.2019.1674570

Ruiz, Sandra. *Ricanness: Enduring time in anticolonial performance*. New York: New York University Press, 2019. http://ebookcentral.proquest.com/lib/aut/detail.action?docID=5784038

Russeth, Andrew. 'Art About Waiting — and What It Takes to Endure'. *New York Times*, 17 September 2020. https://www.nytimes.com/2020/09/17/t-magazine/Tehching-Hsieh-endurance-art.html

Rutledge, Louise. 'Editorial | Enjoy Contemporary Art Space'. *To Find A Place*, 2018. https://enjoy.org.nz/publishing/the-occasional-journal/to-find-a-place/editorial

Shalson, Lara. *Performing Endurance: Art and politics since 1960*. Cambridge, UK: Cambridge University Press, 2018.

ST PAUL St Gallery, AUT. 'Still, Like Air, I'll Rise'. 2017. https://stpaulst.aut.ac.nz/all-exhibitions/still-like-air-ill-rise

The Dowse Art Museum. 'Lifting My Mother for as Long as I Can'. 2012. https://dowse.org.nz/exhibitions-and-events/exhibitions/2012/lifting-my-mother-for-as-long-as-i-can

Tonga, Nina. 'Roaming All Levels'. *Off the Wall* 6 (August 2014). https://tetuhi.art/wp-content/uploads/2020/06/Te-Papa_Roaming-all-levels.pdf

'Kalisolaite 'Uhila: Life set aside'. Interview by Bruce E. Phillips, 2015. https://bruceephillips.com/writing/life-set-aside

Vaioleti, Timote Masima. 'Talanoa Research Methodology: A developing position on Pacific research'. *Waikato Journal of Education* 12 (2006): 21–34.

Vea, John. 'Exploring Pacific Talanoa Research Methods in Visual Arts Installation and Performance Art Practices'. PhD thesis, Auckland University of Technology, 2021. https://hdl.handle.net/10292/14800

Vea, John and Chris Braddock. 'Moana Nui Social Art Practices in Aotearoa'. *DAT Journal* 3, no. 2 (November 2018): 291–324. https://doi.org/10.29147/dat.v3i2.95

Wakefield, Nik. 'Performing Endurance: Art and politics since 1960 by Lara Shalson (review)'. *TDR: The Drama Review* 64, no. 2 (Summer 2020): 177–80.

'Anna-Marie White in Conversation with Kate Brettkelly-Chalmers'. *Ocula*, 18 January 2014. https://ocula.com/magazine/conversations/anna-marie-white

Wynne-Jones, Victoria. *Choreographing Intersubjectivity in Performance Art*. Cham, Switzerland: Palgrave Macmillan, 2021.

12

THREE TYPES OF TIMEPASS

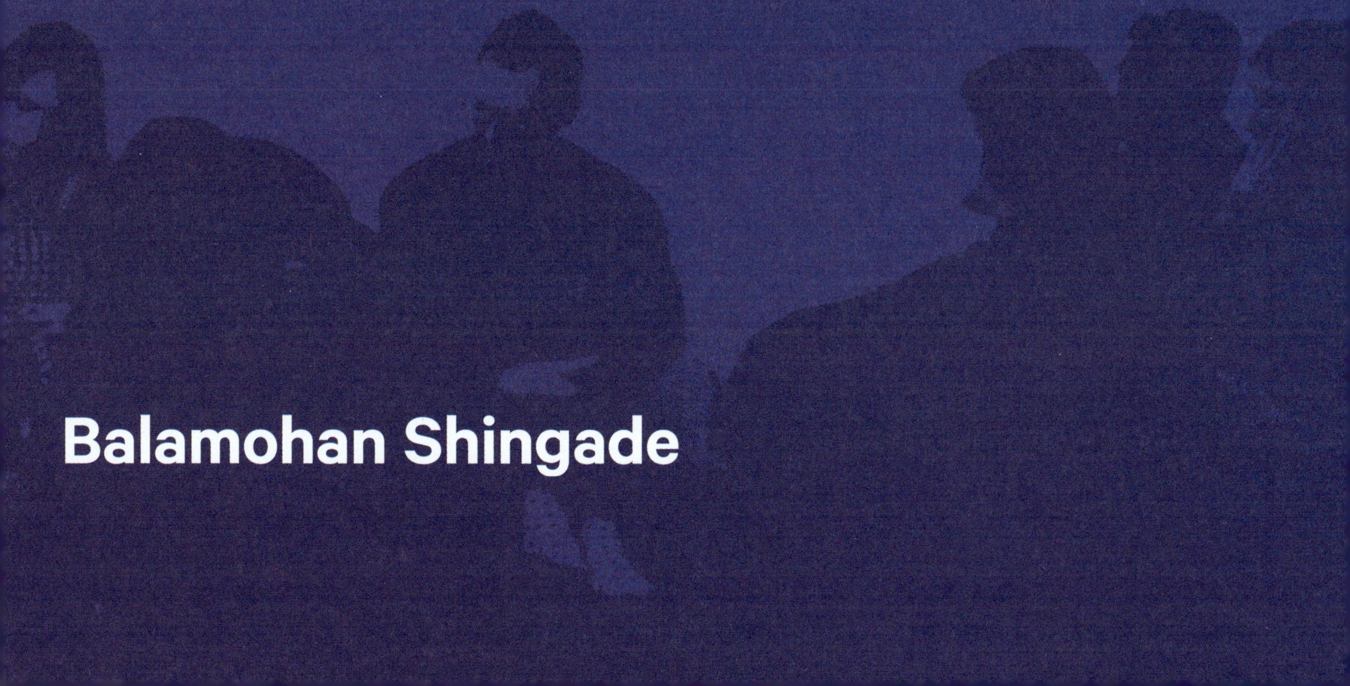

Balamohan Shingade

Performance art is often declared an unequalled medium for social engagement and politics of resistance.[1] The history of Aotearoa New Zealand presents us with plenty of examples, such as artist-activist Tame Iti's 2005 action of firing a shotgun into a flag as a demonstration of Tūhoe anger over the government's treatment of iwi since the nineteenth century. Or we might recall *Te Karanga a Hape Hīkoi* in 2017, an event organised by artist Rebecca Ann Hobbs with members of Ngāti Whātua Ōrākei, the collective Save Our Unique Landscape (SOUL) and artists from Karangahape Road in Tāmaki Makaurau Auckland. Symbolically connecting Ihumātao with Karangahape Road through the story of Hape, the hīkoi advocated for the protection and future management of the Ihumātao whenua and awa by mana whenua.

Such works might be conjured by our minds when we think of performance at the interface of politics. They are action-oriented and speak truth to power. Perhaps for this reason, performance art, more than any other medium, is proclaimed by its advocates as a means to remedy the motivational deficit for socio-political engagement in contemporary liberal democracies.

In this chapter I turn to performance artworks of a different tenor: ones that use the inverse strategies of worklessness and withdrawal, refusals and retreats, passivity and purposelessness. In the context of social engagement and politics of resistance, the significance of such works may be easily overlooked, but they can in fact have important political meaning.

I discuss recent performances by Kalisolaite 'Uhila, Chris Braddock with Dialogue Group,[2] Layne Waerea, Poata Alvie McKree and James Tapsell-Kururangi. All of them embrace the Indian English concept of 'timepass', an expression for doing nothing or doing something non-specific. This chapter is organised into three parts that correspond with the three types of timepass I discuss: temporal, discursive and relational. I write from the point of view of an interlocutor, as an accompanist of these artists, and as curator of an exhibition titled *How to Live Together*, where some of the performances discussed in this chapter were first presented (ST PAUL St Gallery, Auckland University of Technology [AUT], 2019). I draw on conversations with the artists and interpretations of their artworks to show the quieter side of their socio-political performances.

WASTING TIME, BEING USELESS

Tea stalls, rooftops and street corners are popular places for timepass in the subcontinent. Timepass connotes being-in-wait; it is the deliberate passing, wasting or even killing of time. Perhaps for this reason, it is frequently seen as an irresponsible or morally reprehensible activity, and anyone doing timepass is chided for being *bekār*, worthless or workless.

I did not see Kalisolaite 'Uhila's performance *Maumau-taimi* at ST PAUL St Gallery in November 2016. The one-day performance was a rumour that friends in Tāmaki Makaurau recounted to me. 'Uhila was studying for his master's but appeared to be doing timepass: wandering the hallways of the School of Art & Design at AUT, loitering in the stairwell and perching on benches for hours on end. For his end-of-year performance art exam, he sat idly in the window of ST PAUL St Gallery, 'wasting time, being useless'. When art critic Anthony Byrt asked 'Uhila what drove his thinking, 'Uhila replied, 'Wasting time.'[3]

On the day of 'Uhila's end-of-year performance, artist and writer Christopher Braddock was among the group looking into the ST PAUL St Gallery window. On

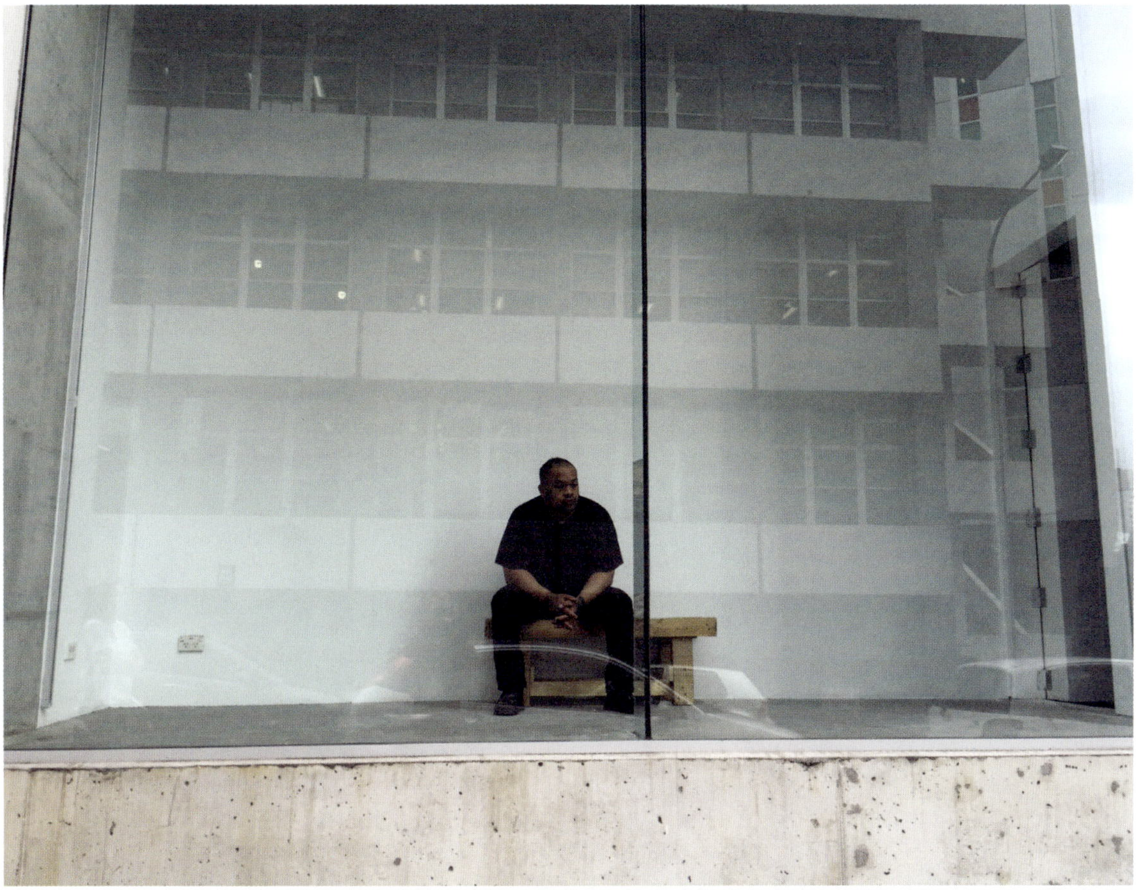

Kalisolaite ‘Uhila, *Maumau-taimi*, 2016, documentation of performance at ST PAUL St Gallery, Tāmaki Makaurau Auckland. *Courtesy the artist. Photo by Chris Braddock*

Braddock’s reading, *Maumau-taimi* was a performance of ‘radical passivity’.[4] From the street, people saw ‘Uhila turn his alleged laziness, his timepass and unemployability ‘into rituals of slowly nuanced engagement’.[5] A sign at the gallery welcomed visitors to join ‘Uhila in the window, and some people waited their turn to sit with him on the wooden bench and speak, their voices inaudible to the viewers outside.

When there were no visitors or viewers, ‘Uhila just sat. He clasped his hands with his elbows on his knees, or he rested his head against the wall, looking as if he was waiting for someone or something. For one day, ‘Uhila was a timepassing presence inside the front window of ST PAUL St Gallery.

‘Uhila has often worked, as he describes it, in the ‘shadow of time’[6] — ‘outside the daily routines and rituals that marked the passing of the day: the opening and closing of the gallery and the arrival and departure of staff’.[7] His best-known performance is *Mo‘ui Tukuhausia* (2012), in which he spent two weeks living homeless in the southeast suburb of Pakuranga in Tāmaki Makaurau.[8] Two years later, he extended *Mo‘ui Tukuhausia* to three months for the Walters Prize at Auckland Art Gallery Toi o Tāmaki.[9]

‘Uhila has also performed a series of ‘disappearing acts’.[10] In his 2012 performance *Stowaway*, he lived in a shipping container for four days and nights, ‘living on coconuts and shitting in a bucket’,[11] as homage to his uncle’s stowaway journey from Tonga to

Aotearoa. For *Pigs in the Yard* (2011), he lived with a piglet that he named Colonist in an open straw pen in central Auckland's Aotea Square. And for his performance *Family Tree* in a suburban park in Tāmaki Makaurau, he climbed the tallest tree then allowed himself to fall out, hitting as many branches as possible on the way down.

Taken together, 'Uhila's works speak to an attitude of stepping into social and temporal peripheries. But of the many performances described above, the idea of timepass helps to reveal, in particular, the political principle at the heart of his 2016 performance *Maumau-taimi*.

'Uhila cites artist Mladen Stilinović's 1978 performance *Artist at Work* as an inspiration for *Maumau-taimi*.[12] Stilinović once said that 'knowing about laziness is not enough, it must be practiced [sic] and perfected . . . There is no art without laziness.'[13] Eulogising laziness in this way, Stilinović lay in a bed in a gallery in Zagreb in the former Yugoslavia, at times asleep and at times wide-eyed with his arms behind his head. Stilinović aimed to reclaim laziness from its position as a bad temporal object in a global-capital world of fetishised production.

Unlike Stilinović's *Artist at Work*, 'Uhila's *Maumau-taimi* does more than valorise laziness. His timepass seeks to overcome a specific set of relations and identities formed around work. Through his performance, 'Uhila questions a work-oriented vision of human life and, in the context of a university visual arts programme, a workforce-oriented education. After all, the university promises that their master's graduates 'will significantly contribute to the creative sector'.[14] The critique of an education directed at sector growth is not trivial; it is connected to 'Uhila's daily experience as a factory worker stationed on an assembly line in a food-processing factory.[15] Through timepass, 'Uhila asks whether an attempt to define a truly human work and education should not entail first a critique of sector or market-oriented notions.

'Uhila has done plenty of timepass. In 2015 he spent a day from dawn to dusk in Albert Park. Afterwards he was invited to travel to Berlin and timepass there. So, we might object that in the economy of contemporary art, timepass — even Stilinović's sleep — can be made productive, especially when it becomes the subject of projects, exhibitions or book chapters like this one. As art historian Isabelle Graw writes, 'poses, attitudes, or the decision to go on strike . . . have proven to be no less value-generating forms of human labor. Non-labor, even refusal to work, may be measured, especially in art, in categories of labor.'[16]

Graw's point rings true, but what matters for us is to see that *Maumau-taimi* serves as an example of a performance that uses the strategies of worklessness and purposelessness to engage in a politics of resistance. There remains an open question about whether these strategies are effective, but that is a different debate. Using the concept of timepass, we can see that 'Uhila aims to dismiss the apparatuses that set him to work, by himself becoming workless within them.

If *Maumau-taimi* is about an individual's wasting time and being useless, then the participatory performance *5 Minutes* expands timepass to the collective. Based on the freeing potential of timepass, in 2019 'Uhila crafted an invitation to office workers and others to the exhibition *How to Live Together*. For the thirteen-week duration of the exhibition, 'Uhila observed silence every Monday at 9 a.m. and invited everyone else to do so also. The silence was sometimes observed together, sometimes alone — as a pause during a commute, a moment of stillness at the office, or quiet time at the rotunda in Albert Park, the designated place of coming together.

INVITATION TO DIALOGUE

In his fieldwork on timepass with college students in India, geographer Craig Jeffrey found chit-chat and conversation to be at the centre of the practice. He saw young women chatting on rooftops and young men hanging out at tea stalls, engaging in horseplay and banter and showing small gestures of friendship.[17] Sometimes Jeffrey observed conversations turning from idle talk, such as gripes about the police harassment of students, to discussions of what should be done. Then, 'young men would often disappear into the bowels of a tea stall to plan their strategy'.[18] But this was after the fact of timepass, after conversations without an agenda.

To onlookers and passers-by, this is the kind of timepass that Christopher Braddock has been doing. Since 2018 he has been engaged in various group formations to converse in a manner proposed by physicist David Bohm. Bohmian dialogue promises that a new form of communication will flow from the collective refusal to speak with an agenda. For *How to Live Together*, Braddock envisaged an hour-long dialogue every Wednesday afternoon for the duration of the thirteen-week exhibition titled *Invitation to Dialogue* (2019). He sent two emails to old and new collaborators, inviting them to join the dialogue group. These emails were also pinned to the gallery wall where they functioned as room sheets to give exhibition attendees information on how to participate.

After removing their shoes outside the carpeted area and drawing square cushions from a stack on one side of the room, participants arranged themselves in a rough circle in readiness. Braddock undertook the role of a facilitator, but with a view to do himself out of that job after introducing Bohmian dialogue.

Braddock introduced the practice in the first email in this way:

> A dialogue group tries to talk together without hierarchies. There are no leaders, no agenda or appointed topics of conversation, and no conclusions for the group to arrive at. People are encouraged not to tell others what they already know, and people try not to judge others and their ideas.

Participants in the dialogue group were encouraged to suspend their beliefs, to avoid pre-planning conversation and arriving at conclusions, and, most curious of all, to withhold from recounting to others what they know. Braddock admits that talking together using this rubric may be challenging. He acknowledges in the second of his two emails: 'In attempting to dialogue, we may encounter difficult moments and the process may appear to fail, but that's part of the exercise. Apparent failure and disappointment become things to observe.'

I was a daily participant in *Invitation to Dialogue* and want to share three observations. First, Bohmian dialogue is an activity without an aim or end-point. It creates a community with no predefined purpose, much like the get-togethers on rooftops and at tea stalls. Except for the arbitrary stopping of the activity, there are no conclusions to these conversations, and participants avoid working towards a goal or reaching a decision.

Second, Bohmian dialogue requires a type of active listening and intentional communication, and here it differs from timepass. In his foreword to Bohm's book *On Dialogue*, Dean Rickles writes that 'dialogue requires *effort* — it is an active procedure, demanding a level of self-denial and ego elimination'.[19] Like fasting or refraining from ordinary indulgences, communicative abstinence requires practice. Refraining from

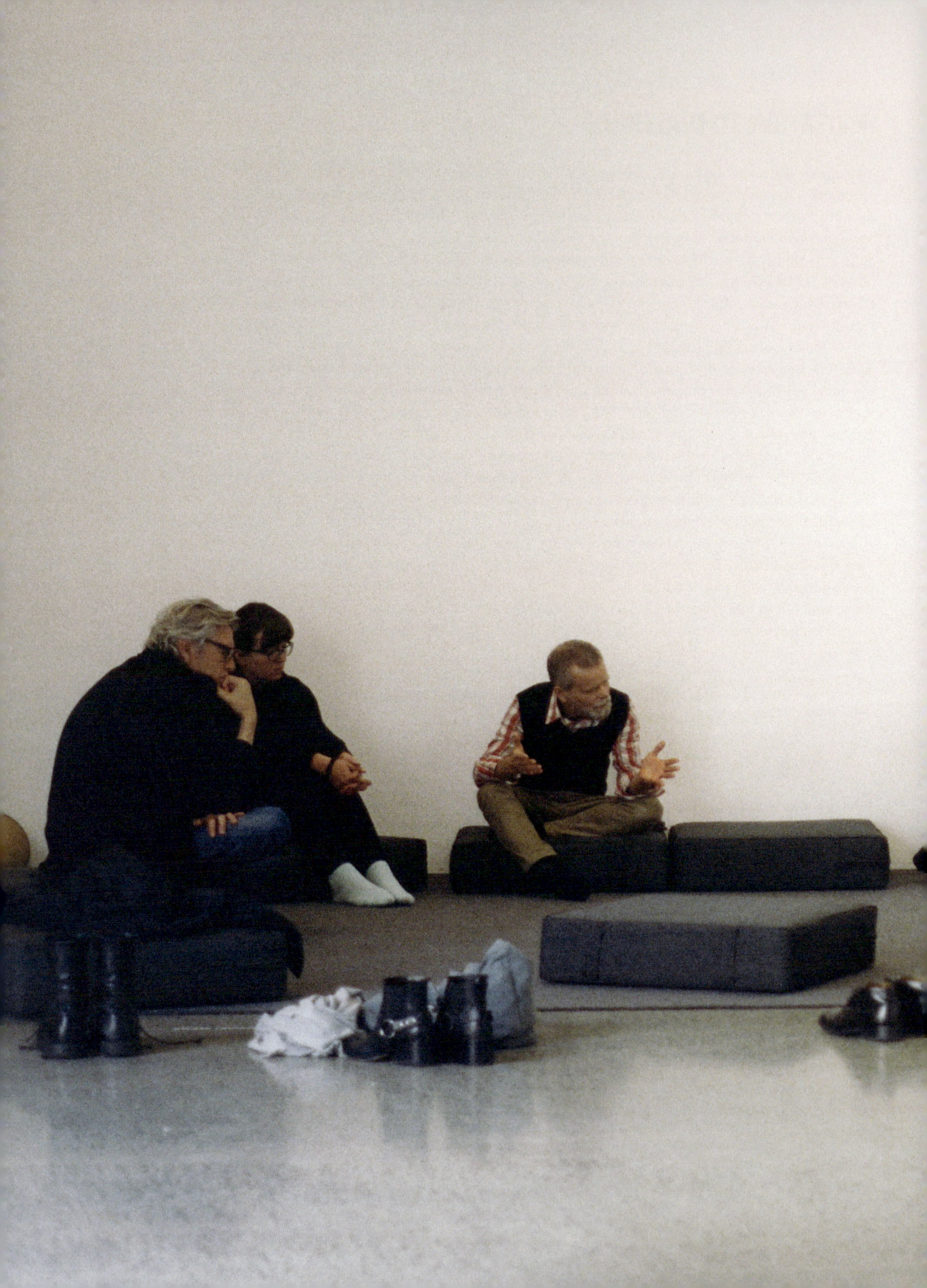

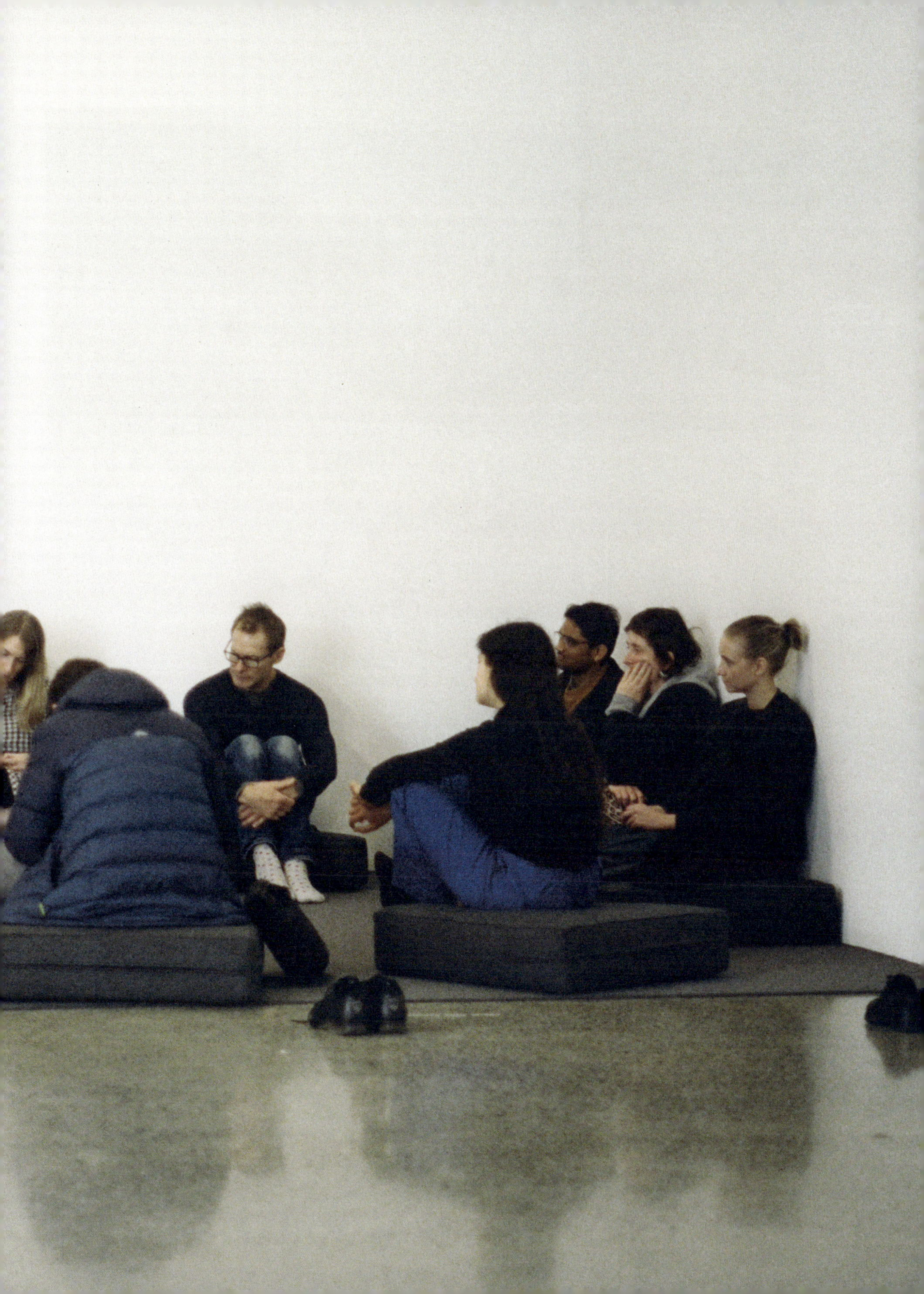

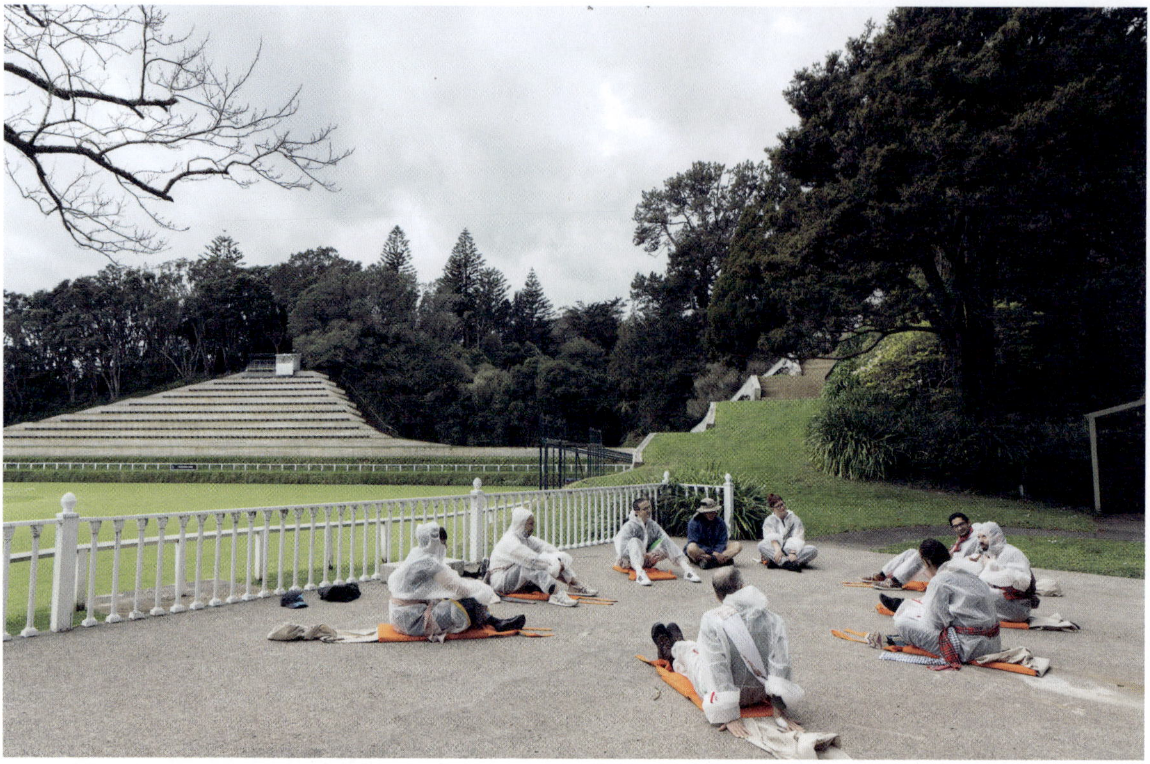

Layne Waerea (Ngāti Wāhiao, Ngāti Kahungunu) and Chris Braddock, *Free Public Sauna: Sweaty conversations in Ngāmotu*, 2022, performance still, Pukekura Park, Ngāmotu New Plymouth. In *Public Relations: A performance series*, curated by Simon Gennard, Govett-Brewster Art Gallery. *Courtesy the artists and Govett-Brewster Art Gallery. Photo by Hayley Bethell*

agenda-based conversations is challenging, and the exercise helps to highlight their centrality in our everyday interpersonal exchanges and social interactions.

Third, Bohmian dialogue shifts the emphasis from the content of thoughts to the process of thinking. Among the participants were Eamon Edmundsen-Wells and Ziggy Lever, members of the artist collective The Observatory Project. They likened Bohmian dialogue to an observatory for communication. As they describe it, the dialogue group functions as a telescope to observe the rising and setting of conversation, the orbits of narratives and the constellation of themes. By paying attention to thought and thinking, both collectively and individually, shared meanings begin to emerge. As Braddock explained in the first of his emails:

> The individual sometimes assumes that their thinking is their own; that they are in control of their thoughts and generate them by themselves . . . In a counter argument to these assumptions . . . thought itself is a process of movement, the content and structure of which is by no means our own, as if the result of an individuated, fragmented knowing self. Rather, thought emerges from a field of discontinuous and entangled experiences, fears, histories and stories.

Using Bohm's idea of dialogue, Braddock creates a setting for opening up participatory thought. Through this process, we might see that insight comes not from individuals but from social activity. In other words, insight is crafted across or between participants; it is not contained within them as stocks to be traded or things to be debated.

In his recent collaborations with artist Layne Waerea (Ngāti Wāhiao, Ngāti Kahungunu), Braddock develops and departs from Bohmian dialogues. Together, Braddock and Waerea devise participatory actions and conversations. Their events combine Braddock's interest in participatory thought with the poetry, playfulness and political orientations characteristic of Waerea's work.

For the exhibition titled *Public Relations*, curated by Simon Gennard in 2022 at the Govett-Brewster Art Gallery, Waerea and Braddock devised two instances for 'sweaty conversations' in Ngāmotu New Plymouth.[20] The first was at Pukekura Park; the second was on the Coastal Walkway a week later. Braddock and Waerea guided participants wearing hazmat-style sweatsuits through gentle exercises designed to generate perspiration. Afterwards, against the backdrop of Ngāmotu, and sitting on orange props made by the artists,[21] their conversations lapped around the topics of public sport, the nature of competition in the art world, the concept of property, and the use, ownership and guardianship of natural resources.

Waerea's own performances can also be interpreted using the concept of timepass. Take, for example, *Free Arguments: [Under Construction]*, first performed in Aotea Square in Tāmaki Makaurau on 15 February 2018. In this performance, Waerea is seen holding a cardboard sign on which is handwritten 'FREE ARGUMENTS'. Among the materials list that forms the documentation of this work is the Trading and Events in Public Places Bylaw 2015, which states that a person must hold an approval issued by Auckland Council when undertaking to carry out an event or when trading in public places.[22]

Waerea is seated on a wooden bench overlooking the square, and she intends to trade arguments freely. In the context of a deterioration of public discourse, of partisanship and political polarisation, the sign invites strangers to timepass with her and to scope the possibilities of disagreement in the public sphere. Drawing on her legal background — as a lawyer interested in exploring the normative foundations provided by Te Tiriti o Waitangi — Waerea is prepared to argue with strangers about the privatisation of natural resources and the socio-legal norms that determine behaviour and relationships. But in the twenty busy minutes she's holding the sign, no one stops to take up this free offer. One young man contests, as he walks away, 'Aren't arguments free anyway?'[23]

PREVIOUS: Chris Braddock with dialogue group, *Invitation to Dialogue*, 2019. Performed at AUT ST PAUL St Gallery, Tāmaki Makaurau Auckland. *Courtesy ST PAUL St Gallery/Te Wai Ngutu Kākā Gallery and the artist. Participant and photographer Emily Parr*

WHAT IS THE INTIMACY WE MUST DEVELOP TO CREATE A COMMUNITY? WHAT IS THE DISTANCE WE MUST MAINTAIN TO RETAIN OUR SOLITUDE?[24]

Poata Alvie McKree (Ngāpuhi, Ngāti Kahu ki Whangaroa, St Vincent, Barbados) often works at the thresholds of human experiences. As a former registered midwife she supported women through labour and birth; more recently she has been called on to care for people in the final stages of their lives. Reflecting on her experiences, McKree asks, 'How do you accompany someone on a journey that you yourself cannot undergo? You walk with them to the threshold, but in the end, while they cross over, you must remain.'[25]

McKree's participatory performances are part of her threshold work. For the exhibition *How to Live Together*, she held three private gatherings for women to pass the time in each other's company. The first was *Hōngongoi*, in which McKree led a movement-as-medicine workshop drawing on ritual practices. The second, *Hereturikōkā*, held on

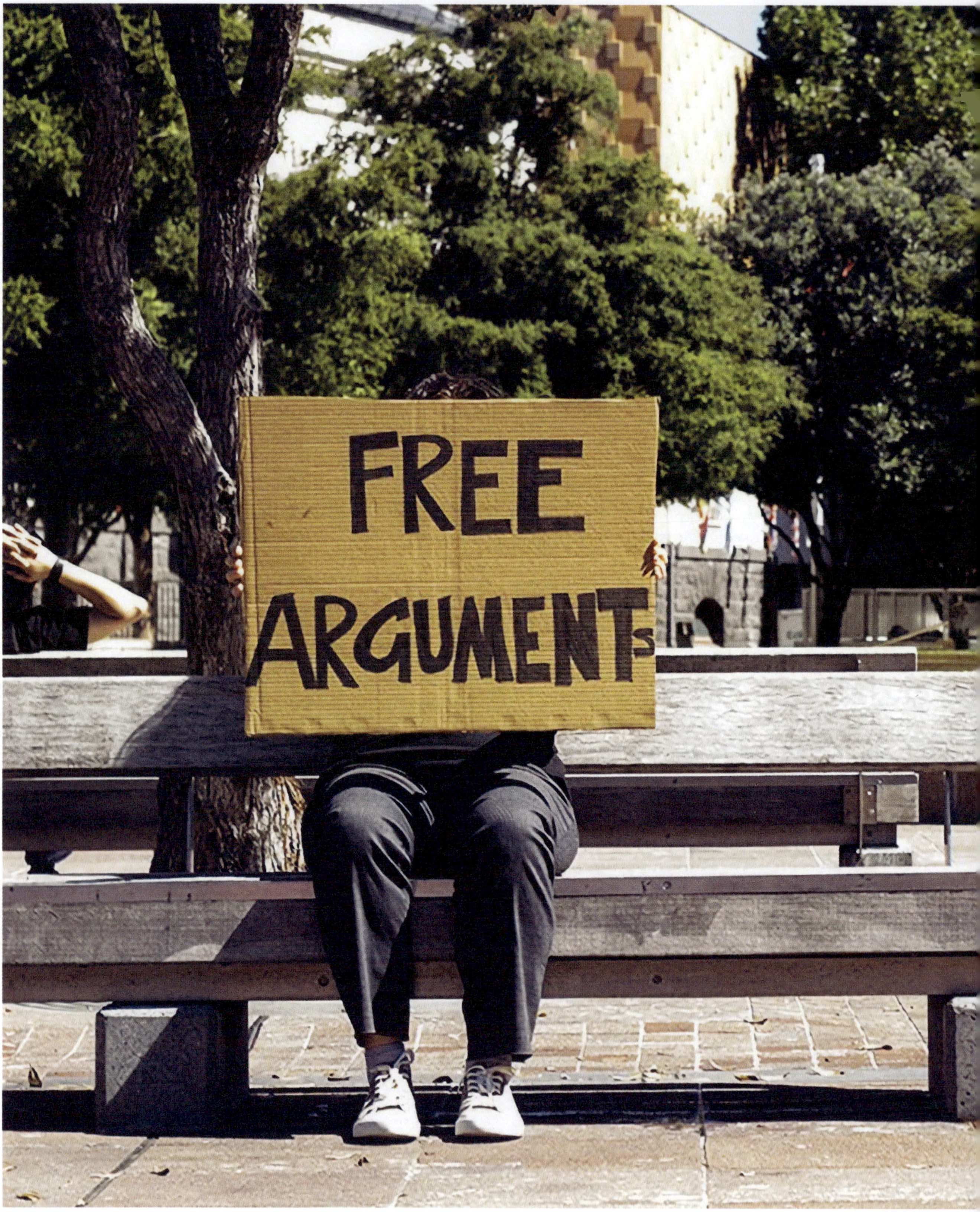
FREE
ARGUMENTs

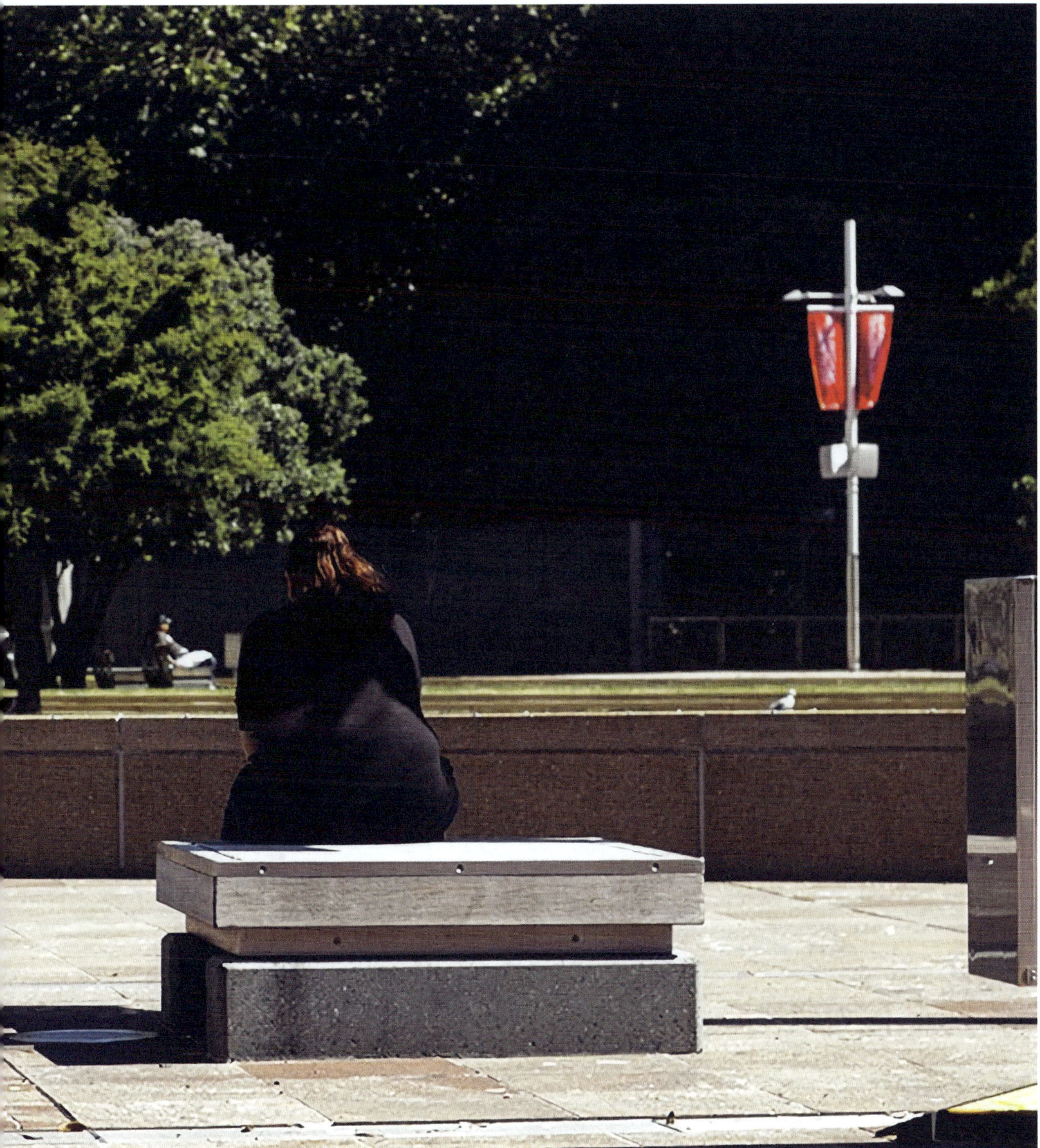

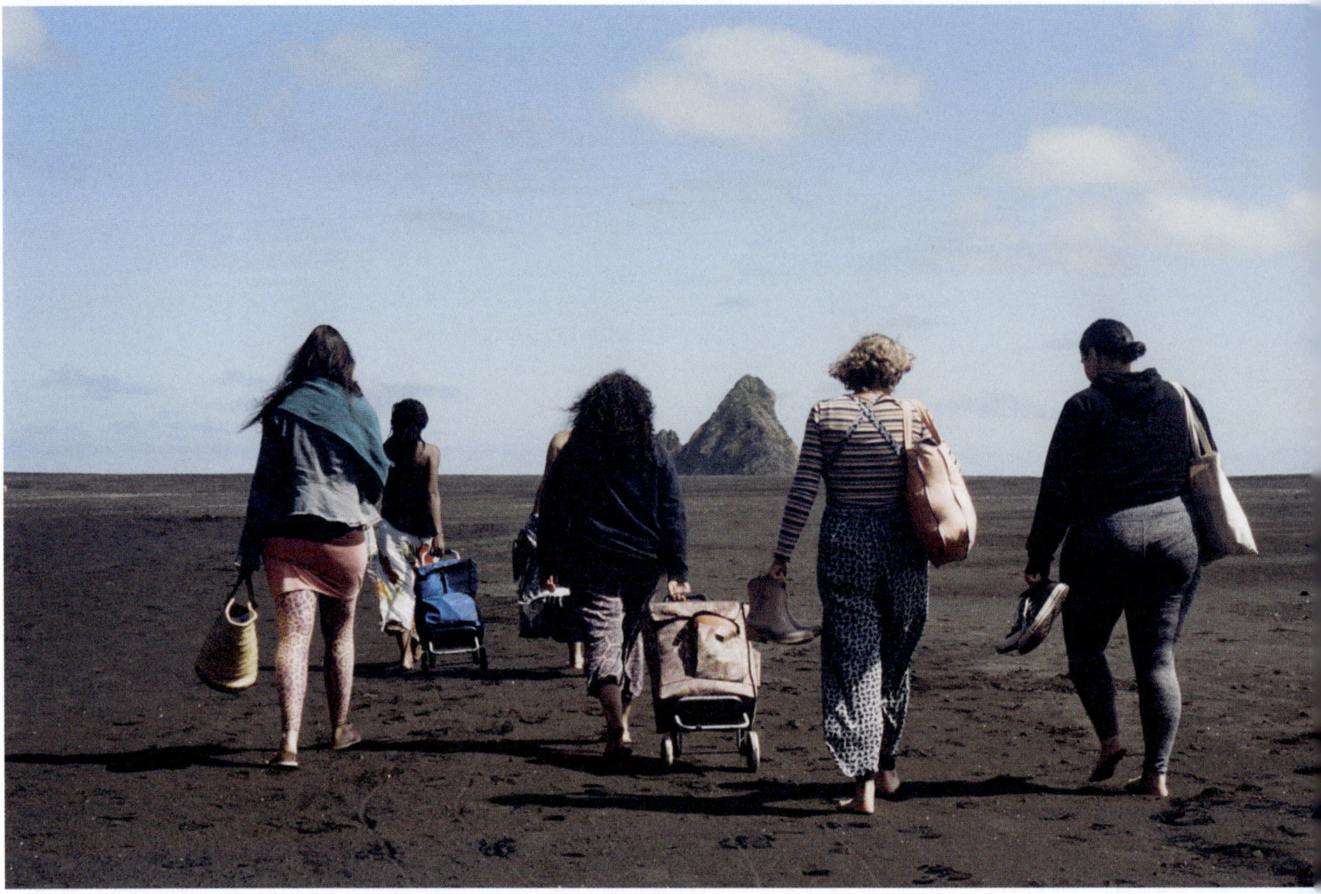

Poata Alvie McKree (Ngāpuhi, Ngāti Kahu ki Whangaroa, St Vincent, Barbados), *Mahuru: E hine e*, 2019. *Courtesy ST PAUL St Gallery/ Te Wai Ngutu Kākā Gallery, Auckland. Photo by Emily Parr*

the occasion of the third lunar month of the Māori calendar, consisted of storytelling and a cacao ceremony. The third was *Mahuru: E hine e*, a beachside gathering for ritual and dance and an invitation to reconnect with the earth as it began to warm beneath the feet in the spring months and as the vegetation and trees showed signs of renewal.

McKree's workshops create an intimacy among participants as they combine their energies to perform a kind of timepass together to expel frustrations and disappointments. She invites participants to withdraw from the mind and connect instead with the wisdom of the body. Those at the intersection of life decisions or experiences are encouraged not to *think* their way through but to *move* through together.

There is an important sense in which being-in-wait is not wholly positive, and McKree's workshops demonstrate a recognition of this. For example, timepass can be enforced rather than voluntarily performed, such as when one is prevented from achieving a goal. During his fieldwork in the subcontinent, Jeffrey saw timepass emerge as an expression of the suffering of young, educated people who faced repeated disappointments in the job market. In Jeffrey's account, timepass can be a collective display of people's painful experiences of dwelling in an extended period of inertia; simultaneously, it can be a collective activity performed deliberately to heal from the permanently provisional feeling of living in limbo. Under the latter definition of timepass,

McKree's workshops could be seen as facilitating the possibility of shared healing.

In gallery settings that have been turned into depoliticised spaces for leisure or merchandising, the value of McKree's performance art might be measured by the institution in terms of consumer satisfaction — that is, by the workshop's capacity to provide pleasurable experiences. But the sort of timepass McKree proposes challenges such consumptive logics by delimiting participation to a small group of women. Then, through ritual and movement, she crafts the workshops as thresholds for participants to cross. By coming together to grieve and celebrate in equal measure, McKree's audience-participants accompany each other through life's substantive and subtle transitions.

In choosing social interaction and intersubjective changes as a medium, performance artists like McKree turn spectators into participants. McKree jettisons any possibility of passive observers being present — demonstrating the genre's capacity to critique spectacle and spectatorship. Here, the artist could be seen to exemplify one of the popular capabilities of performance art: to go beyond the representation of issues to direct engagement. Artist Guillermo Gómez-Peña praises this ability when he writes, 'Performance is about presence, not representation; it is not (as classical theories of theatre would suggest) a mirror, but the actual moment in which the mirror is shattered.'[26]

Like McKree, artist James Tapsell-Kururangi (Ngāti Whakaue, Ngāti Mākino, Ngāti Pikiao, Te Whānau-a-Rakairoa, Ngāti Raukawa) challenges the consumptive expectations of gallery-goers with an artwork that requires active commitment and participation. Tapsell-Kururangi's proposal was perhaps the most radical response to the driving question of *How to Live Together*. The invitation to artists and others in 2019 read as follows: 'Let us inhabit *How to Live Together* as an ongoing enquiry, and this exhibition as a scene or a course guided by the coupled question: What is the intimacy we must develop to create a community? What is the distance we must maintain to retain our solitude?'[27]

The title of Tapsell-Kururangi's performance makes his intentions clear: *Living with My Grandmother for One Year*. For the duration of the exhibition and beyond, the artist moved to Rotorua to live in the home of his late grandmother, Helen Jean Linton. The house contained a lifetime of his grandmother's effects, and Tapsell-Kururangi hesitated to change the order of things: he reshelved linen just as she had in the linen cupboard and learned to use her cookware. When her clock stopped, he wondered whether it would be appropriate to replace the battery.

Of course, the casual visitor to ST PAUL St Gallery in Tāmaki Makaurau Auckland could not immediately experience Tapsell-Kururangi's work. For almost everyone, it remained a rumour accompanied by some text in the exhibition guide. As one reviewer complained, 'In my view — literally! — this project exists only as a name, a catalogue entry.'[28] That the audience could not consume the artwork readily and in an undifferentiated manner reveals an important principle at the heart of Tapsell-Kururangi's work: What would it mean to shift the emphasis of art from the study and materialisation of knowledge and the making of things to the practice of art as a study of being and becoming? That is, to reframe the question of art from 'what to do?' to 'how to be?' As the artist puts it:

> You're not supposed to make art about —. It was a year spent living . . . I do not want to aestheticise her or my life and family as —. I do want to ask: Can a year living at my grandmother's house be an artwork?[29]

When Tapsell-Kururangi lived in the home of his late grandmother, all of life became encompassed in the idea of art, including his day job at the Rotorua City Council.

PREVIOUS: Layne Waerea, *Free Arguments: [Under Construction]*, 2018, documentation of performance at Aotea Square, Tāmaki Makaurau Auckland. *Courtesy the artist*

I visited the artist twice during his artwork residence. His invitation was to pass the time in each other's company and build common ground, even if briefly, at the residence of Helen Jean Linton. After all, he said, for a show titled *How to Live Together*, it made little sense to work with someone whose values and motives he wasn't familiar with.

The invitation was also open to ST PAUL St Gallery-goers for the show's duration. If visitors asked the gallery guides for more information, they were told that visiting Rotorua and staying with Tapsell-Kururangi was possible. The intimacies or distances between the artist and the visitor would determine the visitor's experience of the artist's work.

Living with My Grandmother for One Year was a work about relational commitment — between Tapsell-Kururangi and his grandmother, between staff at ST PAUL St Gallery and Tapsell-Kururangi, and between the visitors to the exhibition and Helen Jean Linton's house in Rotorua. This way, visitors' perspectives became uneven, partial and inconsistent, especially because the artwork was not defined and contained *a priori*. Rather than an object within the gallery space for consumption or contemplation, it was an experience to be lived through, a landscape to sketch in, and an approach for building relationships.

Beneath Tapsell-Kururangi's question about what distinguishes an aesthetic event from a non-aesthetic one, at least two more concerns can be opened for interpretation using the concept of timepass, since most obviously, the accusation against 'Uhila of wasting time and being useless could be levelled at Tapsell-Kururangi too. What is more, Tapsell-Kururangi de-links his performance from the practices of exhibition-making, so the allegation may also come combined with the wasteful use of resources.

The objection may be that Tapsell-Kururangi's timepass seems no different from the hearsay of activities of friends from out of town. After all, as the performance is hidden from the purview of the gallery-goers, then it is without their checks and balances and quality control.

In responding to why Tapsell-Kururangi's retreat to Rotorua might be noteworthy, we must first distinguish timepass from 'time off'. The timepass that Tapsell-Kururangi proposes is different from downtime, from rest between bouts of exertion, in the same way that Sunday golfers are unlike the frequenters of tea stalls and rooftops in their passing of time. Whereas the golfer may carry a sense of deserving the well-earned leisure time against a backdrop of time used well, real timepass intervenes in and interrupts the so-called 'useful' passages of time.

Second, and perhaps more importantly, Tapsell-Kururangi's performances invite reflection on how the desire for community is fulfilled in the context of galleries and museums. The instrumentalist rationalities of mainstream gallery and museum practices, such as the programming of replicable experiences aimed at consumer comfort and mediated by facilitators or interpreters, risk severing artworks from the relationships and communities within which they are embedded. As a consequence, the social and relational commitments of performers and performances are cast aside.

Tapsell-Kururangi's timepass unsettles the assumptions built into the exhibition-making practices that threaten to rearrange our desires along the lines of efficient consumption. In this context, his work helps to re-educate us towards the formation of desires in community — desires that we can't know to have as yet, and which require us to collapse spectatorship into more participatory roles. As if to demonstrate an answer to the question of 'how to live together', Tapsell-Kururangi constrains the readership of his work to those who are willing to co-create it.

Helen Jean Linton's residence continues to anchor Tapsell-Kururangi's artistic-curatorial practice beyond *Living with My Grandmother for One Year*. For the

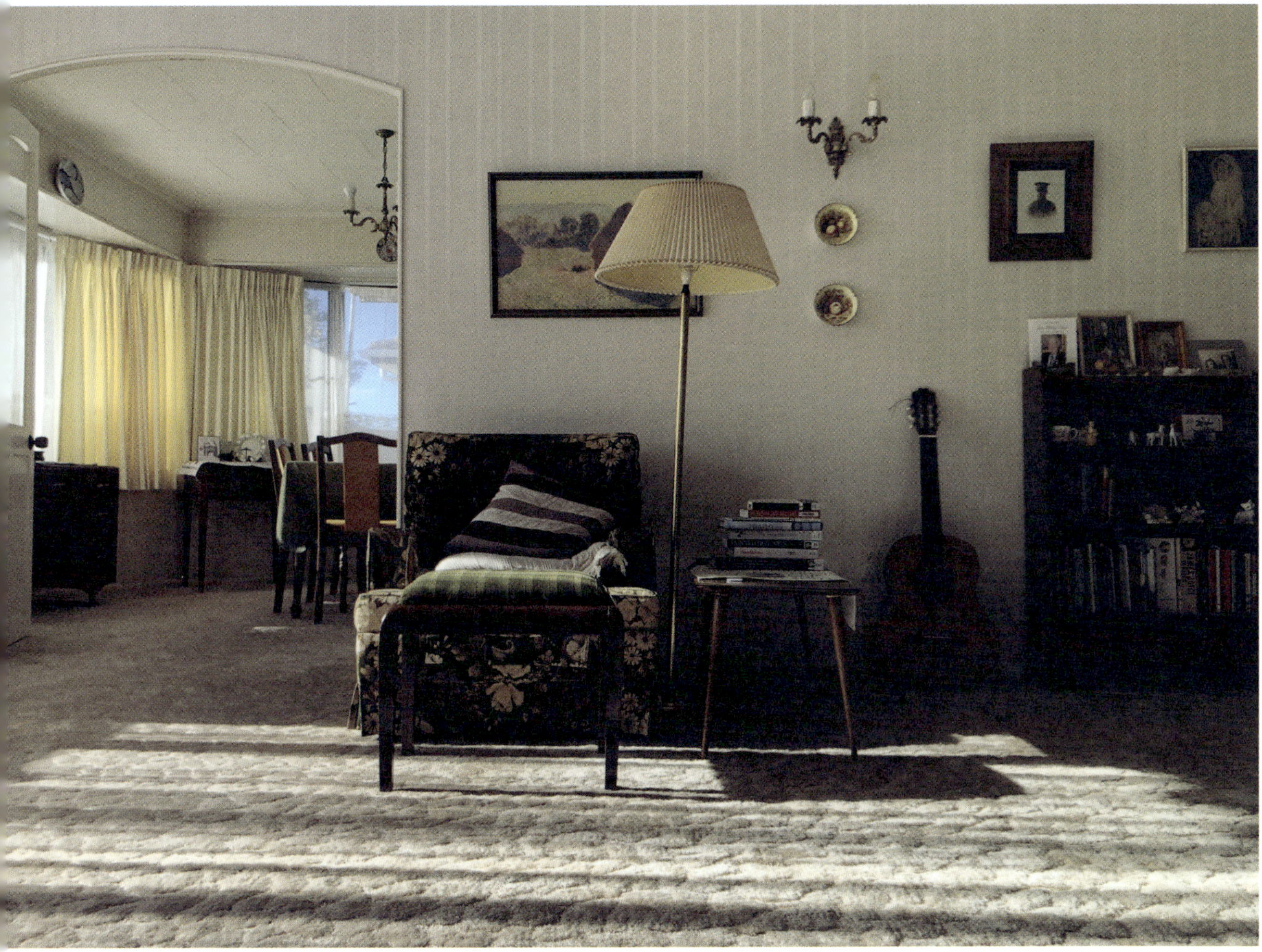

development of the exhibition *Te Pō* (Papatūnga, 2022), Tapsell-Kururangi hosted the artists at his grandmother's house. It became a site to reconfigure artist–curator engagements. In alignment with artist and curator Taarati Taiaroa's maxim for conversational research, the house allowed Tapsell-Kururangi to engage in 'an on-going and potentially immeasurable relational commitment . . . Geared towards a deceleration of outcomes, conversational research is a conscious decision to engage dialogically as a means to facilitate the emergence of knowledge, as opposed to focusing on the production of a predetermined outcome.'[30]

James Tapsell-Kururangi (Ngāti Whakaue, Ngāti Mākino, Ngāti Pikiao, Te Whānau-a-Rakairoa, Ngāti Raukawa), *Living with My Grandmother for One Year*, 2019. *Courtesy the artist*

CONCLUSION

It is sometimes difficult to read the socio-political relevance of performances that, unlike marches, strike or protests, use the inverse strategies of worklessness and withdrawal, refusals and retreats, passivity and purposelessness. But such performances' oblique relation to social engagement and politics of resistance does not render them insignificant.

Whether timepass unfolds as inaction, agenda-less conversation or a coming together without *telos*, an ultimate object or aim, each artist poses challenges to institutional practices and the behaviours of individuals. From an individual's point of view, the performances offer a form of methodological training to orient oneself towards openness, listening and insight. From an institutional perspective, the performances resist the instrumentalist rationalities of mainstream galleries and museums, which sever artworks from the communities they are embedded within to make them available for market circulation.

There remain questions about the strength of timepass as a social-political strategy and how artists might resist the commodification of their performances by galleries and museums motivated by consumerist ideals. But if we read these questions of timepass and performance art as intrinsically social-political, intertwined with social engagement and a politics of resistance, then the task of this chapter is fulfilled.

NOTES

1 Claire Bishop, *Artificial Hells: Participatory art and the politics of spectatorship* (London: Verso, 2012).
2 The name 'Chris Braddock with Dialogue Group' extends authorship to all possible participants.
3 Anthony Byrt, 'How Artist Kalisolaite 'Uhila Made a Statement by Vanishing into the Streets', *Noted*, 10 April 2017, https://web.archive.org/web/20180223083436/https://www.noted.co.nz/culture/arts/how-artist-kalisolaite-uhila-made-a-statement-by-vanishing-into-the-streets
4 Christopher Braddock, 'Radical Silence in Performance Art: Kalisolaite Uhila's Maumau-Taimi', *The Occasional Journal* (April 2018), Enjoy Contemporary Art Space. The term 'radical passivity' comes from Thomas Carl Wall, *Radical Passivity: Levinas, Blanchot, and Agamben* (New York: State University of New York Press, 1999).
5 Ibid.
6 Kalisolaite 'Uhila in Bruce E. Phillips, 'Discussing Mo'ui Tukuhausia' in *What do you mean, we?*, edited by Bruce E. Phillips and Rebecca Lal, exhibition catalogue (Auckland: Te Tuhi, 2012), 48.
7 Nina Tonga, 'Roaming All Levels', *Off the Wall* 6 (August 2014): 3.
8 When curator Bruce E. Phillips approached 'Uhila, 'he was engaging in opposing aspects of participatory research into homelessness by spending the odd day or night living on the street while conversely working as an inner-city security guard often required to move homeless people off private property'. See Bruce E. Phillips, 'Curator's Response: Kalisolaite 'Uhila's Mo'ui Tukuhausia', Auckland Art Gallery Toi o Tāmaki, 21 August 2014.
9 For an extended discussion of Kalisolaite 'Uhila's Mo'ui Tukuhausia (2012, 2014), see Chapter 11 of this volume, 'Either For a Moment or For as Long as Possible' by Christopher Braddock and Ioana Gordon-Smith.
10 Byrt, 'How Artist Kalisolaite 'Uhila Made a Statement'.
11 Scott Hamilton, 'The Artist as Haua', *EyeContact*, 14 October 2014, https://eyecontactmagazine.com/2014/10/the-artist-as-haua
12 Kalisolaite 'Uhila, 'Maumau-Taimi: Wasting time; being useless' (Master's thesis, Auckland University of Technology, 2016).
13 Mladen Stilinović, 'Praise of Laziness', trans. Marija Marušić, 4 October 2013, https://mladenstilinovic.com/works/10-2
14 Auckland University of Technology, 'Qualification Details: Master of Visual Arts', https://arion.aut.ac.nz/arionmain/courseinfo/Information/Qualifications/Details/QualDetails.aspx?id=1801
15 Kalisolaite 'Uhila, 'Kalisolaite 'Uhila: I Use My Tongan Knowledge and Identity as Resources', interview by Magnus Rosengarten, *Contemporary And (C&)*, 29 July 2016, https://contemporaryand.com/magazines/i-use-my-tongan-knowledge-and-identity-as-resources
16 Isabelle Graw, 'The Value of the Art Commodity: Twelve theses on human labor, mimetic desire, and aliveness', *TEXTE ZUR KUNST* 88, 'The Question of Value' (December 2012): 38.
17 Craig Jeffrey, *Timepass: Youth, class, and the politics of waiting in India* (Stanford: Stanford University Press, 2010), 94.
18 Ibid., 120.
19 Dean Rickles, 'Foreword', in *On Dialogue*, by David Bohm (London: Routledge, 2014), xvii. Emphasis in the original.
20 These performances took place on 10 and 17 September 2022 and were titled *Free Public Sauna: Sweaty conversations in Ngāmotu — Pukekura Park*; *Free Public Sauna: Sweaty conversations in Ngāmotu — Coastal Walkway*.
21 These sculptures or props are titled *Free sweat cushion-bags* and are designed to be worn as backpacks or folded to be used as cushions.
22 Layne Waerea, 'Free Arguments: [Under Construction]', edited by Louise Rutledge, *The Occasional Journal*, April 2018, Enjoy Contemporary Art Space, https://enjoy.org.nz/publishing/the-occasional-journal/to-find-a-place/free-arguments-under-constructio
23 Ibid.
24 Claude Coste, 'Preface', in *How to Live Together: Novelistic simulations of some everyday spaces. Notes for a lecture course and seminar at the Collège de France (1976–77)*, by Roland Barthes, trans. Kate Briggs (New York: Columbia University Press, 2012), xxii.
25 Poata Alvie McKree in conversation with the author, 25 March 2019.
26 Guillermo Gómez-Peña, *Dangerous Border Crossers: The artist talks back* (London: Routledge, 2000), 9.
27 Balamohan Shingade, 'How to Live Together', ST PAUL St Gallery, 2019, https://stpaulst.aut.ac.nz/exhibitions/past-exhibitions/2019/how-to-live-together
28 Ralph Paine, 'A Very Precise Kind of Rhythm', *Art + Australia*, 2019, www.artandaustralia.com/online/online/disruptions/very-precise-kind-rhythm.html
29 James Tapsell-Kururangi, 'Gains? Grandmother. Grey Street.', in *As Needed, as Possible*, edited by Sophie Davis and Simon Gennard (Wellington: Enjoy Contemporary Art Space, 2020), 3, https://enjoy.org.nz/publishing/other/as-needed-as-possible/gains-grandmother-grey-street
30 Taarati Taiaroa, 'Conversational Research: Praxis & emergence', in *A Year of Conscious Practice* (Dunedin/

Christchurch: The Physics Room and Blue Oyster Art Project Space, 2016).

REFERENCES

Auckland University of Technology. 'Qualification Details: Master of Visual Arts'. https://arion.aut.ac.nz/arionmain/courseinfo/Information/Qualifications/Details/QualDetails.aspx?id=1801

Bishop, Claire. *Artificial Hells: Participatory art and the politics of spectatorship.* London: Verso, 2012.

Braddock, Christopher. 'Radical Silence in Performance Art: Kalisolaite 'Uhila's Maumau-Taimi', edited by Louise Rutledge. *The Occasional Journal* (April 2018). https://enjoy.org.nz/publishing/the-occasional-journal/to-find-a-place/radical-silence-in-performance-art-kalisolaite-uhi

Byrt, Anthony. 'How Artist Kalisolaite 'Uhila Made a Statement by Vanishing into the Streets'. *Noted*, 10 April 2017. https://web.archive.org/web/20180223083436/https://www.noted.co.nz/culture/arts/how-artist-kalisolaite-uhila-made-a-statement-by-vanishing-into-the-streets

Coste, Claude. 'Preface'. In *How to Live Together: Novelistic simulations of some everyday spaces. Notes for a lecture course and seminar at the Collège de France (1976–77)*, by Roland Barthes, trans. Kate Briggs, xxii. New York: Columbia University Press, 2012.

Gómez-Peña, Guillermo. *Dangerous Border Crossers: The artist talks back.* London: Routledge, 2000.

Graw, Isabelle. 'The Value of the Art Commodity: Twelve Theses on human labor, mimetic desire, and aliveness'. *TEXTE ZUR KUNST* 88, 'The Question of Value' (December 2012): 30–38.

Hamilton, Scott. 'The Artist as Haua'. *EyeContact*, 14 October 2014. https://eyecontactmagazine.com/2014/10/the-artist-as-haua

Jeffrey, Craig. *Timepass: Youth, class, and the politics of waiting in India.* Stanford: Stanford University Press, 2010.

Paine, Ralph. 'A Very Precise Kind of Rhythm'. *Art + Australia*, 2019. www.artandaustralia.com/online/online/disruptions/very-precise-kind-rhythm.html

Phillips, Bruce E. 'Curator's Response: Kalisolaite 'Uhila's Mo'ui Tukuhausia'. Auckland Art Gallery Toi o Tāmaki, 21 August 2014. www.aucklandartgallery.com/article/curator-s-response-kalisolaite-uhila-s-mo-ui-tukuhausia

——— 'Discussing Mo'ui Tukuhausia'. In *What Do You Mean, We?*, edited by Bruce E. Phillips and Rebecca Lal. Exhibition catalogue, 47–48. Auckland: Te Tuhi Centre, 2012. https://issuu.com/tetuhiart/docs/what_do_you_mean_we

Rickles, Dean. 'Foreword'. In *On Dialogue*, by David Bohm, xvii. London: Routledge, 2014.

Shingade, Balamohan. 'How to Live Together'. ST PAUL St Gallery, 2019. https://stpaulst.aut.ac.nz/exhibitions/past-exhibitions/2019/how-to-live-together

Stilinović, Mladen. 'Praise of Laziness'. Trans. Marija Marušić. 4 October 2013. https://mladenstilinovic.com/works/10-2

Taiaroa, Taarati. 'Conversational Research: Praxis & emergence'. In *A Year of Conscious Practice.* Dunedin/Christchurch: The Physics Room and Blue Oyster Art Project Space, 2016. www.ayearofconsciouspractice.com/texts/conversational-research-praxis-emergence

Tapsell-Kururangi, James. 'Gains? Grandmother. Grey Street.' In *As Needed, as Possible*, edited by Sophie Davis and Simon Gennard. Wellington: Enjoy Contemporary Art Space, 2020. https://enjoy.org.nz/publishing/other/as-needed-as-possible/gains-grandmother-grey-street

Tonga, Nina. 'Roaming All Levels'. *Off the Wall* 6 (August 2014): 3.

'Uhila, Kalisolaite. 'I Use My Tongan Knowledge and Identity as Resources'. Interview by Magnus Rosengarten. *Contemporary And (C&)*, 29 July 2016. https://contemporaryand.com/magazines/i-use-my-tongan-knowledge-and-identity-as-resources

——— 'Maumau-Taimi: Wasting time; being useless'. Master's thesis, Auckland University of Technology, 2016. https://hdl.handle.net/10292/10323

Waerea, Layne. 'Free Arguments: [Under Construction]'. Edited by Louise Rutledge. *The Occasional Journal* (April 2018). https://enjoy.org.nz/publishing/the-occasional-journal/to-find-a-place/free-arguments-under-construction

13

IT'S A WORK: SPECTACULAR SECRECY IN PRIVATE AND UNANNOUNCED PERFORMANCES

Christopher Braddock
& Victoria Wynne-Jones

How might artists challenge the expectations that performance art is transgressive, excessive and spectacular in its delivery and eagerness to seek attention? This chapter explores visual arts performances that are somewhat reticent and modest in scale: examples that evoke complex discussions about the significance of audiences as witnesses, that adopt a playful approach to posterity as well as documentation or recording of performance art for future audiences.

Secret, private, one-on-one or unannounced performances that place less value on immediate, large-scale, public exposure and communication enable engagement that is in fact radically altered through the limited access to audiences and participants. The artists discussed toy with relationships between performance artist and art historian, action and trace, display and documentation. Additionally, unique approaches to temporality are taken — in particular, ideas of delay and trace.

BREAK AND ENTER

Naarm Melbourne-based art writer Tessa Laird recalls how, in 1996–97, artist Daniel Malone conducted 'a series of breaking and entering actions in abandoned buildings'.[1] His performance *Break and Enter* involved entering private properties around Tāmaki Makaurau Auckland 'but never vandalising or stealing, only ever leaving a rather crypto-poetic personal trace: blue balloons filled with the artist's own breath'.[2] As Laird suggests, the work alludes to Marcel Duchamp's *Air de Paris* (1919), a readymade sculpture that consisted of a glass phial filled with genuine Paris air that acted as a type of portable souvenir. The sole record of Malone's actions were photographs taken with a flash using slide film. The artist was working in the dark, frequently in locations without mains power, and Laird points out that the flashes of light 'were the only moments Malone could see where he stood: often in physically precarious conditions'.[3]

Malone's slide images were later shown as a continuous sequence in a darkened room at TESTSTRIP gallery in Tāmaki Makaurau in 1996, in order to immerse viewers in a similar experience.[4] There is no documentation of this event in any publications, and the artwork was first drawn to our attention through the recollections of performance artist Mark Harvey. Harvey described the work, embellishing it with his own recollection that in the late 1990s when it took place, the blue of Malone's balloons could be read as the same shade as the helmets of United Nations peace-keeping troops in the Yugoslav Wars.[5] Intrigued, we continued to interrogate elders from the fine arts community and received further information about the performance from Laird, arts writer Gwyn Porter and designer Warren Olds.[6]

In the 2000s, US-based performance theorist Philip Auslander reflected on the significance of what he called 'the performativity of documentation itself', and the functions of performances (like those of Malone) 'not available to an audience in any form apart from its documentation'.[7] Auslander proposed a mutual dependence of performance and document, and that any photographic record ultimately replaces the very reality it documents: 'the act of documenting an event as performance is what constitutes it as such'.[8] Not only does documentation produce an event as performance, it also produces a performer as an artist. Auslander posits performance 'as a mode of communicative display, in which the performer signals to an audience'.[9]

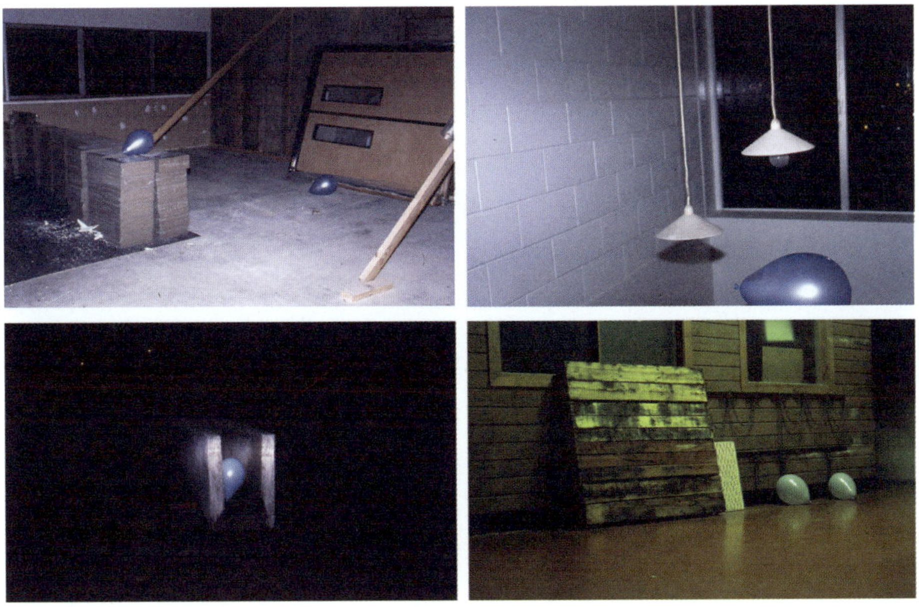

Daniel Malone, *Untitled (Break and Enter)*, 1995. *Courtesy the artist and Warren Olds*

> [T]he act of expression itself is framed as display: objectified, lifted out to a degree from its contextual surroundings, and opened up to interpretive and evaluative scrutiny by an audience both in terms of its intrinsic qualities and its associational resonances . . . The collaborative participation of an audience, it is important to emphasize, is an integral component of performance as an interactional accomplishment.[10]

Photographic documentation of a performance allows actions to be framed as display and to be lifted from their contextual surroundings. The audience of the performance becomes those who perceive an artist's actions solely by means of the documentation — a crucial point for secret, private or unannounced performances. According to Auslander, it is only documentation that allows an audience to interpret and evaluate an artist's actions as a performance: 'The actions undertaken by the artist and depicted in the images become available to an audience as performances solely through their documentation.'[11]

As soon as an artist decides to document their performance, they send out their signals, assuming a kind of speculative responsibility to an audience, one that will exist across a variety of spatio-temporal locales. Auslander summarises: 'It is not the initial presence of an audience that makes an event a work of performance art: it is its framing as performance through the performative act of documenting it as such'; performance art 'is constituted as such through the performativity of its documentation'.[12] Of paramount importance is 'interactional accomplishment',[13] the relationship between the document and its audience, so that any so-called authenticity of the performance document 'resides in its relationship to its beholder rather than to an ostensibly originary event'.[14]

Malone's decision to show his slide photographs as a continuous sequence in a darkened room was an attempt to involve his audience in his clandestine and precarious break-ins. In this respect, an audience's sense of 'presence, power, and authenticity' of performance artworks derives 'from perceiving the document itself *as a performance* that directly reflects an artist's aesthetic project or sensibility and for which we are the present audience'.[15]

BAD OMEN

Another example of secret or private performance that can be accessed solely through documentation is *Bad Omen* (2009), a work executed by London-based Aotearoa artist Sriwhana Spong. For this work, Spong took on the persona of a crow who appears in Balinese Legong dances as a bad omen, foreshadowing death. The artist donned cardboard wings and held ballet poses remembered from lessons she had taken as a teenager, all the while being filmed by her mother with a Super 8 camera. Spong reflects that perhaps the performance was only ever meant to be for her mother:

> Growing up, we never ever discussed the complexities of being mixed heritage, growing up in a Pākehā family, and perhaps it was my way of getting her to try and see me? Literally performing this mixed-bird creature of legong and ballet representing a bad omen (or perhaps I've just done too much Lacanian analysis lol).[16]

Still photographs of the performance were taken by artist Edith Amituanai, and a 1-metre-square framed print still exists in the artist's parents' house. Spong recalls that she only ever showed the Super 8 film once, and that somewhere there may also be digital footage of her performing the work in a friend's studio while he filmed it, though it is likely this video is now lost. So, *Bad Omen* consisted of two private performances for two different cameras and operators as well as for Amituanai. It persists in time through Amituanai's documentation.

Spong's and Malone's private performances hark back to earlier artworks by Andrew Drummond. Many of Drummond's performances resounded with 'the political implications of responsible land usage'.[17] Drummond's *Filter Action* (1980) was performed on the mud flats of Aramoana at the mouth of the Otago Harbour in the South Island of Aotearoa. On the southwestern side of the village, expansive salty mudflats extend from the Aramoana Spit around the harbourside to the settlement of Te Ngaru. In the late 1970s Aramoana was proposed as the site of a major aluminium smelter by a consortium including New Zealand-based Fletcher Challenge. The smelter would have destroyed the villages of Aramoana and Te Ngaru and a local wildlife reserve.

In protest, residents announced the 'Independent State of Aramoana' on 23 December 1980, establishing a 'border post' complete with flag, seal and printed passports. To raise funds for the anti-smelter campaign, they issued stamps featuring the painting *Puketotara, Twice Shy* by Aotearoa painter Don Binney. Many other artists contributed to the protest, including prominent Māori artist Ralph Hotere with his *Aramoana* series of paintings. By late 1981 the consortium had disbanded and the proposal was withdrawn.

Drummond joined these artistic protests with the private ritual *Filter Action*, documented by Nicholas Spill, who was the only other person present. Influenced by the performance art of German artist Joseph Beuys, who referenced the role of shamanistic ancient healers,[18] Drummond wore a white cotton boiler suit with a white cotton cloth helmet (similar to what pilots used under their leather helmets in the Second World War) and a bespoke frontpack for carrying performance elements, which included three animal kidneys, lengths of muslin, small divining rods made from willow, and copper rod and chimes to signal sequence changes as the performance developed.[19] Lita Barrie wrote for *Art New Zealand* in 1987 that Drummond put his body to 'allegorical use . . . to upturn

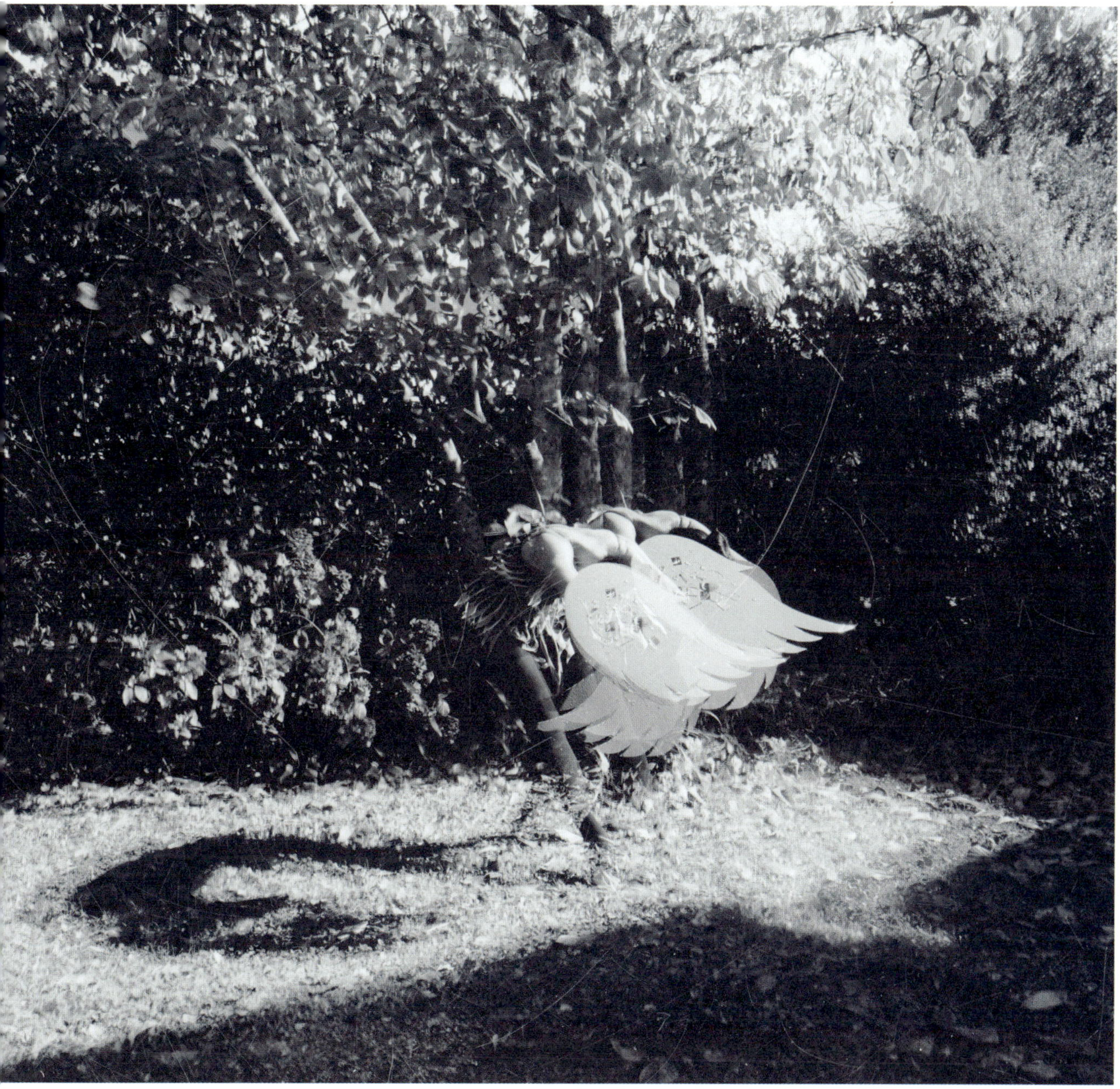

Sriwhana Spong, *Bad Omen*, 2009. *Courtesy the artist. Photo by Edith Amituanai*

a number of "master narratives"'. His performance works embodied a 'non-oppositional relationship between human beings and the physical world they inhabit'.[20]

Barrie describes Spill's images as 'haunting . . . incomplete fragments'[21] of Drummond as he explored ways of protecting and healing the Aramoana mudflats through the power of ritual. Within a large circle inscribed in the mud, Drummond laid long strips of muslin as filters on the mud's surface, inserted the willow divining rods around the perimeter of the circle, and walked barefoot around the circle. Throughout the performance he placed the kidneys in his mouth and dropped them into holes excavated in the sand. Drummond then carried all the performance materials back to his arrival point, leaving the kidneys to rot away.[22] All this was symbolic of a body filtering toxins and the landscape's inability to filter industrial waste.[23]

Australian art theorist Anne Marsh writes that any 'insistence on the audience having to be there in real time, to experience the event . . . privileges presence (speech over writing)'.[24] Marsh rightly observes that performance art has a legacy in its resistance to commodification by the art market (which is true of Drummond's private ritual for *Filter Action*); however, such resistance has been quietly diluted through commodification of its documentation in the form of photographs, video and so on.[25] While on a visit to Aotearoa in 2004, celebrated American performance artist Vito Acconci recounted that he regretted the sale of his black and white photographs of his early performance art works.[26] He believed that they had undermined the vitality and effect of the live events; yet the sale of these photographs had helped to bankroll his architectural business, Acconci Studio, and also enabled Acconci to be written into art history. Photographic and written documentation of Acconci's performances, as well as Nicholas Spill's photographs of Drummond's *Filter Action*, are testament to Auslander's thesis that an event is framed as a work of performance art through the performative act of its documentation and its subsequent reception as such by those who see it.

Acconci's stance echoes that taken by performance theorist Peggy Phelan in her book *Unmarked: The politics of performance* (1993), in which she celebrates the impermanence and lack of durability of performance, arguing that this constitutes its political resistance as it thwarts the commodification of capitalist exploitative regimes.[27] Yet as artist Myriam Van Imschoot argues, Phelan's valorisation of performance as disappearance 'stays within the frame of the archival logic it precisely seeks to thwart'.[28] In contenting itself with dwelling outside of the archive, with its 'practice of conservation', which is also 'a matter of patriarchal conservatism',[29] it poses no challenge to the existing order of things.

The intricate relations between archive and performance have been examined in more detail by theorist Rebecca Schneider. Focusing on the trace, Schneider emphasises performance as memory, 'a physicalised relational field of interaction, intensities, techniques, histories, traces, and relics of experienced information'.[30] Van Imschoot takes this further, arguing that performers are 'mobile body-archives'.[31] Indeed, this idea resonates with the way in which Malone's performance persists in the memories and narratives of his friends and peers, and the way those recollections have allowed an artwork to travel through time and space.[32] Drummond's performance can also be thought of as a private mobile body-archive as he physically relates to the Aramoana mud flats, leaving traces to wash away and rot, together with Spill's haunting photographic traces that seem to gain a life of their own.

An interest in documentation of performance and its possibility to possess 'an entity with a life of its own'[33] was characteristic of the 2015 exhibition *Embodying the Archive*, curated by Anneke Jaspers and Melanie Oliver at project space The Physics

Room in Ōtautahi Christchurch. As Warren Feeney notes, this exhibition 'circled around the nature of performance art, placing emphasis upon its presence as archival records: transcripts, film, documented texts, recorded spoken-memories and notes'; this gives importance to documentation and archiving that is 'as significant as the performance itself'.[34] For this exhibition, artists and collectives such as Alex Martinis Roe, Emma Fitts, Brown Council and the Newspaper Reading Club challenge Auslander's causal relationship between performance and documentation by activating archival materials through performance, including video, reading aloud and fabric constructions: all activities that were then re-incorporated into revitalised archives once more.

For example, the Newspaper Reading Club, established by Aotearoa artists Fiona Connor and Michala Paludan in 2011, contributed to *Embodying the Archive* with a month-long residency, during which they invited participants 'to meet and read from the newspaper in order to articulate the familiar process of skimming, commenting and editing that occurs when reading the news'.[35] In relation to the re-construction of the city following the 2011 earthquake, this participatory performance explored how reading the news (as a powerful social archive) aloud 'reflexively moderates between the past and potential future of the city' and exposes 'the state of the news within our knowledge-based economy'.[36] In this way, reading aloud operates as a trace structure for social memory, further entangling the relationship between archives, documentation and performance.

Projects like *Embodying the Archive* point to core problems of modernist epistemologies that rest on fundamental oppositions — live versus document, present versus past, nature versus culture, subject versus object, straight versus queer, and so on. The possibility of secret, private and unannounced performances — where access is denied to 'rightful' audiences other than through a culture of trace — deliberately problematises these dichotomising epistemologies.[37] We argue for something much more radical than the sometimes-to-and-fro arguments about live performance art and its documentation. By highlighting possible occurrences of secret, private and unannounced performances along with an array of possible traces (including writing or even talking about an event over unspecified time periods), we are saying that we cannot distinguish live performance from its material trace.

'The challenge here is to consider all signification as delayed trace and all trace as animate.' In this sense, each 'iteration of "liveness" always already becomes trace'.[38] To be clear, we are not interested in turning the tables, in creating another dichotomy that says, like Auslander, that documentation is as important, or more, than live performance. We are suggesting, more radically, that these categorisations disappear when an ontology of trace is acknowledged. Highlighting the significance of secret, private and unannounced performances is a way of contesting imperative and dichotomised understandings of live art practices and their so-called documentation.

NIGHT PIECE

As Amelia Jones has argued, 'there is no possibility of an unmediated relationship to any kind of cultural product, including body art'.[39] Secret, private and one-on-one performances challenge how mediation of an event might unfold. The way in which Malone's performance relied on first-person accounts by friends and colleagues has a precedent in an earlier performance from the 1980s by Linda Buis and Peter Roche. *Night Piece* began in the ruins of the old gasworks by the harbour bridge, on the city side of

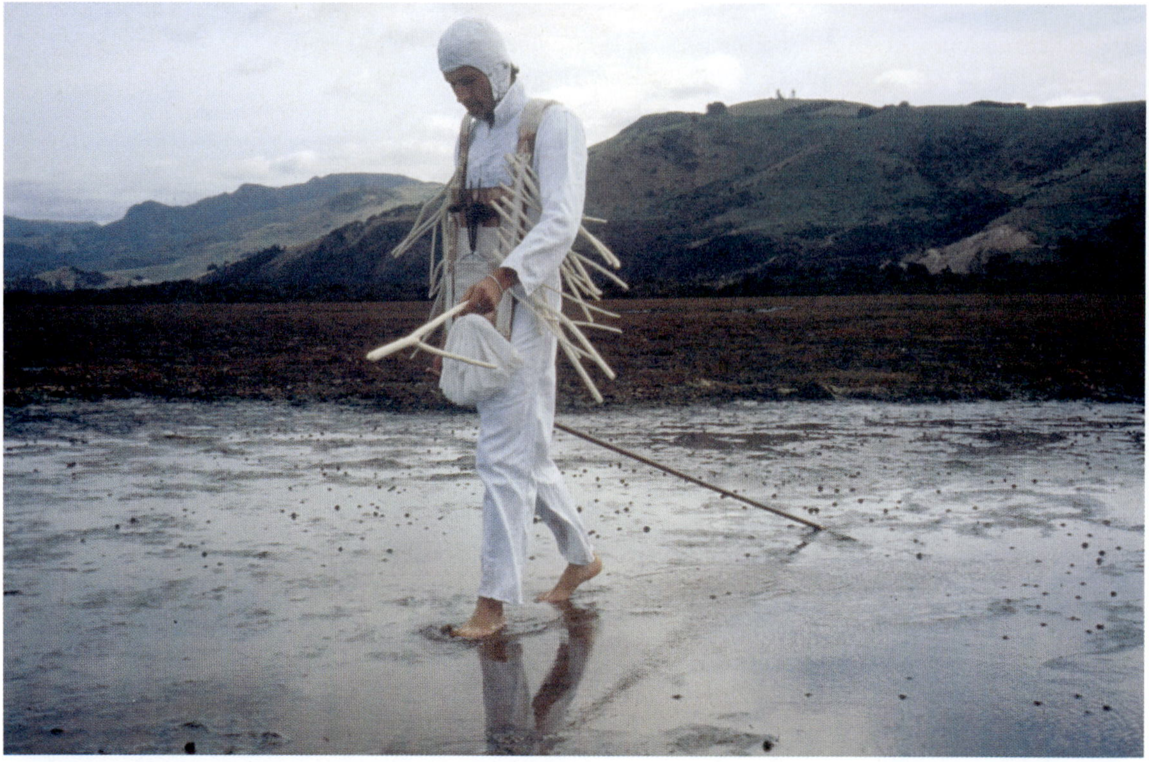

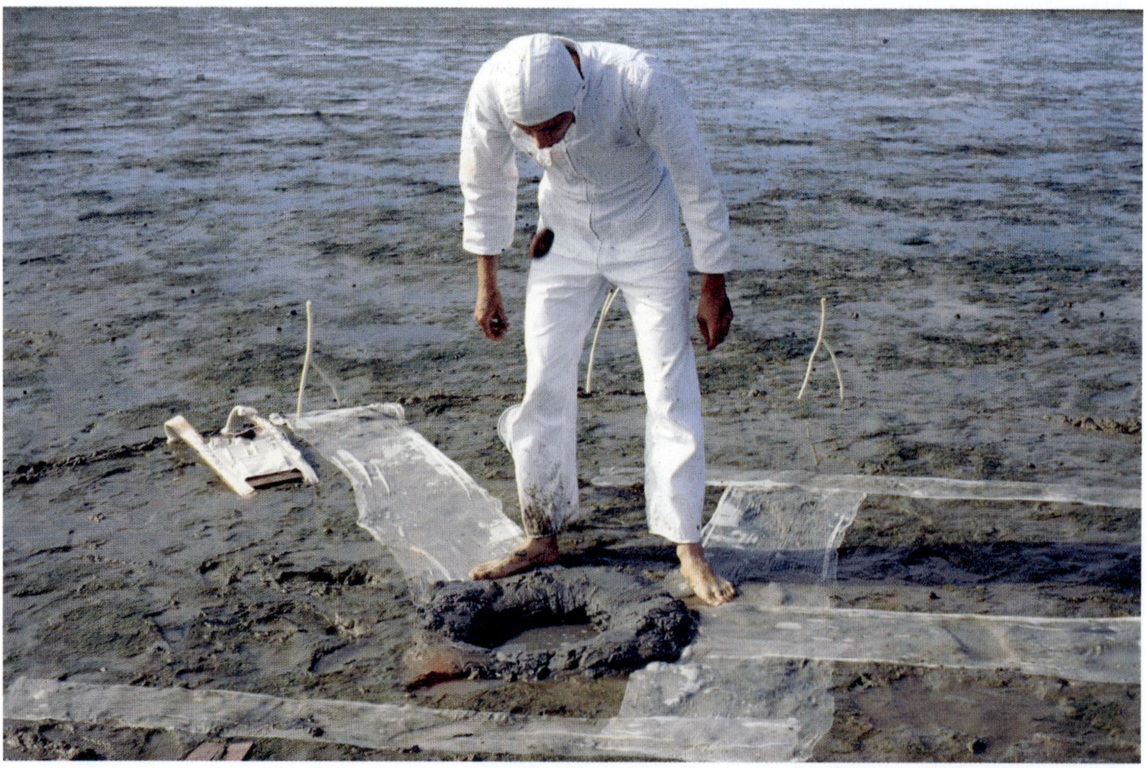

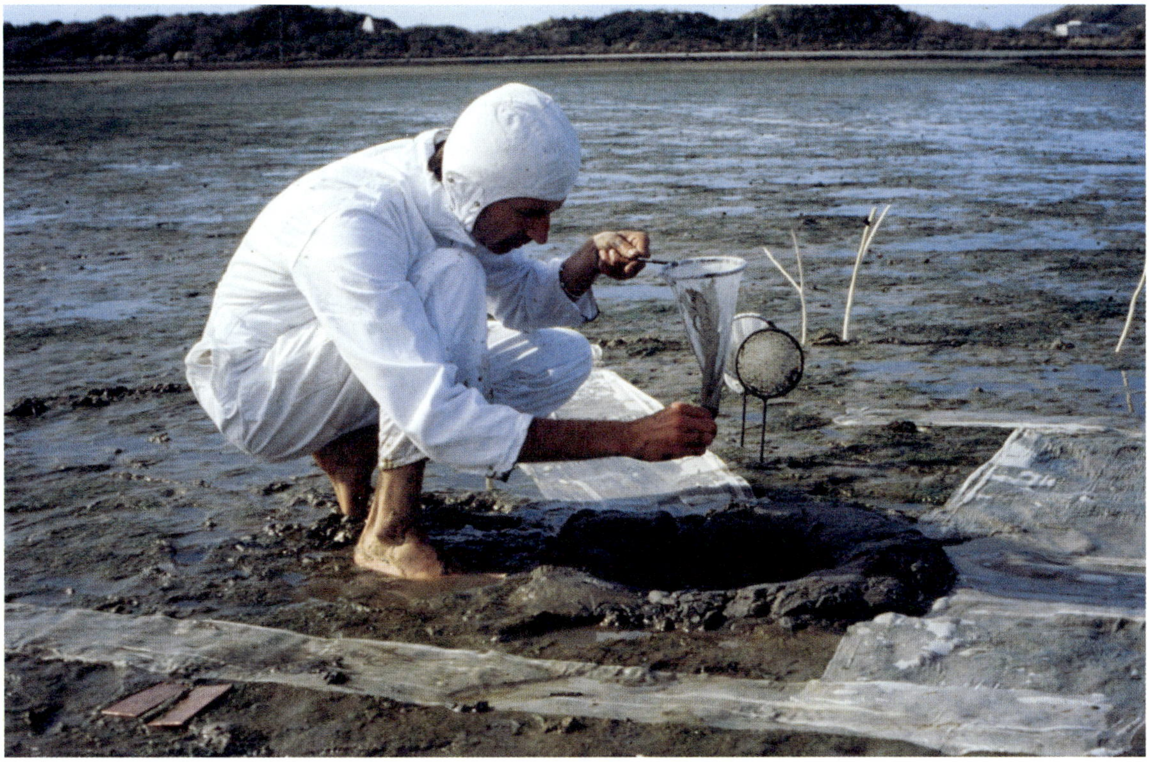

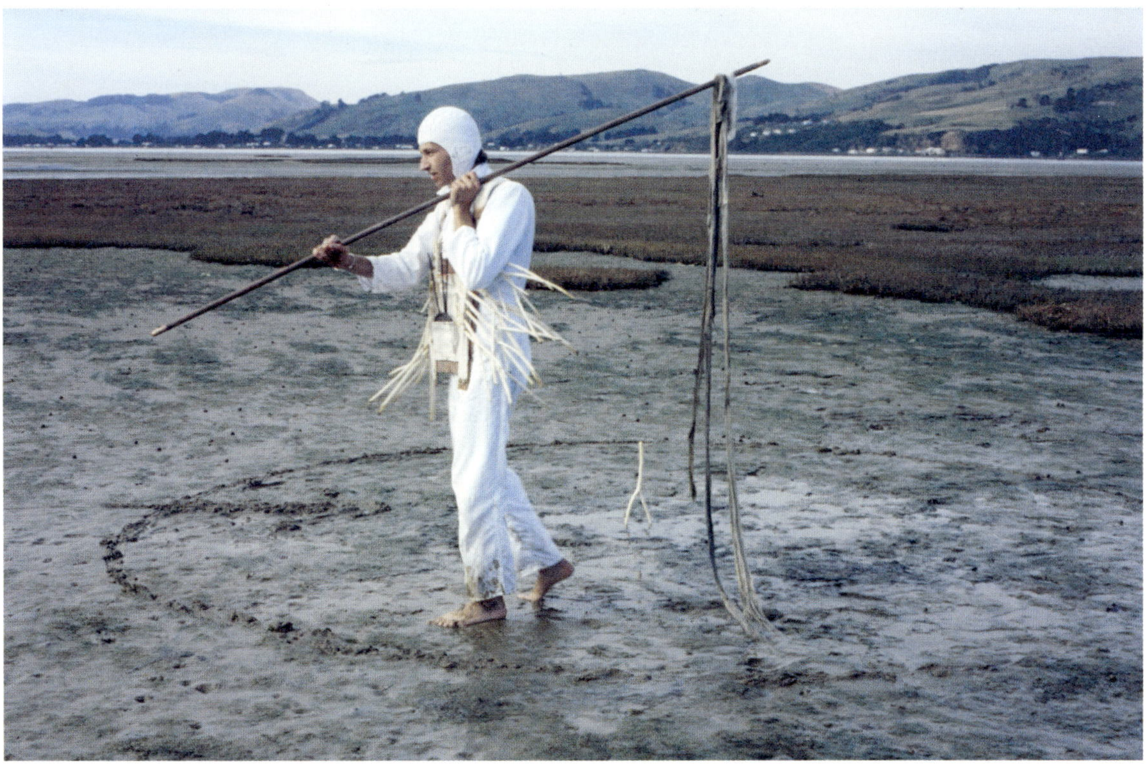

Tāmaki Makaurau, on 14 July 1981 at 7.42 p.m., when art critic Wystan Curnow got off the bus and illegally entered the site. It finished at 8.50 p.m. when he left to catch the Maritime Terrace bus from Victoria Street back home.[40]

The old gasworks had been derelict for years; Roche & Buis had unsuccessfully requested access from the owners, the Assembly of God church, but decided to press on anyway.[41] Passing the 'Trespassers will be prosecuted' signs, Curnow clambered through concrete rubble and overgrown gorse, twisting his ankle on the way, before eventually spotting Buis, who was crawling perilously along the top of a crumbling 15-metre-high concrete wall for some 180 metres.[42] Far below, Roche was marking out Buis' highly dangerous passage with a trail of fourteen candles. Curnow's published account of the performance included reflections by Roche as part of a deliberate collaboration that merged critic and artist voices:

> We were quite alone. The wall was a formidable sight that night. The more we dwelled upon the piece, the larger it seemed to become. From the top of the wall, I would say there'd be a sixty- to seventy-foot [18–21 metres] drop to the base of the site . . . Well, things by this stage had gone too far to even think about turning back. There was nothing to be done but for one of us to climb the ladder. I went up first and lay on top of the wall . . . It took a lot to keep myself from panicking. Shit, it was not pleasant being up there. Well, I got down quick and put on a brave face for Linda . . . Up she went and lay there. The ladder the only link between us now.[43]

Curnow's writing becomes an embodiment of fear as he witnesses the scene that unfolds in front of him: 'All of a sudden, my feelings about the work change. I feel fear. I feel the idea of the work enlarged to a point where it might be said to take on the entire site.'[44] As part of this artist/critic collaboration, or writing-as-participating, Roche explicitly describes the performative relationship at work as a 'three-way relationship' as witness to the work: 'A silent relationship. All of us intent upon our roles. Each performing.'[45]

Night Piece was one of twenty-five performances produced by Roche & Buis between 1979 and 1985.[46] We described the performance as beginning and ending with Curnow's bus trips because he was an audience of one; his writing for *Parallax* as the only witness of this event was 'documentation'. As Curnow wrote for the first edition of *Parallax* in spring 1982: 'Content is to be discovered not in the work, but in our interaction *with* the work. All observations are participations.'[47] In effect, our engagement with *Night Piece* is only possible *and* radically altered through this limited means of access.

The performance was carried out in the secrecy of nightfall. The two performers and audience-of-one entered the site illegally. We know of the existence of this artwork only because of the trusting and private relationship between the performers and Curnow, which cements a special and intimate witnessing of the work that is, in turn, our access to the transgression and fear embodied in Roche & Buis's performance. This reminds us that site and audience are significant in actions that happen only once, thus making written recordings of an event even more pertinent. As Helen Cole has noted in 'This Secret Location':

> Live Art creates intimate and radical exchanges with context, site and audience, and it only ever occurs once. In this uniqueness and site-specificity, a single work may teeter on the edge of familiarity, but it can

PREVIOUS: Andrew Drummond, *Filter Action*, 1980, documentation of performance. *Courtesy the artist. Photos by Nicholas Spill* never be repeated, as it relies on interaction in each new meeting with each new person, place and time.[48]

Questions about how secret, private and unannounced performances are related to others evoke a seemingly contradictory position: the necessity to tell a secret undoes its secrecy.[49] Adam Alston explores secrecy in theatre marketing strategies, as well as secrecy as the framework for audience participation in the context of contemporary theatre, and suggests that theatre, as the 'home of spectacle and of public scrutiny . . . is surely the last place one would expect to find a turn towards secrecy'.[50] As with contemporary performance art practices discussed in this chapter, only when secrecy or privacy are partially broken can the experience be shared. A secret is no longer a secret 'once concealment of a secret is coupled with an advertisement of secrecy'.[51] As Alston asks, 'What do secrets become once packaged and sold to anyone who is able and willing to forward disclosure?'[52] With reference to the writing of Beryl L. Bellman, Alston explores the paradoxes surrounding secrecy in that 'a secret becomes itself through its own negation'.[53] In other words, we know about secrecy and privacy only through its revelation or a threat of revelation.[54] 'The paradox of secrecy . . . is about striving to involve prospective audiences, rather than exclude them', Alston continues, giving rise to his term 'spectacular secrecy'.[55] For our chapter, spectacular secrecy means that private moments or unannounced performances are revealed through their revelation or threat of revelation.

In recalling Malone's performance artworks, Laird posited that Malone was constantly performing actions, recounting these to his fellow artists and explaining, 'it's a work'. Such activities, which included suspending ballpoint pens from the Grafton Bridge adjacent to Elam School of Fine Arts, occurred every day and gradually accreted over time.[56] More than two decades later, Laird wondered whether Malone still engaged in such activities, as historically he was 'always doing a range of iterative things'. For Laird, these actions operated as a kind of hoarding, as though the artist were accumulating them for future use, as though 'even secret performances get their pay off'. Perhaps this chapter is proof that Malone was right all along. When reflecting on these performances, Laird wondered aloud whether they demonstrated brilliance or a kind of fraud. With no outcome in mind, they were 'purely wilful', made with a 'personal belief that eventually it will get noticed'.[57]

Curnow's experience as an audience-of-one for Roche & Buis's *Night Piece* was testament to the discursive function of his art writing that was being framed in performance terms, which, he wrote, 'suggests a common impulse not unrelated to the decentred and dialogic tendencies of the works'.[58] As Christina Barton puts it: 'Curnow sees writing as a task of transference in which the "being" of the work is restored in the "body" of the text.'[59] Here then, performative writing as performance explores the power of a forbidden site as light fades and an overwhelming sense of fear pervades the atmosphere. It could be argued that to experience this performance as an invited viewer among many others, seated somehow in observation, would profoundly diminish and alter any experience of this artwork.

In terms of 'spectacular secrecy', Curnow's account of *Night Piece* escalates the clandestine nature of the performance, exploring his participation as if ours in poetically poignant prose: holding and exposing the event such that the promise of secrecy becomes a key factor in the work. As second-hand witnesses, we know that we should, or could, never have been there that night. Yet, paradoxically, we are involved, not excluded. The same might be said of Drummond's *Filter Action*. We could, and should, never have been present. Drummond as private mobile body-archive would have been diluted. Yet,

Spill's photographs explore this ritual healing of the Aramoana mud flats, paradoxically intensified for us through their spectacular disclosure.

This paradoxical involvement of possible audiences is complex. For example, the possible face-to-face advantages shared by audiences of a live performance art event are withheld from a secret or private performance; or, if it is an unannounced performance, are perhaps given over to unsuspecting passers-by in the public domain. The viewer is denied what Amelia Jones calls the live situation's 'phenomenological relations of flesh-to-flesh engagement'. But, as she also argues, the 'documentary exchange (viewer/reader<—> document) is equally intersubjective'.[60] Secret, private or unannounced performances are a way of further exploring the intersubjective nature of the traces of performance, executing what Bauman, via Auslander, called 'interactional accomplishment'.[61]

Malone's performance comes to us not only through his 35mm slides projected in a darkened room, but through the rumours, anecdotes and storytelling of his fellow artists and peers. Such 'interactional accomplishments' as complex traces of performance are indistinguishable from any previous so-called live performance. Having just experienced Tino Sehgal's performance *Yet untitled* (2013) at Auckland Art Gallery Toi o Tāmaki while writing this chapter, we are confronted by this turn of events.[62] The performance was presented live, every day for six weeks, by two to three dancers and singers in the gallery's atrium. Sehgal refuses documentation of his live performances in order to prioritise the live moment in the moment and as memory. This falls in line with Jones's comment that we are always recalibrating previous live performance based on hindsight and reappraisal.[63]

But more than a simple denial of documentation, Sehgal explores questions such as 'How live is a live work?' and 'What is progress?', especially given that what is enacted in live performance is often pre-determined by score or script.[64] He notes how his dancers, whom he calls 'interpreters', evolve through their performances over time, 'moving differently in the work over two weeks'; and how, for *Yet untitled,* 'interpreters' were 'singing into someone rather than into the room, sometimes with their eyes closed'.[65] In that these experiences are un-documentable, Sehgal suggests we expect too much from material productivity. Thus, he explores what 'openness' to an experience might mean. Yet Sehgal's strategy does nevertheless prioritise our encounter of these artworks in the moment.

As a further counter-move to these debates about live art and its relationship to documentation, secret, private, one-on-one or unannounced performances deliberately question an ontology that privileges presence or document (the artist or performers in the live moment of production as 'speech' or the act of writing/documenting in general) in favour of a myriad of ways life is performed, recounted and re-lived (even speculation about possible performances, letters written about performance and second-hand remarks etc.). These strategies prioritise performance as trace wherever it may be found.

I WOULD LIKE TO BE ATTACHED TO A RANDOM ENTRANT

Severely limiting documentation as well as announcements about live art performances operates on a similar terrain to Sehgal's complete refusal to document. Naarm Melbourne-based Aotearoa artist Alicia Frankovich performed an unannounced and largely undocumented 'private' performance in the public streets of Zagreb on 25 June 2009 as part of *PSi#15:* a worldwide conference on performance art.[66] For her performance

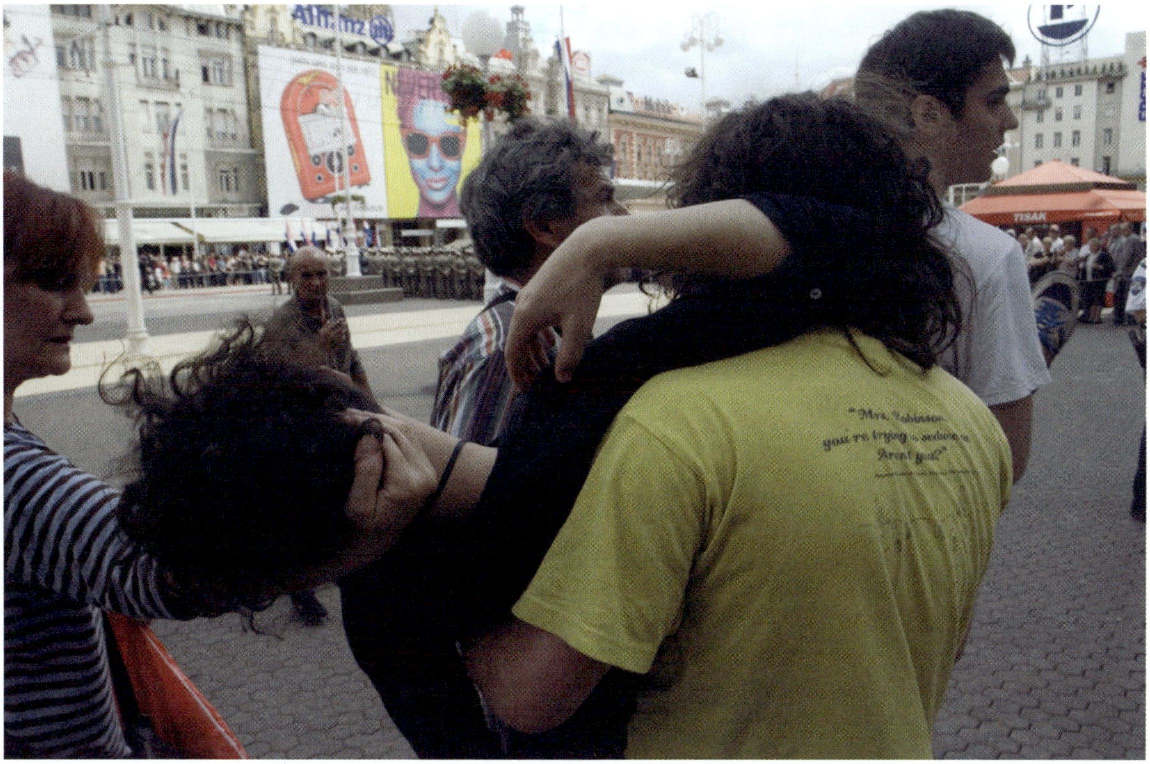

Alicia Frankovich, *I Would Like to Be Attached to a Random Entrant*, 2009, documentation of performance as part of *PSi#15* in Zagreb, Croatia. Curated by Christopher Braddock. *Courtesy the artist. Photo by Bojan Mrđenović*

I Would Like to Be Attached to a Random Entrant, Frankovich enlisted the help of a local Croatian family (who did not know much about art) to physically carry her limp body several kilometres from their home to the *PSi#15* conference venue.

Frankovich had supplied her Croatian family with a limited toolkit, including wheels and ropes that they could use for the task. As was the case with other works by Frankovich, her body was completely limp and at the mercy of her collaborating performers (the family).[67] She was vulnerable and at risk. As she wrote in her project outline, 'The role of the artist is handballed to the viewer.' Curator Christopher Braddock explains, 'We had to notify the Zagreb police. Basically, any unsuspecting passer-by encountered a small group of people carrying a body on and off the tram and through the streets, with some difficulty.' Not only was the spectacle unannounced, but Frankovich also asked the family, on arrival at the conference venue, to carry her body into various conference presentations, thus interrupting proceedings.[68]

In contrast to almost all of Frankovich's other performances to date, *I Would Like to Be Attached to a Random Entrant* never had an audience as such, and never really reached a 'staged' conclusion. The performance was documented with only one photograph, which reveals only a small aspect of a difficult and precarious exercise in which Frankovich's safety was at times called into question.[69] It shows a limp body in the arms of three males, the head supported by a concerned-looking older woman to the left. A man to the middle-left of the composition gestures ambiguously and we are unsure whether he is involved or not. To the extreme right we glimpse a half-view of a police officer, badge and baton visible. In the background we see a military parade in progress and audiences lined up under temporary marquees. This single photograph operates as a tantalising break with the clandestine and unannounced activity, perhaps creating a public desire for truth and disclosure; to know exactly what went on.[70]

Malone's *Break and Enter*, Spong's *Bad Omen*, Roche & Buis's *Night Piece* and Frankovich's *I Would Like to Be Attached to a Random Entrant* challenge how live performance art is mediated through a proliferation of material productivity and, like the performance work of Sehgal, seek out what 'openness' might mean. The artists' radical refusal to invite conventional audiences and enlist more standard forms of documentation is augmented by the illegal (Malone and Roche & Buis), secret and unannounced nature of their activities. But it is only through the paradoxes of secrecy (that a secret becomes itself through its own negation) that the spectral and spectacular nature of these performances, involving all possible audiences across time and space, begins to emerge; here, now, you.

POCKET WORKS

A further example of private performances that evade documentation is a series of works by a contemporary of Sriwhana Spong: Texas-based Aotearoa artist Kate Newby. When questioned as to her engagement with secret performances, the artist replied:

> the closest that I can think of is my pocket works that I keep with me as well. So I always have this quite solid chunk of silver tin foil in my pocket for years. I do that skipping stone thing where I give a stone to a person and they throw it — often the audience is just me and the participant.[71]

The series, known as *Pocket Works*, has persisted since 2011 when Newby exhibited *Just enough to feel stronger and a little bit fond* in a group presentation at City Gallery Wellington, Te Whanganui-a-Tara.[72] This work consisted of silver and bronze casts of objects: stones, a cigarette filter, ring pull, matchstick, cupboard handle, an allen key, hook, tinfoil, drawing pin and a coin. As curator Kate Montgomery explains, the work 'revised the space of encounter from the scale of a gallery, or a public space to the area of an outstretched hand'. For the duration of the exhibition, the small, cast objects were cared for by various people affiliated to the exhibition, including the artist, the curator and members of the gallery's team of visitor hosts.

At first blush Newby's *Just enough to feel stronger and a little bit fond* seems to be merely a sculpture, and a slight one at that. But the more one considers it, the more it seems to operate as an ongoing series of private performances with spectacular secrecy. In order to view the objects during the exhibition, visitors had to perform a series of activities of their own, including approaching, questioning, and acts of attention and examination. These activities contributed to how the artwork was presented; as Montgomery says, the work operates on a human scale, focusing on the area of the palm of a hand, acts of showing, looking, perhaps exclaiming and admiring. Just as Curnow's account of the Roche & Buis work delineates a performance with porous temporal and spatial boundaries (does it start when he is waiting for the bus? When he is wandering around?), Newby's pocket work is unknowable: it moves around, bypassing gallery hours and set locations.

When the exhibition closed at the end of the day, the objects travelled away from the gallery in the pockets of their minders, to 'wherever their respective days or nights might take them'.[73] The peregrinations of minders and objects enable the performances, including the acts of display, to take place; their meandering allows them to initiate small acts of 'interactional accomplishment'. The accompanying exhibition booklet with Montgomery's

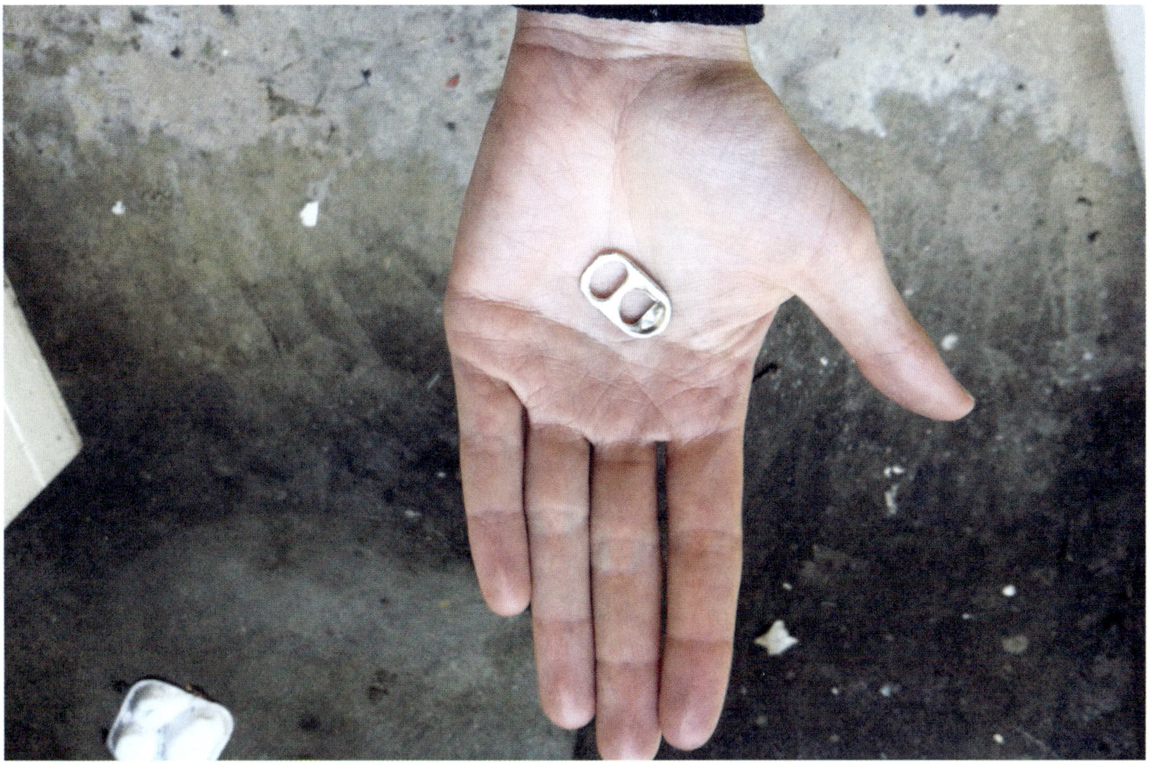

Kate Newby, *Pocket Works*, 2011–ongoing. Courtesy City Gallery Wellington and the artist

notes, as well as our own discussion in this very chapter, enable the objects to persist through space and time for another set of audience members as readers.

Through the secret, private, one-on-one or unannounced performances of Daniel Malone, Sriwhana Spong, Andrew Drummond, Linda Buis and Peter Roche, Alicia Frankovich and Kate Newby, we have traced what Myriam Van Imschoot provocatively calls 'mobile body-archives' — bodies that persist in proliferating elusive memories and narratives. Thinking about secrets, and the paradoxical nature of the need for their disclosure for anything to be revealed, has enabled us to further contemplate the complexities of where and how live performance art exists. Adam Alston's theory of 'spectacular secrecy' offers a paradoxical investment in participation or involvement.[74] It involves all possible audiences rather than excluding them. These performance art practices challenge categories of 'live' and 'documented', allowing them to dissolve as ontologies of trace across time and space.

NOTES

1 Tessa Laird, 'Malone, Animal, Man', unpublished essay, 2011, n.p.
2 Ibid.
3 Ibid.
4 Daniel Malone, email with the authors, 20 July 2023. This solo exhibition was titled *Change the Script*.
5 Mark Harvey, conversation with Victoria Wynne Jones, 1 December 2016.
6 Both Gwyn Porter and Warren Olds were involved in a monograph on Daniel Malone, which was never completed. Laird's unpublished essay was written for this incomplete publication.
7 Philip Auslander, 'The Performativity of Performance Documentation', *PAJ: A Journal of Performance and Art* 28, no. 3 (September 2006): 4, 5.
8 Ibid., 5. Emphasis in the original.
9 Richard Bauman quoted in ibid., 5.
10 Ibid.
11 Ibid., 6.
12 Ibid., 7.
13 Richard Bauman quoted in ibid., 5.
14 Ibid., 9.
15 Ibid. Emphasis in the original.
16 Sriwhana Spong, email conversation with author, 6 March 2022.
17 Allan Smith, 'Mapping Imperatives: Putting the land on

the map at the Govett-Brewster Art Gallery', *Art New Zealand* 52 (Spring 1989): 78.

18 Lita Barrie, 'Andrew Drummond: Towards an allegorical use of the body', *Art New Zealand* 44 (Spring 1987): 66.

19 Jennifer Hay, 'Trans-Marginal: New Zealand performance art 1970–1985', in *Intervention: Post object and performance art in New Zealand in 1970 and beyond* (Christchurch: Robert McDougall Art Gallery & Annex, 2000), 18.

20 Barrie, 'Andrew Drummond', 65.

21 Ibid.

22 Email conversation between Andrew Drummond and Christopher Braddock, 12 February 2024.

23 Hay, 'Trans-Marginal', 18.

24 Anne Marsh, *Performance_Ritual_Document* (Melbourne: Macmillan, 2014), 4.

25 Ibid.

26 Vito Acconci was in Aotearoa for the exhibition *Vito Acconci: Screening architecture & the red tapes*: 4 September–30 October 2004, ST PAUL St Gallery. Acconci made this remark as a visiting critic in a studio critique with visual arts students at the School of Art and Design, Auckland University of Technology.

27 Peggy Phelan, *Unmarked: The politics of performance* (London: Routledge, 1993), 149.

28 Myriam Van Imschoot, 'Rests in Pieces: On scores, notations and the trace in dance', in *Danse: An Anthology*, edited by Noémie Solomon (Dijon: Les presses du réel, 2014), 44–45.

29 Ibid., 41.

30 Schneider quoted in Van Imschoot, 'Rests in Pieces', 44.

31 Ibid., 45.

32 Myriam Van Imschoot's idea that performers are 'mobile body-archives' persisting in the narratives of others also applies to the performance art of Brent Harris. His *Oct Dec Series* with ST PAUL St Gallery occurred in various urban locales in Tāmaki Makaurau from 19 October to 15 December 2011. Harris' repeated emails gave ambiguous instructions, invitations and requests in terms of movements, behaviours and locale. See Brent Graeme Harris, 'Figuring Diachrony: Ethics before the voice' (PhD thesis, Auckland University of Technology, 2013).

33 Warren Feeney, 'Performance and Documentation', *EyeContact*, 30 September 2015, https://eyecontactmagazine.com/2015/09/performance-and-documentation

34 Ibid.

35 'Embodying the Archive', Physics Room gallery room sheet, https://physicsroom.org.nz/exhibitions/embodying-the-archive

36 Ibid.

37 See Cornelius Borck, 'Animism in the Sciences Then and Now', *E-Flux Journal* 36 (July 2012).

38 Christopher Braddock, *Performing Contagious Bodies: Ritual participation in contemporary art* (London: Palgrave Macmillan, 2012), 24, 128. Braddock references Jacques Derrida, who writes that 'there have never been anything but supplements, substitutive significations which could only come forth in a chain of differential references'. See Jacques Derrida, *Of Grammatology* (Baltimore: Johns Hopkins University Press, 1997), 159.

39 Amelia Jones, '"Presence" in Absentia: Experiencing performance as documentation', *Art Journal* 56, no. 4 (1997): 12.

40 See Wystan Curnow, 'Peter Roche/Linda Buis: A gathering concerning three performances', in *The Critic's Part: Wystan Curnow art writings 1971–2013*, edited by Christina Barton, Robert Leonard and Thomasin Sleigh (Wellington/Brisbane: Te Pātaka Toi Adam Art Gallery, Institute of Modern Art and Victoria University Press, 2014), 164–68, for a discussion of *Night Piece*.

41 Curnow, 'Peter Roche/Linda Buis', 164.

42 Ibid., 167.

43 Ibid., 165–66.

44 Ibid., 167.

45 Ibid., 168.

46 See Chapter 5 in this volume by Christina Barton and Gregory Burke for a detailed overview of these performances by Peter Roche and Linda Buis.

47 Wystan Curnow, 'Postmodernism in Poetry and the Visual Arts', in *The Critic's Part*, 149; see also Christina Barton, 'Notes on Method', in *The Critic's Part*, 14.

48 Helen Cole, 'This Secret Location', in *Performance and Place*, edited by Leslie Hill and Helen Paris (London: Palgrave Macmillan, 2006), 18.

49 We assume there are untold secret artworks that will never enter the pages of a book like this, remaining forever significant only to those who carried out a performance at a specific time in history, never to be recounted or relived.

50 Adam Alston, '"Tell No-One": Secret cinema and the paradox of secrecy', in *Performance and Participation: Practices, audiences, politics*, edited by Anna Harpin and Helen Nicholson (New York: Red Globe Press, 2016), 184.

51 Ibid.

52 Ibid.

53 Ibid., 194.

54 Ibid.

55 Ibid., 195. Alston's term 'spectacular secrecy' is borrowed from Jack Bratich.

56 Tessa Laird, Zoom conversation with Victoria Wynne Jones, 18 May 2022.

57 Ibid.

58 Wystan Curnow, 'Writing and the Post-Object', in *The Critic's Part*, 379.

59 Barton, 'Notes on Method', 13.

60 Jones, '"Presence" in Absentia', 12.

61 'Philosophical, sociological and psychological theories help to provide a critical framework for understanding the structure, effects and exchanges produced by performance artworks but, crucially, these works themselves have important contributions to make to the discourse on subjectivity and intersubjectivity, not least by plumbing the depths of this complex and chiasmic relationship between self and otherness.' For more on relationality and intersubjectivity in performance art, see Victoria Wynne-Jones, *Choreographing Intersubjectivity in Performance Art: New world choreographies* (Cham, Switzerland: Palgrave Macmillan, 2021), 4–7.

62 *Yet untitled* was first presented in the 55th Venice Biennale in 2013, where Sehgal received the Golden Lion award for best artist. It was acquired by Auckland Art Gallery Toi o Tāmaki for its collection in 2020 with support from Auckland Contemporary Art Trust. See Auckland Art Gallery, 'Tino Sehgal: Yet Untitled', 1 October 2022, www.aucklandartgallery.com/whats-on/exhibition/tino-sehgal-yet-untitled

63 Jones, '"Presence" in Absentia', 12.

64 Tino Sehgal, Zoom conversation with curator Natasha Conland at Auckland Art Gallery Toi o Tāmaki, 3 November 2022.

65 Ibid.

66 *I Would Like to Be Attached to a Random Entrant* was part of the project *Random Entrant* curated for *PSi#15* (Performance Studies International) by Christopher Braddock. The project also included the inaugural performance of *Pump* (2009) by Australian artist David Cross who was living and teaching in Aotearoa at the time. For an account of *Random Entrant*, see Christopher Braddock, 'Random Entrant and the Force of Failure', *Frakcija Performing Arts Journal* 50 (2009): 26–33. In that essay, Braddock also discuss three other artworks

by Frankovich: *Sempre Meno, Sempre Peggio, Sempre Più* (2008), screened at Artspace Sydney in June 2009; *The Opposite of Backwards* (2008), performed outside Galleria Annarumma404, Naples; and *Lungeing Chambon*, performed in January 2009 in Melbourne with curator Hannah Mathews (2009). For an account of David Cross's *Pump*, see Christopher Braddock, 'Pump', in *Air Supplied: David Cross*, edited by Fiona Lee (punctum books, 2016), 117–19.

67 Frankovich uses this device in other artworks. For *Performance 2* of *A Plane for Behavers* (2009) at Auckland ARTSPACE, Frankovich's prone body was carried into the opening event and then passed around the audience for an hour or so. For a detailed account of Frankovich's *A Plane for Behavers*, see Christopher Braddock, 'The Force of the Text: Alicia Frankovich and Marcel Duchamp', in *Performing Contagious*, 83–97.

68 *PSi#15*, Zagreb, did not give us permission for Frankovich's body to be taken into any conference proceedings but we did it anyhow as a way of engaging with the conference theme of 'misperformance'.

69 Other performance artworks by Alicia Frankovich are also documented with one photograph, such as *Flying Fox* (2008) and *To Veer: A sudden change of opinion, subject or type of behaviour* (2007). However, both these performances involved invited audiences.

70 For an elaboration of this argument and an account of *I Would Like to Be Attached to a Random Entrant*, see Christopher Braddock, 'Alicia Frankovich and the Force of Failure', *Column* 6 (2010): 8–15. Braddock develops this argument in relation to metonymically (part of a possible whole) frustrating a desire for wholeness, functionality and reproduction (all qualities upheld by the conventional museum or gallery context).

71 Kate Newby, email conversation with author, 2 February 2022.

72 *PROSPECT: New Zealand Art Now*, City Gallery Wellington, 26 November 2011–12 February 2012, curated by Kate Montgomery.

73 Kate Montgomery, 'PROSPECT: NEW ZEALAND ART NOW', exhibition notes (Wellington: City Gallery, 2011).

74 Alston, 'Tell No-One', 194.

REFERENCES

Alston, Adam. '"Tell No-One": Secret cinema and the paradox of secrecy'. In *Performance and Participation: Practices, audiences, politics*, edited by Anna Harpin and Helen Nicholson, 184–209. New York: Red Globe Press, 2016. https://research.gold.ac.uk/id/eprint/28084

Auckland Art Gallery. 'Tino Sehgal: Yet Untitled'. 1 October 2022. www.aucklandartgallery.com/whats-on/exhibition/tino-sehgal-yet-untitled

Auslander, Philip. 'The Performativity of Performance Documentation'. *PAJ: A Journal of Performance and Art* 28, no. 3 (September 2006): 1–10, 4–5.

Barrie, Lita. 'Andrew Drummond: Towards an allegorical use of the body'. *Art New Zealand* 44 (Spring 1987): 64–67.

Barton, Christina. 'Notes on Method'. In *The Critic's Part: Wystan Curnow art writings 1971–2013*, edited by Christina Barton, Robert Leonard and Thomasin Sleigh, 13–19. Wellington/Brisbane: Te Pātaka Toi Adam Art Gallery, Institute of Modern Art and Victoria University Press, 2014.

Borck, Cornelius. 'Animism in the Sciences Then and Now'. *E-Flux Journal* 36 (July 2012). www.e-flux.com/journal/36/61266/animism-in-the-sciences-then-and-now

Braddock, Christopher. 'Alicia Frankovich and the Force of Failure'. *Column* 6 (2010): 8–15.

——— *Performing Contagious Bodies: Ritual participation in contemporary art*. London: Palgrave Macmillan, 2012.

——— 'Pump'. In *Air Supplied: David Cross*, edited by Fiona Lee, 117–19. punctum books, 2016.

——— 'Random Entrant and the Force of Failure'. *Frakcija Performing Arts Journal* 50 (2009): 26–33.

——— 'The Force of the Text: Alicia Frankovich and Marcel Duchamp'. In *Performing Contagious Bodies: Ritual participation in contemporary art*, 83–97. London: Palgrave Macmillan, 2012.

City Gallery Wellington. 'Peter Roche: Committed | Wystan Curnow, Art Critic and Witness'. 4 October 2020. https://citygallery.org.nz/blog/peter-roche-committed

Cole, Helen. 'This Secret Location'. In *Performance and Place*, edited by Leslie Hill and Helen Paris, 17–21. Performance Interventions series. London: Palgrave Macmillan, 2006. https://doi.org/10.1057/978023059 7723_2

Curnow, Wystan. *The Critic's Part: Wystan Curnow art writings 1971–2013*, edited by Christina Barton, Robert Leonard and Thomasin Sleigh. Wellington/Brisbane: Adam Art Gallery Te Pātaka Toi, Institute of Modern Art and Victoria University Press, 2014.

Derrida, Jacques. *Of Grammatology*. Baltimore: Johns Hopkins University Press, 1997.

'Embodying the Archive'. Physics Room gallery room sheet. https://physicsroom.org.nz/exhibitions/embodying-the-archive

Feeney, Warren. 'Performance and Documentation'. *EyeContact*, 30 September 2015. https://eyecontactmagazine.com/2015/09/performance-and-documentation

Harris, Brent Graeme. 'Figuring Diachrony: Ethics before the voice'. PhD thesis, Auckland University of Technology, 2013. https://hdl.handle.net/10292/6058

Hay, Jennifer. 'Trans-Marginal: New Zealand performance art 1970–1985'. In *Intervention: Post object and performance art in New Zealand in 1970 and Beyond*, 5–25. Christchurch: Robert McDougall Art Gallery & Annex, 2000. https://christchurchartgallery.org.nz/media/uploads/2016_09/Intervention2.pdf

Jones, Amelia. '"Presence" in Absentia: Experiencing performance as documentation'. *Art Journal* 56, no. 4 (1997): 11–18. https://doi.org/10.2307/777715

Laird, Tessa. 'Malone, Animal, Man'. Unpublished essay, 2011.

Marsh, Anne. *Performance_Ritual_Document*. Melbourne: Macmillan, 2014.

Montgomery, Kate. 'PROSPECT: NEW ZEALAND ART NOW'. Wellington: City Gallery, 2011.

Phelan, Peggy. *Unmarked: The politics of performance*. London: Routledge, 1993.

Roche, Peter, Wystan Curnow and Tony Green. 'Peter Roches/Linda Buis: A gathering concerning three performances'. In *The Critic's Part: Wystan Curnow art writings 1971–2013*, edited by Christina Barton, Robert Leonard and Thomasin Sleigh. Wellington/Brisbane: Te Pātaka Toi Adam Art Gallery, Institute of Modern Art and Victoria University Press, 2014.

Smith, Allan. 'Mapping Imperatives: Putting the land on the map at the Govett-Brewster Art Gallery'. *Art New Zealand* 52 (Spring 1989).

Van Imschoot, Myriam. 'Rests in Pieces: On scores, notations and the trace in dance'. In *Danse: An anthology*, edited by Noémie Solomon, 41–54. Dijon: Les presses du réel, 2014.

Wynne-Jones, Victoria. *Choreographing Intersubjectivity in Performance Art*. New World Choreographies. Cham, Switzerland: Palgrave Macmillan, 2021. https://doi.org/10.1007/978-3-030-40585-4

14

THREADS: MUSINGS ON QUEER PERFORMANCE ART IN AOTEAROA

Ioana Gordon-Smith &
Khye Hitchcock

BOTH, AND; TOGETHER

Queer performance art spans performances that have a clear queer agenda and those made by queer artists.[2] The terms 'queer' and 'art' function both as umbrellas to shelter under and fences that exclude. Collating the threads woven through performance art practices with 'both, and' in mind has produced this chapter. Our writing seeks to acknowledge and archive and, at the same time, to resist the creation of a category defining 'queer performance art' in Aotearoa.

In *The Queer Art of Failure*, Jack Halberstam proposes a 'low theory' approach that draws on eccentric archives. This both 'locate[s] all the in-between spaces that save us from being snared by the hooks of hegemony and speared by the seductions of the gift shop' and 'makes its peace with the possibility that alternatives dwell in the murky waters of a counterintuitive, often impossibly dark and negative realm of critique and refusal'. Halberstam does this 'in order to push through the divisions between life and art, practice and theory, thinking and doing, and into a more chaotic realm of knowing and unknowing'.[3]

We're not sure if we're doing it right, but this text serves as our own eccentric archive. It is a small, non-chronological accounting. However, as Nathan Joe notes in his *Seven Gestures Towards a New Queer Performance in Aotearoa*, we must work 'AGAINST ERASURE: The history of the work is to be archived'.[4] In this respect, our chapter serves as a gesture to an expansive, and even elusive, queer performance art history held through specific works, approaches and contexts that have stayed with us, the authors.

The themes explored are intended to be porous and unbracketed; though formality of writing has produced a series of subsections, it is important to bear in mind that many of the works here could be included in any of the topics explored, and that there is, in fact, a close relationship between protest, resistance, reclamation and joy. It is our hope that some of these reflections and memories may provoke a better awareness of the breadth and refusals of queer performance art in Aotearoa.

QUEER LIKE ESCAPING DEFINITION

The term 'queer' once meant strange or described feeling unwell. It has also been weaponised as a term of homophobic abuse. However, as David M. Halperin notes, the term has been reclaimed and 'now intimates possibilities so complex and rarefied that entire volumes are devoted to spelling them out'.[5]

We refer again to Nathan Joe's manifesto: as we write, we seek to 'ADORE THE AUDIENCE: For the work never to forget the community [that] it is indebted to and designed for.'[6] The title of this section is borrowed from an oft-cited quote from poet Brandon Wint: 'Not queer like gay. Queer like escaping definition. Queer like some sort of fluidity and limitlessness at once. Queer like a freedom too strong to be conquered.'[7] As with any minority group, the queer community has its own histories, rapidly shifting lexicons and cultural reference points.[8]

We seek to prioritise queer artists and readers. We have tried to be generous in the footnotes for those without contextual experience or knowledge. We reject the notion of a singular definition of terms. Contemporary queerness is still shifting, sliding and refusing definition while being simultaneously co-opted by academia, popular culture and capitalism.[9] This text does a bit of both.

'Queer performance art' could encompass contemporary artists, choreographers, dancers, slam poets, drag artists, burlesque babes, activists, kapa haka group and theatre queens. It could include the daily performance of those not out, or the transitioning folks documenting their journey on Instagram Live, or the community marching in protests or pride. Maybe every queer is a performance artist, even if they don't identify as queer or an artist.

The notion of daily life as a performance is well-trodden territory. Judith Butler said gender was a performance, or something like that, and lots of queers ran with it.[10] Many Indigenous cultures held space for queerness long before that. We practise code-switching as required to survive day to day.[11] On her website, Lindah Lepou lists her first 'performance' as *Riding a Duck* (c. 1975).[12] The entry comprises just the title and an image of a child, presumably a younger Lindah Lepou, on a playground duck at Cannons Creek, Porirua, Te Whanganui-a-Tara Wellington.

A multidisciplinary Samoan fa'afafine[13] artist, Lepou is an icon — one of Aotearoa's leading queer artists.[14] *Riding a Duck* offers an important consideration for queer performance histories: How do performances by queer artists fit within an anthology of performance art in Aotearoa? If performing is a social act, and not just an artistic one, how do we frame and historicise work by queer performance artists where queerness is located not in the intentions, subject or methods of the work but in the fact that their makers are queer? To claim that they are about queerness, or alternatively to ignore the queerness of the performer or producer, are both unsatisfactory positions. Perhaps a better resolution lies in the works of Samoan artist Shigeyuki Kihara. In speaking about *Taualuga: The last dance* (2006), Kihara says: 'I don't really separate art and performance from my life because I think every day is a performance, and I think life is a performance.'[15]

Since queerness resides both in works and in artists, the visibility of queer artists often relies upon overt queer themes and framings in exhibitions. Some Tāmaki Makaurau-based exhibitions that have foregrounded an overtly queer theme or focus on queer artists include *Queer Resistance* (2014) at RM Gallery; *The Bill* (2016) at Artspace Aotearoa; *Queer Algorithms* (2020) at Gus Fisher Gallery;[16] and *Queer Pavilion* (2020) at Rangipuke Albert Park, facilitated by artist Richard Orjis. While not all the artists in all these exhibitions are queer, exhibitions organised around queer identity have doubled as both an act of visibility for queer artists and a type of mapping or networking tool for recognising queer artists.

The problems of canvassing or archiving queer art was illustrated in a Tumblr post by curator Daniel Sanders, in which they document a search of the Auckland Art Gallery Toi o Tāmaki archives using a list of search terms that include 'LGBT', 'gay', 'lesbian', 'queer', 'takatāpui' and 'fa'afafine'. The search yielded slim results, suggesting a lack of queer representation within Auckland Art Gallery's programming or collections. As Sanders notes, however, this also reflects a way of recognising, cataloguing, archiving and historicising queer art. They write:

> The results of these searches are flawed in that they do not represent the actual number of LGBTQ+ people who have exhibited at the Auckland Art Gallery. There are variables such as whether the exhibited artwork is concerned with LGBTQ+ issues or experiences, whether the artist openly identifies as LGBTQ+, etc.[17]

The categorising of art under labels such as 'LGBT(QIA+)', 'gay', 'lesbian', 'queer', 'takatāpui' and 'fa'afafine' is to some extent also generational — identities repressed through colonisation and reclaimed through civil rights, the rise of decolonisation and an embrace of Indigenous gender norms. Not only have these issues risen to prominence within contemporary arts discourse, but so too have the social contexts of queerness more generally shifted over time. A few generations ago it was not socially or publicly acceptable for people to be openly queer. However, the 2021 Ipsos LGBT+ Pride Global Survey showed that in Gen Z (those born since 1997), 18 per cent of people responded as identifying within the rainbow community, compared with 6 per cent in Gen X (1965–80) and 10 per cent of Millennials (1981–97).[18]

In the last decade or so, the notation of pronouns and claiming of queerness has increased as a form of positionality in artist biographies, introducing queer identifiers even beyond queer group exhibitions. However, the visibility or framing of performance artworks as queer continues to reveal a contingency on either overt biography, exhibition frameworks, or queer themes or references within artworks. Together, although these signifiers might capture a section of queer performance, the cataloguing, archiving and historicising of queer art remains — as Sanders' own attempts to recover queer exhibition histories indicate — incomplete.

A SPACE IN WHICH TO TWIRL

Living as a queer person often feels like there's a constant hum of static. It's your awareness of potential danger, of being other, of being outside. That hum hasn't entirely gone away with law changes,[19] and the volume fluctuates wildly. Aotearoa is not the safe haven it likes to pretend it is[20] even though in te ao Māori, takātapui have always been part of the whānau.[21] It's a daily struggle against the insidious impact of Eurocentric, colonial and religious ideologies. Luckily (sadly), queer folk are really good at protesting and at making their own families and spaces.

We've been practising. Decades of steady progress towards civic equity in Aotearoa has created a wider visibility of queerness; and in the context of queer performance, art practice remains one of courage and resilience. The international rise of far-right ideologies and anti-trans propaganda has also been evident here, conditioning both performance art and its reception.

Sam Duckor-Jones's *Gloria of Greymouth* project is somewhere between an installation, a home, a (somewhat unwilling) political statement and a performance venue. The former church has been transformed into a camp, sculptural and entirely pink dwelling — Gloria — in which Duckor-Jones likes to twirl and host the occasional drag show. The quiet courage of the work is that it is located on the West Coast of the South Island of Aotearoa in Māwhera Greymouth, a small town not known for being particularly culturally progressive, nor for having a significant rainbow population. In June 2022 Gloria was attacked: vandals left a burned rainbow flag out front and scrawled homophobic and antisemitic graffiti all over the walls.[22] *Gloria of Greymouth*, or more specifically the response to it, reveals the very tangible dangers within which queer performance art is still situated. Duckor-Jones writes:

> It was frightening. I was all alone. My family & all of my old heart friends are still up north. I am all alone. I phoned the police & they turned up quickly & took

the hate crime seriously. Am I all alone. I phoned some new
local friends, a little apologetically. Word spread then & folks showed
up in droves. With flowers & cards & hugs & tears & support & outrage
Gloria's pink icing flanks were restored by noon [. . .]
We continued to be vividly outraged &
We continued to be queerly defiant &
We put on our silk robes & our big hats & our gumboots &
We watched the sun go down & the glorious coast was lit up as pink as a
lullaby
We twirled.[23]

The Māwhera community rallied around Gloria: the community restored the damage the same day and in time to host a touring drag show. The visiting performers had recently been subjected to small but aggressive protests around the motu (islands) as the drag queens had been reading storybooks to children. They welcomed the kind reception at Gloria.

DECOLONISE AND MOISTURISE[24]

A strong thread across performance is the desire to reclaim queer identity as one that exists within Indigenous cultures and pre-colonial contexts. Niuean fakafifine and queer rights activists, for instance, recently coined MVPFAFF+ as an acronym for various gender identities across the Moana: mahu, vakasalewalewa, palopa, fa'afafine, akava'ine, fakaleiti or leiti, fakafifine and more.[25] This Indigenous reclamation reasserts not only a Moana presence within queer discourse but also a queer presence within Moana histories, presents and futures. Reclaiming queer and trans identities as an experience that existed long before the colonial context and has its own culturally specific understandings is apparent in the work of many artists.

Embracing 'the power of body adornment to affirm their takatāpuitanga', artist Louie Zalk-Neale (Ngāi Te Rangi, Pākehā) uses recycled fabrics and materials gleaned from 'forests, beaches and gutters' in a multifaceted practice that '[adds] meticulously crafted extensions to their body . . . [immersing] their audience in ritualistic performances, bringing queer visions of the past and future abruptly into the present moment'.[26] Zalk-Neale's recent exploration of twisting taura tī kōuka (cabbage tree-fibre rope) is informed by mātauranga Māori and 'attempts to bind the sacred transgender experience with the transformative powers of taniwha and tipua — spiritual beings from pūrakau Māori [Māori legends] that can change gender and form'.[27]

The use of natural materials is a constant refrain across Zalk-Neale's practice. In their 2020 video *kei matairangi tōku kāinga ināianei*, the artist lies and writhes on a grassy ledge. The artist likens this burrowing action to the transformation found within nature (specifically plants, worms and fungi), and notes: 'transformations are more blatant when they don't align with the majority'.[28] Here, Zalk-Neale reclaims shifting, transformation, queerness and changing as natural phenomena. In performing and connecting with natural materials and locations, queerness is reaffirmed as a state that pre-exists any heteronormative construct.

Those who are arguably making some of the most interesting works are taking the biggest risks by being visible as trans women and gender-nonconforming people of colour.

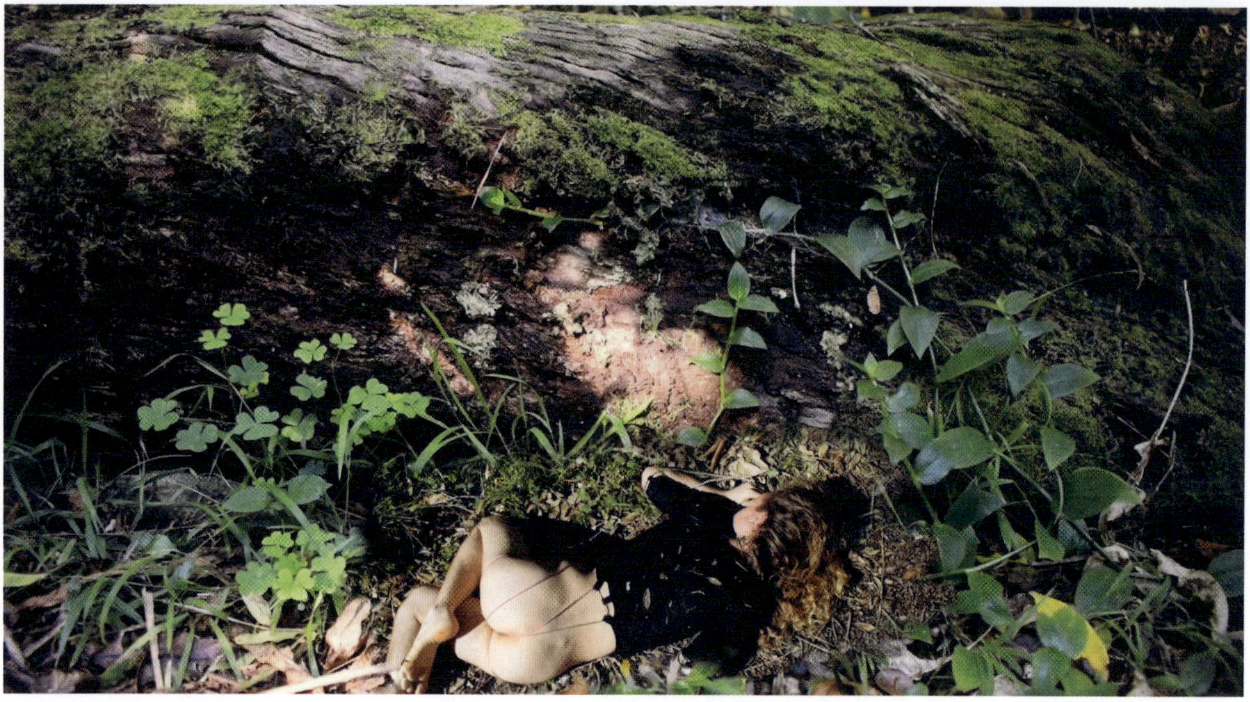

Louie Zalk-Neale, *kei matairangi tōku kāinga ināianei*, 2020. Single-channel digital video, duration 1 minute 26 seconds, colour, sound. *Courtesy the artist*

American civil rights activist Kimberlé Crenshaw popularised intersectionality as a lens that identified and illuminated how different modes of identity overlap to create specific experiences of discrimination. This lens allows an understanding of how homophobia affects bodies of colour in particular and specific ways. For queer performance artists of colour, this often means negotiating the dual visibility of being both queer and brown.

Aotearoa has a long history of MVPFAFF+ performance collectives.[29] Fine Fatale, Pure Funk and the Pasifika Divas were all collectives which paved the way for greater Moana queer representation. The Pasifika Divas' participation in the 4th Asia Pacific Triennial in 2002 marked a milestone not only for queer performance art from Aotearoa but also for Moana art from Aotearoa. During their performance, the Pasifika Divas members took turns to occupy the spotlight. In its programme of multiple performances, the act had the format of a talent show; however, as Kihara warned: 'Don't expect just a cabaret drag show, because this is beyond drag, this is beyond performance.'[30] Kihara's comment seems to suggest that queer performance exceeds the brackets of 'performance art' as something far more embodied and affirming.

Perhaps the most visible brown and queer artist collective in Aotearoa is FAFSWAG, which first emerged in October 2012 as a Facebook page. Founded by visual artists Tanu Gago and Pati Solomona Tyrell, the FAFSWAG Facebook page provided a digital portal for MVPFAFF+s to meet and connect. Many of those contacting the page were creative producers — filmmakers, dancers and photographers who then became regular collaborators. With little access to or interest from mainstream institutions, FAFSWAG began curating their own exhibitions. In 2012 FAFSWAG staged *No Fruit Without Labour* at the Methodist church close to Karangahape Road in Tāmaki Makaurau; and in 2014, Gago curated *Poly-Typical* for Fresh Gallery, Ōtara, also in the city.

Despite a long exhibition history that often foregrounds photography as a corrective tool for brown, queer representation, FAFSWAG is perhaps best known for cultivating Aotearoa's ball scene. FAFSWAG member and iconic ball MC Akashi coined the phrase 'decolonise and moisturise'. Akashi was often MC of the balls, a role that is part schedule-keeper, part audience-engager and 100 per cent hype-person. In their commentating on the ball, they often proclaim the political or social significance of the event. The phrase 'decolonise and moisturise' captures the ballroom's dual mission of undoing the work of colonial gender constructs and simultaneously living out one's best, most glow-up self without the colonial baggage. Akashi repeated the phrase often, like a percussive soundtrack or spoken manifesto for those strutting the catwalk.

FAFSWAG's balls are modelled after the Harlem drag balls in New York City, which themselves emerged from a politics of colour. In the early 1900s, American queer events consisted mainly of white men putting on drag fashion shows and pageants. Black queens rarely participated; when they did, they were expected to lighten their faces. Feeling racism and rejection from the white ball community, Harlem balls emerged from the 1960s onwards as a haven for queers of colour to 'walk' in different runway categories before a judging panel.

FAFSWAG's balls localise this queer politics of colour by foregrounding Indigenous references. The Aitu Ball hosted by the performance collective House of Aitu, for example, is a deliberate reference to a Samoan belief in deities who rule the underworld, a spiritual belief that existed before the introduction of Christianity. FAFSWAG's earliest balls also took place in South Auckland, and implicitly point to a politics of colour within Tāmaki Makaurau's gay scene. In the central city, the pride parade and the gentrifying gay clubs in the CBD have side-lined concerns about physical safety for Māori and Moana queer peoples. By contrast, the high demographics of Moana peoples living in South Auckland rendered the geography a type of Moana queer home turf.

From 2016 FAFSWAG began staging more events in central Tāmaki Makaurau. In 2017 they presented Disruption Vogue Ball at Artspace Aotearoa, and for the 2018 Pride Festival in Auckland they presented a ball at Auckland Art Gallery Toi o Tāmaki. FAFSWAG's move into central-city spaces coincided with an institutional move towards diversifying gallery programming and audiences, particularly concerning Indigenous practices and publics.

In 2021, however, FAFSWAG formally announced their exit from ballroom, acknowledging that the scene was now self-sustaining. FAFSWAG's withdrawal perhaps also reflects a frustration with the politics of art institutions, however. In a critique of the documentary *Paris Is Burning*, American cultural critic bell hooks argued that the spectacle of the documentary did not do enough to de-establish the racial hierarchies that were apparent in the early days of drag balls, and reproduced brown bodies as a spectacle for white audiences.[31] Similarly, FAFSWAG expressed concern that simply occupying gallery spaces was not doing enough to decolonise institutions. As FAFSWAG member Tapuaki Helu writes:

> We are always very cautious about being invited to major institutional exhibitions as our practice is sometimes tokenised and sometimes, we are booked as entertainment. The thirst for diversity within civic arts programming often means some public arts programming will include us as a means of ticking boxes.[32]

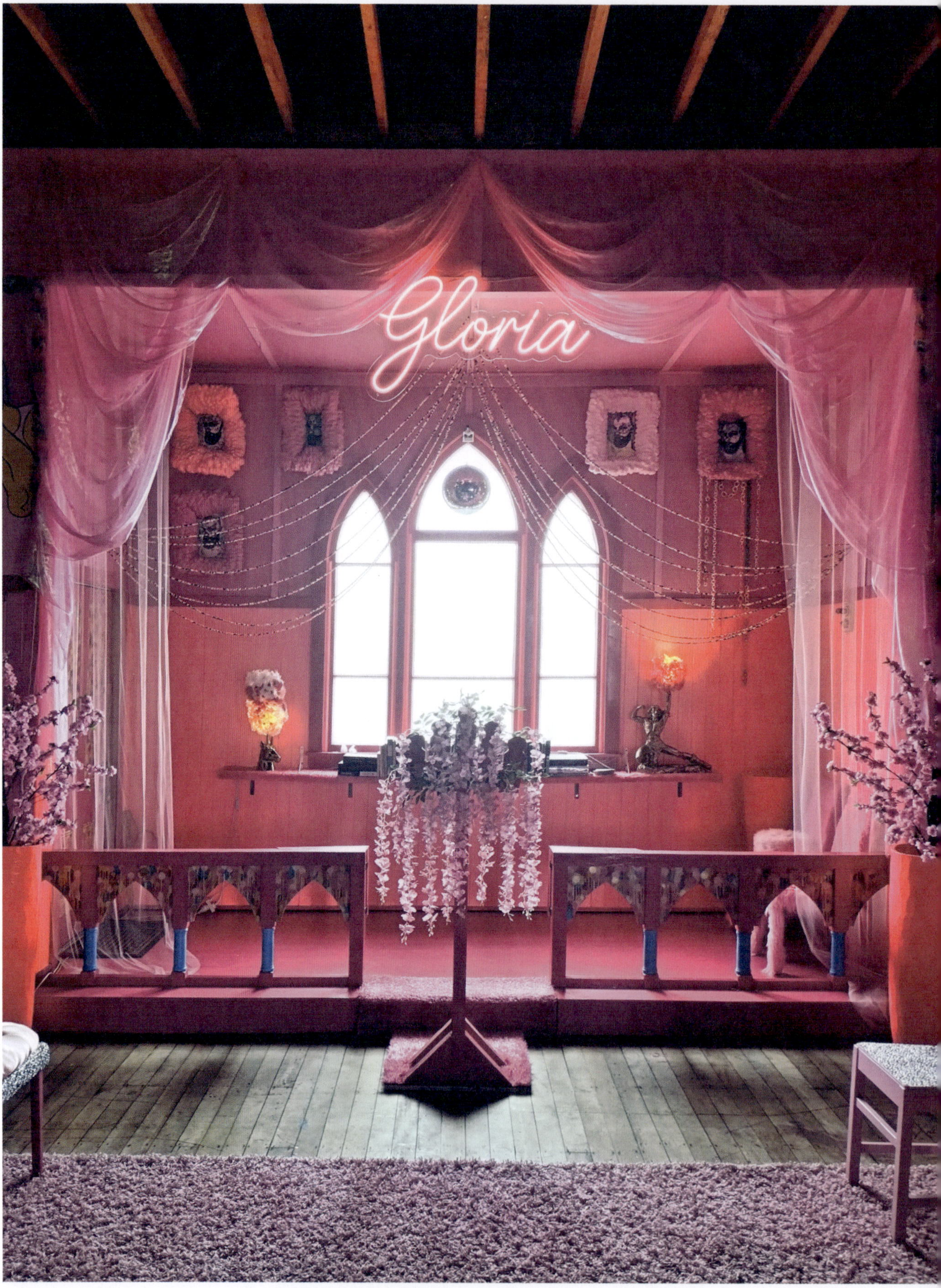
Gloria

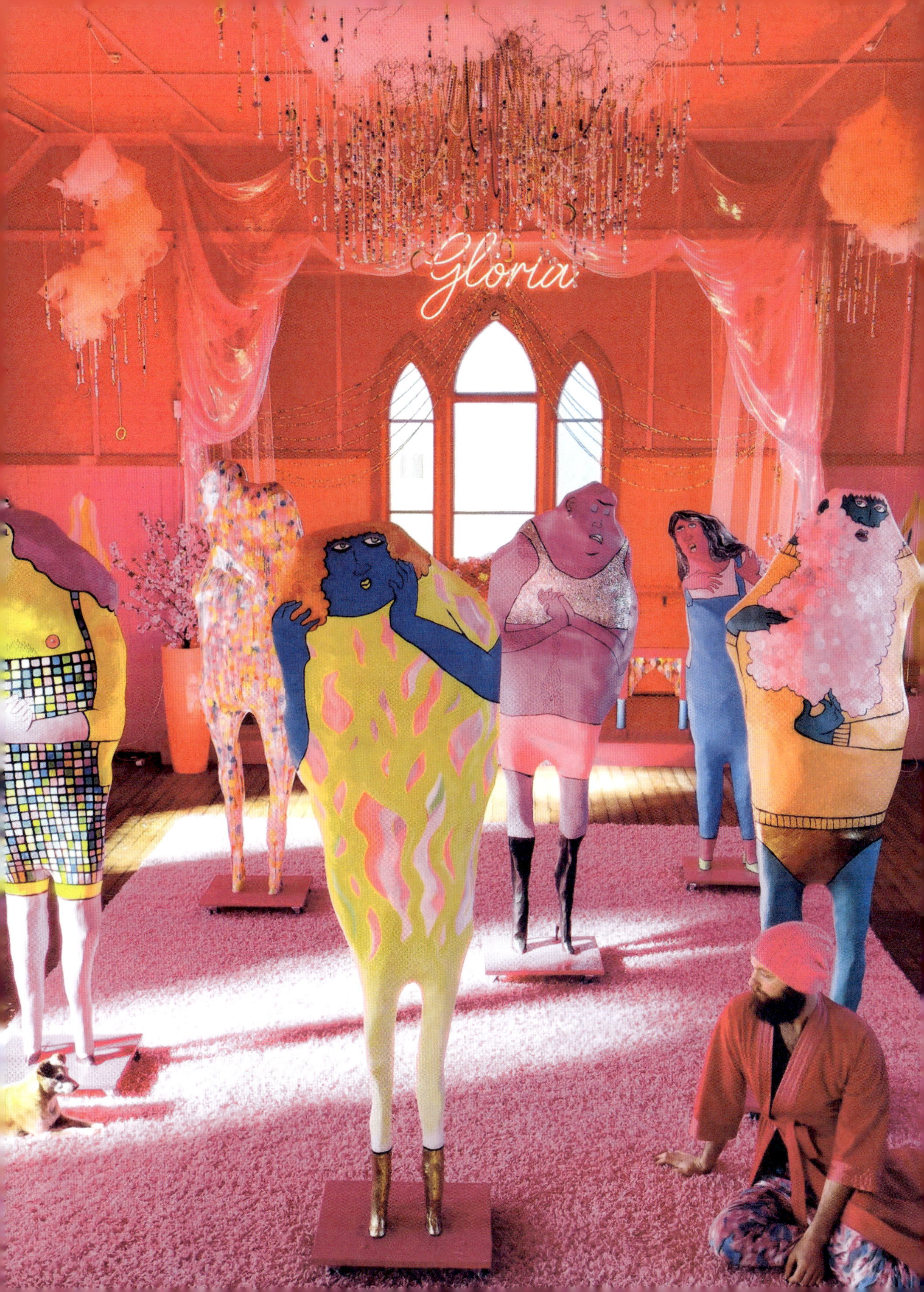
Gloria

Beyond their significant work in reframing bodies according to an affirmative, queer, brown self-defined expression, FAFSWAG's institutional appearances reveal the somewhat facetious distinction between gallery culture and street culture when it comes to queer performance art. As curator Sanders notes, the programming of queer art in institutional spaces can have the effect of essentially cordoning queerness, especially with the concurrent closing of queer spaces beyond the gallery. As Sanders writes:

PREVIOUS: Sam Duckor-Jones, *Gloria of Greymouth. Courtesy the artist. Photos by Sam Duckor-Jones*

> **I noticed that LGBTQ+ artists started occupying institutional spaces. Suddenly, queer night space became restricted to a public programme or exhibition schedule . . . I feel like more than often, 'queerness' as a conceptual framework is now beholden to institutions.**[33]

LITTLE MOMENTS OF JOY

Joy and humour are often utilised as both a mode of critique and a vehicle for bypassing institutional containment and politics by minority groups. *Thanks for All the Fish* (2021), a collaborative three-channel video by Elisabeth Pointon and Christopher Ulutupu, was conceptualised by the artists as their 'big coming out party'. The work was informed by several overlapping realities: the absence of brown bodies within pride spaces in Aotearoa; the artists' experiences of being included in ethnically organised but rarely queer-themed exhibitions; and the commodified spectacle of identity through issues such as the corporatisation of pride festivals. In response, Ulutupu and Pointon planned their own pride parade.

The video work feature three vignettes playing side by side that juxtapose the image of queerness with opulence. Filmed largely on or near the water, the videos co-opt symbols of luxury, scale and spectacle: a yacht, jet-skis and an industrial crane. The work was originally intended to culminate in a pride parade down the streets of Porirua, Te Whanganui-a-Tara, but Covid-19 restrictions put a halt to the public work. Nonetheless, these foiled attempts are incorporated into the work as a type of tragic comedy and offer an insight into the ways in which joy, humour and collaborative practice circumnavigate issues affecting queer artists of colour.

D.A.N.C.E. Art Club is a collective of artists who similarly produce and embrace joy in protest of hierarchical and exclusionary systems. D.A.N.C.E. stands for 'Distinguished All Night Community Entertainers', and both this name and the 'dance' it spells out indicate the social bent of the collective. Also seeking an alternative mode of engaging with art, the collective consists of Chris Fitzgerald, Ahilapalapa Rands, Tuāfale Tanoa'i aka Linda T, and Vaimaila Urale. Both Rands and Tanoa'i identify as queer.

The four visual artists met while studying art at Auckland University of Technology in Tāmaki Makaurau and found they shared a disillusionment with the individualistic studio culture, the clear social hierarchies between the different year groups, tutors and lecturers, and between the art school and other university departments. D.A.N.C.E. Art Club's events emphasise hospitality and use music and free food to create democratic spaces that break down social barriers. Multiple performances initiate social interactions, such as their kava circle at Snake Pit in Tāmaki Makaurau, or their Romance at Enjoy in Te Whanganui-a-Tara.

Perhaps their most ambitious performance/relational work was *GWR (Guinness World Record Attempt)* in 2014 at Artspace Aotearoa. Here, Tuāfale Tanoa'i attempted to break the record for the longest public DJing marathon. The gallery was converted into a dance space, complete with a dance floor, lights, DJ set up and a green room. The Guinness World Record rules stipulate that two dancers and two timekeepers must always be present to legitimate the attempt. This necessitated enormous audience participation. It also brought an effervescence of community, chaos and the everyday into this contemporary art space above Karangahape Road, a space that had predominantly been one of conceptual and esoteric exploration.

The act of endurance that followed was not only experienced by Tanoa'i as DJ and the other D.A.N.C.E. Art Club members supporting her, but also by a community of volunteers who looked after them. People slept at the gallery, children ran around, crock pots were constantly on the go with boil-up, and so many espressos were made the coffee machine gave up the ghost soon after.

This collective approach to production speaks to both queer support networks and extended kinship networks that resist white hegemonic individuality. Volunteers supporting the production included artists' whānau and friends, the existing Artspace Aotearoa volunteer cohort,[34] and those interested in the kaupapa[35] who were drawn in by an open call for volunteers. The round-the-clock roster of dancers, sometimes sought at the last minute, meant the gallery space was constantly in motion with groups of friends coming to dance their shift together.

On one night a group of fa'afafine calling themselves The Black Barbies danced the shift from 3 to 6 a.m. At another time, a senior Creative New Zealand (New Zealand's government arts funding body) administrator danced with a first-year art student. Many of those who participated in this endeavour had never been to the gallery before, and perhaps have not been again since, but for the 84 hours of the attempt, the gallery was a much more open communal space.

RAIL AGAINST HYPOCRISY[36]

Another thread weaving through queer performance art is one of (at times excruciating) self-reflection and resistance to the commodification of capitalism and gay culture. This can be seen in Nathan Joe's *Gay Death Stock Take*, which premiered at Tiny Fest in Ōtautahi in 2021, where it was performed by the artist, then was performed by five gay men at Auckland Fringe Festival in 2022, all with no prior rehearsal. Somewhere between performance art, theatre and poetry, the work offers both insight into and critique of the concept of 'gay death': the notion that a gay man's participation in a certain type of gay culture ends at age thirty.

For *Gay Death Stock Take*, a stage was set with thirty helium balloons. Each one was numbered and containing an instruction, a question or a piece of writing to be read aloud. The performance lasted only 60 minutes, and the aim was to complete all thirty tasks within the timeframe. The performer asked the audience to choose a number then popped the chosen balloon to reveal its contents. The snippets of performance traversed the endearing nature of personal reflection, to pure smut, to the absurdist act of being tickled by an audience member while reading a rant about the privilege of cis-white men. It was a messy, unapologetically queer take on existing in a capitalist society that values you not as you are but for what you do, and a celebration of becoming a queer elder.

val smith's performance work also highlights the complexities of queer culture. *Gay Shame Parade* (2014) took place as part of the *to and fro* exhibition at Artspace

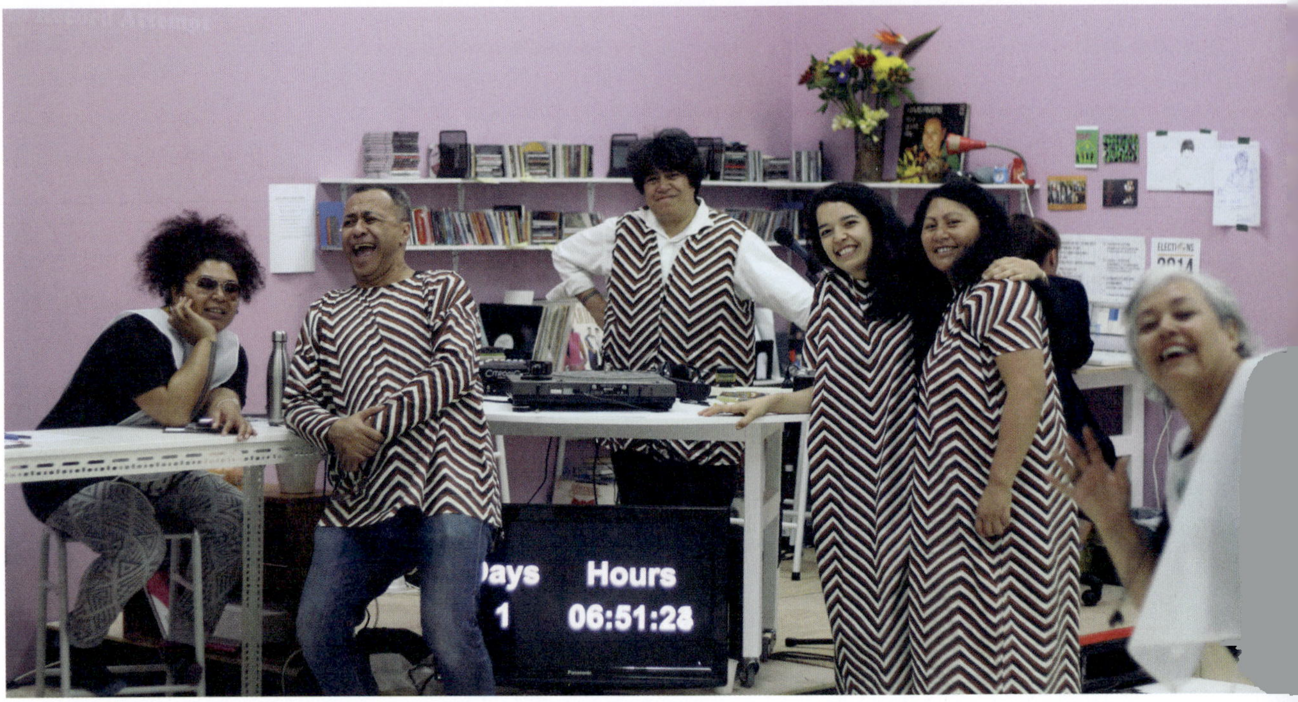

Aotearoa on Karangahape Road — a street that is historically a site of queerness and conflict, where marginalised communities congregate. In 2014 the Auckland Pride Parade was scheduled to march down Ponsonby Road, avoiding Karangahape Road — the pinkwashing was particularly strong that year.[37] smith began the performance literally lying on the street; a taped outline of a body indicated where an audience member should lie, darkly referencing crime scenes and violent ends. smith, in a grubby masc drag replete with scruffy mullet, moustache and gold jacket, lay with audience members in the rain, shining a tiny torch down into the gutter.[38]

A second queer performer, Magdalena O'Connor, was dressed in high-vis and held a sign made of rough cardboard — a material associated with protests and pleas — with a big arrow drawn on it announcing the 'gay shame parade'. After an hour of one-on-one interactions, smith slowly crawled, rolled and edged their way into the gallery space, bedraggled tinsel pom poms trailing in their wake. O'Connor followed behind, sweeping up the scattered glitter. smith eventually made it into one of two adjacent human-sized packing boxes, with mini disco lights inside, for an 'introvert's afterparty'.

smith's performance work *formations for reciprocal justice and further sad attempts to punish you or make some kind of a difference: i. Making the club gay again ii. Ensuring no pride is a positive outcome of the protest* (2016) sat in conversation with Jamiee Stockman-Young's *Spectres of Violence* (2016), which referenced the impacts of homosexual law reform and the physical destruction of queer spaces. Stockman-Young's work referred to the 1986 suspected arson of The Dorian Club in Ōtautahi, which existed before homosexual law reform days.[39] The work included archival photos of the damage caused by the fire, courtesy of the Lesbian and Gay Archives of New Zealand Te Pūranga Takatāpui o Aotearoa.

D.A.N.C.E. Art Club crew pictured during *GWR (Guinness World Record Attempt)* at Artspace Aotearoa, 2014. From left: Reina Sutton, Teokotai Paitai, Tuāfale Tanoa'i, Ahilapalapa Rands, Vaimaila Urale, Ella Grace McPherson-Newton and Melanie Rands. *Courtesy the artists. Photo by Janet Lilo*

In 2016 Ōtautahi was still in post-earthquake disarray and many of its queer venues had been demolished. smith set up a hidden space between a false gallery wall and the exterior wall of the building; a liminal space into which one had to squeeze, and which could only be occupied by two dancers at a time. Soft music, a disco ball and coloured lights created the atmosphere of a tiny club eking out an existence in secret. During the opening, smith, dressed in a femme-drag persona, kicked a hole in the wall so they could shout through it using a megaphone and creating a peephole so people could look in. They connected a line of queer conspirators across the gallery, all wearing cardboard tub cuffs to disguise and protect their hand-holding, and smith directed their actions with the megaphone.[40] It was chaotic, riotous and celebratory all at the same time.

For her performance installation *Para-* (2014), Jennifer Katherine Shields constructed a wooden bar with a shiny piece of copper sheeting nailed on the top. During the opening event she assumed the role of a barmaid, bantering with the audience. The bar separated her from the crowd, both protecting and constraining her movements. In her accompanying essay, Shields notes that 'parasexuality' is a term used to describe social mechanisms that 'allowed for the expression of sexual energy in a channelled and safe manner, in contexts where the usual social rules did not apply'.[41]

She drew a scathing comparison between the role of a Victorian barmaid, allowed to be flirtatious and sexual while working behind a bar, and the contemporary experience of trans artists like herself: celebrated for a limited time and space within the institution, after which they are abandoned to fend for themselves again in a world that is often hostile to trans people. The bar's copper top captured the fingerprints of people who engaged with Shields during the evening and oxidised over the duration of the exhibition, posing questions about complicity, allyship and remembrance.

Sung Hwan Bobby Park's *BTM Live* (2023), performed as part of Auckland Pride Festival 2023, was a live performance of sculpture-making. Park, dressed in full 'Dom Leather Daddy' get-up, lovingly fisted a large cylinder of clay for a couple of hours, hollowing out a cavity within. Park asserts that popular culture's representation of queer sex acts is often designed to 'stir disgust and fear in the larger population . . . even our rainbow community has developed a hesitancy to make references or associate with these sex practices, and the groups that openly embrace them'.[42] The gentle, considered gestures in this performance were designed to counter these narratives. The performance ended with the artist pouring plaster of Paris into the cavity he had created, and the resulting sculpture was replicated in a fundraising edition to support RainbowYOUTH's work supporting the homeless community.

SELF-INFLICTED

One specific genre of queer performance art tends to push at the edges of pain tolerance and endurance, kink, sex and taboo.[43] Audrey Baldwin and Pat Parkin performed *Assent // Ascent* (2017), in which both artists were suspended cross-legged from the ceiling wearing nothing but matching grey panties.[44] The performance started as Parkin was suspended by their flesh, with hooks in their knees, calves and shoulders. Baldwin was then ensnared in a cocoon of thin, white paracord. They floated opposite each other as Baldwin slowly cut herself free, cord after cord, with each cut putting more of her body weight onto the remaining threads. The performance ended when Baldwin fell to the ground, at which point Parkin was lowered and released. The work touched

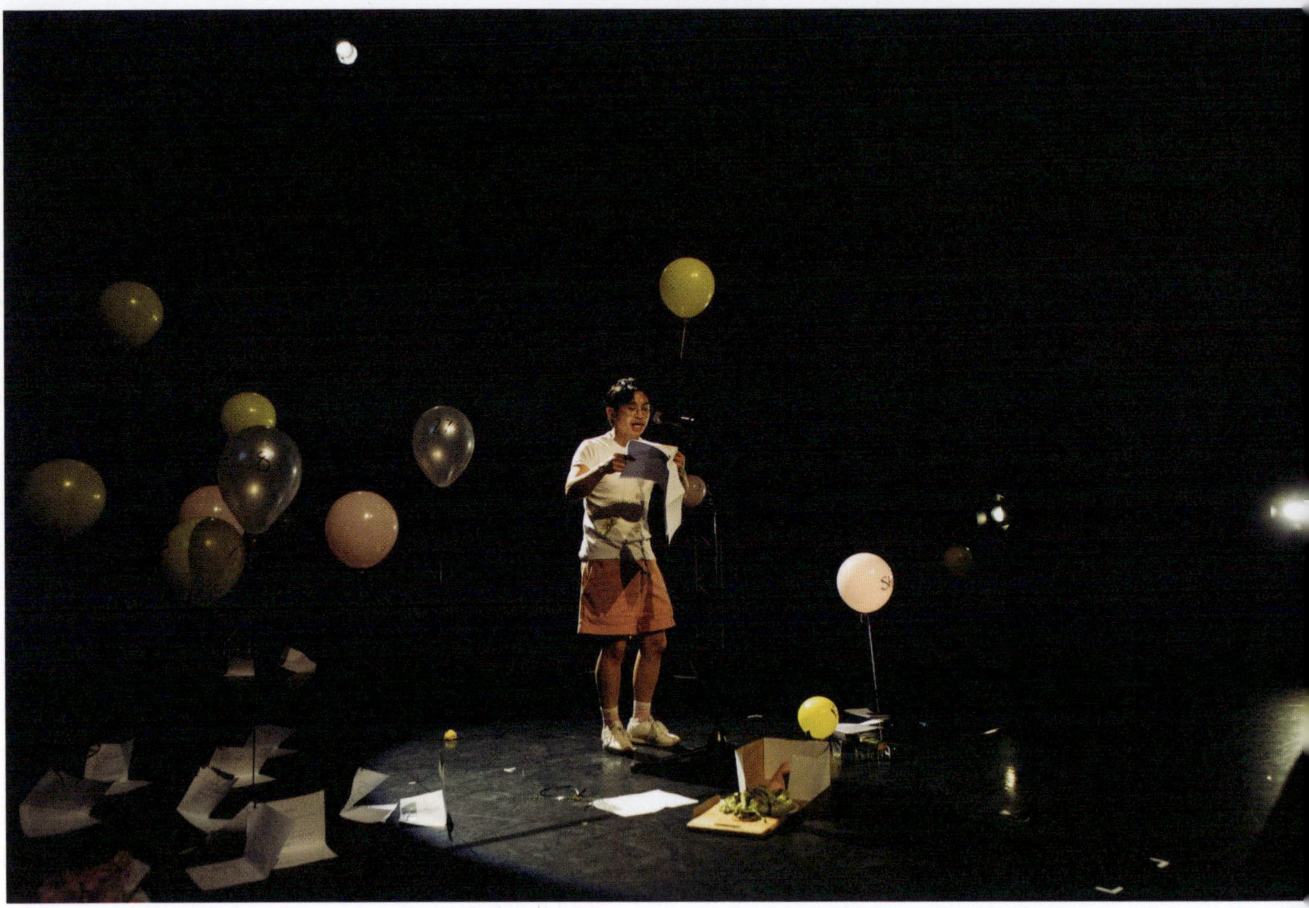

LEFT: Nathan Joe, *Gay Death Stock Take*, performance at Tiny Fest 2021, Ōtautahi Christchurch. *Courtesy the artist. Photo by Petra Mingneau*

BELOW: Audrey Baldwin and Pat Parkin, *Assent // Ascent*, 2017, documentation of performance held at a pop-up exhibition at XCHC (Exchange Christchurch), Ōtautahi Christchurch. *Courtesy the artists. Photo by Lison Colin*

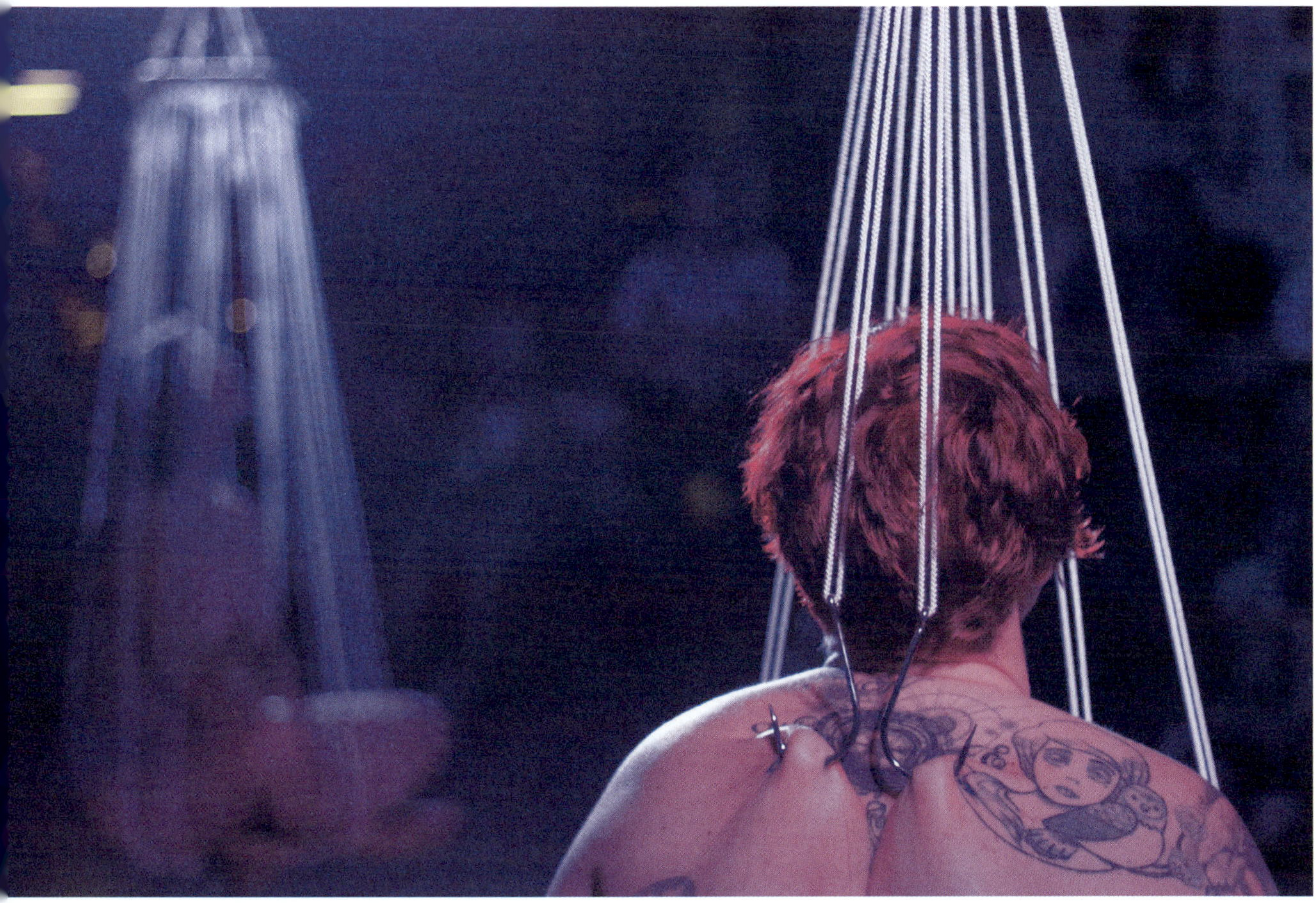

on vulnerability, agency, consent, solidarity, and the complexity of the artists' mutual experiences in the queer kink scene. Baldwin still bears scars from this performance.

Modes of self-inflicted endurance were also a characteristic of Jo Bragg's durational performance *Forecasting* (2018), in which the artist was strapped to the bonnet of a car on top of a shipping container, where he endured the weather for a four-day durational piece as part of The Performance Arcade, an annual offsite performance-dedicated exhibition on Te Whanganui-a-Tara Wellington's waterfront promenade.[45] The accompanying video work, *And Again*, showed the artist strapped to a car, this time being driven around in circles by an ex-lover. A soundtrack repeats: 'And again, the sun rose on the next day. When your back is turned, the day does not turn away, always the same. Love is absolution, persecution, ejaculation, always the same.'[46]

Ivan Lupi often puts his body on the line, too. In *X* (2018–19) Lupi stood behind a custom-made polling booth at several events and invited audience members to use a tattoo gun to 'secretly' mark his hands with an X. The resulting tattoos are a permanent reminder of the collectively created work, which highlights the importance of individual responsibility at the polling booth and how it affects gender equity. Lupi shared conversation with the individuals tattooing him as they marked his skin. In *Salut* (2022), the artist repeatedly tattooed his own palm with a '+' sign, with no ink, in a performance that lasted an hour. Performed on World AIDS Day, the plus symbol refers to being HIV positive. The artist states:

> While drugs have mitigated the former death sentence for most in the developed world, for many in the world a positive result will still bring stigma and the likelihood of an early, miserable death. This action on World AIDS Day draws attention to the inequality inflicted on so many in our world.[47]

WITHOUT BEGINNING OR END

The works in this chapter are but a slim selection of queer performance art in Aotearoa. The limits of defining and cataloguing queer performance are matched only by the refusal of the fixed definition queerness itself implies. In the 2022 group exhibition of video art by queer artists, *Wild Once More*, Te Tuhi's guest curator Christopher Ulutupu draws on Jack Halberstam to foreground the false narrative of discovering or rediscovering the wild.[48] In particular, Ulutupu referenced Halberstam's caution against the false binary logic of believing that the wild either comes into or out of existence.

In a similar manner, the works discussed here evade a bracketing of any time or place where queerness did or did not exist. Queer performance art moves in and out of the institution, public spaces, the canon and even biography. Rather than reproducing a containment that queer performance rallies against, this chapter suggests that any account of queer performance can, at best, follow (some of) the threads.

NOTES

1 This text sutures together two positions: that of a non-binary queer Pākehā and that of a cis straight Moana woman in diaspora, through a friendship formed during an internship at Artspace Aotearoa that spans a decade of sporadic, deep-diving catch ups. We have both practised as curators, from the margins and within the institution. We have different relationships to 'queerness' and have allowed the text to unfurl in ways that reflect this.

2 'Queer' is a term with a multifaceted history. We acknowledge that it has been a term used to inflict violence and that it is not a comfortable term for everyone. In the context of this piece, we are using it with pride. It is primarily being used as a shorthand to refer to people with diverse SOGIESC — an umbrella term for all people whose sexual orientations, gender identities, gender expressions and/or sex characteristics place them outside culturally mainstream categories.

3 Jack Halberstam, *The Queer Art of Failure* (Durham, NC: Duke University Press, 2011), 2.

4 Nathan Joe, 'Seven Gestures Towards a New Queer Performance in Aotearoa', *BLOT* 1 (September 2022), www.blot.online/journal/1/seven-gestures-towards-a-newqueer-performance-in-aotearoa

5 David M. Halperin, 'The Normalization of Queer Theory', *Journal of Homosexuality* 45, no. 2–4 (September 2003).

6 Joe, 'Seven Gestures'.

7 Brandon Wint, 'Not Queer like Gay. Queer like, Escaping . . .', Facebook post, 7 February 2013, https://www.facebook.com/brandon.wint/posts/not-queer-like-gay-queer-like-escaping-definition-queer-like-some-sort-of-fluidi/10100296731275845

8 Khye Hitchcock: defining 'community' in relationship to LGBTQIA+ peoples is complex and requires far more nuance than is possible within a chapter of this length. Our 'community' is somewhat united by our, but is still divided by other social structures such as gender, ability, race and class. We're a nebulous, fractured demographic.

9 Joe, 'Seven Gestures'.

10 Judith Butler, *Gender Trouble: Feminism and the subversion of identity* (New York: Routledge, 1990). Judith Butler's theory of 'gender performance' proposes that gender is something created through daily practices, and that these practices are learned and performed by individuals based on cultural norms of femininity and masculinity. This could be briefly summarised as: gender is what you perform, not who you are.

11 As Madeleine Holden writes: 'Code switching is a sociolinguistic concept that once simply described the practice of alternating between multiple languages or varieties of language in conversation, but which is now used in discussions about how members of marginalized communities adjust their voices, speech patterns, mannerisms, and behavior to blend in across various social settings.' Madeleine Holden, 'The Exhausting Work of LGBTQ Code-Switching', *Vice*, 13 August 2019, www.vice.com/en/article/evj47w/the-exhausting-work-of-lgbtq-codeswitching.

12 Lindah Lepou, 'Aotearoa, New Zealand. My First Performance (c. 1975): "Riding a Duck"', 2023.

13 Fa'afafine is often translated as 'in the manner of a woman', and is a Samoan-specific term. Many other terms specific to different languages for living as a woman are found across the Moana.

14 Lepou was recently the recipient of The Arts Foundation's inaugural Toi Kō Iriiri award in recognition of her services to Aotearoa's creative queer, LGBTQI+ and MVPFAFF+ communities. She is particularly known for her work as a fashion designer, but is also a performer, and was part of notable collectives such as Pure Funk and Pasifika Divas.

15 Museum of New Zealand Te Papa Tongarewa, *Shigeyuki Kihara — Taualuga: The Last Dance*, 2015.

16 *Queer Resistance* featured work by Cameron Ah Loo-Matamua, Léuli Eshraghi, Kiran Foster, Tanu Gago, Cecilia Kavara Verran, Moe Laga, Emilie Rākete, Molly Rangiwai McHale, David Roil, Sangeeta Singh, Tuafale Tanoa'i (aka Linda T.), Ron Te Kawa, Luisa Tora, Pati Solomona Tyrell and Anna Vo. Exhibiting artists at *The Bill* included Billy Apple, Amy Blinkhorne, Black Cracker and GFS, Teghan Burt and George Rump, Léuli Eshraghi, Tom of Finland, Alicia Frankovich, Nan Goldin, Nilbar Güreş, Dale Harding, Samuel Hodge, Lonnie Hutchinson, Paul Johns, William E. Jones, Yuki Kihara, Grant Lingard, Alex Monteith, Catherine Opie, Emily Roysdon, Aykan Safoğlu, Ava Seymour, Jennifer Katherine Shields, Jaimee Stockman-Young, Zackary Steiner-Fox, Brian Tennessee Claflin and Wolfgang Tillmans. Exhibiting artists at *Queer Algorithms* included John Walter, Evan Ifekoya, Ursula Mayer, Aliyah Winter, Shannon Novak, Yuki Kihara, Shu Lea Cheang, Bronte Perry, Micha Cárdenas, Martine Gutierrez and essa may ranapiri.

17 Daniel Sanders, *P4r451t3* (blog), https://artspace-aotearoa.nz/reading-room/a-conversation-between-bronte-perryand-daniel-john-corbett-sanders

18 Nicholas Boyon, 'LGBT+ Pride 2021 Global Survey Points to a Generation Gap around Gender Identity and Sexual Attraction,' Ipsos, 9 June 2021, https://www.ipsos.com/en-us/news-polls/ipsos-lgbt-pride-2021-global-survey

19 Progress as a result of protest for takatāpui, LGBTQIA+ and MVPFAFF+ people in Aotearoa over the last fifty years includes the Gay Liberation movement sparked by Ngāhuia Te Awekōtuku (1970s); Homosexual Law Reform (1986); the Civil Union Act (2004); same-sex marriage through the Marriage (Definition of Marriage) Amendment Act passed in 2013; Births, Deaths, Marriages, and Relationships Registration Act Amendment allowing the change of sex marker on birth certificates (2021). See: PrideNZ, 'Timeline: Politics', www.pridenz.com/timeline/politics.html.

20 See Will Hansen and Kerryn Pollock, who argue that discrimination against diverse genders and sexualities was introduced to Aotearoa by Europeans, who brought their conservative Christian values and introduced British laws criminalising homosexuality after the signing of Te Tīriti o Waitangi. British colonisation led to the adoption of British laws, 'including the law which criminalised sodomy'. Will Hansen and Kerryn Pollock, '50 Years of Gay Liberation in Aotearoa', *The Spinoff*, 28 February 2022, https://thespinoff.co.nz/society/28-02-2022/50-years-of-gayliberation-in-aotearoa

21 Originally meaning 'intimate companion of the same sex', the term takatāpui was reclaimed in the 1970s as an identity in response to 'Western ideas of sex, sexuality and gender, and emphasises one's identity as Māori as inextricably linked to their gender identity, sexuality or variation of sex characteristics'. Rainbow Youth Inc & Tīwhanawhana Trust, 'Definition of Takatāpui', Takatāpui: A resource hub, https://takatapui.nz/definition-of-takatapui.

22 The same month, The RainbowYOUTH Hub in Tauranga was arsoned (the judge ruled 'not a hate crime', despite both perpetrators' use of homophobic slurs to the police). See: Sandra Conchie, 'Arsonists who torched Tauranga Rainbow Youth and Gender Dynamix building sentenced', *New Zealand Herald*, 29 November 2022, www.nzherald.co.nz/bay-of-plenty-times/news/arsonists-who-torched-tauranga-rainbow-youth-and-gender-dynamix-building-sentenced/O6WBUFV5CZFDRFVPKYJOHTFRME.

23 Sam Duckor-Jones, 'How Gloria of Greymouth Rose

Again', *The Spinoff*, 12 June 2022, https://thespinoff.co.nz/society/12-06-2022/how-gloria-of-greymouth-rose-again

24 This phrase was used by FAFSWAG MC Akashi and also features heavily in the work of the performance collective Hot Brown Honey. See Alex Casey, '"Decolonise and Moisturise": How the Hot Brown Honeys are changing the face of theatre', *The Spinoff*, 7 February 2017, https://thespinoff.co.nz/hot-brown-honey/07-02-2017/decolonise-and-moisturise-how-the-hot-brown-honeys-are-changing-the-face-of-theatre

25 MVPFAFF+ is an acronym for mahu, vakasalewalewa, palopa, fa'afafine, akava'ine, fakaleiti or leiti, fakafifine and more. It was coined to enhance Moana-specific terms for diverse genders and was intended to provide additional terminology to the acronym LGBTQI+.

26 Louie Zalk-Neale, 'Louie Zalk-Neale: Ngā Manuhiri Taura', Govett-Brewster Art Gallery | Len Lye Centre, 11 August 2022, www.circuit.org.nz/work/kei-matairangi-t-ku-kainga-inaianei

27 Ibid.

28 Louie Zalk-Neale, 'Louie Zalk-Neale: *kei matairangi tōku kāinga ināianei* (2020): Artist's statement', CIRCUIT Artist Moving Image, 2020, https://web.archive.org/web/20220811235711/https:/govettbrewster.com/events/performance/louie-zalk-neale-ngamanuhiri-taura-the-visiting-r?date=2022-08-27.

29 Included within this history are collectives who sit beyond the art world's definitions of performance art, most notably kapa haka and Moana performing arts groups.

30 *APT4 Performance: An introduction to the Pasifika Divas*, 2018, www.youtube.com/watch?v=f-jX96w0pQY

31 bell hooks, 'Is Paris Burning?', in *Black Looks: Race and representation* (Boston, MA: South End Press, 1992), 145–56.

32 Tapuaki Helu, FAFSWAG at Documenta 15: Interview with Tapuaki Helu by Pacific Cooperation Foundation, 2022, www.pcf.org.nz/news/fafswagatdocumenta15-aeg5k-tpp9x.

33 Daniel Sanders and Bronte Perry, 'A Conversation between Bronte Perry and Daniel John Corbett Sanders,' Artspace Aotearoa, 8 December 2021, https://artspace-aotearoa.nz/reading-room/a-conversation-between-bronte-perryand-daniel-john-corbett-sanders

34 At the time, Khye Hitchcock was curatorial assistant at Artspace, and Ahilapalapa Rands was public programmes intern. Whether coincidentally or because of their presence, a large number of Artspace volunteers at that time were queer.

35 In this context, 'kaupapa' encapsulates the concept and activity of the artwork.

36 Joe, 'Seven Gestures'.

37 Pinkwashing is a marketing/communication strategy that serves to slap a rainbow on organisations, governments and systems as a marker of inclusivity even as those organisations continue to perpetuate systemic injustices and oppression against both queer folk and people of colour.

38 Khye Hitchcock: I have used the terms 'masc' and 'femme' to describe two different instances of smith's drag. The use of 'drag king' or 'drag queen' in this instance did not feel appropriate as both these terms come with a particular intention and aesthetic that is different from what smith does. It's not a fantasy of royalty; it's intentionally occupying the gutter. 'Masc' and 'femme' refer to culturally accepted masculine and feminine signifiers. Drag bogan might also be a term that could work for smith. 'Bogan' is New Zealand slang for a person whose speech, clothing, attitude and behaviour are considered unrefined or unsophisticated.

39 The Dorian Club was a private members club located on the second floor in Cashel Mall in central Christchurch and created space for queer people in the time before homosexual law reform. I strongly suspect a link to The Dorian Society, which was a group in Te Whanganui-a-Tara from the 1960s to the late 1980s. Members provided mutual support for each other and were a driving force in homosexual law reform. They set out to 'promote a social life amongst its members, to promote mutual helpfulness, tolerance, and respect, and to afford amenities to its members for mental and moral improvement and rational recreation of every kind'. See: Museum of New Zealand Te Papa Tongarewa, 'The Dorian Society: An entrée into Wellington's homosexual world', 26 September 2019, www.tepapa.govt.nz/discover-collections/read-watch-play/lgbtqi-histories-aotearoa-new-zealand/dorian-society-entree

40 This references protest lines in which people often link hands with their arms in rigid tubing so it is harder for people to break the line by forcing hands apart.

41 Jennifer Katherine Shields, 'Para-: A contemporary working of parasexuality', 29 August 2014, https://jenniferkshields.nz/essay/para--a-contemporary-working-of-parasexuality

42 Sung Hwan Bobby Park, 'BTM Live', Auckland Pride Festival, 4 February 2023, https://2023.aucklandpride.org.nz/shows/btm-live

43 International examples include artists such as MC Coble, senVoodoo/Fiona McGregor, Catherine Opie, Cassils and S. J. Norman.

44 Audrey Baldwin's *Tether/Reel* (2014) and *Hobble* (2018) also both engaged with body suspension/modification.

45 The work references Chris Burden's *Trans-Fixed*, in which the artist was crucified on top of a Volkswagen beetle.

46 'And Again', X PA 2021 Archive, https://theperformancearcade.wixsite.com/website-3/2018-1/and-again

47 Robyn Peers, '"Salut": An essay by Robyn Peers', 16 February 2023, https://ivanlupi.com/index.php/2023/02/17/salut

48 Christopher Ulutupu, 'Wild Once More', Te Tuhi, 2022, https://tetuhi.art/art-archive/digital-library/read/wild-once-more

REFERENCES

'And Again'. X PA 2021 archive. https://theperformancearcade.wixsite.com/website-3/2018-1/and-again

APT4 Performance: An introduction to the Pasifika Divas. 2018. www.youtube.com/watch?v=f-jX96w0pQY

Boyon, Nicholas. 'LGBT+ Pride 2021 global survey points to a generation gap around gender identity and sexual attraction'. Ipsos, 9 June 2021. www.ipsos.com/en-us/news-polls/ipsos-lgbt-pride-2021-global-survey

Butler, Judith. *Gender Trouble: Feminism and the subversion of identity*. New York: Routledge, 1990.

Casey, Alex. '"Decolonise and Moisturise": How the Hot Brown Honeys are changing the face of theatre'. *The Spinoff*, 7 February 2017. https://thespinoff.co.nz/hot-brown-honey/07-02-2017/decolonise-and-moisturise-how-the-hot-brown-honeys-are-changing-the-face-of-theatre

Conchie, Sandra. 'Arsonists who torched Tauranga Rainbow Youth and Gender Dynamix building sentenced'. *New Zealand Herald*, 29 November 2022. www.nzherald.co.nz/bay-of-plenty-times/news/arsonists-who-torched-tauranga-rainbow-youth-and-gender-dynamix-building-sentenced/O6WBUFV5CZFDRFVPKYJOHTFRME

Duckor-Jones, Sam. 'How Gloria of Greymouth rose again'. *The Spinoff*, 12 June 2022. https://thespinoff.co.nz/

society/12-06-2022/how-gloria-of-greymouth-rose-again
Halberstam, Jack. *The Queer Art of Failure*. Durham, NC: Duke University Press, 2011.
Halperin, David M. 'The Normalization of Queer Theory'. *Journal of Homosexuality* 45, no. 2–4 (September 2003): 339–43. https://doi.org/10.1300/J082v45n02_17
Hansen, Will and Kerryn Pollock. '50 years of gay liberation in Aotearoa'. *The Spinoff*, 28 February 2022. https://thespinoff.co.nz/society/28-02-2022/50-years-of-gay-liberation-in-aotearoa
Helu, Tapuaki. 'FAFSWAG at Documenta 15: Interview with Tapuaki Helu by Pacific Cooperation Foundation'. 2022. www.pcf.org.nz/news/fafswagatdocumenta15-aeg5k-tpp9x
Holden, Madeleine. 'The Exhausting Work of LGBTQ Code-Switching'. *Vice*, 13 August 2019. www.vice.com/en/article/evj47w/the-exhausting-work-of-lgbtq-code-switching
hooks, bell. 'Is Paris Burning?'. In *Black Looks: Race and representation*, 145–56. Boston, MA: South End Press, 1992.
Joe, Nathan. 'Seven Gestures Towards a New Queer Performance in Aotearoa'. *BLOT* 1 (September 2022). www.blot.online/journal/1/seven-gestures-towards-a-new-queer-performance-in-aotearoa
Lepou, Lindah. 'Aotearoa, New Zealand. My First Performance (c. 1975): "Riding a Duck"'. 2023. www.lindahlepou.com/faafafineartist/performance-art
Museum of New Zealand Te Papa Tongarewa. 'The Dorian Society: An entrée into Wellington's homosexual world'. 26 September 2019. www.tepapa.govt.nz/discover-collections/read-watch-play/lgbtqi-histories-aotearoa-new-zealand/dorian-society-entree
——— *Shigeyuki Kihara — Taualuga: The Last Dance*. 2015. www.youtube.com/watch?v=ev-vIeSDb4I
Park, Sung Hwan Bobby. 'BTM Live'. Auckland Pride Festival, 4 February 2023. https://2023.aucklandpride.org.nz/shows/btm-live
Peers, Robyn. '"Salut": An essay by Robyn Peers'. 16 February 2023. https://ivanlupi.com/index.php/2023/02/17/salut/
PrideNZ. 'Timeline: Politics'. www.pridenz.com/timeline/politics.html
Rainbow Youth Inc & Tīwhanawhana Trust. 'Definition of Takatāpui'. Takatāpui: A resource hub. https://takatapui.nz/definition-of-takatapui
Sanders, Daniel. 'Untitled', *P4r451t3* (blog). https://p4r451t3.tumblr.com/?og=1
Sanders, Daniel and Bronte Perry. 'A Conversation between Bronte Perry and Daniel John Corbett Sanders'. Artspace Aotearoa, 8 December 2021. https://artspace-aotearoa.nz/reading-room/a-conversation-between-bronte-perry-and-daniel-john-corbett-sanders
Shields, Jennifer Katherine. 'Para-: A Contemporary Working of Parasexuality'. 29 August 2014. https://jenniferkshields.nz/essay/para--a-contemporary-working-of-parasexuality
Thomas, Melody. 'BANG! Season 2 Episode 6: Takatāpui'. *RNZ*, 2 July 2018. www.rnz.co.nz/programmes/bang/story/2018651794/bang-season-2-episode-6-takatapui
Ulutupu, Christopher. 'Wild Once More'. Te Tuhi, 2022. https://tetuhi.art/art-archive/digital-library/read/wild-once-more
Wint, Brandon. 'Not Queer like Gay. Queer like, Escaping . . .'. Facebook post, 7 February 2013. www.facebook.com/brandon.wint/posts/not-queer-like-gay-queer-like-escaping-definition-queer-like-some-sort-of-fluidi/10100296731275845/
Zalk-Neale, Louie. 'Louie Zalk-Neale *kei matairangi tōku kāinga ināianei* (2020): artist's statement'. CIRCUIT Artist Moving Image, 2020. www.circuit.org.nz/work/kei-matairangi-t-ku-kainga-inaianei
——— 'Louie Zalk-Neale: Ngā Manuhiri Taura'. Govett-Brewster Art Gallery | Len Lye Centre, 11 August 2022. https://web.archive.org/web/20220811235711/https:/govettbrewster.com/events/performance/louie-zalk-neale-nga-manuhiri-taura-the-visiting-r?date=2022-08-27

15

THE SKIN OF DISPLACED EVENT IN AOTEAROA PERFORMANCE ART

Lisa Samuels

As mental propositions, concepts are commonly considered intangible. This chapter proposes its starting concept as sensory: art skin is a term for the distributed membranes of polyvalent materials and experiences in performance art. As a sense concept, art skin is both physical — tangible, dimensional, ephemeral, interactable — and ideational, thick with material's ideas. The energy fields of the making and interpreting of art perform deformable exchanges in this tactile conceptual view. Such tactile conceptuality invokes a dialectic energy that multiplies its vectors in relation, akin to topological fields of touch with always differencing touch and concept, concept with always altering concept and touch. Art skin is protective and exposing, interior-facing and exterior-facing, and mediative matter and force. These complementary and inverting descriptions of art skin indicate how it opens different interpretive directions, including wondering about emplaced performance art as simultaneously displaced.

To be displaced is to hover and refract what are contextually proposed and queryable notions of emplacement. 'Displaced' signifies not out-of-place but forms of placement that implicate the transferences that are 'place'. Places are ground sky water outside, are cultures ideas community region, are house flat car sidewalk, are shifting bounded altered moved through, and are any of these in activated combinations. Some art places are repurposed sites or established gallery rooms, some are conjured by events and acts. Place imagines inside, and exteroceptively projects with, the experiences and materials of the art's making; places ('here' and 'there') form part of any art event; and place expresses interactively with any art perceiver. Displacement's *dis*, the English-language formative prefix, attaches with the word it inverts, a bound morpheme waving its alternative and provisional attachability.

In performance art something moves and sounds in provisional place and time. Breath, temperature, context inveigle. Performance art events always involve locale, and in this chapter the examples occur in Aotearoa New Zealand, a location both illimitable in its interpretability and compassed by many considerations. These considerations include what we are where 'we' is many, our consciousness of the flora, fauna, and elements who lived here without humans prior to the last millennium, the deep contingency-commitment complexes of human arrivals and the values of their earlier lived places, the suffusions of epicolonialism and faster travel, our relations with symbols, and how we make art for and with the other-than-human. In Aotearoa, place interacts with the Te Awa Tupua Act of 2017 and subsequent similar legal moves that recognise and protect the being rights of waterways and land areas. In Oceania, place and displace also interact with two 1884 inventions that reoriented planetary space-time imaginaries: first, the abstract line of the prime meridian, 'over there' in the United Kingdom, and second, the mapped irregular angles of the international date line, 'over here' near New Zealand. These contingent materialised topologies bear on the making and perception of any art in Aotearoa.

Some art-makers here experience their emplaced embodiment tethers as spiritual, (or) as granular elemental connectedness, coaxing or shocking the art material to connect with realms that are not of the everyday. Some propose embodiment as wet electric human decorated with clothes and other symbols and performing with art as socius. Many makers look both ways, as with Tāwhanga Nopera (Te Arawa, Ngāti Tūwharetoa, Ngāpuhi), whose complex performance I witnessed in the Gus Fisher Gallery in Tāmaki Makaurau Auckland on 25 June 2020. My other example is an experimental moving image installation curated by Elle Loui August, titled *Mercury*, and including contributions from Elena Betros López, Juliet Carpenter and Nell Thomas. *Mercury* lifted a large screen from normative flat-wall

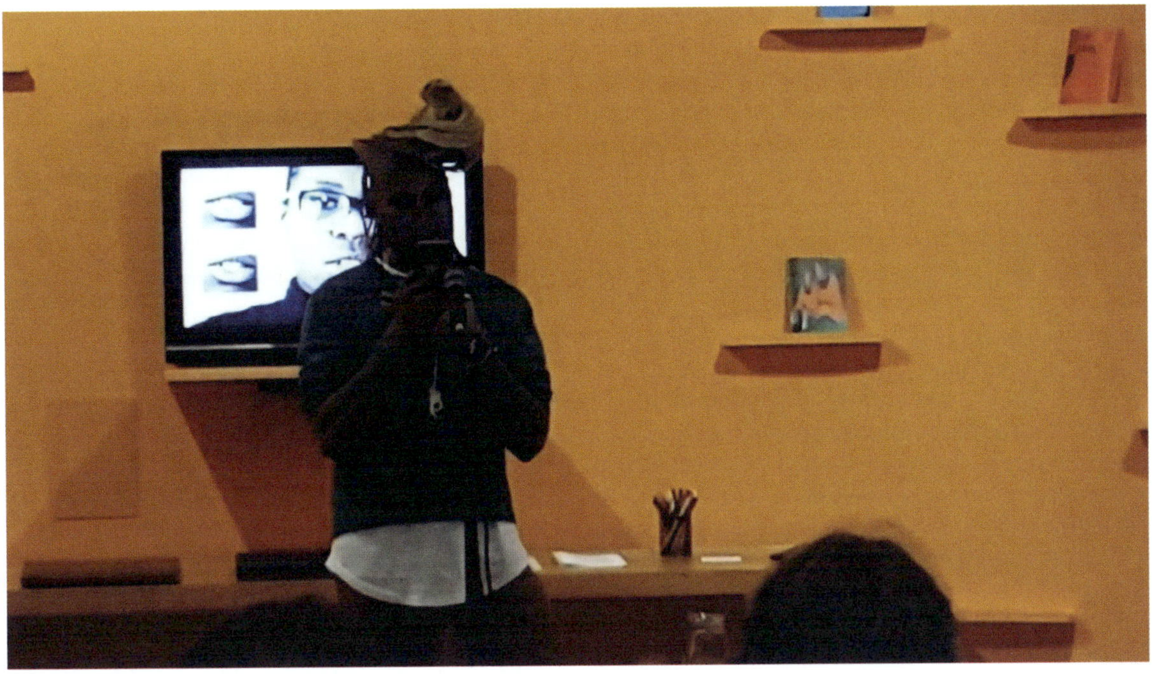

Tāwhanga Nopera (Te Arawa, Ngāti Tūwharetoa, Ngāpuhi), Gus Fisher Gallery, Tāmaki Makaurau Auckland, 25 June 2020. *Courtesy the artist. Video still by Lisa Samuels*

emplacement into a re-angled shimmering. I didn't experience the *Mercury* installation when it played in Tāmaki Makaurau on 2 July 2016; I've now observed a version of the work repeatedly in an online storage form. These two performances are the art examples of this chapter. Each of them opened up tactile concepts of art skin and event idea.

EACH WORK OF ART WAS TEMPORALLY EMPLACED, AND YET

Each work of art was temporally emplaced, and yet Tāwhanga Nopera is an artist whose presences conjure in multiple ways. Tāwhanga connects to their 'whānau, hapū and iwi, or family, subtribes and tribes'.[1] A performance transports and performs such connections, which are displaced from their multi-temporal, embodied and geophysical contexts into the art skin event. So time opens: blood history present and future, loved relations, ghosts and incipient generations co-perform their appearances. Tāwhanga also connects with the other-than-human in their work with 'raranga, a traditional Māori weaving process'.[2] In the June performance, Tāwhanga is wearing a raranga headpiece, whose botanical times are also in the event. Weaving's botanical fabric and processes connect plant, water, land, air and human experiences. Craft knowing happens as humans employ the woven botanical fabric. Meanwhile, the botanical fibres perform their own motives, tactility, movement and timespan. They hold and release soil, interact with air and water and transpire plant breath; they transport the weathers in which they've grown, and they connect with their botanical forebears and futurities. So Tāwhanga is bearing and wearing the plant's land, water and air. The weaving is like a resonance chamber attached symbiotically, prosthetically, with the human body time of the performance event.

Each work of art was temporally emplaced, and yet a storage version of *Mercury* can be digitally experienced, with permission and in an altered format: with pause buttons, on a screen unlike the installation's screen heft, time, dimensions and venue. The work's July 2016 site-specific moment is partly recorded by Victoria Wynne-Jones, whose response ('Sparkling Winter Tonic: Elle Loui August's "Mercury"') indicates how *Mercury* was situated in the repurposed building area that midwinter day. In the accompanying images, photographed by Jennifer French, you can see how the untethered screen lifts away from the habitual flat-wall emplacement of video and film, an emplacement associable with museums where wall art hangs. Normatively presented straight-walled films flatten out and cancel the back space 'behind' them: the representation portal postulates your looking into a set otherness. By contrast, *Mercury* is untethered. It lifts its sizable screen from any background, displacing film's orientations, to which it also connects. Film and other moving image work can be projected onto many surfaces, and the manifestation surface of these projections exists conceptually as a kind of skin. In the *Mercury* performance, the tilted and floating position of the screen evokes a sense of hovering image skin as dimensionally deep-surface, both evidently present and happening elsewise. The moving image skin becomes a performance art. Behind and around the screen of *Mercury*'s performance is you, walking.

OUT OF THE BACKGROUND

Out of a back room Tāwhanga Nopera appeared walking through the close crowd gathered in the gallery. Already bearing other places as proposed above, Tāwhanga carries those places in multiple ways to the front of the venue. Displacing genre expectations — the event is billed as a poetry reading — this performance from the start embodies multiple tactile concepts. On Tāwhanga's head the crown of weaving is cracking the air in tiny sonic cracks, the flowing raranga-woven braids flicking nearly to the floor. On Tāwhanga's upper body there is normative urban shirt- and jumper-type wear, displaced street identity human walk clothes. Below Tāwhanga's hips there is no evident clothing; the human legs and feet establish skin time, tangible concept dis-placing by comparison the clothed audience's covered flesh. In the performer's front position, defined by cleared floor area and a microphone, Tāwhanga lifts a mobile phone. Displaced from ordinary utility (making a call or an online search) to an unidentified channel, the phone begins an audio reading and Tāwhanga's mouth moves. The poetry reading begins, and continues, as a lip-sync to a recorded voice. This recording — of someone else in voice and time place, with a biologically female human pitch and a North American accent — comes from an unannounced source.[3] The performance turns the recording from that other person's voice, now relayed through mobile phone technology across time via the soundwaves present in the performance embodiment, with a leap. The leap is the displacement of lingualism across the multi-part co-presented aspects of the art body, the voice of Tāwhanga not a voice but connected with voice, holding and carrying like a translation (from *translatio*, Latin's 'to carry across'). Each genre, each type of act, is lifted and displaced in and with another. In their work and life, Tāwhanga identifies with and performs the two-spirit energies of takatāpui, which names gender and sexual identity fluidity. Each identity is lifted and performed in the other. The weaving of layers intensifies.

Out of its online storage, the archive version of the moving image work *Mercury* starts (for one second) and ends (for ten seconds) as black-screen. This screen is visual nothing-saturation, if we take visual art's black to be the absence of light and colour. Conceptually, the work's archived black-screen start and end are the same, where sameness equals alterity in identity: that is, when something starts and ends in material similitude, both end and start can be said to share and switch, dialectically, position across their occurrences. Yet a going-forward directionality is also performed in *Mercury*, by propulsions of diachronic visual increments and, eventually, by two sustained deliveries of spoken words. In the archive version of the (6 minutes 55 seconds) work, the opening 20 seconds perform three black-screens that interact with six different increments of kinetic visuals. The split-edit presentation is of recurred envelopes of perception in an ethos that both cuts and connects. As throughout *Mercury*, real-world things — or 'positive' visual percepts — are filmed in heat-sensing infrared, appearing as silvery greyscale. These first 20 seconds of 'positive' visuals show sky-cloud-tree up, ground-tree out laterally, car window framing passing sky and trees, and in one second a human hand image. Part-way through *Mercury*, we see the torso, framed from shoulders to hips, and also the arms and hands of a gesturing person among park-like trees and ground; another time, the same actor's sun-glint hair displaces and joins the leaf effects of sun-glint trees. The appearance of light in hair and leaf inverts via infrared what is darkness — dark hair, dark leaves — in the filmed percepts. The interplay of positive and negative image skin intensifies in four sustained times when another layer emerges in *Mercury*'s art skin: computer-generated colour screens occur and hold the entire visual field as they internally dissolve. These colour screens perform another whole position within the image skin's other focalisations and black-screens. The digital colour fields displace and also embody as alterity the filtered normate percepts, the swatches of black-screen and the representational kinetic images (outdoor and car scenes) captivated in the camera work. The colour screens simulate crepuscular shifts, the changes in light when the part of Earth where we're standing shifts toward or away from the sun. The colour fields are — somewhere else and here. The art skin's layers intensify as thickenings and sheaved displacements.

SOMEWHERE ELSE AND HERE

Mercury's colour fields can be seen as having drunk the colour that is (present) occluded in the greyscale representations hovering in other zones of *Mercury*'s skin. The colour fields and black-screens also propose a-teleological, non-determinate, positive negations of the parts of *Mercury* we can recognise as action in two fields: the visuals and the sonic layers. In terms of the mimetic visuals, moving images of trees, water reflection, sky, torso, hand and arm actions, and focalised car window observation all occur as outer skin of normate filmed perception. The black-screens and the colour fields are inner or other skin, digital dermis and hypodermis, technically conceptual fleshes transferring and infusing with the artfully representational flesh of the mimetic place and body action images. Within and across what might seem to be sharp separations, these visual art skin types bleed and overlap. For example, the black-screens in *Mercury* do move: not (perceptibly) visually, but temporally and sonically, because moving image work necessarily moves with time and this work almost always includes sound. Non-visually-moving black-screen performs the continuity of non-event, and other-event, existing in a here-and-elsewhere relation with the apparent event images. We are somewhere elses and heres. The colour fields move markedly, morphing their colour tones — in

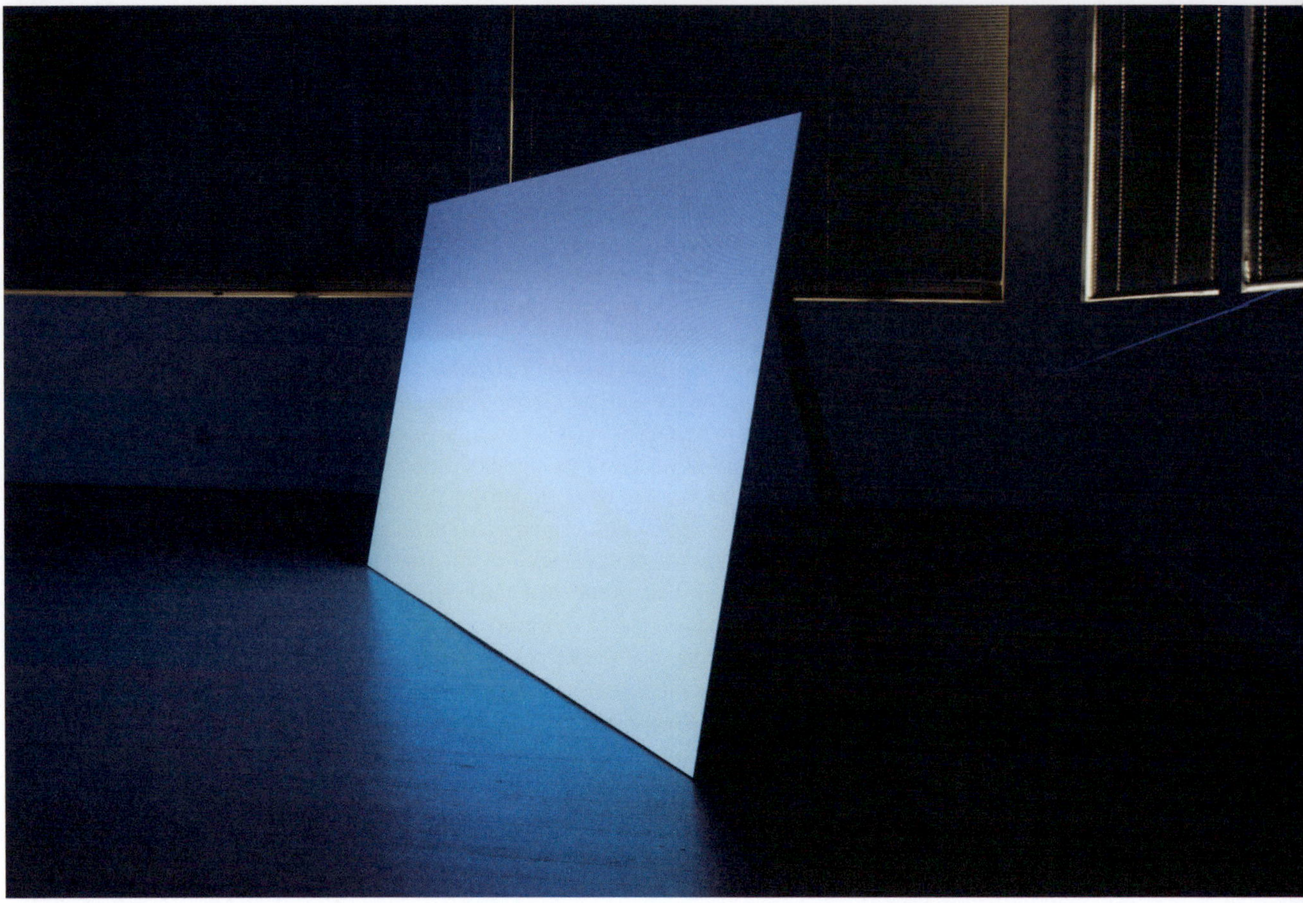

Elle Loui August, *Mercury*, 2016, with Juliet Carpenter, Nell Thomas and Elena Betros López. *Courtesy the artist. Photos by Jennifer French*

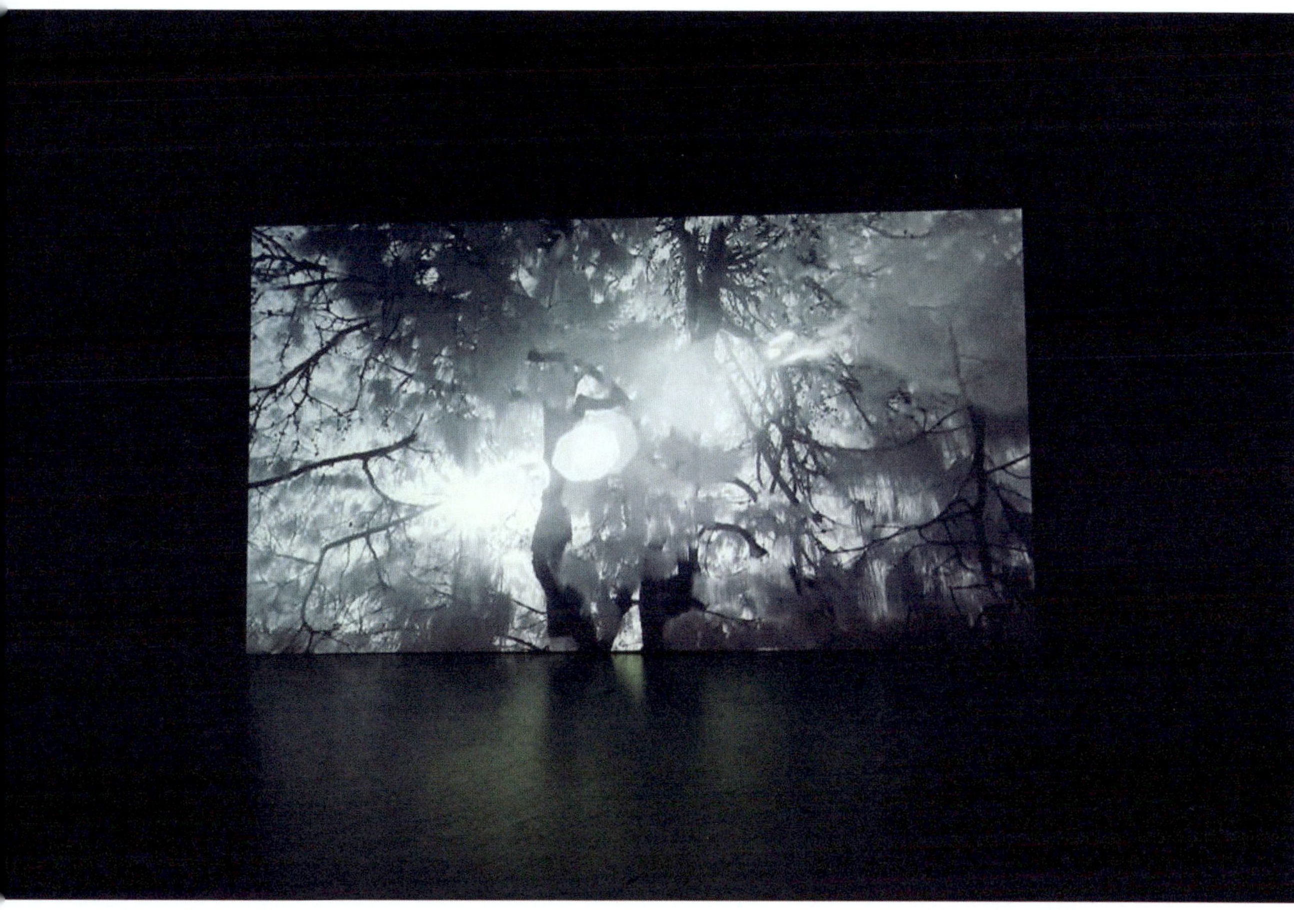

film terms they shift with dissolve. They are conceptually simultaneous inherences with the skin of the 'positive' event images and the skin of the black-screen 'negatives'. A triangulated dialectic moves among these three primary visual ingredients, slanted in the hovering screen of the *Mercury* installation. The art event displacedly shifts its visual skin. The work's friction can be interpreted as a topological field suturingly perforated by increments of displacing force: in terms of friction, the visual manifestations hold together in the overall artwork; in terms of force, the visuals pull free in the individual increments. In energy terms, conjoining friction is (almost) overcome by revelatory force. The circulation of the ecology of the work is tensed opening, not only allied with how film and moving image work always beckon to their made places, geophysical and editing suite alike. *Mercury* cycles its ingredients across and through each other: colour fields and black-screen propose source and target sites in relation to each other and in dialectical relations with the moving, representationally resolved image increments that are staged from point perspective. Each ingredient performs as either/or, both/and source and target, so the dialectics are kinetic and displacing, structurally intact and relationally inverting. This interpretable situation especially obtains in the 2016 installation version of *Mercury*, when the work cycled continually with no marked beginning or end.

Tāwhanga Nopera's June 2020 performance occurred in a place dis-placed from it, an art gallery whose layers irrefragably co-imbued the extended moment. This chapter's image shows a still from a video clip made spontaneously with my phone. I was magnifying to get a closer visual recording of Tāwhanga's moving (unspeaking yet co-reticulating) mouth and apparently casual (experienced as ceremonially struck) posture. In this image, the evident dialectics are in a stretched relation between exterior and interior. The art skin is multi-part: there are the weaving crown and body presentations, discussed earlier. There is also the sublimation of the exterior recorded voice's affect into a postural co-performance — the hand on the chest performs as affectively connected, across disconnection, with the emotive expression of the phone-transmitting voice. Bridges across (cultures, times, technes, bodies) are performed as art skin imbued. The voice is somewhere else and here. Simultaneously, a co-incidental gallery accompaniment became integral, in the way that context can imbue, frame or flood art's performance. On the back wall behind Tāwhanga, a video spun out multiple symbol-pattern and kinetic human-form images. At the moment of the image, another human face speaks behind, also without audible words. Embedded in the same video image are two mirror mouths of the same video head, mouths displaced to the side and doubled. None of the three on video are audible, all are actively articulating. This context threw up perpendicular co-occurrences with Tāwhanga's lip-syncing displacement. Somewhere elses and heres, mouths in motile constellating dialectics, intensified in this performance art.

BREATHING EVERYPLACE

The mouth is a skin transition with wetness and potential for sounds and forming words, with potential for drinking liquid, eating sustenance, kissing, stretching, closing together to hold in interior body darkness and opening to let in light and air, holding and framing laughter, vomiting out toxicity. And for taking in and pushing out air and breath. Words necessarily involve breathing, because organic human bodies cannot speak without breath. In Tāwhanga Nopera's performance, breath occurs in the performing body, in the technologically conveyed words of a different body speaking via the phone device, in the recurrently cycling video bodies, and in the bodies of the gallery audience. Transpiration also occurs in the breath of the plants that grew and were turned into weaving that crowns the performer. The breath of connections with whānau, hapū and iwi coexist alongside conjurations of prior and future breath of all these present, and present-absent, beings. Simultaneous multi-breath accompanies the recorded words we hear, especially since words are never exclusively focalised as objects for semantic or ontological singularity. Words are also jointure and panoply, and their multi-place connectivity is rendered overt in the art skins of this performance. These skins of respiration, of actual and potential presence, of multi-layered articulatory embodiments, infused and displaced the skin of this art event, where displacement is layering of place-time-bodies tangibly and conceptually present. Displacement manifests in multiple, imbricated, embodied contexts that demonstrate the transferences of place. The mouth of the non-speaking performing artist co-performs the recorded voice, which is the only normative vocal we ever hear in Tāwhanga's performance. At the same time, the artist's own somatic voice is performed as pure potential: its absence opens a resonant gap. We expect that a performer of poetry will activate vocal cords, will 'speak'. To speak without speaking is to rupture vocality with a displacement that both occurs the potentiality of voice and strains to hear the invisible. A synaesthesia of habitative energy shunts through itself as we listen, our audience bodies expectant. We perform our own not-speaking more loudly because our performer is not speaking. Our not-speaking also displaces the potential of speaking, making us both more aware of its absence and more aware of the breath it takes to make speech summon and abate and multiply. Tāwhanga's not-speaking transfers vocal energy outside of the performing body: in a conceptually somatic revisioning of ventriloquism, Tāwhanga's performance *throws the voice*. This situation intensifies the outside sense of bodies and sounds and also the plural fostering vacuum of the performing body. Tāwhanga is holding the voice that emerges in the sound apparatus of the phone-screen, throwing and catching it again in a tactile conceptual loop.

In the archive version of *Mercury*, the sonic inter-occurrences are resolutely somatic: first off, there is a breath: *hhhh*. The first visual image seems suddenly brought into being by the sound of that forced exhale puff of human lungs, very near to an articulation of affective significance though it speaks no word. Breath is the suffusive sonic of this moving image work: there are single and multiple breath notes, expressive and sometimes nearly anxious intakes and exhales. At times we hear sharp co-deflecting chorales of breath, multiple human lungs 'speaking' breath-points quickly across and with each other. The inhabitable range of co-breath is dimensionally mimetic with any human observer who is breathing, both here and 'there'. Experiencing *Mercury* can prompt any hearing human observer to become conscious of human breath. For a non-hearing and sighted observer, human breath is present in the body, known to be present in the work and its makers, and perhaps affected responsively by the often swiftly cycling images. For the hearing but non-sighted or low-vision witness, the sonic skin of *Mercury* can blow into the body. (For non-hearing observers, one could wish for a print score of the work's sonics, not sub-titles so much as a parallel piece with the scripted words and with sonic action descriptions — like 'rising intonation inhale' and 'declarative exhale'. Similarly, a descriptive audio score of the image action could be fashioned for blind/low-vision witnesses.) A critical ingredient of human speech and life, breath mostly performs in *Mercury* without resolved words and without correlative visual figuration: the skin of the inner lungs and vocable physiology is mostly non-denotatively performed. The skin of displaced event happens where skin is not only outer but inside, in the nerves of the bronchioles, the receptors of the inner eyes, the canals of the ears. *Mercury*'s art skin performs awareness of positioning in both co-present elsewheres and receptive perceptions. Simultaneously, *Mercury* can be interpreted to propose its technological artifice as coextensive with organic bodies: the work breathes where technology does not need oxygen. The dislocated, displaced breaths, not correlated with 'actors', become the moving image work's own sound skin. *Mercury*'s techne then is conceptually organic, conjuring and distributing its outer and inner life forms. *Mercury* inverts the nature of art's oxygen in a techno-somatic cycling that suggests our inner skins are also, as we witness, technological. That is one way we join the work while we are under way with its performance.

INTERIOR SKIN AND CONTEXT BOUNDS

The interior skin of Tāwhanga Nopera's performance is partly in the ears, in hearing and in the conduit of hearing and sounding that is the whole body. Yet because Tāwhanga is lip-syncing, not speaking aloud, the present body is displaced from the sound event with which it co-occurs. The silent mouth is more acutely an interior skin: when an ontology is displaced from normative function, its absoluteness swerves to a different awareness of what it is and what it might be 'for'. A non-speaking mouth performatively allied with speakingness opens negative space in the function and force of the mouth. Correlatively, in the tactile conceptuality of this performance event, the cave of the gallery room also shifts its perceptible nature as the context in which Tāwhanga's performance is ephemerally embedded. This performance occurs as part of an exhibition titled *Queer Algorithms*. My copy of the paper flyer, available at the gallery that day, says the exhibit ran 'Feb 15–~~May 2~~June 27' and that it was 'FREE'. What the flyer calls the 'intimate poetry reading' held in connection with the exhibit was scheduled for 29 April and then re-scheduled to 25 June, in line with that month's easing of the Covid-19 pandemic lockdown restrictions in Tāmaki Makaurau Auckland. The interior skin of Tāwhanga's performance folds into itself not only what this chapter is interpreting about its displaced layers but also the energy of that public time: the pressure of emerging from a strict pandemic lockdown into looser possibilities like shared public art space. As I've already emphasised, an art event is never separable from its occurrence: its own skin co-imbues with the contextual implications and material of its staging. Again and always differently, context reveals and creates bodily contiguities with the framed event. Emerging from the contagion severity of Covid-19 Level 4 lockdown into permitted art sociality made the overall embodiment of the performance even more, arguably acutely more, body-conscious for everyone present. Here we were maskless together while elsewhere, including in the North America of the thrown recording voice, humans were in the thick of masked contagion and death. Especially from June 2020 to August 2021, when Covid-19 had no free purchase on our public breathing, the *here* of Aotearoa was in a bend of time, situated in what I elsewhere call an 'umbral poetics'.[4] The interior skin of our lungs and throats was a zone of mortal awareness. What it meant to hear each other close together, released from strict lockdown, was intensely 'intimate'.

The mimetic kinetic visuals of *Mercury* are liminal and intimately shot; and, simultaneously, their openness is interiorised. They present the bodies of trees, ground, water and sky in a park-like area; they present partial views of a person — torso, arms, hands and hair — moving in that outdoor area; and they present exterior visuals shot from and framed in the window of a moving car, at times from one side of the back seat,

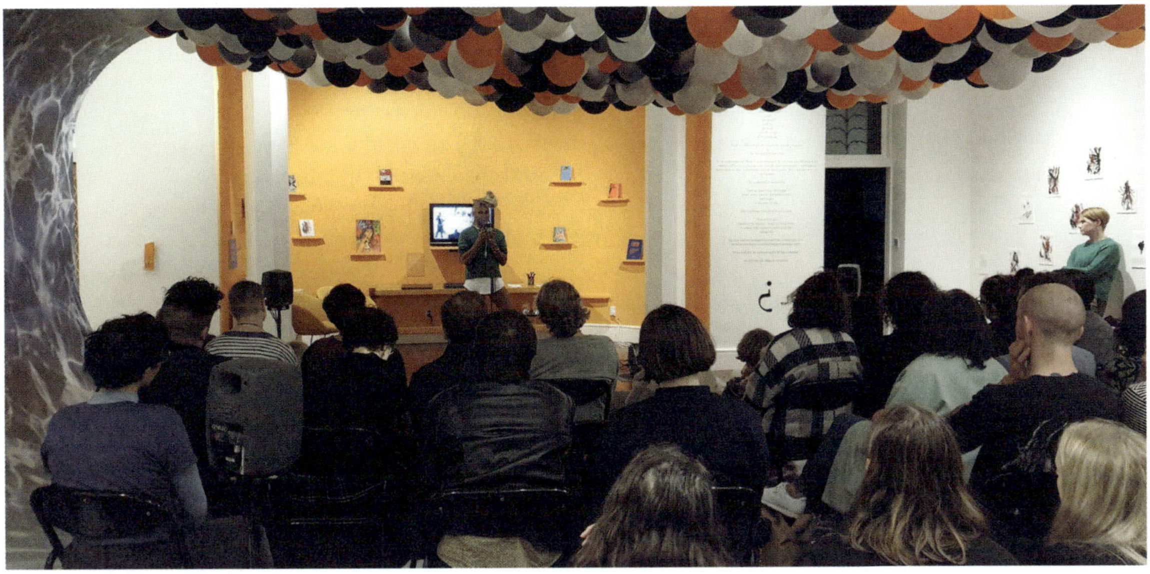

at times from the other side. Point of view is dispersed in the first case, optative in the second, and focalised in the third, where we sense the eye of a not-visible camera and camera holder looking out the window at the occasionally peopled passing road and sidewalk. Here the context of the outdoors — what and where they are — is dispersed and non-identified, not tightly held as in the Tāwhanga Nopera event with its Covid-19 framing. Yet *Mercury*'s context is partly rendered in the types of trees, and suggested in the long-haired human, all cast with infrared's black-white, naturalistically inverted. What can be taken as representationally normative in its real-time happening, inhabitable as action in liminal (moving automobile) and outdoor areas, is not precisely or wholly re-presented in the forms on screen. The occurrences are not recapturable from agentive perspectives nor situated in a known film-like tale. Like the colour screens that co-form the interior skin of *Mercury*, these situationally mimetic figurations are lifted from their correlative naturing and co-imbued with the techno-skin of how moving image work can project its senses, principally those of hearing and seeing. The cycling of conceptual sight cross-blends the human hair with the tree-leaves as hair, for example. Each becomes the other's hair, enmeshed and performed as perforable. Cycling with them, chemically speaking, are the black-screens and the digital colour screens, movement and visual hover, exemplifying this chapter's point about ontological co-imbuing in the skin of displaced event. The techne conjoins the differential figures, whose location specifications fleetingly anchor in a sight of the volcanic island of Rangitoto and, more steadily, in the leaves of pōhutukawa and other trees of the North Island of Aotearoa. We can consider the distributed curation and the geophysically blended sources of *Mercury* as dialectically co-constituted with these depictive filmic inter-correlations. The suturing chiasmatic connections of the topological continue to revolve.

Tāwhanga Nopera, Gus Fisher Gallery, Tāmaki Makaurau Auckland, 25 June 2020. *Courtesy the artist. Photo by Lisa Samuels*

VOICE BOXES

In *Mercury*, an unseen human voice sometimes produces words. The voice is both proximal and distal to the vocalising norms of Aotearoa, because the speaker, artist Elena Betros López, comes from Naarm Melbourne, Australia. In the archive version of *Mercury*, the first soundtrack moment of a human speaking is at 2.52. Here is a transcription of the words from 2.52 to 3.34 (forward slashes indicate short pauses):

> pensive **[rising intonation]** / yeah **[longer pause]** / pensive; internal, condescending, neutral, analytical, mannered, hesitant, understanding, generous, warm, hidden, considered / her eyes, breath.

The pace is measured, slow, and the articulation is distinct. From 5.12 to 6.35, further words come into hearing, again some with a slight lilt toward question inflection:

> often / often, yes / often her body moves quickly and suddenly, shifting in to different moods / she's heaten / heaten **[rising intonation]** / yes / as her moods are shifting, she is shifting. / constantly, yes / her posture, mouth, hands, breath, eyes / temperature moving between warm and cool, but never gives anything to hot or cold / she meanders / yeah.

The listening experience is of a reflective delivery, and the words indicate that this is speaking as response: answers to posited near-questions, and the affirmation ('yeah') of what's been declared, operate in the zone of dialogue response. The female-identified voice is singular, natural, not treated sound but human voice. In consultation with Elle Loui August in the end stages of writing this chapter, I learned that the words spoken are re-assemblages of some unidentified portions of Simone de Beauvoir's 1954 novel, *Les Mandarins*. Beauvoir's words are selected, rewritten and recorded by Elena Betros López and transposed into and through the technological skin surface, the breath skin, of the moving image event that is *Mercury*. As with Tāwhanga Nopera's performance, dictation and translation effects are on the move. Words are uttered without situated explanation, and without the context of any apparent need for explanation to occur. Speech, then, is displaced; it lifts from its norms of instrumental act-event and situates as part of the performance art. If speech is commonly socially emplaced — one speaks to someone who is presumed capable of a measure of understanding in order to effect some communication — then this art speech reframes that speech placement and expands zones of lingual similitude. Simone de Beauvoir's printed female character in a fictive room is transported as the translated vocalised fragments of another woman recording in a different room, both of whose (dis)placements become, elsewhere in Oceania, part of a blend of motion, sound, circumambient and navigable screen and depictive images in a new room where the *Mercury* installation occurs. This is a performance of linked and diffracted intertextuality, whose unlabelled sources indicate and add to the embeddedness of known and unknown art and place co-texts. Moreover, in these *Mercury* zones, the speaking voice, using the breathing, emblooded human body, exists alternatively in this performance art as a distributed speaker who joins the apparatus, the symbiotic mechanisms, of this recorded and re-coded art. This performance art aspect transposes human biomechanics into technical energy mechanics. The technological skin of *Mercury* is conceptually somatic, and the human skin of *Mercury* is repletely technologised. The speech of life is perfused into, translated as, the speech of art.

The words captured on my video clip from Tāwhanga Nopera's phone-speaking voice partake of the discourse of uplift. Even before I learned of their source, they were readily recognisable as words from the introduction to a self-improvement retreat or self-service uplift message. Having their source identified as Esther Hicks (see endnote 3) intensifies the displacement effects in this performance. Hicks identifies as a conveyor of messages from a spirit guru she calls 'Abraham', whose invocations are to positive energy, to aligning with what are termed the Laws of Attraction. The actual and apparent distal relation of these words — somatically, technologically, locationally, lingually, culturally — with Tāwhanga's performing presence opens a potential critique of the possibility of their content, a message encouraging acting with desire. Yet this distance is legible as the tearing open of alterity into jointure. From start to end of this performance event, the art skin is stretched past identity and into dialectics of relation across dimensions of bodies, places and times. Most of the words recorded in my (necessarily selective) 1 minute 32 second phone clip are distinctly audible. I watch Tāwhanga mouthing those words and phrases with performed confidence, with what seems either a rehearsed familiarity or the ability to look at phone words on the screen and translate them instantly into a correlating lip-sync. Here is an excerpt:

> . . . we would ask that the question that you hold in your mind is — rather than I *should* do this, I should meet with these people or I need to meet with these people, we would encourage you to ask a question that is pure to its very core: I *want* to do this, it is my desire to do this.

Different understandings can be brought to the effects of this kind of discourse as embodied by Tāwhanga, to how the recorded voice's advice — allow desire to be the leading principle of participants in the referenced event — imbues this performance art. One consequence is a kind of shock within the scene: alterity, in dialect, apparent gender, discourse situation and distance, is inhabited as identity, as Tāwhanga becomes a mouthpiece for the otherness we hear. What is the position of this performance art event toward the recorded words? Is Tāwhanga's performance body in accord with these messages? Perhaps displacement is constitutive in the semantics as well as in the other aspects of this performance. But it is not part of this art's necessity, it seems to me, that we know whether to 'believe' these recorded words or resolve them in the performance. The words are lifted in; they whirr. At the same time, the recorded voice's message is that one should conjure desire to mesh with the activities one carries out. There should be a coming together of act and intent. So far as a message goes, then, the recorded voice both underscores the segregation of act and wish — because it is the topic of redress, the topic of what needs to be changed — and also introduces it. In this measure of Tāwhanga's performance, too, the skin of displaced event is riveted as polyvalent.

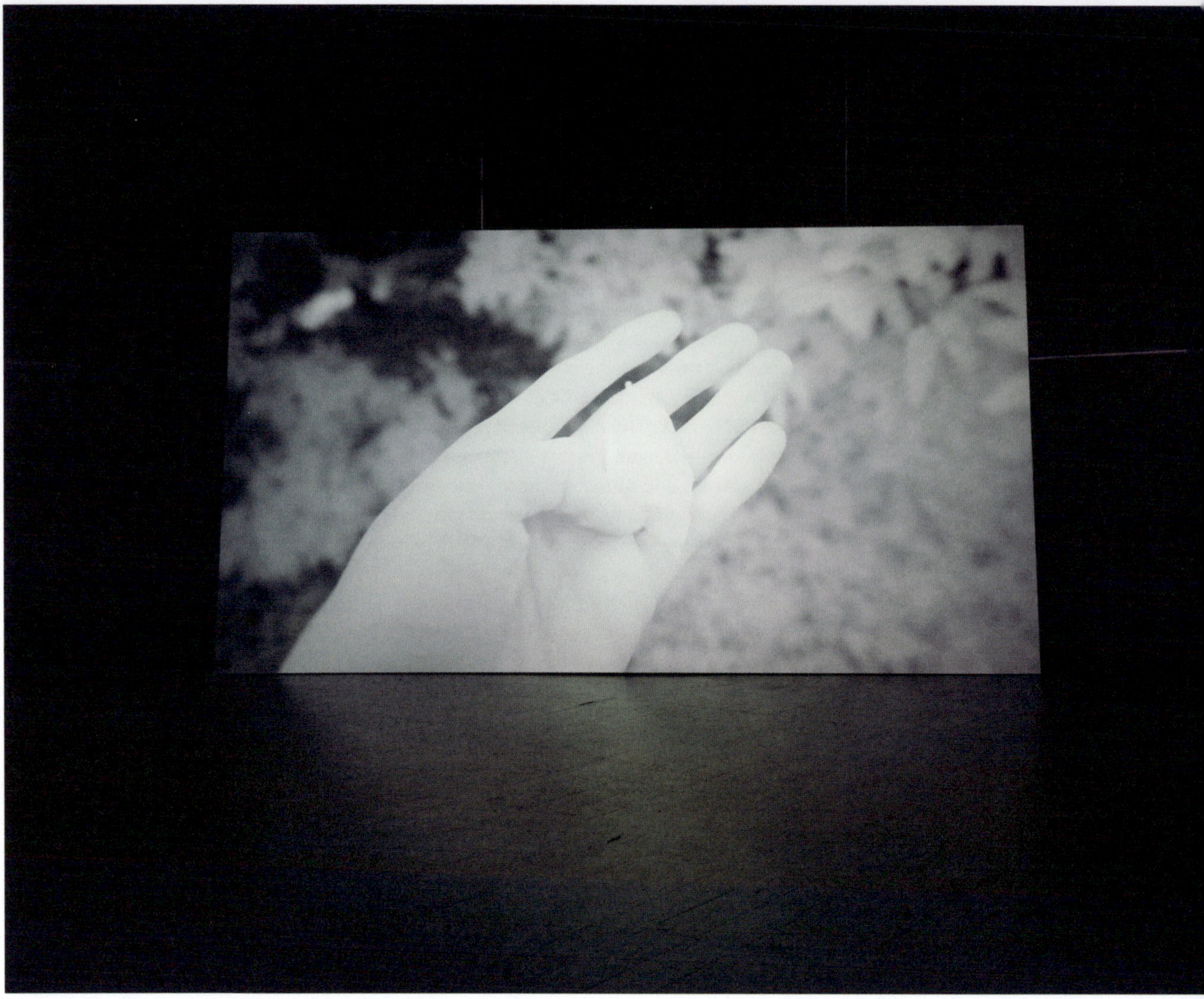

Elle Loui August, *Mercury*, 2016, with Juliet Carpenter, Nell Thomas and Elena Betros López. *Courtesy the artist. Photo by Jennifer French*

OUTRO

Sound is a constitutive aspect of the art skin concept and for the performance works attended to here. Yet even while treating of breath and speech, this paper chapter is silent unless a reader, or a reading software, speaks it aloud. Art writing in print is constrained as word and image signs interacting with sampled documentation. Archival and post-event access, such as what's happening here, displaces — thickens, differentiates, multiplies — the sensory situations of performance events. The deferrals are infinite after the performance and prove the rule that deferral also characterises 'the occurrence' as it occurs.

So the energy of making and interpreting art performs exchange, which can provoke the happy thought that your own reading body becomes the re-play zone for the conceptual and sensory information of art writing. You reanimate the words as sound and significance, and the documentary images and sensory performance as imagined projection, based on lived experience. The skin of displaced event co-occurs with you. Insofar as Aotearoa performance art happens in the epicolonial circumstances of our pervading close distances, such co-occurrence is part of what it feels like to negotiate art life here.

NOTES

1 Tāwhanga Nopera, 'ASHM Report Back', http://web.archive.org/web/20221201121725/http://ashm.info/report-back/blogger/listings/tawhanganopera

2 Ibid.

3 When I presented this material as a lecture at Wake Forest University in November 2022, Dr Tiffany Judy suggested the voice is that of positivity guru Esther Hicks. Although the broadcast wording is not identical, a sample recording from 20 March 2020 (www.abraham-hicks.com/#single/0) indicates that the voice and message type are the same as that in the mobile phone part of Tāwhanga's performance. See also www.abraham-hicks.com/about/

4 See Lisa Samuels, 'Umbral Poetics', in *Imagining What We Don't Know: Creative theory and critical bodies* (Goleta: punctum books, 2024). Also in that book, as in the present chapter, I use the term 'epicolonial' to signify our formation and imbrication with ongoing colonial values of takeover, extraction, inequality and othering.

REFERENCES

August, Elle Loui. *Mercury*. With contributions from Elena Betros López, Juliet Carpenter and Nell Thomas. Moving image installation, 2 July 2016.

Nopera, Tāwhanga. 'ASHM Report Back'. http://web.archive.org/web/20221201121725/http://ashm.info/report-back/blogger/listings/tawhanganopera

——— 'Huka Can Haka'. 19 June 2019. https://hukacanhakadotcom1.wordpress.com

——— *Performance*. Gus Fisher Gallery, 25 June 2020.

Samuels, Lisa. *Imagining What We Don't Know: Creative theory and critical bodies*. Goleta: punctum books, 2024.

Wynne-Jones, Victoria. 'Sparkling Winter Tonic: Elle Loui August's "Mercury"'. *The Pantograph Punch*, 8 September 2016. www.pantograph-punch.com/posts/mercury

16

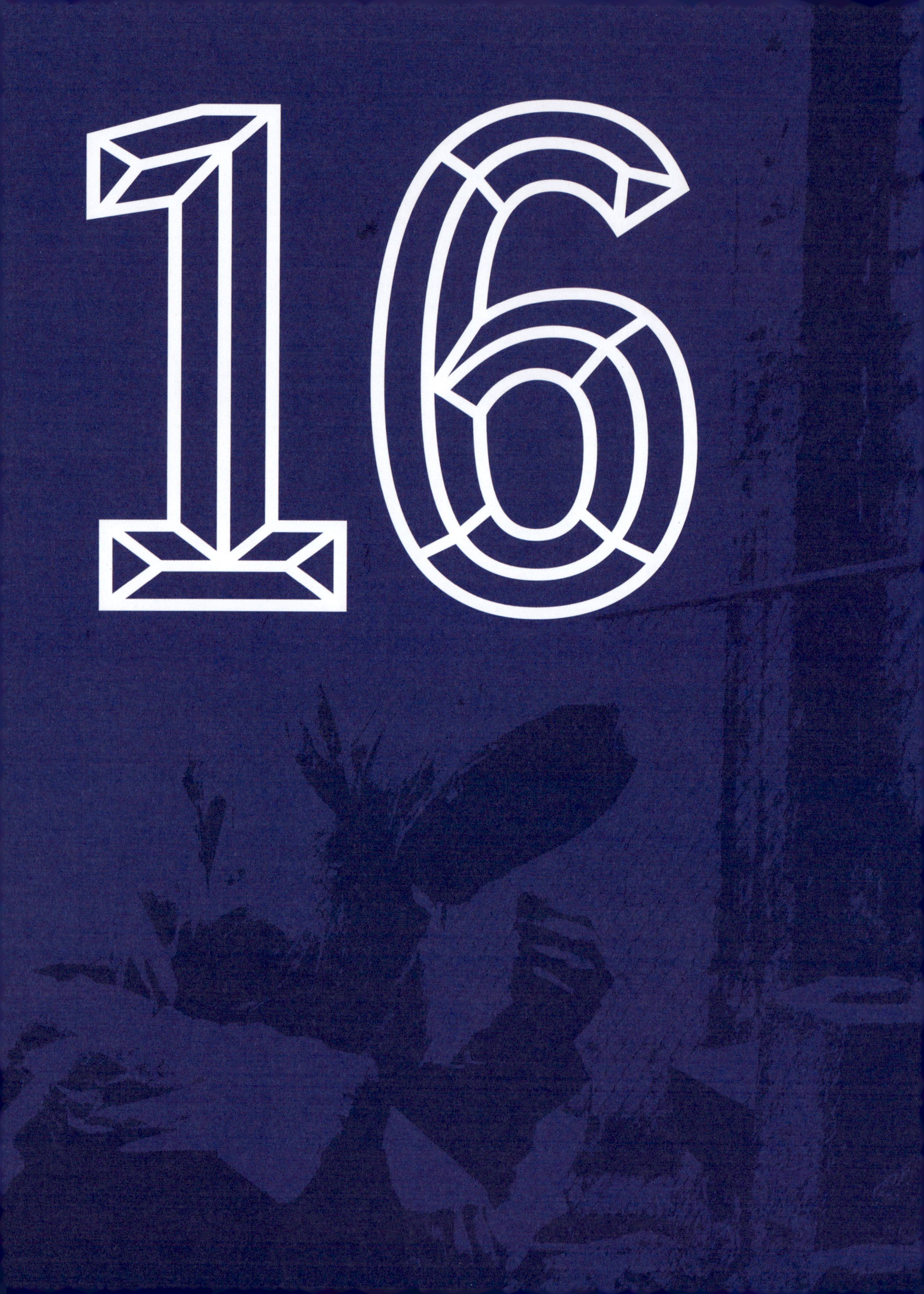

PERFORMANCE ART IN POST-QUAKE ŌTAUTAHI CHRISTCHURCH

Audrey Baldwin & Khye Hitchcock

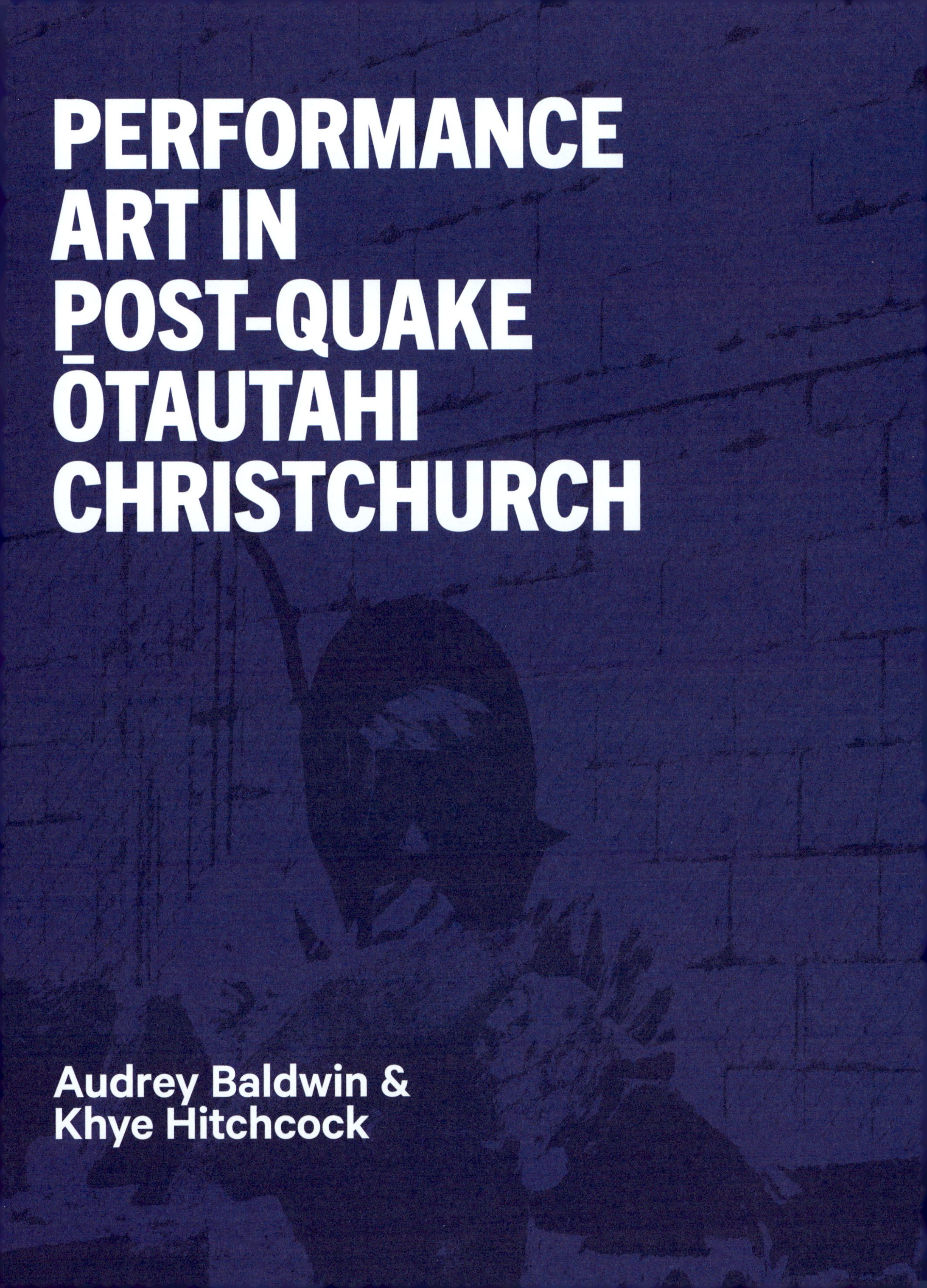

A post-disaster context gives rise to a search for meaning and a new identity beyond, but inextricably tied to, the thing(s) that happened. From 2010 to 2011, Ōtautahi Christchurch experienced several major earthquakes and tens of thousands of small ones. The most significant quake struck on Tuesday, 22 February 2011 at 12.51 p.m. and resulted in the deaths of 185 people and countless injuries and was ultimately responsible for the levelling of over three-quarters of the central city.

Since the quakes, the city's identity has been in constant flux. Te Rūnanga o Ngāi Tahu was made a statutory partner to the recovery, moving the city closer to a more meaningful Te Tīriti partnership, which has had lasting effects on the physical and social rebuild.[1] The population of the city has altered too: many people left, and those who stayed share a communal sense of solidarity, cynicism, enthusiasm and experience of trauma.

Ōtautahi has since been impacted by the horror of a terrorist attack, on 15 March 2019, against the local Muslim communities worshipping at Masjid Annur and the Linwood Islamic Centre.

Against this background, artists have continued to practise. Most galleries and civic spaces closed after the earthquakes, and as a result there has been a proliferation of direct artistic intervention into the fabric of the city. In this chapter, friends and long-time collaborators artist Audrey Baldwin (Zimbabwe-born, Ōtautahi-raised) and curator Khye Hitchcock (Pākehā; Whanganui-born and raised) discuss some of these artworks and their broader context, and explore a number of themes that have emerged in Ōtautahi performance art practices.[2]

SHAKING UP SWAMP CITY

Khye Hitchcock (KH): In early 2015 at New Brighton beach on the edge of the city, I was captivated by a tideline of flowers. As a newcomer to the city, I wondered if I'd stumbled on the remains of an art intervention. I later learned it was the remnants of River of Flowers, an annual event to commemorate the Canterbury earthquakes in which people meet along the Ōtākaro Avon River and throw flowers in the water.[3] It's a public performance (of sorts) that connects the community. In 2021, during the ten-year anniversary commemorations of the 22 February quake, I joined friends working in the Ōtākaro river corridor and contributed my own flowers to the islands of blooms heading downstream.[4]

For those who have stayed, and those of us who have joined them in this regenerating city, the creation of new narratives, new landmarks and new meanings of place is a constant activity. Pausing to remember what was lost and to acknowledge the struggles between then and now is still necessary. Since moving here I've become entangled in a community of people who think deeply about what it is to be a part of rebuilding a city in Aotearoa.

Audrey, on the other hand, was here when all the studios in the central city literally fell down and the galleries closed, and has played a significant role in collaborations and collectives that have enabled art to go on in Ōtautahi. In October 2014, artist Gaby Montejo created a performance awards ceremony entitled *Mothers*. Montejo presented Audrey, Jessica Halliday, Chloe Geoghegan, Melanie Oliver and Coralie Winn with enormous trophies for their role as the 'Founding Art Mothers of New Christchurch'. In speaking about the performance, Montejo noted 'that he had grown tired of waiting for someone of higher authority . . . to honour these people and their accomplishments'.[5]

Audrey Baldwin (AB): Pre-quake Ōtautahi had a reputation as a conservative city that focused on rugby and gardens and viewed contemporary art with suspicion — particularly public art. Although performance art was by no means a new genre for the city, attitudes to 'the arts' shifted after the quakes.[6] The arts became a way for us to respond and come together because we were so beyond words. In this context, performance art had a particular appeal because of its immediacy. An ongoing example is Henry Sutherland's simple yet poignant act of inviting all people to place a flower in a road cone, an action that continues every year.[7] Invitations to put forward proposals, and funding from Christchurch City Council, made me realise that perhaps I could operate more effectively as an artist in Ōtautahi.

KH: That pre-quake conservatism seems amplified by the historical folly of the city's location. Mana whenua sited their pā on solid ground to the north or south of the current city location and on Banks Peninsula. Europeans settlers thought they knew better, however, and here we are: swamp city.

Christchurch is sometimes called 'Little England', shorthand for the prevalence of British ideals in the urban design of the city and its demographic makeup. In 2013 the population was 83.9 per cent Pākehā; in comparison, the Pākehā populations of Tāmaki Makaurau Auckland and Te Whanganui-a-Tara Wellington were 59.3 per cent and 76.4 per cent respectively. Demographically, Ōtautahi is a divided place, with wealth in the west on stable ground and poverty in the east on reclaimed land. The communities rarely mix. At the time of writing, some lower socio-economic suburbs remain in states of disrepair; in the well-off suburbs, all signs of earthquake damage have been removed. Interrupting the dominant white narrative takes time and constant repetition, but the disaster does seem to have given it a nudge.

The quakes changed more than the physical landscape; demographics and attitudes in the city are shifting slowly.[8] Mana whenua — Ngāi Tahu, and specifically Ngāi Tūāhuriri — were made a statutory rebuild partner with the Crown, which meant the Christchurch Earthquake Recovery Authority (CERA) and local and regional councils were required to work closely with them. This legislative change ensured mana whenua were always at the table in planning the recovery, which created noticeable cultural shifts in local governance. Perhaps influenced by these changes, some post-quake performance art practices have pushed back directly at the 'colonial Christchurch' narratives and have infiltrated local institutions in ways they would not have done prior to the quakes.

Juanita Hepi's (Kāi Tahu, Ngāti Wai, Moriori, Ngāti Kahungunu, Ngāpuhi) *Ariā I* and *Ariā II* (2022) were performed at the Centre of Contemporary Art Toi Moroki (CoCA) and Canterbury Museum respectively. In these works, Hepi (Kāi Tahu, Ngāti Wai, Moriori, Ngāti Kahungunu, Ngāpuhi) responded to existing exhibitions and the institutions in which they were hosted. Embodying several characters of different ages, Hepi seemed to time travel, weaving a multifaceted wahine Māori narrative into spaces where it has been absent. Performing with a large piece of black and white parachute-like material, she traversed emotions and ritual, exploring loss, grief, birth and death in a manner that both confronted the audience and drew them in. Daring and inviting active participation in her resistance to colonial narratives, within colonial institutions, the piece finished in a collective grounding of the parachute/dress with river stone anchors placed by audience members. A watching wahine Māori placed the final stone.

Canterbury Museum has been the site of many performances that question its depiction of Māori, including artist Ana Iti's *Treasures Left by Our Ancestors* (2016).

In this work, Iti filmed herself in front of dioramas built in 1989, described by some as offensive and reductive, which ostensibly depicted 'pre-colonial Māori'.[9] Iti noted that they 'reinforce colonial narratives around Indigenous bodies and relationships with the environment'. In what she described as 'an act of empathy and endurance', Iti crouched like the figures in the diorama, posing herself in relation with those depicted.[10] In 2023 the museum closed for significant refurbishment in collaboration with Papatipu Rūnanga, the rūnanga of Waitaha (Canterbury) area. Museum chairperson David Ayers notes, 'The museum acknowledges that dioramas presented a colonial view of Māori in Te Waipounamu. The figures have been removed as a tangible acknowledgement of this.'[11]

Nina Oberg Humphries' work *I CALL TO HER* (2016) also responded to the site of Canterbury Museum. Oberg, who is second-generation Aotearoa-born with Cook Islands heritage, critiqued the common museum practice of storing taonga from across Te Moana-nui-a-Kiwa the Pacific Ocean in sterile and temperature-controlled environments, sometimes with little access by Indigenous peoples. *I CALL TO HER* combined performance, spoken word, recordings and dance to reference a fictional ancestress whom Oberg embodied.

The work spoke to her difficulty in connecting directly with her heritage as diaspora, and the production of pan-Pasifika signifiers such as 'Pasifika'.[12] In a reclamation of space, the work began outside the museum, followed by a slow procession through the exhibits to one of the rooms containing colonial artefacts. The performance called to the taonga housed in the museum, activating the vā through movement and sacred threads that continue to bind cultural taonga from the past with the living today.[13]

Leafā Wilson's work engaged explicitly with the quakes and social demographics.[14] In *Me and My Salu Lima* (my hand brush) (2016), Wilson donned professional business attire and swept the streets of Christchurch with her salu lima between the Cardboard Cathedral and the original, earthquake-damaged cathedral in the Square.[15] Her performance referenced the sacrifices her parents' generation made in order for her generation to be successful in Aotearoa. Wilson sought to challenge problematic stereotypes. The action represented her sense of pride associated with the hard work carried out by migrant workers such as her parents, and drew attention to the presence of new migrant workers during the city's rebuild.

All of these performance artworks have a connection to the social (and artistic) shifts that have happened relatively quickly over the post-quake years; the shift in gaze from the colonial 'mother England' towards a contemporary, multicultural city (re)built in partnership with mana whenua. It is difficult to pin down the links and trajectories of this change, as a network of interconnected political decisions, actions and discourses has led to the opening up of space for a multiplicity of narratives. Perhaps the loss of so much of the physical fabric of the city allowed more space to ask questions of what remained, what would be rebuilt, and for whom.

IF YOU DON'T ART, YOU'LL CRY

KH: In the years immediately following the quakes there was a proliferation of performances and interventions. These performances were made while Ōtautahi residents were literally shitting in buckets, fighting for insurance claims and living through thousands of aftershocks. There was public consultation and a reshaping of civic government. It was a messy time.

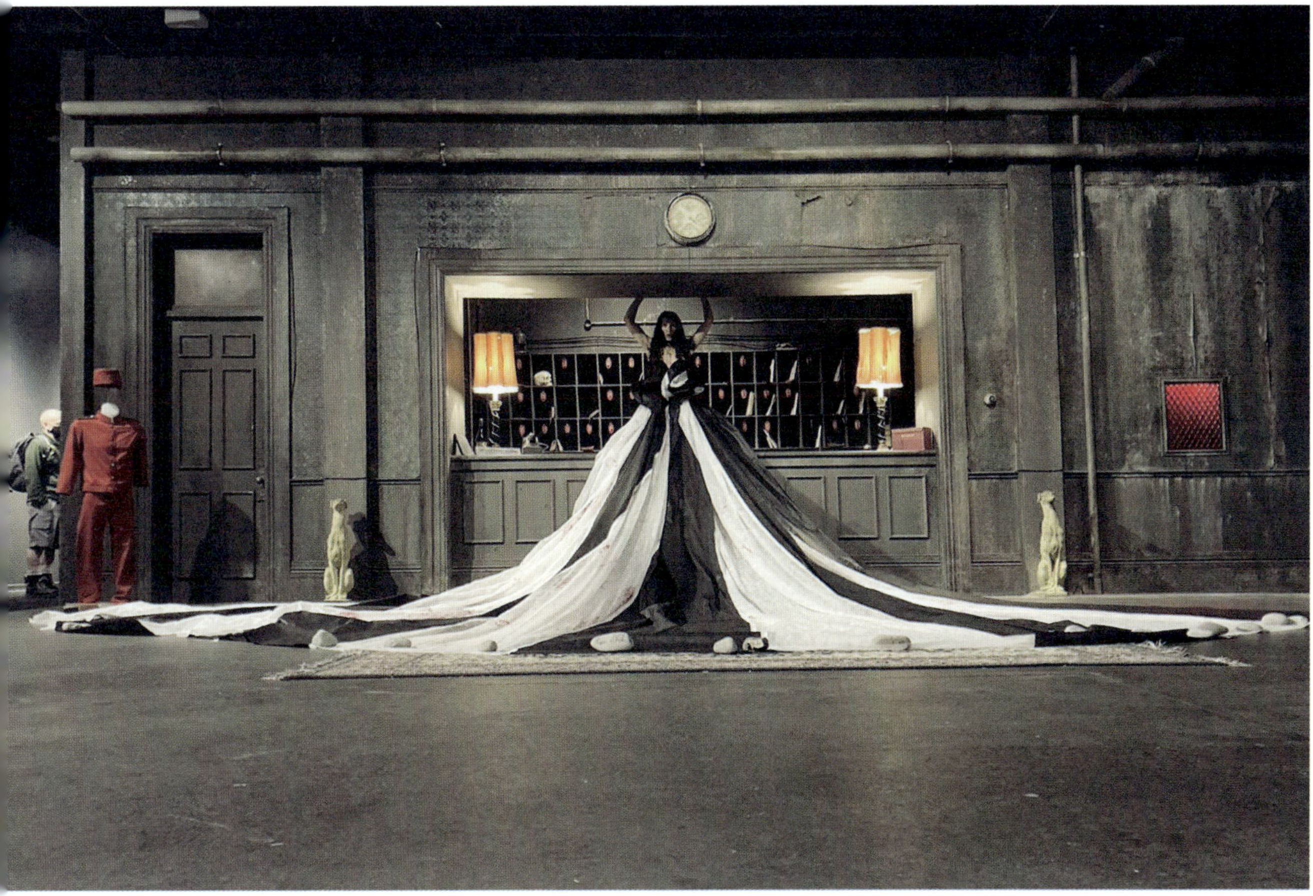

Juanita Hepi (Kāi Tahu, Ngāti Wai, Moriori, Ngāti Kahungunu, Ngāpuhi), *Ariā I*, 2022, documentation of performance at Canterbury Museum, Ōtautahi Christchurch. *Courtesy the artist. Photo by Holly Chappell-Eason*

The particular brand of dark humour that these experiences spawned can be seen weaving its way through the artworks. Art became a necessary counterpoint to disaster, and this was recognised by Christchurch City Council and Creative New Zealand, both of whom enabled specific funding for creativity in Ōtautahi during that period. Without going too deeply into the quake trauma, nor romanticising the necessity of creative responses, we want to record some of the works that happened. I know from digging about in various archives that it was quite a wild time — one of army tanks and seed bombs, cordons and community care. Audrey lived it.

AB: Going back to 2011 is a bit blurry. I was in deep trauma and in denial. We were all reeling from losses — I'd lost a lover; everyone knew someone who knew someone who'd passed away. In the immediate aftermath of the first quake, I spent a couple of weeks helping to dig out liquefaction-clogged houses, gardens and paths around the city with old school friends, inspired by the Student Volunteer Army.[16] The physicality of the work helped me to process the trauma before I could conceptualise anything into an artistic action. There was a drive to do something tangible instead of doom scrolling.

In terms of live art, there were many music gigs. The band The Eastern were ever-present; Von Klap scandalised audiences wherever they played; and numerous metal bands played memorials for musician Matti McEachen, who lost his life in the 22 February quake.[17] We shared live music in parks, at bars in Hornby and in bowling clubs, and had tearful carpark reunions.

I couldn't even think about making new artwork for at least six months. When I

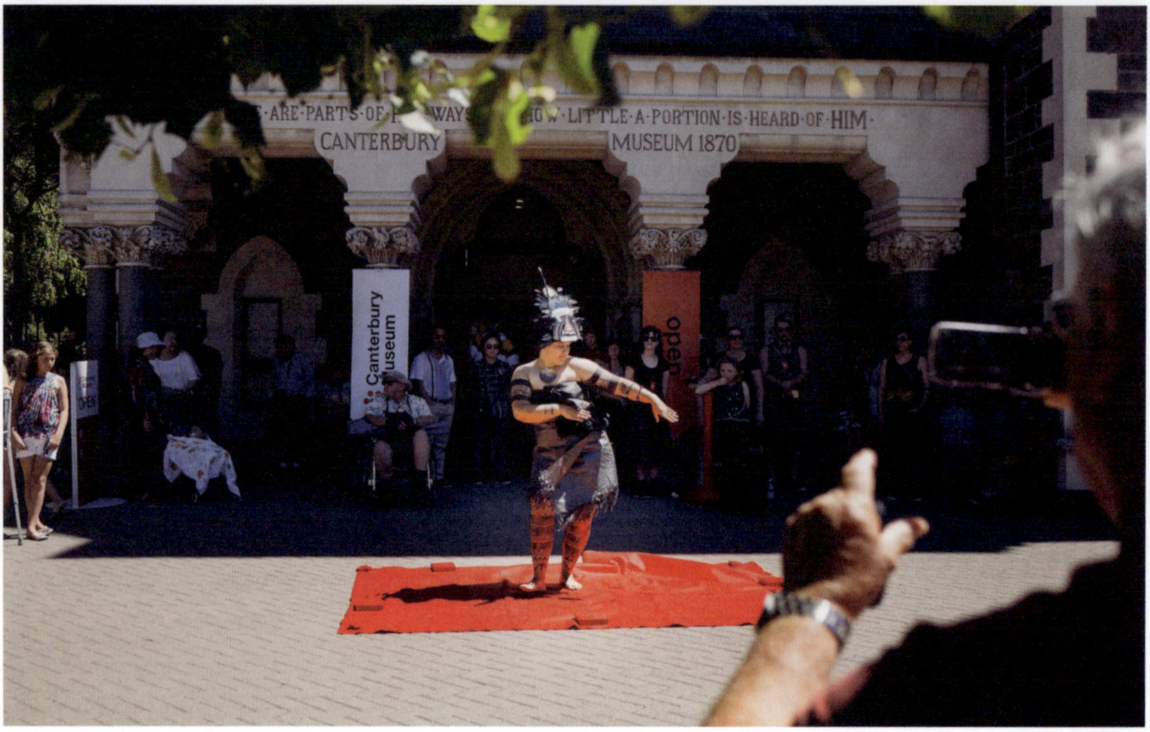

did, one of the first new works I presented was *End of the Line* (2012). A collaborative work with Annie Mackenzie and Dave Marshall, it highlighted the frustrations of red tape and bureaucracy. We had wanted to place a little tram cart on the unused lines in Re:START Mall, but the health and safety restrictions were wild.[18] Despite it being a pedestrian precinct, we were required to present a traffic management plan. So instead, we threw a very absurd, tongue-in-cheek 'parade', pushing the cart repeatedly through a 'finish line' of red crepe paper held across the tracks as the audience let off party poppers around us. Upon reaching the literal end of the line — Colombo Street was walled off — we lit some old sparklers in the daylight and quietly pushed the cart back to a waiting trailer, sweeping up behind us. It felt good to be able to *do* something and to share that with other people, even though it was anticlimactic and absurd.

The immediacy and often embodied nature of performance was, for me, an ideal way to respond to things that felt too big to cope with, even as time went on. In this context, the curation of group art exhibitions and event production, often self-funded with help from the Social Arts Collective and Arts Voice Christchurch, had a quick gestural quality: get it done, get it out there.[19]

KH: That sense of urgency and a desire to 'just get it done' is definitely one that I saw rippling through many of the post-quake performance practices, and in the proliferation of groups like Gap Filler,[20] FESTA,[21] Life in Vacant Spaces[22] and The Green Lab[23] that were interested in direct creative interventions in the fabric of the city, and/or supporting others to do that work. All of these organisations were supported by the local council in some way, and this civic investment in creative responses to the rebuild of the city seems to have shifted the public perceptions of the value of art and creativity. In some ways the city itself became a performance venue for a few years as more traditional venues fell away. Many of these works connected directly with the effects of the disaster and post-disaster bureaucracy.

Nina Oberg Humphries, *I CALL TO HER*, 2016, documentation of performance for the Summer Performance Series at Centre of Contemporary Art Toi Moroki, featuring Pasifika artists and curated by Khye Hitchcock, Ōtautahi Christchurch. *Courtesy Centre of Contemporary Art Toi Moroki. Photo by Janneth Gil*

AB: As part of a response to post-disaster bureaucracy, many performances were united by a sense of absurdity: that if you can't laugh about it all, you'll just keep crying. A coping mechanism of sorts. Ana Iti (Te Rarawa) and Alissa Gilbert presented *Make Doubt Your Friend* (2011) in a stall in the Re:START Mall, where people could write down their fears anonymously in exchange for a screen-printed poster. The work played on 'sincere cynicism and optimism'[24] and trading something unpleasant for a more pleasant memento. I collaborated with them a few months later in *Catharsis*, in which we held a symbolic 'airing' of these collected fears, reading them aloud into a megaphone on a rooftop then swallowing the paper on which they were written.

The Loss Adjusters (2012), also located at the mall, was an interactive performance by Jamie Hanton and Alex Lovell-Smith that poked fun at the insurance claim process. The work was strangely soothing in its absurdism and delivered with impressively straight faces. Each 'claimant' — members of the public — was met by a panel of Loss Adjusters in suits and dark glasses. A Stenographer took notes on what had been lost, another performer sketched it, and one ventured out to take a Polaroid photograph of an approximation of the object or something symbolising it. A fourth performer loomed as a Supervisor — like a stony security guard at one end of the line-up. Finally, a blindfolded Adjudicator stamped each claim as either accepted or rejected.[25] The paperwork was then sealed in an envelope and given to the claimant to take home. I spent a day in the role of sketch artist and was fascinated by what people claimed as lost — from courage to a pet rat and faith in local government.

Stuck (2013) took place on a rubble-strewn vacant site on Gloucester Street. A collaborative performance by Julia Croucher and myself, it was more visceral than some. We collected rubble from various parts of the central city and took it upon ourselves to construct a chaotic cairn or low stone wall between ourselves and the footpath where our audience stood. We used chewing gum and our physical labour as a symbolic way of re-inserting the fragile (femme) body into the harsh environment. Hubba Bubba gum, pink and saccharine, sweated out our spit between layers of aggregate, an oozing ineffectual mortar in an absurdist attempt to build something out of the chaos.

It rained for the afternoon of the performance, so we donned pink rain ponchos and persevered while our audience stood beneath umbrellas in solidarity with our efforts. There was a sense of reinserting the soft, squishy and feminine into the city with all its rubble and sharp edges; all the hi-vis and steel-capped boots and bulldozing of buildings felt distinctly masculine. That and the ever-present gaze of tradies on our bodies as we went about our business.

KH: I remember reading Brie Sherow's review of *Stuck*, saying it was the only new build she'd seen on Gloucester Street that year.[26] A lot of your work relates quite directly to the rebuild. As another example, *Target* (2013) connected with women's experiences in a city populated by male construction workers.[27] Standing on a vacant site, you painted your white underwear with orange dazzle — the ubiquitous fluorescent spray-paint used in construction throughout the city to draw attention to hazards or plans. Even your work *tether/reel* at Artspace Aotearoa in the exhibition *to and fro* in 2013, where you were connected to the wall with hooks through your back, seemed to relate to that frustration of being at the whim of whatever decisions others made, be they policy-maker or curator.

Despite not seeing these performances in person, it strikes me that they've become emblematic of that era — to the point where I reference some of them in creating new projects and exhibitions. We still talk about these projects in a canon of new Ōtautahi

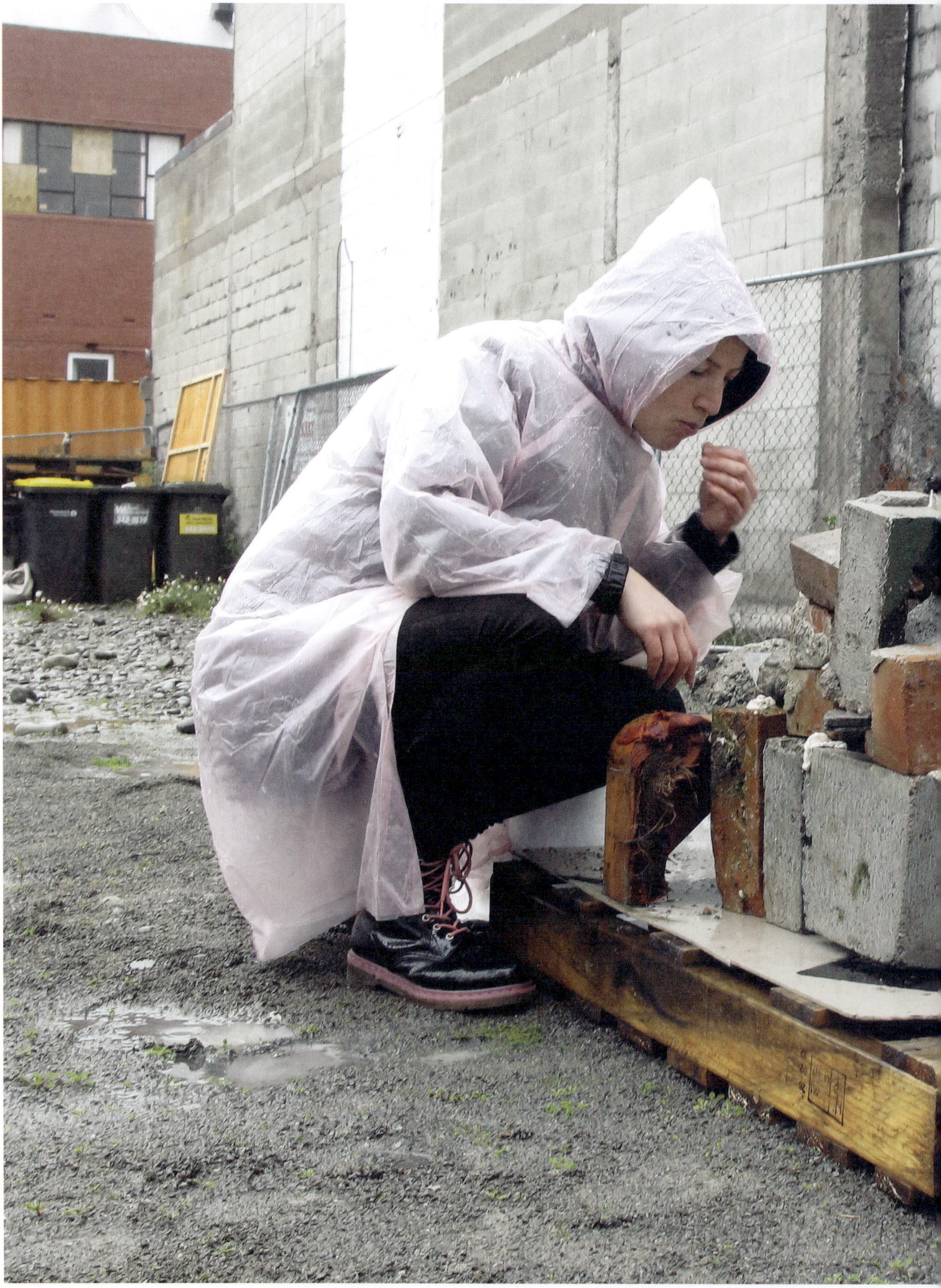

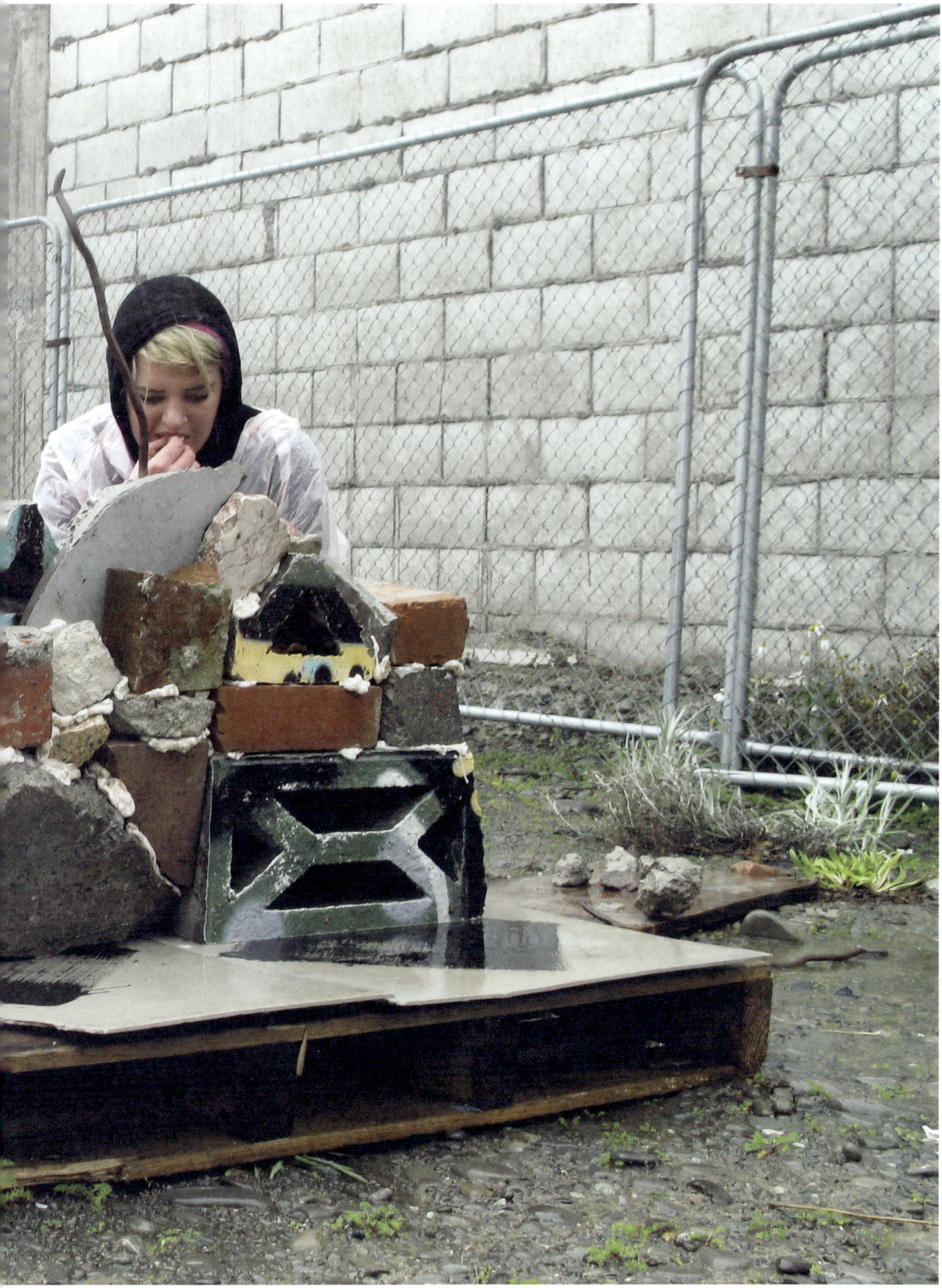

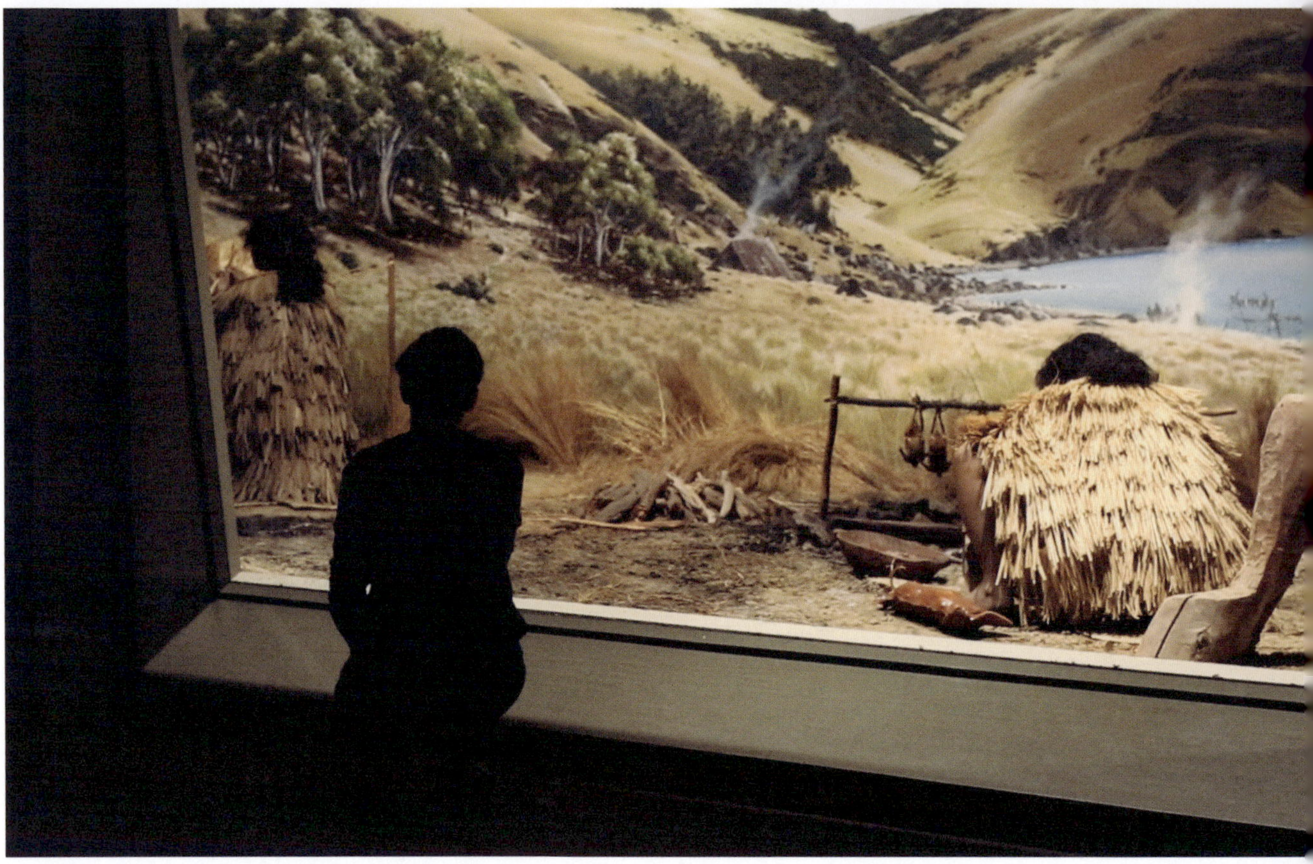

Ana Iti (Te Rarawa), *Treasures Left by Our Ancestors*, 2016 (still). Single-channel HD video, colour, sound, duration 15 minutes 10 seconds. *Courtesy the artist*

art. There is a power in their immediacy, in the re-enactment with a different ending and of changing the narrative, which groups these works and links them to a time that was both physically and politically fraught.

PREVIOUS: Audrey Baldwin and Julia Croucher, *Stuck*, 2013, documentation of performance. *Courtesy the artists. Photo by Alex Wootton*

COLLECTIVE LOW-FI: THE SOCIAL

KH: The Social was an artist collective begun by Lucy Matthews and Gaby Montejo in 2012. Their nebulous organisational structure expanded and contracted between 2012 and 2018, offering any opportunities they were given to the wider Christchurch arts community. This kind of collective approach to art-making is more often seen in groups that share a marginalisation or are othered by dominant systems. In Ōtautahi, it was a response to a disaster.

AB: The purpose of The Social was to stimulate conversations about art in Christchurch between artists and the wider public in a way that was meaningful, relevant and fun. It was to be 'low frills', playful, socially engaged, and able to take place outdoors. It was an important opportunity for emerging artists to establish a presence for their work in a city where our main gallery, Te Puna o Waiwhetū, had been taken over by Civil Defence, where our artist-run spaces were almost non-existent and our community needed art more than ever. The Social is the reason that I stayed in Ōtautahi — I became the group's administrator, which was the stepping stone to my ongoing practice in art production and community engagement today.

A key element of The Social was a non-hierarchical and collaborative approach to curation. Open calls were held for proposals and guest panels selected artworks. These panels were made up of a range of individuals — someone's grandma, a child, a visitor to the city, some local artists.

KH: As one of The Social projects, from 2013 to 2017 Gaby Montejo instigated A Place to Build Art Projects, aka The Christchurch International Art Residency. It was an artist workshop/residency in a caravan, installed on vacant sites in the central city, with the purpose of offering artists a unique opportunity to be part of the transitional period of demolition, planning and rebuilding that the city was undergoing. While the very act of occupying a rubble site was a performance work in itself, many artists made site-specific performance works as part of this project.

AB: The caravan residency hosted a number of out-of-town artists for three- to five-day stays on empty sites in the central city. These ranged from Agropolis on High Street, to Kilmore Street where the old convention centre used to be and, eventually, on the forecourt at Christchurch Art Gallery Te Puna o Waiwhetū when we showed at CoCA.[28]

Hana Pera Aoake performed *Meat Prize* (2013) as part of their caravan residency. The work was concerned with subverting dominant gender norms by engaging with the sexual politics of meat: narratives amplified by the vulnerability of their body in the context of the central city rubble. After being garnished with oil and the herbs that usually accompany roast chicken, Hana was wrapped in clingfilm. Curled into a face-down ball, they were carried onto the site and deposited on the ground, breathing through a straw until they gradually broke through the plastic and left the site.

Another work of which I have strong memories is Leafā Wilson/Olga Krause's *Tu'u Mai Lou Lima* (2017), in which she wore a poncho created from a silver emergency blanket and conducted one-on-one intuitive and healing hand-holding performances in that intimate space. The residency was less about artistic outputs and more about offering a

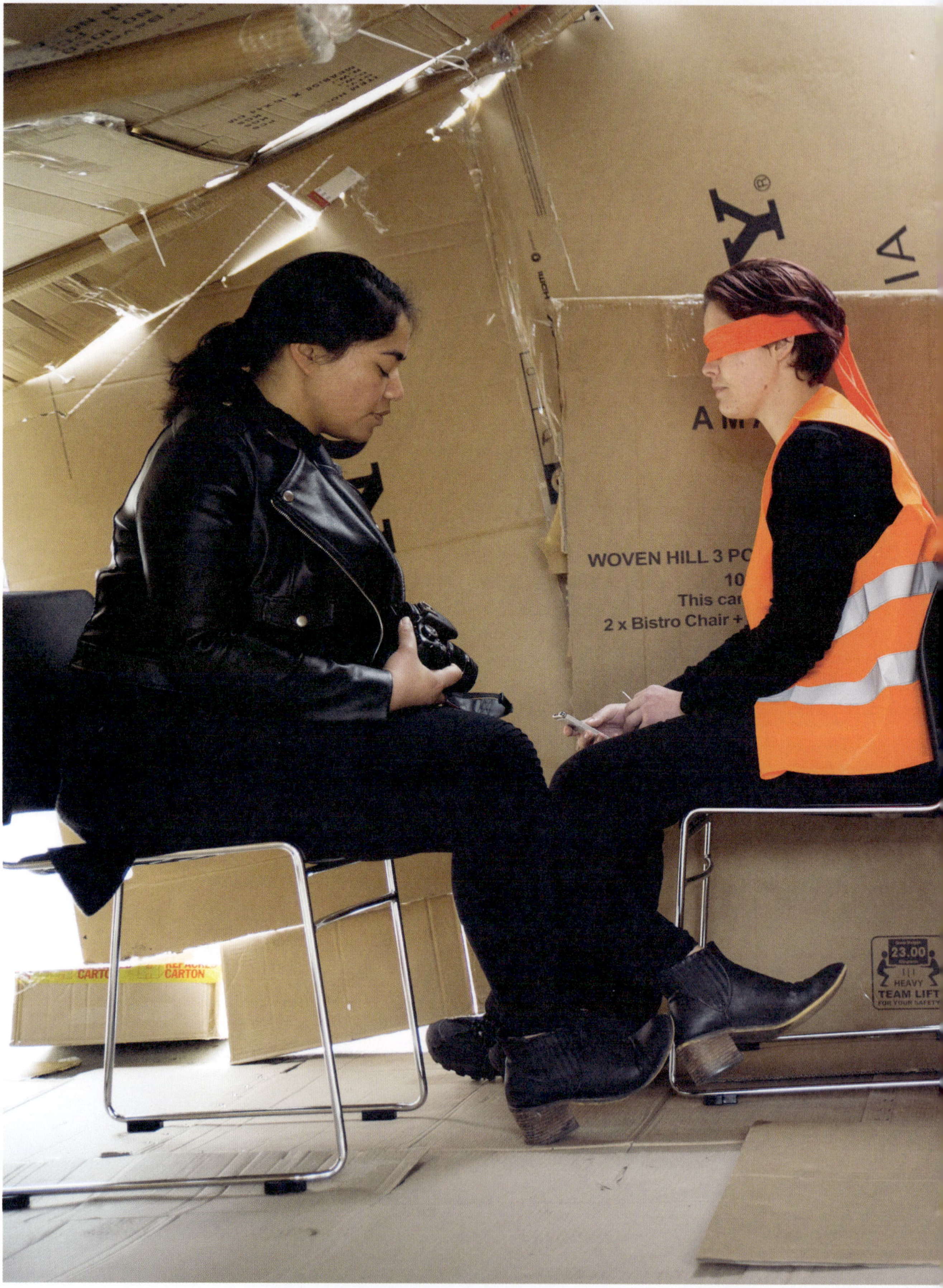
WOVEN HILL 3 PO
10
This ca
2 x Bistro Chair +
A M
23.00
HEAVY
TEAM LIFT
CARTON

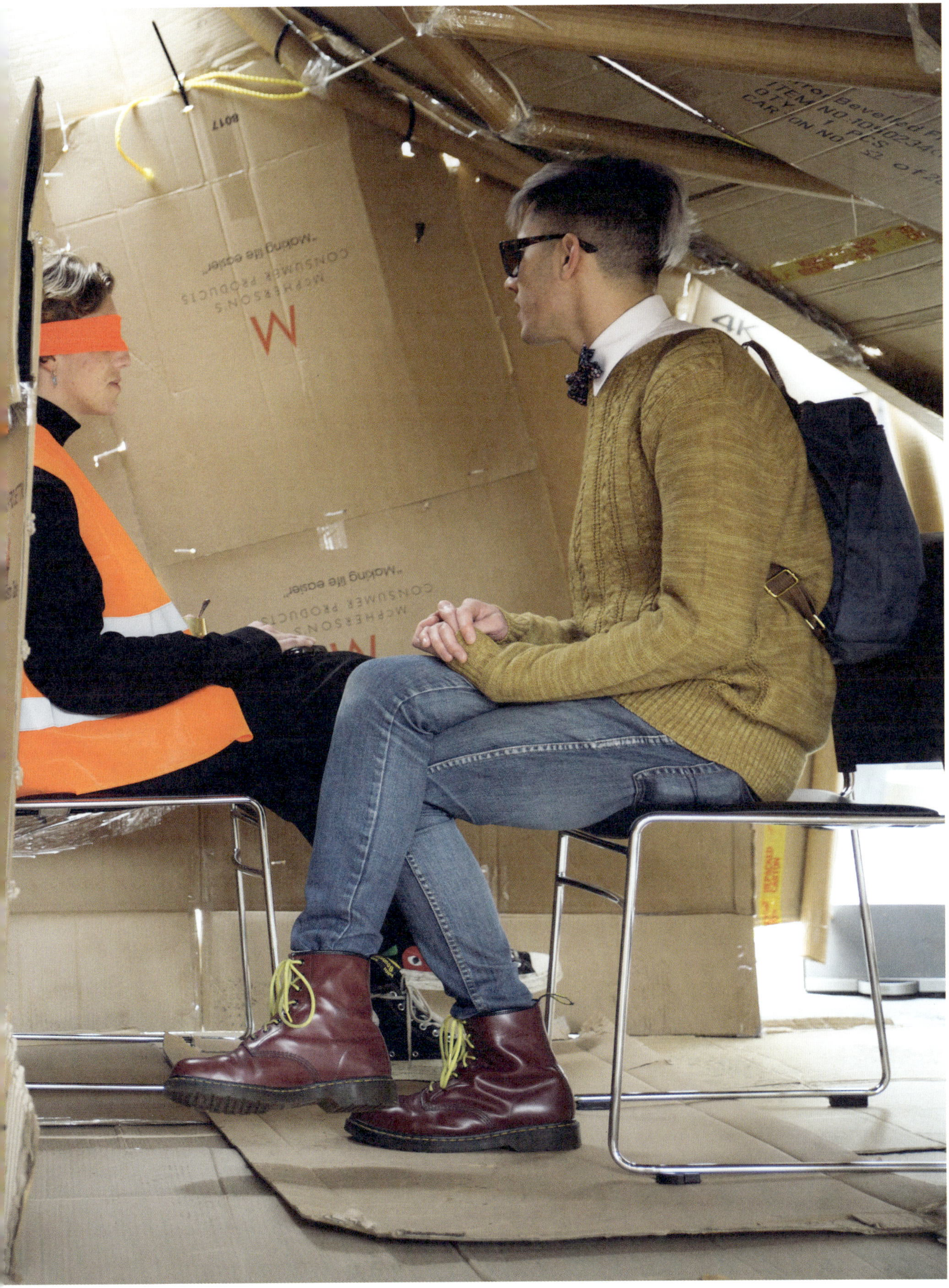
McPHERSON'S
CONSUMER PRODUCTS
"Making life easier"

visitor a unique perspective of post-quake Ōtautahi, a chance to be present and reflective.

Montejo played host and guide to the artists, and they had open studios in the caravan. Locals were encouraged to visit them on site.

PREVIOUS: Audrey Baldwin, Oscar Bannan, Bridget Harris, Neil MacLeod, Annemieke Montagne, Pat Parkin, Jennifer Katherine Shields, *Cardboard Confessional*, 2016, documentation of performance for the Centre of Contemporary Art Toi Moroki programme, Ōtautahi Christchurch. *Courtesy Centre of Contemporary Art Toi Moroki. Photo by Janneth Gil*

CREATIVE CURE-ALLS

KH: There was a strong desire from artistic creatives to contribute to the city's wellbeing, and a sense of creating safety and spaces and offering healing can be seen in many post-quake performances. On the surface most appear soft, but when you look a little deeper, they have sharp conceptual edges. For example, Julia Harvie's performance of *Nest*, at *FESTA: Lean means* (2016), was a literal creation of a space for herself. Harvie wove a nest of hazelwood branches while suspended from a gantry behind CoCA for the six hours of the festival. The work was a test of endurance for an individual practitioner, and the weaving of a space of safety by any means possible felt apt at a time where people were struggling to get insurance pay-outs to have their homes rebuilt. A beautiful performance, but with a pithy core.

Olivia Webb's *Voices Project* (2014) took place at three earthquake-ruined churches in Ōtautahi: the Catholic Basilica in central Christchurch, Holy Trinity Church in Lyttelton and Our Lady of Fatima in Mairehau. A trained choral singer, Webb invited local residents and parishioners to attend a series of singing sessions. She rehearsed with these communities, creating sonic sung 'monuments' for these lost spaces. The recordings from each singing session formed the basis of a one-day performance/installation: an ambient four-channel sound work situated at the sites of these former churches on Sunday, 29 June 2014. On this day, participants encountered themselves and their communities in places of worship so recently made unrecognisable.[29]

Another event aimed at contributing to the city's wellbeing was the youth performance mentored by Audrey in 2016. Six young artists — Oscar Bannan, Bridget Harris, Neil MacLeod, Annemieke Montagne, Pat Parkin and Jennifer Katherine Shields — signed up and were asked to determine a performance exploring a theme of their choice. The result was an ambitious performative sculpture, *Cardboard Confessional*. The artists spent a morning building a large-scale cardboard shelter redolent of a refugee or crisis tent — perhaps with a nod to the Cardboard Cathedral — on a vacant site on Hereford Street.

There was a tea and biscuit station outside the structure, and inside was a small cleansing shrine where audiences could wash their hands and two confession booths. Wearing hi-vis vests and blindfolds, the performers took turns hearing confessions — anything that the public wanted to bring. The advice they gave was beautifully considered and caring. The work was deeply connected to the site and to their experience of living in post-quake Ōtautahi.

AB: The hosting in *Cardboard Confessional* resonated with me. The performers weren't performing so much as holding space and being kind to strangers. And instead of inviting aspirations, they invited people to share their frustrations. We were sick to death of #goodvibesonly and being 'resilient Cantabrians'. Giving people permission to whinge, complain and vent their frustrations was unexpected, and audiences appreciated the gesture.

Together with this emphasis on care, a strong thread of mending and potential cure was at the forefront of works created by artists in Ōtautahi. Shared Lines Collaborative (SLC)[30] was established in 2011 in response to earthquake events that devastated Canterbury, Aotearoa as well as Tohoku, Japan. Artists in Ōtautahi and Sendai, Japan, connected to support each other and share experiences of disaster. Since then, SLC has provided a platform for exchange, exhibitions, performances and discussions in and between cities that have experienced quakes, including Te Whanganui-a-Tara Wellington, Kaikōura and Shiogama, also in Japan.

Social Soup (2012), by Heather Hayward and Tessa Peach, was a heart-warming work that took place in the Re:START Mall. The artists approached dining as a social interaction that humans perform together. As the summer sun set behind the Bridge of Remembrance, 100 people shared leek-and-potato soup and bread on trestle tables that ran the length of the disused tram tracks. The tables acted as a stage, blurring boundaries between performer, participant and spectator. It was free, it was wholesome, and as the first performance to take place on this site it was a symbolic starter. This work led to further iterations in later years that retained a focus on community connection and support.[31]

Rosalee Jenkins ran an interactive performance called *Phone Check* at one of the 2012 night markets that were part of the ArtBeat summer programme. She invited people to leave their mobile phones with her in a custom-made glass-topped case, with a slip of paper detailing how long they'd be apart from their digital extensions — from 30 minutes to 2 hours or more. The work was a gentle encouragement for people to connect and engage with each other in a conscious, analogue way. She also ran *Share a Smoothie with (insert name here)* (2012), in which people pedalled a cycle-powered blender to create a smoothie to share between friends.

For *Making Space* at CoCA in 2017, Lucy Matthews offered *The Department of Art Relations and Therapy (ART)*, a fictional organisation, in which a dozen hot-water bottles were fitted with a variety of soft white covers and filled with hot water to encourage a soothing art experience as people hugged them while exploring the gallery. The exhibition information referenced the work using science and business jargon: 'Using the latest hot [water] bottle research and technology the department offers a nostalgia-infused heated core with white cube-inspired covers.'[32] Matthews wore a white lab coat to refill each bottle carefully and helped people to select one that suited them.

In the same exhibition I presented *Cup of Tea and a Lie Down Clinic* (2017), an interactive work in which I created a therapeutic space replete with soft furnishings, blankets in pastel hues and a caddy full of tea. I offered one-on-one consultations that included a cup of tea and engagement with soft sculptures which worked as objects to complicate a moment of connection between two people. These included a 'snood' that enabled eye contact through a tunnel of mink blanket; a velvet-covered 'secret funnel' that blindfolded and gagged the receiver; or the spooning divider, a piece of violet PVC with a hole cut through it for an arm to drape over the 'little spoon' while keeping bodies separated.

There were also contemplation hoods — seafoam-green woven baskets that went over the heads of the activators as they tried blindly to mirror each other's movements. I was aiming for a playful ambiguity in the work — the sculptural elements referenced orifices and interiors — linking to the role of women in gendered emotional and sexual labour.

This work was very much in response to the overwhelmed mental health sector in Aotearoa, especially in Ōtautahi. It was a jibe at the bureaucratic processes that make accessing care so hard for many people already struggling with mental health, a problem exacerbated by the earthquakes.

Cup of Tea and a Lie Down Clinic was a tongue-in-cheek but earnest work that offered a moment of connection as a pathway to wellbeing. This has since evolved into the performance work *Art Chemist*, in which I more directly reference the structure and

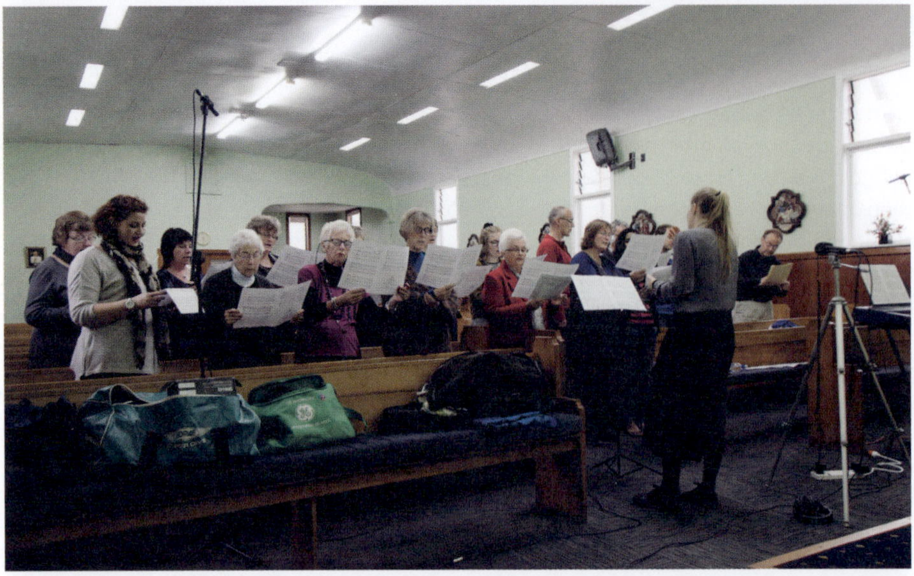

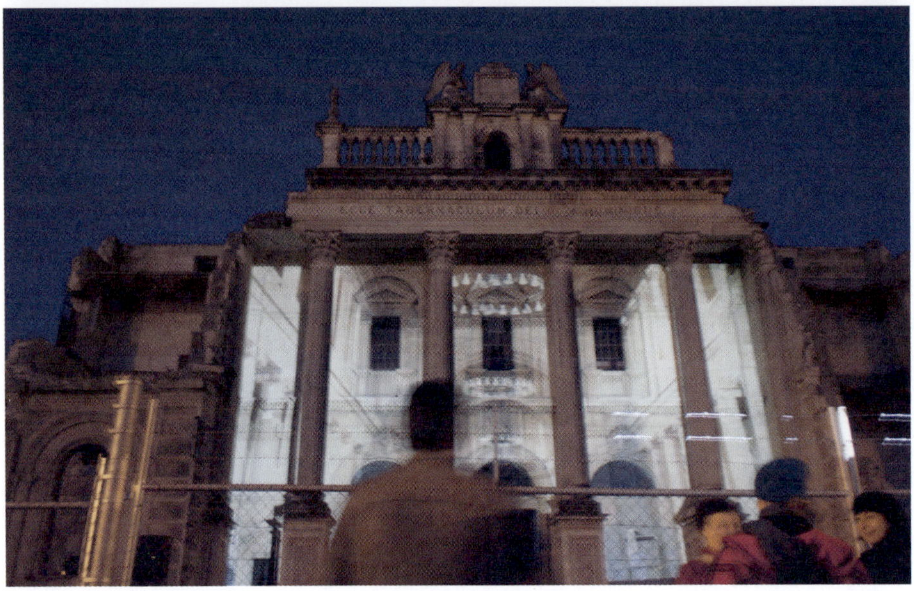

Olivia Webb, *Voices Project*, 2014, a one-day performance/installation at Our Lady of Fatima with the Mairehau Parish community (above), the Catholic Basilica in central Christchurch (below), and Holy Trinity Church in Lyttelton (not pictured), Ōtautahi Christchurch. *Courtesy the artist. Photos by Mitchell Bright (above) and Deagen Wells (below)*

branding of a pharmacy — but again, adding a pastel hue and softening the hard edges of the health industry.

KH: First performed in a vacant shop in Ōtautahi in 2021, *Art Chemist* redirects 'patients' to local art experiences, selected for them by the Art Chemist following a one-on-one consultation in which they are asked 'How are you doing?' or 'What ails you?'.[33] Conceived in the context of Ōtautahi just coming out of the first year of Covid-19 interruptions, part of its purpose was to increase public awareness of the art offerings of the city. Much like the operation of The Social, other local performers were invited to become Art Chemists. This work has now toured around Aotearoa and offers audiences a bit of healing balm everywhere it goes. It's very camp — everything is shades of pink pastel and parody — with an undertone of politically loaded. Mental health care is no easier to access in 2023 than it was immediately after the quakes.

NEW FOUNDATIONS

Just over a decade after the quakes, most artists in Ōtautahi are now back working with and in galleries and making artworks about anything but disaster. But the threads of ideas in the performances discussed in this chapter have continued to weave through artworks being created both locally and nationally. It is undeniable that the earthquakes were tragic, life-shattering events. Our creative community experience suggests, however, that the seismic shifts did ripple out into a cultural shift. For several years directly following the quakes there was a communal sense of rebuilding and generosity; landowners supported creativity; and funding enabled artists to respond quickly and provide moments of joy and healing.

We have come to know the value of the arts in building resilient communities in the face of disaster, and the creative responses in Ōtautahi have been widely recognised for the important role they have played in reimagining a devastated city.[34] In 2023, after three years of the Covid-19 pandemic on top of the existing frustrations of the post-quakes rebuild, there is definitely an air of cynicism and a longing to return to normality.

It is important not to create a rose-tinted nostalgia for the community connection in the days in the immediate aftermath of the quakes, but in the wake of natural disasters happening around the motu and around the world, we think it vital to remember this experimental and reactive time in performance art (and artistic practice in general) in Ōtautahi. We hope the foundations laid over this period continue to foster artistic practice that is generous and responsive. This is a small offering to those similarly affected by disasters. These recounted moments of performances that created interaction and relationships between artists and viewers, collectives and communities, demonstrate that art is worthwhile and deeply necessary in difficult times.

NOTES

1 A rūnanga is a council of members from a hapū (sub-tribe) or iwi (people of a tribe). Ngāi Tahu is an iwi located in Te Waipounamu. Ōtautahi is in the area taken care of by Te Ngāi Tūāhuriri Rūnanga.

2 We acknowledge that, in a post disaster context, those who are initially able to respond creatively or conceptually often have a degree of social privilege that allows them to do so. Ōtautahi has a statistically higher proportion of Pākehā (and therefore privileged artists) than other major cities in Aotearoa. As Pākehā writers, we have done our best to represent a diversity of practices.

3 Waka Toa Ora, 'River of Flowers — Te Waitohi Maumahara', www.healthychristchurch.org.nz/focus-areas/river-of-flowers.aspx

4 The Ōtākaro Avon River Corridor is a new name for the Residential Red Zone: large areas of land, predominantly along the Ōtākaro, which were deemed unsuitable for building after the 2011 earthquakes. Housing in this area was demolished, creating a wide green swath from city to sea. Charlie Mitchell et al, 'Red to Green: The stark evolution of a city's abandoned acres', *Stuff*, September 2019, https://interactives.stuff.co.nz/2019/09/christchurch-red-zone-to-green

5 Melissa Reid, 'Mothers: A Gaby Montejo performance', *Project Freerange*, 24 March 2016, http://web.archive.org/web/20160324131730/http://www.projectfreerange.com/mothers-a-gaby-montejo-performance

6 There was an intense period of experimental performance work between 1970 and 1985, as referenced in the exhibition *Intervention Post Object and Performance Art in New Zealand in 1970 and beyond*. See Bruce Barber et al., *Intervention: Post Object and performance art in New Zealand in 1970 and beyond*, edited by Jennifer Hay, exhibition catalogue (Christchurch: Robert McDougall Art Gallery and Annex, 2002). Pre-quake performance art was mostly seen in designated art spaces such as High St Project, The Physics Room and Nibelheim (now the dealer gallery The Central at the Arts Centre Te Matatiki Toi Ora). Together with these spaces, Free Theatre has been around since the late 1970s, and the prolific Tagata Moana group, Pacific Underground, formed in 1993.

7 Bennett Barnaby, Eugenio Boidi and Irene Boles, eds, 'Flowers on Road Cones', in *Christchurch: The transitional city Pt IV* (Christchurch: Freerange Press, 2012), 230–31.

8 The 2018 census showed a drop to 77.9 per cent European population.

9 Jake Kenny, 'Complaints Lead to Covering of Māori Exhibit at Canterbury Museum', *Stuff*, 12 June 2020, www.stuff.co.nz/national/121802557/complaints-lead-to-covering-of-mori-exhibit-at-canterbury-museum?rm=a

10 Ana Iti, 'Treasures Left by Our Ancestors', 2016, https://

anaiti.art/Treasures-left-by-our-ancestors-2016

11 Canterbury Museum, 'Museum Makes Changes in Māori Galleries', 17 August 2022, www.canterburymuseum.com/explore/latest-news/museum-makes-changes-in-m%C4%81ori-galleries

12 Nina Oberg was deliberately using the term 'Pasifika' as a cultural signifier that would be recognised as being generally from the 'Pacific' by people in Aotearoa. See Ioana Gordon-Smith, 'Terms of Convenience', 20 September 2015, https://ioanagordonsmith.com/2015/09/20/terms-of-convenience, for a more detailed discussion.

13 Traditionally, in multiple cultures across Te Moana-nui-a-Kiwa, sacred relationships exist between people, as well as between people and the environment, ancestors and the heavens. It is both spatial and relational. To nurture the vā is to respect and maintain the sacred space, harmony and balance within relationships.

14 Aka Olga Krause. See Chapters 10 and 11 in this volume for further discussion of Leafā Wilson's art practice.

15 The Cardboard Cathedral, formally 'The Transitional Cathedral', was built in 2013 as a temporary replacement for the badly earthquake-damaged Anglican Cathedral in central Christchurch. It is designed by Japanese architect Shigeru Ban. See New Zealand Story Group, 'A Cathedral Made out of Cardboard?', www.nzstory.govt.nz/stories/a-cathedral-made-out-of-cardboard

16 The Student Volunteer Army, led by Sam Johnson, was made up of thousands of volunteers who came together to help the wider community in the immediate aftermath of the February earthquakes, primarily helping dig and shift liquefaction using wheelbarrows and shovels. Sally Blundell, 'Call to Arms', *New Zealand Geographic* 114 (April 2012), www.nzgeo.com/stories/call-to-arms

17 Matti McEachen was a tattoo artist and musician, a much loved member of the creative community. He was killed trying to flee a building where he should not have been; the building was deemed structurally unsafe for occupancy by an engineer from the September quake, but tenants had not been informed. His family were instrumental in advocating for the families of quake victims and the instatement of the earthquake memorial. See Vicki Anderson, 'The Strands of Grief', *Stuff*, February 2018, https://interactives.stuff.co.nz/2018/02/strands-of-grief/part1.html

18 Re:START was a temporary shopping mall built from colourful shipping containers in central Christchurch, which opened in 2011. It was driven by Re:START The Heart Trust and initiated by the Christchurch Central Business Association with the aim of bringing retail back into the largely cordoned off central city, and proved a popular spot for tourists and locals alike. Initially planned as a short-term project, its popularity saw it maintained until January 2018.

19 The Social, initiated by Gaby Montejo and Lucy Matthews in 2012, was a rotating collective of artists engaged in a practice of interactive and site-specific performances in Christchurch. They focused on critical public dialogue and setting up environments for social connections to take place within the urban centre of the post-quake city. See chchsocial, 'The Social', https://chchsocial.tumblr.com; Khye Hitchcock, 'Making Space: The Social', Centre of Contemporary Art Toi Moroki, 2017, https://coca.org.nz/exhibitions/makingspace_thesocial. Arts Voice Christchurch was a group of arts industry elected representatives created in 2011 with the aim of creating a vision and strategy for the arts in Christchurch. They gave out small amounts of funding to local artists and collectives such as The Social. https://creativenz.govt.nz/News-and-blog/2022/06/15/02/23/40/Arts-Voice-Christchurch

20 Gap Filler is a placemaking group that formed to create playful public spaces in the many gaps left by the quakes in the central city. They are most well known for their Pallet Pavilion and the Dance-o-Mat — both of which facilitated public performance and connection. Gap Filler, 'A Creative Placemaking Social Enterprise', 2023, https://gapfiller.org.nz

21 The Festival of Transitional Architecture (FESTA) worked with architectural students from around Aotearoa and Australia, as well as with artists, to create pop-up one-night festivals in a vacant city block between 2012 and 2018. FESTA always had a theme and was deliberately designed to offer opportunities for residents to think about how the city was being rebuilt.

22 Life in Vacant Spaces is a non-profit that brokers creative and entrepreneurial use of vacant sites, both indoor and out, in Ōtautahi. They take care of the legal side of securing project sites, and are supported by Christchurch City Council to offer rates rebates to landowners who support temporary projects on their site. This has been in place since 2012, and enables pop up projects, including performance art, across the city. LiVS, 'Life in Vacant Spaces (LiVS): Breathing life into empty corners of Ōtautahi Christchurch', www.livs.org.nz

23 The Green Lab (formerly Greening the Rubble) creates temporary gardens/parklets that encourage community connection in vacant sites in the central city. These often have an educational or environmental theme. The Green Lab, 'Welcome to The Green Lab', https://thegreenlab.org.nz

24 The Social, Christchurch, https://chchsocial2.tumblr.com/doubt

25 Performers included: Jamie Hanton, Alex Lovell-Smith, Aaron Hawkins, Anya Sinclair, Francis van Hout, James Dann, Gaby Montejo, Audrey Baldwin, Rohanna Weaver, Lucy Matthews, Jed McCammon and Clarke Hegan.

26 Brie Sherow, 'Creative Thinkers of Christchurch: Audrey Baldwin', *The Pantograph Punch*, 23 October 2014, https://pantograph-punch.com/posts/audrey-baldwin

27 This work also took place in the national context of the 2013 'Roast Busters' case, in which it came to light that a group of young men in West Auckland were boasting online about their sexual assaults of underage girls. Despite many people coming forward, no arrests were made until 2021. *1 News*, 'More charges laid against two men in Roast Busters scandal', 31 March 2021, www.1news.co.nz/2021/03/31/more-charges-laid-against-two-men-in-roast-busters-scandal

28 In 2017, at the exhibition *Making Space* at CoCA, The Social brought the caravan back into use and it was hosted on the forecourt of Te Puna Waiwhetū, Christchurch Art Gallery. The gallery was keen to acknowledge The Social's significant contribution during the quakes. Several out-of-town artists held residencies during this period. The residencies ran in parallel to Martin Schick's *Nomad (thinking) Residency* in a camping ground in Switzerland; communication and exchanges were encouraged between artists taking part in both residencies.

29 See: Olivia Webb, 'Voices Project', 1 July 2014, https://oliviawebbartist.com/portfolio/voices-project

30 The collective was co-founded in 2011 by Ngaroma Riley, Aya Takada, Kim Lowe and Linda Lee, and has included over 140 collaborators from Japan and Aotearoa. Shared Lines Collaborative, 'Kaupapa', www.sharedlines.org.nz/kaupapa

31 Chch Soup ran from 2013 to 2018 and was based on the format of Detroit Soup, where people come together and contribute cash to a community pot. A selection of ideas was pitched to the diners ,and one of them was awarded the funds from said pot. The first Chch Soup was held

at Gap Filler's Pallet Pavilion in autumn, where pumpkin soup was shared.

32 Centre of Contemporary Art Toi Moroki, 'Lucy Matthews: Hot Bottle lunch with the Department of Art Relations and Therapy, 2017', https://coca.org.nz/exhibitions/makingspace_thesocial/ms_thesocial-15

33 With the disclaimer that performers are artists, not mental health professionals, and with mental health resources on hand, just in case.

34 Amanda Monehu Yates and Kelly Dombroski, 'The City as Laboratory: What post-quake Christchurch is teaching us about urban recovery and transformation', *Architecture Now* (blog), 22 September 2022, https://architecturenow.co.nz/articles/the-city-as-laboratory-what-post-quake-christchurch-is-teaching-us-about-urban-recovery-and-transformation

REFERENCES

1 News. 'More charges laid against two men in Roast Busters scandal'. 31 March 2021. www.1news.co.nz/2021/03/31/more-charges-laid-against-two-men-in-roast-busters-scandal

Anderson, Vicki. 'The Strands of Grief'. *Stuff*, February 2018. https://interactives.stuff.co.nz/2018/02/strands-of-grief/part1.html

Baldwin, Audrey. 'Art Chemist Series'. https://audreybaldwin.art/Art-Chemist-2021-22

Barber, Bruce, Blair French, Tony Green, Nicholas Spill, and Jennifer Hay. *Intervention: Post Object and Performance Art in New Zealand in 1970 and Beyond*, edited by Jennifer Hay. Exhibition catalogue. Christchurch: Robert McDougall Art Gallery and Annex, 2002.

Barnaby, Bennett, Eugenio Boidi and Irene Boles, eds. 'Flowers on Road Cones'. In *Christchurch: The transitional city Pt IV*, 230–31. Christchurch: Freerange Press, 2012.

Blundell, Sally. 'Call to Arms'. *New Zealand Geographic* 114 (April 2012). www.nzgeo.com/stories/call-to-arms

Canterbury Museum. 'Museum Makes Changes in Māori Galleries', 17 August 2022. www.canterburymuseum.com/explore/latest-news/museum-makes-changes-in-māori-galleries

chchsocial. 'The Social'. https://chchsocial.tumblr.com

——— 'Stuck: Audrey Baldwin and Julia Croucher'. https://chchsocial.tumblr.com/post/57512021741/hubba-bubba-bubble-gum-chew-drool-blow-lick-spit

Centre of Contemporary Art Toi Moroki. 'Lucy Matthews: Hot Bottle lunch with the Department of Art Relations and Therapy, 2017'. 2017. https://coca.org.nz/exhibitions/makingspace_thesocial/ms_thesocial-15

——— 'Cardboard Confessional'. 2016. https://coca.org.nz/exhibitions/beyond-the-visual/cardboard-confessional-2016

——— 'Leafâ Wilson: Me and My Salu Lima'. 2016. https://coca.org.nz/exhibitions/summer-performance/me-and-my-salu-lima

——— 'Nina Oberg Humphries: *I Call to Her*, 2016'. 2016. https://coca.org.nz/exhibitions/summer-performance/i-call-to-her

——— 'Making Space'. 2017. https://coca.org.nz/exhibitions/makingspace

——— 'The Social Caravan Residency, 2017'. 2017. https://coca.org.nz/exhibitions/makingspace_thesocial/ms_thesocial-24

Feeney, Warren. 'Op Shop Paradise'. *EyeContact*, 10 March 2017. https://eyecontactmagazine.com/2017/03/op-shop-paradise

Gap Filler. 'A Creative Placemaking Social Enterprise'. 2023. https://gapfiller.org.nz

Gordon-Smith, Ioana. 'Terms of Convenience'. 20 September 2015. https://ioanagordonsmith.com/2015/09/20/terms-of-convenience

Harrington, Erin. 'Review: Ariā I and II: Voices of longing, absence and connection'. *Flat City Field Notes* (blog), 23 January 2022. https://flatcityfieldnotes.com/2022/01/23/review-aria-i-and-ii-voices-of-longing-absence-and-connection

Hitchcock, Khye. 'Making Space: The Social'. Centre of Contemporary Art Toi Moroki, 2017. https://coca.org.nz/exhibitions/makingspace_thesocial

Iti, Ana. 'Treasures Left by Our Ancestors'. 2016. https://anaiti.art/Treasures-left-by-our-ancestors-2016

Kenny, Jake. 'Complaints Lead to Covering of Māori Exhibit at Canterbury Museum'. *Stuff*, 12 June 2020. www.stuff.co.nz/national/121802557/complaints-lead-to-covering-of-mori-exhibit-at-canterbury-museum?rm=a

LiVS. 'Life in Vacant Spaces (LiVS): Breathing life into empty corners of Ōtautahi Christchurch'. www.livs.org.nz

Mitchell, Charlie, Iain McGregor and Alden Williams. 'Red to Green: The stark evolution of a city's abandoned acres'. *Stuff*, September 2019. https://interactives.stuff.co.nz/2019/09/christchurch-red-zone-to-green

Napier, Abbie. 'Conquering Your Fears'. *Stuff*, 16 January 2013. www.stuff.co.nz/the-press/christchurch-mail/lifestyle/8185846/Conquering-your-fears

New Zealand Story Group. 'A Cathedral Made out of Cardboard?'. www.nzstory.govt.nz/stories/a-cathedral-made-out-of-cardboard

Reid, Melissa. 'Mothers: A Gaby Montejo performance'. *Project Freerange*, 24 March 2016. http://web.archive.org/web/20160324131730/http://www.projectfreerange.com/mothers-a-gaby-montejo-performance

Shared Lines Collaborative. 'Kaupapa'. www.sharedlines.org.nz/kaupapa

Sherow, Brie. 'Creative Thinkers of Christchurch: Audrey Baldwin'. *The Pantograph Punch*, 23 October 2014. https://pantograph-punch.com/posts/audrey-baldwin

SOUP. 'About'. https://detroitsoup.buildinstitute.org/about

The Green Lab. 'Welcome to The Green Lab'. https://thegreenlab.org.nz

Vares, Julian. *FESTA Promotional Video: UC Quake Studies*, 2014. https://quakestudies.canterbury.ac.nz/store/object/322348

Waka Toa Ora. 'River of Flowers — Te Waitohi Maumahara'. www.healthychristchurch.org.nz/focus-areas/river-of-flowers.aspx

Webb, Olivia. 'Voices Project'. 1 July 2014. https://oliviawebbartist.com/portfolio/voices-project

Yates, Amanda Monehu and Kelly Dombroski. 'The City as Laboratory: What post-quake Christchurch is teaching us about urban recovery and transformation'. *Architecture Now* (blog), 22 September 2022. https://architecturenow.co.nz/articles/the-city-as-laboratory-what-post-quake-christchurch-is-teaching-us-about-urban-recovery-and-transformation

17

CRY FOR ATTENTION: POST-INTERNET PERFORMANCES BY NATASHA MATILA-SMITH AND SIONE TUÍVAILALA MONŪ

Victoria Wynne-Jones
& Lana Lopesi

Cut. Choral music. A mid shot from a low angle of Sione Tuívailala Monū, head raised. One of their cloud-shaped artworks can be seen on the wall behind them. From beneath the crown of a black beanie emerge scores of dripping blue beads forming a glamorous fringe, a kind of elaborate head-gear. The effect is vaguely imperial, also recalling something that would be worn by a 1920s screen star. The camera flickers with slow-motion. Monū slowly blinks, looking away, aloof. Lowering their eyes, tilting their head forwards, the beads cascade downwards like water. They appear to be wearing a garment made of black and white gingham. The lighting conditions indicate it is night-time. The frame orientation is vertical, indicating this was filmed with an iPhone.

This is an account of the digital performance-to-video *Mangere Bridge* (2020) by Tongan-born and Tāmaki Makaurau Auckland-based Sione Tuívailala Monū (b. 1993), an artist working in adornment, drawing, performance art, video, animation and community art workshops.[1] Alongside their production of distinctive, colourful, sculpted artworks adapting techniques of *nimamea'a tuikakala*, Tongan floral design, Monū also works across social media platforms, particularly Instagram. Their image-making often presents slices of life that are light-hearted yet existential. Tinged with longing and imagination, they can oscillate between the mundane — waiting for the bus to the laundromat — to the dramatic — staging back-yard glamour shots with the aid of elaborate gowns made from mass-produced mink blankets (in lieu of kafu, customary handmade Tongan blankets).[2]

Monū's performance-to-videos frequently involve suburban settings in Tāmaki Makaurau, such as Māngere with its distinctive volcanic reserve; and everyday activities like going for a walk, making art, cooking in the kitchen, commuting on the train, vaping, daydreaming, hanging out with friends, spending time with family, scrolling through their phone or drawing on an iPad.

Focusing in this chapter on Monū's *Mangere Bridge*, as well as *If I die, please delete my Soundcloud* (2019) by Natasha Matila-Smith (b. 1984, Ngāti Kahungunu, Ngāti Hine, Samoan, Pākehā), we argue that both artists engage in what American artist Audrey Wollen, in 2014, named Sad Girl Theory, to acknowledge the acts of resistance and protest in expressions of female sadness.[3] In their performances, Monū and Matila-Smith destigmatise female sadness, often disregarded as passivity, and instead position it as a kind of resistance, and in doing so make space for all modes of femme expression. Although both artists employ digital technologies as well as online social media platforms for structure and content as part of their image-making practices, in fact their work harks back to a broader history of performative photography and self-imaging that stretches back into twentieth-century art and performance studies discourse.

Within the performance-to-video artworks that we discuss, Monū and Matila-Smith demonstrate theorist Melissa Gronlund's assertion that, with social media, 'users tend now to perform themselves, rather than assuming other identities'.[4] According to Gronlund, there is a fascination with the performance of identity and the autobiographical: 'Identity on the web remains in a mode of performance, although at present the performance — perhaps more anxiously — comes as an attempt to perform one's real self.'[5] Gronlund asserts that, currently, representation of oneself online involves a 'self' as 'a number of subject positions represented in a public field' rather than a 'psychologically coherent whole'.[6] We argue that Gronlund's thesis of 'identity as constructed through a social field, and the specific conditions of interacting on the internet' assists in discussing Monū and Matila-Smith's artworks.[7]

Historically, post-internet art practice has a specific genealogy that stretches from Len Lye's technical innovations in the first half of the twentieth century to post-object practice of the 1970s as exemplified in part 1 of Jim Allen's *Contact* (1974) — *Computor Dance* — to new media art experiments with a diverse range of hardware and software in the 2000s, as exemplified by the *Aotearoa Digital Arts Reader* (2008). Platforms provided by big tech have proved useful for artists in Aotearoa to explore their own relationship to technology and art-making, investigating the formal qualities of online performativity, specificities of various media, digital technologies and the internet. For example, artist Rachael Rakena (Kāi Tahu, Ngāpuhi) conceived of the internet as a 'fluid medium' of liquidity and flow.[8]

A current generation of artists co-opts the internet, a medium where the audience and modes of distribution are built into the making practice. In Aotearoa, these artists include Te Whanganui-a-Tara Wellington-based Claire Harris, who has used early streaming technologies to transmit long-durational acts of fandom. Using the UStream platform for *Happy Birthday Lindsay Lohan* (2012) on the occasion of the starlet's twenty-sixth birthday, Harris streamed herself for twenty-six hours watching all of Lohan's films, back-to-back; she provided live commentary, ate popcorn, and fell asleep. Tāmaki-Makarau-based Zarah Butcher-McGunnigle (like Matila-Smith) uses Instagram in tandem with the self-timers on her hand-held devices to explore self-imaging and performative photography. Tāmaki-Makarau-based Karin Hofko performed live for *iTrash/youTrash/weTrash* (2013) at The Physics Room, Ōtautahi Christchurch. As a mediated rendition of Bonnie Tyler's pop song 'Holding out for a Hero' (1984) through her laptop (assisted by image libraries and text-to-voice software), this performance was a compilation of karaoke and a televised talent competition.

Cognisant of these various artists, but with a focus on Monū and Matila-Smith, this chapter discusses contemporary post-internet performance of Aotearoa in the performing of selves as a way to connect to authenticity, sadness and vulnerability, particularly in the context of late capitalism, the 24/7 ubiquity of the internet/digital technologies and the 'Tinderfication' of daily life.

We will argue that a further way of reading our two main artworks discussed (*Mangere Bridge* and *If I die, please delete my Soundcloud*), while taking into consideration their engagement with post-internet aesthetics and tendencies, is via a thesis taken from novelist Leslie Jamison's 2014 essay 'Grand Unified Theory of Female Pain'.[9] Complementing Wollen's Sad Girl Theory, premises relevant to Monū and Matila-Smith's performative video works include the idea that women are always-already wounded; the pain of women is fertile, generative and must not be dismissed: 'Pain that gets performed is still pain.'[10] Jamison posits: 'Pain only reaches beyond itself when its damage shifts from private to public, from solipsistic to collective.'[11]

Jamison's thesis has implications for both performer and beholder:

> We should watch. She's hurting, but that doesn't mean she'll hurt forever — or that hurt is the only identity she can own. There is a way of representing female consciousness that can witness pain but also witness a larger self around that pain — a self who grows larger than its scars without disowning them, who is neither wound-dwelling nor jaded, who is actually healing.[12]

Cut. Brassy marching music. In the foreground are white-framed doors and windows. In the background is the brick façade of a building. A mid shot in slow motion, Monū slowly walks towards the camera, eyes downcast, casual, in a pale blue oversized singlet, what appears to be a long brown wig and a blue beanie. Stepping towards the light. When golden slants of sunlight hit their face, they look wistfully into the distance. Electronic synth sounds cut in.

Cut to a profile shot of Monū before a white background wearing the same wig pulled back into a messy ponytail and a collared sweatshirt. The camera zooms in. They look straight ahead, staunch. Electronic sounds play. Fun jazzy music. Monū runs through a suburban garden gate, making a dramatic entrance.

Throughout *Mangere Bridge*, Monū tries out various accessories and costumes and inflects these using a soundtrack made up of different genres of music that alternate with ambient sound. In another video work, *Returning Traces: Our ancestors left us clues* (2020), a high-contrast shot of them in golden light, resembling *Bacchus* (c. 1598) by Michelangelo Merisi da Caravaggio, is accompanied by chamber music played on a solo violin.

In their video works Monū performs themself, toying with a number of subject positions and the way these can be represented or interpreted in a public field. How might a woollen beanie and oversized singlet signify masculinity? Is such a reading altered by a long, brown wig? And what happens when these are accompanied by coy, doe-eyed facial expressions and wistful glances off camera and into the distance? Challenging what Gronlund refers to as a 'psychologically coherent whole', *Mangere Bridge* frequently involves instances of trying-on various personae, using the camera phone as a way to capture these.[13]

The identities are then tested with various soundtracks as well as entrances and exits in and out of frame. Tāmaki Makaurau-based curator Ane Tonga has argued that in their works Monū 'physically and metaphorically' inscribes leitī within the domestic. She asserts that Monū playfully reinterprets and re-presents domesticity and the home 'as a space where gender can be simultaneously learned, exposed and disrupted'.[14] A broader social environment that is all too often heteronormative and/or adheres to conservative Christian attitudes to gender and sexual orientation means that such a ludic approach is always-already radical and subversive.

Gronlund uses the term 'dialogic' — a concept by theorist Mikhail Bakhtin in which any utterance, image or video implies a response in its very construction — to describe the way in which online self-imaging, the kind also enacted in Monū's video works, means that 'the spectre of a respondent' is 'always on the horizon'.[15] In the case of *Mangere Bridge*, this begs the question of who such a respondent might be. What values do they ascribe to? Are they fellow members of Rainbow Pasifika communities, supportive family members, or those adhering to more conservative values?[16] Regardless, for Gronlund, one performs for a social field as the audience of the internet/video. There is an 'emphasis on picturing a relationship with someone else', suggesting:

> a focus on the gap between one's notion of one's own identity and its representation out in the world; this involves a movement away from fusion, towards a split subject and object and towards a character for whom the look of others is constitutive of [oneself].[17]

There is a sublimation of a body into an 'acted character' and a transition away from the body as a site of authenticity towards an aesthetics of representation. One way this is

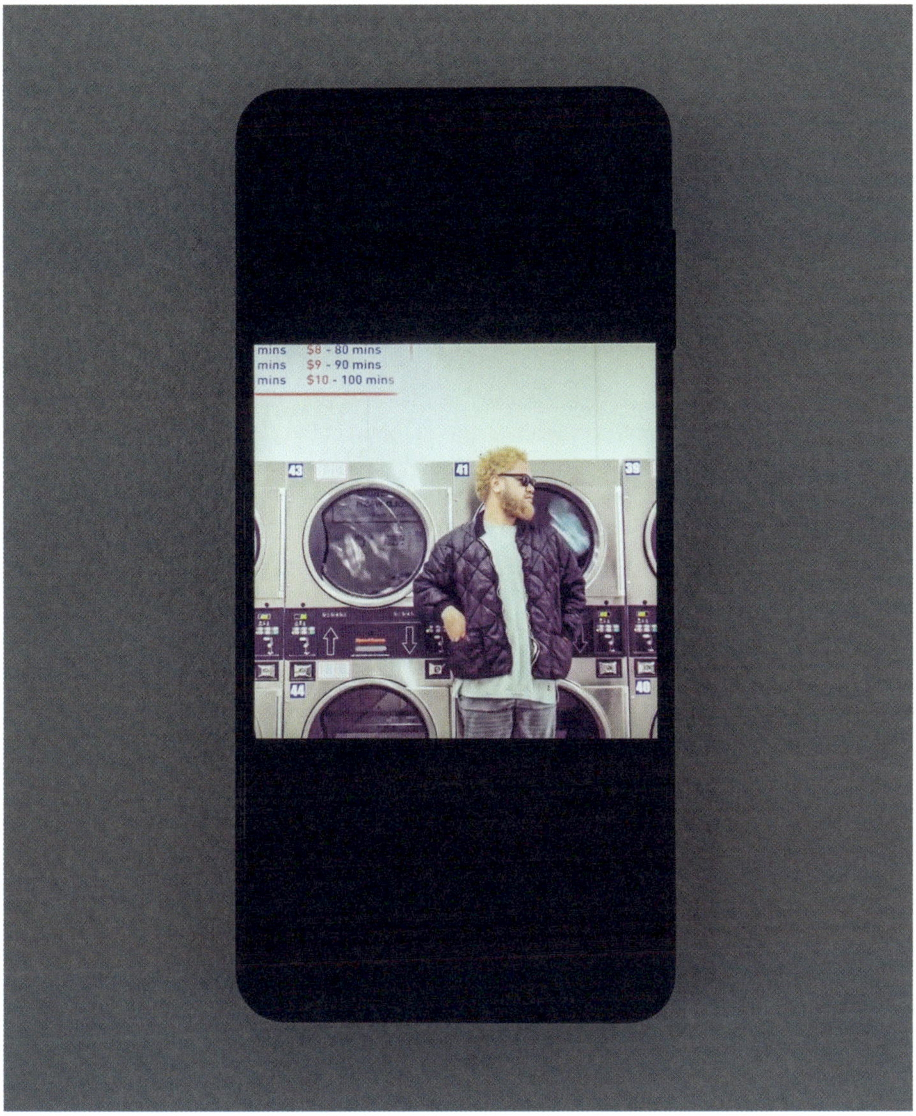

Sione Tuívailala Monū, *Laundromat*, 2018, digital video on Samsung Galaxy A22, duration 24 seconds. *Courtesy the artist and Robert Heald Gallery, Wellington*

achieved is through 'the accumulative temporality of identity's presentation', where the 'full picture is never available'.

Cut to bathroom tiles. The camera tilts, rights itself and pans across Monū's naked body. Knee, thigh, hand with cigarette, buttocks, upper body. Taking a shower and looking bored and urbane, they have a drag of their cigarette. They wash themselves with one hand, turn their head and blow smoke towards a window. The soundtrack stutters.

European folk music takes over. There appear to be two mirrors. In one framed surface we see Monū's reflection. Shirtless, they tilt their head back and take a tincture, placing droplets on their tongue. Is it CBD oil? Rescue Remedy? Echinacea oil? A flash of a rainbow, psychedelic frog animated sticker appears, superimposed, then vanishes.

Slow fade to Monū sitting on a bus. Streetlights can be seen reflected on glass before them. Another animated sticker, this time one of the Disney animated version of Alice in Wonderland as she falls into the underground, appears before Monū's face.

The use of animated stickers in *Mangere Bridge* is a feature taken from short videos — reels or stories — used on Instagram. In *Volver,* a 2022 exhibition at Robert Heald Gallery in Te Whanganui-a-Tara, Monū screened ten video works on iPhones attached to the gallery walls. Such conventions and display link Monū's artworks to the way in which users craft videos on the social media platform. From a different perspective, Monū's self-imaging (as well as that of Matila-Smith) is part of a broader narrative in the history of art from Aotearoa.

An important precedent is work by Shigeyuki Kihara (b. 1975), an artist of Samoan and Japanese descent who recently represented New Zealand at the 59th Biennale di Venezia with her project *Paradise Camp* (2022). Since the early 2000s, Kihara has made performative photographs of herself in order to challenge the ways in which, historically, those from Te Moana-nui-a-Kiwa have been presented in colonial photography. In the 2004–05 work *Fa'afafine: In the manner of a woman, Triptych 1,* in the collection of the Metropolitan Museum of Art, New York, Kihara posed upon a chaise longue as a 'dusky maiden', in various stages of undress, in a re-constructed nineteenth-century photography studio.

For the past two decades she has also made live performances, videos and performative photographs as her alter-ego, Salome, a persona based on nineteenth-century portraits of a Samoan woman in Victorian mourning costume who dances and surveys landscapes ravaged by colonialism. In a recent interview, Kihara reflected that the roots of such a practice lay in fa'afafine beauty pageants of the 1980s and 1990s — in particular, the production *My Girls* in the 1990s led by the late Moefa'auō Tanya To'omalātai, who produced, directed and choreographed the pageant — as well as in learning about the power of mise-en-scène to create narratives after working as a freelance costume designer and wardrobe manager for theatre, film, television and raves.[18]

We would argue that the performance-to-video works of Monū and Matila-Smith can be considered as part of a broader history of what performance theorist Philip Auslander has called 'performed photography' — productions of the self for posterity through orchestrated visual representations.[19] Similar artworks have also been created in Aotearoa, such as Rosanna Raymond's *Full Tusk Maiden* (1999) and Greg Semu's series *Battle of the Noble Savage* (2007), which hark back to intriguing historical examples such as the self-representation by painter Tony Fomison the year before his death in Shirley Grace's *Double Portrait of Tony Fomison* (1989). In this double-exposed photograph the artist appears as both artist and subject, a painter from the European Renaissance as well as a soga'imiti, or tattooed one.[20]

An even earlier precedent would be Billy Apple's *Billy Apple Bleaching with Lady Clairol Instant Crème Whip, November 1962* (1962/2002). This black and white print made from a 35mm colour slide shows the artist with newly bleached hair looking at himself in a mirror, illuminated by a partially visible lightbulb: a subject 'split, literally, by the act of representation', as described by art historian Christina Barton.[21]

Cut to a view of Māngere Mountain. A paddock, grass, a cow and fence. A figure can be seen in the distance walking along the side of the paddock and the end of a cul de sac. Cars pass. A pipe organ plays an aria from Bizet's Carmen. *The camera pulls back, past a fence, to reveal Monū climbing the side of the mountain wearing blue jeans and a green knitted hoodie over a grey long-sleeved T-shirt. They carry supermarket bags and wear a colourful mask made of red flower petals on the chin and forehead, yellow-green petals on the cheeks and purple petals for eyebrows, with incisions for eyes and nose. From the chin dangle strings of colourful beads.*

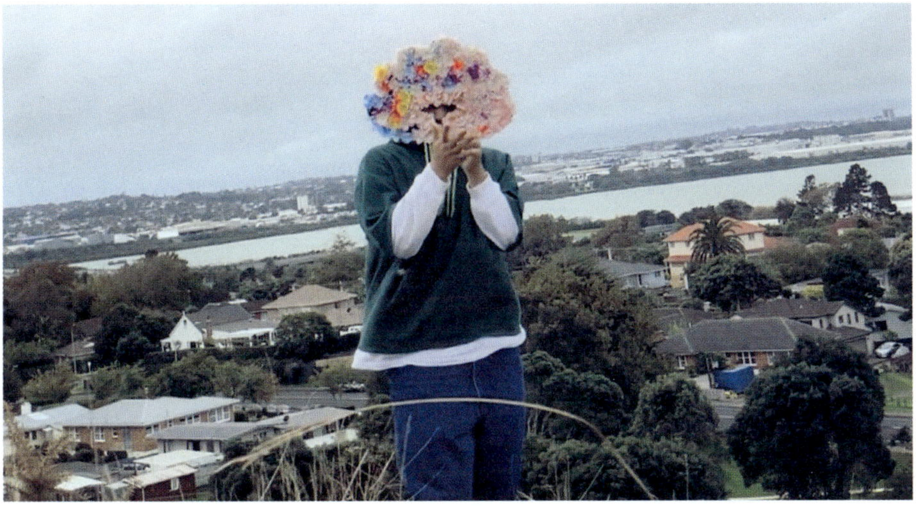

Sione Tuívailala Monū, *Mangere Bridge* (iPhone screen-capture), 2020. Single-channel HD digital video, colour, sound, duration 3 minutes 55 seconds. *Courtesy the artist*

Cut to Monū walking away from the camera, proceeding up the mountain with the mask strapped to their face. They pause and survey the geological formations and wild grasses of the terrain. Cut to a closer shot: they turn and look dramatically towards the camera.

Monū's instances of performed photography and imaging of the self (as well as those of Matila-Smith, which we discuss shortly) tie into performance art discourse, particularly from the 1990s and early 2000s. Performance theorist Amelia Jones, for instance, argued that artists use technologies of visual representation to objectify/render/confirm the self, the body's never-ending 'thereness', 'so as to prove existence as a subject' in all fullness and truth, though such technologies only 'expose the inexorable failure of representation to offer up the self as a coherent knowable entity'.[22]

It is interesting to see the way the discourse has shifted, from Jones and her discussion of artists like Renée Cox, Laura Aguilar and Pipilotti Rist, to Gronlund's discussion of the way in which social-media users constantly attempt to perform their real selves, though these are selves that occupy multiple subject positions in a public, social field and are enacted through interaction on the internet.

For audience members, the space between these multiple subjectivities of real selves and performed selves is ambiguous. Within the panopticon of digital surveillance, ambiguity becomes a tool or a protective force from the disciplining that occurs from perceived narcissism of self-imaging. As scepticism of social media self-representation has grown over the past decade, critiques of authentic-selves have also increased. The presentation of one's authentic self (both real and perceived), often presented as earnest, then becomes the expectation; any other self-performance open for scrutiny is often labelled as attention-seeking. We see a resistance to this policing of self-expression through Wollen's Sad Girl Theory. Jamison states:

> A cry for attention is positioned as the ultimate crime, clutching or trivial — as if 'attention' were inherently a selfish thing to want. But isn't wanting attention one of the most fundamental traits of being human — and isn't granting it one of the most important gifts we can ever give?[23]

As noted, Sad Girl Theory responds to acts of resistance and protest in expressions of female sadness. Wollen uses Instagram to post photos that encapsulate her sadness alongside commentary about feminism and art world patriarchy. The platform enables Wollen to broadcast ideas, photos and artworks to more than 24,000 followers. The idea is that Sad Girl Theory destigmatises female sadness, often disregarded as passivity — positioning it as a kind of resistance, making space for all modes of female expression. Arguably, female sadness could also be read as anti-capitalist in the way it prioritises emotional expression, rather than suppression for the sake of capitalist productivity.

The long-standing critique on the performance of self on video as narcissistic, articulated by art historian Rosalind Krauss in her 1976 essay 'Video: The aesthetics of narcissism', has itself since been critiqued. Dismissing self-images as narcissistic stems from the long reach of Western philosophy (the domain of white men), which sees a separation of the mind from the body, a kind of transcendence reserved exclusively for men. In contrast, in the history of feminist theory one's body is a central part of theoretical work, as it enables one to theorise from one's own position. While arguably all philosophy is created from one's own position, feminist and feminist of colour work specifically makes this explicit. This is autotheory, a way of moving between theory and philosophy that values the experiential and the embodied.

Lauren Fournier's discussion on autotheory brings to light the way many artists work autotheoretically through practice. Drawing from performance art of the early 1990s, with reference to Wollen's Sad Girl Theory, Fournier discusses how performance can be a way of embodying theory.[24] Arguably, the work of Natasha Matila-Smith (and Monū) can be connected to this 1990s history of feminist performance art.

Cut to the corner of a room in view through the lens of a locked-off shot. More than half the frame is taken up with a bed, flooded with pink lighting. The walls of the room are bare except for two images stuck to the wall above the head of the artist, who is lying in the bed. The artist's face and body are covered by blankets; we see only the top of her head and her arm. She appears to be scrolling through her phone. Next to the artist is a laptop playing something that we cannot see: short passages of text appear on the screen:

These days, I get quite excited about the prospect of going to bed
Men not being able to handle emotions or an iota of honesty is so boring to me
I wish someone would buy me flowers
Dreaming about crying then not actually crying when you're awake
I'm ready to have my heart broken again
My loneliness is manageable but I think I'm just a bit tired of doing things on my own
Men on dating apps . . . I don't care if they ski or mountain climb or go to the gym or partake in adventure sports. I just wish they had a personality
I just wanna be spooned
I leave my laptop running all night long because it makes me feel less alone
If I die, don't worry about the porn, it's tasteful . . . Just delete my Soundcloud
I always feel like I annoy people but I don't really care
'Bubbly' is my least favourite adjective
When I wake up in the morning it feels like I haven't slept at all
CAPITALISM IS FAILING
Are my heart palpitations from drinking too many fizzy drinks?
wanna date me?

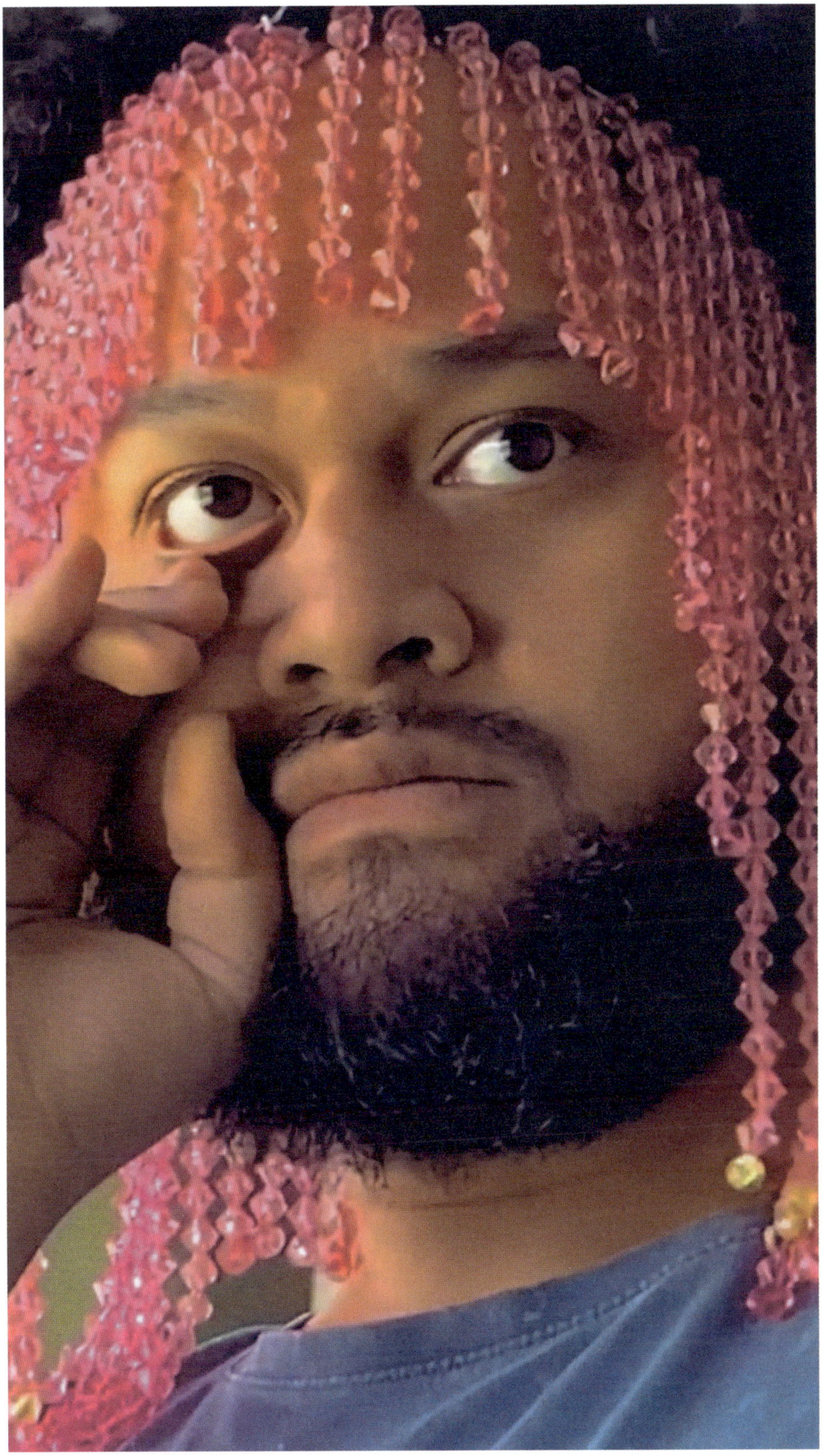

Sione Tuívailala Monū, phone screen-capture from a selected video shown at the exhibition *Stories*, City Gallery Wellington Te Whare Toi, 2023, showing large-scale multiple projections. Digital video on Samsung Galaxy A23s, duration 10 minutes 21 seconds. *Courtesy the artist*

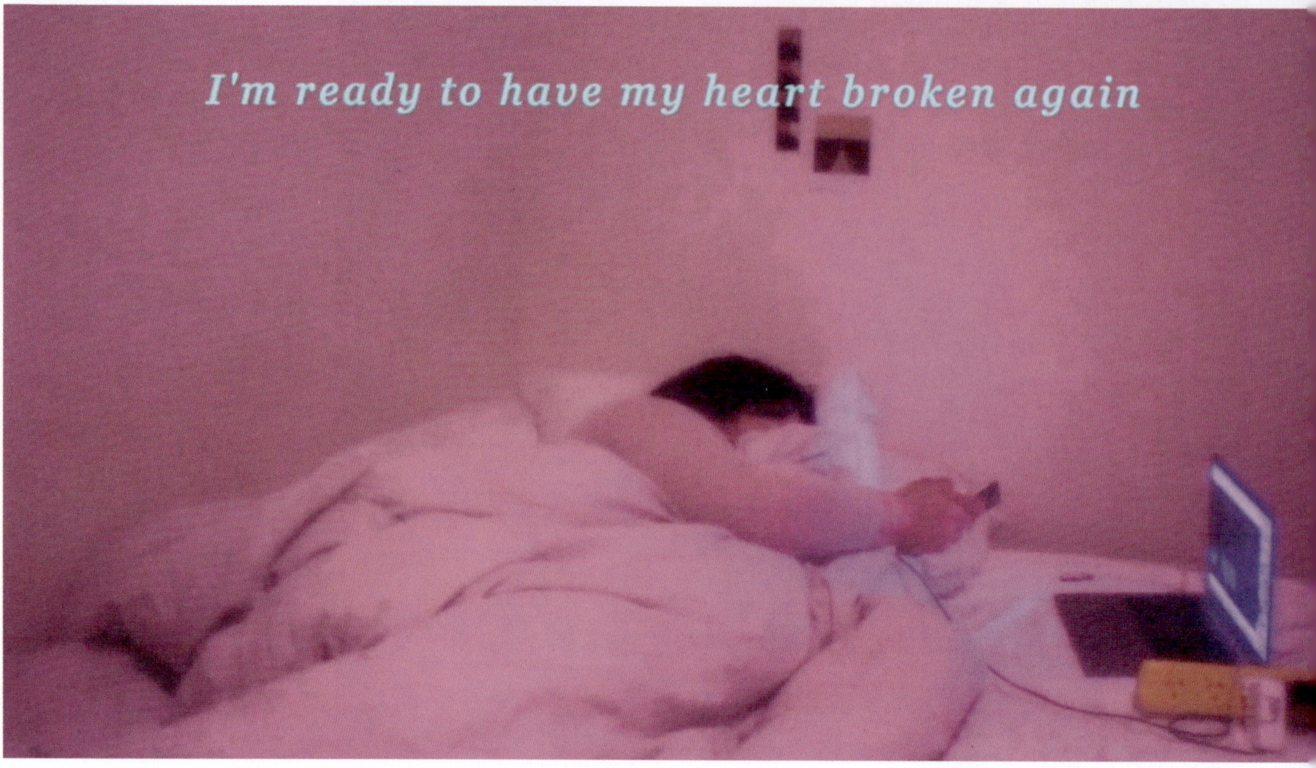
I'm ready to have my heart broken again

LEFT: Screenshot of Natasha Matila-Smith (Ngāti Kahungunu, Ngāti Hine, Samoan, Pākehā), *If I die, please delete my Soundcloud*, 2019. Single-channel digital video, colour, sound, duration 7 minutes 37 seconds. Commissioned by CIRCUIT Artist Moving Image with the support of Creative New Zealand. © *Natasha Matila-Smith*

BELOW: Installation view of *If I die, please delete my Soundcloud*, on display at the NGV Triennial 2020, 19 December 2020–18 April 2021, NGV International, Naarm Melbourne. © *Natasha Matila-Smith. Photo by Tom Ross*

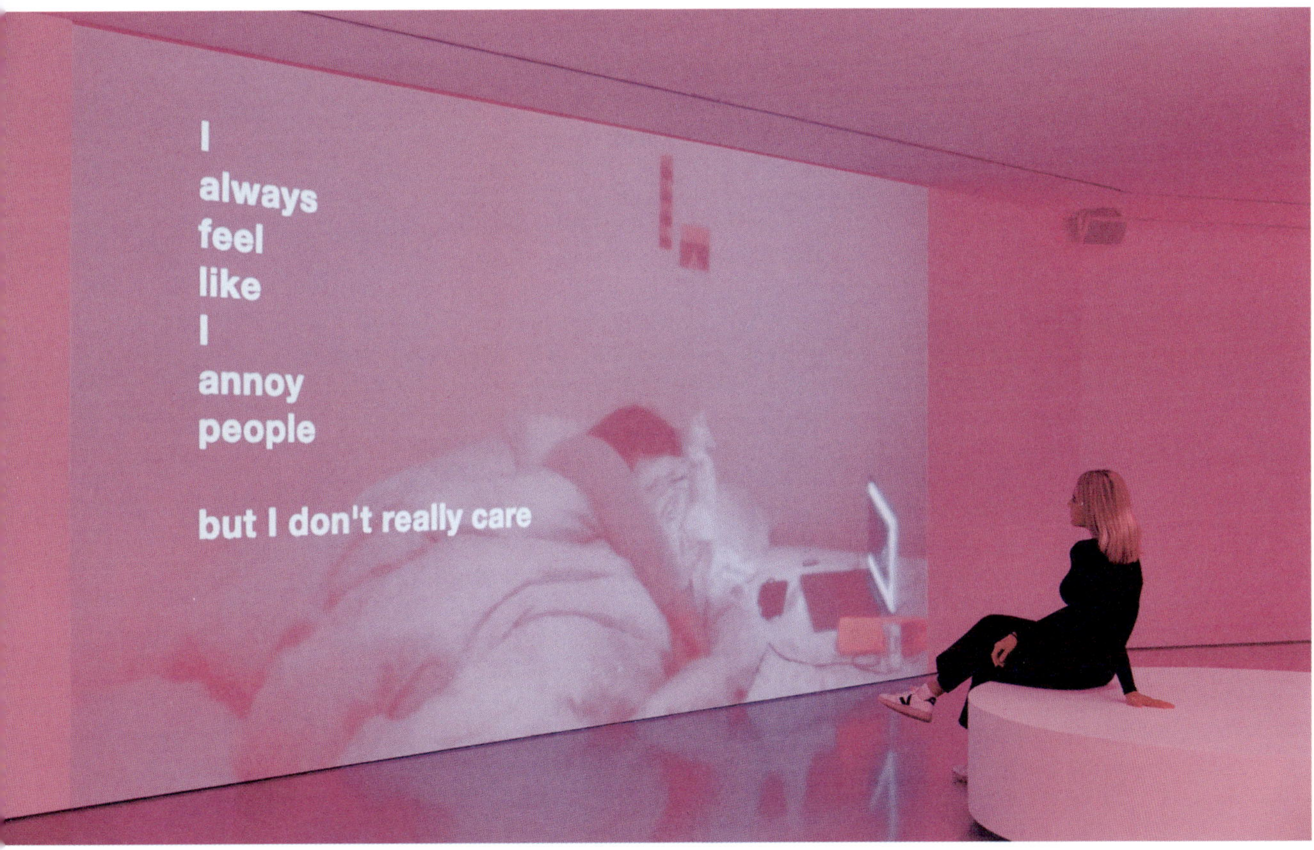

I fell like I'm not a typical Aquarian but then again, that is something an Aquarian would say
Was it bad that I had a nap at 5pm?
The neverending period
2 UGLY 2 DATE
lol
Feel like I need to urgently bag a boyfriend before I get uglier. You?
Why am I always attracted to men who look like they're ill?
I forget not everyone is as good at whining as I am

The continuous text reads like tweets or Instagram captions, all of them focused on loneliness and desire for intimacy. This work is emblematic of Matila-Smith's 'sad girl confessional'-style of making, which examines tensions between online performances of self and our physical desires for intimacy.[25]

This work, titled *If I die, please delete my Soundcloud* (2019), and other works in the artist's 'sad girl confessional' genre, are a culmination of the artist's own use of social media. Over the past decade Matila-Smith has played with self-portraiture and oversharing. Initially, using the mediums she had access to — a phone and Instagram — she would overlay selfies with text and illustration in an early 2000s Microsoft Paint aesthetic. In an interview for *Metro* magazine, Matila-Smith noted that sharing online, coupled with her love of romance shows, became a kind of compulsion and strategy for coping with the world.[26] This playfulness with subjectivity occurred early, when creating online profiles was in its infancy and most people using social media were not yet thinking about it critically.

Matila-Smith took the language she was using on social media into her practice through a series of paintings on velvet, in which she used confessional phrases that often focused on love, loneliness and insecurity. In many ways the confessional paintings said things that perhaps could not otherwise be voiced, mirroring the degree of separation and protection that occurs online, a literal screen between two bodies.

As Joanna Walsh notes, the online confessional in its various forms can be connected to a genealogy of the diary: 'The diary used to be for thoughts that were unspeakable. The blog made it about sharing them with as many people as possible. The digital diary put onscreen the screened-off "private" self.'[27] Breaking privacy offers possibilities, and the genre of the diary offers protection. The revelations of Matila-Smith's confessionals are ambiguous in intent. It is difficult to ascertain whether they are jokes or earnest truths, and whether the audience response should be laughter or empathy. In previous conversations the artist has noted an interest in the fantasy of the romance genre. The real and performed self of Matila-Smith is blurred and catches audiences in the same tangle.

Like Wollen's Sad Girl Theory, which asserts that sadness is not passive or shameful but rather is an active mode of articulation, Matila-Smith's work uses sadness to comment on the seriousness of loneliness, and the significant need for acts of care in a hyper-capitalist society that diminishes the value of care work and has a rapacious hunger for online consumption. As writer Huni Mancini notes, using the language of technology, Matila-Smith 'creates space to contemplate herself outside the need for a function'.[28]

Reasserting the figure of the Sad Girl, whether lying in bed or smoking in the shower, Sione Tuívailala Monū and Natasha Matila-Smith offer self-performances that reclaim the range of female expression and present the passive as a refusal.

NOTES

1 *Mangere Bridge* (2020) was screened as part of the exhibition *Spheres: An online video project*, curated by Nathan Pōhio and Melanie Oliver at Christchurch Art Gallery Te Puna o Waiwhetū, 2020.
2 Sione Tuívailala Monū's *#BlanketCouture* (2016) was exhibited in *Social Matter*, curated by Louisa Afoa at Blue Oyster Project Space, Ōtepoti Dunedin in 2016. *Kafu Couture* (2014–ongoing) was also included in *Declaration: A Pacific feminist agenda*, curated by Ane Tonga at Auckland Art Gallery Toi o Tāmaki in 2022.
3 Benjamin Barron, 'Richard Prince, Audrey Wollen, and the Sad Girl Theory', *I-D*, 12 November 2014, https://i-d.vice.com/en/article/nebn3d/richard-prince-audrey-wollen-and-the-sad-girl-theory
4 Melissa Gronlund, *Contemporary Art and Digital Culture* (London/New York: Routledge, 2017), 151.
5 Ibid., 152.
6 Ibid., 155.
7 Ibid.
8 Janine Randerson, 'Sampling Tradition: The old in new media', in *The Aotearoa Digital Arts Reader*, edited by Stella Brennan and Su Ballard (Auckland: Clouds and Aotearoa Digital Arts Trust, 2008), 94. https://clouds.co.nz/the-aotearoa-digital-arts-reader
9 Leslie Jamison, 'Grand Unified Theory of Female Pain', in *The Empathy Exams: Essays* (Minneapolis: Graywolf Press, 2014), 373–440.
10 Ibid., 380.
11 Ibid., 435.
12 Ibid., 436–37.
13 Gronlund, *Contemporary Art and Digital Culture*, 155.
14 Ane Tonga, ed., *Declaration: A Pacific feminist agenda*, exhibition catalogue (Auckland: Auckland Art Gallery Toi o Tāmaki, 2022), 105. Leitī is a Tongan term for a biologically male person who embodies female gender traits.
15 Gronlund, *Contemporary Art and Digital Culture*, 155.
16 See Victoria Wynne-Jones, 'From Elsewhere to Here: Rebecca Hobbs' networked and post-internet choreographies', in *Choreographing Intersubjectivity in Performance Art* (Cham, Switzerland: Palgrave Macmillan, 2021), 145–77.
17 Gronlund, *Contemporary Art and Digital Culture*, 155–56.
18 Shigeyuki Kihara, 'Shigeyuki Kihara in Conversation with Natalie King', in *Paradise Camp by Yuki Kihara*, edited by Natalie King (Wellington/Melbourne: The Arts Council of New Zealand Toi Aotearoa and Thames & Hudson, 2022), 61.
19 Philip Auslander, 'The Performativity of Performance Documentation', *PAJ: A Journal of Performance and Art* 28, no. 3 (September 2006): 3.
20 Peter Brunt, 'Framing Identity', in *Fomison — What Shall We Tell Them?*, edited by Ian Wedde, exhibition catalogue (Wellington: City Gallery Wellington, 1994), 73.
21 Christina Barton, *Billy Apple® Life/Work* (Auckland: Auckland University Press, 2020), 56–59.
22 Amelia Jones, *Self/Image: Technology, representation, and the contemporary subject* (London/New York: Routledge, 2006), xvii.
23 Jamison, 'Grand Unified Theory', 385.
24 Lauren Fournier, *Autotheory as Feminist Practice in Art, Writing, and Criticism* (Cambridge, MA: MIT Press, 2022).
25 Natasha Matila-Smith, 'Natasha Matila-Smith: Kaituhi Tūtahi | Contributing Writer', *The Pantograph Punch*, 2023, www.pantograph-punch.com/writers/natasha-matila-smith
26 Lana Lopesi, 'The Inner World of Artist Natasha Matila-Smith', *Metro*, 26 April 2021, www.metromag.co.nz/arts/the-inner-world-of-artist-natasha-matila-smith
27 Joanna Walsh, *Girl Online: A user manual* (London/New York: Verso, 2022), 89.
28 Huni Mancini, 'The Dark Intimacies of Online Romance in Natasha Matila-Smith's Artwork', *The Pantograph Punch*, 10 January 2020, https://pantograph-punch.com/posts/touching-the-veil

REFERENCES

Auslander, Philip. 'The Performativity of Performance Documentation'. *PAJ: A Journal of Performance and Art* 28, no. 3 (September 2006): 1–10, 4–5.

Barron, Benjamin. 'Richard Prince, Audrey Wollen, and the Sad Girl Theory'. *I-D*, 12 November 2014. https://i-d.vice.com/en/article/nebn3d/richard-prince-audrey-wollen-and-the-sad-girl-theory

Barton, Christina. *Billy Apple® Life/Work*. Auckland: Auckland University Press, 2020.

Brennan, Stella and Su Ballard, eds. *The Aotearoa Digital Arts Reader*. Auckland: Clouds and Aotearoa Digital Arts Trust, 2008.

Brunt, Peter. 'Framing Identity'. In *Fomison — What Shall We Tell Them?*, edited by Ian Wedde. Exhibition catalogue, 63–75. Wellington: City Gallery Wellington, 1994.

Fournier, Lauren. *Autotheory as Feminist Practice in Art, Writing, and Criticism*. Cambridge, MA: MIT Press, 2022.

Gronlund, Melissa. *Contemporary Art and Digital Culture*. London/New York: Routledge, 2017.

Jamison, Leslie. 'Grand Unified Theory of Female Pain'. In *The Empathy Exams: Essays*, 373–440. Minneapolis: Graywolf Press, 2014.

Jones, Amelia. *Self/Image: Technology, representation, and the contemporary subject*. London/New York: Routledge, 2006.

Kihara, Shigeyuki. 'Shigeyuki Kihara in Conversation with Natalie King'. In *Paradise Camp by Yuki Kihara*, edited by Natalie King, 61. Wellington/Melbourne: The Arts Council of New Zealand Toi Aotearoa and Thames & Hudson, 2022.

Lopesi, Lana. 'The Inner World of Artist Natasha Matila-Smith'. *Metro*, 26 April 2021. www.metromag.co.nz/arts/the-inner-world-of-artist-natasha-matila-smith

Mancini, Huni. 'The Dark Intimacies of Online Romance in Natasha Matila-Smith's Artwork'. *The Pantograph Punch*, 10 January 2020. https://pantograph-punch.com/posts/touching-the-veil

Matila-Smith, Natasha. 'Natasha Matila-Smith: Kaituhi Tūtahi | Contributing Writer'. *The Pantograph Punch*, 2023. www.pantograph-punch.com/writers/natasha-matila-smith

Tonga, Ane, ed. *Declaration: A Pacific feminist agenda*. Exhibition catalogue. Auckland: Auckland Art Gallery Toi o Tāmaki, 2022.

Walsh, Joanna. *Girl Online: A user manual*. London/New York: Verso, 2022.

Wynne-Jones, Victoria. 'From Elsewhere to Here: Rebecca Hobbs' networked and post-internet choreographies'. In *Choreographing Intersubjectivity in Performance Art*, 145–77. Cham, Switzerland: Palgrave Macmillan, 2021.

18

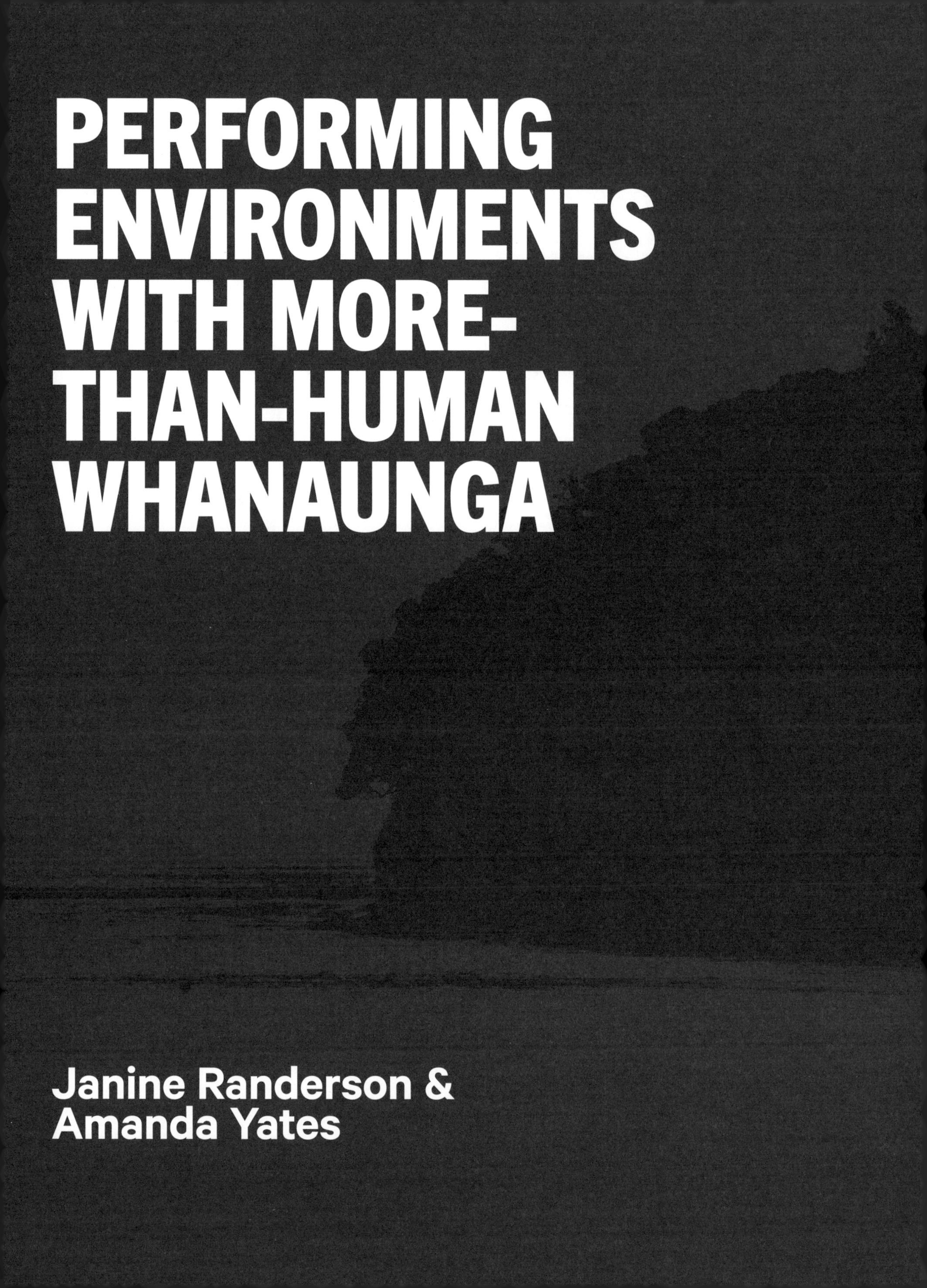

PERFORMING ENVIRONMENTS WITH MORE-THAN-HUMAN WHANAUNGA

Janine Randerson &
Amanda Yates

The environment does not perform for us. Human lives are incidental to a cyclone, yet we become co-performers as a virus inflames our bodies, or when the same wind that topples the giant pūriri trees outside agitates our bodies as well, or the waters rise around our knees in the back yard. In February 2023, the deep barometric low of Cyclone Gabrielle brought the heaviest rains on record to Aotearoa New Zealand. It followed floods and severe coastal erosion from ex-tropical Cyclone Hale a month earlier, and all as people continued to navigate the long tail of a pandemic.

Under the weight of ancient pōhutukawa trees that could no longer grasp the sodden soil, cliffs crumbled, awa breached their banks and roads became impassable. Water and earth surged into all the spaces expunged by human infrastructures and systems.

In Titirangi we lived without power and water for a week, feeling grateful that the floods and slips that had so powerfully affected others had not reached us. In a time of compounding disaster, enmeshed in the nature–culture tumult of the climate catastrophe and Covid-19, how best to write about environmental performance art?

In what follows, we recognise our shared ecology, other species and environmental entities as whanaunga — our kin. But for the human late-comers to the world, the biophysical reality created by the colonial–capitalist complex has thrust our relationships with our ecosphere into chaos. The ecological crisis is, in part, a crisis of relationships and how we perform them. In this chapter we attune to Māori practices of whanaungatanga, and relation-making with lively ecologies.

Whanaungatanga — as a relational practice between living entities — can be traced in performance practices that perform ontological and eco-political agitations. We find artists immersed for hours in the sea, wading through public baths, carrying saplings through the rain, conversing with plants and battling with weeds: performing with our more-than-human whanaunga.[1] The work of care is an expression of whanaungatanga and involves the maintenance of relationships. Environmental performance is not for the faint-hearted; we are in it for the long haul.

We draw on and interweave our discussion of whanaungatanga with kaitiakitanga, care-giving practices that also encompass whakapapa, a more-than-human genealogy. To be whanaunga, a cousin to other entities such as insects, birds and rocks, is related but qualitatively different to Euro-American, post-humanist notions of the more-than-human kinship.[2]

Some performers discussed in this chapter weave between Indigenous whakapapa and settler histories in collaborative relations between tangata whenua and the descendants of colonisers; the members of HIWA kapa haka group and supporters of New York-based artist Sarah Cameron Sunde uphold their connection to Te Manukanuka ō Hoturoa Manukau Harbour, affirming their relationships with this ocean while participating in *36.5/A durational performance with the sea* (2013–22); and val smith and Forest Vicky Kapo collaborate across Te Tai o Rehua the Tasman Sea. In the performers' movements we find the ebb and flow of tides, diurnal cycles of growth, decay and regeneration: performative modes that attune, move with and tend to and, at times, also rebel against nature–cultural forces, in resistance to the wilful damage to the Earth in the age of the Petrocene.

This chapter traverses seven performance moments that express whanaungatanga as a way to face this turbulent ecological moment and epoch manufactured by capitalist and colonialist culture. The carrying of young saplings and the exchange of seeds between participants in Jeremy Leatinu'u's *Mauria* (2020) expresses the caregiving practice needed at present and, at the same time, a retracing of a migration story. We walk with him, looking forward and backward to his ancestor maunga Ōwairaka/Te Ahi Kaa o Rakataura (the latter the Tainui name), later called Mount Albert by colonial settlers. We find a queer(y)ing of environmental discourse that challenges nature–culture binaries in the work of val smith and Forest Vicky Kapo in *i'll grow back* (2020), a 'human*plant communing'. We follow the ecological crisis of rising sea levels and the specific struggles for land and water sovereignty in *36.5/A durational performance with the sea* (2013–22).

In Tru Paraha's collusions with Te Pō, the originary darkness in *KARE: kind artificial real experience* (2016), the kūmara plays a part in Māori cosmogeny and an implicit critique of neo-coloniality; and in Mark Harvey's *Group Weed Wrestle* (2016), the invasive Australian wattle proves a worthy adversary. The gentle cyclical flows and embodied attunements with the more-than-human appear in Angela Tiatia's *Lick* (2015), in which her body becomes fishlike, returning softly to oceanic whanaunga, fish kin. Most of these performances take place outdoors, but in Alicia Frankovich's water-based performance *The Eye* (2022), nature becomes interiorised in the Brunswick Baths in Naarm Melbourne. The body language of a frantic escape from flood — performers weighted down by clothes and a few possessions — is familiar across the cyclone-drenched isles of Te Moana-nui-a-Kiwa.

Contemporary ecological performance in Aotearoa often contains echoes of deeper cosmologies or lines of whakapapa and whanaungatanga, even in relationships between performers of Pākehā descent who work in collaboration with tangata whenua, such as smith and Kapo.[3] Alicia Frankovich and Jeremy Leatinu'u have whakapapa connections to Te Moana-nui-a-Kiwa but create collective stories for and with people from many different lineages in conjunction with more-than-human entities. Mere Roberts and her co-authors discuss how the sustainable principles behind plant and animal Māori whakapapa have been underexplored, and use the whakapapa of the kūmara as a case study. In te ao Māori, they continue,

> there is no disjunction between the spiritual and material worlds. Insects and humans, fish and ferns, stars and stones all descend from the spiritual realm of the atua, and thus all possess spiritual qualities (such as mauri) in addition to their own unique material attributes. This dual inheritance applies to all things and, in this context, establishes and emphasises complementary relationships, rather than the oppositional ones that exist between more modern juxtapositions, such as the 'natural and the supernatural', the 'living and the nonliving', and the 'nature–culture' divide.[4]

Importantly, whakapapa narratives connect our bodies to the plethora of entities in the environment and cosmos as both ancestors and kin, opening our imaginations to shared coexistences. In the contemporary performances we describe, we find traces of the cosmogonies that connect human to more-than-human through descent lines and relationships, whakapapa lineages or papa, the layers that connect the generations. From a very different paradigm, with Rosi Braidotti, we suggest that new social formations are imagined in performance that generate 'ontological relationality', or radical ways of being together. This fostering of relationality exceeds former definitions of the human.[5]

We adopt the term 'more-than-human' from cultural geographer Sarah Whatmore,[6] along with the notions of kinship that are fundamental to mātauranga Māori and notably utilised by Donna Haraway and Rosi Braidotti. Performance does not always present an affirmative ethos, however, and there are undercurrents of desperation in works that probe our fraught and often harmful relationships with the more-than-human.

TRU PARAHA, KARE: KIND ARTIFICIAL REAL EXPERIENCE (2016)

> things perform in a collaboration of human–nonhuman perpetrators. The bite-marked remains of a choreographic ménage à trois, the flesh of moemoe is absorbed of post-vital powers, each of us — unidentified subjects — transfusing, sucking, impaling. What could be so sweet about a potato kissed to its hour of death, penetrated by, and penetrating into monstrous dancing mouths? [7]

Moving slowly at arm's length, two performers circle each other in a slow, intent walk. One, a female, holds a kūmara in her mouth; the other is male and has no kūmara.[8] Their eyes are fixed on each other in some kind of stand-off. After some time they come closer, sharing breath or hā energy, not in hongi but in the passing of the kūmara between them, mouth to mouth, hands behind their backs. The passing of the homely, root-studded starchy vegetable is slow, awkward and seismic. This vegetable is kai, sustaining food, a signifier of resilience, but, as Paraha (Ngāti Hineāmaru, Ngāti Kahu o Torongare) writes, this exchange is also a little death. The kūmara is passed between their mouths reluctantly, resistantly, less a fetish object than a plant-actant that arrives and dies in the mouth of the descendant-coloniser.

In the basement depths of Tāmaki Makaurau Auckland's Kenneth Myers Centre, the audience huddles on the fringe of the dark room: this is the '3 am cosmos // asbestos ash' of Paraha's imaginary.[9] She describes the performance field as a 'blackening choreosphere', where the darkness is full of generative potential; where cosmologies of Te Pō and Te Kore contain 'inhuman darknesses of Māori oral traditions'.[10] Half-remembered recollections of this performance include strained relations, psycho-physical conflicts that build and diminish between human bodies that struggle, fall, are dragged away and rise again.

Yet the more-than-human presence of the kūmara in the chiaroscuro of the choreography remains strong in body-memory. The kūmara resonates with a cosmology of migration stories and earthly burial and tendrils of regrowth. The homeliness of the kūmara lends focus to this gritty, uncomfortable darkness, full of edges and depths, an un-colonising by stealth.

For Paraha, the trope of the brightly illuminated gallery or theatre is a hangover from the hyper-visuality of white enlightenment. Instead, her performers emerge and disappear from the shadow world, away from artificial light.[11] Writer André Lepecki suggests that the darkness in contemporary performance offers 'a much needed space of potentiality' within neo-capitalist mores and codes of constraint and erasure.[12] The collusion with darkness in Paraha's *KARE: kind artificial real experience* is part of a later trilogy of darkness and 'astrochoreography'[13] in *blackOut* (2018) and the *5th Body* (2019–21).

'Kare' is te reo Māori for waves, where the kūmara floats buoyantly in the waves of darkness, a migrant vegetable that lies dormant in the earth until harvest. One version

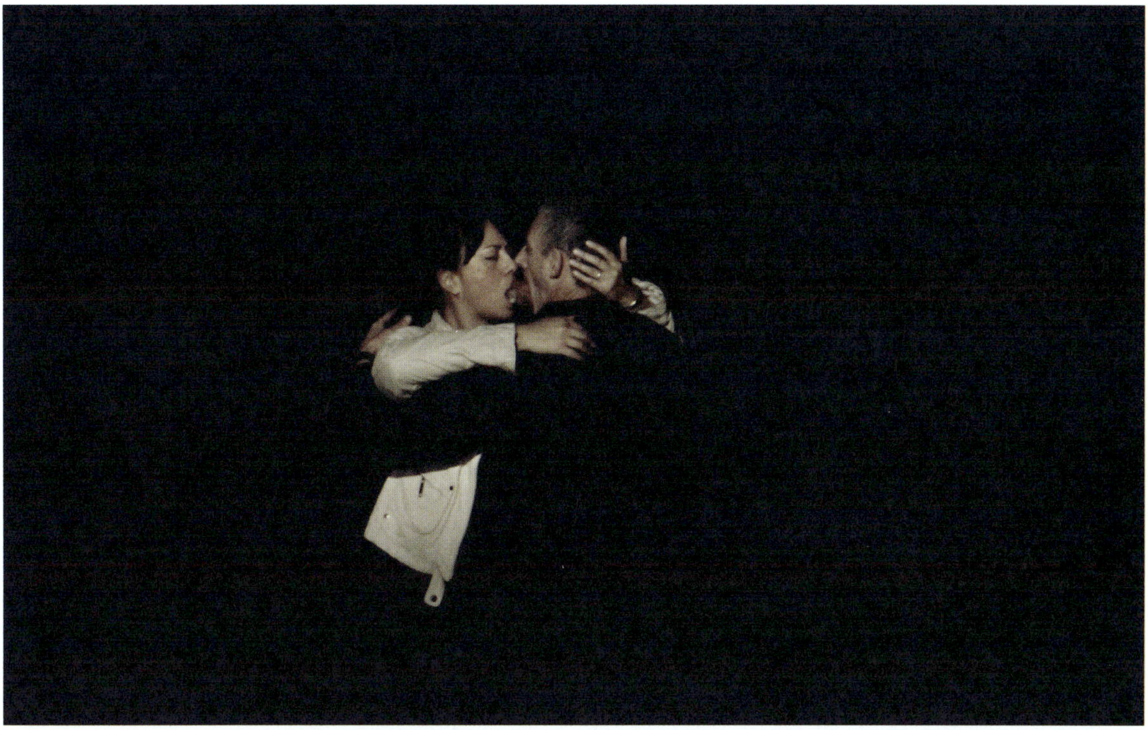

Tru Paraha (Ngāti Hineāmaru, Ngāti Kahu o Torongare), *KARE: kind artificial real experience*, 2016, documentation of performers Sean Curham and Tru Paraha, Kenneth Myers Centre, Tāmaki Makaurau Auckland. *Courtesy the artist*

of a kūmara narrative, recounted by Mere Roberts and her co-authors, begins with Uru-te-ngangana, the tutelary deity of celestial bodies, including stars and Whānui (the star Vega), the elder brother of Rongo-māui, a small star close to Whānui:

> Rongo-māui's wife Pani-tinaku (tinaku means to germinate, sprout, conceive) was the foster mother of the five Māui brothers, who were fishermen. When the brothers reproached Rongo-māui for his indolence in failing to procure food supplies, he set off to obtain the celestial kūmara held in the care of Whānui. Rongo-māui was forced to steal the celestial kūmara and brought them back to earth, carrying the tubers in his scrotum. He then impregnated his wife Pani and told her to go to the Wai o Mona-Ariki (the waters or stream of Mona-Ariki) and give birth to their offspring, the earthly form of the kūmara. The underwater birth of the kūmara is 're-enacted' in the practice of placing stored tubers in water to stimulate the sprouting of shoots prior to planting. Pani's children — Nehutai, Pātea, Waihā, Pio, Matatū, Pāuārangi, Toroa-māhoe, Anurangi, and Aka-kura — are all names of different varieties of kūmara, thus recounting a performative narrative of connection.[14]

While Paraha's choreography does not explicitly reference such narratives of whakapapa human-non-human lineage, implicitly the kūmara is an uncanny relation in her cosmic horror story. For Paraha, the active darkness of the performance negotiates an estranged territory, a remembrance of the black-out, night-time wānanga: 'a shadow

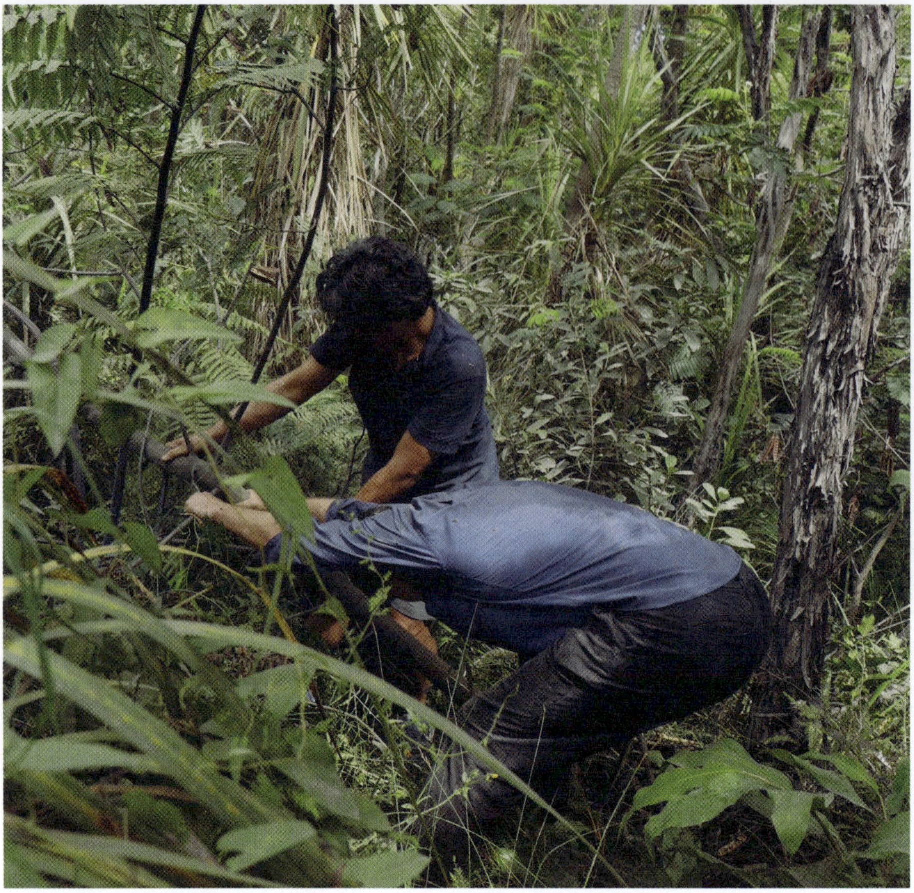

Mark Harvey, *Group Weed Wrestle*, 2016. Pictured are Charles Koroneho and Mark Harvey. *Courtesy the artist. Video still by Daniel Strang*

side of life, unbearable recesses in a cracked world, toward even more bewildering notions of a world without human'.[15]

For the next performance artwork to which we turn, the non-human weed is an adversary; the relationship *is* in crisis.

MARK HARVEY, GROUP WEED WRESTLE (2016)

On a roadside in the Waitākere Ranges a wattle tree's thin branches shake as performance artist Mark Harvey (Ngāti Raukawa ki te Tonga, Clan Keith) wrestles with the weed. Participants join the struggle, pulling together at the snaggly roots of the Australian wattle, one of many that infest the native bush of the Waitākere Ranges. Roots that encroach upon native plants and dig into Papatūānuku tear and are wrenched into the air. Clods of soil scatter onto human limbs and clothing and fall back to earth. The violence of this performative action registers broadly; branches snap, people fall. Scattering dark seeds, colonising vectors, are caught on a dropcloth and carefully contained to limit the ongoing spread of this ecological outsider to Aotearoa.

Starting in the suburb of Titirangi, *Group Weed Wrestle* unfolds as a caravan of participant-performers travelling by car, following Harvey through Woodlands Park and into Laingholm. At each new site of encroachment of the Australian wattle, the participants gather, assess and discuss a strategy for removal before beginning to engage. The afternoon's heat builds and humidity rises as participants gather seeds and collect greenery into piles that over time will rot down and return to the earth.[16] Harvey acts as guide and motivational leader, exhorting more! and harder! and the participants pull together as if in a tug of war. Whanaungatanga — relational practice — is performed here as a robust act of service to the mauri and ecological integrity of place. As weeds are removed, ancient relationships, between bird and seed, river and tree, are strengthened and attenuated ecological webs cohere.

JEREMY LEATINU‘U, MAURIA (2020)

While Harvey arrested weeds, in Jeremy Leatinu‘u's (Tainui, Samoan) social performance *Kawea* (2019), walkers were given five rākau: tōtara, kōwhai, tītoki, kahikatea and pōhutukawa seedlings less than a metre high. They took turns to carry these against their bodies, walking stoically through a rainstorm. They were instructed to bring herbs, seedlings and vegetable seeds of their own to exchange. Leatinu‘u's performance artworks operate in a careful social practice of exchange, activating walking/hīkoi as a performative mode. *Mauria* (2020) is the companion piece to *Kawea*. In *Kawea*, which took place in spring, each participant's precious personal taonga was carried by another, and each navigated their own path from the maunga to the sea. In *Mauria*, participants moved as a body, described by Leatinu‘u as a ‘human waka’, from the sea to the maunga.

Mauria and *Kawea* are named from instructional passive verbs — to carry or take, and to bring — leading us back to the voyages of early waka and their precious cargo and intertwined stories. The relationship between sapling and human kaitiaki is intimate. Leatinu‘u says: ‘Plants are living, they have their own mauri, each of them asks to be handled differently.’[17]

The twin performances took place as part of *About Walking*, curated by Christina Houghton and Melissa Laing in 2020 and supported by Te Uru Waitākere Contemporary Gallery.[18] The assembled group met on the maunga of Ōwairaka/Te Ahi Kaa o Rakataura Mount Albert. A year later in a cyclical return, *Mauria* took place in October in torrential rain. At the time, Ōwairaka was a lightning rod for a social furore about the felling of non-native rākau by descendants of settlers who occupied the area in resistance to the intergenerational plan of replanting by the Tūpuna Maunga Authority. Instead of bringing the group carrying the trees into direct conflict with the protesters, they concluded their walk near the maunga rather than on its side.[19] They followed a path from Waterview Reserve toward the mountain along Te Auaunga Oakley Creek.

Leatinu‘u had in mind the story of a waka carried along Te Auaunga Oakley Creek and buried by the waterfall. He speculated: What was carried in the waka in migrations? What plants or taonga might aid you when you arrived? He had also recently participated in the custom of gifting rākau from his iwi lands as koha to the rightful occupiers at Ihumātao on Makarau marae. In an earlier work, *Earthpushers* (2017), performed for Headlands Sculpture on Waiheke Island in the Hauraki Gulf, audience-participants carried 700 hessian sacks of soil across from Tāmaki Makaurau by ferry.[20] Both works give participants the opportunity to become kaitiaki (caregivers) of soil from one place to another, a taste of the experience of migration and the need to maintain connection.

Mauria ended with a blessing, an exchange of young trees and their stories for each participant to plant to create space for something new, something unforeseen. As well as ancient voyages by waka, Leatinu‘u recalls his Samoan heritage and the

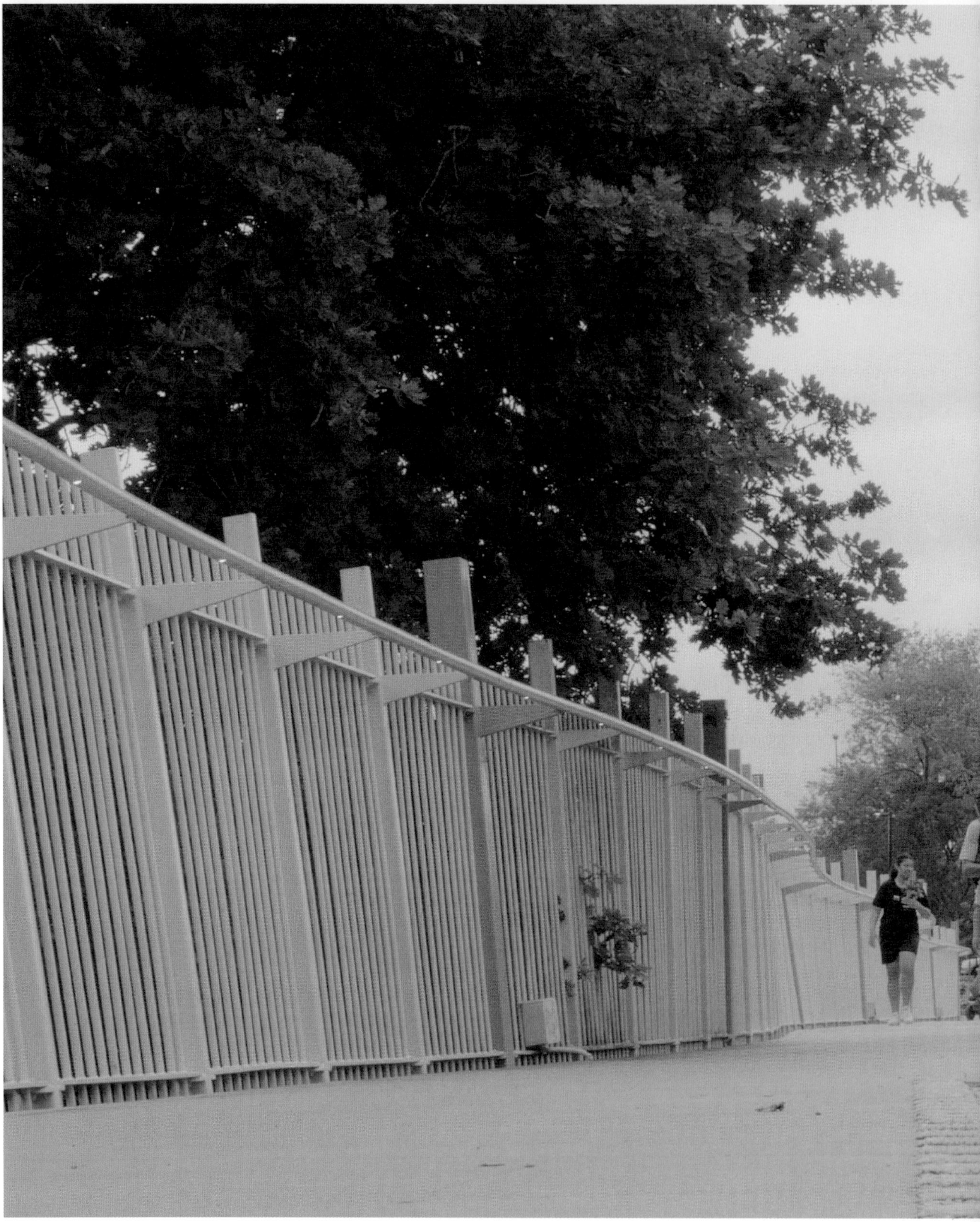

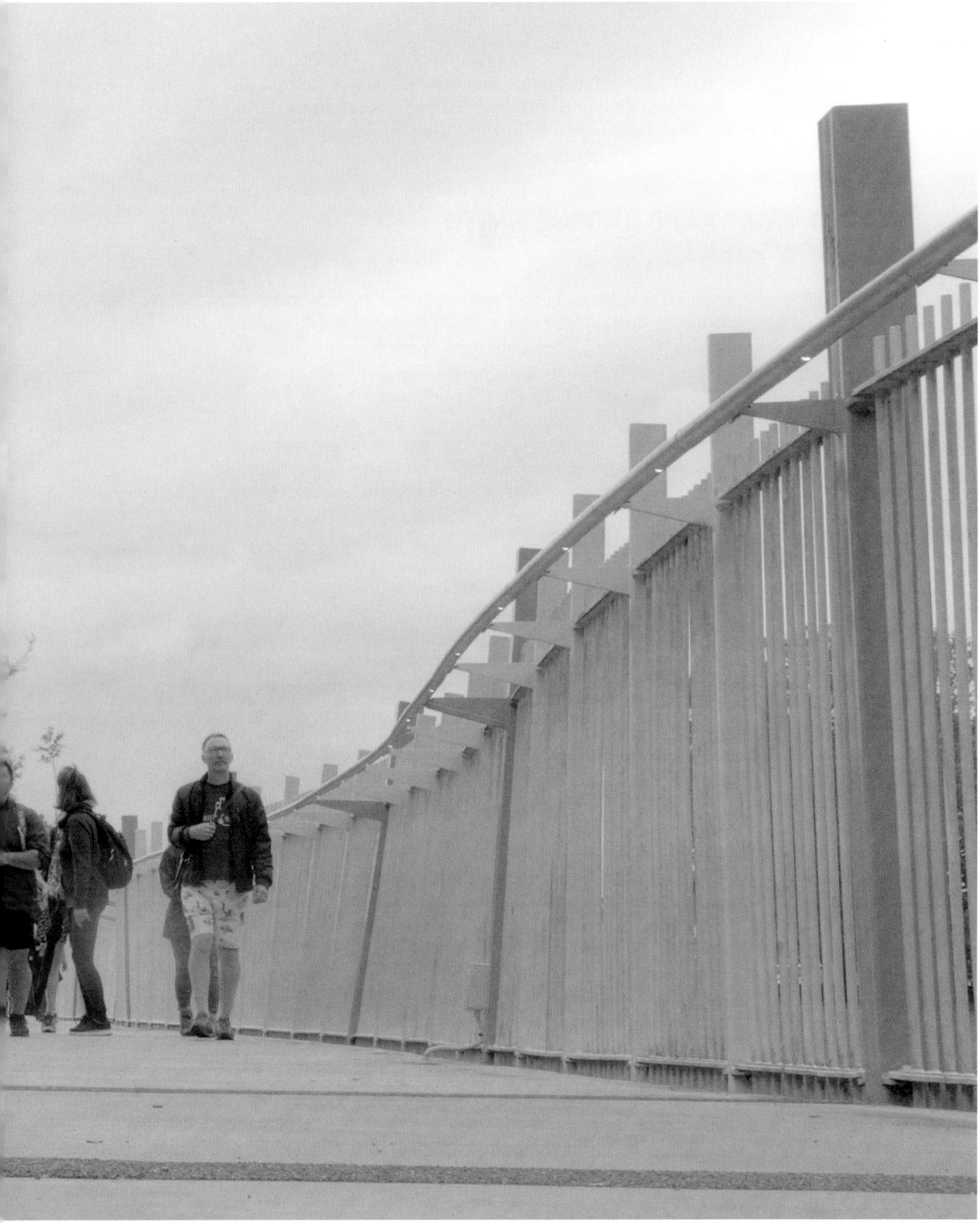

continuation of customs in the diaspora through 'fa'a Sāmoa' in the back yards, at church and community halls, making do in a human waka in relation to a new environment.[21]

As we will see in the next performance artwork discussed, the notions of whakapapa and whanaungatanga span oceans and countries.

FOREST VICKY KAPO AND VAL SMITH, I'LL GROW BACK (2020)

Several oak saplings, growing in an industrial bucket wound with tape, stand on stage next to an oval full-length mirror. Wrapped in a tartan blanket at the edge of the stage at Tāmaki Makaurau's Basement Theatre, in Experimental Dance Week Aotearoa 2020, val smith crouches over a battered laptop. They are tinkering with their Zoom livestream to Facebook; they look about the same size as the plant. The plants are central, the human is to the side working on a technical set-up.

At their home in Naarm Melbourne, Forest Vicky Kapo is standing near a full-length mirror, reading tarot cards to a row of house plants that stand waving next to an open window. The two human performers, separated by the travel protocols occasioned by the Covid-19 pandemic, are projected on a screen on stage in Basement Theatre in a Zoom diptych livestream, connected by unstable electrical exchanges, flickering and delayed. The plant 'performers' are immune to the Covid virus.

smith is also attempting to communicate with one of the plants. But how is it that we can 'speak' to the more-than-human? A disco light animates the oak saplings so they shimmer with light and appear responsive to human voice. Out loud, smith probes with awkward questions to find out what the plants think about the aging/gendered body. smith has grown the oak saplings from found acorns. A blackboard propped against the bucket bears the words: 'Acknowledging Ngāti Whātua Ōrākei and all iwi affiliated with this land and Waihorotiu'. Kapo is internet-connected to their iwi homeland in Aotearoa. Writer Amit Noy describes the performers' presence as: 'queerly doubled, their screen presence always reflecting their actions 20 seconds ago'.[22]

The glitchy conversation is full of plant and human dependencies: the potted plant relies on us for water yet supplies us with oxygen. We wonder whether dialogue with a potted plant is any more absurd than our limited human interactions with strangers through screen interfaces. Kapo and smith create a milieu for 'a human*plant communing', as smith calls it. For smith, the asterisk is a modifier of both human and plant, allowing a form of tactile, bodily, haptic connection.[23] This is a more-than/human performance riffing on gender, where smith emphasises the differences between Indigenous and settler, abiotic experience in the 'slash' rather than the easy flow of dashes in more-than-human.

Building on Eva Hayward, smith offers the tentacular process of transit*ioning as imbricated in the interactions of humans and plants or human*plant. The plants are carried in the performance, devices are carried and moved, the mirrors reflect the performers obliquely. They relate to each other and the plants through song, gesture and disrupted conversation: 'What colour is your gender?/ Green/ but there's probably more to it than that/ Where do you hide your maleness?'

The plants are interviewed by two large vocal microphones. In a distracted way, smith rubs one of the microphones against the oak sapling's bucket, a techno–plant pleasuring. Kapo's undulating hands become leaf-like for a moment. smith disappears under their blanket and reads through their performance notes. In turn the performers ask:

PREVIOUS: Jeremy Leatinu'u, *Mauria*, documentation of twin performances held as part of *About Walking*, 2020, curated by Christina Houghton and Melissa Laing, Te Uru Waitākere Gallery of Contemporary Art, Tāmaki Makaurau Auckland. *Courtesy the artist. Photo by Ian Powell*

RIGHT: val smith and Forest Vicky Kapo, *i'll grow back*, 2020, documentation of performance at the Herald Theatre for Experimental Dance Week Aotearoa, Tāmaki Makaurau Auckland. *Courtesy the artist. Photo by Courtney Rodgers*

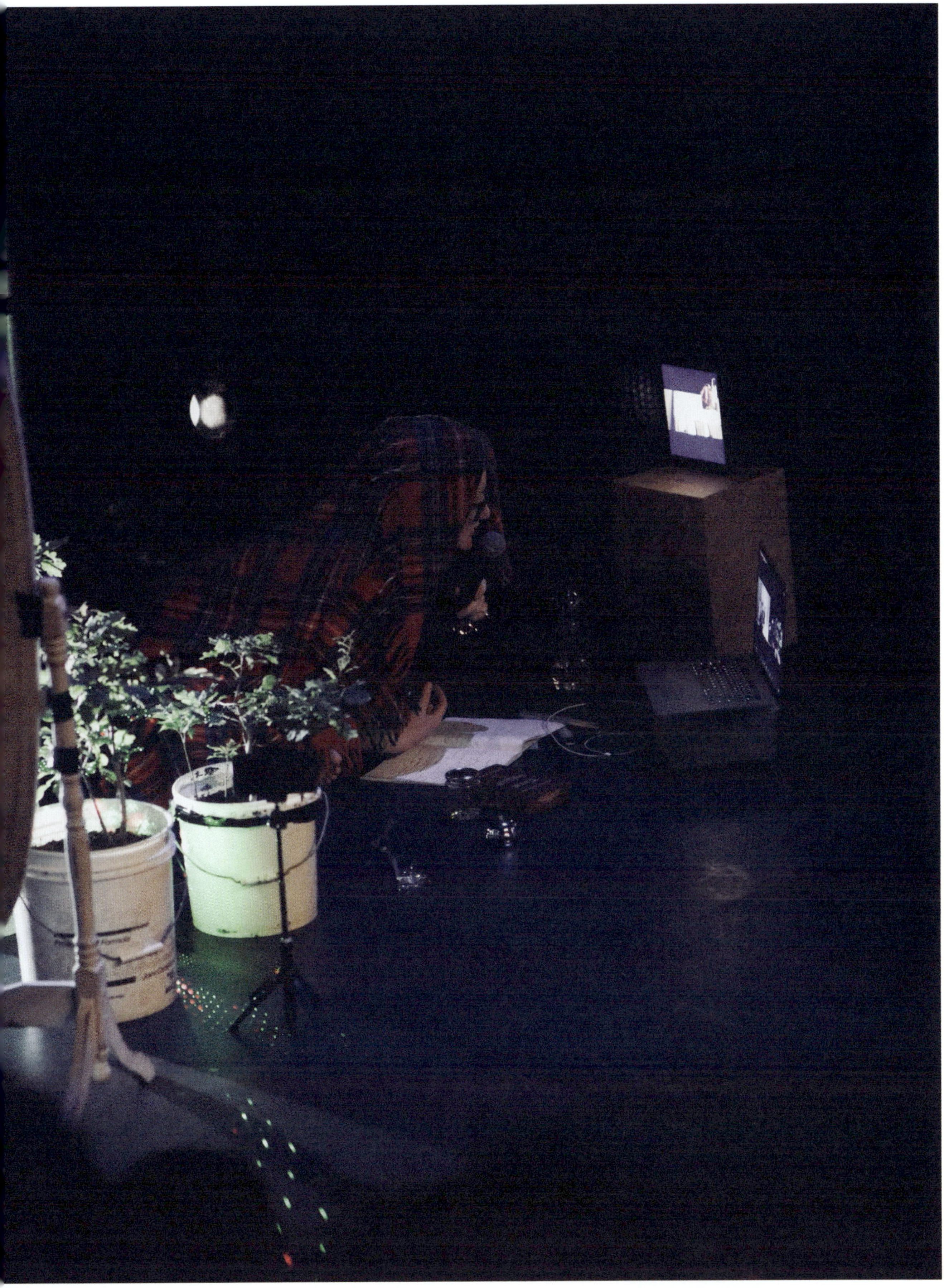

smith: Maybe it's that family and kinship thing/ I'm keen to do a reading for the back plant.

Kapo: This one? I'll just see if it wants to actually, it's been quite a passive performer this whole time/ the passionfruit is completely, always up for it, thyme, totally up for it. I can totally answer on behalf of this plant.

smith: Harold I am interested in your thoughts on kinnn . . . ship and gennnderrr . . .

They speak using long, slow drawn-out consonants. Kapo moves waveringly while more-or-less rooted to the floor, their arms moving like the shadow on a sundial as plants follow the path of the sun. smith remains under the blanket. The whanaungatanga web of relations surges, ebbs and flows across the sea and in scratchy pixels, through plant*human performers.

ANGELA TIATIA, LICK (2015)

Angela Tiatia's four limbs hang, tentacle-like, suspended in seawater in the frame of an underwater camera in this fixed-camera video. Small reef-fish dart around the gentle seaweed-slow sway of arms and legs in a lagoon's swell. Tiatia's head and torso are above the surface at first, but gradually her whole body sinks and drifts backwards until she is out of the camera's view. The fish carry on with their business, unperturbed by the body carried away by the tide. In this lush lagoon ecosphere, resisting a hyper-sexualised treatment of a Pacific woman's body, Tiatia becomes more fish-like than human gendered.

Neither we nor our fish cousins can survive the acidification of waters when the sea can no longer absorb the carbon produced in lands far away.[24] We pay the carbon debt of the Global North. *Lick* was made on Tuvalu, a small archipelago of reefs and atolls to the northeast of Sāmoa, and a country that is rapidly losing habitable land. Cyclonic storms, salination of drinking water, erosion and rising sea levels are already impacting Tuvaluans, many of whom are leaving for the relative safety of Aotearoa. Is Tiatia letting go or departing for an underwater existence?

SARAH CAMERON SUNDE, WITH AMIRIA PUIA-TAYLOR, NETTIE NORMAN AND KINGI PETERSON, 36.5/A DURATIONAL PERFORMANCE WITH THE SEA (8TH WORK IN THE SERIES: 36.5/TE MANUKANUKATANGA Ō HOTUROA, AOTEAROA NEW ZEALAND, 2020–22)

Rather than drifting supine under the water, the next performance of climate realism involves a collective of upright bodies that face the rising seas with an outward gaze. In letting go, or in taking a stand, these performing bodies direct attention to the biophysical world, performing within the warming, rising seas.

New York artist Sarah Cameron Sunde, performer-activist Amiria Puia-Taylor (Ngāti Te Ata Waiohua, Ngāti Tipa, Hamoa, Kuki Airani, Tahiti) and Kingi Peterson

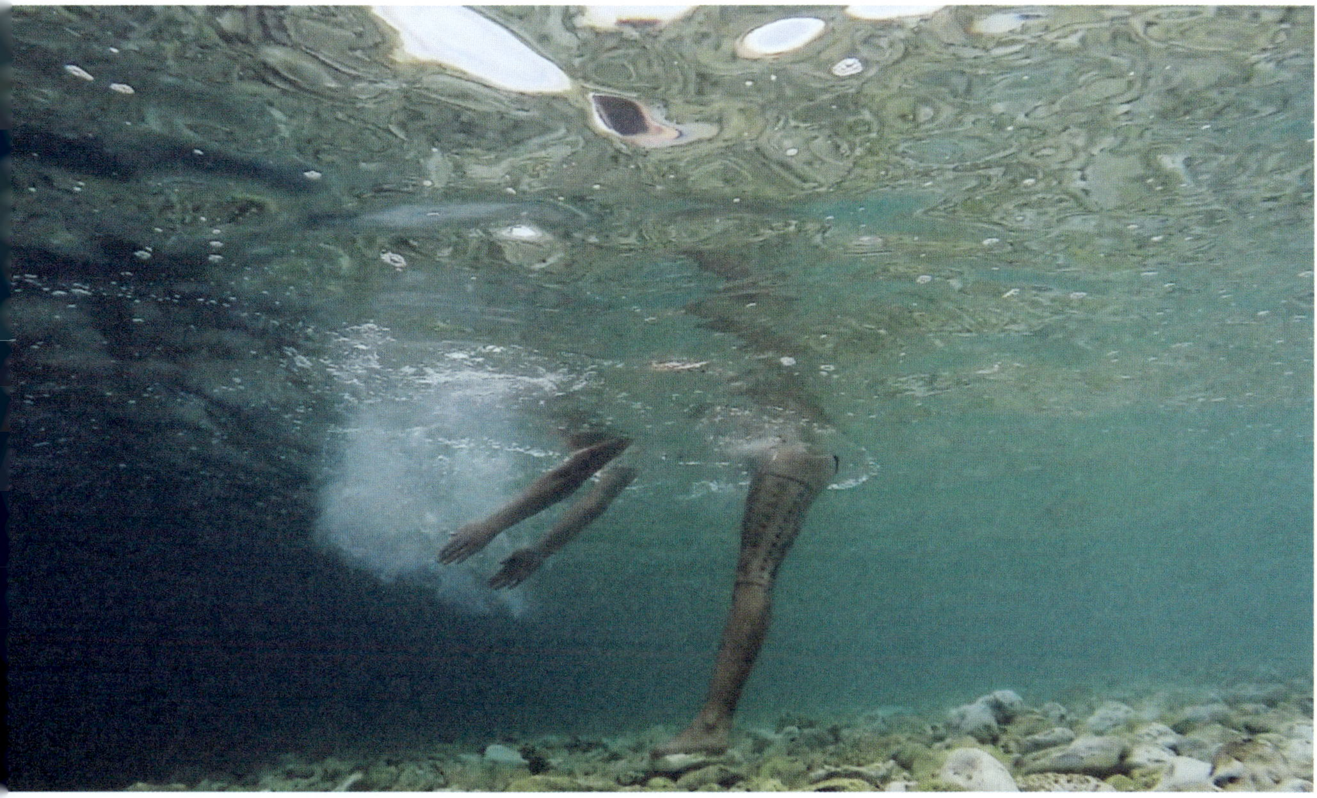

(Ngāti Kahu ki Whangaroa, Ngāpuhi, Ngāti Maniapoto) are in their fifth hour in the waters of Te Manukanuka ō Hoturoa at Kaitarakihi Beach in May 2022. I (Janine) am standing with them, now up to my chest in the water with four others. The sea is unusually warm as the result of a marine heatwave, and the tide is coming in.[25] My feet are numb, my hands feel warmer in the water than out, and my toes dig into the iron sand of Kaitarakihi Beach for stability. Sunde, Peterson and Puia-Taylor are supported by mānuka tiripou, wooden staffs plunged into the sand to stop their bodies being pushed around in the waves; they are stoic, they bear witness to the relentless press of the incoming tide.

Angela Tiatia, *Lick*, 2015. Still image from single-channel digital video, colour, sound, duration 6 minutes 33 seconds. *Courtesy the artist and Sullivan+Strumpf*

We stood with water up to our necks at first, allowing ourselves 'to be acted on' by the sea, to reference Stacey Alaimo.[26] We were so still that seaweed began to build up around our thighs. A kāruhiruhi, pied shag, swims up to Peterson, then visits each of us. This is the closest I have ever been to this fish-like bird, who fixes her white-rimmed eye on me then dives for many minutes before surfacing next to a different human. At this moment we too have become sea-plant-like, fixed points in a moving ocean, and the bird weaves a web between us.

Leaves also drift around us in the current. Peterson picks one up and appears to read a sign, a tohu from the water. I watch the way light winds change the directional shimmer of the waves, and the play of light across the Mahanihani headland. At the top of this wāhi tapu is a radio tower with a transmitter that livestreams these waters to the other side of the world.

Puia-Taylor wears a black coat with 'WAI08' painted on the back in white lettering. The letters are revealed bit by bit as the tide begins to recede. WAI-8 is the Waitangi Tribunal claim brought by Puia-Taylor's great-aunt, Dame Ngāneko Minhinnick (Ngāti Te Ata Waiohua), and representatives of several iwi who called for the return of this harbour,

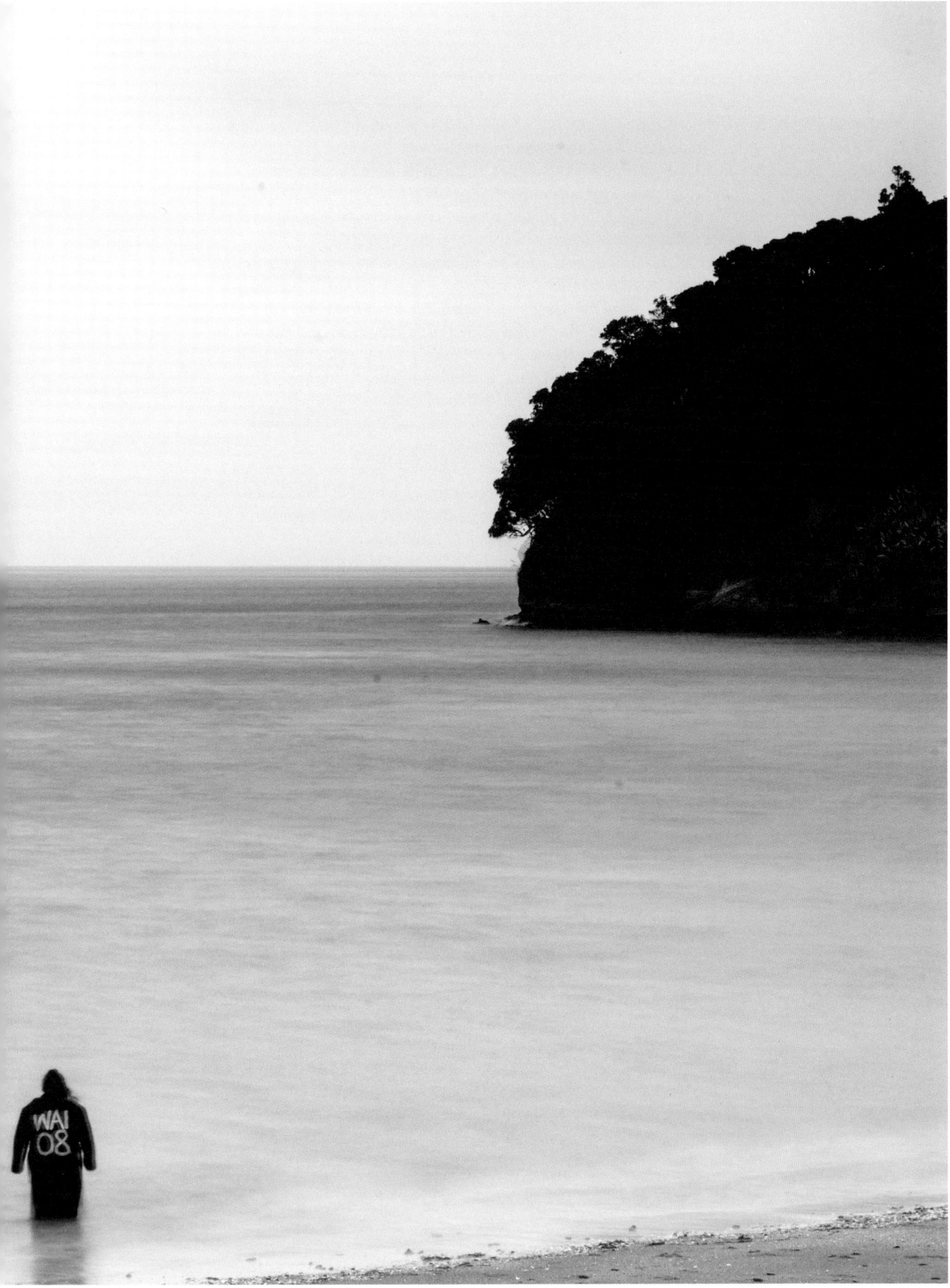
WAI
08

Te Manukanuka ō Hotoroa, and their ancestral sovereignty. Minhinnick brought this claim on behalf of Te Kaitiaki Whānau o Manukau (the Guardian Families of the Manukau) with the support of Te Waiohua, Kawerau and Ngāti Whātua.[27] The claim is still not settled, and Puia-Taylor stands as whanaunga of both the waters and the Waitangi claim.

Puia-Taylor and Peterson remained immersed in the ocean with Sunde for the entire tidal cycle, from before dawn until sunset on 16 May 2022: 4.08 a.m. to 4.31 p.m. They were the first and only participants to remain in the water for the entire duration of one of Sunde's global series of performances, which she first began in 2013.

On the beach at Kaitarakihi, the performers are watched and tended to by Nettie Norman (Ngāti Kuri, Ngāpuhi, Ngāti Whakahotu), who has whakapapa ties to this ocean and coastline and is an integral part of the event's realisation. Every hour, members of HIWA, Norman's kapa haka group, wade into the ocean or stand on the shore singing a waiata to the ocean and the performers in the sea. I hear the sound of the pūtātara conch followed by the vocal strains of 'Wairua tapu, wairua . . .' as we stand facing the open ocean. I think about how Sunde, an American, and myself — both descendants of settlers — feel protected here, and how the mana whenua of this coastline rescued British soldiers from these same waters as their ship, the HMS *Orpheus*, sank into these waves in 1863.

Large wave surges cause Sunde to falter in her red wool dress as she also battles physical pain, but she is held by the water and her collaborators. In my short time in the water, my body begins to know intimately the impressive feat of endurance it takes to stand amid the endless waves, in the chill of late autumn, for a full tidal cycle.

Aotearoa is the seventh country in which Sunde has collaborated with Indigenous participants for her vigil in coastal waters for a full tidal cycle, to draw attention to sea level rise by sensorial means.[28] Alaimo writes that Sunde performs our ontological relationality between the body of a human being and the vast body of the ocean: 'Sunde's striking and prolonged stillness — she does not float, swim, or tread water — removes this encounter from practices of resource extraction as well as familiar cultural frames of aquatic experience, such as the athletic, adventurous, sublime or touristic. Nothing is taken from the water; nor is the water put to use.'[29]

The project creates parallels between very different shorelines, yet it is still possible for specific politics to be foregrounded. It was crucial to Sunde and Puia-Taylor to spend time with those with ancestry to these waters, and wānanga took place over a two-year period prior to the performance. Sunde received a blessing to enter the water from kaumātua Jeff Tukua (Te Waiohua, Ngāti Tahinga). For Puia-Taylor's part, the project was an act of care:

> *A Durational Performance with the Sea* is a reminder and an opportunity to give back some love and light to our harbour. To remember we are nothing without our Moana, our oceans. Participating will honour the mauri of the Manukau and all those caretakers who have helped to preserve its mana (power). Participating helps to reinforce for us all the need to care for what we have now.[30]

Peterson and Puia-Taylor support Sunde's fatigued body when the time comes to leave the boisterous grip of the Manukau Harbour. Sunde is manuhiri and she is welcomed and looked after. She realises, along with myself and all the other participant-settler descendants here, that we are part of the longer, painful history that the coat painted with WAI-8 invokes. Puia-Taylor, Peterson and Norman, and many others who participated

PREVIOUS: Sarah Cameron Sunde, *36.5/ Te Manukanukatanga ō Hoturoa*, 2020–22. Site-specific participatory performance and HD video, duration 12 hours 23 minutes. Around 4 hours into the performance, Sunde (in red) is flanked by Kingi Peterson (Ngāti Kahu ki Whangaroa, Ngāpuhi, Ngāti Maniapoto) (left) and Amiria Puia-Taylor (Ngāti Te Ata Waiohua, Ngāti Tipa, Hamoa, Kuki Airani, Tahiti) (right). Photo captured by Raymond Sagapolutele for 36.5. *Courtesy the artist*

in this performance in their own way, demonstrate that the ecological crisis cannot be separated from the long catastrophe of colonisation.

How might we relate to our shared seas while neo-colonial structures and corporations still continue to excrete carbon that the oceans can no longer absorb? We share the ongoing effects — of seabed resource extraction of the iron sands at Glenbrook steel mill at the other end of the harbour, overfishing of the tarakihi fish this bay is named after, and the wastewater this harbour absorbs — as either allies of mana whenua or those with deep whakapapa connections. Yet wai, the waters, foster healing in such acts of collectivity; ānga whakamua, momentum gathers as we move forward together.

ALICIA FRANKOVICH, THE EYE (2022)

The final performance we consider enacts current and future crises of flood and dislocation. In the artificiality of a municipal swimming pool, the chlorinated water and concrete tiles barely echo a sea or lake. The audience waits in anticipation of a performance, accompanied by the dull noise of a water pump. Although wintry outside, in the steamy 33-degree-heat and in amber light, the Brunswick Baths in Naarm Melbourne begin to resemble a natural body of water, removing us from our common experiences of pool entertainment or exercise. In a day-lit public swimming pool we would usually find sleek or clumsy human bodies plunging into the chlorinated blue. But in the low light, diffused by red gels, the performing bodies transmute into creatures like reptiles and marine mammals, immersed in water to play, find food, cool down or flee.

In the choreographed performance *The Eye* (2022) by Alicia Frankovich, the thin membrane of separation between us and other creatures dissolves. At first, an oddly familiar, crocodilian creature drags itself along the edge — they are clothed like us but reptilian, slow and hesitant. Other creature–human hybrids slip-sink into the water and drift around the pool. Their noses are just out of the water, their shadows creep after them. Another creature leaps into the water; although they mostly ignore each other, there is a tussle, a splash and a brief territorial squabble. The water becomes still again — this is 'the eye' of the storm, the all-too-familiar experience of our world becoming water. Ripples are reflected upside down around the walls.

We hear the muffled, amniotic sounds of a womb-like enclosure. The creatures' legs wiggle like fins. Seals were dogs that left the land, and a reminder of this evolution is visible in their awkward hauls from the water. Three bodies jerk in a sudden change of direction like a school of fish. Our furless human skin provides no advantage on land, but in water, hominids are well adapted to the aqueous life.[31] Like Tiatia's *Lick*, this performance invites speculation that we might one day relinquish our ties to land to devolve into semi-aquatic creatures.

As a point of departure, Frankovich described the repurposing of municipal buildings at times of crisis. Christchurch Art Gallery Te Puna o Waiwhetū became an emergency centre after the February 2011 Canterbury earthquake; what other public spaces might transform into life-support hubs?[32] At sites of plural purpose, in this case in the reimagined baths, the hominoid–animal–environment boundary breaks down. A civic pool might also become a survival shelter in which we could perhaps hide away from the apocalypse in a temperature-controlled environment with water to cool us.

Frankovich has staged other performances in enclosed vitrines: a butterfly house became the backdrop for human experience in the video *Defending Plural Experiences*

(2014), and she employed a large orange Perspex box in *AQ/2020*, commissioned by Auckland Art Gallery Toi o Tāmaki in 2020, in which human animality was revealed inside a glasshouse. These vitrines suggest our shared spaces as collective negotiations between human and more-than-human whanaunga at times of crisis. Her pieces often involve large choreographies of social groups — a mix of people from her friendship network, trained and untrained performers.

Swimming was part of Frankovich's childhood in Tauranga, Aotearoa, on a coastline where seals venture from the sea to bathe in rocky inlets and a large aquatic complex is central to town life. Deeper still, her Samoan grandmother's whakapapa binds her ancestry to the sea of islands of Te Moana-nui-a-Kiwa. During *The Eye*, three performers read out scripts of their own watery experiences. We hear personal testimonies, amplified in ten speakers throughout the pool complex, of violent storms and of water as a peaceful, fluid zone. One swallowed river water: 'It felt like the storm was *in* me, not around me.' When paired with recounted floods or near drownings, the voice-over repositions the joyous reptilian-performers cavorting in a watery playground. These scenes and stories are familiar; Frankovich calls them 'quasi-fictive stories', precarious moments of suspension.[33]

In the last movement of the hour-long performance, a steady stream of people starts to wade through the pool as if crossing an expanse of water. Some are lifted or dragged. They rise from their seats within the audience, enter the pool and wade purposefully to the other side. They are clothed in winter coats, dresses and glasses and some wear shoes or carry a handbag. Some rush through, scale the pool ramps, then battle their way around the side of the pool to wade through again. Some hold bags above their heads. Some are running now, becoming more desperate. They are migrants crossing waters, refugees close to drowning, scenes from floods in Gadigal lands, Sydney and Tāmaki Makaurau.

These humanoid creatures once again become other: reptilian, viral life, fungal life — communities of difference immersed in water, air or fire; clinging collectives in states of environmental chaos. After a long while, some of the performers lie floating like seaweed, or scull, kicking softly at first then fading as they become lifeless, floating belly-up, their hair streaming out around them. Then one by one they wade to the side of the pool.[34] Hesitantly, the remaining audience begins to clap.

Rosi Braidotti says of interspecies, gender–intercultural relations in the twin crises of the Fourth Industrial Revolution with the Sixth Extinction: 'We swim or sink together, but keep looking for the adequate way to actually connect and be together.'[35] Cathartic performances such as Frankovich's *The Eye* reveal the fragility and specificity of our ecological and climatic niche and the need for collaborative alliances with each other. They work on us to tackle the inner bias toward human exceptionalism, a task that demands emotional as well as intellectual and practical resources, an affirmative ethics as argued by Braidotti.

It takes artists, activists, scientists and school climate strikers to sound the alarm, to keep climate change present on the agenda of defenders of the status quo. In post-disaster reportage and governance, beyond cows floating down flooded rivers or horses on roofs, how little we hear about the animal lives that are lost. What of the native eels that became a feast for imported crocodiles at Auckland Zoo after the river flooded their enclosure in February 2023? Creatures are thrown into strange relations as anthropogenic storms rage. And then there is the lull in between, *The Eye*, where species collapse into each other in the febrile Noah's ark of the Brunswick Baths.

**

Alicia Frankovich, *The Eye*, 2022, documentation of performance at *Take Hold the Clouds*, curated by Tara McDowell and Fleur Watson. Performers: Rebecca Jensen, Raina Peterson, Lilian Steiner, Daniela Accary, Rowena Archer, Stephanie Bradford, Melanie Field-Pimm, Jane Hinwood, Nia Le, Kim Northmore, Gabrielle O'Brien, Elena Osalde, Sahra Stolz and Linda van de Wall. *Courtesy the artist and Open House Melbourne. Photo by Nick Bebbington*

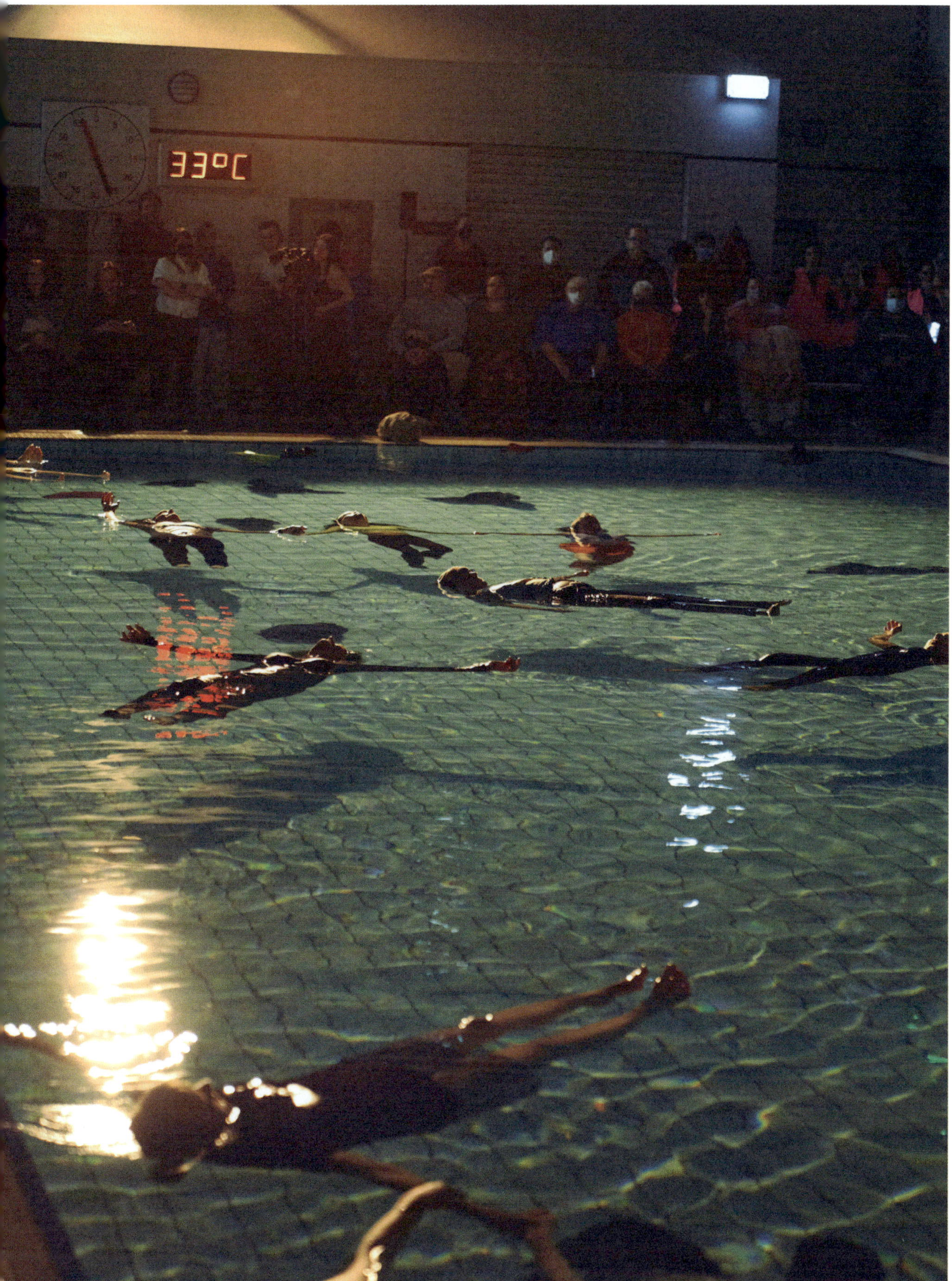
33°C

Each performance artwork discussed in this chapter builds our understanding of whanaungatanga, of the inherent, indissoluble relations between ourselves and the other entities of this living planet. The contemporary performances described and experienced here return us to an enveloping sense of environmental performativity; human bodies, fish, plants, seawaters and waves are all part of a larger planetary cycle. This is found in wavering, co-dancing and communing with gendered plants in Kapo and smith's *i'll grow back*, and in the wrestling of exotic weeds to allow indigenous plants space to grow in Harvey's *Group Weed Wrestle*. In Leatinu'u's *Kawea*, participants in a more-than-human waka transport precious rākau as taonga, reinscribing an ancestral journey that fuses reparative politics with ancient migrations.

Paraha's choreography takes us into the deep dark of Te Pō, the fertile environment that predates humanity and the astro-futures that will go on without us. Sunde and Puia-Taylor's collaboration traces how international performance artists respond to the aftermath of colonialism carried in the rising seas, the embodied pain between human and more-than-human described by Paraha as the 'flesh of moemoe'.[36] Frankovich and Tiatia also open us to an expansive, watery imaginary generating cathartic or anticlimactic moments respectively that return us to our animality, our whanaunga.

In shared experiences of more-than-human whanaungatanga, we attune more deeply with te taiao, our vibratory world. Performance art invokes emergent modes of togethering and dwelling as it brings multi-entity difference into correlation. This is the great opportunity of our time, to better perform with, sustain with, thrive with this living world, our kin.

NOTES

1 Amanda Monehu Yates, 'Transforming Geographies: Performing Indigenous-Māori ontologies and ethics of more-than-human care in an era of ecological emergency', *New Zealand Geographer* 77, no. 2 (July 2021): 101–13. https://doi.org/10.1111/nzg.12302

2 For instance, Rosi Braidotti, Donna Haraway, Stacy Alaimo and Astrida Niemanis.

3 Although our focus here is on Indigenous performativity through whanaungatanga connection, the authors recognise the ecological performances of many Pākehā New Zealanders including Phil Dadson's performance events *Earthworks* (1972), *Solar Plexus* (1970) and *Echo Logo* (2003), and John Cousins' experimental sonic performance using natural rhythms in the 1970s. In the last two decades, Amy Howden-Chapman's participatory bell-ringing alarm in *You Can't Unring a Bell/The Flood My Chanting* (2008), the attention to waterways in Julieanna Preston's *Moving Stuff* (2013), HOOPLA's *Flotilla Whau* and Kathy Waghorn's interdisciplinary *The Fluid City Roaming Laboratory* (2013–), Christina Houghton's choreographies of yellow lilos in collective social assemblages in *Survival Tours* (2015–17),Carol Brown's collaboration with Tia Reihana in *LungSong* (2019) at Te Uru Waitakere Contemporary Gallery, Alys Longley's *Mistranslation Laboratory* (2019), Brydee Rood's *Please Return Me to the Earth*, in her 'We Are The Weather' series (2017), TEMP festival, many works in Sam Trubridge's *Performance Arcade*, Catherine Bagnall's animal embodiments in for participatory tramps *Alpine Walking With Tails and Ears* (2013), and Caro McCaw and scientific collaborators' *Sounding Walks* on eroding coastlines in Ōtepoti Dunedin are among many performance works that attune to coal mining, whales, rising seas and cyclonic winds to generate performative dialogues with more-than-human kin.

4 Mere Roberts et al., 'Whakapapa as a Māori Mental Construct: Some implications for the debate over genetic modification of organisms', *The Contemporary Pacific* 16, no. 1 (Spring 2004): 1–28. They note that renewed interest in whakapapa in Aotearoa arises directly from recent worldwide controversy over the genetic modification (GM) of plants and animals and, in particular, of transgenic modifications.

5 Rosi Braidotti, 'Posthuman Relational Subjectivity and the Politics of Affirmation', in *Relational Architectural Ecologies: Architecture, nature and subjectivity*, edited by Peg Rawes (London/New York: Routledge, 2013), 21–39.

6 Sarah Whatmore, 'Materialist Returns: Practising cultural geography in and for a more-than-human world', *Cultural Geographies* 13, no. 4 (October 2006): 600–09.

7 Tru Paraha, 'Colluding with Darkness', *Performance Research* 23, no. 2, 'On Writing & Performance' (February 2018): 49–54.

8 The performers are Tru Paraha and Sean Curham.

9 Paraha, 'Colluding with Darkness', 54.

10 Ibid., 49.

11 See also performances by Moana Nepia and Charles Koreneho that embrace darkness.

12 André Lepecki, *Singularities: Dance in the age of performance* (London: Taylor & Francis, 2016), 58.

13 Tru Paraha, 'Astrochoreography', *Choreographic Practices* 11, no. 2 (December 2020): 231–44.

14 Roberts et al., 'Whakapapa as a Māori Mental Construct'.

15 Tru Paraha, '& Darkness', in *Undisciplining Dance in Nine Movements and Eight Stumbles*, edited by Carol Brown

and Alys Longley (Cambridge: Cambridge Scholars Publishing, 2018), 119–37.

16 The leftover wattle foliage breaks down and is later turned into compost, further feeding the soil, the ngahere (bush) and continuing to nourish ecological cycles of the Waitākeres.

17 Jeremy Leatinu'u, email interview with authors, 31 January 2023.

18 Christina Houghton, Melissa Laing and Becca Wood, eds., *About Walking: 15 months of artist walks in Tāmaki Auckland* (Auckland: Te Uru Waitākere Contemporary Gallery, 2021).

19 Jeremy Leatinu'u, email interview with authors, 31 January 2023.

20 For more detail see https://tetuhi.art/exhibition/jeremy-leatinuu-earthpushers

21 Jeremy Leatinu'u, email interview with authors, 31 January 2023.

22 Amit Noy, 'Glitches & Sweat: A response to Experimental Dance Week Aotearoa', *The Pantograph Punch*, 16 December 2020, www.pantograph-punch.com/posts/glitches-sweat

23 val smith, 'Promiscuous Emplacements: Performing with marginal urban places' (Auckland: Auckland University of Technology, 2022), https://hdl.handle.net/10292/15644

24 Zoe Todd, 'Fish, Kin and Hope: Tending to water violations in amiskwaciwâskahikan and Treaty Six territory', *Afterall: A Journal of Art, Context and Enquiry* 43 (March 2017): 102–07.

25 This section is written from co-author Janine Randerson's experience as a participant in the performance. Prior to the event, Randerson hosted a talk and workshop at AUT with Sarah Cameron Sunde, Dr Marama Muru-Lanning (James Henare Research Centre, University of Auckland), Dr Nicholas Vigar (scientist and Safeswim programme manager, Tāmaki Makarau). *Tidalectic Rhythms: A durational performance with Te Manukanuka ō Hoturoa*, AUT, 6 March 2020. The performance was postponed until 2022 due to the Covid restrictions. The event was produced at different stages by Ariane Craig-Smith and Diane Blomfield and filmed by Mairi Gunn, Amarbir Singh and Fergus Milner (2022) and Ian Powell (2020). Supported by Te Uru Waitakere Contemporary Gallery.

26 Stacey Alaimo, in Una Chauduri, ed., 'Signaling through the Waves', a special issue of *Resilience: A Journal of the Environmental Humanities* (University of Nebraska Press), 228.

27 'Report of the Waitangi Tribunal on the Manukau Claim (WAI-8)' (Wellington: Waitangi Tribunal, Department of Justice, 1985).

28 Other locations include the North Sea, Netherlands; Bay of All Saints, Brazil; Bay of Bengal, Bangladesh; Bodo Inlet, Kenya; and New York Bay.

29 Alaimo, 'Standing', 227.

30 Press release: 'New York artist presents all-day tidal performance in Tāmaki Makaurau', 9 May 2022.

31 Astrida Neimanis, *Bodies of Water: Posthuman feminist phenomenology* (London/New York: Bloomsbury Academic, 2017). See also Karl Ove Knausgaard, 'Aquatic Apes', in *Winter* (London: Harvill Secker, 2017), 21–23.

32 Alicia Frankovich, informal conversation with Janine Randerson, Tāmaki Makaurau, 13 December 2022.

33 Ibid.

34 We are reminded of another water-based performance: Rachael Rakena and Samoan artists Fez Fa'anana and Brian Fuata's *Pacific Washup* (2006) during a residency at Sydney's Performance Space, where performers wearing the oversize, plaid, cheap plastic carry-bags often used by migrants washed up in the waves on Sydney's Bondi Beach.

35 Rosi Braidotti, 'Entities of All the Living World, Unite!', in *Alicia Frankovich: Outside before beyond*, edited by Eva Birkenstock (London: Koenig Books, 2020).

36 Paraha, 'Colluding with Darkness'.

REFERENCES

'Report of the Waitangi Tribunal on the Manukau Claim (WAI-8)'. Wellington: Waitangi Tribunal, Department of Justice, 1985.

Alaimo, Stacy. 'Standing'. *Resilience: A Journal of the Environmental Humanities* 7, no. 2–3, 'Signaling Through the Waves: Essays on *36.5/A Durational Performance with the Sea* by Sarah Cameron Sunde. A special section guest-edited by Una Chaudhuri' (Spring–Fall 2020): 227–31.

Braidotti, Rosi. 'Posthuman Relational Subjectivity and the Politics of Affirmation'. In *Relational Architectural Ecologies: Architecture, nature and subjectivity*, edited by Peg Rawes, 21–39. London/New York: Routledge, 2013.

——— 'Entities of All the Living World, Unite!'. In *Alicia Frankovich: Outside before beyond*, edited by Eva Birkenstock. London: Koenig Books, 2020.

Houghton, Christina, Melissa Laing and Becca Wood, eds. *About Walking: 15 months of artist walks in Tāmaki Auckland*. Auckland: Te Uru Waitākere Contemporary Gallery, 2021.

Knausgaard, Karl Ove. 'Aquatic Apes'. In *Winter*, 21–23. London: Harvill Secker, 2017.

Lepecki, André. *Singularities: Dance in the age of performance*. London: Taylor & Francis, 2016.

Neimanis, Astrida. *Bodies of Water: Posthuman feminist phenomenology*. London/New York: Bloomsbury Academic, 2017.

Noy, Amit. 'Glitches & Sweat: A response to Experimental Dance Week Aotearoa'. *The Pantograph Punch*, 16 December 2020. www.pantograph-punch.com/posts/glitches-sweat

Paraha, Tru. 'Astrochoreography'. *Choreographic Practices* 11, no. 2 (December 2020): 231–44. https://doi.org/10.1386/chor_00020_1

——— 'Colluding with Darkness'. *Performance Research* 23, no. 2, 'On Writing & Performance' (February 2018): 49–54. https://doi.org/10.1080/13528165.2018.1464754

——— '& Darkness'. *In Undisciplining Dance in Nine Movements and Eight Stumbles*, edited by Carol Brown and Alys Longley, 119–137. Cambridge: Cambridge Scholars Publishing, 2018.

Roberts, Mere, Brad Haami, Richard Benton, Terre Satterfield, Melissa L. Finucane, Mark Henare and Manuka Henare. 'Whakapapa as a Māori Mental Construct: Some implications for the debate over genetic modification of organisms'. *The Contemporary Pacific* 16, no. 1 (Spring 2004): 1–28. www.jstor.org/stable/23722949

smith, val. 'Promiscuous Emplacements: Performing with marginal urban places'. Auckland University of Technology, 2022. https://hdl.handle.net/10292/15644

Todd, Zoe. 'Fish, Kin and Hope: Tending to water violations in amiskwaciwâskahikan and Treaty Six territory'. *Afterall: A Journal of Art, Context and Enquiry* 43 (March 2017): 102–07. https://doi.org/10.1086/692559

Whatmore, Sarah. 'Materialist Returns: Practising cultural geography in and for a more-than-human world'. *Cultural Geographies* 13, no. 4 (October 2006): 600–09. https://doi.org/10.1191/1474474006cgj377oa

Yates, Amanda Monehu. 'Transforming Geographies: Performing Indigenous–Māori ontologies and ethics of more-than-human care in an era of ecological emergency'. *New Zealand Geographer* 77, no. 2 (July 2021): 101–13. https://doi.org/10.1111/nzg.12302

GLOSSARY OF MĀORI AND PACIFIC TERMS

ABOUT THE AUTHORS

ACKNOWLEDGEMENTS

INDEX

GLOSSARY OF MĀORI AND PACIFIC TERMS

Place names are written first in Māori, followed by the Pākehā name, e.g., Aotearoa New Zealand, a convention employed as a way of acknowledging both Indigenous and settler relationships to this land.

Words are in Māori unless noted otherwise.

ʻāiga	(Samoan) family, often denoting immediate family
ānga whakamua	to drive forwards, gather forward momentum
Aotearoa	the Māori name for New Zealand. Historically it was the name for the North Island only
atua	supernatural being, deity, ancestor(s) with continuing influence over particular domains, spiritual/non-human being with influence in the physical realm
awa	river, stream, creek, canal, gully, gorge
āwhā	storm, heavy or torrential rain, gale, cyclone
fa'afafine	(Samoan) often translated as 'in the manner of a woman'
fa'a Sāmoa	(Samoan) the Samoan way, or in the manner of Sāmoa
fakafifine	(Vagahau Niue) third gender
gafa	(Samoan) lineage or genealogy
hā	breath, essence
haka	to dance, perform, perform haka
Hape	a Tainui ancestor who famously travelled from Hawaiki to Aotearoa on the back of a stingray
hapū	kinship group, clan, tribe, subtribe — section of a large kinship group and the primary political unit in traditional Māori society
Hawaiki	ancient homeland — the original homelands/places from which Māori migrated across the ocean to Aotearoa
Hereturikōkā	third lunar month of the Māori year, approximately equivalent to August
hīkoi	step, stride, march, walk
hīkoi te whenua	walking the land

hongi	to press noses and exchange breath in greeting
Hōngongoi	second lunar month of the Māori year, approximately equivalent to July
hula	(Hawaiian) a dance
'ie faitaga	(Samoan) a wrapped fabric worn at the waist by men, which is usually black, reaches the shin and has pockets. Often described as a formal lavalava
Ihumātao	an historical pā (fortified village) site of cultural and archaeological importance, in the suburb of Māngere, Tāmaki Makaurau Auckland
iwi	tribe(s), extended kinship group descended from a common ancestor
ka mua, ka muri	a Māori proverb translating as 'walking backwards into the future' which refers to looking to and learning from history in order to inform the future
kafu	(Tongan) customary handmade blankets
kahikatea	*Dacrycarpus dacrydioides*, white pine — a tall coniferous tree, the leaves are scale-like and soft to touch
kai	food, sustenance, a meal
kaitiaki	caretaker, keeper, steward
kaitiakitanga	stewardship, governance, guardianship, trusteeship
kapa	rank, row, line. Also refers to a team, group or company of people
kapa haka	haka group, Māori cultural performance group
karanga	formal call, ceremonial call, welcome call — a ceremonial call of welcome to visitors onto a marae, or equivalent venue
kare	ripple, surface of the sea
kāruhiruhi	pied shag, a large native shag found in coastal areas
kaumātua	elder, elderly man or woman, a person of status within the whānau (family) and hapū (subtribe)
kaupapa	topic, matter for discussion, purpose, intention, proposal, agenda, subject, theme, issue, initiative, concept
kaupapa mana wāhine	topics, matters for discussion, proposals, issues and initiatives pertaining to mana wāhine (women)
kava	(Fijian) a beverage or extract made from the *Piper methysticum* plant
koha	gift, present, offering, contribution, donation — given in the spirit of maintaining social relations
kōrero	discussion, discourse, conversation
koru	spiral motif, traditionally found in carving and kōwhaiwhai patterns
kōwhai	small-leaved native trees of the genus *Sophora*, common along riverbanks and forest margins, produces hanging clusters of large yellow flowers in early spring
kuia	grandmother, female elder, elderly woman
kūmara	*Ipomoea batatas*, sweet potato

lavalava	(Samoan) a garment worn around the legs
leitī	(Tongan) third gender
Mahuru	fourth lunar month of the Māori year — approximately equivalent to September. Also refers to the star Alphard, whose reappearance in the night sky heralds the start of this month
mana	authority, control, power, influence, prestige, status, spiritual power and/or charisma — a supernatural force or essence in a person, place or object that is palpable
mana motuhake	independence, sovereignty, autonomy, self-determination, self-rule, self-governing, authority; also, separate identity
mana wāhine	authority, power, influence, status, spiritual power, charisma which is unique to women and inherent in the female body, particularly because of its potential for childbirth — whether or not this right is enacted; mana wāhine intersects with feminism but has broader implications, and acknowledges an authority that is ancestral and spiritual in origin
mana whenua	local Māori people (hapū and iwi) who have authority and jurisdiction over land or territory that is derived from genealogical ties to the land
manuhiri	visitor(s), guest(s)
mānuka tiripou	supporting pole/stick made from a mānuka tree
Māori	Indigenous New Zealander, Indigenous person of Aotearoa New Zealand
marae	meeting ground, the courtyard in front of a wharenui where formal interactions and discussions take place; a focal point of hāpu/iwi interactions
mātauranga Māori	Māori knowledge, originating from Māori ancestors, a Māori worldview, or a Māori perspective; Māori creative and cultural practices
mau	(Samoan) to keep, retain, hold fast, stick firmly; the name of Sāmoa's independence movement
maunga	mountain
mauri	vital essence, life principle, special nature; the life force that animates all living things; the essential quality of a being or entity
measina	(Samoan) treasures
mere	a short, flat, hand-held weapon made of stone, often greenstone
Moana	the great ocean and its descendants; an alternative to colonial terms for the region, such as Pacific or Oceania. Moana has been used widely in the last decade as an abbreviated term for the great ocean found in many Indigenous Moana languages (te reo Māori, gagana Sāmoa, 'Ōlelo Hawai'i, and Rarotonga Māori to name a few). While the term is not without its problems, foremost its Polycentric bias, its use here signals the need to keep alive the debates around colonial naming of the Moana region and its peoples

moemoe	a variety of Māori potato with a purple skin and reddish-yellow mottled flesh
mōteatea	traditional chant, lament, sung poetry
motu	island, country, land
MVPFAFF+	acronym for mahu, vakasalewalewa, palopa, fa'afafine, akava'ine, fakaleitī or leitī, fakafifine, and more. Coined to enhance Moana-specific terms for diverse genders and intended to provide additional terminology to the term LGBTQI+
Ngāpuhi	a tribal group comprising much of the Northland province; the largest tribe in Aotearoa New Zealand
Ngāi Tai ki Tāmaki	a tribal group of the Auckland region
Ngāti Porou	a tribal group of the East Coast region north of Gisborne extending to Tihirau
Ngāti Whātua o Orākei	a hapū (subtribe) of Ngāti Whātua, the tribal group of the area from Kaipara to Tāmaki Makaurau; the hapū tribal area is mostly in Tāmaki Makaurau Auckland
nimamea'a tuikakala	(Tongan) floral design
oriori	a lullaby sung to a child. Traditionally composed at the birth of a child and told the story of their whakapapa (genealogy), the feats of their tupuna (ancestors) and their tribal history
Ōwairaka/Te Ahi Kaa o Rakataura	a mountain in central Auckland
pā	fortified village
pakapaka	dryness, drought, arid conditions
pākē	a traditionally woven rain cape made of undressed kiekie leaves or flax
Pākehā	New Zealander of European descent
papa	layer, level; colloquial contraction of paparanga or papanga
Papatūānuku	earth, earth mother, wife of Ranginui — all living things are the fruit of this relationship
Parihaka	a coastal Māori settlement located in western Taranaki. The settlement and the movement which was forged there have come to symbolise peaceful resistance to the confiscation of Māori land
Pasifika	coined by government agencies to describe Moana peoples living in Aotearoa New Zealand as well as their descendants. Recognised as being generally from the 'Pacific' by people in Aotearoa
pātaka	traditional storehouse raised upon posts, pantry, larder
pātere	a traditional chant, fast in tempo; sometimes a chant of derision in response to an insult or slander
pāua	*Haliotis*, abalone — edible molluscs of rocky shores; a much-valued delicacy
pōhutukawa	*Metrosideros excelsa, Metrosideros kermadecensis, Metrosideros bartlettii* — trees found in coastal areas which bear large, red flowers in summer, leaves are velvety-white underneath.

	Metrosideros bartlettii has white flowers and is found in the far north of the North Island
pou	pillar, support, literal or metaphorical supporting post
pou rāhui	rāhui post — a post marking a temporary prohibition on access to land or water
pūrākau	myth, tale, ancient legend, story
pūriri	*Vitex lucens* — a large spreading tree of the northern North Island, produces pinkish-red flowers; the nectar attracts tūī; the fruit appeals to kererū
pūtātara	conch shell trumpet with an attached short, wooden mouthpiece
rākau	tree, plant, stick
Ranginui	god of the sky, husband of Papatūānuku — from their union all living things originate
raranga	traditional Māori weaving using plant fibre
rohe	tribal territory, area, region, district
Rongo-māui	younger brother of Whānui; responsible for stealing celestial kūmara from Whānui and bringing it down to earth. Also written as Rongomāui
Rūaumoko	Māori god of seismic, volcanic and geothermal activity
rūnanga	council, board, tribal council, tribal authority
rūruhi	an elderly woman; a female elder; tribal-specific usage may denote a particular relationship role
salu lima	(Samoan) hand brush or a type of broom made from the midribs of coconut leaf
Soga'imiti	(Samoan) man who wears a pe'a, a Samoan tatau (tattoo)
takatāpui	lesbian, gay, homosexual, queer, bisexual; intimate friend of the same gender
takatāpuitanga	(colloq. noun) lesbian, gay, homosexual, queer, bisexual; intimacy with the same gender
takiwā	tribal territory, area, region, district
talanoa	(Tongan, Fijian, Samoan) to chat, talk, have conversation, sometimes without a rigid framework
tangata moana	contemporary term for people who have genealogical ties to Te Moana-nui-a-Kiwa (the Pacific Ocean)
tangata Tiriti	non-Māori who acknowledge Te Tiriti o Waitangi (the Treaty of Waitangi) as the nation's founding document and who identify as Treaty partners with Māori
tangata whenua	people of the land, the Indigenous people of this country, local people, hosts
taniwha	water spirit, powerful water creature, monster, awesome being
taoka puoro	traditional (Ngāi Tahu) Māori musical instruments. In other tribal dialects: taonga puoro

taonga	objects of cultural significance; treasures, anything prized or highly valued
tapa	(Fijian, Samoan, Tongan) bark cloth
tapu	sacred, restricted, set apart for a specific purpose, untouchable, not for common use
taura tī kōuka	a rope made from the fibre of cabbage tree leaves
tautoko	to support, advocate for, provide assistance
te ao Māori	the Māori world, a Māori worldview
te ao mārama	the world of light and life, the physical realm, this earthly realm
te ao Pākehā	the Pākehā world
Te Awa Tupua Act 2017	Whanganui River Claims Settlement Act 2017
te hinengaro	mind, intellect, thought, consciousness, awareness
Te Kaitiaki Whānau o Manukau	the Guardian Families of the Manukau, committed to fulfilling their kaitiaki (guardianship) responsibility to protect the Manukau harbour and its natural resources
te kore	the realm of potential being, the realm of nothingness, the potent void from which creation comes forth
te mahara	thought, memory, recollection
Te Manukanuka ō Hoturoa	the Manukau Harbour, Tāmaki Makaurau Auckland
Te Moana-nui-a-Kiwa	the Pacific Ocean. In contemporary usage often translated as Oceania
Te Pāpaka o Māui	Australia
te pō	darkness, night
te reo Māori	the Māori language
Te Rūnanga o Ngāi Tahu	the governing council of the Ngāi Tahu iwi (tribe)
Te Tai o Rēhua	the Tasman Sea
te taiao	the natural world, environment, nature
Te Tiriti o Waitangi	the Treaty of Waitangi, the 'founding document' of Aotearoa, signed by representatives of the British Crown and a number of Māori iwi on 6 February 1840. There are two versions of the document, one written in English the other in te reo Māori. The interpretation of the Treaty is contentious as there is significant variation in terminology between the English and Māori language versions. The principles of Te Tiriti o Waitangi are articulated by the Waitangi Tribunal and include: reciprocity, active protection, partnership, equity and equal treatment
Te Wānanga o [te] Tai Tokerau	Wānanga of the northern region of the North Island
Te Whiti-o-Rongomai	Te Āti Awa leader and prophet who helped establish Parihaka and employed passive resistance against Pākehā land confiscation

tikanga	correct procedure, custom, lore, method, manner, rule, way, meaning, practice, convention, protocol — the customary system of values and practices, developed over time and deeply embedded in the social context
tinaku	to germinate, sprout, conceive; also refers to tubers for planting, cultivation ground
tino rangatiratanga	sovereignty, self-determination, autonomy, self-government, domination, rule, control, power
tipua	supernatural being, strange or otherworldly being
tīpuna	ancestors; also written as tūpuna
tītoki	*Alectryon excelsus* — a tree common on river flats
Tohu (1828–1907)	Te Āti Awa leader and prophet who helped establish Parihaka and a passive resistance movement against Pākehā land confiscation
tōtara	*Podocarpus totara, Podocarpus cunninghamii* — large forest trees with prickly, olive-green leaves, found throughout Aotearoa New Zealand, popular for carving
Tūpuna Maunga Authority	the statutory authority established under the Ngā Mana Whenua o Tāmaki Makaurau Collective Redress Act 2014 to govern the fourteen Tūpuna Maunga (ancestral mountains) of Tāmaki Makaurau Auckland
uiaki fono	(Tongan) a type of town crier that vocally relays messages from the King or village authorities
Uru-te-ngangana	the eldest of the children of Ranginui and Papatūānuku (the primordial parents); the atua of light and celestial bodies
vā	(Samoan) the space or relation between two things or entities. Vā is often a prefix found across different terms that describe a particular set of relations or things in relation
waahi tapu	sacred place, a sacred site subject to long-term ritual restrictions on access and/or use. Also written as wāhi tapu
waha kōhatu	a learning technique, whereby initiates, at the direction of a tohunga, place a stone in their mouth and keep it there while reciting the oral histories they are acquiring
wahine/wāhine	woman, female/plural
wai	stream, river, creek, body of water
waiata	song, psalm, chant
waiata wawata	a song of yearning or longing; includes love songs and laments
waikohu	mist, fog
'Wairua tapu, wairua . . .'	lines of a well-known Māori song written by Ngapo Wehi
Waitangi Tribunal	a a standing commission of inquiry that makes recommendations on claims brought by Māori relating to legislation, policies, actions or omissions of the Crown that are in breach of the promises made in the Treaty of Waitangi

waka	canoe
waka taua	war canoe
whē	essential sound form; the substance or shape of word/thought
wānanga	tribal knowledge, lore, learning; meetings discussions, deliberations privileging Māori tribal knowledge, lore, and learning
whaikōrero	oratory, formal speech-making
whakaaro	thought, understanding, idea, opinion, insight
whakapapa	genealogy, lineage, descent; recitation of whakapapa is an important skill in Māori society and central to all Māori institutions
whānau	extended family, family group, the primary economic unit of traditional Māori society; in contemporary contexts, sometimes a form of address to a familiar group of people who are not relatives
whanaunga	relative, relation, blood relative, kin
whanaungatanga	relationship, kinship, a sense of familial connection, reciprocal relationship
Whānui	Vega — the brightest star in the constellation of Lyra; fifth brightest star in the sky
whare karakia	church, any building used for religious services
whare rangatira	carved/decorated house of a chief
whare tapere	traditionally a place where people gathered for entertainment
whare whakairo	carved house, decorated meeting house
wharekai	dining hall
whenua	land, country, nation, state

ABOUT THE AUTHORS

Jim Allen (MNZM) (1922–2023) was a pioneer of post-object and performance art in New Zealand in the 1970s and is regarded as the most influential art educator of his generation, both in New Zealand and Australia. He was head of the Elam Sculpture Department, University of Auckland, before taking up the position as founding head at Sydney College of the Arts (1977–87). Since 2000 Allen restaged several early works, such as the two-part installation *O-AR* (1974) and the early performances *Contact* (1974), *Poetry for Chainsaws* (1976), *News* (1976) and *On Planting a Native* (1976), in Adelaide, Sydney, Auckland, New Plymouth and Wellington. He held honorary doctorates from Sydney University and Auckland University of Technology.

Audrey Baldwin is a Zimbabwe born, Ōtautahi-based performance artist, curator and event producer. She graduated from Ilam School of Fine Arts, Canterbury University, in 2009 and has shown in galleries nationally as well as in Japan, India, Zimbabwe, Australia and the Netherlands. Audrey has been on the forefront of enlivening and activating public spaces in Ōtautahi since 2010, particularly in the central city through pop-up artworks and events such as First Thursdays Chch, Shared Lines Collaborative and the Social Artists Collective. Her interactive performance works have been included in SCAPE Public Art, The Performance Arcade, Nelson Arts Festival, Auckland Pride, Taranaki Arts Festival and Performance Art Week Aotearoa. Baldwin has held roles in public programming with The Physics Room Contemporary Art Space and WORD Christchurch.

Christina Barton is one of the first art historians to have documented a history of post-object art in New Zealand between 1969 and 1979, in her MA thesis (University of Auckland, 1988). Through her work as a curator and writer, and as director of Te Pātaka Toi Adam Art Gallery at Victoria University of Wellington (2007–23), she has contributed substantially to the survival of and interest in the history of conceptual and critical art in Aotearoa. In 2023, with Gregory Burke, she co-curated *In Relation: Performance works by Peter Roche & Linda Buis 1979–1985* (Adam Art Gallery, Wellington).

Christopher Braddock, artist and writer, is professor of visual arts in the School of Art & Design, Auckland University of Technology. He is director doctoral studies and co-leads the Art & Performance Research Group. He has written extensively on performance art in Aotearoa. He is author of *Performing Contagious Bodies: Ritual participation in contemporary art* (Palgrave Macmillan, 2013) and editor of *Animism in Art and Performance* (Palgrave Macmillan, 2017). His performance and installation works have been included in *Public Relations* at the Govett-Brewster Art Gallery, curated by Simon Gennard (2022); *How to Live Together* at ST PAUL St Gallery, curated by Balamohan Shingade (2019); and *Material Traces: Time and the gesture in contemporary art*, curated by Amelia Jones in Montréal (2013). Key research terms include: animism, dialogue, silence, contagion, material trace, ritual, spirituality, performance and participation. See www.christopherbraddock.com

Gregory Burke is a Toronto/Berlin-based curator and writer. Formerly an artist, Burke collaborated with Roche & Buis, photographing many of the couple's performances as a friend and fellow Elam School of Fine Arts graduate. Burke has continued to curate and publish artists working in performance and live situations, including Marina Abramović, Reza Afisina, Ei Arakawa, Fiona Banner, Sophie Calle, Andrea Fraser, Maria Hassabi, Thomas Hirschhorn, Matt Mullican and Ben Patterson. In 2023, with Christina Barton, he co-curated *In Relation: Performance works by Peter Roche & Linda Buis 1979–1985* (Adam Art Gallery, Wellington).

James Charlton is an artist whose work includes video, object-based sculpture, stereo-lithography, installation, robotics and interactive screen-based and performance work. He has lectured on post-material practices and interactive installation, topics that parallel his PhD on digital materiality with Plymouth University (UK). Recent projects include: *Thrown* (Te Uru, Auckland, 2020), *Rebound* (KARST, Plymouth, UK, 2017), *Three Actions in 56 Bytes* (Berlin, 2014) and *Waiting event: 64 bytes* (Lisbon, 2014). Recent publications include: *Pocket-calls: Point(s) of contact between art practice and philosophy* (*Kaiak: Journal of Philosophy*, 2020); *No More and Less: The withdrawal of speculation* (*MaHKUscript: Journal of Fine Art Research*, 2019); *Catch / Bounce: Towards a relational ontology of the digital in art practice* (Plymouth University, 2017); *Stack Overflows and Digital Actions, Digital Movement* (Palgrave Macmillan, 2015); and *Add to Shopping Basket* (ARPA for Transmediale, Germany, 2015).

Andrew Clifford is a writer and curator and is the director of Sarjeant Gallery Te Whare o Rehua Whanganui. He was the director of Te Uru in Tāmaki Makaurau 2013–23. His research interests follow the worlds of contemporary art, performance, new media and music, particularly where their orbits overlap and collide, notably with the 2018 touring exhibition *From Scratch: 546 moons*. Clifford has produced music programmes for Radio New Zealand and 95bFM and contributed articles and essays to books and publications throughout the Asia–Pacific region. He is a trustee for the Len Lye Foundation, the Contemporary Art Foundation and the Edith Collier Trust, has been a trustee for CIRCUIT and the Audio Foundation, and holds an MFA from the University of Auckland.

Natasha Conland is senior curator of global contemporary art at Auckland Art Gallery Toi o Tāmaki. She has over twenty years' experience developing exhibitions of contemporary art, and has written for a number of contemporary arts journals and catalogues in the Asia–Pacific region. She co-edited *Reading Room*, a peer-reviewed journal of contemporary art published annually by the E H McCormick Research Library, Auckland Art Gallery, 2006–18. She has a long interest in performance, art in public space and the dissemination of the historic avant-garde.

Blair French is CEO of Murray Art Museum Albury located on Wiradjuri land in NSW Australia. He was previously CEO of Carriageworks, Sydney; director, curatorial and digital at the Museum of Contemporary Art Australia; executive director of Artspace, Sydney; and associate director of Performance Space. Blair was curatorial convenor of the sixth (2010–11) and curator of the seventh (2013) iterations of *SCAPE Public Art: Christchurch Biennial*, and a co-curator of the first edition of *The National: New Australian Art* biennial exhibition in 2017. His publications include contributions to books on performance and post-object art in Aotearoa, Australia and Canada. His most recent books (as editor or co-editor) are *Civic Actions: Artists' Practices Beyond the Museum* (2017), *Mischa Kuball: Solidarity Grid* (2017) and *Shaun Gladwell: Pacific Undertow* (2019).

Heather Galbraith is a contemporary art curator, writer, and professor of fine arts at the College of Creative Arts Toi Rauwhārangi, Massey University, Wellington. Galbraith has held curator roles at the Museum of New Zealand Te Papa Tongarewa, City Gallery Wellington and ST PAUL St Gallery at Auckland University of Technology. She was involved in New Zealand's representation at the Venice Biennale as a co-curator in 2009, deputy commissioner in 2013 and commissioner in 2015. Recent projects include *Judy Darragh: Competitive plastics* (Objectspace and Centre of Contemporary Art Toi Moroki), and *Deep Material Energy* (the Suter Art Gallery and Australian Design Centre). She is a board member for Contemporary HUM Arts Trust and Experience Wellington. She holds a BFA, Elam School of Fine Arts, University of Auckland, and an MA Arts Administration and Curatorship, Goldsmiths' College, London.

Ioana Gordon-Smith (New Zealand/Sāmoa) is an arts writer and curator. She has held roles at Artspace Aotearoa, Objectspace, Te Uru Waitākere Contemporary Gallery and Pātaka Art + Museum. Gordon-Smith is a co-curator of the international Indigenous triennial *Naadohbii: To draw water* in Canada, and together with Lana Lopesi is the co-founder and co-editor of *Marinade: Aotearoa journal of Moana art*. She is a trustee for Enjoy Contemporary Art Space. Consistent throughout her curatorial process is a priority on close working relationships with artists.

Khye Hitchcock (they/them; Pākehā) is a producer/curator/community organiser based in Ōtautahi. They are interested in generosity and experimental modes of practice that prioritise community and unsettle hegemonic systems. Hitchcock has an MFA from Elam School of Fine Arts (2012) and has held various curatorial roles including at Artspace Aotearoa, SCAPE Public Art and the Centre of Contemporary Art Toi Moroki.

Lana Lopesi is an author, editor and assistant professor in indigenous, race and ethnic studies at the University of Oregon. She is the author of *False Divides* (2018) and *Bloody Woman* (2021), and editor of *Pacific Arts Aotearoa* (2023). Her writing has featured extensively in magazines, journals and publications in print and online. In 2021 Lopesi was the writer in residence at the Michael King Writers Centre, and she has served as a judge for the Best Writing by a New Zealand Māori or Pacific Islander category for the Art Association of Australia and New Zealand Awards (2018) and the Illustrated Non-Fiction Award for the Ockham New Zealand Book Awards (2020).

Melanie Oliver is a curator at Christchurch Art Gallery Te Puna o Waiwhetū. Previously she was senior curator and programme manager at The Dowse Art Museum, director of The Physics Room Contemporary Art Space, assistant curator at the Govett-Brewster Art Gallery and Artspace Sydney, and was gallery manager at Enjoy Contemporary Art Space and Blue Oyster Art Project Space. Melanie has a PhD in curatorial practice from Monash University, Melbourne.

Bruce E. Phillips (neurodivergent, he/him, Pākehā) is an independent creative practitioner from Aotearoa based in Edinburgh, Scotland, whose practice is dedicated to working alongside others to seek out unrealised potential, overlooked histories or to confront social inequalities. He holds a PhD from Massey University focusing on cooperative exhibition-making and curatorial practice, and has held curatorial positions in public galleries such as the South London Gallery, Te Tuhi Centre for the Arts in Auckland. From 2022 to 2023 Phillips was a member of Neuk Collective and since 2018 he has been a member of The chronicle of <_______> collective. He has worked with many performance artists such as Tania Bruguera, Phil Dadson, Mark Harvey, Amanda Heng, Tehching Hsieh, William Pope.L, Santiago Sierra, Kalisolaite 'Uhila and Sally J. Morgan.

Janine Randerson is associate professor in the School of Art & Design, Auckland University of Technology. She is an artist and writer from Aotearoa. Her moving image and performance works are exhibited in the Asia–Moana region and internationally. She often practises in collaboration with artists, performers, community groups, mana whenua and environmental scientists, from urban meteorologists to glaciologists. Janine's book *Weather as Medium: Toward a meteorological art* (MIT Press, 2018) focuses on modern and contemporary art and performance works that engage with our present and future weathers. She recently curated the programme *fathomless: artists converse with the more-than-human* for the Australasian Association for Art, Science and Literature (2021), she is currently curating the programme *Huarere: Weather Eye, Weather Ear* for Te Tuhi (Auckland, 2022–ongoing) as part of the World Weather Network platform for contemporary art. is also a LASER (Leonardo Art Science Evening Rendezvouit's esps) talk chair.

Lisa Samuels experiments with writing, art and relational theory in transnational life. She is the author of fifteen books, from *The Seven Voices* (1998) to *Livestream* (2023), many poetry pamphlets, and essays on theories of art, interpretation and the body. She collaborates with composers and movement artists, edits literary work and performs internationally. A book of her selected essays, *Imagining What We Don't Know: Creative Theory and Critical Bodies*, is forthcoming in 2024 with punctum books. Lisa is a professor in the Faculty of Arts at the University of Auckland.

Rachel Shearer (Rongowhakaata, Te Aitanga ā Māhaki, Pākehā) is an artist and academic. Shearer's work and research investigates sound as a medium through a range of practices: writing, moving image, installations, composing, recording, performance. As well, she collaborates as a sound designer and composer for moving image and live performance events. Shearer is kaiwhakatere in Huri te Ao/The School of Future Environments at AUT, from where she holds a PhD.

Balamohan Shingade is a doctoral candidate in philosophy at the University of Auckland. From 2020 to 2022 he worked as a researcher with the Center for Culture-Centered Approach to Research and Evaluation (CARE), Massey University, andfrom 2017 to 2020 as a curator at ST PAUL St Gallery, Auckland University of Technology. He was the inaugural manager and curator of Malcolm Smith Gallery, Uxbridge Arts and Culture 2015–16. Shingade holds an MLitt (Philosophy) from the University of Auckland, and is also an MFA graduate of Elam School of Fine Arts, where he was formerly a teaching fellow. He is a singer of Hindustani music. See balamohanshingade.com

Layne Waerea (Ngāti Wāhiao, Ngāti Kahungunu) is a Tāmaki Makaurau-based artist and educator whose practice involves carrying out performance art interventions that seek to question and challenge social and legal ambiguities in the public sphere. As a former lawyer and lecturer in law, Waerea uses this experience to inform her performance interventions, with a particular focus on how Te Tiriti o Waitangi could continue to play a critical role in the developing cultural fabric of Aotearoa. In 2016 Waerea completed her PhD at Auckland University of Technology, titled 'Free Social Injunctions: Art interventions as agency in the production of socio-legal subjectivities not yet imagined or realised'.

Victoria Wynne-Jones, art historian and curator, is an honorary research fellow in art history at the School of Humanities at the University of Auckland. She currently lectures in the disciplinary areas of art history, fine arts and dance studies, and collaborates with artists on written commissions and exhibition-making. Her research focuses on the intersections between dance studies and performance art as well as curatorial practice, feminisms, contemporary art theory and philosophy. She is author of *Choreographing Intersubjectivity in Performance Art* (Palgrave Macmillan, 2021), part of the series 'New World Choreographies'.

Amanda Yates (Ngāti Rangiwewehi, Ngāti Whakaue, Te Aitanga a Māhaki, Rongowhakaata) is associate professor in the School of Art & Design, Auckland University of Technology. She works with councils, iwi and communities exploring place-based, Indigenous-led strategies and actions for urban transformation in an era of climate and biodiversity emergency. Yates is director of He Puna Wai-Papa-Ora | Emergent Ecologies Lab, an urban mauri ora research and activation lab. She is co-programme leader and principal investigator of the Urban Wellbeing Research Programme in New Zealand's Building Better Homes, Towns and Cities National Science Challenge. Her current research focuses on the city as puna ora/living labs testing regenerative strategies. She co-curated 'Sea-change: Performing a fluid continent' for the Oceanic Performance Biennial in 2015 and the art and performance event *Heat: Solar revolutions* at Te Uru Waitākere Contemporary Gallery in 2017.

ACKNOWLEDGEMENTS

Huge thanks go to all the artists represented in this book who corresponded with us and generously assisted with the development of each chapter. You are the source of and inspiration for this volume.

We acknowledge and admire all the contributing authors in this book. Thank you for your ongoing dedication to performance art of Aotearoa, and for your patience as we worked with you on each chapter.

We gratefully acknowledge funding from the School of Art & Design and the Faculty of Design and Creative Technologies at Auckland University of Technology (AUT), as well as from Creative New Zealand: Arts Council of New Zealand Toi Aotearoa.

Special thanks go to students and staff in the Art & Performance Research Group of the School of Art & Design (AUT), as well as Mandy Smith (head of school) and Greg Bennett (head of research) for their support. Colleagues in the Department of Visual Arts at AUT are an engaged group of teachers and artists and we thank them all for their support.

We thank Chris Braddock for his role as lead-editor.

We thank Ena Kosovac (artist and PhD candidate, AUT) for her sterling work as research assistant.

We thank Poata Alvie McKree for her translation work in the glossary.

A number of individuals have discussed this project with us and been generous with their time and helpful in their engagement. We want to thank in particular: the late Jim Allen, Bruce Barber, Christina Barton, James Charlton, Wystan Curnow, Phil Dadson, Natasha Francois, Sally J. Morgan, Stuart Page, Albert Refiti, Balamohan Shingade, Bridget Sutherland and Jane Sutherland.

We acknowledge the generous assistance of the Auckland Art Gallery Toi o Tāmaki for this publication, and thank the staff of the E H McCormick Research Library including image rights and permissions officer Geoffrey Heath and librarian Tamsyn Bayliss. Thanks also to Catherine Hammond, Hannah Mathews and Ngarino Ellis for writing letters of support in the proposal stages of this book, and to Natasha Conland for acting as 'reader' for the Introduction and Chapters 1, 4, 6 and 7.

Finally, we thank the staff at Massey University Press, especially publisher Nicola Legat, managing editor Anna Bowbyes and editorial assistant Anna Jackson-Scott, and editor Imogen Coxhead, for their guidance through the process of publishing.

INDEX

Entries in **bold** indicate images

MASSEY
UNIVERSITY
PRESS

First published in 2024 by Massey University Press
Private Bag 102904, North Shore Mail Centre
Auckland 0745, New Zealand
www.masseypress.ac.nz

Design by Seven
Cover image: Shannon Te Ao, *two shoots that stretch far out*, 2013–14. Courtesy the artist.

A catalogue record for this book is available from the National Library of New Zealand

Printed and bound in Malaysia by Papercraft

ISBN: 978-1-99-101654-6

The assistance of Creative New Zealand and Auckland University of Technology is gratefully acknowledged by the publisher

AUT

creative nz
ARTS COUNCIL OF NEW ZEALAND TOI AOTEAROA